EARLY MOVEMENT EXPERIENCES AND DEVELOPMENT

Habilitation and Remediation

JOSEPH P. WINNICK

Professor, Physical Education
State University College
Brockport, New York

1979

W. B. SAUNDERS COMPANY
Philadelphia   London   Toronto

W. B. Saunders Company: West Washington Square
Philadelphia, PA   19105

1 St. Anne's Road
Eastbourne, East Sussex BN21 3UN, England

1 Goldthorne Avenue
Toronto, Ontario M8Z 5T9, Canada

Early Movement Experiences and Development:
Habilitation and Remediation   ISBN   0-7216-9465-9

Last digit is the print number: 9   8   7   6   5   4   3   2   1

*This book is dedicated to those with me
during its preparation. . . .*
To
EVELYN, VALERIE, AND JASON WINNICK

PREFACE

This book may be separated essentially into five sections. The first section, consisting of the first chapter, introduces the reader to the role of movement and play experiences in the development of selected areas of human development. Also, a skeletal outline of developmental areas and their components that serves as the structure for the second section is presented.

The second section of the book, the developmental section, presents information to help professionals habilitate or remediate physical, motor, perceptual, academic, and cognitive development through play, physical recreation, and physical education activities. The five chapters (one for each area) have similar formats. Specific physical and motor activities are suggested for program components that have been drawn from a theoretical base.

In the third section, handicapping conditions affecting movement are identified and described. Information pertaining to nature, incidence, treatment, cause, general characteristics, and general needs of special pupils is presented for each of the major handicapping conditions affecting physical and motor performance.

The relationship of these conditions to physical and motor performance is presented in the fourth section. The abilities and limitations of special pupils in movement activities are discussed. Unique needs of special pupils, methods of teaching to be emphasized, and appropriate activities for programming are then presented.

The fifth section deals with assessment. Content-referenced, criterion-referenced, and standardized-referenced standards and tests are distinguished, and their particular use in the development of individualized education programs is identified. A discussion of criteria for the development and selection of tests is followed by a review of several standardized or developed tests pertaining to the physical, motor, and perceptual-motor functioning of special populations. The tests are analyzed in terms of validity, reliability, and the availability of norms. The components of development measured by each test are presented and, where possible, individual test items are described. Readers are provided with sources for the procurement of test materials.

The final section of the book is a review and analysis of research regarding the effects of physical and motor experiences on physical, motor, perceptual-motor, academic, and cognitive variables. It focuses on research pertaining to the effects of physical and motor experiences on the habilitation and remediation of physical, motor, and perceptual development. This is an important aspect of the book, since research pertaining to the effects of training on special children has, until now, not been available in a single source.

This work is primarily designed to be a graduate text in Special Physical Education. However, it may be used as an undergraduate text if it is supplemented with a book dealing with the corrective and adapted phases of Special Physical Education. It may also serve well as a text for a course in developmental movement or as a resource for early childhood educators. It may be used as a text or resource for special education teachers, special physical educators, and regular physical educators involved in bringing the handicapped into the mainstream of physical education and recreation.

ACKNOWLEDGMENTS

Many people have contributed to the development of this book. First and foremost, I am sincerely indebted to all the "special" children with whom I have worked for the past several years. They have provided me with the inspiration to be concerned with them.

Several people and institutions have helped in obtaining pictures used in the book. I am indebted to Gabe Galgo and Frank Westover for their expert filming. For their assistance in obtaining pictures, I want to thank Mike Reif and Pam Bartemus of Monroe Development Services; Luke Kelly and Garth Tymeson of the School of the Holy Childhood, Rochester; Sam Paradise and Sharon Garski of the New York State School for the Blind in Batavia; Eileen Corcorran of the State University College at Brockport; and Robert Reynolds and his staff of the Second Supervisory District, Board of Cooperative Educational Services (BOCES), Monroe County. Appreciation is extended to the Audio-Visual Center, State University College at Brockport, for filming and development.

I want to express gratitude to Dorothy Goldsmith Jansma for reviewing and proofreading the material related to learning disabilities and to Paul Jansma for his help in selecting materials for various figures used throughout the book.

Finally, I wish to thank the people of New York State and the State University College, Brockport, for enabling me to take a sabbatical leave to begin the book.

CONTENTS

INTRODUCTION

Movement Experiences and Development

Human Development

The optimal development of the human organism is the chief responsibility and concern of those professions that are established to affect the environment of children. Their mission is to nurture the basic endowments of the individual. Just as a seed needs soil, air, water, and sunlight to grow, a child needs a rich environment in order to develop optimally. Certain anatomical and physiological human traits appear involuntarily and are predetermined by heredity. The timing and patterning of the appearance of these innate traits is known as maturation. Although the unfolding may be hindered by severe deprivation, it is relatively unaffected by practice, special instruction, or other techniques of environmental manipulation designed to accelerate it. The growth of an individual is an indication of changes in maturation. These changes in growth may be expressed quantitatively, i.e., by increases in height, weight, and girth. Development is an evolutionary *process* by which an individual attains maturity. It is influenced by maturation and learning.

Movement and Play in Total Human Development

Play has often been referred to as the "business" or "work" of childhood. It is through play that children learn about their abilities, nurture them, and use them to learn about their surroundings. Play is a volitional, spontaneous, and socially acceptable vehicle for exploration and learning. It is the primary tool for early development. Although play may involve non-observable movement, movement experiences have an important role in play and in development. Through movement, the child develops the body and improves the ability to play and to move through the environment, thereby enhancing learning and development. The importance of movement is demonstrated by the continuous involvement of children in movement experiences during their early years. It is obvious that much of a child's initial learning and development involves learning to move. With increases in age, movement capabilities and experiences change. As the child enters school, movement experiences become more structured and organized. Children become involved in games, sports, aquatics, dance, gymnastics, stunts and tumbling, and exercises. Movement experiences include all of these activities. The contribution of movement activities to physical, motor, academic, cognitive, and perceptual development is a key aspect of this book.

Movement Experiences for "Special" Children

Although development of the human generally follows an orderly and continuous pattern, there are variations in rate within an individual and among members of a group. Developmental attributes that appear to emerge naturally and spontaneously in one child need to receive special attention in another. Severe developmental lags may occur as a result of human deviance or of lack of opportunity for nurturing. When these lags may be ameliorated by movement experiences, it is important that such experiences be provided.

"Special" children, those individuals who are impaired, disabled, or handicapped, often exhibit severe developmental lags. Their anomalies often affect participation in movement experiences. Although the basic needs of all humans are the same in type, the needs of special children are "special" in degree. Thus, for example, the blind need greater than normal attention to maximize use of their other senses. Children with postural deviations need activities to enhance body alignment. The American Association for Health, Physical Education and Recreation (1971b) defines impaired, disabled, and handicapped individuals as follows:

> *Impaired* individuals have identifiable organic or functional conditions; some part of the body is actually missing, a portion of an anatomical structure is gone, or one or more parts of the body do not function properly or adequately. The condition may be permanent, as in the case of amputation, cerebral palsy, brain damage, or retrolental fibroplasia. It may be temporary — functional speech defects, some learning disabilities, various emotional problems, certain social maladjustments, or specific movement deficiencies.
> *Disabled* individuals, because of impairments, are limited or restricted in executing some skills, doing specific jobs or tasks, or performing certain activities.
> *Handicapped* individuals, because of impairment or disability, are adversely affected psychologically, emotionally, or socially. Handicapped persons reflect an attitude of self-pity. Some individuals with impairments and disabilities are handicapped, some severely.

Figure 1–1. Movement experiences play an important role in the total development of the child.

Others with severe impairments or disabilities adjust extremely well to their conditions and live happy and productive lives. In their eyes they are not handicapped even though society continues to label them handicapped. (American Association for Health, Physical Education and Recreation, 1971b, p. 63.)

A major focus of this book is to develop an understanding of special children and the relationship between deviance and movement experiences. The principal handicapping conditions will be described, and abilities and limitations of special children, in terms of movement experiences, will be presented.

Development and Education

The Developmental Component of Regular and Special Physical Education

Movement activities may be employed in pre-school and school programs for a variety of purposes. They are, of course, included in regular programs as well as in programs for special pupils. Movement activities are considered developmental when they are selected for the primary purpose of enhancing physical, motor, cognitive, academic, perceptual, and social development.

The facet of physical education attending to the needs of special children has been termed *adapted physical education* by the American Association of Health, Physical Education, and Recreation (AAHPER). In 1952, this organization defined *adapted physical education* as "a diversified program of developmental activities, games, sports, and rhythms suited to the interests, capacities, and limitations of students with disabilities who may not safely or successfully engage in unrestricted participation in the vigorous activities of the general physical education program." This statement has been of great assistance in identifying the role and function of this kind of physical education. The fact that the definition identifies the population that the program is intended to serve helps to establish criteria for the placement of pupils in appropriate settings. However, some confusion has occurred in the use of the word *adapted.* Many feel that it is too restrictive to be used as an umbrella term for this subdiscipline of physical education. They prefer to use the term *special physical education,* which more closely aligns itself with the Special Education—Regular Education relationship.

In this book, *special physical education* will be used as an umbrella term for that part of the program of Physical Education described by the 1952 AAHPER definition of *adapted physical education.* It includes the three component parts identified and described as follows:

1. *Adapted:* the phase of special physical education that emphasizes the modification or adaptation of physical education activities or methods in order that impaired, disabled, and handicapped children may participate in physical education activities safely and with success.
2. *Developmental:* the phase of special physical education that emphasizes total development through habilitative physical activities for those exhibiting developmental lags. It emphasizes the use of movement activities for physical, motor, academic, cognitive, social-emotional, and perceptual development. The unique aspect of developmental physical education is the use of movement activities for developmental purposes. The primary function of the developmental phase is physical and motor development. However, the emphasis given in a particular program varies with pupils' needs.
3. *Corrective:* the phase of special physical education that emphasizes the correction, restoration, or rehabilitation of human conditions through movement activities. It focuses upon the appropriate use of movement activities for the cor-

rection of postural deviations and the rehabilitation of muscular functioning. This phase of the special physical education program must often be conducted under appropriate medical guidance.

It should be recognized that this notion of special physical education will not be universally accepted. The component parts are not mutually exclusive or exhaustive. However, the descriptions presented here should serve to clarify the use of the terms in this book.

Subject, Child, and Teacher-Centered Approaches in Education

Over the years, educators have debated subject, child, and teacher-centered approaches to education. The approaches are not mutually exclusive; a subject-centered approach emphasizes structuring of experiences around the component parts of a subject area. Although instruction may be individualized, most children are taught similar content in accordance with the normative characteristics of their group. In a child-centered approach, content is selected according to the immediate needs and interests of the child. Children are the primary determiners of content. In a teacher-centered approach, needs of the child are determined by the teacher subjectively or through relevant assessment techniques. Content appropriate to fulfillment of the child's needs is selected by the teacher. Detailed analysis of the various approaches is beyond the scope of this book. However, it is important to realize that the concepts that follow stress the interrelationship of subject, teacher, and child. It is assumed that subject matter or experiences are provided to the child according to assessed needs, which are determined by teachers with the benefits of assessment techniques.

The Use of Movement Experiences in Educational Settings

Movement experiences may be employed in physical education as well as in other subject areas. Since in physical education the priority areas of development are physical and motor, physical educators will, obviously, select movement experiences that will attain physical and motor objectives. However, since movement experiences may be used to develop perceptual, academic, and cognitive abilities, teachers of other subjects may incorporate them in their programs. In addition, physical educators may be asked to contribute to perceptual, academic, and cognitive development in their programs through movement activities. It must be stressed that perceptual, academic, or cognitive development will ordinarily not take priority over physical and motor objectives in physical education programs. Generally, movement experiences that are employed by physical educators for associated objectives should be offered in conjunction with or in addition to movement activities employed for physical and motor objectives.

The developmental or educational objectives to be stressed in a program and the type of activities employed to attain those objectives will vary with pupil needs. If the goal of physical development has the highest priority for a particular child, this area should be emphasized in the total developmental or educational program planned for the child. If the principal needs are academic, cognitive, or social-emotional objectives, then activities to attain these objectives should be emphasized. It is assumed that emphasis should and will be placed where it is needed. The role that a particular subject area or teacher plays will depend on the needs of the individual. The role that movement experiences play will depend on the needs of the child, the objectives of the program, and the ability of teachers to employ them in their programs.

Developmental-Educational versus Medical-Pathological Models

Traditionally, professional programs designed to prepare special educators for the teaching of special pupils have structured knowledge and experiences along medical-pathological categories. Units, courses, and programs have been built around mental retardation, emotional disturbance, visual or auditory handicaps, speech and hearing defects, and a variety of physical handicaps. The limitations of such an approach, which have been discussed in detail by Winnick (1972), include: the perpetuation of segregation and dehumanization, the limited value in implementing programs, and the development of preconceived notions about the learning ability, needs, and interests of certain groups of children. The labels that have been associated with such an orientation have tended to place responsibility for educational failure on the child, the parents, or factors unrelated to school experiences.

There is a need to develop alternative models that fulfill the educational needs of special children. There is a need to develop models that stress developmental and educational concepts. The focus in such models should be on experiences relevant and meaningful to education in general and to physical education in particular. The models should focus on the abilities rather than the disabilities of children and should attempt to meet their individual needs, interests, and abilities. Models based on developmental and educational needs are only beginning to emerge, and the specific nature of each varies. There will certainly be no *one* acceptable developmental-educational model. Although a comprehensive model is not presented here, the outline of developmental areas and components presented in the next section may serve as a springboard for the development of comprehensive models.

Individualized Education Programs

Special children are an extremely heterogeneous group. They exhibit great variation in development, and no one program will meet all their needs. Education programs must be individualized to the greatest extent possible in order to meet their needs most effectively.

Movement experiences, paces of instruction, methods, materials, time allotments, settings, and standards must be adjusted for each child in order to achieve individualization in the purest form possible.

One of the most significant occurrences in the education of the handicapped was the passage of the Education for All Handicapped Children Act of 1975 (PL 94–142). This act was designed to ensure that all handicapped children have available to them a free appropriate public education that emphasizes special education and related services designed to meet their unique needs. The term *special education* includes instruction in physical education, and the term *related services* includes recreation. The Act also requires the development of an individualized education program (IEP) for each handicapped child. PL 94–142 specifies that the individual education program shall include a statement of the child's present levels of educational performance; a statement of annual goals, including short-term objectives; a statement of the specific educational services to be provided and the extent to which the child will be able to participate in regular educational programs; the projected date for initiation and anticipated duration of such services; and appropriate objective criteria, evaluation procedures, and schedules for determining whether instructional objectives are being achieved.

The information presented in subsequent chapters should be very useful to development and implementation of individual education programs in physical education and recreation. Theoretical knowledge regarding physical and motor development, sequences of development, and the relationship of age and sex to physical and motor development is presented. The relationship of some deviances to physical and motor development is analyzed, and activity needs and methods for instruction of special children are recommended. Research related to the effectiveness of physical and motor experiences is reviewed, and methods of assessing pupil performance are suggested.

Outline of Developmental Areas and Their Components

Table 1–1 presents an outline of the developmental areas and their components that will be covered in this book. We will be exploring the contribution of movement experiences to each of these areas. In the outline, it is readily apparent that five areas of development are identified: physical, motor, perceptual, academic, and cognitive. This is not to suggest that these are the only areas that should be covered or identified. Others, such as social-emotional development, should be developed. Further, it should not be assumed that these five areas are discrete entities. Although a child's progress in one developmental area may occur without advances in another, each area either directly or indirectly relates with and affects other areas. The assumption of this interrelationship is, in fact, the basis for this book. Interrelationships between areas of development are expressed in the outline in Table 1–1 by the two-directional arrows between developmental areas.

Although all the developmental areas are assumed to be inter-

Table 1-1. Outline of Developmental Areas and Their Components

TOTAL DEVELOPMENT

Physical	Motor	Perceptual	Academic	Cognitive
Static Strength	*Phylogenetic Locomotor Movements*	*Visual Perception*	*Language Arts Concepts*	*Play*
Dynamic Strength	rolling	visual figure-ground	reading	*Physical and Motor Knowing*
Explosive Strength	crawling and creeping	spatial relationships	writing	*Perceptual Activity*
Cardiorespiratory Endurance	walking	perceptual constancy	listening	*Logico-Mathematical Thinking*
Speed	running	visual-motor coordination	language and communication	*Spatial-Temporal Thinking*
Agility	jumping			*Representation and Social Interaction*
Flexibility	galloping	*Auditory Perception*	*Mathematical Concepts*	*Physical Knowledge*
	hopping	figure-ground	number recognition	*Problem Solving*
	skipping	discrimination	counting	
		sound localization	computing	
	Non-Locomotor Phylogenetic Movements	temporal auditory perception	measurement	
	throwing		basic geometric concepts	
	catching	*Haptic Perception*	other logico-mathematical operations	
	kicking	body awareness		
		laterality	*Science Concepts*	
	Balance	tactual perception	effects of gravity	
			laws of motion	
			types of motion	
			levers	
			projectiles	
			absorption of force	
			equilibrium	
			physiological concepts	
			other basic concepts	

related, the focus here is on the use of movement experiences for total development. Thus, only the role of physical and motor activities for the five areas will be examined in detail. The importance of cognitive and academic abilities in physical or motor development, for example, is not fully discussed.

Each area of development comprises several components. For example, the physical area includes static strength, dynamic strength, explosive strength, cardiorespiratory endurance, speed, agility, and flexibility. As is true with the development areas, it should not be assumed that these are the only acceptable components. In the perceptual area, for example, it is obvious that other components (olfactory, gustatory) as well as subcomponents could have been identified. In the academic area, other subject areas and their components could be included. The motor area could be and has been structured in many different ways. The point to be stressed is that the outline is a guide for the structure of this book. The components and subcomponents that have been selected are considered most important and most relevant to our purposes.

Although primarily written for the physical educator, this work does not imply that total development is the sole responsibility of physical educators. It is also assumed that other educators can employ movement experiences to attain developmental objectives. It is not assumed that the five areas of development are or should be of equal importance for the physical educator. In fact, the principal function of the physical educator should be the development of physical and motor abilities. As programs are implemented, however, they may be arranged to contribute to the other areas of development. Since perceptual, academic, and cognitive development are usually the responsibility of other professionals, the physical educator will generally serve as a resource for movement activities for the attainment of skills in these areas. However, determination of the exact role of the teacher and the specific program objectives to be stressed should be based on student needs rather than on subject area priorities.

Habilitation and Remediation

This book deals with habilitation and remediation of the developing child through movement experiences, with the primary emphasis being on habilitation. The term *habilitation* is used to stress the use of movement experiences as a stimulus for development. Appropriate movement experiences are suggested that will enable the individual to develop his or her innate endowments. The key purpose of habilitation is to provide quality experiences for optimal nurturing of the individual. It is hoped that a quality movement environment will forestall developmental failures and lags. In cases in which injury, deformities, or developmental lags have already occurred, habilitative movement experiences should be designed to maintain optimal functioning and to prevent further malfunctioning or developmental lags.

The term *remediation* is used to describe programming whose purpose is to restore the individual to normal functioning, to ameliorate disease conditions, or to correct faulty function or structure.

In other words, activities are considered remedial if they are employed to bring the individual back to previous levels of functioning, if they are used for the primary purpose of alleviating disease, or if they are used primarily to correct deviance. As it is used here, *remediation* is associated most often with the corrective aspect of Special Physical Education. However, all aspects of corrective physical education are not covered herein.

2

PHYSICAL DEVELOPMENT

Although the amount of emphasis on physical development and physical fitness has changed throughout the twentieth century, the professions of physical education and recreation have invariably been concerned with this phase of development. Many physical educators believe that physical development is their functional priority — the unique contribution of their field to education — and therefore the reason for the field's existence. They have advocated physical fitness for a healthy body and a healthy mind. They have recognized the importance of physical fitness to successful participation in games, sports, play, and work for both children and adults.

Kraus and Hirschland (1954) published results of a study indicating that the physical fitness of American children was found to be inferior to that of European children. Although the validity of the test used in the study has been questioned, the report was significant because it generated a great deal of attention. In 1956, President Eisenhower established the President's Council on Youth Fitness (now called the President's Council on Physical Fitness and Sports) to promote physical fitness in the United States.

Within the last decade, the importance of the physical in overall development has received increased attention from special educators, psychologists, and physicians. They have supported the need for physical development for the handi-

11

capped, particularly the severely handicapped. Many educators now recognize that basic physical fitness is necessary for children to move through and explore their environment and to sustain their performance in everyday tasks. For example, Barsch (1965) established a curriculum entitled "Movigenics," designed to provide children with the "physiological readiness" to learn from the environment.

The importance of physical activity and physical fitness has long been considered vital in programs for the blind. Blindisms have been associated with repressed urges for physical activity. Thus, schools for the blind have incorporated physical activity programs to allow these urges to be satisfied. It is also generally believed that the blind need greater than average stamina if they are to compete with the normally sighted; they frequently utilize more energy to accomplish a task. The blind also need strength, endurance, flexibility, and agility to move with and control a Seeing Eye dog and to move effectively in the environment using a cane.

Physical development is also critical in habilitating, rehabilitating, or remediating other types of handicapping conditions. For example, the cerebral palsied need physical activity to strengthen appropriate muscle groups and to stimulate the development of controlled movement. Victims of muscular dystrophy need physical activity to develop, maintain, or prolong the usefulness of their musculature. Learning disabled, mentally retarded, and emotionally disturbed youngsters need physical development to be able to move through and learn from the environment. Since these children are often physically awkward, physical development increases the likelihood of their successful involvement in play, games, sports, and other motor activities. Exercise is particularly beneficial to the diabetic because it helps to maintain muscle tone, improve circulation to extremities, and keep body weight under control. Scientific evidence is available indicating that individuals require less insulin to reduce blood sugar levels when they exercise than when they do not. Victims of poliomyelitis often benefit from activity to "re-educate" muscles and restore them to normal functioning.

Physical Fitness and Physical Development

Physical educators, physicians, and physiologists have attempted to define physical fitness for many years. The literature abounds with both similar and varying views. Most professionals agree, however, that it is the physical aspect of total fitness and implies freedom from disease. Further, an individual is generally considered physically fit when he or she is able to meet the physical requirements of daily tasks without undue fatigue. For this condition to be met, the individual must have attained an accepted level in certain physical abilities or components. Again, there are differences of opinion as to what the components of physical fitness are. For the purposes of this text, the components of physical fitness are static strength, dynamic strength, explosive strength, cardiorespiratory endurance, agility, flexibility, and speed. In essence, then, a person is considered physically fit when the components of physical fitness are developed to the degree that he or she is able to meet the physical requirements of his or her daily tasks without undue fatigue.

Physical fitness, thus, is a state of being that may vary for different individuals. For example, a child of 5 years and a man of 30 years may both be physically fit although their strength may differ considerably. However, one would expect greater similarity in strength if two male children of 5 were compared or two men of 30 were compared. When children are not within acceptable norms in their physical fitness and they need experiences to bring them within acceptable norms, there is need for physical development. Such children are not physically fit. There is also a need for habilitating the physical area of development. *Physical development* in this text is the process of stimulating and enhancing physical fitness. *Physical habilitation* is the process of stimulating the acquisition of normal levels of physical fitness.

Development of the Components of Physical Fitness

Static Strength

Muscular strength has been traditionally explained as the maximum amount of force that can be exerted by a muscle in a single contraction. Fleishman (1964a), after conducting a factor analysis study of the components of physical fitness, identified this factor as *static strength.*

Static strength, as well as other types of strength, may be increased by using one of two types of exercises. The first of these is known as *isotonic exercise,* which consists of two types of muscular contraction, *concentric* and *eccentric.* Isotonic exercises* are characterized by muscle shortening and lengthening and result in observable movement by the body. Examples include arm curls, sit-up exercises, and push-ups. *Concentric* contractions occur when a muscle shortens during tension. *Eccentric* contractions occur when a muscle lengthens or releases its contraction but also remains under tension. For example, in the execution of an arm curl, the barbell is lifted by the elbow flexors (biceps femoris, brachialis, brachioradialis). During flexion of the elbow, these muscles shorten and are in a state of tension (active) as the barbell is lifted. During the upward movement of the barbell, the elbow extensors (triceps) are considered the con-

---

*Some authors distinguish between isotonic and isokinetic movements under the rubric of *dynamic strength exercises* and, subsequently, distinguish between isometric and dynamic strength. In isotonic movements, resistance is constant, but the tension exerted by the muscle varies throughout the entire range of motion. In isokinetic movements, resistance varies, the muscle contracts at its capacity or at a constant percentage of capacity, and movements are made at a constant speed throughout the full range of motion.

tralateral muscles of this movement and release their contraction to enable the flexors to perform the task. Since the elbow extensors are not tensing, however, they are not in eccentric contraction. Some writers refer to such muscle action as *relaxing* or *stretching.* It is important to note that, in terms of gain in static strength, the muscles benefiting from the upward movement of the arm are the elbow flexors, not the elbow extensors. When the barbell is returned to the starting position, the movement is caused by a releasing or a gradual lengthening of the elbow flexors rather than by a concentric contraction of the elbow extensors. Thus, the elbow flexors are still in a state of tension while the elbow extensors are in a state of "relaxation." Typically, then, the muscles being developed in arm curls are the elbow flexors.

If the participant wishes to develop the strength of the elbow extensors using an arm curl, the extensors would need to contract concentrically and move the barbell downward at a speed greater than that of gravity. On the other hand, if the participant simply released the barbell or allowed it to be returned to the starting position at a force equal to gravity, the elbow flexors would be in a relaxing state rather than in a state of eccentric contraction. Whenever a participant engages in isotonic exercise, care must be taken to understand which muscles are under tension and which are being developed. Involving muscles of a joint in activity does not mean that strength will be gained in all the muscles of that joint. For a muscle to gain strength, tension must occur in it.

The second type of exercise that may be used to increase strength is an *isometric exercise.* Isometric exercises are characterized by muscle tension or static contraction with no resultant movement exhibited by the body. Isometric contractions occur when an individual pushes against immovable objects or attempts to lift a weight that he or she cannot move. In the performance of such exercises, the muscles exerting tension are the muscles in which strength is being developed.

THE OVERLOAD PRINCIPLE AND RESISTANCE

Basic to the development of strength is application of the "overload principle." *Overload* means a progressive increase in tension over that previously exerted by a muscle. In terms of static strength development, strength gains will occur only when a muscle exerts progressively more work per unit of time. The overload principle is met when tension is increased. Tension is increased to improve static strength by increasing the velocity of exercise or by increasing load or resistance. In other words, to increase static strength, one may perform the same exercise at a faster rate, or keep the same rate of exercise and increase resistance or load. In both cases, the work per unit of time is increased, thus satisfying the overload principle.

Load or resistance may be supplied in a variety of ways. In weight training, load is easily and efficiently provided by the use of barbells or dumbbells. However, in exercises such as push-ups or sit-ups, individuals may provide their own resistance. In isometric exercises, "self-resistance" occurs when an individual pushes one hand against the other, one leg against the other, or one arm against one leg. At times, resistance may be supplied by other people. Examples include partner lifting, "piggy back" races, Indian hand and leg wrestling, or tug of war. Resistance also may be supplied by inanimate objects other than barbells or dumbbells. For example, youngsters may lift stuffed animals, medicine balls, or chairs. In isometric exercises, resistance may be applied against walls, doorways, floors, or balls.

SELECTION AND IMPLEMENTATION OF STATIC STRENGTH ACTIVITIES

Isotonic exercises selected for static strength development should provide opportunity for tension to be increased by increases in velocity of exercise and in load or resistance. By such selection, progression is made more conducive and motivating. In selecting isometric exercises, the physical educator must take care to select exercises that allow for maximum contraction. Recent research, contradicting earlier findings, indicates that the maximum strength gains occur with maximum contraction.

Strength may be developed in conditioning programs, in play, and in activities such as games, sports, combatives, gymnastics, or aquatics. Although gains will generally be greater in conditioning programs explicitly designed to improve static strength, it may be sufficient and generally is more fun to develop static strength in situations other than formal conditioning programs (Fig. 2–1).

Dynamic Strength

Clarke (1967) defines muscular endurance as "the ability to continue muscular exertions of a submaximal magnitude." Such muscular exertions would be localized exercises rather than "whole body" activi-

Figure 2–1. The cargo net — a fun way of developing strength.

Figure 2–2. Using a medicine ball to develop strength.

ties, which are generally associated with cardiorespiratory endurance. In his work, Fleishman (1964a) designates essentially the same concept as *dynamic strength.* Regardless of the terms used, it is important to recognize that static strength and dynamic strength are related. This being the case, both isometric and isotonic exercises are helpful in developing dynamic endurance. Isotonic exercises are preferred, however, since they involve inherent repetition of activity.

Since it is vital to continue muscular exertions to develop dynamic strength, the individual must work at submaximal effort. It is not possible to perform activity for a sustained period of time when working at maximal effort. Exercises selected to develop dynamic strength should generally involve at least 15 repetitions. The maximum number of repetitions will depend upon the objectives of the program. Thus, the principle underlying the selection of activities for the development of dynamic endurance is to choose those activities in which a muscle or muscle group works against a relatively light load so that many repetitions may be performed. Progression for development of dynamic strength is essentially accomplished by increasing the number of repetitions, the load of an activity (do not select a load that will lead to less than 15 repetitions), or the duration of the workout session.

As was true for static strength activities, resistance for dynamic strength development may be supplied by inanimate objects, self, or others. Dynamic strength may be developed within various exercise systems or in play, games, sports, gymnastics, and aquatics (Fig. 2–2).

Explosive Strength

Explosive strength, or muscular power, is the amount of force that can be exerted by a muscle or muscle group in a short length of time; thus, it combines strength and speed. The greater the force exerted in a short period of time, the greater the power of the individual. Power is useful in activities such as broad jumping, line playing and offensive back-field running in football, shot-putting, and a variety of throwing and kicking activities for distance. In each case, strength needs to be exerted quickly for the most effective results.

Since muscular power is closely related to static strength, many writers do not select muscular power as a separate component of physical fitness. Fleishman (1964a, 1964b) did identify this component in his factor analysis study. He appropriately named this factor *explosive strength* and included the shuttle run and the softball throw as items in his battery of tests measuring this component. Many tests of physical fitness utilize the standing broad jump as an indicator of explosive strength.

Explosive strength is developed by increasing strength and exerting it over progressively shorter periods of time (with more speed). In order to continue such activity, the development of dynamic strength is also necessary. Therefore, static strength and dynamic strength exercises should accompany the training for explosive strength. In "pure" (static) strength development, the goal is essentially to perform a single maximum contraction (single contraction with maximum load). In the development of dynamic strength, the goal is essentially to repeat movements of a submaximal nature (light load with a large number of repetitions). In the development of explosive strength, it is important to perform heavy loads with few repetitions. Since a time factor is involved, training for explosive strength should be aimed at performing the task as quickly as possible. Progression in the development of explosive strength is essentially accomplished by increasing load, repetitions (no more than ten), speed of execution (decreasing the time taken to perform a task).

Speed

Speed is the ability to execute or repeat a movement rapidly. Speed is enhanced by increasing the ability to incur oxygen debt when necessary. For example, in sprinting, a participant is able to run 100 yards without breathing. However, at the end of the sprint, the body seeks oxygen to replace that used in the sprint. The body has incurred, in effect, a debt that must be repaid. This physiological phenomenon is known as *oxygen debt* and is measured by subtracting normal oxygen usage from that utilized during recovery from exercise. Since the body performed "without oxygen" and must replace the oxygen supply, the body metabolizes anaerobically. Anaerobic metabolism, less efficient than aerobic metabolism, must occur to replace the oxygen debt incurred. Anaerobic metabolism may be improved by providing the body with exercise opportunities to adapt to oxygen debt. Through exercise, the body may be trained to incur larger debts of oxygen.

The ability of a muscle to move rapidly is enhanced by increasing its elasticity and strength. Elasticity and strength allow rapid muscle contraction and relaxation. Thus, strength activities are recommended for the development of muscle strength up to the point of excessive hypertrophy, which may interfere with rapid movement.

Thus, speed training requires maximal effort, opportunity for the stimulation of anaerobic metabolism, and strength development. As with the other components of physical development, speed may be developed directly in programs of exercise or indirectly in play, games, sports, gymnastics, or aquatics.

Agility

Agility is generally defined as speed in changing directions. It is a component thought to combine speed, power, and coordination for the purpose of changing the position of the organism. In his work, Fleishman (1964a) found that agility did not emerge as a separate factor but was acounted for by the explosive strength factor.

Agility is developed by selecting activities that require changes in body position and direction (Fig. 2–3). Progression may be made by increasing the speed of the activity and by selecting gradually more demanding activities. In addition, agility may be improved by developing the components of speed and power.

Flexibility

Flexibility has generally been associated with the range of movement in a joint. In his work, Fleishman (1964a, 1964b) identified two types of flexibility, *extent* and *dynamic. Extent* flexibility is the range of

Figure 2–3.   A fun way of developing agility.

movement possible in a joint, and *dynamic* flexibility is the ability to make repeated rapid flexing movements.

Unlike most other components of physical development, flexibility can be overdeveloped. It is possible for the individual to be "too flexible." Flexibility is excessive when it causes lack of muscular support in a joint and makes it susceptible to strain or injury. A common example is hyperextension of the knees in gymnasts and dancers. When such a situation occurs, the muscles surrounding the joint should be strengthened under the direction of medically qualified personnel.

Those of low physical fitness usually need to increase their range of movement. This is accomplished by selecting activities that involve joint movements in appropriate directions, gradually increase the range of movement, and demand more and more flexibility in a joint. To increase dynamic flexibility, such movements should be made at progressively increasing rates.

Cardiorespiratory Endurance

Cardiorespiratory endurance is the ability to perform large muscle or whole body activities continuously for a sustained period of time. Such ability is dependent on healthy cardiovascular and respiratory systems. Since it would not be possible to continue activity for a sustained time period if one worked at maximal effort, the intensity of exercise for the development of cardiorespiratory endurance must be submaximal. Activity performed for the purpose of improving cardiorespiratory endurance should be conducted for at least ten minutes and preferably for much longer periods of time. Since the purpose of training is to improve cardiovascular and respiratory function, it is necessary to employ activities that will stimulate the organs to adapt significantly. Therefore, large muscle group or whole body activities conducted for a prolonged period are recommended.

Improvements in cardiorespiratory endurance are designed to produce better functioning of the cardiovascular and respiratory systems. Stimulation of the cardiovascular system is designed to increase capillarization, develop a hypertrophied heart capable of increasing its efficiency, reduce resting heart rate and increase stroke volume, and increase the number of red blood cells in the cardiovascular system. Stimulation of the respiratory system is designed to improve the transportation and absorption of oxygen throughout the body. This is accomplished by increasing lung aeration, leading to more efficient breathing (reduced rate and increased depth of breathing).

Within the past decade, many exercise physiologists have supported the contention that the ability to take in oxygen and make it available for use in physical activity is the best indicator of one's physical fitness. This concept is referred to as maximum oxygen intake ($\dot{V}O_2$ intake). The greater the amount of oxygen the individual can take in, the longer he or she may work without "borrowing" oxygen and thereby incurring oxygen debt. When it incurs an oxygen debt, the body metabolizes anaerobically. When the supply for oxygen is less than or equal to demand, the body metabolizes aerobically (with oxygen). Since $\dot{V}o_2$ varies according to the sex, weight, and age of the individual, norms are provided for males and females of different ages. When it is desirable to account for body weight, norms are expressed in $\dot{V}o_2/kg/min$.

Cooper (1968) designated the term "aerobics" to encompass his training program for the development of maximum oxygen intake, or aerobic capability. One of his greatest contributions has been to make the physiological concept of aerobic metabolism meaningful and applicable to the everyday use of individuals. He translates maximum oxygen intake capability to time required to perform tasks and thus makes goals easy for participants to understand.

For clarity, this author feels that the goals and programs for the development of cardiorespiratory endurance and maximum oxygen intake, or aerobic efficiency, are essentially the same. Aerobics is a system of exercise for attainment of cardiorespiratory endurance.

Cardiorespiratory endurance may be developed by formal programs of exercise or by physical recreation activities. It is recommended that both be utilized to produce the best results and to provide optimal motivation for participants. Progressions for the development of cardiorespiratory endurance are developed by increasing the intensity or duration of work, albeit the work is of submaximal magnitude.

Training Systems for Habilitating Physical Development

Physical development may be enhanced through participation in appropriate exercises, games, sport, and play. Training systems used for exercise purposes include circuit training, calisthenics, weight training, interval work, Fartlek training, speed training, continuous training, and aerobics. Since there are advantages and disadvantages to using each of the various systems, it is necessary to analyze them and to select the appropriate system for desired objectives. A description of the various training systems is presented.

Circuit Training

In circuit training, exercises are individually executed at different stations placed throughout a relatively large area (Fig. 2–4). Participants move from one station to the next until they complete the circuit or until the available time has elapsed. Progress can be determined by counting the number of circuits completed or recording the time required to complete the circuit. When the circuit is changed, progress is made by increasing the number of repetitions and the intensity of exercises at each station.

The following guidelines are recommended for development of a circuit:

1. Exercises selected should relate to program objectives. For example, if the objectives of the circuit include the development of static or dynamic strength in the arms, then activities

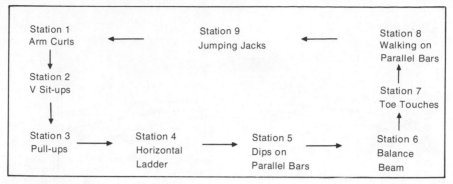

Figure 2–4. Sample circuit training course.

to improve this area, such as arm curls, must be included in the circuit.

2. Provision should be made for individual differences at each station in the circuit. Although exercises may be basically the same, modifications should be available. For example, at a station for improvement of balance, provision should be made to utilize balance beams of different widths and lengths.

3. Exercises selected should enable participants to perform independently.

4. In order to prevent "bottlenecking" or waiting at stations, duplicate exercise stations and passing stations should be established.

5. Exercises selected should be of such a nature that workload may be increased.

6. Generally, each circuit should consist of nine stations: three weight training exercises, three freestanding exercises, and three exercises using some type of apparatus.

7. For youngsters, it is motivating to develop a circuit based on an attractive theme. For example, to facilitate a theme of "A Trip to the Woods," a balance beam may be conceived of as a bridge over dangerous water (Figs. 2–5 and 2–6).

Circuit training is a desirable system of exercise because activity can be individualized, participants can perform at their own rate, relatively large classes can be effectively accommodated, progressions can easily and effectively be incorporated, the system can be designed to meet any component of physical development, the system provides opportunity for continuous activity, the setting of individual goals is inherent in circuit training, and the system provides for a built-in motivating force. Quality implementation, however, depends to a great extent upon student initiative. Participants must be motivated to perform exercises correctly and encouraged not to avoid exercises they dislike. Since circuit training is continuous, it logically follows that participants generally work at submaximal levels. To counteract this characteristic, activities that develop strength should be incorporated. One of the major drawbacks of circuit training is that it is relatively complicated and thus difficult for young, retarded,

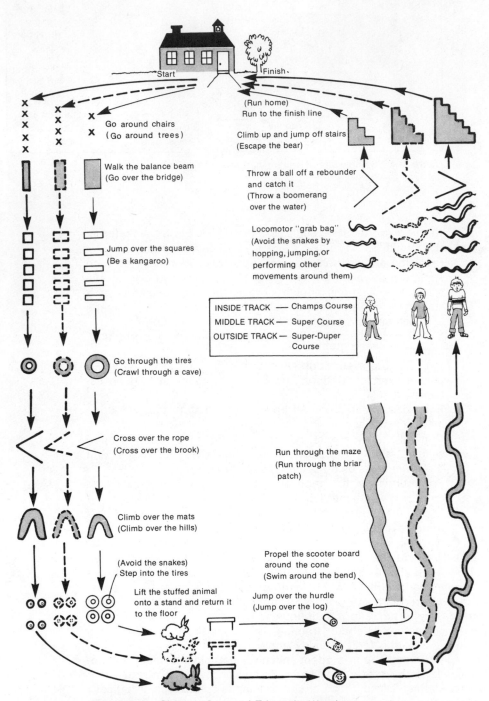

Figure 2–5. Obstacle Course: A Trip to the Woods

Figure 2-6. Pretending one is "Tarzan" makes exercise seem like play.

or emotionally disturbed pupils. To prepare them for circuit training, the following progression is recommended:

1. *Simon Says or Do This, Do That.* In such games, children learn to repeat a motion demonstrated by a leader.

2. *The Sea is Rough or Follow the Leader.* In these games, children move and repeat the movements of children directly in front of them.

3. *Obstacle Course.* In an obstacle course, participants are required to move to obstacles or stations and to perform one response at the station or obstacle. Obstacle courses can be successfully employed with severely retarded youngsters.

4. *Station-to-Station.* After the concept of moving to different stations has been established, the participants should be ready to perform more than a single repetition at each station. When using station-to-station procedures, each participant exercises at a station until a signal is given to move to the next one.

5. *Initial Circuit.* In the initial circuit, exercises are prescribed at each station and each participant performs one to three circuits. Participant times for completing the circuit are recorded and "target times" are established.

6. *Second Circuit.* This is the same as the initial circuit except that exercises at the stations are more strenuous.

7. *Individual Circuit.* In this circuit, exercise dosages are determined individually. The number of repetitions to be executed at each station is based on the participant's ability. Participants are individually tested to determine the maximum repetitions they can perform in a specified time. The training dosage is half this number. The participant is then timed for three laps of the circuit at this training dosage. The "target time" is two thirds of this time. When the participant reaches the target time, he or she is retested, and the process is repeated.

Calisthenics

Traditionally in calisthenics, participants execute in unison exercises that have been selected by a leader. Progression of activity is based on a standard selected by the leader, and therefore the approach is less conducive to individualizing progress and allowing pupils to perform at their own rates. Thus, the system is often frustrating to participants who are unable to meet the selected standards and is of little or no challenge to pupils able to exceed the selected standard with ease. Since time is generally taken for the leader to explain exercises and how they are to be performed, the activity is interrupted. On the other hand, traditionally administered calisthenics facilitate the control of large and undisciplined groups. In addition, students can easily grasp what is expected of them, and any component of physical development may be improved.

Weight Training

Weight training is a conditioning program that utilizes weights to develop primarily static and dynamic strength. Since static strength enhances speed, the system is often used to increase speed of movement. Progress is made by gradually increasing resistance or by performing repetitions of exercises. Although weight training is recommended for habilitation, it has been particularly popular for rehabilitation purposes. A system of progressive resistance exercises for use in weight training has been developed by DeLorme and Watkins (1951). The system is highly recommended and serves as a basis for rehabilitation programs in hospitals today.

Since weight training relies primarily on the use of barbells and dumbbells, it is expensive to begin such a program, and youngsters frequently lose interest in moving such objects. Barbells are often too heavy, and steps in progression are too big. Innovative leaders have responded to such problems by making barbells and dumbbells for their programs. This not only saves money but also makes available barbells that are lighter and allow for smaller increases in weight. Lounsberry (1971) reported on a program in which medicine balls and animals stuffed with buck shot were utilized as replacements for barbells and dumbbells. Such objects were used in games as well as in weight training sessions. Such an approach is inexpensive and motivating and provides for smaller increments in weight, making weight training both successful and fun.

Interval Work

Interval work is a training system in which exercise is interrupted by rest. It is essentially a modification of interval training, which is often employed for the training of varsity or champion athletes. Interval work is primarily utilized to increase cardiorespiratory endurance and dynamic strength by increasing work, decreasing rest, or both during a work session. For example, assume that a participant desires to perform 30 step-ups per minute for a five-minute period. Initially, the participant may begin by performing 15 step-ups for 30 seconds, then resting 30 seconds, and repeating this sequence for five minutes. The participant then may progress to performing 30 step-ups per minute, then resting for 30 seconds, and repeating the process. Eventually, by increasing work and decreasing rest, the participant reaches the target task of 30 step-ups per minute for five minutes.

Interval work may be regarded as a separate system of exercise. However, its principles may be applied to other exercise systems and to games, relays, aquatics, gymnastics, or other movement activities.

Fartlek Training

Fartlek is a Swedish word meaning "speed play" or "play of speed." It is a training method characterized by running at various speeds on various surfaces and in a variety of environments. Participants are encouraged to run on grass or sand, in and out of woods, and up and down hills. The greater the variety, the better. Interspersed with the running are periods of jogging, walking, sprinting, or calisthenics. Depending on how it is organized, Fartlek training may contribute to any component of physical development. Progressions may be easily made by increasing the nature, intensity, or duration of workout sessions. Although Fartlek training may be very demanding, the frequent change in terrain, routine, and environment inherent in the program makes it attractive to youngsters.

Speed Training

Speed training is a system of exercise that improves speed by increasing the rapidity of the participant's movement. It is designed to strengthen a muscle and enlarge its diameter in order that the rapidity of contraction and relaxation is enhanced. Speed training also contributes to the development of anaerobic capabilities for running. The stimulus in speed training is simply to run or to move a part of the body as rapidly as possible for as long as possible. In effect, speed training involves maximum effort at all times. The system of speed training can be used with any age group and should be used when speed is an objective of physical development.

Continuous Training

Cureton (1967) advocated and popularized a nonstop system of exercise for the development of physical fitness. As the name of the system suggests, physical activity is conducted continuously during a workout session lasting 30 minutes to an hour. As in the Fartlek system, continuous running, jogging, skipping, bench stepping, hopping, jumping, or other activities are interspersed with short periods of calisthenics. During the workout, emphasis is placed on deep breathing. In addition, each workout session begins with a mildly stressing warm-up, progresses in intensity until a peak is reached about halfway through the session and then gradually diminishes as the workout ends. Especially in the beginning, rhythmic activities such as running, rowing, swimming, jogging, or cycling are advocated rather than activities done in spurts such as weightlifting and handball.

In order to provide progression, Cureton designated three categories of exercise, Low Gear, Middle Gear, and High Gear, to identify easy, medium, and intense levels. Thus, participants may work at the gear most suitable for them, and further provisions are made to allow adaptations within each level (gear). Although the system may be utilized to develop all components of physical fitness, it is particularly suited for the development of cardiorespiratory endurance. The continuous training system can be easily and appropriately adapted for use with children of low fitness.

Aerobics

A system of exercise called *aerobics* has been recently developed and popularized by Cooper (1968, 1970). This system is primarily designed to improve an individual's maximum oxygen intake and is therefore especially useful for the development of cardiorespiratory endurance. Aerobics is designed to stimulate heart and lung activity for a period long enough to produce beneficial changes in the body. The amount of oxygen processed by the body is increased by improving the ability to breath large amounts of air, to deliver large volumes of blood forcefully and efficiently and to supply oxygen effectively to all parts of the body.

In aerobics, exercise programs are designed according to an established point value system for exercises such as walking, running, cycling, swimming, rope skipping, handball, basketball, squash, stationary running, stair climbing, and treadmill walking or running. The intensity of a workout or the number of points selected as a target depends on the level of fitness of the participant. Gradual increments are considered the key to the conditioning program. Participants may begin in a starter program and proceed to conditioning programs at progressively more demanding levels.

The system of aerobics presented by Cooper is particularly effective because it is based on medically sound rationale, it is safe, the participant's initial status is determined, assessment of fitness is built into the system, points are awarded for various intensities of activity (a motivational as well as safety factor), and workouts are conducted progressively according to the level of the participant's ability.

Performance in Selected Measures of Physical Fitness

Normative Data

In Table 2–1, central tendency values on selected measures of physical fitness are presented according to age and sex. In selection of sources, preference was given to those most widely used, those providing data on American children, and those employing the broadest and most recent sample in data collection. For some measures, the available data are limited.

The measures of physical proficiency presented in Table 2–1 and discussed here relate to groups of children. The data reported are generally based on cross-sectional studies of childhood performance, limiting analysis of individual and group changes. As is true with many human abilities, it should be recognized that there is a great deal of variation in the maturation and development of physical and motor abilities. Developmental changes are subject to environmental influences such as instruction, opportunity for activity, nutrition, and interests of children. In addition, hereditary factors play a role in influencing the rate of change in physical performances of a child. Longitudinal studies have been conducted to provide insight on individual and group variations related to physical and motor variables. Rarick (1973) gives a detailed description of stability and change in motor and physical abilities.

STATIC STRENGTH

Based on their review of research, Fisher and Birren (1947) report that the development of muscular strength follows a systematic trend, with an increase in strength up to the late twenties and a decline, usually at an increasing rate, from that time on. Maximum strength occurs between the ages of 25 and 30, according to these investigations. Rodahl and associates (1961) report that increases in strength are attributable to muscle size. This association of strength and muscular size explains, in part, why boys tend to be stronger than girls of the same age.

In her survey of several studies in which grip strength of children was tested, Metheney (1941) found increases in grip strength from age 3 to age 18. Keogh (1965), comparing his data on Santa Monica children with those from previous investigations, summarized that mean age increases occur for boys to at least age 17 and for girls to age 15. He also reported that boys are generally superior to girls on grip strength, with differences increasing at adolescence. His data indicate that strength increases between the ages of 5 and 11 for both boys and girls with differences in grip strength favoring boys.

DYNAMIC STRENGTH

Although changes in dynamic strength or muscular endurance have not been studied as extensively as some other measures of physical proficiency, some indications may be drawn from norms established in association with standardized tests. Fleishman (1964a) reported steady group median gains in the ability of boys to execute pull-ups from age 12 to age 17 and little change in girls' ability to execute pull-ups during this same period. AAHPER norms (1975) indicate that median group gains are evident in the ability of boys to execute sit-ups between the ages of 10 and 14, but there is a plateau between the ages of 14 and 17. For girls, median values for sit-ups increase slightly between the ages of 10 and 13 and generally stabilize between 12 and 17.

Text continued on page 31

Table 2–1. Central Tendency Values on Selected Measures of Physical Fitness.

Flexed Arm Hang (test scores in seconds)

Measure	Sex	Source	9–10	11	12	13	14	15	16	17
						Age				
Median	Girls	AAHPER (1975)	9	10	9	8	9	9	7	8

Pull-ups (number of pull-ups)

Measure	Sex	Source	9–10	11	12	13	14	15	16	17
						Age				
Median	Boys	AAHPER (1975)	1	2	2	3	4	6	7	7
Median	Boys	Fleishman (1964a)				3	5	7	8	9

Hand Grip (scores in pounds)

Measure	Sex	Source	5	6	7	8	9	10	11	12	13	14	15	16	17
								Age							
Median	Girls	Fleishman (1964a)									42	43	55	59	63
Median	Boys	Fleishman (1964a)									78	93	106	109	114
Mean (right grip)	Girls	Keogh (1965)	18.3	23.5	26.3	31.3	37.3	40.1	45.2						
Mean (right grip)	Boys	Keogh (1965)	16.6	19.3	22.9	28.0	30.8	35.3	45.8						
Mean	Girls	Metheney (1941)	18.5	20.2	23.5	27.5	32.1	36.3	42.0						

Flexed Leg Sit-ups (number performed in 60 seconds)

Measure	Sex	Source	9–10	11	12	13	14	15	16	17
						Age				
Median	Girls	AAHPER (1975)	27	29	29	30	30	31	30	30
Median	Boys	AAHPER (1975)	31	34	35	38	41	42	41	41

Shuttle Run (scores in seconds)

Measure	Sex	Source	9–10	11	12	13	14	15	16	17
						Age				
Median	Girls	AAHPER (1975)	11.8	11.5	11.4	11.2	11.0	11.0	11.2	11.1
Median	Boys	AAHPER (1975)	11.2	10.9	10.7	10.4	10.1	9.9	9.9	9.8

Standing Broad Jump (scores in inches)

Measure	Sex	Source	9–10	11	12	13	14	15	16	17
						Age				
Median	Girls	AAHPER (1975)	4'8"	4'11"	5'0"	5'3"	5'4"	5'5"	5'3"	5'5"
Median	Boys	AAHPER (1975)	4 11	5 2	5 5	5 9	6 2	6 8	7 0	7 2
Average	Girls	Espenschade (1960)	4 4	4 4	5 2	5 2	5 3	5 3	5 3	
Average	Boys	Espenschade (1960)	5 1	5 1	5 5	5 9	6 1	6 8	7 4	7 4
Median	Girls	Fleishman (1964a)					5 0	5 0	5 1	5 3
Median	Boys	Fleishman (1964a)				5 8	6 2	6 10	7 1	7 1

Standing Broad Jump (scores in inches)

Measure	Sex	Source	5	6	7	8	9	10	11
Average	Girls	Espenschade (1960)	31.6	36.2	40.0	45.9	51.3	54.7	
Average	Boys	Espenschade (1960)	33.7	37.4	41.6	46.7	50.4	57.3	
Mean	Girls	Keogh (1965)	33.1	41.2	48.6	49.9	52.7	61.4	61.9
Mean	Boys	Keogh (1965)	35.9	42.9	49.1	55.2	56.6		66.5

50-Yard Dash (scores in seconds and tenths)

Measure	Sex	Source	9–10	11	12	13	14	15	16	17
Median	Girls	AAHPER (1975)	8.6	8.3	8.1	8.0	7.8	7.8	7.9	7.9
Median	Boys	AAHPER (1975)	8.2	8.0	7.8	7.5	7.2	6.9	6.7	6.6
Median	Girls	Fleishman (1964a)				7.8	7.7	7.2	6.9	6.8
Median	Boys	Fleishman (1964a)				8.6	8.5	8.4	8.3	8.6

Run (yards per second)

Measure	Sex	Source	5	6	7	8	10	11	12	13	14	15	16	17
Average	Girls	Espenschade (1960)	3.6	4.1	4.4	4.5	5.8	6.0	6.1	6.3	6.2	6.1	6.0	5.9
Average	Boys	Espenschade (1960)	3.8	4.2	4.6	5.1	5.9	6.1	6.3	6.5	6.7	6.8	7.1	7.2

30-Yard Dash (scores in seconds)

Measure	Sex	Source	5	6	7	8	9
Mean	Girls	Keogh (1965)	7.67	6.69	6.17	6.10	5.81
Mean	Boys	Keogh (1965)	7.47	6.78	6.28	5.94	5.66

600-Yard Run (scores in minutes and seconds)

Measure	Sex	Source	9–10	11	12	13	14	15	16	17
Median	Girls	AAHPER (1975)	2:56	2:53	2:47	2:41	2:40	2:37	2:43	2:41
Median	Boys	AAHPER (1975)	2:33	2:27	2:19	2:10	2:03	1:56	1:52	1:52
Median	Boys	Fleishman (1964a)				2:30	2:20	2:12	2:04	2:04
Median	Girls	Fleishman (1964a)	Median for girls aged 12–18 is 3:12							

9-Minute, 1-Mile Run

Yards Run in 9 Minutes

Measure	Sex	Source	10	11	12
Median	Girls	AAHPER (1975)	1514	1537	1560
Median	Boys	AAHPER (1975)	1717	1779	1841

Time to Run 1 Mile

Measure	Sex	Source	10	11	12
Median	Girls	AAHPER (1975)	10:29	9:58	9:24
Median	Boys	AAHPER (1975)	9:07	8:44	8:21

Table continued on the following page

Table 2-1. Central Tendency Values on Selected Measures of Physical Fitness. *(Continued)*

12 Minute, 1½-Mile Run, Age 13 and Older

Measure	Sex	Source	Yards Run in 12 Minutes	Time to Run 1½ Miles
Median	Girls	AAHPER (1975)	1861	16:57
Median	Boys	AAHPER (1975)	2592	11:29

Maximum Oxygen Intake (ml/kg/min)*

Measure	Sex	Source	*Mean Age*									
			6.1	*10.4*	*14.1*	*17.4*	*24.5*	*35.1*	*44.3*	*51.0*	*63.1*	*75.0*
Mean	Male	Robinson (1938)	46.7	52.1	47.1	52.8	48.7	43.1	39.5	38.4	34.5	25.5

Working Capacity (kg M/min)

Measure	Sex	Source	*Age*								
			6	*7*	*8*	*9*	*10*	*11*	*12*	*13*	*14*
Mean	Girls	Adams, Linde, and Miyake (1961a)	265	287	343	337	406	488	483	564	542
Mean	Boys	Adams, Linde, and Miyake (1961a)	331	368	438	472	551	650	703	739	964

*Many studies have determined mean maximum oxygen consumption values for young boys. Data emanating from these studies are summarized by Stewart and Gutin (1976).

EXPLOSIVE STRENGTH

Most standarized tests have employed the standing broad jump as an indicator of explosive strength, or muscular power. Espenschade (1960) compiled the results of several investigations of the standing broad jump and reported increases for boys between the ages of 5 and 17 and for girls between 5 and 12 or 13. From ages 13 to 16, girls evidently change little in broad jumping ability. Keogh (1973) found similar results in his review of literature. He reported increases in the broad jumping performance of boys between ages 7 and 17 and of girls between the ages of 7 and 12. At age 12 and continuing until age 17, girls' performance scores remained relatively unchanged. Median values on the standing broad jump item of the AAHPER Youth Fitness Test (1975) reflect improvement for boys and girls between 10 and 17. The performance scores for girls, however, appear to reach a plateau at age 13.

SPEED

Generally, speed has been assessed by measuring the performance of children on 35-, 50-, 60-, or 100-yard dashes. Espenschade (1960) reviewed research on running speed and transformed data emanating from a number of studies to yards per second. Espenschade reported that the speed of running increased for boys between the ages of 5 and 17, and for girls she noted increases at every age between 5 and 13. Following age 13 and continuing to age 17, girls showed a decline in running speed. Median points for boys on the AAHPER test (1975) indicate that performance improves on the 50-yard dash between the ages of 10 and 17, whereas for girls, performance improves on the 50-yard dash between 10 and 14 and decreases slightly between 14 and 17.

FLEXIBILITY

In regard to flexibility, Buxton (1957) found that the ability of children to touch their toes generally decreases between the ages of 6 and 12 and is followed by improvement until age 15. She also found that girls were able to perform the task better than boys. This finding was supported in a study conducted by Kirchner and Glines (1957), in which 1195 elementary school children were given the Kraus-Weber test. The percentage of children between 6 and 12 failing the flexibility item (touching toes) increased with age. In an earlier study, Phillips and associates (1955) tested 1456 elementary school children between the ages of 6 and 12 on the Kraus-Weber test. These investigators also reported a general decline in the percentage of older boys and girls passing the flexibility item, and they also found that the performance of girls was definitely better than that of boys at corresponding age levels. Median points for extent and dynamic flexibility in norms provided by Fleishman (1964a) for individuals between the ages of 15 and 18 generally show little change.

AGILITY

A very popular indicator of agility has been performance on a shuttle run. Median values of shuttle run performance for boys on the

AAHPER Test (1975) indicate an increase between the ages of 10 and 17. Median values for girls on the same test indicate improvement up to age 14 and little change from 14 to 17. Median points on the shuttle run reported by Fleishman (1964a) for boys and girls between the ages of 12 and 18 indicate improvement for boys but no improvement for girls. Improvements in performance at ages 5, 13, 16, and 17 are balanced by decreases in performance from previous years, at 14, 15, and 18.

Another test of agility that has been frequently used is the side step. Keogh (1965) found that his results and those of other studies agree that the performance of boys and girls increases from age 6 to age 11 and that the ability of boys exceeds that of girls at most ages.

CARDIORESPIRATORY ENDURANCE

A common method of measuring cardiovascular endurance in non-laboratory settings has been performance on long distance runs. Median values associated with the 600-yard run-walk on the AAHPER Youth Fitness Test (1975) indicate a definite improvement for boys between the ages of 10 and 17 and very little change for girls between these ages. In fact, a decline in the performance of girls begins at age 16.

Robinson (1938) compared the maximum oxygen intake per minute of 79 male subjects ranging in age from 6 to 75 years. This investigator reported an increase in maximum oxygen intake per minute for subjects during their developmental years (up to 17.4 years old), but he found little change during these years when differences in body size were considered. Adams, Linde, and Miyake (1961a) determined the physical working capacity for 243 California boys and girls, ages 6 to 14. The working capacity (expressed as kg M/min) of boys increased at each age between the ages of 6 and 14. The working capacity of girls increased at each year of age between 6 and 8, decreased from 8 to 9, increased from 9 to 13, and declined at 14. Adams and associates (1961b) found that the working capacity of Swedish school children increased with age, height, weight, surface area, heart volume, and degree of physical training and that the working capacities of Swedish boys were greater than those of Swedish girls of the same age. In reviewing literature related to factors affecting the working capacity of children, Adams (1973) indicates that body size and not age should be used in evaluating work capacity.

On the basis of their research and a review of other relevant research, Astrand and Rodahl (1970) indicate that there is no significant difference in the maximal oxygen uptake, as expressed in ml O_2/kg gross body weight, for boys and girls before puberty. There is a gradual increase with age that peaks at 18 to 20 years and is then followed by a decline (Fig. 2–7).

The 1975 revision of the AAHPER Youth Fitness Test includes the 9-minute, 1-mile run and the 12-minute, 1½-mile run for boys and girls aged 13 and older. Median times for girls in the 1-mile run are 10:29, 9:58, and 9:24 for ages 10, 11, and 12, respectively. Median times for boys are 9:07, 8:44, and 8:21 for the same ages. The median times for girls and boys aged 13 and older on the 1½-mile run are 16:57 and 11:29, respectively. Thus, boys are expected to surpass girls on these measures of cardiorespiratory endurance.

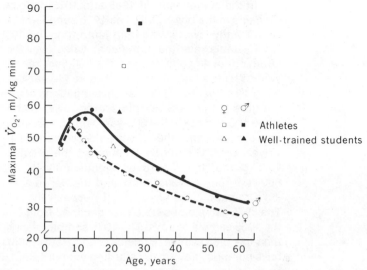

Figure 2--7. Mean Values for Maximal Oxygen Uptake (Expressed in ml O₂/kg gross body weight. The standard deviation is between 2.5 and 5 ml O₂/kg body weight.) *From:* Astrand, Per-Olaf, and Eric H. Christensen, "Aerobic Work Capacity," in *Oxygen in the Animal Organism,* edited by Frank Dickens and Eric Neil. Oxford, England: Pergamon Press, 1964, p. 298.

SUMMARY

On the basis of the literature review in this section, the following generalizations regarding group changes on selected measures of physical fitness seem warranted:

1. Normal boys tend to improve their physical performance throughout the development years. The one possible exception is in flexibility.
2. Normal girls tend to improve in measures of physical fitness until the ages of 12 to 14, at which time their performance frequently stabilizes and sometimes declines.
3. With the exception of flexibility, the test scores of boys generally exceed those of girls of the same age on measures of physical proficiency.

Changes in Physical Fitness 1958–1965–1975

Hunsicker and Reiff (1977) compared the 1958, 1965, and 1975 test results of boys and girls in the continental United States on the AAHPER Youth Fitness Test. The study population included public school children in the fifth through twelfth grades. On the basis of the results, percentile norms were established for each test item for boys and girls ages 10 through 17 inclusive. In the comparison of 1958 and 1965 data, girls made significantly higher scores in 39 out of 48 age and test item comparisons; boys made significantly higher scores in 54 out of 56 age and test comparisons.

In the comparison of 1965 and 1975 national samples, there were no gains in the boys' data. The 1975 sample of 14-year-old boys scored significantly lower in the long jump than the 1965 sample. Girls in the 1975 sample revealed significant gains over the 1965 sample in only seven out of 40 comparisons: the 600-year run by 13-, 14-, 15-, and 17-year-olds; the long jump by 13- and 14-year-olds; and the flexed-arm hang by 14-year-olds. These investigations also reported that 10-year-old girls in the 1975 sample scored lower than the 1965 group of the same age and sex in the 600-yard run. In endurance events, girls did not improve with age; the 10-year-olds performed about the same as the 17-year-olds. Girls aged 14 showed the greatest improvement of the 1975 group; they improved significantly in three of five items, the 600-yard run, the long jump, and the flexed-arm hang.

Dramatic gains were found between the 1958 and 1965 samples. The 1975 sample of boys either declined from or remained the same as the 1965 sample of boys. The 1975 sample of girls scored slightly better than the 1965 sample. Hunsicker and Reiff (1976) indicated that neither boys nor girls showed any startling overall gains.

Guidelines for the Implementation of Programs for Physical Development

Programs for physical development need to be implemented according to sound educational and medical principles for all children. In addition, certain diseases, conditions, or environmental factors create unique situations warranting special attention in program implementation; these are presented and discussed in detail in later chapters. Following are guidelines for implementing programs designed to enhance physical development of all participants.

1. Pre-school children should not be involved in physical development programs without the consent of their family physicians. Fait (1972) recommends medical examinations four times during the school career of a student: at time of entry, in the intermediate grades, at the beginning of adolescence, and at the end of school.
2. Physical activity or exercise with rehabilitative or other medical purposes must be conducted under the supervision of a physician.
3. Physical activity tolerance levels should be established for all participants. Initially, exercise should be mild and should progress gradually to more intensive activity.
4. Activity periods should progress from short, mild sessions to longer, more strenuous sessions.
5. Activity should be regular rather than sporadic. Participants should exercise at least three to four times per week.
6. Physical activity should be individualized, allowing participants to develop at their optimal rates, to meet their individual needs, and to work independently at times.
7. Efforts should be made to make physical activity fun by employing games or other experiences enjoyed by participants.
8. Programs designed to enhance physical development should ensure success and self-satisfaction for each participant.

9. Program leaders should set reasonable goals and plan activity so that optimal progress is made.
10. Program leaders must have a positive and enthusiastic attitude toward physical activity and toward participation. Praise of the children rather than reproof or ridicule is preferred.
11. Program leaders should arrange a desirable environment for physical activity, i.e., comfortable temperature, background music, showers.
12. In planning physical activity, provision should be made to involve as many parts of the body as possible and to develop the components of physical fitness appropriately and as needed.
13. Leaders and teachers should participate in exercise sessions whenever possible and reasonable. Such participation is motivating to participants.
14. Leaders and teachers should keep records of participant progress and should involve the children in record keeping.
15. Awards should be provided for participation and other accomplishments.

Activities for Physical Development

Activities to Develop Static, Dynamic, and Explosive Strength

WEIGHT TRAINING

Static strength can be developed through weight training including static strength activities in the program, increasing the tension exerted by increasing the velocity of shortening, and increasing tension by increasing the load. Dynamic strength can be enhanced through weight training by including dynamic strength activities in the program, increasing the repetitions involved in each activity, and increasing the load. Explosive strength may be developed by including explosive strength activities in the program, exerting movements in progressively shorter time periods, increasing the load, and increasing static strength. In implementation of programs, it is often helpful and motivating to have the children begin by lifting stuffed animals, moving to medicine balls and other inanimate objects, and finally using barbells and dumbbells:

1. For children of low fitness, use stuffed animals weighted with buckshot. This is a desirable method of beginning a progression program because relatively small weights can be included, small progressions are possible, and the program is more motivational. Examples of such activities are:
   a. Lift animals over the head with the hands while standing.
   b. Bend and lower animal to the floor with two hands from standing.
   c. Lift the animal over the head with one hand while standing.
   d. Bend and lower animal to the floor with one hand from standing.
   e. Perform one and two-handed arm curls while sitting.
   f. Raise and lower animals using the arms from the supine position.
   g. Raise and lower animals using the legs from the supine position.

h. Pass animals in circle group exercises.
i. Carry animals in relay games.
j. Throw animals at various targets.
k. Play "catch" using animals by throwing them over an obstacle like a net.
l. Throw animals as far as possible.
m. Place animals in a container as quickly as possible.

2. Use a medicine ball. The following are examples of activities that utilize a medicine ball:
a. Lift the ball over the head with two hands while standing.
b. Bend the body and slowly lower the medicine ball to the floor.
c. Pick the medicine ball up from floor.
d. Roll the medicine ball at duck pins.
e. Kick the medicine ball to a partner.
f. Pass the medicine ball overhead, between legs, from the chest, underhand and overhand in circle group exercises.
g. Carry the medicine ball in relay games.
h. Play "over and under" relay games.
i. Throw the medicine ball at various targets.
j. Play "catch" with the medicine ball by throwing it over obstacles like a net.
k. Throw the medicine ball as far as possible; use progressively heavier balls.
l. Play "catch" with a medicine ball using various passing techniques and gradually increasing the passing distance.
m. Play "self-catch," throwing the ball overhead, catching it when it returns, repeating as fast and as long as possible.
n. Raise and lower the medicine ball using the arms from a supine position.
o. Place the medicine ball on the front of both ankles and attempt to raise and lower the legs while lying.
p. Hold the medicine ball on the head and perform 3/4 knee bends.
q. Hold the medicine ball on the head and perform heel raising exercises.

3. Design similar programs using inanimate objects such as benches and chairs

4. Utilize activities in which a partner is carried or lifted, such as:
a. See how high a partner can be lifted.
b. See how high a partner can be lifted and held.
c. See how far a partner can be carried.
d. Play "piggy back" races.
e. See how many times a partner can be lifted.
f. See how fast a partner can be lifted.

5. For children at higher levels of ability, establish an isotonic strength training program using standard equipment.

CALISTHENICS

Dynamic strength may be developed through calisthenics by including dynamic strength activities in the program and by increasing the tension exerted in these exercises by making the velocity of shortening higher and by supplying greater resistance. It should be noted that for dynamic strength development, repetitions should not exceed ten. Dynamic strength may be developed through calisthenics, including exercises that require dynamic strength, progressively increasing the number of repetitions and making the calisthenic workout longer. Explosive strength may be developed by including explosive strength activities in the program, exerting movements in progressively shorter periods, increasing the load, and increasing static strength.

A sample program showing a progression beginning with an exercise period of relatively short duration, using mild activities, few exercises, and few repetitions is presented below:

1. Beginning:
   10 knee touchers
   10 sit-ups with knees flexed
   10 three-quarter knee bends
   12 modified push-ups
   12 vertical jumps
   24 repetitions of running in place.
2. Progression through increase in the number of repetitions:
   12 knee touchers
   12 sit-ups with knees flexed
   12 three-quarter knee bends
   12 modified push-ups
   12 vertical jumps
   24 repetitions of running in place.
3. Progression through increase in the vigorousness of exercise and the duration of workout:
   12 toe touchers
   12 V sit-ups
   12 three-quarter knee bends with weight on head
   12 push-ups
   12 vertical jumps
   24 repetitions of running in place
   12 squat-thrusts.
4. Progression that includes grass drills. Continue the same program, interspersing each exercise with a series of grass drills.

CIRCUIT TRAINING

Static strength may be progressively developed through circuit training by including static strength exercises within the circuit and progressively increasing tension by making the execution of each exercise faster and or supplying greater resistance. Dynamic strength may be progressively developed through circuit training by including dynamic strength exercises within the circuit, progressively increasing the number of repetitions of each exercise, progressively adding load (do not inhibit the performance of at least 15 repetitions), adding exercises requiring greater dynamic strength, increasing the distance between stations, increasing the number of stations, increasing cycles required for completion, or increasing the time spent on circuit training. Explosive strength may be progressively developed by including explosive strength exercises in the circuit, progressively adding load, executing exercises faster and running between stations as fast as possible, and increasing the number of circuits required in the same time period.

In addition to those activities listed in other parts of this section on strength development, the following examples of activities may be included in the circuit.

1. Example showing progression through increased resistance:
   a. Grasp a horizontal ladder and hang.
   b. "Walk" a horizontal ladder forward.
   c. "Walk" a horizontal ladder backward.
   d. "Walk" a horizontal ladder forward and backward.
2. Example showing progression through increased resistance and increased velocity:
   a. Grasp chinning bar.

  b. Hang from chinning bar with arms extended (increased load).
  c. Hang from chinning bar with arms flexed.
  d. Perform a chin-up (increased load).
  e. Increase chinning repetitions (increased load).
  f. Perform 10 chins, noting the time required.
  g. Attempt to perform 10 chins in a shorter time (increased velocity).
3. Example showing progression by increasing the vigorousness of the exercise, the resistance, and the velocity of shortening:
  a. Knee push-up.
  b. Increase repetitions to 10, noting time required (increasing load).
  c. Attempt to perform 10 knee push-ups in shorter time (increased velocity).
  d. Perform regular push-ups (increased load).
  e. Attempt to perform 10 push-ups, noting time required (increase load).
  f. Attempt to perform 10 push-ups in 10 seconds (increased velocity).
  g. Perform push-up, clap, push-up (increase vigorousness of exercise).
  h. Attempt to perform 10 repetitions (increase load) of push-up, clap, push-up
  i. Attempt to perform 10 repetitions in 10 seconds (increased velocity).
4. Example of activities conducted between stations:
  a. Run (increase distance between stations).
  b. Hop (increase distance between stations).
  c. Carry objects such as stuffed animals or medicine balls between stations.
  d. Run on toes between stations.
  e. Run uphill to stations.
  f. Jump obstacles or hurdles between stations.
  g. Rope swing to stations.

INTERVAL WORK

Interval work is a conditioning method in which stress is increased, rest is decreased, or both. Although it may be utilized with other activities, interval work is usually associated with running. Stress can be increased by increasing the distance of the run, the speed of the run, or the number of runs. Rest may be decreased by shortening rest periods, by changing the activity conducted during the pause, or both. For example, the performer may lie, sit, stand, walk, or jog during the "rest" periods. Examples of how the principles of interval work may be applied to running, running games, running relays, and circuit training for the development of dynamic endurance are presented below. Interval work is usually not employed for the development of static or explosive strength.

1. Running:
  a. Run 50 yards at half speed at the beginning and end of a 30-minute class.
  b. Run 50 yards full speed at the beginning and end of a 30-minute class (increasing the speed of the run).
  c. Run 50 yards at the beginning, middle, and end of a 30-minute class (increasing number of runs and decreasing rest periods).
  d. Run 75 yards at the beginning, middle, and end of a 30-minute class (increasing the distance of runs).

2. Running games:
   a. Play Red Rover with 20 players.
   b. Play Red Rover with 10 players (shorter rest periods between runs).
   c. Play Midnight (shorter rest periods than Red Rover).
   d. Play Crows and Cranes (shorter rest periods).
   e. Play Crows and Cranes with greater distances between goals (greater distance of runs).
3. Running relays:
   a. Begin a 25-yard running relay with eight players on each team.
   b. Increase the distance to 50 yards (increase distance of runs).
   c. Increase the number of runs in a relay.
   d. Decrease the number of players on each team (decrease rest period).
4. Circuit training:
   a. Establish a circuit consisting of nine stations.
   b. Move the stations farther apart (increase the distance of the run).
   c. Motivate pupils to complete the circuit as fast as possible (increase speed of the run).
   d. Make activities at stations more vigorous (less rest at stations).
   e. Have pupils perform activities at stations faster, thus decreasing the time spent at each station (shorten rest period between stations).

FARTLEK AND CONTINUOUS TRAINING

Dynamic strength may be developed through varieties of Fartlek or continuous training by increasing the intensity and duration of a workout. This may be done by progressively increasing the number of activities executed requiring muscular endurance and the number of repetitions completed, and by switching the exercises requiring more dynamic strength. The following is an example of progression for the development of muscular endurance through Fartlek or continuous training.

1. Beginning program: Following a warm-up, run 100 yards as fast as possible down a road or around a building; walk two minutes; perform three minutes of calisthenics; sprint for 50 yards; jog for 100 yards; run up a hill; walk down the hill; sprint 50 yards; walk one minute; jog one minute; sprint 50 yards; jog home.
2. Progressive Program: Following a warm-up, run 125 yards as fast as possible down a road or around a building; walk two minutes; perform three minutes of calisthenics; sprint 75 yards; jog 100 yards, run up and down a hill; walk 50 yards; sprint 50 yards; jog two minutes, sprint 50 yards; jog home.

ISOMETRICS

Isometric exercises may be useful in developing strength, since they can be done quickly and do not require elaborate equipment. Tension is increased in isometrics by exerting maximal effort for six to eight seconds. The contraction should be repeated six to eight times. Thus, progression is inherent in the form of the activity. The following are examples of isometric exercises:

1. Using playground balls:
   a. Squeeze the playground ball between the hands at various positions.

   b. Squeeze the ball against the ground or floor with both hands.
   c. Squeeze the ball against the ground or floor with one hand.
   d. Squeeze the ball against the wall with both hands.
   e. Squeeze the ball against the wall with one hand.
   f. Squeeze the ball between the legs (adduction) while lying.
   g. Squeeze the ball between the legs (adduction) while standing.
   h. Squeeze the ball against the floor with the leg while lying.
2. Using towels or jump ropes:
   a. Step on a towel or jump rope with one foot, grasp the opposite end of the towel or jump rope with one hand, take up the slack, and flex the arm against the resistance of the towel or jump rope.
   b. Step on towel or jump rope with both feet, grasp the ends of the towels or jump ropes and take up the slack, and flex both arms against the resistance of the towel or jump rope.
3. Design similar exercises for other muscle groups:
   a. Push against a wall or tree with hands supinated.
   b. Push against a wall or a tree with hands pronated.
   c. With side to wall or tree, abduct arm against resistance.
   d. While in prone position with elbows flexed, push against the ground or floor.
   e. Placing palms of hands together in front, push one hand against the other.
   f. With interlaced fingers behind neck, extend neck against resistance created by the hands.
   g. With interlaced fingers on forehead, flex head against resistance created by the hands.
   h. Inhale as much as possible, hold for six to eight seconds, and exhale slowly.
   i. While sitting, place hand on thigh and attempt to flex the thigh against resistance applied by the hand.
   j. Perform a push-up while a downward resistance is supplied by a partner to neutralize movement.
   k. Perform a sit-up while a downward resistance is supplied by a partner to neutralize movement.
   l. Perform movements against resistance supplied by an Exergenie.

PLAYGROUND ACTIVITIES

Select playground activities that require strength. Some examples follow:

1. Hang from a horizontal ladder, chinning bar, or rings with arms extended.
2. Hang from a horizontal ladder, chinning bar, or rings with arms flexed.
3. Mount parallel bars with straight arm support and walk forward and backward.
4. Climb jungle gym, horizontal ladder, or other equipment.
5. Move along a horizontal ladder hand-over-hand forward, backward, and sideways.
6. Perform chin-ups on various pieces of equipment.
7. Grasp chains of a swing and move feet over and back of the seat.
8. Execute inverted hang from rings.
9. Skin the cat on rings.
10. Hand-walk a rope hung between two poles.

11. Knee hang from rings.
12. Straddle parallel bars, perform a hammock hang.

COMBATIVES

These exercises offer an especially excellent medium through which strength may be developed. Examples are suggested:

1. Indian hand and leg wrestling.
2. Tug of War against a partner.
3. Team Tug of War.
4. Chicken Fighting.
5. Pushing a cage ball against a partner.
6. Team cage ball pushing.
7. King of the Hill.
8. Steal the Bacon (using a medicine or cage ball).
9. Wrestling.

ELEMENTARY GAMES AND ACTIVITIES

Games

Commando
Relays
Cross the Brook
Red Light
Pom Pom Pullaway

Activities

Frog Stand	Wheelbarrow Walks
Burpee	Jack In the Box
Coffee Grinder	Chinese Get-up
Animal Walks	Leap Frog
Scooter activities	Obstacle courses
Parachute Play (group)	Cargo Net activities
Rope Jumping	Tumbling
Crawling and Creeping	Swimming activities
Running in Place (Sewing Machine)	Movement Education activities

SPORTS, AQUATICS, GYMNASTICS, AND RHYTHMS

Swimming	Parallel Bar	Archery
Canoeing	Rings	Fencing
Rowing	Ropes	Tennis
Skiing	Ballet	Handball
Skin Diving	Tap Dance	Paddleball
Diving	Basketball	Squash
Bowling	Field Hockey	Track and Field
Stunts	Ice Hockey	Wrestling
Tumbling	Lacrosse	Weightlifting
Trampoline	Soccer	
High Bar	Baseball	
Horse	Football	

Activities to Develop Cardiorespiratory Endurance

CALISTHENICS

Progress in the development of cardiorespiratory endurance through calisthenics is ultimately based on increasing the intensity or duration of a calisthenic workout. The intensity of a workout may be increased by increasing the vigorousness of activities, increasing the speed of execution of exercises, increasing the number of activities included, increasing the number of repetitions of each exercise, and decreasing rest periods between exercises. The following is an example showing progressions that may be utilized for the development of cardiorespiratory endurance through calisthenics. Although the sample progression begins with a five-minute workout, it should be emphasized that longer workouts should be designed for the development of endurance.

1. Beginning level, conducted for five minutes:
   10 knee touchers
   10 sit-ups with knees flexed
   10 three-quarter knee bends
   10 modified knee push-ups
   10 vertical jumps
   20 repetitions of running in place
2. Progression by increasing number of repetitions and speed of execution (five-minute workout):
   12 knee touchers
   12 sit-ups with knees flexed
   12 three-quarter knee bends
   12 modified push-ups
   12 vertical jumps
   24 repetitions of running in place
3. Progression by increasing number of activities and speed of execution (five-minute workout):
   12 knee touchers
   12 sit-ups with knees flexed
   12 three-quarter knee bends
   12 modified knee push-ups
   12 vertical jumps
   24 repetitions of running in place
   12 squat-thrusts
4. Progression by increasing vigorousness of activity (five-minute workout):
   12 toe touchers (from knee touchers)
   12 sit-ups with knees flexed twisting right and left
   12 three-quarter knee bends with a weight on the head
   12 push-ups
   12 vertical jumps
   12 squat-thrusts
   24 repetitions of running in place
5. Progression by increasing the duration of the calisthenic program to six minutes, for example. Additional activities or repetitions might need to be added to maintain the intensity level.

INTERVAL WORK

Cardiorespiratory endurance is developed through interval work by progressively increasing stress while progressively decreasing rest.

Although it may be utilized with other activities, the progression that follows may be easily applied to running. Stress can be increased by increasing the distance of runs, increasing the speed of runs, and increasing the number of runs. Rest may be decreased by shortening the time of rest periods or by changing the intensity of activity performed during rest or both. For example, the performer may progressively lie, sit, stand, walk or jog during rest periods.

Apply the principles of interval work to active games.
1. Shorten rest periods:
   a. Begin with Red Rover with 20 players.
   b. Progress to Red Rover with 10 players.
   c. Play Midnight (shorter rest periods between runs).
   d. Crows and Cranes (progressively shorter rest periods between runs).
2. Increase distance of runs:
   a. Crows and Cranes.
   b. Crows and Cranes with increased distance between goals resulting in greater running distance.
   c. Crows and Cranes with further increase in distance between goals.
3. Increase speed of execution:
   a. Jump rope at a cadence of 15 jumps per minute.
   b. Progressively decrease the time allowed for 15 jumps.
4. Increase number of repetitions:
   a. Jump rope at a cadence of 15 jumps per minute.
   b. Jump rope at the same cadence for two minutes.
5. Increase speed of execution and number of repetitions:
   a. Jump rope at a cadence of 15 jumps per minute.
   b. Complete 30 jumps in one minute.

Apply the principles of interval work to relays as depicted by the following example.
1. Shorten rest periods — decrease the number of players on a relay team.
2. Increase the distance required in the relay.
3. Increase the number of repetitions — provide longer period for relay races, thereby running more relays.

Apply the principles of interval work to conditioning activities. The following is an example of how the principles of interval work may be applied to the development of cardiorespiratory endurance through the medium of running:
1. Begin with two 100-yard runs at 3/4 speed separated by an interval of 15 minutes.
2. Increase speed of the run — progress to two 100-yard runs at full speed separated by an interval of 15 minutes.
3. Increase the number of runs — progress to three 100-yard runs at full speed separated by intervals of 15 minutes.
4. Decrease the rest period — progress to three 100-yard runs at full speed separated by intervals of 12 minutes.

It should be noted that although running is used as an example, it is not the only medium through which cardiorespiratory endurance may be enhanced through interval work. Other activities include hopping, jumping, rope skipping, galloping, cycling, and swimming.

FARTLEK TRAINING

Cardiorespiratory endurance may be developed through Fartlek training by progressively increasing the intensity and duration of a workout. The following is an example showing the progression that can be used for the development of cardiorespiratory endurance through Fartlek training.

1. Run 100 yards as fast as possible down a road or around a building; walk for two minutes; perform three minutes of calisthenics; sprint for 50 yards; jog for 100 yards; run up a hill; walk down the hill; jog for two minutes; walk for two minutes; sprint for 50 yards; walk to home position.
2. Run 125 yards as fast as possible down a road or around a building; walk for one minute; perform four minutes of calisthenics; sprint for 75 yards; jog for 150 yards; run up and down a hill; jog for two minutes; walk for one minute; sprint 50 yards; alternately walk and jog to home position.
3. Run 125 yards as fast as possible down a road or around a building; walk for one minute; perform six minutes of calisthenics; sprint for 75 yards; jog for 200 yards; run up and down a hill; jog for two minutes; walk for one minute; sprint 100 yards; alternately walk and jog to home position.

In establishing a program of Fartlek training, it is necessary to consider the needs and interests of those for whom the program is designed.

CIRCUIT TRAINING

Cardiorespiratory endurance is developed through circuit training by increasing the intensity and duration of activity. The intensity of activity is increased by including more vigorous activities at each station, increasing the speed of execution of exercises at each station, and increasing the number of repetitions. The duration of activity can be increased by increasing the time spent on circuit training, increasing the number of stations, or increasing the number of cycles. In addition to those activities listed in other parts of the cardiorespiratory endurance section, the following are given as examples of activities that may be included in the circuit with examples of how progression for the development of circulatory endurance may be attained in each.

1. Organizational progression:
   a. Begin with a relatively easy circuit in which exercises are mild and involve few repetitions; include no more than nine stations, and require the completion of only one cycle.
   b. Gradually increase the number of repetitions executed at each station.
   c. Add another station.
   d. Gradually include more vigorous exercises.
   e. Increase the distance between stations.
   f. Ask participants to complete as many cycles as possible within a given time.
   g. Require additional completions of the circuit.
   h. Continue increasing the intensity or duration of activity by repeating these processes on a higher level and by motivating pupils to attain "target times," "target cycles," or "target stations."
2. Specific activities:
   a. Running (increase distance between stations).
   b. Hopping (increase distance between stations).
   c. Run hurdles (increase repetitions).
   d. Include a long distance run in the circuit and gradually increase distance.
   e. Bench stepping (increase cadence and duration).

  f. Run or hop over, under, and around obstacles (increase number of obstacles).
  g. Rope jumping (increase cadence and duration).
  h. Running in place (increase cadence and duration).
  i. Pedaling a stationary bicycle (increase cadence, resistance, and duration).

AEROBICS

Aerobics is a popular and effective system for developing cardiorespiratory endurance. Activities recommended in the program include walking, running, cycling, swimming, rope skipping, handball, basketball, squash, stationary running, stair climbing, and treadmill activity. Participants begin in "starter" programs and proceed to conditioning programs in progressively more demanding categories. Points are awarded for varying types and intensities of exercise for daily or weekly participation. Intensity of workouts is individualized according to the participant's level of fitness. Specific programs are described by Cooper (1968, 1970), and Cooper and Cooper (1973).

CONTINUOUS TRAINING.

Cardiorespiratory endurance is developed in continuous training by progressively increasing the intensity and duration of a workout. In this program, rhythmical exercises are particularly stressed in the beginning. As the individual reaches high gear, more time is devoted to test exercises, competition, and exercises done maximally in spurts. A typical program of moderate intensity would begin with a warm-up of 15 to 20 minutes, alternating hard and light exercises, including rhythmic endurance exercises for all parts of the body. The more intensive exercises are followed by periods of forced breathing. Following the warm-up, participants may engage in activities such as swimming, cycling, jogging, running, skating, skiing, canoeing, or rowing. In addition, intermediate tests of performance may be taken. Wind sprints may be run but without full effort.

ELEMENTARY GAMES AND ACTIVITIES

Lists of suggested games and activities for development of cardiorespiratory endurance follow.

Games

Crows and Cranes	Simple Tag
Midnight	Partner Tag
Hill Dill	Japanese Tag
Run, Rabbit, Run	Red Light
Relays	Commando
Brownies and Fairies	Pom Pom Pullaway
Charlie Over the Water	

Activities
Scooter activities
Obstacle courses
Rope Jumping
Swimming activities
Running in Place (Sewing Machine)
Movement Education activities

SPORTS AQUATICS, AND RHYTHMS

The following activities enhance cardiorespiratory endurance.

Cycling	Soccer
Canoeing	Badminton
Skiing (all types)	Track
Jogging	Wrestling
Square Dancing	Rowing
Clog Dancing	Skating (all types)
Basketball	Swimming
Field Hockey	Cross Country Running

Activities to Develop and Maintain Speed

SPEED TRAINING

The aim of speed or sprint training is to enlarge the diameter of a muscle and improve nerve performance so that the individual may contract and relax muscles more rapidly and consequently move faster. The implications for training are to develop these aspects primarily by exercising at maximum effort as fast as possible. For running progressions, increase the distance of runs (up to 200 yards) and the number of runs. The following is an example of the type of progression that may be utilized for the development of speed through speed training.

1. Assume that the starting level is running 25 yards as fast as possible without stopping.
2. Progress through increasing the number of runs — run a 25-yard sprint, recover, and run a 25-yard sprint.
3. Progress through increasing distance — run a 35-yard sprint, recover, and run a 35-yard sprint.
4. Progress through increasing the number of runs — increase the number of 35-yard sprints.
5. Subsequent progressions follow the sample pattern.

EXERCISE PROGRAMS

The following exercise programs may be used to develop and maintain speed.

1. Circuit training provides an opportunity for participants to run from one station to the next as fast as possible, includes exercises that develop neuromuscular coordination, and encourages participants to perform exercises as quickly as possible.
2. Calisthenics offer participation in exercises that develop neuromuscular coordination.
3. Weight training increases strength and provides exercises that develop neuromuscular coordination.
4. Fartlek training and continuous training provide an opportunity to run at maximal effort and offer exercises that develop neuromuscular coordination.

ELEMENTARY GAMES AND ACTIVITIES

The following games and activities are recommended for development and maintenance of speed.

Games

Hill Dill	Partner Tag
Midnight	Japanese Tag
Crows and Cranes	Red Light
Brownies and Fairies	Commando
Charlie Over the Water	Steal the Bacon
Simple Tag	Pom Pom Pullaway
Busy Bee	Beater Goes Round
Hide and Seek	

Activities

Scooter activities
Obstacle courses
Wheelbarrow
Rope Jumping
Animal Walks
Crawling and Creeping
Swimming activities
Relays
Running in Place (Sewing Machine)
Movement Education activities

SPORTS AND AQUATICS

Any of the following sports and aquatics enhance the development of speed.

Swimming	Football
Canoeing	Volleyball
Rowing	Table Tennis
Skiing	Track
Basketball	Wrestling
Soccer	Weightlifting
Baseball	

Activities to Develop Agility

CALISTHENICS

Agility may be developed through calisthenics by including exercises that require agility, increasing the speed with which they are executed, and progressing to higher levels. A program of such locomotor activities follows:

1. Run in place.
2. Run sideways.
3. Run forward—sideways—forward—sideways.
4. Run backward.
5. Run forward—backward—sideways—forward.
6. Shuffle forward.
7. Shuffle sideways.
8. Shuffle forward—sideways—forward—sideways.
9. Shuffle backward.
10. Shuffle forward—backward—forward—backward.
11. Shuffle forward—backward—sideways—forward.
12. Hop.
13. Hop forward.
14. Hop sideways.
15. Hop forward—sideways—forward—sideways.
16. Hop backward.

17. Hop forward–backward–forward.
18. Hop forward–backward–sideways.
19. Jump.
20. Jump forward.
21. Jump backward.
22. Jump forward–backward–forward.
23. Jump sideways.
24. Jump forward–backward–sideways–forwards.

CIRCUIT TRAINING

Agility may be developed through circuit training by including in the circuit exercises that require agility, increasing the speed with which these are executed, and progressing to a higher form of agility exercise. An example of activities follows.

1. Jump objects:
   a. Walk over a small object like a balance beam.
   b. Run over the object.
   c. Increase the size of the object to a 15-inch bench.
   d. Step onto the bench and step off.
   e. Jump onto the bench and jump off.
   f. Jump over the bench.
2. Jump over a rope:
   a. Walk over a rope raised 6 inches off the ground.
   b. Run over the rope.
   c. Jump over the rope.
   d. Increase the height to 10 inches.
   e. Run over the rope.
   f. Jump over the rope.
   g. Continue raising the height of the rope.
3. Jump over two ropes:
   a. Place two ropes parallel to each other 6 inches apart.
   b. Walk over the two ropes.
   c. Run over the two ropes.
   d. Jump over the two ropes.
   e. Continue increasing the distance between the two ropes and attempt to walk, run, and jump across the two ropes.
4. Step under ropes:
   a. Begin with a rope raised 5 feet off the ground.
   b. Walk or run under the rope.
   c. Lower the rope to 4½ feet.
   d. Walk or run under the rope.
   e. Continue lowering the rope.
5. Perform serpentine runs:
   a. Place objects like duck pins or chairs in a row with 10 feet between each.
   b. Run, weaving through the objects.
   c. Decrease the distance between objects and add more objects.
6. Use the New York State Agility Test at an exercise station.
7. Run or hop around objects.
8. Include a tunnel in obstacle courses or circuit programs.
9. Run backward using the serpentine.
10. Hop around serpentine course.
11. Crawl through bicycle tires.
12. In advanced stages, use agility exercises such as the squat-thrust.

GRASS DRILLS

The following drills may be used to develop agility.

1. Stand, sit, lie, stand, run in place, jump, sit.
2. Stand, sit, lie on front, lie on back, lie on front, stand.
3. Stand, sit, lie, sit, stand, sit, lie, sit, stand, squat-thrust.
4. Stand, squat-thrust, stand, lie, stand, squat-thrust, push-up, squat-thrust, push-up, sit.

ACTIVE GAMES

Play active games and relays involving agility. An example of a progression using the game of dodgeball follows:

1. Bombardment: Roll one ball — ball coming from one direction.
2. Bombardment: Roll two balls — balls coming from one direction.
3. Bombardment: Throw one ball — ball coming from one direction.
4. Bombardment: Throw two balls — balls coming from one direction.
5. Bombardment: Add more balls — balls coming from one direction.
6. Greek Dodge Ball: Use one ball — ball coming from two directions.
7. Greek Dodge Ball: Use two balls — balls coming from two directions.

ELEMENTARY GAMES AND ACTIVITIES

Any of the following games and activities help develop agility.

Games

Jack Be Nimble	Busy Bee
Dodge Ball	Japanese Tag
Hopscotch	Bombardment
Hill Dill	Steal the Bacon
Charlie Over the Water	The Huntsman
Simple Tag	

Activities

Animal Walks	Cargo Net activities
Scooter activities	Tumbling
Tire activities	Crawling and Creeping
Chinese Get-Up	Swimming activities
Leap Frog	Relays
Hula Hoop activities	Heel Click
Trampolining	Movement Education activities
Rope Jumping	

SPORTS, AQUATICS, GYMNASTICS

All of the following can be used to enhance agility development.

Stunts	Folk Dance	Badminton
Tumbling	Tap Dance	Fencing
Trampoline	Basketball	Skiing
High Bar	Field Hockey	Table Tennis
Horse	Ice Skating	Track
Parallel Bars	Soccer	Wrestling
Rings	Baseball	Cross Country Running
Ropes	Volleyball	

Activities to Develop and Maintain Flexibility

CALISTHENICS

Flexibility may be developed through calisthenics by including exercises that require a comparatively great range of movement, progressively increasing the range of movement in these exercises, progressively changing to those exercises that require a greater range of movement, and performing exercises at progressively increasing rates. An example of activities for the development of flexibility in selected joints follows:

1. Hip and vertebral joints:
   a. Bend body forward — stand erect.
   b. Bend body sideward—stand erect.
   c. Bend body forward — sideways stand erect.
   d. Increase range of movement by "swaying like trees."
   e. Touch toes with slight knee bend — stand.
   f. Bounce toward toe touch keeping knees straight — stand.
   g. Touch toes.
   h. Progress to windmill and wood-chopper exercises.
2. Ankle joint
   a. Dorsal flex ankle while sitting.
   b. Plantar flex ankle while sitting.
   c. Dorsal flex and plantar flex ankle while sitting.
   d. Heel- and toe-touch to the floor while sitting.
   e. Walk on toes.
   f. Walk on heels.
   g. Place a one-inch thick object on the floor and place toes on object while heels remain on floor; raise onto toes.
3. Knee joint (it should be noted that hyperflexibility of the knee joint is not recommended):
   a. Flex and extend knee joint through entire range of motion while sitting.
   b. Conduct three-quarter knee bends.
   c. Gradually move to complete knee bend (do not continue for many repetitions).
   d. Run in place.
4. Shoulder joint:
   a. Flex, extend, hyperextend shoulder throughout complete range of motion.
   b. Abduct and adduct shoulder throughout complete range of motion.
   c. Circumduct shoulder.
   d. Execute exercises involving shoulder joint.

CIRCUIT TRAINING

Flexibility may be developed through circuit training by including in the circuit exercises requiring flexibility, progressively increasing the range of motion in these exercises, and changing to those exercises that require a progressively greater range of movement. In selecting exercises, consideration should be given to establishing which joint is to be developed. Examples of activities that may be used follow:

1. Toe touching progressions.
2. Sit-up progressions.
3. Running on toes.
4. Running under a rope or other object.
5. Crawling through bicycle tires.
6. Jumping jacks.

7. Back extension progression from prone position.
8. Walking in high "inchworm" position.
9. Mimetic activities such as lame dog walk, elephant walk, and bear walk.
10. Crawling through a tunnel.
11. Jumping over objects.

OTHER EXERCISE SYSTEMS

Continuous and Fartlek Training may be utilized to develop flexibility, provided that appropriate activities are selected within the programs.

ELEMENTARY GAMES AND ACTIVITIES

The following games and activities help to develop flexibility.

Games

Hopscotch	Simon Says
Hide and Seek	Bombardment
Japanese tag	Do This, Do That

Activities
Forward and Backward Rolls
Cartwheels
Handstands
Animal Walks
Limbo Walk
Wheelbarrow Walks
Scooter activities
Obstacle courses
Trampolining
Walking and Crawling through Barrels and Tunnels
Tumbling
Crawling and Creeping
Swimming activities
Wring the Dishrag
Playground activities
Relays
Seesaw
Thread the Needle
Heel Click
Movement Education activities

Basic Equipment for Physical Development Programs

Very sophisticated and elaborate equipment is available in laboratories for the assessment and development of physical fitness. Although most leaders would like to have such equipment, economic considerations make that impossible. Fortunately, very satisfactory programs may be conducted with a minimum of equipment. In addition to the items listed below, it is strongly recommended that the utmost attention be given to the establishment of quality developmental playgrounds in communities. If playgrounds were designed to include developmental equipment, less attention would need to be given to formal conditioning programs in schools. Basic equipment suggested for physical development includes:

2 grip manuometers or dynamometers
1 leg and one back dynamometer
2 push-pull dynamometers
1 cable tensiometer
2 stop watches
2 adjustable chinning bars
3 exercise mats
Measuring tape
2 parallel bars differing in height and width
2 5-foot benches
Variety of weights
1 full-length mirror
1 height and weight scale
Calipers for the determination of anthropometric measurements
Medicine balls
1 jungle gym
Hurdles
Rope climbing system
1 parachute
1 universal gym
1 goniometer
1 pulmonary function analyzer
2 horizontal ladders of different height
1 cargo net

MOTOR DEVELOPMENT   3

The ability to move, balance, and master fundamental motor skills is important for play, exploration, and learning from the environment. The mastery of these abilities contributes to the physical, motor, social, and psychological development of the child. In addition, motor abilities serve as the basis for childhood and adult participation and success in sport, dance, exercise, and play. The relationship of motor development to other areas of development is discussed elsewhere in this book.

In the first section of this chapter, some general trends in motor development are identified and briefly discussed. Components of motor development are grouped into three categories and are discussed in detail in the second section. Selected phylogenetic locomotor movements are treated in the first category, non-locomotor phylogenetic motor abilities in the second, and the development of balance in the third. Based on the research presented in the second section, a schedule of motor development is presented in the third section. The final section contains examples of specific activities for the habilitation or remediation of motor development.

Some General Trends in Motor Development

A number of general trends in motor development have been identified on the basis of the characteristics of children. Although not unbending rules, these trends help to describe or explain the development of controlled motor development of the child — particularly during the first year or two of life. These trends are characteristic of the human species, rooted in the growth process, and generally independent of child-rearing practices or cultural influences. They serve to shed some light on the complexities of motor development. The five trends briefly presented here should aid the understanding of motor development and guide professionals in planning motor sequences for youngsters.

Cephalocaudal Trend

The cephalocaudal trend relates to a directional sequence of growth and development. It implies that muscular control and coordination proceeds in an orderly sequence from head to foot. Upper body muscular control precedes lower body muscular control.

Proximal–Distal Trend

The proximal–distal trend implies that parts of the body closest to the torso or center are controlled before those in peripheral or more distal portions. Thus, control of trunk movement and shoulder functioning precedes controlled functioning of the elbow, wrist, and fingers. At the lower extremity, motor control proceeds from the hips to the legs, feet, and toes.

Mass-to-Specific Trend

The mass-to-specific trend refers to the emergence and differentiation of specific patterns of movement from general or mass responses. For example, during early writing or manipulation of crayons, the child contorts feet, legs, head, trunk, lips, tongue, shoulder, elbow, wrist, and fingers. The manipulation of toys with the fingers and hand emerges from total or near total body involvement. Out of general responses, specific patterns of movement develop.

Bilateral-to-Unilateral Trend

The bilateral-to-unilateral trend describes the development of one-side preferences in motor activity from bilateral activity (activity involving both sides of the body). Thus, during the early years children may eat with either or both hands, strike or kick objects with either hand or foot, or cut paper with either hand. From such bilateral activity, preferences and "handedness" develop. In general, children experiment with both sides of the body before a preference is made.

Large-to-Small Muscle Trend

The child gains control of large muscle groups before control of small muscle groups is gained. In other words, gross motor control precedes fine motor control. In tossing a ball for accuracy or shooting a basketball, controlled movement proceeds from the relatively large muscles of the shoulder to the relatively small muscles of the elbow, wrist, and fingers. Writing and cutting are examples of fine motor activities that follow controlled movements of the shoulder, elbow, and wrist.

Components of Motor Development

Locomotor Phylogenetic Abilities

In the literature on this subject, basic movement abilities have been appropriately categorized in a number of ways; classifications are based on certain assumptions and reflect the views and purposes of the writer. For our purposes, basic movement abilities are separated into two groups. The first group consists of locomotor phylogenetic abilities and includes rolling, crawling, creeping, walking, running, jumping, galloping, hopping, and skipping. The second group encompasses non-locomotor phylogenetic abilities consisting of throwing, catching, and kicking. The list of abilities in each group is not intended to be exhaustive. Those discussed here, however, are the abilities commonly involved in play, physical recreation, or physical education, and they have been studied from a developmental perspective. The emphasis is placed on tracing the development of each of these basic abilities and, when considered necessary, on identifying basic mechanics important to successful performance.

ROLLING

One of the early locomotor abilities developed by the infant is the ability to roll. Bayley (1935) noted the ability to turn from back to side at 5.0 months and Gesell and associates (1950) report that children are able to roll over on their sides at 20 weeks. The ability to roll from back to stomach is placed at 7.0 months by Bayley (1935) and at 29.0 weeks by Shirley (1931).

CRAWLING AND CREEPING

Developmentally, creeping is preceded by crawling, and walking by creeping. One of the most complete studies of prone progressions was conducted by Ames (1937), who not only identified stages of prone progression but also provided data relative to the occurrence of each stage. In Figure 3–1, the 14 stages of prone progression are depicted, and in Table 3–1, the median age for each stage is presented. Ames indicates that the mean age for crawling is 34 weeks (crawling is defined as moving the abdomen in contact with the floor), for creeping 40 weeks, and for quadrupedal progression 49

Figure 3–1. Prone progression: summary view of stages one to fourteen. *From:* Ames, Louise B., "The Sequential Patterns of Prone Progressions in the Human Infant," *Genet. Psychol. Monogr.* 19:411–460 (1937), p. 436.

Table 3–1. Mean Ages for Stages of Prone Progression.

Stage of Progression	Age in Weeks
1. Knee and thigh forward beside body	28
2. Knee and thigh forward, inner side of foot against the floor	28
3. Pivoting	29
4. Attaining inferior low creep position	30
5. Attaining low creep position	32
6. Crawling	34
7. Attaining high creep position	35
8. Retrogression	36
9. Rocking	36
10. Creep-Crawling	36
11. Creeping	40
12. Creeping, near step with one foot	42
13. Creeping, step with one foot	45
14. Quadrupedal progression	49

Ames, Louise B. "The Sequential Patterns of Prone Progressions in the Human Infant," *Genetic Psychology Monographs* 19:411–460, 1937, p. 425.

weeks. Defining *creeping* as any means of locomotion whereby the body covers ground, Shirley (1931) reported the median age of creeping as 44.5 weeks. Thus, the data reported by these two investigators are relatively close.

WALKING

One of the major accomplishments of the young child is the ability to walk alone. During the first year of life, the child gradually increases postural control in a variety of movements that later help the child make controlled motor movements during walking. In addition, children generally follow a developmental progression leading to the ability to walk alone. Shirley (1931) found that children stand while holding onto furniture at 42 weeks, walk when led at 45 weeks, pull to a stand at 47 weeks, stand alone at 62 weeks, and walk alone at 64 weeks. Bayley (1935) found ages of 10.6 months for standing up, 11.6 months for walking with help, 12.5 months for standing alone, and 13 months for walking alone. Gesell and associates (1950) indicate that the period at which children begin to walk varies from about 12 to 18 months. Based on their research, Frankenburg and Dodds (1967) have developed normative data indicating that 25 per cent of all children are expected to walk well at 11.3 months, 50 per cent at 12.1 months, 75 per cent at 13.5 months, and 90 per cent at 14.3 months. In Figure 3–2, data from Shirley and the California Infant Growth Study (Bayley, 1935) related to motor abilities preceding and involving walking are identified and compared.

Figure 3–2. Comparison of data from Shirley (1931) and from California Infant Growth Study (Bayley, 1935) on the median age of first passing certain motor ability items. *From:* Bayley, Nancy, "The Development of Motor Abilities During the First Three Years," *Soc. Res. Dev. Child Developm. Monogr.* 19 (1935), p. 81.

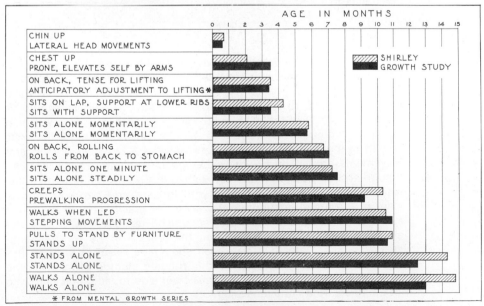

Following the ability to walk alone, variations and improvements in walking develop. Bayley (1935) reported ages of 16.5 months for walking sideways, 16.9 months for walking backwards, and 30.1 months for walking on tiptoe. Shirley (1931) indicates that speed of walking and length of step increase during the early stages of walking. Gesell and associates (1950) indicate that by the age of 3 years, heel and toe progression is well incorporated, and the child can take walking and running steps on his toes, walk in a straight line, and walk a long distance. Guttridge (1939) indicates that "the art of walking" is not perfected until 50 months.

In efficient walking, weight is transferred from the heel to the outside edge of the foot and finally to the foot itself. The arch enables the foot to absorb force over a greater distance and period of time, thereby decreasing the shock that results from contact with the ground. Forward movement is enhanced by pushing from the toes, moving the center of gravity forward and lengthening the stride (to a point). Arms swing easily and in coordination with movement of the legs. Toes are pointed forward and feet placed so that their inner borders touch an imaginary line straddled by the walker. Faults frequently observed in walking include walking with toes pointed outward, placing feet too far apart (waddle), pointing toes inward (pigeon toes), and taking too large a stride or pushing vertically to excess (bouncing walk).

Unless extreme deprivation is a factor, evidence supports the contention that age at which a child walks is dependent on growth and maturation rather than environmental conditions, experiences, or practice. Dennis (1960), comparing the motor development of children in three Iranian institutions, found that the children in institutions that restricted opportunities to play and move freely were retarded in beginning to walk. Studies by Dennis (1941) and McGraw (1935) support the contention that walking will develop without special teaching.

RUNNING

Running is a locomotor movement characterized by a period of nonsupport, i.e., there is a brief period in which neither foot touches the ground. There is no period of double support as there is in walking. According to Broer (1973), the first contact in running should be made on the ball of the foot or on the whole foot in such a way that the weight rolls across the foot to the ball. During running, the arms should swing to balance rotary effects of the body, and such arm movements should be coordinated with movements of the legs. Although arm swings are made across and in front of the body to some extent, they should not interfere with forward and backward movement of the arms. In running, the center of gravity should be ahead of the back foot, and the trunk should be upright. The knees and elbows should be bent to shorten the length of the lever and increase angular velocity. The knees should be brought straight forward and upward. Faults observed in running include running on the heels, excessively swinging the arms from side to side, and failing to lift the knees to a sufficient extent.

Figure 3–3. Running. *From:* Espen-schade, Anna, "Motor Development," in *Science and Medicine of Exercise and Sports,* edited by Warren R. Johnson. New York: Harper and Broth-ers Publishers. 1960, p. 432.

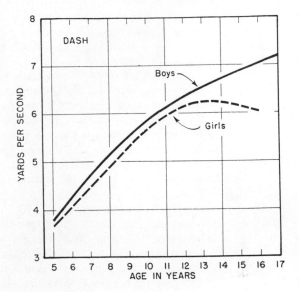

Between 18 and 24 months, the child begins to make rapid leg movements that are more a fast walk than a true run since they contain no period of non-support. Between the ages of 2 and 3, running begins, and Gesell and associates (1950) report that at 30 months the child is able to take short running steps on his toes. Between 4.5 and 5 years, the running of the child begins to more fully approximate that of an adult.

A number of studies have been conducted to determine running speed from age 5 to adulthood, and many tests of locomotor ability include items to measure performance in 30-, 35-, 50-, 60-, or 100-yard dashes. Espenschade (1960) has summarized the data from a number of investigations, and her summary appears in Figure 3–3. The scores reported for children aged 5 through 17 (except for age 9) indicate that performance of boys is consistently faster than that of girls, and that girls' scores begin to decline at age 14. Keogh (1965), on the basis of his own studies and his review of other studies of the running performance of children aged 5 to 11, reports similar results.

JUMPING

Studies of jumping ability have investigated the ability of the child to jump down from an elevation, to jump in place, to perform standing and running broad jumps, to jump over barriers or hurdles, and to jump and reach. One of the early forms of jumping is a kind of stepping down from or jumping down with one foot leading from some elevation. Gesell and associates (1950) indicate that the child is able to jump down a distance of 12 inches with one foot leading between 1.5 and 2 years. Wellman (1937) reports that children are able to jump down 12, 18, and 28 inches with one foot leading at 27, 31, and 43 months, respectively. In regard to the ability to jump down with both feet together, Gesell and associates (1950) report similar data. They indicate that the child is able to jump down 8 inches at about 3 years and 28 inches at about 4. The ability to jump from a height with both feet is preceded by the ability to jump off the floor with both feet, which Bayley (1935) places at about 28 months.

The ability to perform a standing broad jump of 8 to 10 inches by age 4 was reported by Gesell and associates (1950). The standing broad jump performance of children aged 5 and over has been investigated in many studies. Based on her summary of research, Espenschade (1960) reports that boys progress from 33.7 inches at age 5 to 88.4 inches at age 17. The average increase is about 4.5 inches per year. Jumping distance for girls progresses from 31.6 inches at age 5 to 63.0 inches at age 16. The performance of girls reaches a plateau at about age 13, resulting in a widening gap between the sexes from this age onward. Keogh (1973), comparing his data on standing broad jumping with summarized data from seven other studies done between 1960 and 1968, reports results similar to those of Espenschade (see Figure 3–4). He found that group performance on the standing broad jump increases 3 to 5 inches per year for both boys and girls from ages 9 to 11. He also reports that group performance for boys during those years exceeds that of girls by 3 to 5 inches per year. However, Keogh points out that learning and participation may affect performance, and he cautions against generalizing these results to apply to children in other cultures or populations.

In regard to performance on the running broad jump, Gesell and associates (1950) indicate that the child is able to perform a running broad jump of 23 to 33 inches at age 4, 28 to 35 inches by age 5, and 40 to 45 inches by age 6.

One of the jumping abilities that have been investigated in a number of studies is the vertical jump and reach. The score of the child on this task is the difference between the height a child can reach while standing and the height touched during a vertical jump. Gesell and associates (1950) report that the child is able to jump and reach 2.5 inches at age 5 and 3.5 inches at age 6. This is in general agreement with the review of literature by Espenschade (1960), who reported that boys were able to jump and reach 2.5 and 4.0 inches at

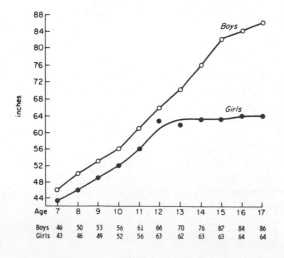

Figure 3–4. Standing broad jump performance based on data from seven studies (Keogh). *From:* Keogh, Jack, "Fundamental Motor Task," in *A Textbook of Motor Development,* edited by Charles B. Corbin. Dubuque, Iowa: Wm. C. Brown, Publishers, 1973, p. 59.

ages 5 and 6, respectively, and girls 2.2 and 3.5 inches at ages 5 and 6, respectively. Espenschade also reports that the ability of boys increases from 6.1 inches at age 7 to 12.2 at age 12. These findings agree with those of Johnson (1962), who reported values of 6.07 inches and 11.70 inches for first and sixth grade boys, respectively. Espenschade reports that girls progress from 5.7 inches at age 7 to 11.2 inches at age 12, and Johnson reports that girls progress from 5.67 inches at first grade to 10.51 inches at sixth grade.

In regard to high jumping, Gesell and associates (1950) found that the child of 4 can crouch for a high jump of 2 inches and at 6 can perform a standing high jump of 8 inches. Bayley (1935) found that children were able to jump over a rope less than 20 centimeters high at 41.5 months. It is apparent that jumping for height is influenced by practice, and, for children aged six and upward, generalizations of data must be made with considerable caution.

Although there are a variety of jumps, application of basic principles may be generally relevant in enhancing jumping performance. In jumping, force is enhanced by quick extension of the legs from a flexed position. The amount of flexion depends upon the strength of the legs. Crouching places the body in a position that enables the individual to exert force in a straight line through the joints and allows force to be generated through a greater distance. In jumping, a forceful and coordinated arm swing in the direction of the desired movement significantly enhances performance. When height is the goal, the center of gravity should be directly over the base of support and the feet should be only slightly spread, with one foot a little ahead of the other. When jumping for distance, the center of gravity should be projected at slightly less than a 45-degree angle. This means that the center of gravity must be ahead of the feet at take-off (body leaning forward). The feet should be spread at about shoulder width, and force should be executed equally from them. The toes should be pointed forward. After take-off, the knees should be bent to keep the center of gravity as high as possible and to avoid touching the ground prematurely. In a running broad jump, horizontal force is converted to vertical force by the lifting of the knees. In this jump, distance is enhanced by keeping the center of gravity over the take-off foot. The absorption of force during landing is enhanced by flexing the joints and falling on padded or other absorptive surfaces. Faults observed in jumping include failure to use the arms or to use them properly, to crouch to sufficient degree before take-off, to bend the knees during the running broad jump after take-off, and to place the center of gravity over the base upon take-off in the standing broad jump. Leaning too far forward is a commonly observed fault in preparation for a jump for height.

GALLOPING

Galloping is a forward motion of the body in which the same foot leads on each stride and the opposite foot is brought adjacent and parallel to it. Although this movement has not been studied as extensively as some other locomotor abilities, it is generally accepted that galloping appears before the ability to skip. Guttridge (1939) reported that 43 per cent of children in her observations were able to gallop at age 4 and 78 per cent at age 5. Gesell and associates (1950) indicate, however, that children are able to gallop at 30 months. It is possible that differences in the results of these studies may be partially explained by a difference in the quality of movement accepted as galloping.

HOPPING

Hopping is elevating the body off the ground from a standing position by one foot and then landing on the same foot. It may be done "in place" or in some direction. Studies of hopping consider the ability to balance on one foot, the number of hopping steps executed, rhythmic hopping, and precision hopping. The ability to hop depends on the ability to balance on one foot. Bayley (1935) indicates that this ability is attained at approximately 29 months and Gesell and associates (1950) indicate that the child attempts to stand on one foot at about 30 months. Frankenburg and Dodds (1967) report a median age of 3.4 years for hopping on one foot, and Wellman (1937) reports that the child is able to execute 1 to 3 hopping steps at about 43 months. Gesell and associates (1950) indicate that children are able to hop 4 to 6 steps on one foot at 4.5 years, 16 feet at age 5, and 50 feet in 9 seconds at age 6.

Keogh (1968a) investigated the ability of youngsters aged 5 through 7 to hop 15 feet on both the right foot and the left foot. He found passing rates of 37 per cent, 63 per cent, and 87 per cent for boys aged 5, 6, and 7, respectively. In comparison, the passing rates were 73 per cent, 93 per cent and 93 per cent for girls aged 5, 6, and 7, respectively. In an investigation of rhythmic hopping, Keogh (1968b) also found results favoring girls. In this study, Keogh administered 2–2 (hop twice on the right foot and twice on the left foot) and 3–2 hopping patterns. For boys, a 10 per cent success rate at age 6 increased to 67 per cent at age 9; for girls, a success rate of 50 per cent at age 6 increased to 87 per cent at age 9. For the 3–2 pattern, a 10 per cent success rate at age 6 increased to a 77 per cent rate of success at age 9 for boys, and a 37 per cent success rate at age 6 increased to 83 per cent for girls at age 9. In comparing these data with those in two of his other studies, Keogh (1968b) indicates that the data for boys in the 2–2 hop patterns are very consistent and indicate approximately 15 per cent success at age 6, which increases to 65 per cent at ages 8 and 9. He reports that girls perform about 17 to 40 per cent better than boys on the 2–2 hopping pattern. Investigating the ability of children to hop 50 feet, Keogh (1965) found that 31 per cent of boys and 19 per cent of girls were unable to complete the task at age 5; 13 per cent of boys and 1 per cent of girls were unable to complete the task at age 6; 6 per cent of the boys and 7 per cent of the girls were unable to complete the task at age 7. Girls performed the task faster than boys throughout the 5 to 11 range. By age 9, the median completion time for boys and girls was below six seconds.

SKIPPING

Skipping involves alternating a step and hop with one foot with a step and hop of the other. Successful performance thus requires the ability to step and hop, motorically cross the midline of the body, shift weight appropriately, and execute movements in an uneven but rhythmical fashion. Wellman and McCaskill (1938) place the ability to perform a kind of shuffle step at 38 months, the ability to skip on one foot at 43 months, and the ability to alternate feet at 60 months. Gesell and associates (1950) also indicate that the child is able to skip at age 5. However, the quality of the 5-year-old's performance may be questioned. Guttridge (1939) reported that 14 per cent of 4-year-olds, 22 per cent of 5-year-olds, and 90 per cent of 6-year-olds were able to skip well. Research indicates that the ability to skip appears at about age 5, that it is perfected between the ages of 5 and 6, and that even at 6 years there is a great variation in quality of performance.

Non-Locomotor Phylogenetic Abilities

THROWING

The ability to throw is important for successful performance in many sports and games in which a variety of objects are thrown in a variety of ways for a variety of purposes. For example, youngsters play games in which they throw overhand, underhand, or sidearm. They throw objects of varying sizes, textures, shapes, and weights. They may throw for distance, speed, or accuracy. In each case, at least a minimum amount of momentum must be generated, and in most cases the amount of momentum applied to an object is critical to optimal performance. The generation of momentum is enhanced by applying certain mechanical principles to throwing. These principles are evidenced by certain movements employed in the act of throwing and are generally constant even when the nature of the object, the type of throw, or the purpose of the throw varies.

When throwing for distance or for speed, it is particularly important to generate as much momentum as possible in order to project an object with as much speed as possible. The speed at which an object travels is directly proportional to the speed of the hand upon its release. Maximum speed is attained by employing a large backswing, rotating the body during the throw, transferring the weight of the body from the rear to the forward foot, and following through after release so that the musculature is not activated to inhibit motion prematurely. As the throw is made, each body part comes into action after the preceding body part has reached its maximum speed. When throwing for speed (attempting to project an object from one point to another point as fast as possible), the angle of projection should be as small as possible. The angle of projection is directly related to the speed of the object. When throwing for distance, the object is projected with backspin (if possible) at an angle of slightly less than 45°. When accuracy is paramount, the importance of speed is diminished, and the direction of the hand at release becomes critical. Objects move in a line tangent to the arc of the arm's motion at the point of release. Regardless of the purpose of the throw, adjustments to air resistance and spin must be made. Common faults associated with throwing include failure to bend the rear foot slightly during backward rotation, lack of body rotation, poor coordination and involvement of major parts of the body, failure to coordinate release with other bodily movements, failure to transfer body weight, failure to step forward, short backswing, poor follow-through, and holding the object in the palm of the hand.

At birth and during the first four months or so, the infant exhibits the grasp reflex, which evidently is a vestigial remnant of prehension. Touching the infant's palm elicits flexion of the hand. With increased age, voluntary manual manipulation or prehension develops. Halverson (1931) identifies ten stages in the development of grasping. From the first stage at about 16 weeks to the tenth stage at about 52 weeks, the child focuses on an object, makes contact with it, squeezes it, uses the forefinger in grasping, and begins to coordinate thumb and forefinger in the grasping function. Forefinger grasping appears at about 36 weeks and forefinger-and-thumb grasping at about 52 weeks. By 14 months, the child's grasping abilities are much like those of an adult. Gesell and associates (1950) indicate that the child brings prehension into practical use as early as 18 months and, at 2 years, begins to hold a crayon in the fingers.

In regard to the release of objects, Gesell and associates (1950) indicate that the advertent release of objects begins at about 44 weeks, and by 52 weeks the child attains considerable proficiency in dropping. These authors report that difficulties in the release of objects may be observed throughout the first 4 years. In regard to throwing, Gesell and associates (1950) indicate that the child tests his release abilities at 52 weeks by occasional throwing and at 18 months can throw, but generally with an inappropriately timed release that results in poor throwing direction. At 18 months, throws are made from an erect standing position and are preceded and followed by walking movements. At age 2, throwing posture does not change to a great degree but there is improvement in the timing of the release and some body rotation with the forward thrust of the arm. These researchers report that differences in ability favoring boys are apparent by 3.5 years and increase with age. It is clear from the literature that a variety of throwing patterns are exhibited prior to age 5. At about age 5, throwing patterns begin to approximate those of an adult.

A comprehensive and frequently cited study of the development of throwing patterns was conducted by Wild (1938). Using cinematographic records, she identified four throwing patterns. The first, occurring at ages 2 to 3, is characterized by movements of the arm conducted in the anteroposterior plane with a relatively erect body facing the direction of the intended throw. The second pattern is typical of children between 3.5 and 5 years of age. At this age, the body rotates to the right and then to the left as the feet remain in place. Thus, arm and body movements occur more in a horizontal plane than in the first stage. In the third pattern (ages 5 and 6), the child steps forward with the right foot while throwing with the right hand, rotates the body to the left, and completes the throw with a follow-through in which the body faces partially to the left following release. In the fourth pattern, the weight is transferred to the right foot during the preparatory phase, and the trunk rotates as the left foot moves forward and receives weight during the delivery. Wild reported that

Table 3–2. Ball Throwing Achievements of Preschool Children.

Distance of Throw in Feet	Motor Age in Months	
	Small ball (9½ in)	Large ball (16¼ in)
4 to 5	30	30
6 to 7	33	43
8 to 9	44	53
10 to 11	52	63
12 to 13	57	above 72
14 to 15	65	
16 to 17	above 72	

Wellman, Beth L. "Motor Achievements of Preschool Children," *Child. Educ.* 13:311–316, 1937, p. 311. Reprinted by permission of the Association for Childhood Education International, 3615 Wisconsin Avenue, N.W., Washington, D.C.

boys attained the fourth pattern by 6.5 years; however, girls of this age had not completely developed the arm movements associated with this stage.

In analyzing throwing ability, a number of investigators have studied the distance of throwing. In Table 3–2, results reported by Wellman (1937) relative to the throwing distance of youngsters aged 30 months to 72 months are presented. Gesell and associates (1950) indicate that 5-year-old boys and girls are able to throw a baseball

Figure 3–5. Ball throw mean scores for boys and girls ages 6 through 11 (Santa Monica 1963–1964). *From:* Keogh, Jack, "Motor Performance of Elementary School Children," Los Angeles: Physical Education Department, University of California, 1965, p. 22.

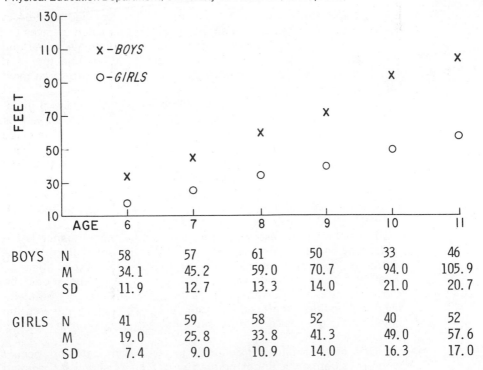

		AGE 6	7	8	9	10	11
BOYS	N	58	57	61	50	33	46
	M	34.1	45.2	59.0	70.7	94.0	105.9
	SD	11.9	12.7	13.3	14.0	21.0	20.7
GIRLS	N	41	59	58	52	40	52
	M	19.0	25.8	33.8	41.3	49.0	57.6
	SD	7.4	9.0	10.9	14.0	16.3	17.0

about 24 feet and 15 feet, respectively. Like Wild (1938), Gesell and associates (1950) note sex differences in the ability to throw. In summarizing studies conducted on the throwing distance of boys and girls aged 5 to 17, Espenschade (1960) found that scores of boys exceeded those of girls throughout this age range. In addition, she found that the scores of boys increase with increasing age, but that the scores of girls reach a plateau at age 13 and decline slightly at 16. Keogh (1965) found that boys were able to throw a 12-inch softball, without a running start, a distance of 34.1 feet at age 6 and progress to 105.9 feet at age 11 (Fig. 3–5). He reported that girls averaged throws of 19.0 feet at age 6 and 57.6 feet at age 11. In the AAHPER Youth Fitness Test (1965), the norms on the softball throw for distance place median performances at 96 feet for boys aged ten, 190 feet for boys aged 17, 50 feet for girls aged 10, and 75 feet for girls aged 17.

Although not nearly as extensive, some research has been conducted to determine the accuracy and velocity of throwing as a function of age. However, methodologies of the various researchers have varied considerably, and valid comparisons are difficult to make. The few studies conducted relative to velocity and accuracy of throwing indicate improvement with age. In addition, research is available indicating that throwing accuracy of boys exceeds that of girls. For example, Keogh (1965) found that the throwing accuracy of boys exceeded that of girls between the ages of 7 and 9. However, the performance of both boys and girls improved with age.

CATCHING

Like throwing, catching is an important skill for participation in various childhood games and sports. The ability to catch involves the ability to track objects, to move the body, to coordinate visual and motor abilities for interception of an object, to judge trajectory, and to move the hands, arms, and elbows in order to absorb force most effectively.

In catching, there are certain basic principles of receiving impetus that should be incorporated. The force of an object should be absorbed over as great a distance and time as possible. This is made possible by "giving with" a ball or other object as it makes contact with the hands. Children frequently do this naturally as they pull their hands back in catching an object. Time and distance are increased by using body parts to absorb force, i.e., the fingers, wrist, elbow, and shoulders. In addition, absorption of force is enhanced by catching with a padded object such as a baseball mitt.

In catching, it is also critical to maintain balance. Balance is enhanced by enlarging the base of the body in the direction of the object, lowering the center of gravity, and spreading the legs at somewhat less than shoulder width. In catching, the knees should be slightly bent and a "forward and backward" stance should be maintained. In addition, the catcher should keep the body in line with the object to the greatest extent possible instead of reaching to one side or the other for it.

One of the injuries frequently involved with catching occurs when a ball strikes a finger pointed at it. Fingers should be pointed upward for receiving balls above the waist and pointed downward when balls are received below the waist, and the palms should be held up when receiving an object from overhead. The fingers should be held apart and slightly curved. Faults associated with catching include pointing the fingertips toward the object to be caught, failing to maintain a stable position, failing to "give with" the ball, failing to keep the body in line with the ball, failing to coordinate visual and motor movements, and failing to relax and hold the elbows away from the body during the catch.

A child's first motor ability related to catching appears during the first year and generally involves stopping a gently rolled ball while sitting. By 34 months, Wellman and McCaskill (1938) report, the child is able to catch a large ball (16 1/4 inches in circumference) with the arms straight. This finding is in agreement with that of Gesell and associates (1950), who indicate that the child can catch a large ball at age 3 with the arms stiffly extended. At 44 months, Wellman and McCaskill (1938) report, the child is able to catch a large ball with elbows in front of the body. Gesell and associates (1950) indicate that the child is able to catch a large ball with the arms flexed at the elbows and move in accordance with the direction of the ball by age 4. Wellman and McCaskill (1938) report that the child is able to catch a small ball (9 1/2 inches in circumference) with elbows in front of the body at 50 months and to catch a large ball with elbows at the sides of the body at 68 months. Gesell and associates (1950) found that children judge trajectory at age 5 considerably better than at 4, and that, at age 6, the child can catch a ball tossed chest high from a distance of one meter with one hand in two out of three trials. Cratty (1970c) found that the average 5-year-old child is able to catch a playground ball 8 inches in diameter from three to four times out of

Figure 3–6. A microcephalic child learning to roll and to stop a large ball.

five attempts when the ball is bounced to him at chest height from a distance of 15 feet. Cratty reports that girls are more proficient than boys in this task.

Methods of research on catching ability of 6- to 12-year-old children have varied considerably — thus inhibiting comparative analysis. Cratty and Martin (1969c) studied the ability of children to intercept, with the first finger, a ball on a string swinging through a 180° arc before the ball completed its third swing. These investigators found that, in five trials, children could usually touch the ball one time at age 6, two times at age 7, three times at age 8, and four times at 8.5 to 11 years of age.

Keogh (1968a) tested the catching ability of children on three different tasks. In the first, he tested the ability of children aged 5 to 7 to drop a tennis ball with one hand and catch the ball with two hands (two-hand catch) after one bounce. Children were given 10 trials with the right hand and 10 trials with the left hand (total of 20 trials). Keogh found that the mean number of catches for the 20 trials was 10.9 at age 5 and 15.4 at age 6. In addition, he found that only 2 per cent of the 7-year-olds scored less than 5 on individual trials of 10. In another test (one-hand catch), Keogh recorded the number of times the child was able to drop or throw a tennis ball down with one hand and catch it with the same hand after one bounce. The 20 trials given consisted of 10 with each hand. Keogh found that the mean number of catches for the trials was 7.3 at age 5 and 14.2 at age 6. Only 8 per cent of the children scored less than 7 on individual trials of 10 for the one-hand catch. Keogh noted that girls performed as well as boys on these tasks. In the third test (table tennis ball catch), the child was given six chances (three with each hand) to catch a table tennis ball dropped on a table top by an examiner. Using the criterion of two catches in three attempts for both hands, the passing percentages were 22 per cent of 6-year-olds, 45 per cent of 7-year-olds, 70 per cent of 8-year-olds, and 83 per cent of 9-year-olds.

KICKING

Although important to certain games and sports, kicking ability has not been studied to the extent that throwing and catching abilities have. Gesell and associates (1950) point out that in attempting to kick at 18 months, the child typically steps on the ball. They found that the ability to kick appears between 18 and 24 months of age. Based on their research, Frankenburg and Dodds (1967) have established norms relative to the child's ability to kick a ball forward. They indicate that 25 per cent of all children are expected to successfully complete the task at 15.0 months, 50 per cent at 20 months, 75 per cent at 22.3 months, and 90 per cent at 2 years. These investigators also report that kicking abilities appear earlier in boys than in girls. Gesell and associates (1950) found that the child can kick a soccer ball through the air a distance of 8 to 11.5 feet at age 5 and 10 to 18 feet at age 6. Johnson (1962) conducted a study of kicking for accuracy. Children in grades one through six were asked to kick a soccer ball to a target area at distances of 10, 20, and 30 feet. Results indicate that the performance scores generally increased at higher grades. Johnson provides percentile values for boys and girls in grades one through six.

As was true in throwing, the generation of momentum is important in kicking. Momentum is enhanced by a backswing of the kicking leg during which the swing is made from the hip. During the backswing and prior to contact with the ball, the knee is bent to increase angular velocity. However, when contact is made, it is extremely important for the knee of the kicking leg to be completely extended (straight). Contact is generally made with the instep of the foot at a point slightly below the center of gravity. When kicking for distance, the angle of projection should be slightly less than 45°. Other things being equal, the speed of the projected ball will be directly proportional to the speed of the foot upon contact with the ball. For maximum force, actions of the various body parts must be coordinated. The arms should be involved to generate force and to help maintain balance during the kick. Follow-through is important so that movement is not inhibited prior to contact with the ball.

Although it is not dealt with to a great extent in the literature, the qualitative dimension is as important in kicking as in other skills. For example, early kicking abilities rarely exhibit a suitable range of motion in the leg's follow-through. Early attempts require placement of the ball directly in front of the child. Balance, power, and range of motion gradually develop as the child matures. In addition, improved performance is expected as children are taught how to kick in elementary school programs.

Balance Abilities

The ability to balance undergirds virtually every movement an individual engages in. Balance is necessary for relatively simple tasks such as holding the head erect, sitting, standing, and walking as well as for successful performance in sport, dance, exercise, and play. In view of the need to create muscular tension to maintain equilibrium, balance activities have been advocated by Kephart (1971) for the development of "laterality" and "directionality" in children. Basically, balance involves the ability to make postural adjustments in order to maintain the center of gravity over the base of support or to maintain equilibrium. Balance depends upon the vestibular apparatus, basic reflexes, and unconscious as well as conscious abilities to make postural adjustments.

Balance tasks are generally separated into two categories: *static* and *dynamic*. *Static* balance is the ability to maintain equilibrium while the body is stationary, and *dynamic* balance refers to the ability to maintain equilibrium during movement. Keogh (1965) reports that correlation coefficients between static and dynamic tests often range from .4 to .6. In determining balance abilities, investigators have employed both static and dynamic tasks. Static tasks that have been used include the ability to stand (for infants), standing on one foot (with eyes open or closed), standing on one foot on a narrow base of support, and balancing on tiptoe. Dynamic balance tasks generally employed in developmental studies include walking straight or curved lines or walking balance beams of various heights, widths, and

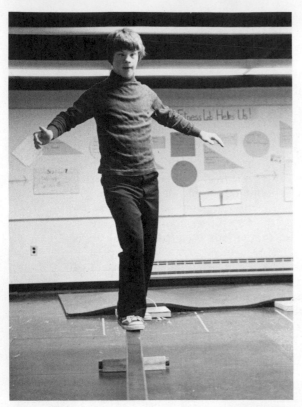

Figure 3–7. Balance: an important skill for sports participation.

Figure 3–8. A basic balance task.

lengths. In more recent years, balance abilities have been studied with the benefit of stabilometers and ladders.

One of the early indicators of the child's ability to maintain static balance is, of course, evidenced by the ability to stand alone. As was mentioned previously, this ability appears shortly after the first year. The next major phase occurs at about 2.5 years. Bayley (1935) places the ability to stand on one foot at 29 months and the ability to stand on a walking board with both feet at 31 months. Frankenburg and Dodds (1967) place the ability to balance on one foot for one second at a median of 2.5 years. Gesell and associates (1950) report that the child attempts to stand on one foot at 30 months, is able to hold the position for two seconds at 42 months, can balance on one foot for four to eight seconds by age 4, and can balance on one foot indefinitely at age 5. Cratty has conducted several studies of static balance, and Cratty and Martin (1969c) report that 5-year-old children cannot balance on one foot with eyes closed but can hold a balancing position on one foot with eyes open and arms folded across the chest from four to six seconds. These investigators also found that the balance performance of boys exceeded that of girls at ages 6 and 7, but that the performance of both sexes is similar in older children; a plateau tends to develop in the performance of boys between the ages of 6 and 8 years. Fleishman (1964a), studying the static balance performance of youngsters aged 13 to 18, found relatively little change at these ages and the performance of boys to be slightly better than that of girls. In his test, the subject balances for as long as possible on a 3/4-inch wide rail with hands on hips, eyes closed, on whichever foot she or he prefers. Keogh (1968a), surveying the ability of 5-year-old children to stand on tiptoe for ten seconds with hands on hips, found that this test was passed by 70 per cent of boys and 100 per cent of girls tested in his study.

Dynamic balance has been a subject of study in many investigations. In summarizing results, care must be taken to account for the various procedures used in testing children. Using a walking board 6 centimeters wide, 10 centimeters high, and 2.5 meters long, Bayley (1935) found that children stand on the board at 31 months, attempt to step while on the board at 32.8 months, and take two or more alternating steps on the board before stepping off at 38 months. Gesell and associates (1950) indicate that by age 4, the child is able to negotiate a walking board 4 centimeters wide, 10 centimeters high, and 2.5 meters long in about 14 seconds, stepping off no more than twice at age 5, and in 9 seconds, stepping off less than once per trial, at age 6.

Several studies have been conducted to determine the dynamic ability of children between 5 and 18 years. These have generally indicated spurts and plateaus in balance performance. In one of the earliest studies, Seashore (1947) measured the dynamic balance performance of boys (aged 5 to 18) on the walking board test. He found a steady improvement in the performance of the boys from ages 5 to 11 and a subsequent leveling-off until 18 years of age. He found an average gain of about 10 points per year between the ages of 5 and 11. Espenschade, Dable, and Schoendube (1953) measured the walking board performance of schoolboys between 11.5 and 16.5 years of age. Their data indicate that the rate of change from 13 to 15 is

Figure 3–9. Throwing and catching while maintaining balance.

much less than that occurring earlier or later. These authors hypothesized that growth in dynamic balance is retarded during puberty. They speculated that this retardation may be due to the rapidity of change in physique and body proportions during this time.

Keogh (1968) compared the results of his studies of beam walking with those of other investigations of boys and girls between the ages of 5 and 11. He found that performance on beam walking is not rectilinear and that the timing of spurts and plateaus varies in different studies. In Keogh's 1964 data, dynamic balance performance scores of boys consistently improved except for a leveling-off period from ages 7 to 9. For girls, a significant increase in performance from 7 to 8 was followed by a leveling-off from 8 to 10. These plateaus and spurts resulted in similar performances for boys and girls at ages 5, 6, 10, and 11 and slightly better performances for girls between 7 and 9.

Bachman (1961) measured the stabilometer and vertical ladder performances of 320 subjects to determine the influence of age and sex on motor performance and on the amount and rate of learning. He found similar scores for boys and girls in the preadolescent years. However, he noted an apparent adverse effect in adolescence that occurred earlier for females than for males.

In helping children to improve in balance activities, several basic principles may be applied in various settings. First, balance depends upon keeping the center of gravity over the base of support. The base of support may be the feet (in walking), the two hands and head (in executing a headstand), or the hands (in performing a frog stand). The greater the distance of the center of gravity from the center of the base, the more difficult it is to execute a balance movement. In addition, a force applied a greater distance away from the center of the base has a greater effect than the same force applied toward the center of the base. For example, individuals of different weight may balance using a seesaw if the heavier of the two moves closer to the fulcrum or the lighter person moves further away from the fulcrum. The distance necessary for the lighter person to move away diminishes proportionately the further he or she sits from the fulcrum. When balancing or lifting weights, it is easier (takes less effort) to balance or lift an object held closer to the body than one held away from the body. Further, compensations can be made when handling different weights. In carrying objects, the individual compensates for carrying a pail of water by lifting the opposite arm. In motor activities, a child may compensate for a prosthetic device by correspondingly adjusting movements on the opposite side of the body.

Second, balance is enhanced by the lowering of the center of gravity. The importance of this principle is evidenced when one compares standing and sitting in a canoe. By bending the knees and slightly flexing other major joints of the body, balance is enhanced in ice skating, wrestling, catching, fencing, and other activities in which impact is received from another person or object. In addition, balance is enhanced by broadening the base of support (to a point). The precariousness of balance on a narrow base is evidenced in ice skating or in walking a narrow balance beam.

Balance may also be enhanced by enlarging the base in the direction of the force to be received. For example, a child runs into the wind by leaning forward, receives a blow from the left by striding to the left, catches a ball with a forward-backward stance, and stops running with a forward-backward stance. In each case, the possibility of maintaining balance is increased by enlarging the base in the direction of the force and by causing the center of gravity to shift toward the force, thus requiring the center of gravity to move a greater distance before disequilibrium occurs. The greater the distance, the greater the possibility of maintaining equilibrium, other things being equal.

Balance is enhanced by those sensations or perceptions that aid individuals in orienting themselves in space. Thus, auditory and visual perceptions may be employed to enhance balance. It is well known that it is easier to maintain balance in twirling if the eye is focused on a point in space. Blind children orient themselves on the trampoline by attending to the voice of an instructor at the head of the trampoline. It is much more difficult to balance on one leg with the eyes closed than with the eyes open. Any doubters are invited to cross a swaying footbridge to its middle, close their eyes, move their heads toward the sky and then toward the water, open their eyes, and attempt to maintain balance. It is recommended that those attempting such a task be expert swimmers!

Table 3–3.   Schedule of Motor Development.

Year	Ability	Specific Age	Source of Data
0–1	Rolls from back to side	5 months	Bayley (1935)
		20 weeks	Gesell et al. (1950)
	Rolls from back to stomach	7 months	Bayley (1935)
		29 weeks	Shirley (1931)
	Grasps with forefinger	36 weeks	Halverson (1931)
	Crawls	34 weeks	Ames (1937)
	Creeps	40–45 weeks	Shirley (1931)
			Ames (1937)
	Begins advertent release of objects	44 weeks	Gesell et al. (1950)
	Grasps with forefinger and thumb	52 weeks	Halverson (1931)
	Shows considerable proficiency in dropping objects	52 weeks	Gesell et al. (1950)
1–2	Stands alone	62 weeks	Shirley (1931)
		12.5 months	Bayley (1935)
	Walks alone	12.1 months	Frankenburg and Dodds (1967)
		64 weeks	Shirley (1931)
		13 months	Bayley (1935)
	Grasps with approximately adult ability	14 months	Halverson (1931)
	Walks sideways	16.5 months	Bayley (1935)
	Walks backwards	16.9 months	Bayley (1935)
	Throws from erect standing position	18 months	Gesell et al. (1950)
2–3	Jumps down from a 12-in elevation with one foot leading	27 months	Wellman (1937)
	Jumps off the floor with both feet	28 months	Bayley (1935)
	Balances on one foot	29 months	Bayley (1935)
		30 months	Gesell et al. (1950)
	Takes short running steps on toes	30 months	Gesell et al. (1950)
	Throws a 9.5-in or 16.25-in ball 4 to 5 ft	30 months	Wellman (1937)
	Walks on tiptoe	30.1 months	Bayley (1935)
	Jumps down from 18-in elevation with one foot leading	31 months	Wellman (1937)
	Stands on walking board 6 cm wide	31 months	Bayley (1935)
	Attempts to step while on walking board	32.8 months	Bayley (1935)
	Catches a 16.25-in ball with arms straight	34 months	Wellman and McCaskill (1938)
3–4	Jumps down from 8-in elevation with both feet together	36 months	Wellman (1937)
			Gesell et al. (1950)
	Hops on one foot	3.4 years	Frankenburg and Dodds (1967)
	Jumps over a rope less than 20 cm high	41.5 months	Bayley (1935)
	Executes 1–3 hopping steps	43 months	Wellman (1937)
	Throws a 9.5-in ball 8 to 9 ft	44 months	Wellman (1937)
	Catches a 16.25-in ball with elbows in front	44 months	Wellman and McCaskill (1938)
4–5	Jumps down with both feet together from 28-in elevation	4 years	Gesell et al. (1950)
	Balances on one foot for 4–8 sec	4 years	Gesell et al. (1950)
	Performs broad jump 8–10 in	4 years	Gesell et al. (1950)
	Performs running broad jump 23–33 in	4 years	Gesell et al. (1950)
	Catches a 9.5-in ball with elbows in front	50 months	Wellman and McCaskill (1938)
	Throws a 9.5-in ball 10–11 ft	52 months	Wellman (1937)
	Throws a 9.5-in ball 12–13 ft	57 months	Wellman (1937)
5–6	Catches a bounce pass 3–4 times out of 5	5 years	Cratty (1970c)
	Kicks a soccer ball through the air a distance of 8–11.5 ft	5 years	Gesell et al. (1950)
	Steps while throwing	5 years	Gesell et al. (1950)
	Stands on tiptoe for 10 sec	5 years	Keogh (1968a)
	Alternates feet in skipping	5 years	Wellman and McCaskill (1938)

Table 3–3. Schedule of Motor Development. *(Continued)*

Year	Ability	Specific Age	Source of Data
	Balances on one foot 4–6 sec	5 years	Cratty and Martin (1969c)
	Most children are able to gallop	5 years	Guttridge (1939)
	Most girls hop 15 ft on both right and left feet	5 years	Keogh (1968a)
	Runs: Boys—3.8 yd/sec Girls—3.6 yd/sec	5 years	Espenschade (1960)
	Performs standing broad jump: Boys—33.7 in Girls—31.6 in	5 years	Espenschade (1960)
	Performs jump and reach: Boys—2.5 in Girls—2.2 in	5 years	Espenschade (1960)
	Throws a 9.5-in ball 14–15 ft	65 months	Wellman (1937)
	Catches a 16.25-in ball with elbows at side of body	68 months	Wellman and McCaskill (1938)
6–7	Skips well	6 years	Guttridge (1939)
	Throws softball for distance: Boys—34.1 ft Girls—19.0 ft	6 years	Keogh (1965)
	Walks a balance board 4 cm wide and 2.5 m long in 9 sec, stepping off less than once per trial	6 years	Gesell et al. (1950)
	Runs: Boys—4.2 yd/sec Girls—4.1 yd/sec	6 years	Espenschade (1960)
	Performs standing broad jump: Boys—37.4 in Girls—36.2 in	6 years	Espenschade (1960)
	Performs jump and reach: Boys—4.0 in Girls—3.5 in	6 years	Espenschade (1960)
	Performs standing high jump of 8 Inches	6 years	Gesell et al. (1950)
	Kicks a soccer ball in the air a distance of 10–18 ft	6 years	Gesell et al. (1950)
	Girls can perform 2–2 hopping pattern	6 years	Keogh (1968b)
	Boys can hop 15 ft on right and left feet	6 years	Keogh (1968a)
7–8	Runs: Boys—4.6 yd/sec Girls—4.4 yd/sec	7 years	Espenschade (1960)
	Throws softball for distance: Boys—45.2 ft Girls—25.8 ft	7 years	Keogh (1965)
	Performs standing broad jump: Boys—41.6 in Girls—40 in	7 years	Espenschade (1960)
	Performs jump and reach: Boys—6.1 in Girls—5.7 in	7 years	Espenschade (1960)
	Most girls can perform 3–2 hopping pattern	7 years	Keogh (1968b)
8–9	Throws softball for distance: Boys—59 ft Girls—33.8 ft	8 years	Keogh (1965)
	Runs: Boys—5.1 yd/sec Girls—4.6 yd/sec	8 years	Espenschade (1960)
	Performs standing broad jump: Boys—46.7 in Girls—45.9 in	8 years	Espenschade (1960)
	Performs jump and reach: Boys—8.3 in Girls—7.7 in	8 years	Espenschade (1960)
	Most boys can perform 2–2 and 3–2 hopping patterns	8 years	Keogh (1968b)

Schedule of Motor Development

On the basis of the research presented in the previous section, a schedule of motor development is presented in Table 3–3. From this information, it is relatively simple to construct a screening survey for use in a particular situation. However, care must be taken in using the schedule, because it presents data from a number of investigations, and the expression of developmental age or performance varies to some extent. Generally, the values presented in the schedule are based on median and mean ages or median and mean performances at a particular age. Some items are listed as being accomplished by "most" children. In those cases, the percentage of children passing an item exceeds 50 per cent. Since means and medians are the basis for most of the data, readers are reminded that it is normal or "average" to be above or below an average or a median. Although the schedule identifies specific ages, they should be interpreted as approximate. Readers also must be reminded that although children follow similar stages in development, it is "normal" for the rate of development to vary. The schedule serves to shed light on motor development, but a great deal of caution must be taken in using it as an assessment tool.

Specific Activities for Motor Development

Locomotor Abilities

Since by their nature physical education, play, and physical recreation activities are largely characterized by kinds of movement, the number of activities that may be selected to enhance locomotor abilities is unlimited. Some examples are given below:

GAMES AND RELAYS

Games that involve locomotor activity include:

Red Light	Busy Bee
Brownies and Fairies	The Huntsman
Duck, Duck, Goose	Drop the Handkerchief
Cat and Rat	Old Mother Witch
Run, Rabbits, Run	Freeze
Hill Dill	Fire Engine
Tag (all kinds)	

An almost limitless number of relays involve or can be arranged to involve running, walking, creeping, leaping, galloping, and hopping.

RHYTHMS AND DANCES

Examples of activities involving many locomotor activities and their variations are listed. Children may also perform various movements stimulated by different beats of a drum or by music.

How Do You Do My Partner (walking, skipping)

I See You (walking, skipping)

Farmer in the Dell (walking, skipping)

Bunny Hop (jumping)

Twinkle, Twinkle, Little Star (walking on tiptoe)

Chimes of Dunkirk (walking, running)

Oats, Peas, Beans, and Barley (walking, skipping)

Schottische (running, hopping)

Did You Ever See a Lassie (various movements)

Hansel and Gretel (heel-and-toe movements)

Seven Jumps (walking, hopping)

Jolly Is the Miller (walking, skipping)

STUNTS AND TUMBLING ACTIVITIES

Many stunts and tumbling activities involve rolling. Examples are presented in the section on balance activities.

MOVEMENT EXPLORATION ACTIVITIES

Activities that may be conducted with movement exploration include:

1. Walking, running, hopping, and jumping forward, backward, sideways, and zigzag.
2. Walking on tiptoes, on heels, with long steps, with short steps, with legs stiff, with knees high.
3. Running on tiptoes, around objects, under objects, up and down hills, and through a maze.
4. Jumping off, over, and across objects.
5. Hopping on one foot as fast as possible, with a partner, and in various patterns while switching feet.
6. Creeping forward, backward, under a rope, through a tunnel, on a line, and on a balance beam.
7. Leaping over a rope, a tire, a box, a partner, and other obstacles.

OTHER ACTIVITIES

1. Animal walks.
2. Balance beam activities.
3. Obstacle courses.
4. Rope jumping.

Non-Locomotor Abilities

THROWING AND CATCHING

GAMES

There are a great number of elementary games in which throwing and catching are involved. These games may be played with a variety of objects and may involve different types of throwing and various types of catching. Examples include:

Call Ball

Spud

Simple Dodge Ball

The Huntsman

One-Base Kick Ball

Newcomb Ball

Guard the Pin

Hot Potato

Bowling (plastic pins
  and playground balls)
Teacher Ball

Keep Away
Circle and Stride Ball

OTHER ACTIVITIES

1. Throw, catch, and dodge balls of yarn.
2. Throw, catch, and volley balloons.
3. Roll and catch hula hoops.
4. Bounce and catch playground balls.
5. Throw a ball in the air, clap hands, and catch it.
6. Throw, catch, and bat Wiffle Balls.
7. Throw and catch a cage ball in groups.
8. Shoot baskets with various objects (lower the basket).
9. Throw beanbags at a target or throw and catch beanbags with a partner.
10. Intercept swinging balls (tether ball).

KICKING

GAMES AND RELAYS

Examples of elementary games include:

Line Soccer
Kick Ball
Dribble Relay
Circle Soccer
Dribble Maze Relay
One-Base Kick Ball
Line-up Ball

OTHER ACTIVITIES

1. Have children kick a ball to each other for accuracy and for distance.
2. Have children pass the ball to each other in a circle formation.
3. Have children kick a ball rolled to them by a partner.
4. Have children kick a ball through a goal.
5. Have children "bowl" by kicking a playground ball at plastic pins.
6. Have children dribble down a field, blow a whistle as a signal for them to stop, and see if they can have control of the ball by a count of three after the whistle is blown.

Balance Abilities

BALANCE BEAM AND BALANCE BOARD ACTIVITIES

1. There are over 100 activities that may be conducted on balance beams. The examples that follow may be conducted on beams of various base sizes, heights, and slants.
   a. Walking forward.
   b. Walking forward, turning, and walking forward.

    c. Walking forward and backward.
    d. Moving sideways.
    e. Walking forward, bending a knee to the beam, and rising.
    f. Walking with an eraser on the head.
    g. Walking on the beam, and ducking under an object extended over it.
    h. Walking while carrying various weights.
    i. Creeping on the balance beam.
    j. Playing catch while standing on the beam.
    k. Hopping on the beam.
    l. Standing on the beam, jumping up, and landing on the beam while maintaining balance.
    m. Walking the beam with a partner.

2. On a balance board, the child may practice movements such as those listed below. In obstacle courses or such games as Stepping Stones, children may be asked to traverse a balance board.
    a. Standing on the board.
    b. Standing on the board while catching and throwing a ball, balloon, or beanbag.
    c. Standing on the board and holding objects of various weights.
    d. Standing and balancing objects on various parts of the body (head, outstretched arm, shoulder).
    e. Attempting to touch a swinging ball while standing on the board.

TRAMPOLINING

Activities to encourage balance development on a trampoline include:

1. Walking or creeping around on the trampoline.
2. Jumping and stopping while maintaining balance.
3. Performing seat, knee, front, and "doggie" drops (back drops are recommended only for skilled performers)
4. Swiveling hips and performing "ins and outs" with legs while jumping.
5. Moving the arms in various ways while jumping.
6. Jumping up and clapping hands or touching feet.

STUNTS AND TUMBLING ACTIVITIES

These activities require positioning of the body in unique ways, and thus they stimulate the child's need to maintain equilibrium. Examples include:

1. Rolling: forward, backward, and three-man rolls.
2. Inverted bicycle pedal.
3. Toe touches to the floor behind one's head from the supine position (precursor to the backward roll).
4. A dive over a rolled mat, followed by a forward roll, donkey kick, cartwheel, or headstand.

MIMETIC ACTIVITIES

Children enjoy imitating animals and objects, and some mimetic activities stimulate maintenance of equilibrium. While performing a

Stork Stand, for example, a child may be asked to: open or close the eyes, switch to the other foot, place hands on hips or thighs, fold arms across the chest or hold them in various positions, hold or balance objects, bounce a ball, or play catch. Other mimetic activities involving balance are:

Bunny Walk	Wheelbarrow Walk
Seal Walk	Bear Walk
Puppy Walk	Crab Walk
Three-Legged Doggie Walk	Beetle Walk
Kangaroo Walk	Inchworm Walk

GAMES AND RELAYS

Examples of elementary games that depend to a great extent on balance are:

Hopscotch
King of the Hill
Crossing the Brook
Modified Wrestling
Stepping Stones
Leap Frog

Relays in which children hop, jump, or imitate animals and vehicles may be selected to stimulate balance.

RHYTHMS AND DANCES

Rhythmic and dance activities involve fundamental movements and thus may be utilized to supplement programs designed to enhance balance.

MOVEMENT EXPLORATION ACTIVITIES

Activities to promote balance may be stimulated by the following questions:

1. Can you balance on one part of the body? On two parts? On three parts?
2. How long can you balance on two parts of your body?
3. Can you balance on one foot with your eyes open? With your eyes closed?
4. Can you balance on one foot as you change the position of a body part when you hear the beat of the drum?
5. Can you walk this line without falling off? (Children may be stimulated to walk straight or curved lines of varying width and length.)
6. Can you balance on one foot as you make yourself as small as possible?
7. Can you balance on one foot as you make yourself a twisted tree?

OTHER ACTIVITIES

Other activities that involve balance include:

1. Scooter board activities.
2. Indian hand wrestling.
3. Chicken fighting.
4. Coffee Grinder.
5. Rope jumping activities.
6. Jumping and turning.
7. Walking logs on a playground.
8. Pogo stick activities.
9. Jumping with a "lemon twist."
10. Skating.
11. Walking on various-sized tires laid horizontally or buried partly in the ground and secured vertically.

4

PERCEPTUAL
DEVELOPMENT

In the last 20 years, a great deal of attention has been given to the relationship of perceptual and motor development. A number of theories have been developed about this relationship and the role of perceptual and motor activities for academic achievement and intellectual development. In their eagerness to help children, educators have developed programs based on these theories. Particular attention has been focused on designing programs to help learning disabled, mentally retarded, emotionally disturbed, culturally deprived or disadvantaged, and cerebral palsied children. The results of such programs have varied. Although not all the answers are yet known, research is slowly helping educators to place perceptual-motor development in proper perspective. In this chapter, some of the more prominent theories relative to perceptual-motor development are briefly presented. The theories are then analyzed, and components of perceptual development are suggested. Finally, guidelines and specific activities for development are recommended.

Contemporary Theories of Perceptual-Motor Development

The importance of movement in the development of sensory or perceptual abilities to enhance academic achievement and intellectual development has long been recognized. Itard (1962) and Seguin (1907) pioneered sensory education programs in the nineteenth century. In her writing, Maria Montessori (1964a, 1964b, and 1965) has advocated the development of the senses in order that children may explore and become acquainted with the environment. In working with "backward" children, Montessori developed an action program that she contends lays the foundation for intellectual development. On the basis of research conducted during the second quarter of the twentieth century, Gesell (1950) reports that the early motor abilities of the child are an important and effective indicator of normal child development. Piaget (1963), in presenting his theory of cognitive development, contends that sensory-motor experiences lay the foundation for cognitive development. Piaget (1967a) and Piaget and Inhelder (1967b) recognize a unique and close relationship between perceptual activity and movement. Careful to distinguish perception and conception, Piaget indicates that perceptual activity becomes quite apparent during the *intuitive* period (ages 4 through 7). There is little question that contemporary theories, which are presented in detail, have drawn from these and other works.

KEPHART'S THEORY

In *The Slow Learner in the Classroom* (1960 and 1971) and many subsequent writings, Newell C. Kephart presents his theory of perceptual-motor development. The theoretical constructs underlying his theory are presented in Figure 4–1. According to Kephart, perceptual-motor development begins in infancy. Reflex activities become integrated and combine with generalized movements, which then become differentiated to form controlled movement patterns. Concurrently, sensory manipulations become differentiated to permit the child to recognize differences and similarities between sensory im-

Figure 4–1. Theoretical constructs. *From:* Roach, Eugene G., and Newell C. Kephart, *The Purdue Perceptual-Motor Survey.* Columbus, Ohio: Charles E. Merrill Publishing Co., 1966, p. 3.

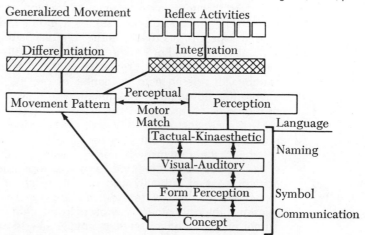

pressions. As sensory mechanisms become refined, they supply data for perception. Perception subsequently combines with controlled movement patterns to form perceptual-motor "matches," in which perceptual information and motor information come to mean the same thing. The first perceptual systems to be matched include the tactual and kinesthetic. Later, visual and auditory systems are integrated and are built into the earlier tactual and kinesthetic systems. Kephart states that perception supplies the information upon which behavior is based, and motor responses supply the movements that are the overt aspects of behavior. Out of perceptual-motor matching, laterality and directionality develop. An analysis of similarities and differences among perceptions forms the basis for the categorization of perceptions. Initial concepts *(percepts)* consist of a pattern of commonalities (categories among perceptual elements). Abstract concepts consist of a "pattern of patterns" among perceptual elements. Thus, concepts follow the manipulation of perceptual data. Each sequence of development depends on an earlier stage. Concepts rest on percepts, and percepts are based on motor patterns. This, then, is the role of movement in conceptual development.

Kephart (1971) illustrates perceptual-motor matching by using eye-hand coordination as an example. In the early stages of development, the child moves the hand and watches it as it moves. The hand is used for exploration and provides the major input of information. Eye movements follow the hand, and information from it is coordinated with that from the eye. As Kephart indicates, the eye is taught to see what the hand feels (hand-eye coordination). Since they are more efficient, the eyes begin to lead and the hands to follow. Although the eyes may depend on the hands for verification from time to time, the hand is used less and less as the eye becomes more adept (eye-hand coordination). As perceptual information and motor information become more closely connected, the two types of information become the same (perceptual-motor match). Perceptual data and motor data are so closely matched that one type can be translated into the other. Kephart stresses that perceptual is matched to motor data, not the reverse. He stresses that children must make many such connections between perceptual and motor data. When they are not prepared to do this, they exhibit learning disabilities, which need to be improved through his developmental training approach.

The Kephart program assumes a motor premise for learning. A critical aspect of his theory is the role of postural adjustment in conceptual formation. For Kephart, postural adjustment involves the ability to innervate muscle groups so that the body's position is maintained with reference to its center of gravity. Postural adjustments enable the individual to experiment with movement of the two halves of the body, observe and compare differences, ascribe different qualities to each side, and distinguish the two sides. Activities of balance provide the primary patterns for such distinction. Through balance activities, the organism becomes aware of the center of gravity, which serves as a reference for the coordination of space and the development of laterality and directionality. In innervating muscles and creating muscular tension, the individual becomes aware of the relationship of his other body parts to the center of gravity. Following numerous motor encounters, the individual develops laterality.

Laterality is an internal awareness of the two sides of the body and their differences. Kephart points out that laterality proceeds from bilateral to unilateral activity, since distinctions between sides cannot be made unless two sides are recognized. He indicates that the primary pattern out of which the differentiation of right and left occurs is balance. When balancing, the child must learn to distinguish right and left, to innervate one side against the other, to detect which side has to move, and to move in order to maintain equilibrium. Out of such activities, the child learns to differentiate the right from the left side. Such ability is basic to the attainment of *directionality,* which is the ability to translate laterality into right-left discrimination among objects in space.

The development of directionality proceeds from the location of objects relative to oneself (egocentric localization) to the location of objects in relationship to each other (objective localization). A particularly important factor in the development of directionality is control of the eyes. It is normally through the eyes that laterality is projected into space. Through numerous encounters, the child learns that when the eyes are directed toward a given point, the object lies in that direction. A "match" is created between the direction of the eyes and the position of the hand. Thus, there is a transfer of kinesthetic information from the hand and the eye. When the transfer has been made, the eyes are used to determine direction in space.

Kephart indicates that we must have a point of reference around which to organize the relative impressions that we receive. Since the location of objects is made in reference to the body and oriented in space with reference to it, the child uses the body as this point of reference. Thus, a child must have a clear, accurate, and complete picture of the body and its position in space. Kephart states that the development of body image is particularly important in this process. Body image involves knowledge and awareness of one's body parts and the relation beween them, and the ability to innervate parts of the body when so desired. Body image thus serves as the point of origin for developing spatial relationships outside the body. Awareness of spatial relationships will be disturbed if body image is not adequately developed.

According to Kephart (1971), the most significant aspect of motor activity in the child lies in its implication for gathering data about the environment. To explore and learn about the environment, the child must move. The purpose of movement must be contacting and interacting with the environment. To permit the type of exploration needed, Kephart (1971) indicates, four basic movement generalizations are required:

1. *Balance and Posture.* The child needs to understand the nature of gravity, its direction, and its point of application relative to the body. Through postural adjustment and balance activities, the child develops a point of origin from which right-left gradients and then laterality are developed. As balance and posture are mastered, the child gains freedom to further explore the environment.

2. *Locomotion.* Through locomotion, the child is able to explore the relationship *between* objects in space. In order that maximum attention may be given to exploration, locomotor activities such as walking, running, skipping, and jumping should become automatic.

Kephart stresses the need for an intensive repertoire of locomotor movements that become available when needed to obtain information from the environment.

3. *Contact.* Whereas locomotor generalization permits the child to explore relationships *between* objects in space, contact generalization permits exploration of relationships *within* objects. Contact generalization includes movements related to the handling and manipulation of objects: reaching, grasping, and releasing. As the child learns the nature of objects, form perception and figure-ground concepts emerge.

4. *Receipt and Propulsion.* With a knowledge of the space between objects and the relationships within objects, the child is equipped, according to Kephart, to deal with static environment. However, things change positions in relation to the child and to each other. There is a need to distinguish between the movements of objects in the environment and the self. This requires systematic information about movements in the environment, which is supplied through the receipt-and-propulsion generalization. *Receipt* involves activities such as catching, dodging, and trapping through which contact is made with objects coming toward the child. *Propulsion* includes activities such as throwing, batting, and pushing, which involve moving objects away from the child. The interpretation of movements that do not involve the child directly is made through a coordination of receipt and propulsion activities.

Kephart traces the development of form perception, space discrimination, and knowledge of temporal dimensions to show their importance in academic pursuits and the role of movement in their development. *Form perception* is perceiving a figure on a background and applying meaning to it. Again, although seemingly simple, this process involves learning, for the infant perceives vague, ill-defined masses or globular forms at beginning stages of development. Eventually the child is able to differentiate (separate the units in a form) and integrate (build units into a meaningful whole) forms. Weakness in either differentiation or integration causes problems in learning. For example, differentiation problems prohibit breaking words into parts. Integration problems inhibit the ability to put parts of words together to form the entire word. According to Kephart, forms consist of elements existing in space; since the learning of coordinates of space is based on laterality and postural adjustment, sensory-motor activity is important in the development of form perception.

The concept of space is considered important in Kephart's theory, and he presents the motor basis for the development of space as well as activities to develop space discrimination. He states that our most direct information concerning space comes about through movement. For example, the infant gains information about the distance of an object by learning the amount of movement required to reach for or move to it. However, the learning of the coordinates of space and spatial discrimination through movement only is inefficient, and thus is coordinated with other processes, the most important of which is vision. Since movement is coordinated with visual functioning and, in addition, places the individual in a variety of positions for unique perspectives, the role of motor activity is critical.

Another aspect of space discrimination is the development of a space structure in which objects are placed in proper relationship to the child and to each other. In Kephart's view, the development of space structure proceeds from egocentric and objective localization. The development of a space structure depends to a great extent on ocular mechanisms, since the eyes receive input signals on the basis of which the image of an object is generated in the cortex. Thus, he places great attention upon ocular control and vision in the development of space structure.

Kephart (1971) indicates that if a child wants to locate the series of events that represent his present and that can be used to extrapolate backward into the past and forward into the future, a temporal dimension similar to a spatial structure must be developed. Such a temporal dimension not only must provide for the location of an event in time but also must provide for the preservation of the relationships between events and time.

In the development of the temporal dimension, a "zero point" on the temporal scale is necessary. This point of origin for the temporal dimension is referred to as *simultaneity.* Simultaneity occurs when the temporal dimension between events is zero. Kephart indicates that simultaneity is first experienced when two movements are made together. For example, as the child moves in a crib, two arms or two legs move together. In addition, the child makes alternate movements in a sequence, which then helps to contrast movements of parts together with movements of parts in succession. From this beginning, the child learns to distinguish between auditory and visual events that occur together and those that occur successively.

Kephart (1971) indicates that the unit of extension on the temporal scale is rhythm. *Rhythm* involves the awareness of equality among temporal intervals, and a constant rhythm is a series of temporal intervals. Kephart notes that a high percentage of poor readers lack consistent rhythmic patterns. Rhythm is involved in many areas. Motor rhythm is necessary for the child to perform movement tasks in a series. Auditory rhythm is included in the effective receipt of auditory stimuli. Visual rhythm is important for the organization of various single visual fixations so that they may be integrated into a single visual impression. Motor, auditory, and visual rhythm all play an important role in successful academic achievement.

In further discussing the time dimension, Kephart stresses the importance of pace, sequence, and temporal-spatial translation. Through *pace,* there is an alteration in the size of temporal units. Children unable to change pace must do everything at a standard pace, which may be ineffective for certain tasks. *Temporal sequence* is the placement of events on a temporal scale so that time relationships and the order of events are apparent. Children experiencing difficulties with temporal sequence often exhibit difficulty in motor and academic tasks that require "sequencing" in performance. *Temporal-spatial translation* includes the ability to correlate temporal and spatial dimensions and to translate one dimension to the other with ease. For example, when children study the details of a picture within the context of the whole, they translate space to time. When children listen to a series of words and phrases in time and organize and put them together to recognize a scene, they translate time to space. In his theory, Kephart presents the need for pacing, sequencing, and temporal-spatial translation and illustrates how they are involved in motor experiences.

For Kephart, all the perceptual processes operate together as a totality. Just as input in the perceptual process cannot be separated from output, perceptual data cannot be separated from motor data. He therefore presents the hyphenated terms *perceptual-motor* and indicates that learning experiences should be designed in terms of the total process. Thus, movement experiences become the basis for academic and intellectual activities. Roach and Kephart (1966) developed the Purdue Perceptual-Motor Survey as an instructional aid for assessing the perceptual-motor abilities of children. The components included are: balance and posture, body image and differentiation, perceptual-motor match, ocular control, and form perception. Kephart (1971) suggests activities for the development of various components of perceptual-motor development.

GETMAN'S THEORY

Getman (1962) originally developed a theory and suggested program activities relative to the contribution of movement and vision to the development of reading and culturally influenced intellectual abilities. The purpose of the program is to develop readiness skills on the basis of six sequential but interrelated stages of childhood development. The first is the development of general movement patterns, which Getman states lays the foundation for all performance and all learning. Through general movement patterns, a child uses the head, arms, legs, feet, and other parts of the body to move and to assist in learning to use the eyes as the steering mechanism to guide these movements. General movement patterns provide an opportunity for exploration and are developed through activities such as Angels in the Snow, stomach rolls, sit-ups, toe touches, obstacle courses, balance beam activities, and trampolining.

The second level is the development of special movement patterns of action. A derivation and extension of the previous general movement pattern, this level enables the child to use the body and its parts to control and manipulate things in the world. Eye-hand coordination plays an important role at this level. Some activities suggested for the development of manipulative skills include playing with percolators, cupboards, drawers, jigsaw puzzles, and balls. The third level is the development of eye movement patterns. The objective is to develop the eye movement skills necessary for quick and efficient visual inspection of the world and for reading. Activities suggested for the development of eye movement patterns include those that require eye shifting, ocular tracking, and peripheral vision. Specific examples are following dots on a page and a swinging ball with the eyes.

The fourth level of Getman's program is the development of communication patterns to replace actions. This process aims to help children use their visual and movement experiences for communication with others. A relationship between vision and language is established to permit an exchange of information through speech. According to Getman, undeveloped eye movement abilities can act as a restriction upon language development. Activities suggested for the development of communication patterns include talking about interests, classifying objects, and playing games that involve verbs (*walk, run*), adverbs (*walk quickly*), prepositions (*on, over, under*), and adjectives (*hard, soft*). Getman states that the child lacking full freedom of eye movements will have more than usual difficulties with words such as *up, down, right, left, near,* and *far.* The child learns to talk by imitating and by learning to describe or name what is seen.

The fifth level is the development of visualization patterns to substitute for action, speech, and time. Getman (1962) states that "these are the processes that assist a child in learning the visual interpretation of the likeness and differences in objects, numbers, and words." This level includes the memory of things, people, or places previously learned (visual memory); the recalling of a happy weekend would be an example. Getman states that visualization is a learned ability and suggests activities involving visual comparison to enhance visualization patterns. Examples are comparing chairs, tables, or other objects and putting together jigsaw puzzles.

The development of visual-perceptual organizations is the purpose of the sixth level of Getman's program. It includes the ability to interchange body mechanisms with interpretation, understanding, and concept formation of the world and its contents. An example of eye-hand interchange occurs when the child feels an object and describes its appearance without looking at it. More complex examples given by Getman are using words, formulas, or maps rather than relying on movements or actions of the hand.

According to Getman, meeting the demands of each developmental step will provide the basic abilities necessary for success in reading. He indicates that primary visual abilities are essential to reading skill and that "vision is intelligence." Getman (1962) holds that "experience is the best teacher only when the experience involves movement use of the neuromuscular system (general movement patterns), practice and repetition for the coordination of parts and body mechanisms (special movement patterns), and the resulting interpretation of all information thus received and integrated by all body mechanisms (perception)."

Getman's theory and training program have been further developed since his original work. Getman and Kane (1964) and Getman, Kane, Halgren, and McKee (1968) revised and expanded Getman's original training program. They suggested specific activities to develop skills within the following categories: general coordination, balance, eye-hand coordination, eye movements, form perception, and visual memory.

Getman (1965) presented a "visuomotor model" to illustrate, in a simplified way, the manner in which perceptual and higher level intellectual abilities are normally developed from lower level motor systems (Figure 4–2). As the illustration depicts, skills are arranged in a hierarchy, with higher level skills dependent on lower level skills. As the model illustrates, innate responses, on the bottom row, serve as a base for all further learning and include the *tonic neck reflex* (TNR), the *startle reflex* (S), the *light reflex* (L), the *grasp reflex* (G), the *reciprocal reflex* (R), the *stato-kinetic reflex* (SK), and the *myotatic reflex* (M). The second row represents the general motor systems of loco-

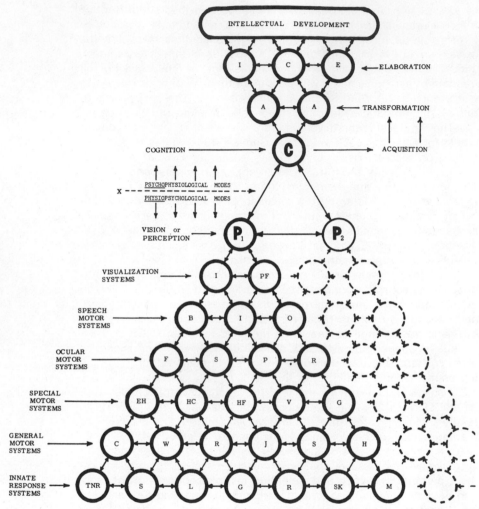

Figure 4-2. The visuomotor complex. *From:* Getman, G. N., "The Visuomotor Complex in the Acquisition of Learning Skills," in *Learning Disorders,* edited by Jerome Hellmuth, Vol. 1. Seattle, Washington: Special Child Publications, 1965, p. 60.

motion and includes, but is not limited to, *creeping* (C), *walking* (W), *running* (R), *jumping* (J), *skipping* (S), and *hopping* (H). These processes enable the child to move through and explore the environment, and they provide the basis for the development of special motor systems. Special motor systems (third row) include *eye-hand relationships* (EH), *combination of the hands* (HC), *hand-foot relationships* (HF), *voice* (V), and *gesture relationships* (G). The fourth row represents ocular motor systems for development of controlled movements of the eye; they include *fixations* (F), the ability to fixate on a target; *saccadics* (S), the ability to move the eyes from one target to another; *pursuits* (P), the ability to follow a moving target with both eyes; and *rotations* (R), the ability to move the eyes in all directions. The fifth row includes speech motor systems: *babbling* (B), *imitative* speech (I), and *original speech* (O). The sixth row, representing visualization systems, includes two types of visualization: *immediate* (I), and *past-future* (PF). Getman uses the example of "seeing" a coin in a purse or pocket by the feel of it to illustrate *immediate* visualization. *Past* represents the space-time relationships that enable the individual to review what occurred yesterday, and *future* represents a previewing of the details of what will occur. The six rows of skills lead to *perception* or, as Getman calls it, *vision.* Intellectual development is based on the interrelationship and integration of several perceptions and a variety of cognitive processes.

BARSCH'S THEORY

Another theory and program related to perceptual-motor development was developed by Barsch (1968). He calls his theory *Movigenics* — the study of the origin and development of patterns of movement in humans and the relationship of these movements to their learning efficiency. The theoretical basis for his approach encompasses ten constructs. Barsch contends that humans are designed to move (not just in the muscular sense but also in social, psychological, and cognitive senses), are propelled to move, and must be prepared to move efficiently to survive in an energy surround. Efficiency of movement as well as learning from the environment is derived from the perceptocognitive system, which includes visual, auditory, kinesthetic, tactual, olfactory, and gustatory modes of obtaining and processing information. A system of feedback enables the mover to enhance performance in a climate of stress. Movement efficiency, developed in segments of sequential expansion from simple to complex, is communicated to others through symbols. The terrain for movement is space. The domain of space includes *milieu interior* (the human physiologic system), *physical space* (world of objects and events), *milieu space* (space of social identification), and *cognitive space* (terrain of symbols, thoughts, ideas, and conceptualizations). The fields of space include *right, left, back, front, up,* and *down,* and the zones of space include *near space, mid-space, far space,* and *remote space.* The goal of the individual is to reach maturity as efficiently and as comfortably as possible.

From his basic constructs, Barsch (1967) established 15 components of movement efficiency. The first five are postural-transport orientations, which prepare the individual for moving efficiently and building a posture. These include muscular strength, dynamic balance, body awareness, spatial awareness, and temporal awareness. The next six components of movement efficiency give meaning and information to the moving organism and are designated as the perceptocognitive modes. They are the gustatory, olfactory, tactual, kinesthetic, auditory, and visual modes. Barsch contends that development of these modalities is hierarchial and that each has its period of developmental dominance. The last four components, designated *degrees of freedom,* serve to enhance and enrich performance, allowing it to increase in range and breadth. The first, *bilaterality,* increases movement patterns on both sides of the body. The second, *rhythm,* involves proper timing of movements for grace and agility. *Flexibility,* the third component, increases the repertoire of responses with modifications in speed, direction, and time. The last, *motor planning,* is concerned with the ability to plan and execute movement tasks.

Finally, Barsch (1968) suggests activities to attain the components of movement efficiency. Included are activities such as rolling, crawling, walking, stair climbing, running, jumping, hopping, rope jumping, trampolining, obstacle courses, cognitive stress and movement activities, chalkboard activities, graphic space exercises for the classroom, and metronome-pacing activities. In conducting activities, emphasis is placed on mobility, on development rather than remediation, on awareness of the self and the environment, and on diversity.

According to Barsch (1968), the core of the curriculum is perceptual-motor in substance. It is designed for use by parents in their child's infancy, as an orientation for child-rearing parents during the pre-school and elementary years, as a model for spatial emphasis in pre-primary programs, as a model for daily activities for all school units in Special Education, as an orientation to the organization of learning experiences for the elementary school child, and as an orientation to secondary school sequences.

THEORIES OF FROSTIG AND HER ASSOCIATES

Based on their work at the Marianne Frostig Center of Educational Therapy, Frostig and her associates have developed, refined, and presented a visual perception training program that has received considerable attention (Frostig and Horne [1964b], Frostig and Maslow [1970], Frostig, Horne, and Maslow [1973b] and Frostig and Maslow, [1973a]). Frostig and Maslow (1973a) define visual perception as "the ability to recognize and discriminate between visual stimuli and to interpret those stimuli by associating them with previous experience." The program focuses on five perceptual skills. The first, *figure-ground perception,* refers to the ability to distinguish between figure and ground and involves abilities to shift attention appropriately, to concentrate on relevant stimuli and screen out obtrusive stimuli, to scan adequately, and to display attentive and organized behavior. The second, *perception of position in space,* refers to the ability to perceive the relationship of objects to the observer and is associated with reversal difficulties in reading letters and numbers. The third, *perception of spatial relationships,* is the ability to perceive the position of two or more objects in relation to the observer and to each other. Inadequate perception of spatial relationships is associated with difficulties in sequencing in such activities as spelling and certain arithmetic processes. The fourth, *perceptual constancy,* refers to the ability to perceive an object as possessing invariant properties in spite of variability of the sensory impression, i.e., recognizing an object despite changes in its shape, position, and size. The last, *visual-motor coordination,* is the ability to coordinate vision with movements of the body or with movements of a part or parts of the body. Although not regarded as a visual-perceptual ability per se, visual-motor coordination is considered important in the Frostig program.

Movement plays an important role in the Frostig program. Frostig and Maslow (1973a) indicate that movement education is used to develop sensory-motor functions, which serve as a foundation for later perceptual skills. Movement activities are used for the development of visual-motor coordination, body movement abilities, manipulation, body awareness, and the basic movement skills of coordinating, agility, balance, flexibility, strength, speed, and endurance. While moving, the child learns to recognize distance, spatial relationships and position in space. In addition, movement activities contribute to temporal and spatial awareness.

The program is geared to children in kindergarten and first grade, any children with visual-perceptual problems, culturally deprived children with poor reading readiness skills, and deaf, mute, and mentally retarded children. In addition, the program may be adapted for blind children.

In addition to their work relative to visual-perceptual abilities, Frostig and Maslow (1973a) have identified the components of auditory perception included in their program and have presented recommendations for training. According to these authors, "auditory perception is the ability to interpret auditory stimuli, to associate them with stimuli earlier perceived, and to discriminate among them." The abilities considered important for adequate auditory-perceptual functioning include auditory acuity, auditory awareness, attention to auditory stimuli, auditory figure-ground perception, sound discrimination (this includes but is not limited to auditory-perceptual constancy), sound localization (in space and in time), recognition of auditory sequences, auditory memory and imagery, auditory analysis of words, auditory synthesis (sound blending), and associational functions. Table 4-1 illustrates the similarities between visual-perceptual and auditory-perceptual abilities.

It is interesting to note that the programs developed by Frostig and her associates are eclectic. These researchers do not associate themselves with a particular developmental theory but select elements from various educational viewpoints to form a unified theory of instruction including goals, activities, and methods.

Table 4-1. Similarities Between Visual-Perceptual and Auditory-Perceptual Abilities.

Visual-Perceptual Abilities	Auditory-Perceptual Abilities
1. Awareness of stimuli	1. Awareness of stimuli
2. Attention to stimuli	2. Attention to stimuli
3. Eye-motor coordination	3. Auditory-motor association
4. Visual figure-ground perception	4. Auditory figure-ground perception
5. Visual constancy of perception	5. Auditory discrimination
6. Perception of position in space	6. Perception of sound location
7. Perception of spatial relationships	7. Recognition and discrimination of auditory sequences
8. Analysis of complex patterns	8. Auditory analysis of words
9. Synthesis of patterns	9. Sound blending, necessary for word synthesis
10. Visual decoding (reception)	10. Auditory decoding (reception)
11. Visual closure	11. Auditory closure
12. No corresponding ability to grammatic closure	12. Grammatic closure
13. Visual memory for sequences	13. Auditory memory

Frostig, Marianne, and Phyllis Maslow. *Learning Problems in the Classroom.* New York: Grune & Stratton, 1973, p. 202.

CRATTY'S MODEL

Cratty (1970c, 1972) generally rejects what he calls "layer-cake" theories, which propose that movement serves as the basis for perceptual, academic, and intellectual development. One of his criticisms is that such theories fail to explain the adequate academic or intellectual functioning of physically handicapped children and other children who are very restricted in sensory-motor or perceptual-motor activity. Cratty proposed a four-channel model to study and explain the emergence of various types of behaviors. The four channels of the model are cognitive, perceptual, motor, and verbal abilities (Fig. 4–3). In this model, abilities within the four areas proliferate and subdivide, like branches on a tree, as the child matures. In this way, attributes denoting rather specific ability traits are formed. The emergence and proliferation of abilities may be the result of hereditary or environmental factors.

Cratty further proposes that, as the child matures, functional bonds or connections are formed between various abilities or attribute families (see Figure 4–4). For example, the visual ability of tracking (perceptual) may connect with the ability of grasping (motor), enabling the child to intercept a thrown ball (perceptual-motor bond). Such connections may eventually include the bonding of three or four attributes. Cratty (1972) finds it useful to distinguish between *functional* or *natural* bonds and bonds that are *synthetic* in nature. *Functional* bonds are those that normally emerge in children in activities such as learning to speak or to write. *Synthetic* bonds refer to those that educators may employ in circumventing learning disabili-

Figure 4–3. Four attribute channels illustrating examples of behaviors each contains as well as the manner in which each tends to branch as a function of age. *From:* Cratty, Bryant J., *Perceptual and Motor Development in Infants and Children.* New York: The Macmillan Company, 1970, p. 277.

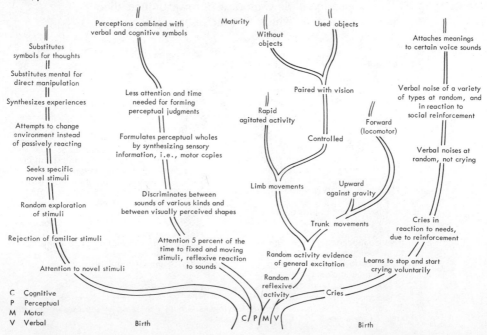

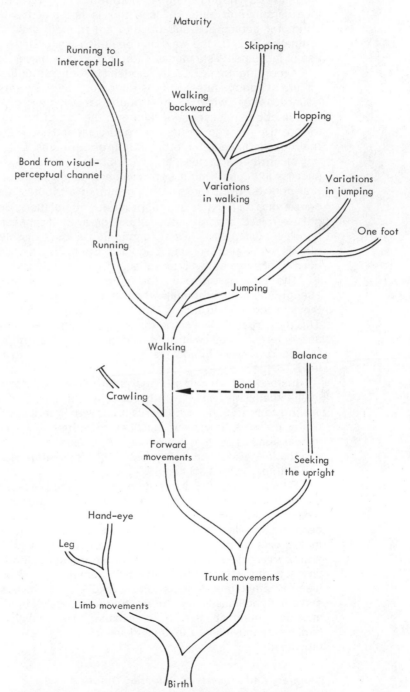

Figure 4–4. The differentiation, diffusion, and bonding that occur within the attribute branch for locomotor and trunk behaviors. *From:* Cratty, Bryant J., *Perceptual and Motor Development in Infants and Children.* New York: The Macmillan Company, 1970, p. 281.

ties. For example, a teacher may help a child learn to add or subtract (cognitive) by having the child hop (motor) a given number of times in a certain grid pattern. Since this is not the usual way that the bonds for adding and substracting are formed, they are considered synthetic. This, by the way, demonstrates what Cratty means by the use of movement as a modality for academic achievement,

According to the Cratty model (1970c), attributes emerge and mature at various rates, and the educators' efforts have the most pronounced effect when such attributes are in their greatest state of flux. In addition, success or failure in the exercise of attributes leads to positive change or to less participation, respectively. Intellectual deficits impede the proliferation of attributes. Delaying or blunting of attributes or families of attributes may be caused by lack of success in coping with the environment, sensory, motor, and intellectual deficits, overexercise of a group of attributes resulting in underexercise of others, or inappropriate stimulation. Bonds that are not exercised become less distinct or even disappear. In addition, bonds that impede efficient functioning should dissolve. For example, as writing or walking becomes proficient, the child does not need to observe body parts while performing the tasks.

The task of the educator is to aid children in forming and strengthening useful bonds when and where appropriate and to aid them in terminating bonds that have become inefficient or useless. This requires the educator to be knowledgeable about the nature and emergence of abilities at various ages, the viable bonds to be formed or dissolved, and the strategies necessary to help the child learn.

Instead of conceiving of movement as a basis for academic and intellectual achievement, Cratty conceives of movement as a modality serving to form bonds with perceptual, verbal, and cognitive abilities. Cratty presents movement activities to enhance bonding with intellectual abilities such as memorization, categorization, language communication, evaluation, and problem solving, with academic abilities, and with perceptual abilities.

For Cratty (1970c), *perception* denotes the process of organizing raw sensory data or input. Perceptual and motor behavior are at times independent from each other and at other times are joined. All perceptual abilities cannot be modified through movement and all movements cannot be modified by perceptual activity. For Cratty, the term *perceptual-motor* "merely denotes the condition in most voluntary acts of a considerable amount of dependency on perceptual abilities." Cratty's model helps him to explain why a person limited in movement abilities is able to function adequately in cognitive, verbal, and perceptual abilities. It is because these abilities may be enhanced by movement but their development is not contingent upon movement.

Summary and Analysis of Selected Theories

The views presented in the previous section are quite involved. It is not possible to analyze each of the theories in detail here; however, the major distinctions can be drawn, identified, and analyzed.

Kephart, Getman, and Barsch assume that movement is the basis for academic and intellectual development. Motor activity lays the foundation for academic success. Kephart and Barsch regard the perceptual and motor as inseparable. When Kephart thinks of movement, he includes external and observable movement as well as movement occurring within the organism. Just as input and output cannot be separated in the perceptual process, so too perceptual and motor cannot be separated. Kephart (1960) indicates that we must use the hyphenated term *perceptual-motor* instead of regarding these entities as separate. Barsch (1968) goes further when he states that the separating hyphen will be declared obsolete in the near future. Barsch indicates that the hyphen should be replaced by a bi-directional arrow (↔) to represent properly the reciprocal relationship between perceptual and motor.

The theories of Kephart, Barsch, and Getman are sometimes called "stage" or "layer cake" theories. In each one, movement experiences constitute the basic stage, or the bottom layer. Children who are unable to develop certain motor abilities are at a definite disadvantage in their academic and intellectual pursuits.

Cratty seems to turn the layer cake theory on its side. Instead of conceiving of movement as a basis for academic achievement and intellect, he regards it as a modality that may be used to form bonds with perceptual, verbal, and cognitive abilities. Although the turning of the "cake" is geometrically simple, the implications are important. For Cratty (1970c), perceptual and motor behavior can be independent from each other He does not believe that all perceptual abilities can be modified through movement or that all movements can be modified by perceptual activity. Thus, at times, the perceptual and motor are combined and at times they are separated. One difficulty in comparing the Cratty model with Kephart's theory is semantic: When Cratty refers to *movement,* he generally means observable movement behavior, whereas Kephart's definition includes observable as well as internal movement.

Although not strictly aligned with any theory, Frostig and Maslow appear to be consistent with Cratty on this point. Frostig and Maslow indicate that it is possible to recognize and discriminate visual stimuli without any movement (except the minimal movement of the eye itself), and it is possible for movement to occur without visual perception. Further, movement depends upon perception and usually occurs as a result of it, but it is not perception itself. Thus, movement is an important adjunct for visual-perceptual training at the Frostig Center of Educational Therapy.

In reviewing some of these and other theories about total child development, Frostig and Maslow (1973a) indicate that the choice of programs for a child will be influenced by the educator's theoretical leaning as well as by the child's specific deficits. They indicate that the emphasis must be shifted from child to child, and from age level to age level. They hold that the best approach is the one that "takes into account the child's total characteristics, the circumstances of his life, and his classroom situation." In the Frostig and Maslow (1970) program, "movement and perception are regarded as different functions."

Components of Perceptual-Motor Development

After reviewing a number of theories, the practitioner is faced with the awesome decision as to what to do. Should one theory or a combination of theories be subscribed to? What is perceptual-motor development? What is the role of movement in perceptual or perceptual-motor development? These and other questions must be answered explicitly or implicitly before one is able to assume that components of perceptual-motor development exist and can be identified. Thus, prior to the identification of components of perceptual development, we present basic notions and assumptions on the basis of which the components are selected and categorized.

It is certainly recognized that humans have available certain senses that serve to provide information about their bodies, the external world, and their relationship to that world. These senses include the tactual, auditory, visual, olfactory, gustatory, proprioceptive, and interoceptive senses. They are activated sometimes by movement and sometimes by environmental stimuli. Sensations derived from such activation are mediated and transmitted through sensory organs to the central nervous system. *Perception* is the monitoring and interpretation of sensory data resulting from the interaction between sensory and central nervous system processes. Perception essentially occurs in the brain and enables the individual to derive meaning from sensory impressions. It enables the individual to interpret stimuli, to associate with stimuli perceived at earlier times, and to discriminate among them. Since perceptions provide information about the world, they are critical to the development of concepts, academic achievement, and environmentally influenced aspects of intelligence. The advantages of sensory and perceptual abilities for the individual are obvious. The child deprived of all senses has no method of interpreting the external world. The blind and the deaf are obviously at a disadvantage in interpreting the external world and need to enhance remaining senses for successful participation in it.

Our discussion of the components of perceptual development and the activities suggested herein is based on the assumption that the various perceptual abilities of the human develop independently at times and in combination at other times. Thus, for example, the child may perceive differences in form without the benefit of observable movement. On the other hand, the perception of form may be enhanced by combining visual, tactual, and kinesthetic perception. Perceptual-motor development is considered a process of enhancing the ability to interpret sensory stimuli arising from or relating to observable movement experiences. It involves the ability to combine kinesthetic and tactual perceptions with and for the development of other perceptions, the use of movement as a vehicle to explore the environment and develop perceptual abilities, the ability to perceive tactually and kinesthetically, and the ability to make appropriate motor responses following the interpretation of sensory data. Depending on the needs of the child, a perceptual-motor training program may involve the development of one of or some combination of these related abilities.

In view of the rather comprehensive notion of perceptual-motor development we have presented, it is possible to categorize perceptual components in a variety of ways. The emphasis here is on the contribution of movement experiences to the development of perceptual abilities. Therefore, it appears advisable to group movement experiences about the perceptual areas most affected by movement. Thus, the components of perceptual development are grouped in three major categories: visual, auditory, and haptic. Within each category, components of perception are identified and types of movement experiences to enhance the development of each are presented.

Visual Perception

VISUAL FIGURE–GROUND PERCEPTION

Visual figure-ground perception refers to the ability to perceive and distinguish a figure separate from its ground. It involves the ability to concentrate on and differentiate parts of objects, to integrate elements within objects to form a meaningful whole, and to appropriately shift attention and ignore irrelevant stimuli. Children with inadequate form perception may exhibit difficulties in such activities as differentiating letters, numbers, and other geometric forms, combining parts of words to form an entire word, sorting objects, engaging in games that involve moving objects or that depend upon attention to lines of boundaries, shifting attention from one stimulus to another as in reading or scanning, and focusing or concentrating on relevant stimuli. Frostig and Horne (1964b) indicate that when children have difficulty in screening out obtrusive stimuli, they may be prevented from separating themselves from a particular stimulus, i.e., the child becomes "stimulus-bound." The child's inability to draw a straight line between boundaries because one of the boundaries captures his or her attention is an example presented by Frostig.

Although it is generally agreed that form discriminations are among the first made by children, complete figure-ground mastery is slow to develop and normally continues into adolescence. Davidson (1935) reported that the up-down orientation of the letters *p* and *q* was not sufficient to prevent confusion and lack of discrimination before a mental age of 6 years, and that left-right orientation of the letters *b* and *d* was not discriminated adequately until the mental age of 7.5 years was reached. Progression in development proceeds from ill-defined globular masses to abilities to differentiate and integrate elements within objects.

Experiences conducted in play, recreation, or physical education involve and may be drawn upon to stimulate the development of visual figure-ground perception. Simple to complex games and activities involving the rolling, throwing, catching, kicking, striking, dodging, and chasing of a variety of objects in a variety of ways may be played. Opportunities may be encouraged and provided for children to move under, over, through, and around perception boxes, tires, hoops, geometric shapes, ropes, playground equipment, pieces of apparatus, and other "junk" (Fig. 4–5). Children may follow or avoid lines associated with obstacle courses, geometric shapes, maps, mazes, hopsctoch games, or grids. To add enjoyment, the lines may

Figure 4–5. Learning perceptual concepts during movement activities.

be followed with scooter boards, tricycles, or other vehicles. Children may step on or avoid foot prints, stones, animals, or shapes painted on outdoor hardtops or floors. Simple to complex activities may be designed in which children imitate movements, such as Leap Frog, Follow the Leader, or Simon Says. Simple rope activities such as moving under and over a rope may eventually progress to complex activities such as rope jumping, jumping-the-shot, and the Lemon Twist. Games and relays that involve sorting of objects may also be found to be stimulating. Specific activities are suggested at the end of this chapter.

SPATIAL RELATIONSHIPS

The perception of spatial relationships involves egocentric and objective localization of objects in space. In accordance with the use of the term by Kephart and Piaget, *egocentric localization* is the ability to locate objects in space in relationship to oneself. Frostig refers essentially to the same ability as *perception of position in space.* Egocentric localization involves the ability to separate oneself from the environment and to perceive the direction of objects from oneself. *Objective localization* is the ability to locate the position of two or more objects in relation to each other. Objective localization proceeds from egocentric localization.

The perception of spatial relationship involves the ability to distinguish distance and depth as well as direction. Thus, perceptions in three-dimensional as well as two-dimensional space need to be developed. The perception of spatial relationships also involves perception of temporal order, or the concepts of sequencing. For example, the individual may look at a word with several letters or a dance with certain patterns and then may be asked to spell the word or to describe or perform the patterns of the dance. Such a task depends on the ability to perceive elements in space and to recall or reproduce them in a temporal sequence. The ability to perceive elements in space and then reproduce them in time is termed *visual-motor translation* by Kephart. It is an ability associated with the development of a space structure that enables the individual to mentally hold and manipulate elements existing in space.

Learning disabilities associated with inadequate visual spatial relationships include reversal or directional problems (such as the inability to distinguish *b* and *d, p* and *q, 36* and *63, saw* and *was, no* and *on* or the tendency to write letters upside down), sequencing problems in arithmetic, spelling, reading, writing, and drawing, difficulties in play and a variety of movement activities, and difficulty with the development of concepts.

Few educators disagree with the view that spatial relationships are enhanced through visual mechanisms available to the organism. Although there is disagreement on the extent and the particular role of movement contributions to the development of spatial relationships, most researchers agree that movement activities enhance the development of spatial relationships. The infant learns about space by moving in it. Perception of distance is enhanced by the kinesthetic information the child receives by reaching for or moving toward or away from objects. Through movement, the child learns to alter visual perceptions, and visual mechanisms are stimulated to steer the body appropriately. Awareness of direction is enhanced by moving up, down, forward, backward, right, and left. During movement, visual perspective, eye movements, size of images, and the location of images on the retina change, thereby stimulating visual-perceptual development. Although not conclusive, there is evidence to support the contention that spatial awareness is enhanced by and even proceeds from awareness of one's own body, i.e., the awareness of relationships in space is enhanced by awareness of the relationships among and the ability to innervate the parts of one's body. In addition, movement enables children to move in "three-dimensional" space, to observe position relative to other elements in space, and to "feel" distances between objects in space.

The types of movement activities that may be selected to stimulate perception of visual spatial relationships are virtually limitless (Fig. 4–6). Directionality is enhanced in activities such as trampolining, swimming, tumbling, rhythms and dances, rope jumping, obstacle courses, and balancing. Activities that develop body awareness are also recommended. Activities using tunnels, tires, ropes, hoops, obstacles, mazes, perception boxes, or partners may be arranged to place and move the body in restricted space environments. The incorporation of different-sized objects will help children discriminate differences in size. Children may move in, out, over, under, through,

Figure 4–6. Developing spatial relationships.

around, behind, and in front of these and other objects. Activities in which movements are imitated stimulate sequencing and the development of spatial-temporal translation. Many games and activities conducted with balls and other objects can be incorporated for the development of spatial relationships.

PERCEPTUAL CONSTANCY

Somewhat related to the development of spatial relationships but considered unique enough to warrant a separate category is perceptual constancy. *Perceptual constancy* refers to the ability to perceive and recognize an object despite variations in its presentation. Perceptual constancy involves recognizing the sameness of an object although the object may in actuality or in appearance change size, color, texture, brightness, or shape. For example, a football is recognized as the same-sized football even when seen from a distance. It maintains the same color in the daylight as in the twilight and it maintains its shape even when only the tip is visible. The development of perceptual constancy involves seeing, feeling, manipulating, smelling, testing, hearing, naming, classifying, and analyzing objects. Inadequate perceptual constancy prohibits the recognition of letters, numbers, shapes, and other symbols in different contexts. This lack of transfer leads to problems in reading, writing, arithmetic, and drawing.

Through movement experiences, objects are manipulated and utilized in a variety of ways and may be viewed from many different perspectives. In addition, children may place their own bodies in a variety of positions and shapes. They may form shapes, letters, and numbers with a partner or with a group. They may run to or play games with various geometric shapes. They may execute and classify their own movements or the movements made by others. Such activity may be stimulated by pictures or by movements demonstrated with dolls. Size discrimination may be enhanced by moving through and ordering different sized objects.

VISUAL–MOTOR COORDINATION

Visual-motor coordination is the ability to coordinate visual abilities with movements of the body. Since visual-motor coordination combines visual and kinesthetic perceptions, it is not exclusively a visual-perceptual ability. Although the coordination of vision and movement may involve many different parts of the body, most attention is given to eye-hand coordination because of its importance in total development and in academic pursuits. Adequate eye-hand coordination is based on the ability to make controlled and coordinated movements of the hand, wrist, arm, and shoulder, the ability to see, follow, and perceive objects, and the ability to match the kinesthetic and visual in the performance of a task.

The development of eye-hand coordination begins virtually at birth as the child begins to briefly fixate and track objects. Later the child is able to use both eyes in concert, to fixate and track objects more effectively and for longer periods of time, to coordinate movements of the eye and head, to volitionally move the hand to the mouth, and to grasp, release, and manipulate objects.

It is generally agreed that controlled movement develops from the midline of the body to its periphery (proximal-distal principle) and from the head to the toes (cephalocaudal principle). Programming based on these principles aims to develop control of the shoulder, the elbow, the wrist, and the hand — in that order. In addition, controlled movements of the head precede those of the spine and lower extremities. Thus, gross motor control precedes fine motor control and dexterity necessary in the hand for activities such as writing. Such motor development is, of course, dependent on the ability to create muscular tensions as appropriate and would be enhanced by activities designed for physical development, body awareness, balance, basic motor development, and motor skill development. The development of these attributes is presented in other parts of this book. Eventually, activities requiring fine motor control of the hands should be selected for developmental purposes.

Although the visual mechanisms available to the organism are obviously critical to the maturation and development of the visual abilities required for visual-motor coordination, participation in movement experiences not only involves and stimulates ocular control, tracking, shifting, peripheral vision, and depth perception but also matches visual and motor abilities. Perhaps the best movement activities for this purpose are games and activities involving the throwing, catching, and striking of balls and other objects. Such activities may be conducted while the object is moving and the individual is stationary, while the object is stationary and the individual is moving, or while both the object and individual are moving (Fig. 4–7). However, since such activities are relatively demanding, activities such as cutting, painting, pasting, finger painting, drawing, tracing, coloring, scribbling, chalkboard activity, bead stringing, puzzles, peg-board ac-

Figure 4–7. Ocular tracking.

tivities, block building, playing with clay, and playing with toys may be used.

Children with inadequate eye-hand coordination will have difficulties not only in certain play activities but also with basic early school activities such as cutting, drawing, coloring, and writing. In addition, they may exhibit difficulty with basic skills such as putting on and tying their shoes, putting on and buttoning their clothes, eating or drinking without tipping glasses and plates, and using simple tools.

Auditory Perception

Auditory perception depends upon learning and is the ability to discriminate, associate, and interpret auditory stimuli in order that such stimuli may become meaningful to the organism. Except perhaps from educators working with blind and deaf children, the contribution of movement experiences to the development of auditory perception has generally not received as much attention as its contribution to visual perception. However, the importance of the receipt and transmission of sound is obvious, and movement experiences may be employed for the development of auditory perception. This section identifies four components of auditory perception that appear to be relevant and responsive to enhancement by movement or physical education.

AUDITORY FIGURE–GROUND PERCEPTION

The ability to distinguish and attend to relevant auditory stimuli against a background of general auditory stimuli is called auditory figure-ground perception. It includes the ability to ignore irrelevant stimuli such as may occur in a room full of noise or one in which different activities are conducted at the same time. The training of auditory figure-ground perception involves improving the ability to attend to relevant stimuli and eventually to do so in situations in which irrelevant stimuli are present. Children with inadequate auditory figure-ground perception have difficulty attending to and concentrating on the task at hand, responding to directions, and comprehending information received during the many listening activities conducted in their daily lives. They may not be able to attend to a honking horn, a shout from their mother, or a whistle in times of danger.

In helping to improve auditory figure-ground perception, methods as well as activities play an important part. For children with difficulties in attending, it may be necessary to reduce distracting stimuli in a classroom. In addition, attention may be drawn to relevant stimuli by changing the rate, tempo, and loudness of speech, speaking softly at certain times so that children must concentrate on listening, touching or coming into close proximity to children when their attention wanders, and verbally emphasizing points. In some instances, earphones have been employed to enhance attention to auditory stimuli. After a child is able to attend to relevant stimuli, opportunities should gradually be provided for the child to learn to function effectively in situations where normal and irrelevant stimuli are present.

There are many movement activities that may be selected and arranged to promote auditory figure-ground perception. Children may follow directions or perform activities while listening to tape recorders or records. They may perform activities suggested by the music itself. For example, the children may walk, run, skip, or gallop to the beat of the music. They may imitate trains, airplanes, cars, or animals according to the sounds suggested by the music. Dances and rhythmic activities in which the rate and beat change are useful. Games and activities may be played in which movement is begun, changed, or stopped according to various sounds. Blind or blindfolded children may move to or be guided by audible goal locators, play with balls with bells attached to them, or be directed in movement or play with triangles, drums, bells, sticks, or whistles.

AUDITORY DISCRIMINATION

Fait (1972) refers to auditory discrimination as the ability to distinguish between different frequencies and amplitudes of sounds. Frostig and Maslow (1973a) include *auditory-perceptual constancy* in their notion of auditory discrimination. According to these authors, *auditory-perceptual constancy* is the ability to recognize auditory stimuli as the same under varying circumstances. Auditory discrimination thus involves the ability to distinguish the pitch, loudness, and constancy of auditory stimuli. Children with inadequate auditory discrimination abilities may exhibit problems in listening activities, games, dances, and rhythmic activities dependent on such skills, and spelling and reading — especially when the phonetic method is used.

Frostig and Maslow (1973a) indicate that teachers will rarely find children with gross deficits in the discrimination of non-speech sound. These authors, however, feel that initial training in sound discrimination should begin with non-speech sounds to give children a feeling of mastery and self-assurance. Many of the movement education activities suggested for auditory figure-ground perception may be used for the enhancement of auditory discrimination. While these activities are being performed, auditory discrimination may be stimulated and expressed as children respond to music, verbal directions, and other sounds at various frequencies and amplitudes. Movement activities are particularly useful because the teacher may immediately determine the effectiveness of discrimination. For example, the child may run when the music is loud, walk when it is softer, and stop when the music stops.

SOUND LOCALIZATION

Sound localization simply refers to the ability to determine the source or direction of sound in the environment. The localization of sound enables one to know the direction of a honking horn, a barking dog, or a crying child. Frostig and Maslow (1973a) consider location of sound in time as well as in space relevant to learning disabilities. They indicate that children sometimes have difficulty locating the position of a sound in a sequence of sounds, resulting in distorted sequences in words, sentences, and paragraphs. It is also well known that sound localization is critical for the blind, who use sound to orient themselves in the environment and to move or stop in response to sounds; the importance of this auditory ability is clearly demonstrated when a blind person crosses a busy intersection.

In cases where the localization of sound becomes an important training goal, blindfolding a child eliminates the advantages of visual perception and increases dependency on auditory perception and thus may be employed for short durations. While blindfolded, children may be asked to move toward or to avoid various auditory stimuli in free play, games, relay races, or obstacle courses. In such instances it is useful to use a variety of stimuli — bells, clapping, voices, triangles, horns, percussion and musical instruments, and whistles.

TEMPORAL AUDITORY PERCEPTION

Temporal auditory perception involves the ability to recognize and discriminate variations of auditory stimuli presented in time. It includes the ability to distinguish the rate, emphasis, tempo, and order of auditory stimuli. Children with inadequate temporal auditory perception may exhibit difficulties with rhythmic movement in dance, singing games, and other physical education activities. In addition, they have problems in appropriately combining syllables to form words because of sequencing problems.

Dance and other rhythmic activities are excellent for the development of temporal auditory perception. It should be stressed that such activities need not always involve music. In fact, beats are much more discernible when made by tom-toms, drums, or other percussion instruments. In developing temporal perception, parts of a movement experience should at first be isolated to the greatest extent possible. Following this, the parts may be integrated and presented in a sequence. Movement patterns may then be performed at varying speeds and beats. In the beginning, simple motor responses should be stressed. For example, the child may simply become as tall as possible when the music gets loud or fast and as small as possible when the music becomes soft or slow. Eventually, progressively demanding patterns may be developed, such as hopping twice on the left foot and once on the right, then hopping twice on the left and twice on the right. It should be noted that such activities require not only temporal perception but also the ability to match motor movements and auditory stimuli.

Haptic Perception

As Sherrill (1976) points out, the term *haptic perception* has been used in recent years to encompass kinesthetic, vestibular, and tactile input. Since kinesthetic and vestibular sense receptors can be grouped together as proprioceptors, *haptic perception* may be regarded as a comprehensive term that includes proprioception and tactual perception.

PROPRIOCEPTION

Proprioception pertains to the memory and awareness of movement and body position (kinesthetic sense), and balance (vestibular sense).

KINESTHETIC PERCEPTION

It is apparent even to the casual observer that the human receives, transmits, organizes, integrates, and interprets information gained through auditory and visual receptors and utilizes such information to move through and learn from the environment. Receptors transmit information to the brain, where a type of integration occurs that enables one to remember sounds, sights, smells, and tastes. Just as one is able to know or remember a smell or sound, she or he is able to remember a movement or a body position. One can "feel" an action before executing it; one can "feel" the correctness of a movement. The memory and awareness of movement and position of the body develop from impulses that originate in proprioceptors. However, proprioceptors may also serve as the basis for reflex actions and inherent movement patterns. Proprioceptors are located in tissues surrounding and adjacent to joints and in joint capsules. Although not all impulses transmitted by proprioceptors are designed to reach the brain, those that do provide the basis for the memory and awareness of movement and body position. It should be remembered that there are movements in the body that are consciously directed (by the decision to move) and those that are not consciously directed. However, even consciously

directed movements do not include detailed directions of joint actions.

The term *kinesthesis* has been defined in a number of ways. Authors have referred to it as the "awareness of movement," "muscle
sense," and the "feeling of motion." Regardless of specific differences,
most definitions of *kinesthesis* generally include information about
movements originating within the body itself. Barsch (1967) applies the
term *kinesthesia* to the cognitive emergent resulting from kinesthetic
feedback. He states, "When movement is perceived by the performer,
kinesthesia is the technical label of the product of such perception." He
indicates that kinesthesia is present when an individual purposely
moves a body part and cognitively directs that movement.

As used in this book, *kinesthetic perception* is considered a rather
comprehensive term encompassing the memory and awareness of
movement. It is basic to the ability to make appropriate muscular tensions, to plan and conceptualize movement, and to internally distinguish right and left (*laterality*). It also includes the ability to interpret
information received from proprioceptors (*kinesthetic feedback*) and
utilize such information in movement. Although unquestionably related
to what is being described here, *tactual perception* is considered separately.

It cannot be stressed enough that kinesthetic perception is basic to
all movement. Kinesthetic feedback is indispensable to the performance of any conscious movement. Therefore, the involvement and
stimulation of kinesthetic perception occur in an unlimited number of
tasks. In terms of organization and discussion for training, two related
components will be considered here: *body awareness* and *laterality*.

Body Awareness. An elusive term, *body awareness* has been
used in a variety of ways by writers representing different but related
disciplines. Used here, it is a comprehensive term that includes: awareness of the position of the body and its parts in space, awareness of the
parts of the body and their relationship to each other, feelings one has
about the body (sometimes referred to as *body image*), the ability to
create appropriate muscular tensions in movement activities, and
awareness of the capabilities and limitations of body parts. The development of body awareness is enhanced by knowledge of the parts of
the body — their names and other factual information (sometimes
called *body concept* or *body knowledge*).

Although the concept is placed here under the rubric *kinesthetic
perception,* it must be pointed out that body awareness as defined here
is influenced by the totality of life experiences including the intellectual, psychological, social, physical, and motor. For example, social
and psychological factors may be involved in the perception of fast,
slow, ugly, beautiful, strong, weak, skilled, unskilled, feminine, and
masculine. The naming of body parts is essentially an academic or
intellectual operation, and it is included with kinesthetic perception
because of its basis, its major thrust, and its importance to kinesthetic
perception.

On the basis of his review of the literature, Cratty (1970c) summarized the developmental trends regarding body perception by children. He reports that the child can identify gross body parts before age
2; becomes aware of front, back, side, head, and feet and can locate
objects relative to these body reference points between ages 2 and 3;

becomes aware that there are two sides of the body and knows their names but not their location at 4 years; knows there is a left and right side of the body but is usually confused concerning their location and can locate the self in relation to objects and objects in relation to the self at 5; begins to distinguish left and right body parts and can locate the body in relation to the left and right of things and objects in relation to the left and right of the body by age 6; establishes the concept of *laterality* between 7 and 8; and adopts another individual's perspective with ease between 9 and 10 years.

The importance of movement for the stimulation of body awareness and of body awareness for movement is obvious. It has also been hypothesized that body awareness, or body image, provides the vehicle for exploration of the environment and is basic to the development of academic and intellectual abilities. Kephart (1960) states that since the body is the zero point or the point of origin for all movements and for all interpretations of outside relationships, these movements and relationships will be disturbed if the body image is disturbed. He supports the contention that perception of relationships in space builds from an awareness of parts of one's own body. Research concerning this contention is not conclusive.

Movement experiences that may be utilized to enhance body awareness include: those in which parts of the body are identified, named, and pointed to, balance activities in which muscular adjustment is necessary to keep the center of gravity over the base, rhythmic or dance activities in which parts of the body are named or involved, trampoline and scooter board activities, mimetic activities, movement exploration, swimming, games and activities conducted in front of a mirror, stunts and tumbling, and isometric, isotonic, and relaxation exercises.

Laterality.   Following the work of Kephart (1960), the term *laterality* received a great deal of attention. Kephart describes laterality as the internal awareness of right and left. He indicates that laterality develops through experimenting with the movement of the two halves of the body, observing and comparing these differences, ascribing different qualities to each side, and thus distinguishing the two sides. Kephart believes that the primary pattern out of which this differentiation grows is balance. Balance requires that the individual keep his center of gravity over the base. The center of gravity thus serves as the reference or distinguishing point for separating the two sides of the body. During balance activities, the individual must make postural adjustment or create muscular tensions in order to place the body in alignment to maintain balance. These muscular tensions help the child learn the sides of the body; the individual needs to innervate the two sides in the same way at certain times and in different ways at other times. Through such postural adjustments, laterality is developed. Since laterality is dependent on movement and may be considered a goal to attain for its own sake, it is included here in our consideration of kinesthetic perception.

Although laterality can be considered a motor goal to be attained for its own sake, there is some controversy over the role that laterality plays in developing academic abilities, particularly reading. For Kephart, laterality is a basis for and thus leads to directionality, and directionality is necessary for reading, writing, spelling, and other academic work. He contends that problems in laterality lead to learning problems in the classroom. Laterality is considered a basic readiness ability. It is hypothesized that when laterality is not attained, children will have difficulty distinguishing *b* and *d, 24* and *42, was* and *saw*, and *p* and *q*. On the basis of his research, Cratty (1970c) indicates that bonds may be formed between perceptual and motor abilities at certain times; however, he would not support the premise of the motor base. This author's review of the literature revealed little disagreement among researchers that directionality is important to reading and other academic functions. Confusion about right and left leads to confusion in reading and writing. Motor activities may be arranged to develop laterality, and the attainment of directionality may be enhanced when laterality is combined with other perceptions. Laterality may be considered a motor goal (like body awareness or strength) to be attained for its own sake. However, the notion of the motor base as "the" base or the "only" base must yet be explored through further research.

According to Kephart, the development of laterality proceeds from bilateral to unilateral activity. One must engage in activities involving both sides of the body in order to distinguish two sides. In addition, activities are not conducted with skill as the paramount objective. The purpose of the activity is to stimulate postural adjustments. When an individual becomes skilled, the developmental value of the activity is reduced. For example, if a child can easily walk a balance beam, some change must be made in the exercise to stimulate greater postural adjustment. By narrowing the base, balance is made more precarious, and increased muscular involvement is stimulated. Activities suggested for the development of laterality include activities that require dynamic balance (balance beam and balance board walking, trampolining, animal walks, stunts and tumbling, jumping from obstacles while maintaining balance, and any locomotor activity), that involve the extremities in joint and separate movements (throwing, catching, scooter board activities, and swimming), that distinguish muscular tensions (relaxation and conditioning exercises), that promote body awareness and involve the ability to name, innervate, and feel the relationship between parts of the body, or that require a knowledge of body parts and of the unique requirements for innervating them (dances and rhythms).

BALANCE

As mentioned previously, proprioception includes sensations pertaining to vestibular sense reception. The vestibular apparatus provides the individual with information about the body's relationship to gravitational pull and thus serves as the basis for balance. In terms of training implications, two aspects of balance are considered and discussed in this book: *static balance* and *dynamic balance*. Since static and dynamic balance are discussed elsewhere, they will not be dealt with here (see Chapter 3).

TACTUAL PERCEPTION

Tactual perception is the ability to interpret sensations from the cutaneous surfaces of the body. Kinesthetic perception is internally related and tactual perception is externally related. Sensations are transmitted to the brain during active and passive contact with the environment (touch). Since tactual perception involves contact with the environment, transmission of impulses to the brain and interpretation of and attachment of meaning to different sensations, it is more than the sensation of touch. Through touching, feeling, and manipulating objects, however, the organism experiences a variety of sensations that not only have a survival value but contribute to a better understanding of the environment. The individual may be attracted to or may attempt to avoid certain sensations. Although sensations come to the organism continually, feeling, touching, and manipulating objects expands the horizons for the developing child. Efficient movement not only enhances active exploration of the environment but has the advantage of combining the kinesthetic and the tactual.

Tactual perception is important for the developing youngster. It enables the individual to distinguish wet from dry, hot from cold, soft from hard, rough from smooth, wood from iron. When touched, the individual may localize the sensation, feel and discriminate between sensations received simultaneously at two points, and perceive the direction of moving stimuli. The importance of touch to the blind is clearly evident when one observes a blind child feeling a lacrosse stick in order to understand what it is, trying to keep on a sidewalk when walking, trying to stay on a cinder track while running, or learning to read braille. All youngsters, especially retarded youngsters, enhance learning by touching, feeling, holding, and manipulating objects. Since it is a relative term, the meaning of *soft* is enhanced when one is able to feel something soft and something hard. Tactual perception enables the child to cope with the world on relatively tangible terms.

Tactual perception also functions and coordinates with other perceptions. Barsch (1967) indicates that tactual perception is the antecedent for kinesthesia. Tactual perception "puts the finishing touches on the early organization of near space and permits the individual to move purposefully into mid and far space." Kinesthesia enables an individual to move his tactual perception to mid and far space. In addition to the association described by Barsch, tactual perception assists the individual to develop fine motor and manipulative abilities. For example, when drawing, writing, sorting, tracing, cutting, or coloring, tactual perception provides information about contact with objects. Tactual perception also combines with kinesthetic sensations in activities such as crawling on the floor or through a tunnel, walking along a balance beam, jumping on a trampoline, climbing up a ladder, wrestling, and tumbling. The combining of tactual, visual, and kinesthetic perceptions is evidenced in activities such as playing with toys, manipulating objects, writing, throwing and catching objects, stringing beads, and walking along a balance beam.

Many movement activities may be conducted during physical education, in classrooms, on playgrounds, and in recreational settings to stimulate tactual perception. Selection of the type of activities obviously requires consideration of the child's abilities and limitations. Types of activities include those involving contact of the hands, feet, and total body with a variety of surfaces. For stimulation of tactual perception through the feet, it is generally advisable for a child to be barefooted. Opportunities then may be provided for the child to walk on floors, lawns, beaches, balance beams, mats, and trampolines and in swimming pools. The child may climb ropes, cargo nets, ladders, and playground equipment. Since they provide unique sensations, swimming activities are excellent. Isometric and isotonic exercises involving increases in resistance are also recommended. Examples of such exercises are presented in our discussion of physical development (see Chapter 2). Games and activities that require the distinction of forms and shapes (balls and other objects) are recommended. Obstacle courses may be arranged to include a variety of different sensations. Games and activities in which various parts of the body are touched by the self or others using a variety of materials are recommended. Other activities include trampolining, scooter board exercises, and stunts and tumbling. When tactual perception is a major goal, it may be advantageous to involve the child in activities while he or she is blindfolded or in a darkened room. Activities conducted while blindfolded, however, should be employed for only brief periods of time.

Guidelines for Program Implementation

1. Perceptual-motor development should be considered a part of physical education programs for pre-school youngsters, youngsters in kindergarten and first and second grades, and handicapped children of all ages. The emphasis placed on perceptual-motor development is dependent upon the needs of the child.

2. Perceptual-motor programs should be considered an adjunct to rather than a replacement for academic activities. Since, at best, perceptual-motor abilities only lay a foundation for academic development, success in these pursuits is not guaranteed. Success in reading, writing, and arithmetic depends on the ability to learn these tasks. Transfer from perceptual abilities to academic and cognitive skills is not automatic.

3. Screening followed by specific testing should precede placement in remedial programs.

4. In programming, the needs of the child rather than the application of a particular theory should be emphasized.

5. Selection of activities should be based on the abilities, age, interests, and limitations of the child.

6. Special perceptual-motor development programs may not be necessary for all children.

7. Perceptual-motor abilities normally develop between 3.5 and 7 years. Differences in ability within this span are extremely varied and need to be considered in programming.

8. Activities selected in programs should be fun, should provide for success, and should relate as much as possible to activities engaged in by all youngsters of the same age level.

9. Emphasis in programs should be placed on development rather than on the perfection of an isolated skill.

10. Perceptual-motor development should involve all professionals who work with the child. The unique contributions of various professions should be identified and coordinated in program implementation.

Specific Activities

Visual Perception

VISUAL FIGURE–GROUND PERCEPTION

GAMES

Games that may be arranged for differentiating and integrating objects, sorting, imitating movements, following moving objects, and shifting attention are recommended. Simple to complex games involving rolling, throwing, catching, kicking, striking, dodging, and chasing a variety of objects in a variety of ways are recommended. Games that may be selected to enhance the development of the various aspects of visual figure-ground perception include:

Simon Says	Leap Frog ·
Do This Do That	Follow the Leader
Spud	Teacher Ball
Tether Ball	Kick Ball
Hot Potato	Simple Dodge Ball
Hopscotch	Laughing Ball
Stepping Stones	Tag Games
Twister	

RELAYS

Relays involving the sorting and matching of objects including geometric shapes are suggested.

MOVEMENT ACTIVITIES

Match movements to geometric forms, numbers, letters of the alphabet, pictures of people, pictures of animals, pictures of vehicles.

MOVEMENT EXPLORATION ACTIVITIES

Opportunities may be encouraged and provided for children to move under, over, through, and around tires, geometric shapes, ropes, playground equipment, pieces of apparatus, and other objects.

LINE ACTIVITIES

Following or avoiding lines associated with obstacle courses, geometric shapes, maps painted on the floor or on "hardtop" outdoor areas, mazes, hopscotch games, or grids. Such lines may be followed by walking, running, or other locomotion or by scooter boards, tricycles, and other vehicles. In addition, children may follow such lines by pretending to be animals, trains, cars, motorcycles, or other objects.

ROPE ACTIVITIES

Rope activities for developing visual figure–ground perception include: moving under or over a rope, broad jumping over two ropes laid parallel to each other, jumping rope, jumping the shot, and the Lemon Twist.

OTHER ACTIVITIES

1. Perception box activities.
2. Imitation of movements and mimetic activities.
3. Obstacle courses.
4. Hula hoop activities.

SPATIAL RELATIONSHIPS

GAMES

Games that involve locating objects in relation to each other or that stimulate a recognition of one's position in space include: Dodge Ball, Hill Dill, Huntsman, Tag Games, Follow the Leader, Jump-the-Shot, Cat and Rat, Hide and Seek, and Steal the Bacon. In addition, nearly any games that involve balls or other objects may be arranged to stimulate spatial relationships.

MOVEMENT EXPLORATION ACTIVITIES

Activities that enhance awareness of spatial relationships are suggested.

1. Have children move under, over, and around each other.
2. Have children move under, over, around, and through tunnels, barrels, boxes, hoops, chairs, tires, cargo nets, ropes, and other objects.
3. Provide children with opportunities to "feel" distances and to view objects from different perspectives.
4. Have children perform tasks in a particular sequence.
5. Involve children in activities that enhance their awareness of direction (up, down, left, right, in front of, and behind).

OTHER ACTIVITIES

Other activities suggested for the development of spatial relationships include:

Rope Jumping
Playground Activities
Scooter Board Activities
Trampolining
Stunts and Tumbling
Obstacle Courses
Mazes
Rhythms and Dances
Swimming

PERCEPTUAL CONSTANCY

GAMES

Select games in which similarities and differences in objects are recognized; those in which objects may be seen from different perspectives (chasing, catching, running to objects); those in which objects are moved or manipulated; those in which differences in distance are perceived; and those in which various geometric shapes, letters, and numbers are used. In order to emphasize perceptual constancy, it may be necessary to modify slightly. Some examples include:

Tag Games
Steal the Bacon
Hopscotch
Tether Ball
Object Relays
Ball Games

Movement Exploration Activities

Opportunities may be provided for children to name, classify, and analyze movements of the body; to form shapes, letters, and numbers with their bodies and with other children; to move through and order different sized objects; and to manipulate objects of different size, color, texture, and shape.

Other Activities

1. Have children run to and from objects.
2. In conducting activities, use different sizes and textures of the same object. For example, different sized footballs or playground balls may be used in the same game.
3. Have children run to, identify, pick up, and carry objects of different geometric shapes. Vary the geometric shapes and their sizes, colors, and textures.
4. Assign children to a "home" position in the gym and ask them to find their "home" when they enter or after certain activities are conducted. Such homes may be animals, letters, numbers, or geometric shapes painted on the gym floor.
5. Have children reproduce movements depicted by pictures or mimic movements demonstrated with dolls.
6. Write directions for obstacle courses, mazes, or exercise stations in different colors and sizes and on different textures.

VISUAL–MOTOR COORDINATION

Ocular Control

1. Most games conducted with an object stimulate ocular control. Some examples include Call Ball, Tether Ball, Simple Dodge Ball, Hot Potato. In addition, games that involve imitation, such as Follow the Leader or Simon Says, may be used to stimulate ocular control. Tag games may be used to stimulate the visual following of moving objects.
2. Imitation of movements enhances ocular control.

Eye–Hand Coordination

1. Elementary games stimulating eye-hand coordination include Tether Ball, Call Ball, Hot Potato, Steal the Bacon, Simple Dodge Ball, Simon Says, Do This Do That, Straddle Ball, and Teacher Ball.
2. Children may roll, throw, catch, strike, or bat balloon balls, cage balls, yarn balls, Wiffle Balls, playground balls, or volleyballs.

3. Children may play with bean bags, hula hoops, punching bags, and scooters.
4. Eye-hand coordination can be enhanced by animal walks and mimetic activities.
5. Combative activities aid in developing eye-hand coordination.

EYE—FOOT COORDINATION

1. Games that may be arranged to stimulate eye-foot coordination: Jump the Shot, Kick Ball, Follow the Leader, Simon Says, Do This Do That, Tag Games, Angels in the Snow, Cross the Brook, Hopscotch, Stepping Stones, Twister, and Line Soccer.
2. Kicking stationary and moving objects.
3. Relays involving animal walks and locomotor activities.
4. Balance beam activities.
5. Movement exploration.
6. Rhythmic and dance activities.
7. Other activities that stimulate eye-foot coordination: activities conducted on tires, obstacle course activities, rope climbing, skating, playground activities, trampolining, stunts and tumbling, and swimming.

Auditory Perception

AUDITORY FIGURE–GROUND PERCEPTION

GAMES

Games in which activity is started, changed, or stopped by an auditory signal may be incorporated to stimulate auditory figure-ground perception. A game that involves a number of such cues is Freeze, in which children are allowed to run around a gym until a signal is given. Then they must "freeze," or stand like statues; they resume running when another signal is given. Other examples include:

Simon Says	Cat and Mouse
Red Rover	Red Light
Back-to-Back	Midnight
Busy Bee	Musical Chairs
Brownies and Fairies	Crows and Cranes
Cowboys and Indians	Have You Seen My Sheep
Call Ball	Hill Dill

RHYTHMS AND DANCE ACTIVITIES

1. March to the beat of music, tom-toms, tambourines, or other percussion instruments.
2. Follow square dance calls.
3. Combine movements to instructions provided in folk dances.
4. While listening to animal sounds, create movements associated with various animals.
5. Participate in various singing games.

OTHER ACTIVITIES

1. Have children jump rope while listening to or reciting various chants or rhymes.

2. Have children run to various sounds during relays while blindfolded. Use a variety of sounds.
3. While using station-to-station teaching techniques, have children change stations on auditory cues.
4. Play "exercise" records for children. Ask them to perform exercises to the tempo of the music.
5. Arrange activities that depend upon the following of directions given by the teacher or leader. While giving directions, change the rate and loudness of speech.
6. For blind or blindfolded children, conduct games and other activities with audible goal locators or balls with bells attached. For example, the game of Steal the Bacon may be played by placing the object to be taken near the audible goal locator. Children may move toward or avoid audible goal locators while playing various games.
7. Give commands to children while they perform on the trampoline or balance beam. Such commands may be conveyed by voice or other auditory signals.

AUDITORY DISCRIMINATION

The activities recommended for auditory figure-ground perception may generally be used to stimulate auditory discrimination. For auditory discrimination, however, attention should be focused on the pitch, loudness, and constancy of sounds. For example, children may be asked to respond with movement to differences in the pitch or loudness of music instead of simply to a sound. Attention may be given to emphasizing certain beats during rhythmic activity.

SOUND LOCALIZATION

Activities for development of sound localization include those that enhance the location of sound in space as well as in time. Some examples follow.

ACTIVITIES FOR LOCALIZATION OF SOUND IN SPACE

These activities may be conducted in a dark room or with blindfolded or blind children.

1. Ask children to move toward or away from a voice or other auditory signal.
2. Provide children with paper cups or other objects. Have them throw the objects a particular distance and then find them as quickly as possible.
3. Have children play games such as Red Light, Midnight, Cat and Mouse, Call Ball, Red Rover, Back-to-Back, or Squirrel in the Trees while blindfolded.
4. While in a restricted space, have children move about without touching each other. They may make their own sounds while moving. Make the activity more difficult by further restricting space.
5. Ask children to roll balls to each other on the grass.
6. Ask children to throw objects at a sound. For example, children may shoot baskets by aiming toward an audible beeper.
7. Arrange an obstacle course in which the order of direction is dependent upon sound. For example, sounds emitted from tape recorders, electronic beepers, or record players may be used. In addition, children may be stationed at various obstacles to lead

youngsters in the correct order by calling, clapping, or creating sounds with objects.

ACTIVITIES FOR LOCALIZATION OF SOUND IN TIME

1. Associate a movement such as hopping, jumping, rolling, or skipping with a particular sound. For example, a clap may mean a hop; a bell may mean a jump; a horn may mean a skip; a strike of a triangle may mean a squat. Make sounds in a particular order and ask children to respond with appropriate movement in the same order.
2. Name a series of stunts or movements for children to perform. Ask children to perform the stunts or movements in the correct order.
3. Ask children to listen to various beats and then to bounce balls, clap, or perform movements to the beats they have heard.
4. Ask children to listen to a whistle, a horn, piano, or other musical instrument as various notes and beats are played. Ask children to represent the sounds by movement in the order in which they were heard.

TEMPORAL AUDITORY PERCEPTION

The types of activities that have been suggested to stimulate other components of auditory perception may be used for the development of temporal auditory perception and thus will not be repeated. For temporal auditory perception, emphasis is placed upon the child's ability to distinguish rate, emphasis, tempo, and order of auditory stimuli.

Haptic Perception

KINESTHETIC PERCEPTION

BODY AWARENESS

1. Games that may be arranged to stimulate body awareness include Simon Says, Angels in the Snow, Where Did I Touch You, Do This Do That, Back to Back, Follow the Leader, and many Tag Games.
2. Rhythmic activities that may be used to stimulate body awareness include Looby Loo, Dry Bones, Hokey Pokey, and the Bunny Hop.
3. A very popular relay with children is the Clothes Change Relay. In this activity, the child dons old clothes at the beginning of the line, runs to a target, returns, and takes the old clothes off while the next person begins to put them on. Relays or line activities involving animal walks, crawling and creeping, and locomotor activities may also be used. A particularly stimulating activity is "Add One," sometimes called "Follow the Leader," in which the first child performs a movement. The next child repeats it and adds one. The third child performs both movements in correct sequence and adds one.
4. While jumping on a trampoline, a child may be asked to touch various parts of the body with the hand, or to touch the trampoline bed with different parts of the body. This can be done while the correct performance of stunts is also encouraged. Examples of actions are: knee drops, seat drops, front drops, swivel hips, and combinations.
5. The scooter board can be used to enhance body awareness. The child is encouraged to move about with the board while assuming

various positions on the board and using various parts of the body to propel the board.

6. During movement exploration, the child may be stimulated to develop body concept and body schema by solving problems such as:
   a. How many different ways can you move your body?
   b. Can you make letters and numbers with your body? Alone? With a partner?
   c. How big and how small can you make your body?
   d. Can you move around a body part? Another body part?
   e. How fast can you move the parts of your body? How slow?
7. Other activities that may easily be arranged to stimulate body awareness include obstacle course activities, playground activities, punching bag activities, and activities involving the imitation of movement.

LATERALITY

1. The balance beam and the balance board are excellent for development of laterality. Examples of activities that may be conducted on the balance beam and balance board are presented in Chapter 3. Balance activities are particularly recommended because postural adjustments are stimulated by the need to keep the center of gravity over the base. Balance beam and balance board activities may be arranged to make balance more precarious and thus to stimulate postural adjustment or muscular tensions.
2. For activities to develop laterality on the trampoline, see list of activities for balance in Chapter 3.
3. Stunts, tumbling, and combative activities may be used to enhance laterality. See activities for the enhancement of balance in Chapter 3.
4. Conditioning and relaxation exercises contribute to an awareness of the location of parts of the body and the ability to innervate or relax muscular tensions.
5. Swimming may involve bilateral and unilateral activity and may place the body in unique positions that stimulate unique muscular tensions.
6. Rhythms and dances require particular responses made in a controlled and rhythmic pattern and therefore require the ability to innervate and differentiate body parts in various ways. These activities generally require crossing the midline of the body.
7. Examples of movement exploration problems that may be posed to children are reflected in the following questions:
   a. How many parts of your body move? Can you name them? Can you touch them?
   b. Where do your different body parts stop and start?
   c. Can you draw a triangle in the air with your feet? With your hand?
   d. Can you make the letter C with your body? The number 7? Can you make letters or numbers with a partner?
   e. Can you touch the floor with one, two, three, four, or five body parts?
   f. Can you make your body look like that of an animal? Can you imitate the animal walk?
8. Other activities for enhancement of laterality are listed.
   a. Have children play games involving various locomotor activities and basic skills.
   b. Have children vault over pieces of apparatus.
   c. Have children jump over and from obstacles and try to hold their balance upon landing.
   d. Have children balancing on one foot and hopping in various directions and following various patterns.
   e. Have children toss a beanbag at various targets.
   f. Have children hit a punching bag.

g. Have children jump rope.
h. Have children play Angels in the Snow.
i. Have children move on scooter boards in a variety of ways.
j. Have children move through an obstacle course.
k. Have children follow lines or maps drawn on the gym floor.
l. Have children climb stairs and ladders.
m. Have children play stepping stones, following foot marks placed on a mat, or play Twister.

TACTUAL PERCEPTION

Except when working with the blind, physical educators generally give relatively little attention to the stimulation of tactual perception in programs emphasizing gross motor development. However, tactual development may be enhanced very conveniently by activities combining kinesthetic and tactual stimuli, and such activities should be utilized when there is a need for tactual development. It is common knowledge that the blind depend upon and maximize their tactual abilities in dealing with the environment. Blindfolding youngsters for brief periods of time or conducting activities in a dark room (the preferred technique) may be productive when tactual perception is an important objective. Some specific suggestions for enhancing tactual perception follow.

1. Touch the various parts of the body of a child with various objects. As the child lies on a mat, ask the child to name or move the parts touched and to identify the characteristics of the object used for touch.
2. Have children move on floors, lawns, beaches, balance beams, and mats while barefooted.
3. Have children perform isometric and isotonic exercises with various objects.
4. Have children climb ropes, cargo nets, ladders, and playground equipment.
5. Have children move through or over a variety of objects, including tires, trampoline beds, mats, playground equipment, and boxes.
6. Activities conducted in a darkened room or for blind or blindfolded children include:
   a. Providing opportunities to feel and discriminate between objects.
   b. Having children feel the position of another person while he or she executes a skill or movement and then ask them to name or reproduce it.
   c. Having children search for objects.
   d. Having children walk or run around a track.
   e. Having children run in the base paths of a softball field.
   f. Having children walk on a sidewalk.
   g. Having children follow tape marks around a floor while barefooted.
7. Other activities that may be employed for the stimulation of tactual perception include swimming, stunts and tumbling, wrestling, and scooter board activities.

5

ACADEMIC
DEVELOPMENT

In earlier chapters, movement activities have been suggested
for the habilitation and remediation of physical fitness and
motor development. The use of physical and motor activities
for this purpose is, of course, widely accepted. In schools,
the responsibility for physical and motor development is
given to physical educators, if such personnel are available,
or is assumed by regular classroom teachers. The development of the physical is generally held to be the priority function in physical education programs regardless of who implements them. That this practice should be continued is not
questioned. However, motor experiences and physical education activities have other values, too. There is a rich potential for education and development *through* the physical as
well as *of* the physical.

The contributions of early movement experiences to cognitive and perceptual development are discussed in other
chapters. If motor activities play a role in cognitive and perceptual development, and if cognitive and perceptual abilities play a role in academic achievement, then, at least an
indirect relationship exists between motor activities and academic achievement. An associated but perhaps more direct
relationship is the focus of this chapter. Here, movement activities are suggested as a *medium* for academic achievement. In essence, the use of motor activities as a medium or
modality rather than as a basis for teaching, reinforcing, and
diagnosing academic abilities related to mathematics, sci-

ence, and language arts is discussed. The focus is directly on academic concepts rather than on the development of perceptual or cognitive abilities which, in turn, influence academic achievement.

It must be emphasized that the use of physical education activities, or the motor activity learning medium (MALM), is not presented as a replacement for the priority functions of physical education. Physical education programs designed to develop the physical and motor should not be replaced by programs designed to enhance academic achievement. However, when the goal or priority for a given child in a particular situation is academic, motor activities may be employed as a method of attaining that goal.

In this chapter, the theoretical basis for and the value of learning academic concepts through motor activities will be briefly considered. Subsequently, examples of motor activities that may be utilized for the attainment of academic abilities will be presented. Research relative to the success with which this approach has been utilized and to its efficacy is discussed in Chapter 14.

Theoretical Basis and Values

The idea of using physical education activities, or the motor activity learning medium (MALM), for the development of academic abilities is not new. However, development, expansion, and refinement of the approach appear to have accelerated in recent years. One partial explanation for this is the growing interest in the education of handicapped children and the need to examine alternative methods of teaching some of them. The MALM has been used successfully with learning-disabled children, slow learners, and children judged to be mentally retarded.

A leader in recent years in the development of the MALM has been James H. Humphrey of the University of Maryland. Humphrey, his collaborators, and his students have developed the MALM concept, have compiled practical activities for program implementation, and have conducted several research studies relative to the effectiveness of the approach. Humphrey (1975) states that this aspect of motor learning "is concerned specifically with children learning basic skills and concepts in the various subject areas in the elementary school curriculum through the medium of motor activity." Humphrey, in many of his writings, holds that the child will "learn better" when learning tasks through pleasurable physical activity. He indicates that when the MALM is utilized, the development of the "total personality" is heightened, and the influence of traditional attitudes tending to separate the mind and body is diminished. In addition, education through the MALM is associated with theories espousing free and natural movements in education.

Humphrey and Humphrey (1974) feel that *motivation, propriocep-*

tion, and *reinforcement* are essential facilitative factors in the MALM approach. They further identify three aspects of motivation that are inherent in the MALM. First, the MALM involves pleasurable play experiences. When activities are pleasurable, they are of interest, and when activities are of interest, the child is eager to participate in them. Secondly, the MALM provides almost instantaneous knowledge of results, or feedback. When knowledge of results is immediately available, the child receives immediate information that tends to accelerate progress, participation, and learning. Thirdly, motivation is enhanced by competition. Many movement activities involve competition and the desire to win. It is believed that such competition motivates participation. Humphrey also indicates that competition encourages cooperation, since winning team games depends on cooperation among members of the same team.

In his writings, Humphrey speculates that *proprioceptive* feedback from the receptors of muscles, skin, and joints contributes in a facilitative manner when the MALM is used for the development of academic skills and concepts. This contention is based on the view that learning takes place in terms of a reorganization of the systems of perception. The sensory systems, consisting of sight, hearing, touch, smell, and taste, are combined with information received from the skin, muscles, and joints (proprioceptors) and are reorganized into functional and integrated wholes in learning. Since movement stimulates proprioceptors, movement facilitates learning. In essence, a greater number of responses are associated with and conditioned to learning stimuli. Sullivan and Humphrey (1973) use the term "motorvation" to describe the combination of the psychological factor of motivation and the physiological factor of proprioception that they feel is inherent in the active game approach to learning.

The third facilitative factor inherent in the MALM identified by Humphrey is *reinforcement.* Humphrey and Humphrey (1974) contend that the MALM reinforces attention to the learning task and learning behavior and so it keeps children involved in the learning activity. MALM accentuates desired behaviors, making them more salient for the purposes of reinforcement, and the gratifying aspect of active games situations provides a generalized situation of reinforcers (Sullivan and Humphrey, 1973).

Although Humphrey is an advocate of the MALM, he is careful to point out that the approach has its limitations. His writing indicates that he prefers to consider this approach as *a* valid approach rather than as *the* approach for teaching academic concepts. He points out that everything cannot be taught through this approach, and he recognizes that children learn differently. Since all children do not learn in the same way, they should not be taught in the same way.[*]

Another advocate of the "active games approach" for the teaching of academic concepts is Bryant Cratty of the University of California, Los Angeles. The basis of Cratty's support of the approach appears to be best expressed in his four-channel model for the study of human maturation, which is discussed in more detail in Chapter 4.

---

[*]Movement activities associated with the MALM are available for reading (Humphrey and Humphrey, 1974; Humphrey and Sullivan, 1970a; Sullivan and Humphrey, 1973), science (Humphrey, 1975; Humphrey and Sullivan, 1970a; Humphrey and Humphrey, 1974), and mathematics (Humphrey and Humphrey, 1974; Humphrey and Sullivan, 1970a).

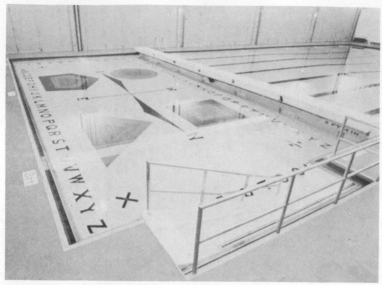

Figure 5-1. Pool bottom designs for academic reinforcement (Yorktown Swimming Pool, Arlington, Va.) From: American National Red Cross. Adapted Aquatics. Garden City, New York: Doubleday & Company, Inc., 1977, p. 121. Illustration, copyright© 1977 by the American National Red Cross, reproduced with permission.

In describing his model, Cratty (1970c, 1972) proposes that at times, various human abilities develop independently and that at other times, bonds are formed between cognitive, verbal, perceptual, and motor abilities to compose functional pieces of behavior. Some of the bonds are considered *natural.* For example, perceptual and motor bonds are naturally formed as the children express themselves in writing. Other bonds are considered *synthetic* and may be used by educators to circumvent learning disabilities. For example, learning to spell by hopping into squares containing letters serves to bond a motor ability (hopping) with a conceptual or perceptual ability. Since this method of teaching spelling is not usual or natural, the bonds so formed are considered *synthetic*. This, then, briefly explains what Cratty means by the use of movement as a "modality" for the attainment of academic concepts or abilities.

Like Humphrey and many other proponents of the motor activity learning medium, Cratty (1972) believes that an advantage of this approach is that it is motivating. Further, the active games approach helps to develop not only the child's academic abilities but also his or her play abilities. Success in play enhances self-confidence, which is, of course, beneficial in play as well as in academic pursuits. In addition to motivation, the active games approach provides an opportunity for children to meet their physical activity needs and to channel them in productive ways. The active game approach also gives those who enjoy and are successful in such activities an opportunity to display and utilize their abilities in learning academic concepts. Cratty (1972) also suggests that is it conceivable that the active games approach may contribute in positive ways to gaining children's attention and maintaining optimum activation levels. To effectively participate in gross motor games, children must direct their attention to the task. In addition, the active games approach allows teachers to easily discern children's inattentiveness and, it is hoped, to arrange experiences so that their attention may be prolonged. Finally, the active games approach may tend to arouse the activation level of children — particularly of those who may be lethargic when other approaches are employed.

Although Cratty is an advocate of the active games approach, he is cautious regarding the expectation of transfer to academic abilities. He indicates that transfer is enhanced when tasks in active games resemble rather closely the academic concepts one attempts to develop. In other words, the academic skills that one desires to enhance should be directly incorporated into the motor activities used as a medium for the development of academic concepts. He would also advocate using the active games approach along with regular classroom instruction.

The integration of physical education with academic concepts is not new. Although not associated with a particular theory or model, the idea that movement activities can contribute to academic functions has been presented by a number of authors — particularly by authors of elementary physical education texts. In addition, teachers have applied some form of the motor activity learning medium for decades. A classic example, of course, are the techniques implemented by Montessori (1964a, 1964b). Action-oriented and tangible movement experiences for the education of all youngsters, including those considered "backward," have been a very important part of her approach.

It is apparent that the motor activity learning medium may be employed as an effective method of teaching academic concepts. Although additional research is necessary to determine its theoretical foundation, effectiveness, transfer enhancement, specific procedures, and use with special populations, the evidence presently available warrants the continued use and exploration of MALM. Logic and some evidence support the contention that the approach is particularly helpful in teaching children who are mentally retarded, those who have certain learning disabilities, and those who succeed in and enjoy motor performance but display lack of interest when more traditional methods are employed.

As mentioned previously, the motor activity learning medium is considered motivating, tends to hold attention of learners, provides an opportunity for physical activity as well as academic learning, is inherently reinforcing, and combines various sensory systems in learning. In addition, the approach may be easily arranged to make learning fun; this is perhaps its most important advantage. It is a change from the usual, more passive learning experience. The fact that learning experiences may be made more "concrete" is a very important part of the approach. In fact, this is certainly an important reason for the effectiveness of the approach with slow learners and mentally retarded youngsters. The approach enables the teacher to observe overt expressions of the thinking process of children, which should help teachers to identify when and where difficulties in the learning process exist. Since the activities are fun, they may be played out of school, thus helping children to learn or reinforce academic concepts to which they were exposed while in school.

Although there are many benefits, there are also shortcomings in the motor activity learning medium. First, academic concepts experienced and learned in movement settings may not always transfer to other academic settings. It is clear that transfer is enhanced when the experiences in the two settings are made as similar as possible. Secondly, all academic concepts do not lend themselves to learning through the motor activity learning medium, and there are times when the use of this approach would be inefficient. For example, there is little question that some concepts may be taught more quickly and more effectively through other approaches. If time considerations become paramount, the use of MALM may not be justified. Teaching abstract concepts may be difficult to arrange through the motor activity learning medium and may not be necessary for learners able to deal with abstractions. Third, the approach may be effectively implemented with certain youngsters and inappropriate for others. Different children learn differently, and teaching methods ought to consider the ways that children learn best. If certain children respond well to the MALM, then it is obvious that the approach should be employed at appropriate times. If not, there is little justification for incorporating it. It is obvious that, in deciding when to implement the approach, the teacher must weigh its advantages and disadvantages in a particular situation. It cannot be emphasized enough that MALM is *an* approach rather than *the* approach.

Components of Academic Achievement

In this section, academic components that may be developed or enhanced through the motor activity learning medium will be identified. In addition, examples of activities will be presented to convey how the MALM may be employed to attain certain academic concepts.

Language Arts Concepts

Early experiences of children in language arts at pre-school or beginning school levels involve learning to speak, listen, write, and read. Each of these is concerned with developing communication skills and involves the ability of the child to decode or encode information, i.e., the ability to meaningfully receive and transmit information for the purpose of communication. Children unable to communicate are at a definite disadvantage and have been labeled as dyslexic, retarded, slow learners, learning disabled, emotionally disturbed, disadvantaged, and aphasic. The motor activity learning medium may be used to help children develop abilities to speak, listen, write, and read. Although the activities that are employed often contribute to more than one ability at the same time, the various abilities will be separated for the sake of discussion. In the first part of this section, the contributions of the motor activity learning medium for the development of reading skills will be discussed. Subsequent sections will deal with writing, speech, and listening.

READING

Pre–Reading Abilities

Regardless of the approach utilized in teaching reading, there appear to be certain skills that the child must master in order to be considered an effective reader. The ability to recognize letters, patterns, and other forms that serve as symbols and the ability to associate sounds with individual symbols or combinations of symbols are early requirements. A number of activities have been employed in movement settings to enhance such pre-reading abilities. A popular one involves children in shaping their bodies to form letters of the alphabet, numbers, or geometric forms. A child may be asked to form such shapes with the whole body, with only certain parts of the body, with partners, with groups of three or more, or with various pieces of equipment. As they become sophisticated, groups of children may form words. Geometric shapes are formed in various dance activities. Another technique, which has been popularized by Cratty (1971a) and used by many educators in a variety of ways, has been to have children play games on grids or hopscotch-type patterns (Fig. 5–2). With this technique, grids or patterns are painted, drawn, or taped on playing surfaces. Children may be asked to spell words by hopping or jumping from one section of the pattern to another. They may also throw objects into a section and then jump into the section to retrieve them, imitate sequences demonstrated by other children, or play traditional games of hopscotch on various patterns (Fig. 5–3).

Games may be developed or modified by teachers to stimulate letter recognition. For example, Humphrey and Sullivan (1970a) have modified the well-known game Steal the Bacon to help children recognize letters of the alphabet. Children are divided into two equal teams facing each other in lines at a distance of 10 to 12 feet. Each child on a team is given a letter that matches a letter assigned to a member of the opposite team. The "bacon" is symbolized by an eraser, an Indian club, or some other object placed between the two teams. The teacher holds up a letter and the children of both teams attempt to "steal the bacon." If a child from one team succeeds in stealing the bacon before being tagged by his opponent, two points are scored for his team. If the child is tagged, the opponent's team scores a point.

The MALM has also been utilized to identify and use various geometric forms. Squares, rectangles, circles, triangles, diamonds, paral-

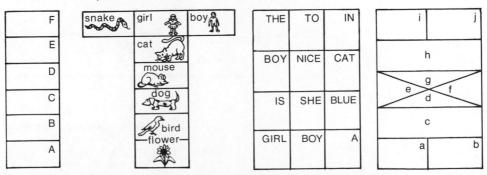

Figure 5–2. Grids and patterns for letter and form recognition.

A

Figure 5–3. A. Hop to numbers. B. Jump to numbers.

B

lelograms, and trapezoids may be painted, taped, or drawn on outdoor surfaces, gymnasium floors, or tumbling mats. Children may run
to these figures in relay races, use them as "safe" areas in tag
games, or jump and hop in, out, and around them. This author has
used such shapes effectively as "home positions" with trainable
mentally retarded children. Shapes are taped on a playing area, and
when children arrive for physical education, they are assigned a form
as a home position for the duration of the class. Children may be
asked to move to certain goals and return to their home positions or
to move to their home positions when directions are to be given or
some activity is to be explained. (The home position is also useful as
a safety measure, to move children to a secure position during an
emergency situation.) Shapes may also be constructed so that they
may be carried in games or moved about for various activities. It is
also possible to collect objects of a variety of shapes and incorporate
them in games, relays, or obstacle courses. For example, tires or
tubes may be used as circles, tumbling mats as rectangles, vaulting
boxes as trapezoids, and boxes as squares. Letters and shapes are
frequently constructed by teachers from blocks of wood or cardboard or are painted on playground balls or other movable objects.
Children may be asked to use these objects as goals, to throw and
catch them, or to carry them in games.

Sight Vocabulary

Games and activities have also been utilized to develop or reinforce *sight vocabulary*, the ability to recognize printed words. Activities to develop sight vocabulary generally involve reading a word or
phrase and performing some action based on it. For example, obstacle courses may be designed in which instructions read from
signs are required for successful completion. Signs may direct the
participant to go over, around, under, or through objects. They may
represent traffic signs such as "stop," "yield," "one way," "no left
turn." They may instruct the participant to hop, jump, skip, leap,
crawl, roll, or climb at various stations of the course.

Activities using grids like those depicted in Figure 5–2 may also
be utilized for teaching or reinforcing sight vocabulary. Children may
be asked to jump to a word or to a picture representing a word
shown on a flash card. For example, the word "dog" is shown on a
flash card and the child is asked to jump to a picture of a dog located within the pattern or grid. In this activity, the child not only learns
to read a word but also learns its meaning.

A very common game that may be modified to teach or reinforce
sight vocabulary is Simon Says. One modification is to have "Simon"
hold flash cards to communicate directions rather than giving directions verbally. For example, Simon may ask the class to jump, hop,
shake, twist, sit, stand, freeze, or stop by showing the appropriate
card. Such commands must be obeyed by the class before another
card is shown. Another modification is to have Simon verbally indicate an action such as "jump" and have children pick out the word
"jump" from their flash cards and perform the action within a specified time limit.

Another game that is quite popular with elementary school youngsters is Red Light. In this game, one child is designated as "it" or the "policeman" (or policewoman). The policeman (policewoman) stands on a goal line on one end of a play area while the rest of the children (the "commuters") stand on a starting line at the other end of the play area. When he (she) yells "green light," the children are allowed to run toward the policeman (policewoman) until he (she) counts to ten. At the count of ten he (she) yells "red light," and the children must stop immediately or be sent back to the starting line. The first player to touch the policeman (policewoman) becomes the next policeman (policewoman). A modification of this game, to involve the reading of words, is to have the policeman (policewoman) hold up action words written on cards such as "jump" or "hop." Such actions would need to be completed before the policeman (policewoman) counts ten and yells "red light."

A similar game, developed by the author, is entitled "Word Race" and may be used to reinforce words from basal readers or other children's books. In this game, all children stand on a starting line. The teacher holds up word cards and calls a child's name. If able to identify the word, the child hops forward the number of hops indicated on the back of the card. If unable to identify the word, the child hops backward the number of hops indicated on the back of the card. Children are called in order, and if a child misses a word, the next child is asked the same word. Of course, movements other than hopping may be employed in the game.

Word Analysis Skills

Relay games may be easily modified to enhance rhyming abilities. For example, the first player of each team runs to a chalkboard or hard-top area and writes a word. Upon returning to the line, the child gives the chalk to the next person, who must now run to the designated area and write a word that rhymes with the previous word. The first team that finishes is declared the winner. Children may get help in this game from members of the same team.

Another game that may be modified for rhyming skill and that is very familiar to classroom teachers is Duck, Duck, Goose. In this game, children sit in a large circle. One child is designated as the "ducker" and says "duck" as he or she walks around the circle and taps each child gently on the head. When the "ducker" taps a child and says "goose," the child tapped chases the "ducker" to the space previously occupied by the tapped player. If the "ducker" is tagged before reaching this point, the "ducker" must go into "soup pot" for one turn. This game may be played by having "duckers" say rhyming words as they move around the circle. If unable to add a rhyming word, the child must say "goose" to the next person. Children may prepare for the game by reading lists of rhyming words prepared by the teacher or by developing lists themselves.

Games may also be used to help children understand word endings. In a game developed by Humphrey and Sullivan (1970) entitled "Plural Relay," children are placed in relay formations facing a chalkboard. The teacher writes a list of nouns on the board in front of each team. On the signal "go," the first player of each team runs to the board and makes a plural out of the first noun. The player then runs back to the next player, who makes a plural out of the second noun appearing on the list. The game continues until one team finishes putting all nouns into plural form. These authors have designed a similar game entitled "Ending Relay," in which the endings s, ed, and ing are used. In this game, each relay team is given a box in which vocabulary words with s, ed, and ing endings have been placed. The children run to the box, pick out three words, one with each ending, pronounce the words, and run to the next person in line. The game continues until all members of one team have completed the task.

Games may also be played in which synonyms and antonyms are emphasized. Again, relay races may be employed for such games. The teacher may write words on the board facing each team (different words should be written for each team). The object of the game is to have the first child run to the board, write a "same" word or an "opposite" word next to the first word, and run and touch the next player, who then repeats the activity with the second word. The game continues until one team has completed its list.

The game Steal the Bacon, which was mentioned previously, may again be modified to learn word "opposites." In this modification, children on teams may be given a word while children on the other team are given an "opposite" word. The teacher then calls out a word and the child with that word from one team and the child with the opposite word from the other team attempt to "steal the bacon."

Word Meaning

Another value of the motor activity learning medium is that it may be employed to help children learn the meaning of words. Several of the activities already mentioned may be used for such purposes. For example, words used for directions in obstacle courses, activities in which children jump to pictures representing objects read by children, or games in which children act on the basis of read words may be employed. In addition, children may be asked to "act out" the names of animals, vehicles, or movements read from cards as they move in a circle around a play area. They may be asked to "act out" words while seated in a circle formation. In circle games, the teacher may call on one or several children to "act out" a word or to imitate actions "acted out" by one child. Since the movements of children are obvious in such activities, there is generally little doubt as to the appropriateness and speed of their responses.

Spelling

Another ability related to reading that may be developed through the MALM is spelling. The first example involves children on relay teams. Each child on a team is given a letter of the alphabet. The teacher calls out a word, which is to be formed by letters held by the children. The children run individually and in proper order to a designated area to form the word. The team that finishes first is declared the winner.

A game referred to as Line-up Ball has been slightly modified by this author to integrate physical education activity with spelling. This game can be used to prepare children to play softball or baseball. Players are separated into two teams that are alternatively "at bat" or "in the field" as in softball. Players are assigned a letter of the alphabet. When at bat the player kicks a stationary playground ball as far as possible and runs to a base and back to home. Players in the field must get the ball and line up at home plate before the kicker runs to the base and back to home. If the kicker completes the run before the fielders line up, he or she scores a run. If not, an out is made. In modifying the game to involve spelling, the teacher selects a word that must be spelled by letters held by the team in the field. Instead of simply forming a line, fielders must line up according to the sequence of letters in the word. Another modification of this game would be to assign letters of the alphabet to the fielders and have them line up in alphabetical order before the player at bat completes the designated run.

Spelling games may also be developed using the grids or patterns previously suggested for letter recognition. Instead of simply hopping or jumping to letters, children may spell words, syllables, or phonics given by the teacher or other youngsters. At times, children may spell words by jumping or hopping to letters and may ask other children to determine the word spelled.

SEQUENCING

Once word skills are reasonably developed, games may be played to help children read and construct phrases and sentences. Nouns, pronouns, adjectives, verbs, prepositions, conjunctions, and disjunctives may be communicated and acted out very concretely in motor activities. For example, the child may be asked to "throw the red ball into the basket as quickly as possible." In this basic sentence, the teacher may change the verb, noun, adjective, or adverb and observe the child's responses.

Relays may also be utilized as a fun way to help children construct sentences. For example, each child on a team may be given a word. Children are then asked to run individually to a sentence tray and put their words in the place appropriate to form a sentence from the words given to the entire team. It is the responsibility of the last player to make any necessary adjustments to form a proper sentence. As children become more sophisticated, they each may be given a sentence instead of only a word. For example, five separate sentences would be given to a team of five members. All sentences given must be part of a story. Children then run individually to a wall or board and tape their sentences in the correct order to form a story. The team that finishes first with all sentences in the right sequence is declared the winner.

COMPREHENSION

One of the major concerns of teachers of reading is that children comprehend what they have read. The ability to read words without understanding them is a very common problem in learning to read.

Related to comprehension is the motivation to read and understand what is read. In a study by Humphrey and Moore (1958b), children read stories describing games and then organized and played games based on their reading. These authors reported that 46 per cent of the children involved showed extreme interest in reading, 24 per cent expressed considerable interest, 27 per cent showed moderate interest, 2.7 per cent showed some interest, and 0.3 per cent showed little or no interest in reading. These investigators concluded that children's natural urge to play stimulated interest in reading about new games that they could play. In a related study, Hale (1940) found that both teachers and students exhibited a great deal of interest in a project in which half the children in third and fourth grade classes wrote descriptions of games and the other half read the descriptions and played the games. In this project, the group that played the games criticized and revised descriptions that were not clear. Although these two studies were not particularly well controlled, they lend some support to the idea of having children read materials related to physical education and sports to create or maintain interest in reading and of having them write descriptions of games for other children to play. There is, of course, an abundance of reading material about famous athletes, sporting events, and descriptions of games that could be read by children. The problem with this approach is the need to match reading materials with the reading levels of youngsters. This problem is diminished, however, if stories are prepared by the teacher or by the youngsters themselves. The possibilities regarding the devising of new games are, of course, unlimited, and the problems of reading are greatly diminished.

WRITING

Before consideration of activities that may be employed to provide writing experiences for children in movement settings, it is important to recognize that writing depends on certain readiness skills that normally develop during the pre-school years. For example, writing involves abilities related to gross and fine motor coordination, visual-motor coordination, figure-ground perception, perceptual constancy, and spatial relationships. It is obvious that a child will have difficulty in writing if his or her ability to appropriately innervate muscles in moving a pencil, to perceive forms, to understand certain relationships between forms and to reproduce forms in time is not developed. Activities to enhance these abilities have been presented in Chapter 4 and will not be repeated here. However, it is important that the teacher consider these "pre-writing" skills when integrating academic and motor activity experiences.

In addition to activities that may be employed to enhance "pre-writing" competency, direct writing experiences may be provided in movement settings. For example, children may write stories about their experiences in play, games, or exercise. They may be asked to write descriptions and rules of games that they themselves devise, or they may write "sports columns." Opportunities may be provided for children to serve as score-keepers and to develop and record their performances on progress charts. Children may write instructions for exercises to be conducted at various stations or lyrics for singing activities. They may develop a file of rope-jumping rhymes that are presented to them or that they themselves create.

Many of the activities suggested previously for the enhancement of reading abilities may also be used for writing abilities. For example, the relay game in which synonyms and antonyms are emphasized involves writing. In this relay, the teacher writes words on the board facing the relay teams, and children run to the board and write "same" or "opposite" words next to the word. They then run and touch the next player, who repeats the activity with the next word. In another relay, children are asked to run to a designated area and write a word that rhymes with the previous word. In still another, the teacher may write a list of words on the board facing each team. Children then run individually to the board and change the word from a singular to a plural, correctly add "ing" to the word, or simply copy and pronounce the word. For a different type of activity, children may be asked to write their own words in grids or hopscotch patterns. They may also write words on cards or on a board for other children to read and "act out."

Drawing is another ability related to reading, and opportunities for drawing may be easily integrated in play and movement settings. Children may draw pictures for grids or patterns, signs and pictures for obstacle courses, or pictures of exercises or of some aspect of a game they have played. They may be asked to develop diagrams of games they have played or devised.

LISTENING

In the chapter on perceptual development, a section was devoted to the contributions of movement experiences to the enhancement of auditory perception. In that chapter, movement experiences to enhance the ability to distinguish and attend to relevant auditory stimuli against a background of general auditory stimuli (auditory figure–ground perception), to distinguish different frequencies and amplitudes of sound and to recognize stimuli as being the same under varying circumstances (auditory discrimination), to determine the source or direction of sound in the environment (sound localization), and to recognize and discriminate variation of auditory stimuli presented in time (temporal auditory perception) were suggested. These abilities are of obvious importance in developing listening skills and must be considered in any program designed to enhance them. Although important for all youngsters, the development of these abilities is especially important for blind children, since they must compensate for their loss of vision by refining their listening abilities.

Humphrey (1974), with the assistance of Robert W. Wilson and Dorothy D. Sullivan, has developed a procedure for teaching reading known as the AMAV (Auditory–Movement–Auditory–Visual) technique. In the first part of the procedure, children listen to and thus receive thoughts and feelings expressed in a story. After this, they engage in movement experiences that are inherent in or are stimulated by the story in some way. Through such experiences, the development of comprehension becomes a part of the child's experience. Following this, auditory and visual experiences are combined as children listen to the story and read along as the story is being read aloud. Humphrey speculates that the movement experience helps the children to bridge the gap between listening and reading and also to comprehend what is read. The creators of the AMAV approach have developed materials related to their technique. Conclusive evidence supporting the technique for the development of reading abilities, however, is evidently not available at present. The technique is mentioned here because it does involve an auditory-movement (A–M) aspect that exemplifies a role of movement in the development of listening abilities. In essence, the child is asked to respond physically, or with movement, to auditory cues. The motor response may be viewed as a rather tangible expression of listening.

In movement settings, children often respond with movement to auditory stimulation. Children respond to verbal directions, whistles, and other auditory signals to start, change, or stop activity, and they move to various rhythmic beats. Games such as Simon Says or Do This, Do That may be arranged so that children listen for directions and attempt to give appropriate motor responses. Children may be asked to listen to stories and to create movements associated with them. Motor responses are made to exercise cadence, exercise records, square dance calls, and signing games. In games such as Call Ball, Crows and Cranes, Red Light, Musical Chairs, Steal the Bacon, and Red Rover, children depend on listening for successful performance. It is quite evident that children who play the game Steal the Bacon must listen carefully for the numbers or words called out If they wish to be successful in the game.

A modification of Crows and Cranes, developed by Humphrey and Sullivan (1970a), is an excellent illustration of how a game may be adapted to stimulate listening as well as to enhance other academic concepts. In this game, a team of players standing side by side and designated as "Crows" faces the other team of players designated as "Cranes" (Fig. 5–4). Each team stands about 5 feet from a center line separating them. If the teacher calls out the word "Crows," the Crows attempt to catch the Cranes before they run to an end line behind them. If the teacher calls out "Cranes," then the Cranes chase the Crows in an attempt to tag them before they reach their end line. Players who are caught must become part of the opposing team. After each chase, the players return to the starting position to repeat the activity.

When the game is used to stimulate auditory discrimination, the teacher emphasizes the initial consonants as "Cr-r-anes" or "Cr-r-ows" is called out. The purpose is to make children aware of these sounds and to develop their auditory perception of the blends in

Figure 5–4. Diagram of the game Crows and Cranes.

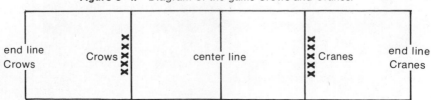

the context of words. Humphrey and Sullivan suggest using other words with beginning consonant blends such as "swans and swallows," "storks and starlings," or "squids and squabs."

The same game may also be used to distinguish words whose beginnings sound the same but are spelled differently. For example, one group of children may be the "k's" and the other groups the "c's". Words such as *kick, cracker, crunch,* or *kettle* may be called out by the teacher. Children learn to listen carefully to words and are motivated to learn the correct spelling of words.

LANGUAGE AND COMMUNICATION

One of the common ways of enhancing language and communication abilities through the MALM has been to develop vocabulary. In movement settings, children are asked to "act out" action words such as *hop, skip, roll, stop,* and *go.* Vocabulary skills are learned or reinforced when words such as *dribble, volley, base, goal, guard, scooter,* and *parachute* are presented. Children learn to associate names with things that are often novel to them, and they have an opportunity to mimic animals, vehicles, moods, or occupations. They apply words such as *in, out, around, through, below, above, over,* and *under* in a variety of games and activities.

Children respond to directions from teachers, records, or tapes when playing games or other activities. Many games are begun, conducted, changed, or ended by language cues. For example, the game of Red Light, which was described earlier, involves language to start and stop movement. Children are guided in rope jumping by verbal rhymes or chants.

Perhaps of greater importance than responding to language is the opportunity to express and communicate. That games stimulate verbal communication is easily demonstrated as one listens to chil-

Figure 5-5. Reciting rhymes while jumping rope.

dren playing games on the playground during recess. When children are members of the same team, they are encouraged to interact verbally. Frequently, their success in a game depends on such verbal communication. In addition, there are some games, such as Have You Seen My Sheep, Farmer in the Dell, Charlie Over the Water, or Ring Around the Rosey, that involve language. Opportunities for expression may also be provided when pupils are asked to explain or demonstrate skills and to evaluate or describe their own performance or others' performance.

The importance of language and communication skills to the developing child is certainly undisputed. Guilford (1967), Bruner (1966), and Piaget (1963) are among the theorists who recognize the value of language in cognitive development. In Chapter 6, specific examples of movement activities that may be employed to enhance representation and communication are presented.

Mathematical Concepts

Since mathematical concepts are involved in many movement games and activities, the MALM may be effectively employed to introduce, develop, or reinforce these concepts. In the literature on the subject, several games and activities have been recommended for the enhancement of number and pattern recognition, concepts of numerical order, counting, number meaning, computing, measuring, geometrical concepts, and other logico-mathematical operations. Once an example or two of an activity to develop a concept is given, the innovative teacher should have no difficulty in developing a repertoire of activities designed to enhance mathematical concepts.

NUMBER RECOGNITION AND NUMERICAL ORDER

Many of the techniques suggested for the recognition of letters and patterns in the previous section on reading may be employed for the enhancement of number recognition. For example, children may be asked to make numbers using their whole bodies or parts of their bodies, and they may run to, from, and around numbers painted, taped, or drawn on play surfaces. They may follow route signs designated on maps drawn on a play area or in obstacle courses. They may be asked to toss objects for accuracy or distance at numbered targets placed on various play areas or walls. Opportunities may be provided in which children identify numbers in grids or hopscotch patterns by hopping or jumping into squares or other geometric forms. Children may be asked to read numbers displayed on large cards or written on a chalkboard by the teacher or other students and to demonstrate their ability to recognize numbers and their meaning by jumping into numbered grids.

There are many games in which children are assigned a number and then are expected to respond in some way when their number is called. An example is the game of Steal the Bacon, which was mentioned previously. In that game, children on the two different teams are assigned the same number and then attempt to "steal the bacon" when the number is called. Another game that has been effectively

Figure 5-6. Throw to the numbers.

employed by this author is Cars. In this game, children stand in a circle formation. The teacher walks around the circle and assigns each child a name of the car for the duration of the game. The first child may be designated as a Ford, the second as a Chevy, the third as a Dodge, and the fourth as a Mercedes. The teacher continues this pattern of assignment until all children are given the name of one of the four cars. When the teacher calls out the name of one of these cars, all of the children representing this car leave their space and run around the circle until they reach their original position. If they tag the "car" in front of them as they run, they score one point. The children return to their position and the teacher calls out the names of other cars. Although the designation of children as cars is motivating, the game may be modified by giving children the numbers 1, 2, 3, and 4. The teacher may then call one number, even numbers, odd numbers, numbers above two, or all numbers to activate the players.

Relay games or their modifications may also be employed to stimulate number recognition. One example might be called Pick Out the Number Relay. In this game, children must run to a designated area and pick out numbers written on cards. The first player picks up number *one,* the second player picks up number *two,* and the game continues until all players on the team have completed a turn. Numbers must be picked in correct order and must be placed in a sequence when the runner returns to the starting line. In another example, Number Erase Relay, a series of numbers are written on a board facing each relay team by the teacher. Children then run to the board and erase a specified number, instead of picking out the number as was the task in the Pick Out the Number Relay.

The last three games mentioned may be arranged to enhance concepts relative to numerical order as well as to enhance number recognition. In fact, the concept of numerical order is inherent in relays in the sense that players perform in order. To heighten this concept, players in relay formation may be numbered and a ball may be passed from the first player to the last player in line. As players receive the ball they may call out their numbers.

Whether in relay formations or in activities in which some kind of race is involved, the concept of numerical order is generally quite clearly demonstrated. In relays, teams finish in a particular order, and in races, there is an order of finish by individuals. In games such as kick ball, where turns are taken, additional opportunities for direct or incidental teaching of numerical order are provided.

COUNTING

Opportunities for counting present themselves very frequently in elementary games and activities. When teams are formed, players are counted so that the number of players on each team is equal. In games such as Crows and Cranes or Cowboys and Indians (Brownies and Fairies), the number of players on each team at the end of the game determines the outcome of the game. Humphrey and Sullivan (1970a) present another game in which children are provided opportunities to practice counting. In this game, entitled Bee Sting, three children are designated as Bees. The three bees attempt to catch (or "sting") the rest of the children as they run within a designated area. When a bee catches a player, that player is taken to the hive of the bee. When all the children are "stung," each bee then counts the number of children in her or his "hive" to determine who is the most successful bee.

Other opportunities for counting include designating the number of times a child must run to a goal and return, the number of laps which must be run, or the number of consecutive times a child and partner are able to successfully throw and catch an object. Certain rope-jumping rhymes require that children perform an activity a certain number of times. At other times, children may be asked to bounce and catch a ball a designated number of times or to count the number of times that they are able to "make" a basket before they miss. Children may be asked to count the number of Indian clubs or duck pins that they cause to fall with a rolled playground ball. In rhythmic activities children are provided with opportunities to count beats in a measure.

A game that this author has employed to enhance counting as well as other mathematical concepts is Busy Bee. In this game, children are generally paired to begin the game. The teacher then calls out instructions such as "face-to-face," "back-to-back," "knees-to-knees," and "elbows-to-elbows." The children perform these activities with their partners. For example, when "face-to-face" is called out, children face each other. When the teacher calls out "busy bee," the children must leave their present partners and secure new part-

Figure 5–7.   Counting the score.

ners before the teacher counts to ten. A modification of this game, which stimulates number meaning, is to have children form different-sized groups. For example, the teacher may precede calling out "busy bee" by stating that children must form groups of three, four, or five, during the next change. They must form such groups before the instructor counts to ten. It is obvious that children must count the players in their groups in order to form groups of appropriate size.

The traditional Easter Egg Hunt may be modified in a number of ways to involve children in counting and motor activities. Objects such as eggs made of plastic or paper cups may be hidden within an area. Children must find and collect the objects as quickly as possible. The child with the most objects is declared the winner. Scavenger hunts involve essentially the same idea, except that a variety of objects rather than same objects become the items for search.

COMPUTING

A very direct and concrete method of enhancing abilities to add, subtract, multiply, and divide is to involve children themselves as units in these operations. For example, in the game of Busy Bee, which was described previously, the children themselves become parts of a group that must be added to or subtracted from to form the appropriate number. In games such as Dodge Ball, Crows and Cranes, Brownies and Fairies, or Bee Sting, the children themselves serve as units to be counted to determine the team with the *most* or *least* number of players. In forming relay teams, the children themselves are counted to determine whether teams are equal in number. If the teams are unequal, the children may be asked what must be done in order to form teams of equal number. Division and multiplication may be stimulated on more advanced levels by asking children to form half or twice as many teams. In the Grand March, children may be asked to form groups of two, four, eight, and sixteen.

A very concrete method of teaching division and multiplication is to ask children to form groups within the total class. For example, children in a class of 15 pupils may be asked to get a partner before the teacher counts to ten. After obtaining a partner, the number of pairs and the remaining number of pupils are counted. In this case, there would be 7 pairs and 1 "left over." Thus, 15 divided by 2 is 7, and 1 left over, or 7½ groups. To stimulate multiplication, the children may be asked to count the number of children in each group and the number of groups. By multiplying these factors, the children learn that 2 times 7 plus 1 equals 15. It is quite obvious that varying the number in each group may stimulate other computations. Through this activity, addition, subtraction, multiplication, and division of whole numbers as well as fractions may be incorporated. Games such as Busy Bee, Squirrel in the Trees, and Three Deep may be modified to include this grouping procedure.

Examples of games involving subtraction and addition are the well-known childhood games Farmer in the Dell, London Bridge, Musical Chairs, and Chain Tag. In these games, children move from one role in the game to another role. There is, thus, a constant subtraction of one and an addition of one as the games are played. In musical chairs, the experience is made very concrete as the number of children remaining in the game becomes progressively smaller. In the game of Chain Tag, in which players are added to the "tagging" chain, the concept of adding is made concrete as the chain becomes larger and larger.

Another favorite game in elementary physical education programs, which needs no modification and may be directly employed to stimulate elementary computing concepts, is Three Deep. In this game, children stand in a circle formation in pairs. One member of the group faces to the center of the circle and the second member lines up behind the first player and also faces toward the center of the circle. A "chaser" and a "runner" stand outside the circle. When the signal to begin the game is given, the chaser tries to tag the runner. The runner attempts to flee and can "save" himself or herself by standing in front of the child closest to the inside of the circle in a paired group. This action forms a group of three, which is not permissible. The child on the outside of the circle but part of the group must leave and become the runner. If the runner is tagged, he or she becomes the chaser.

A final example in which children themselves serve as units for simple computation is the popular game Squirrel in the Trees. It is similar to Three Deep. Children are placed in groups of three. Two children in each group hold hands while the third member stands within the circle made by the other two children. The two children holding hands represent the "trees" and the third member represents the "squirrel." As in Three Deep, there is a runner and chaser outside of the groups. The chaser attempts to tag the runner who, of course, tries not to be tagged. The runner can save himself by moving into one of the groups and replacing the squirrel. The squirrel who was previously in the trees must move out of the group and become the new runner. Again, if the runner is tagged, he becomes the chaser. In this game, concepts of division and multiplication are stimulated by the formation of groups, and the concepts of addition and subtraction are stimulated as children attempt to maintain groups of three.

In other games and activities, children may be asked to physically express their understanding of a number concept. They may run to or around a designated area or repeat an activity a certain number of times. For example, they may hop twice on the right foot and once on the left or bounce a ball three times and then catch it. The instructor may have the children perform a certain number of cycles in an obstacle course or repetitions of an exercise.

A game that has been employed by this author is known as Add One. In this activity, a child observes a movement made by another child and simply imitates it and adds another movement. The next child imitates the two movements and adds a third. The game continues until the sequence is missed or until it becomes too difficult for the children.

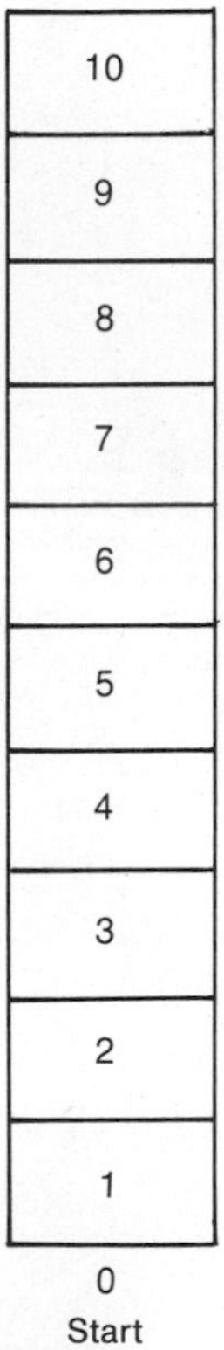

Children may also be asked to perform movements a certain number of times to attain a goal. For example, they may hop, jump, or skip a particular number of times or count the jumps necessary for them to move from one point to another. A mark may be placed on a playing surface after each jump, and the marks are then counted. Another technique involves the use of grids or square patterns to express an understanding of number concepts. For example, using the pattern presented in Figure 5–8, a child may be asked to jump in each square numbered from one to five. The child responds by jumping four times. The child may then be asked the difference between five and one. The child begins at zero and jumps to five, executing five jumps, and the difference between zero and five is expressed and experienced through movement. It is obvious that the technique provides innumerable opportunities to develop and solve addition and subtraction problems.

Patterns presented in Figure 5–2 for letter and form recognition may also be employed for the development of mathematical concepts. Instead of placing letters or words in the patterns, numbers and signs, ($+, -, \div, \times, =$) may be placed within the squares. Children are then asked to jump to numbers called out by the teacher, to develop problems for other children to solve, or to show their own abilities by creating and solving problems. For example, a child may jump into squares representing a two, a plus, a two, an equals sign, and then a four. Then the next child may repeat the problem or create a new problem to be solved.

Games and activities can be used in which action is initiated following the solution of a problem or in which computations become an integral part of the game or activity. Games in which a number is the cue for beginning an activity are the first kind. In Steal the Bacon or Line Soccer, children on two teams are numbered consecutively. When their numbers are called, they must take some action. Instead of simply calling out their numbers, the teacher can devise a problem, the solution of which gives the number to initiate action. For example, instead of calling out the number *four*, the teacher may call out, "six minus two," "one plus three," "two times two," or "eight divided by two."

10
9
8
7
6
5
4
3
2
1

0
Start

Figure 5–8.
Vertical pattern.

Relay games may be arranged in which success depends on solving problems. For example, the first child on each team runs to a chalk board and writes a number. The next child must write another number and add the two numbers together. The game continues until all players have had a turn. Other problems might involve subtraction, multiplication, division, or some combination of these operations. Or children may be asked to write numbers in progressions of two, four, ten, and so on.

Most games involve scoring, and addition and subtraction are obviously involved in computing scores. For example, children add when they toss objects at number targets. They count the number of bowling pins toppled or the number of times they "make" a basket. They add their points in shuffleboard. In relays, the number of times each team wins can be recorded and added. Children may be asked the difference between the number of games won by their team and the number won by another team. They may be asked to keep records and charts of their own performances or the performance of their team.

As their mathematical abilities become more sophisticated, children may involve themselves in computing operations on a higher level. For example, they may compute bowling scores, batting averages, foul shot percentages, or win-loss percentages. To enhance learning fractions, they may be asked to climb one half, one quarter, or three quarters of the way up a pole.

MEASUREMENT

In reflecting on the various motor activities engaged in by children, one realizes that such experiences lend themselves to innumerable opportunities for measurement. The most basic concepts of measurement are evidenced when gross comparisons are made. Children are able to distinguish tall from short, fast from slow, heavy from light, far from near, long from short, and weak from strong. From these "opposites," concepts of measurement become more precise as jumping distance, throwing distance, jumping height, and running speed are measured. Children may measure and compare their height, weight, speed, and strength. They can measure the speed with which they or their relay team can complete a task. They may measure "closeness" in horseshoe-type games, in which rings or bean bags are tossed at some target.

Children may have opportunities to help measure areas, boundaries, and goals used in many games and activities. They may help to establish base distances for Kick Ball or center and end lines for games such as Dodge Ball and Crows and Cranes. They may construct foot and inch scales for measuring broad jumps, maps of a region, patterns for hopscotch, and mazes for agility races. As they become more sophisticated, children may be asked to lay out a softball diamond or a basketball court.

Rhythmic activities may be employed for the enhancement of time concepts. For example, children learn to perform activities according to a particular beat and to move slowly in one tempo and quickly in another tempo. Their movements are short and abrupt or long and sustained. Patterns are conducted for certain periods and are then changed after a certain amount of time.

Learning to "tell time" may also be enhanced in other movement settings. In addition to measuring speed of performance, children can record the number of minutes spent on an activity or the time taken in a particular part of a game. They may also learn that a given period of time remains invariable regardless of the nature of the activity. They learn that time is not dependent on whether or not they enjoy an activity. For example, when station-to-station techniques are employed, children may be asked to spend three minutes on each station in a circuit. They learn that the time is the same even though the nature of the activity is changed.

Crist (1968) employed many methods of teaching time concepts through the motor activity learning medium. In his study, two large clocks were painted on a playing area. In one activity, girls stood on numerals representing hours and boys stood on numerals representing minutes. As different times were called out, children would move in a way that represented the movement of hands on a clock. Subsequently, relays were played to develop or reinforce time-telling concepts. In certain relays, children would run to numerals representing designated times, touch the clock, and return to the starting position. In other relays, team members were numbered from one to twelve, representing various positions on a clock. When certain hours or minutes were called out or displayed on flash cards, the child representing that time would leave his place in line and try to touch the appropriate time on the clock and return to his team before a member of the opposite team completed the same task. Points were awarded to the teams according to the success of their members. In other activities, children stood in circle formations on numerals within the large clock. When a certain time was called out, a ball was passed to the child representing that time. Children of one team attempted to pass the ball to the correct team member before children of another team completed the task. At more advanced levels, two balls were employed in order that hour and minute responses could be demonstrated.

BASIC GEOMETRIC CONCEPTS

Although the formal subject matter of geometry is generally considered an upper level school experience, some forms of geometry as well as certain readiness activities may be developed in early childhood. In other sections of this chapter as well as in other chapters, activities have been suggested for the enhancement of form recognition. In such activities, recognition of circles, squares, rectangles, triangles, diamonds, and other geometric forms is emphasized. Characteristics of such forms, including size, number of points and angles, and symmetry and be demonstrated as children move in, out, around, over, and under objects representing these geometric forms.

Geometry involves the ability to understand relationships between objects existing in space. Three-dimensional as well as two-dimensional perceptual and conceptual relationships are involved. In addition, the child must develop the ability to perceive, hold, and manipulate operations in his mind. The ability to perceive the position of objects in space and their relationship to each other comprises spatial abilities that have been discussed in Chapter 4. In that chapter, movement experiences for the development of spatial relationships have been presented in detail.

In addition to these basic abilities, an understanding of certain elementary geometric concepts may be enhanced through movement games and activities. For example, the concept of perimeter may be developed or reinforced in circle games or in activities in which children move around triangles, squares, rectangles, or diamonds. The concept of a perimeter may be explained in association with boundaries for playing games. Side lines and end lines indicate the perimeter of a playing area; foul lines and outfield fences represent the perimeter of a baseball diamond; side lines and end lines represent the perimeter of a basketball court or football field. In games such as Dodge Ball and The Huntsman, children must stay within the perimeter of the playing area.

In movement activities, children learn to distinguish straight, curved, vertical, horizontal, diagonal, parallel, and intersecting lines. They follow such lines while running races or moving through an obstacle course. Certain games require children to stay within boundaries during play or to perform certain activities within designated areas. In addition, the characteristics of such lines may be demonstrated. For example, the concept that a straight line is the shortest distance between two points may be easily demonstrated by comparing running straight down a playing area with running around chairs placed as obstacles in the runner's path. The characteristics of parallel lines may be easily demonstrated as children run in lanes on a track.

Opportunities to develop or reinforce concepts related to the radius and diameter of a circle are also available in movement settings. A popular activity that may be employed to develop such concepts is the game of Jump the Shot. A rubber ring (or some other soft object) is attached to a rope. Children stand on a circle painted on a playing surface. A child or teacher stands in the center of the circle and swings the rope around the circle at ground level. Children on the perimeter of the circle attempt to jump over the object as it comes towards them. Not only is this fun, but the concept of radius is demonstrated as children learn that the distance between the center of the circle and any point on its perimeter is the same. In the same game, children may be encouraged to jump over the shot at different distances from the center of the circle in order to learn the effects of shortening the radius of rotation as angular velocity remains constant. At more advanced levels, the effects of shortening the radius of rotation may be demonstrated in activities such as jumping and turning while extending the arms outward or bringing them toward the body. Again, at more advanced levels, relationships among the radius, diameter, area, and perimeter may be demonstrated.

OTHER LOGICO–MATHEMATICAL OPERATIONS

Two other operations related to mathematics are classification and seriation. *Classification* is related to set concepts, and the term is defined as grouping things that have common characteristics. In motor games and activities, children are provided opportunities to classify movements, stunts, locomotor activities, the characteristics of abilities of children, shapes, and objects. Games and rhythmic activities may be arranged to stimulate the classification of body parts, body movements, and various objects.

Seriation is another logico-mathematical operation. It is the ability to arrange things according to a dimension along which they differ. For example, children may arrange or order things according to length, width, color, height, weight, or girth. Opportunities may be provided to order or seriate balls, bats, tires, balance beams, targets, and distances. They may seriate forms that they create with their own bodies or that are created by groups of children.

The abilities of classification and seriation have been used by Piaget to demonstrate the mental operations of children at different stages of cognitive development. In Chapter 6, additional examples of movement activities that may be arranged to stimulate these mathematical operations are presented.

Science Concepts

Motor activities by their very nature involve the human in motion. In the early years, the child learns to move in order to play in and learn from the environment. This process of learning continues as the human organism attempts to perfect movement and performance in motor activities. That learning and performance in movement and in sport activities may be enhanced by the application of science concepts is, of course, common knowledge. Institutions preparing teachers of physical education have long included basic and applied science concepts in their programs. Such concepts help in the understanding of the physical world, and methods of improving performance are aimed at enhancing that understanding. In some cases, classroom teachers have used motor experiences as examples when teaching science concepts, and in other cases physical education teachers have attempted to incidentally integrate science concepts with physical eduction. The research available, although quite limited, tends to support these latter practices. It appears that children are motivated to learn science concepts through motor learning. In addition, science concepts may be made concrete and therefore more easily understood, perhaps even retained for longer periods of time, when they are learned or reinforced in movement settings. This section is designed to identify and explain some of the science concepts related to learning through the motor activity learning medium and to provide examples of experiences that may be employed to teach or reinforce them. It is not possible to treat this topic exhaustively in these pages. However, it is hoped that this discussion will stimulate thinking that leads not only to other applications of movement experiences but also to an identification of other science concepts that may be developed through this approach.

EFFECTS OF GRAVITY

Performance in motor activities is, of course, influenced by gravity. Gravitational pull is clearly experienced as children attempt to keep from falling or to jump as high or as far as possible. Gravitational effect may be demonstrated in games and activities in which objects are projected or dropped and in which children attempt to jump for distance. The game of

Call Ball may be used as an example. In this game, children stand in a circle formation. The teacher or one of the pupils stands in the center of the circle, tosses a ball into the air, and calls out the name of a child standing in the circle. The child whose name was called must catch the ball before it hits the ground. In a sense, children must move faster than the force of gravity moves the ball in order to catch the ball.

In another activity, children may be asked to project a ball for distance. As they perform this activity, they should be encouraged to project the ball at different heights and then should be asked which height enabled them to attain the greatest distance. With experimentation, it should become apparent that balls projected at low angles will reach the ground sooner than balls projected at higher angles. Because of the effects of gravity, then, the balls should be projected at higher angles if the purpose is to keep the ball in the air as long as possible. On the other hand, if the purpose is to project an object from one point to another point as fast as possible, then the ball should be projected at lower angles. The best angle, of course, depends upon the velocity of the moving object. A ball thrown at a greater velocity can be projected at a lower angle because it reaches its destination before the effects of gravity force it to touch the ground. This latter concept may also be demonstrated by comparing standing and running broad jumps. In the running broad jump, greater forward velocity enables the jumper to move a greater distance before the effects of gravity force the jumper to touch the ground. Conversely, little distance is attained when a low take-off angle is used in the standing broad jump. In all of these examples, it may be pointed out to children that force is the common factor that projects objects away from the earth's center of gravity.

Another concept related to gravity is that of constant acceleration of gravitational force. Constant acceleration of gravitational force pulls objects downward at a distance of $16.1t^2$ feet (t equals time in seconds during which gravity acts on the object). Thus, in one second, an object falls 16.1 feet and in two seconds 64.6 feet. During the first second the object falls 16.1 feet and during the second second 48.3 feet. Children may feel the effects of accleration as they catch objects from progressively greater heights. This concept may be demonstrated as children drop balls from various heights and observe that, other things being equal, the ball projected from the higher level bounces higher after it strikes the floor.

Conversely, a ball projected upward gradually diminishes in speed (deceleration) until the force at which it was projected is neutralized by the force of gravity. At the point of neutralization, it comes to a stop and begins to fall back toward the earth. As the object falls it accelerates, and when it reaches the point from which it was projected, its speed will be equal to the speed with which it was projected. Thus, the force of projection may be estimated by observing the height of a bounce when the ball returns to the ground as well as observing the height the ball attains when it is thrown straight up.

It must be remembered that the above concepts are based on an assumption of the absence of air resistance. This, of course, is not practical since air resistance is always a factor in the normal environment of the child. Thus, the effects of air resistance on falling objects should also be discussed. Children may project and drop objects of different sizes, shapes, texture, and weight to study the influence of air resistance on projectiles. A shuttlecock cannot be thrown as far as a golf ball, and a softball cannot be hit as far as a baseball, other things being equal. A light object with a large surface area falls more slowly than a heavier, smaller object.

LAWS OF MOTION

During physical activity, force is exerted by the child to begin motion, to accelerate it, to retard it, to change its direction, and to stop it. The effects of such activities are subject to Newton's laws of motion and may be employed to teach youngsters various concepts related to these laws.

LAW OF INERTIA

Newton's first law is that a body at rest tends to remain at rest and a body in motion tends to continue in motion with the same speed and in the same direction unless acted upon by an external force. The law indicates that there is a resistance to change and implies that if a change is desired, some action (force) is necessary to produce it.

In motor activities, it is quite evident that an object or the human body will remain at rest until some force is applied to overcome inertia. For example, a ball remains stationary until it is thrown, struck or kicked. In such activities, the child must generate force in order to overcome the resistance of the object. When an object is rather heavy, like a shot put, the task of overcoming inertia is magnified, and more attention must be given to successful completion of the task. The resistance to change is also evidenced when passengers are thrown forward as a car stops abruptly, or when a child's body on a scooter board moves forward as the child attempts to stop quickly.

Children may learn that once initial inertia is overcome, it is more efficient to continue movement than it is to allow the force to be dissipated, thus creating a need to repeatedly overcome inertia. The instructor may demonstrate and the children may learn that there should be no pause in movements, i.e., there should be a continuity of motion when the goal is continued motion. Children may compare the efficiency of swimming with continuous strokes to that of swimming with a rhythm in which a stroke is executed only after the force of the previous stroke has dissipated. They may find that forward and backward rolls executed from a stand or squat without pause reduce the resistance to motion they experience when they execute rolls from a sitting position. The concept of continuity of motion may also be demonstrated as children compare the ease of executing push-ups or pull-ups continually with that of doing the activity with interruptions.

The principle of transfer of momentum may also be demonstrated in movement activities. Children may learn that momentum developed in a body segment may be transferred to the total body. This principle is demonstrated very concretely in jumping activities. In jumping for distance, the forward swinging action of the arms transfers to the momentum of the total body and results in a longer jump. When a child is on the trampoline, the upward swinging action of the arms results in a transfer of momentum to the whole body, enhancing the attainment of greater height. Similarly, in vertical jumping, the swinging action of the arms also transfers to the total body, making higher jumps possible. In throwing activities, momentum developed in body segments transfers to the whole body and results in greater momentum and improved performance. Children may also know that in order to change the direction of or to stop a moving object, external force must be applied.

The concept that the greater the momentum of an object is, the greater the resistance to change in direction or velocity will be may also be demonstrated. More force must be exerted to stop abruptly when running than when jogging or walking. It may be clearly demonstrated that it is easier to stop a ball that is moving slowly than one moving fast. Since a bowling ball has greater mass, altering its path is more difficult than altering the path of a playground ball. A player running at full speed is more difficult to stop or turn than one running more slowly. A child running at full speed also has more difficulty in changing direction than one running more slowly.

In other motor experiences, attention may be directed to those functions that create resistance to movement. For example, children learn that a ball may be kicked or thrown for a greater distance with the wind than against it. They may compare the effects of different sizes, shapes, textures, and weights on the movement of objects. They may compare the resistance created by different types of swimming suits while swimming, or they may compare running with as opposed to running against the wind. Opportunities may be provided for children to compare rolling a ball in grass of different lengths, in dirt, on hardwood floors, on hard and dry surfaces, and on wet or soggy surfaces.

LAW OF ACCELERATION

Newton's second law states that the velocity of a body is changed when it is acted upon by an external force, and that the change in speed is directly proportional to and in the same direction as the force applied and inversely proportional to the object's mass. Thus, if the same force is applied to two balls of different mass, the ball with the greater mass is affected less. Children soon realize that it is more difficult to change the direction of a heavy runner than a light runner. In experimenting with striking implements, they learn that they are able to swing a light bat much faster than a heavy bat. They also may find that they are unable to run as fast while carrying objects (because velocity is inversely proportional to the mass). They are able to observe that light objects are more affected by air resistance than are heavy objects.

The fact that acceleration (or deceleration) is produced in the direction of the force may be demonstrated or experienced in a variety of situations. Children may strike balls with striking implement making contact at different angles with the ball. They may roll balls to a wall at different angles and study the angles of rebound. They may gently push each other from forward, backward, sideward, or diagonal positions. Opportunities may be provided in which children direct and volley balloons or volleyballs. In each case, they may observe the results of the application of force.

At times, the force may be applied directly opposite to the movement of an object. When children kick a ball coming toward them, they learn that the force they exert must be greater than the momentum of the object in order to make the object reverse its direction. If they stop a rolling ball, they realize that the force applied is at least equal to that of the object. When they roll a ball at objects to make them fall, they are engaged in an experience in which the force of the ball is greater than that of the tumbled objects. By experimentation, they soon learn that some objects fall "easier" than other objects.

LAW OF ACTION AND REACTION

According to Newton's third law, for every action there is an equal and opposite reaction. Although this concept may seem abstract when first presented to youngsters, its meaning generally becomes quite clear with a few concrete demonstrations. When one steps off a rowboat, for example, the backward movement of the boat as it reacts to the force of the foot pushing from it is clearly seen. When one steps off an ocean liner, however, the ship also reacts to the foot's movement, but the reaction is so small that it is not observed. Other examples that clarify the concept include pushing movements in swimming, paddling movements in canoeing, or body movements that produce locomotion.

The amount of counterforce, or reaction, exerted during locomotion is influenced by the nature of the supporting surface. In situations in which forces are dissipated, the counterforce is diminished and propulsion is reduced. Children may experience this sensation when moving on various surfaces. For example, force is dissipated when walking in the sand, making movement more difficult. Ice or water surfaces cause dissipation of force, resulting in less propulsive force. Different types of footwear yield different amounts of friction and counterforce. Efficiency of movement may be demonstrated and compared by running with rubber-soled shoes, sneakers, socks, and bare feet. Differences in footwear may be magnified when children perform activities in which they must change direction quickly or alternately or must stop and go abruptly. The effects of force dissipation may also be demonstrated in striking activities. Children may compare the effects of gripping clubs, paddles, rackets, or bats loosely and firmly. It will become apparent that striking implements held loosely at impact cause dissipation of striking force and a corresponding decrease in propulsive force. Although there are situations for which this may be desired (bunting in baseball), the goal in most games and activities involves increasing the propulsive force.

Associated with the law of action and reaction is the principle that the direction of the counterforce is opposite to that of the applied force. Thus, a pull or push backward in the water causes the swimmer to go forward. To jump vertically, the force should be applied directly downward for maximum results. When a runner in football wishes to run laterally, the runner is aided by a lateral push-off from another player. For a ball to bounce as high as possible, it should be thrown directly downward. Children may be given opportunities to change the angle of starting blocks on a track in order to determine the effect of different angles on their take-off speed.

The importance of surface contact in applying forced to external objects may also be demonstrated in movement activities. When the goal of an activity is to push, pull, or strike, contact with the supporting surface should be maintained until the generation of force is complete. For example, in punting a ball, maximum force occurs when one foot is in contact with the ground during the period that force is generated for the activity. A push or a block is less effective when contact of the foot with the ground is lost. The batter in baseball must maintain contact with the ground for maximum performance. Children may engage in these and other motor experiences in learning about the law of action and reaction.

TYPES OF MOTION

There are two types of motion: translatory and rotary. Both types may be observed and experienced in motor activities. *Translatory motion* occurs when movement takes place over a distance from one point to another. When the movement is in a straight line, it is known as *linear translatory motion,* and if its path is curved, it is referred to as *curvilinear translatory motion.* Rotary motion is characterized by movement about an axis or fulcrum. In rotary motion, the axis of rotation is within the mass of the moving object. In certain activities, an object may undergo both translatory and rotary motion. In addition, a body may experience linear translatory motion as a result of rotary motion of some of its segments.

Motor activities provide many excellent opportunities for the child to observe and experience various types of motion. Linear translatory motion is observed and experienced as a child slides down a slide or pole or coasts on a scooter or skate board. In activities such as walking, running, or jumping, the body experiences linear translatory motion as a result of the rotary motion of its segments. When walking or running along a curved pathway such as occurs in obstacle courses, agility runs, or mazes, the body experiences curvilinear translatory motion. In ball throwing and catching, both curvilinear translatory and rotary motions are evidenced. The ball exhibits rotary motion as it spins and generally follows a curvilinear path as it moves from one point to another point.

The total body or its individual segments may exhibit rotary motion during various types of activities. Rotary movements are experienced during exercise as the child spins, twists, or turns. During forward, backward, and sideward rolls, the individual experiences rotary motion. The spinning movements of skaters exhibit rotary motion. As a child observes or experiences skating, it becomes obvious that shortening the radius of rotation increases rotary speed, and lengthening the radius of rotation decreases rotary speed. The same principle may be observed and experienced as children perform somersaults. They experience rotary motion as they swing in contact with a chinning bar or lie on a Merry-go-round. When performing cartwheels, the child experiences both rotary and linear translatory motion. Rotary movements of individual body segments may be observed and experienced as a child walks (rotation about the hip and knee joints), swims (rotation about the shoulder, hip, and knee joints), or jumps (rotation about the knee and hip joints).

Rotary motion is inherent in certain types of motor activities. In the game of Jump the Shot, for example, a rope with a ring attached to it is swung in a circle and children standing in a circle attempt to jump over the ring as it approaches them. In rope jumping, the rope exhibits rotary motion. The striking of a golf ball and the underhand serve in volleyball are examples of skills in which rotary movements of body segments are exhibited. Pendulum-type rotary movements are exhibited in activities conducted on rings or playground swings.

LEVERS

Body movement is made possible by a system of levers, and movement activities may be employed to demonstrate types of levers and certain basic concepts associated with them. A *lever* is generally defined as a rigid bar that turns about an axis or fulcrum (F), with an effort (E) to move, and a resistance (R) to be overcome. In the human body, bones represent the bar, joints represent the axis, and muscles (point of application of force) serve to move the bone about a joint. There are three types of levers, differentiated by the arrangement of the fulcrum, resistance, and point of application of force. In the first class lever, the fulcrum is located between the force and resistance. In the second class lever, the resistance is located between the force and fulcrum, and in the third class lever, the force is located between the fulcrum and the resistance. Regardless of the type of lever, the resistance arm (RA) is the distance from the fulcrum to the point of resistance. The distance between the fulcrum and the point of force is known as the effort arm (EA). Thus, the RA is always longest in third class levers and the EA is always longest in second class levers. In first class levers, either arm may be longer, depending on the distance from the fulcrum. When $E \times EA$ equals $R \times RA$, the lever balances, and no movement occurs. When $E \times EA$ is greater than $R \times RA$, the muscular effort exceeds resistance, and movement results. When $R \times RA$ is greater than $E \times EA$, the force is not sufficient to overcome resistance. When EA becomes proportionately shorter, the amount of effort needed to cause movement or to overcome resistance increases, but the linear speed with which the lever moves is also increased. When EA becomes proportionately longer, the amount of effort needed to cause movement is reduced, but the speed with which the lever will move is also reduced. Thus, since in second class levers the EA is always longer, this class of lever favors force but sacrifices speed. Conversely, since the EA is always shorter in third class levers, this class of lever favors speed but sacrifices force.

An excellent example of a first class lever in the play environment of children is the seesaw. Children may alter the resistance, effort arm, and resistance arm to demonstrate the principles of levers, and they may observe the effect of such alterations. An example of a second class lever is the wheelbarrow. The force is applied at the handles, the center of gravity of the resistance occurs within the load of the wheelbarrow, and the fulcrum is at the wheel. Children may perform the wheelbarrow walk in experimenting with this lever. Examples of third class levers are, of course, unlimited. Use of third class levers is evident when children strike objects with implements, hands, and legs, lift weights, swim, or walk.

Opportunities may be provided in which children adjust the effort arm of a lever to determine the effect of such a change on the muscular effort required to perform tasks and on the speed and distance of movement. For example, they may compare the amounts of muscular effort required to lift weights held at progressively longer or shorter distances from the body. They may be provided opportunities to study the effects of holding bats, rackets, and other implements at different places while striking objects. A favorite activity of boys is to attempt to hold the arm of a partner down as the partner attempts to flex the forearm against the resistance. The position at which resistance is centered may be altered from near the elbow to near the wrist. After experimentation, children may be asked to decide what positions make movement against resistance most difficult and to explain the mechanical reason for differences.

PROJECTILES

When a body or an object is given an initial thrust and then moves under the influence of gravity and air resistance, it is considered a *projectile.* In motor activities, initial thrusts are applied to objects by throwing, striking, and kicking them. In addition, the body itself is a projectile in jumping, diving, or leaping. Thus, experiences in motor activities may be employed to learn or reinforce concepts about projectiles.

While experimenting with projectiles, children may learn that the distance an object travels is dependent upon the propelling force, gravity, and air resistance. Other things being equal, the greater the initial force, the greater the distance the object will move. Forces applied at the center of gravity of an object result in linear motion. As force is applied away from the center of gravity of the object, spin or rotary motion occurs. Spin causes an object to curve in the same direction as the spin and thus influences the distance the object travels. Because of gravity and air resistance, the angle of projection influences the distance attained by projected objects. In the absence of air resistance, the optimal angle of release is 45 degrees. At that angle, both vertical and horizontal components of force are equal. Because of air resistance, however, this angle must generally be modified. The amount of deviation from 45 degrees is dependent upon the speed, surface area, and weight of the projected object.

Many motor activities may be arranged to teach or reinforce concepts related to the effect of force, gravity, and air resistance on projectiles. Children may project objects with varying amounts of effort. They may be encouraged to kick a ball at, under, over, or to the side of its center of gravity. They may apply spin to the flight of a tennis ball or other light object and observe the effects. They may project a variety of objects such as playground balls, tennis balls, table tennis balls, footballs, medicine balls, or yarn balls. In addition, children may apply various scientific concepts in projecting themselves through space.

Other concepts related to projectiles that may be observed or experienced include the relationship between angles of incidence and reflection, the magnitude of rebound, and the coefficient of elasticity of striking surfaces. Children may roll balls against walls at varying angles and magnitudes to observe the effect of such manipulation. They may use implements of different elasticity for striking, or they may strike objects of varying elasticity with their hands to analyze the coefficient of elasticity of such objects. They may observe the effects of different magnitudes of force on bouncing an object, or of backspin and lateral spin on the velocity and direction of a rolling ball. Children can watch the effects of backspin, top spin, and lateral spin on the rebound angle of a ball as it bounces on horizontal and vertical surfaces. They may observe the effects of varying velocities on spin as objects are rolled or thrown against movable or immovable surfaces. Such activities provide opportunities to observe and apply scientific concepts in a concrete way, thus enhancing the learning and reinforcement of such concepts.

ABSORPTION OF FORCE

The force of impact is diminished if the impact is absorbed over a greater time, distance, or surface area (reducing force per unit area). The receipt of force is inherent in many motor activities, and thus, in such activities children may learn about different methods of force absorption. While catching, children almost naturally "give" with the ball as they pull the catching hand back to receive a throw, thereby increasing the distance and time over which force is absorbed. In addition, a glove is worn to absorb force over a greater time, distance, and surface area. When children land from a jump or fall, force is more gradually absorbed if the various joints of the body are flexed. Children may absorb force more gradually over a greater surface area by rolling after a fall. In trampolining, the performer absorbs force and thus enhances the ability to stop by flexing the knees and other joints of the body. When the goal in trampolining is to gain height, however, the performer avoids flexing the joints. In this case, the greater force exerted on the trampoline bed results in a greater rebound effect.

EQUILIBRIUM

One of the basic elementary concepts that may be taught or reinforced through motor activity is the principle of equilibrium. Balance is involved in virtually every motor activity, and the ability to overcome gravitational forces develops from birth. The human body is balanced when its center of gravity lies over its base of support, and it becomes less stable as the center of gravity moves away from the center of the base. The center of gravity of the human body is sometimes referred to as the *mass center*. It is a point within the body, determined on three planes of mass, about which the gravitational forces are equal. The base of support may be the feet (in walking), the two hands and head (in executing a head stand), or the hands (in performing a frog stand). Certain principles, examples to clarify them, and specific activities to enhance the development of balance have been presented in Chapter 3. It is important, however, to mention here that these principles can be taught or reinforced through the use of movement activities. Thus, the principles that have been formulated to enhance motor performance may, in turn, be learned through the MALM.

PHYSIOLOGICAL CONCEPTS

Experiences dealing with the makeup of the human body are generally included in elementary science programs. As a part of such experiences, children learn fundamental concepts related to the skeletal, muscular, skin, circulatory, and respiratory systems. In the study of the skeletal system, major bones are classified into major groups, the types of bones and their functions are distinguished, and large bones throughout the body are identified. In relation to the muscular system, children learn the purposes of muscles, the kinds and functions of muscles, how muscles work, and how they are attached to bone. Children learn the parts and function of the skin, including the function of sweat glands and how they and the blood vessels help to regulate body temperature. In relation to the circulatory system, children learn the names of parts of the circulatory system and the makeup and functions of blood, blood vessels, heart, and lymph. They also learn how blood circulates throughout the body. They may learn the effects of exercise on the circulatory system and about changes in the beat of the heart pulse. Parts of the respiratory system, the function of different parts, the processes of respiration, and the effects of exercise on respiration are generally included in units dealing with the respiratory system.

It is quite evident that many of the concepts related to the makeup of the human body may be taught or reinforced through activities conducted in movement settings. As children exercise, they are able to feel and observe changes in the structure of their muscles. They observe contraction and relaxation of muscles and the relationship between contralateral muscles during movement. In response to questions dealing with different sizes of muscles, elementary concepts related to the development of strength and endurance may be presented and discussed. In some cases, opportunities may be provided in which children feel the attachment of muscles to bones. As they learn the major types of joints (hinge, ball and socket, and pivot), they may examine the movement possibilities. Opportunities may be provided in which the skull, spinal column, ribs, and limbs may be identified and distinguished according to their movement possibilities. Actions of sweat glands and blood vessels may be contrasted in terms of exercise, temperature, and humidity. During activity, children may observe blood vessels and feel changes in heartbeat. Opportunities may be provided for children to listen to a heart with a stethoscope, to feel and count a pulse, and to feel a chest to count the number of times a child breathes in one minute. Invariably, questions relating to the reasons for differences among children are posed. At such times, basic concepts related to the benefits of training may be taught or reinforced. In addition, the effects of different kinds of activities may be compared. Children may evaluate and account for the strenuousness of different types of exercise.

Writers and practitioners have attempted to integrate the motor activity learning medium with scientific concepts, but relatively little attention has been given to the contributions of motor activities to learning basic physiological concepts. However, it is quite obvious that the association is most direct, that the possibilities for integrating are many, and that movement provides many opportunities for the "teachable moment."

OTHER BASIC SCIENCE CONCEPTS

The opportunities for science experiences in movement settings are virtually unlimited. In fact, it is difficult to identify movement activities that are not related in some way to basic scientific concepts. Humphrey and Sullivan (1970a), in applying the active games approach to learning science concepts, have classified games according to six broad concept areas of elementary school science: The Universe and Earth, Conditions of Life, Chemical and Physical Changes, Energy, Health, and Light. In many cases, they have identified sub-areas within these broad classifications.

For example, the game Light Bounce has been presented by these authors to teach or reinforce concepts relating to light. In this game, two lines are marked on a surface area parallel to a wall. One line (A) is drawn 6 inches from the wall and the other line (B) is drawn 12 feet from the wall.

A team of children stand behind line B and attempt to throw a block so that it lands between the wall and line A. They compare their performance with several other teams engaged in the same activity at other areas. If the block falls outside of line A, each other team gets a point. The team with the highest score is the winner. Humphrey and Sullivan (1970a) indicate that such a game helps children to note that wooden blocks rebound from a wall just as light rays rebound upon coming in contact with a solid object.

These authors have developed a number of similar games to teach and reinforce scientific concepts in all categories they have established. When such games are employed, attention must be given to techniques of enhancing transfer, since children may be so engrossed in the game that they fail to attend to the relationship between the game and its related scientific concept. It also must be recognized that games that are developed often do not give exact replications or examples of scientific concepts. In following the example presented above, one must remember that blocks of wood are not light rays. While there are some similarities in the bouncing reaction, there are also differences that must be considered.

Specific Activities

In the previous section, the use of the motor activity learning medium (MALM) for the enhancement of components related to academic achievement was discussed. Throughout the section, examples of activities to attain this goal were presented. In this section, those examples are summarized and additional ones are suggested. This, of course, is only a partial list of possibilities.

Language Arts Concepts

The list of suggested MALM activities for language arts is divided according to academic ability.

READING

PRE–READING ABILITIES

The following activities are designed to enhance children's pre-reading abilities.

1. Form letters of the alphabet, numbers, or geometric shapes with the whole body, with parts of the body, with partners, and with pieces of equipment.
2. Form parts of the alphabet or words out of letters formed with bodies.
3. Run to, around, and over letters, numbers, and other shapes painted, drawn, or taped on playing surfaces.
4. Play games on grids or hopscotch patterns in which letters and words are written.
5. Make letters, numbers, and shapes out of cardboard, wood, or bean bags and run to them, collect them, or carry them in relay races.

6. Run as fast as possible and in alphabetical or numerical order to letters or numbers placed around a playing area.
7. Play games in which children are assigned letters. For example, in the game of Steal the Bacon, children attempt to steal the bacon when their letter is called. Other games in which activity may be initiated by calling out a letter include Call Ball, Red Rover, and Change Seats.

SIGHT VOCABULARY AND WORD MEANING

The activities listed are suggested for the enhancement of sight vocabulary and word meaning.

1. Place signs within an obstacle course indicating appropriate action to be taken. For example, signs with words such as *hop, jump, under, in, walk,* may be placed at various stations to denote appropriate activity.
2. Have children jump to a picture within a grid depicting a word presented on a chalkboard or flash card.
3. Conduct games in which instructions or names are given on flash cards. Examples of games which may be employed or modified for such purposes include Simon Says, Red Light, Steal the Bacon, Call Ball, Change Seats, Crows and Cranes, Spud, Midnight, and Streets and Alleys.
4. Select relays in which children must pick out movement words (*run, walk skip*) from a pile of words.
5. Have children play Word Race.
6. Ask children to "act out" animals, vehicles, or movements read from cards.

WORD ANALYSIS SKILLS

Children's word analysis skills may be enhanced if they are asked to:

1. Play relays in which players must run to a chalkboard and write words that rhyme with previously written words, make plurals of them, change their endings to "-ed" or "-ing," or write synonyms or antonyms for them.
2. Play a modified version of Duck, Duck, Goose in which the person who is "it" calls out rhyming words as children are tapped on the head.
3. Play games in which activity is initiated by numbers or names. Substitute rhyming words, "same" words, or "opposite" words for numbers or names. For example, in the game of Crows and Cranes, the instructor may call out words that rhyme with Crows or Cranes such as *bows* and *lanes.* Modify the game of Steal the Bacon so that activity is initiated when a word and its antonym are called out.

SPELLING

The activities in the following list will enhance spelling ability.

1. Pass out letters of the alphabet to children on relay teams. Play relays in which children run to a designated area and form words out of their individual letters.
2. Separate children into teams and assign each member of the team a letter. As a word is called out, children line up as quickly as possible in an order representing the word called out.

3. Modify the game of Line-up Ball so that fielders form a line representing the correct sequence of letters in a word.
4. Have children spell words by hopping or jumping to letters placed in grids or hopscotch patterns.

SEQUENCING

Sequencing can be enhanced by the following activities.

1. Write sentences on the board describing movements to be executed by children. Change verbs, nouns, adjectives, or adverbs and ask children to respond with movement to the changes.
2. Give word flash cards to children on relay teams. Play relays in which children run to a designated area and form sentences with their words.

COMPREHENSION

Children's comprehension in language arts can be reinforced by the following activities.

1. Have children read descriptions of games and then organize and play games based on their reading.
2. Have children design games and write descriptions of them, and then have other children read the descriptions and play the games.
3. Provide children with books about famous athletes, sporting events, and descriptions of games.
4. Ask children to write descriptions of their experiences in games and have other children read the descriptions.

WRITING

The following activities are suggested to enhance children's writing abilities.

1. Select, as appropriate, activities to develop gross and fine motor coordination, visual-motor coordination, figure-ground perception, perceptual constancy, and spatial relationships.
2. Write stories about experiences in play, games, or exercise.
3. Have children write rules for games they have devised.
4. Have children develop progress charts and record performances.
5. Ask children to write lyrics to singing games and rhymes that may be used in jumping rope.
6. Play relays in which children run to a designated area and write letters or words.
7. Have children draw grids of patterns or pictures of exercises.
8. Have children draw diagrams of games they have designed or played.

LISTENING

Children's ability to listen can be enhanced by the following activities.

1. Select, as appropriate, activities to develop auditory perception.
2. Read stories to children and ask them to create movement experiences stimulated by the story.

3. Have children perform movements to rhythmic beats.
4. Play games in which activity is started, changed, or stopped according to auditory cues. Examples include: Simon Says, Do This, Do That, Crows and Cranes, Red Light, Red Rover, Brownies and Fairies.
5. Have children listen and respond with movement to exercise records, records of singing games, and square dance calls.

LANGUAGE AND COMMUNICATION

Language and communication skills can be enhanced by the following activities.

1. Provide opportunities for children to "act out" action words.
2. Encourage children to verbally interact as they cooperate as members of teams.
3. Play games involving communication. Examples include: Have You Seen My Sheep, Farmer in the Dell, Charlie Over the Water, Ring Around the Rosey, Cat and Rat, and Red Light.
4. Provide opportunities for children to explain and demonstrate skills.
5. Ask children to verbally explain movements performed by other children.

Mathematical Concepts

NUMBER RECOGNITION AND NUMERICAL ORDER

The following activities are suggested for the enhancement of number recognition and numerical order.

1. Have children form numbers with their whole bodies, with parts of the body, with other children, or with pieces of equipment.
2. When using station-to-station teaching, write the number of repetitions of an activity required at each station.
3. Establish route signs for children to follow in obstacle courses, agility courses, or mazes.
4. Have children play games in which they toss objects at numbered targets.
5. Call out numbers and ask children to jump into squares representing the numbers in grids or hopscotch patterns.
6. Have children play games in which they are assigned numbers and are asked to respond when the numbers are called. Two examples are Steal the Bacon and Cars.
7. Engage children in relays in which they must pick out numbers from a pile of numbered flash cards or in which they must write numbers in a designated order.

COUNTING

There are many games and activities that use counting. Several suggestions follow.

1. Play chasing games in which the winning team is the one with the largest number of players. Examples include: Bee Sting, Crows and Cranes, Brownies and Fairies, Hill Dill, and Red Rover. Have children do the counting.

2. Have children play games in which they must count the number of players on their team or in their group during the game. Examples are: Squirrel in the Trees and Busy Bee.
3. Have children play games such as the Easter Egg Hunt or Scavenger in which they must find, collect, and count objects.
4. Ask children to count the number of jumps executed without error in rope jumping, the number of consecutive catches made of a ball, the number of pins toppled with a ball, or the number of laps run about a given area.
5. Ask children to count beats as they engage in rhythmic activities.

COMPUTING

A number of games and activities are listed that utilize or may be adapted to utilize children's computing abilities.

1. Conduct games in which children themselves serve as units for computation. For example, children in a class may be asked to form dyads, triads, or quadrads. In the games of Busy Bee, Squirrel in the Trees, and Three Deep, children must maintain groups of two or three.
2. Ask children to form teams within a class. Ask them, when appropriate, to form half as many teams, twice as many teams, or teams consisting of a certain number of players.
3. Play games in which children are added and subtracted. Examples include Farmer in the Dell, London Bridge, Musical Chairs, and Chain Tag.
4. Have children physically express their understanding of number concepts by asking them to run around a designated area a certain number of times or to perform a certain number of repetitions of an activity.
5. Play games in which children imitate movements made by other children in a series. An example is "Add One."
6. Make grids in which numbers as well as mathematical signs are placed in squares. Ask children to jump to numbers called out, to develop problems for other children to solve, or to solve problems created by the teacher or other children. For example, a child may jump to a two, then to a plus sign, to a three, to an equals sign, and finally to the correct answer.
7. Play games in which action is initiated following the solution of a problem. For example, in the game of Steal the Bacon, action is begun as a number is called out. Instead of calling out the number, the teacher may call out a problem such as "three minus two equals." The answer is, of course, "one," and the child representing number one would run out in an attempt to steal the bacon. In such games, addition, subtraction, division, and multiplication problems may be employed.
8. Have children add scores obtained in target games.
9. Have children compute scores in bowling games, batting averages, foul-shooting percentages, or win-loss percentages.
10. Have children perform the Grand March in which groups of two, four, eight, and sixteen are formed.

MEASUREMENT

Many motor activities help to develop measurement abilities.

1. Have children compare one another in terms of height, speed, weight, or girth.
2. Have children measure distances of jumping, throwing, or running.

3. Provide opportunities for children to measure distances for goals or areas for play.
4. Employ rhythmic activities for the measurement of time.
5. Provide opportunities for children to measure speed of performance. For example, children may measure the number of seconds required to run from one point to another.
6. Construct a large clock on a playing surface. Ask children to run around the clock or to run to numerals on the clock. Play relays in which children run to numerals representing hours, to times called out by the teacher. Play circle games on the clock in which a ball is thrown to a child representing a particular time. As children become more sophisticated, use two balls: one for the hour and the other for the minute. Have children of one team attempt to pass the balls appropriately before children of another team complete the task.

GEOMETRIC CONCEPTS

Geometric concepts can be taught or reinforced in motor activities. Some suggestions follow.

1. Have children move in, out, around, over and under subjects representing various geometric forms.
2. As children play games, explain and use terms such as *perimeter, circle, radius,* and *diameter.*
3. As straight, curved, vertical, horizontal, diagonal, parallel, intersecting, or perpendicular lines are utilized in games, explain their meanings and characteristics. For example, the concept that a straight line is the shortest distance between two points may be learned or reinforced as children compare their running performance in straight and curved pathways.
4. The concept of radius and the effects of shortening and lengthening the radius of rotation may be developed as children play Jump the Shot, turn themselves around, play rope jumping games, or play on a merry-go-round, swings, or rings.
5. Have children observe the formation of various geometric shapes in dance activities.

OTHER LOGICO-MATHEMATICAL OPERATIONS

Activities to enhance classification and seriation are presented in Chapter 6.

Science Concepts

EFFECTS OF GRAVITY

The following activities can be used to enhance understanding of the effects of gravity.

1. Play games in which children attempt to catch or throw objects before the effects of gravity force the objects to the ground. For example, in Call Ball, children must catch a ball that has been thrown upward when their names are called and before the ball reaches the ground. Ask children to see how far they are able to jump or to throw an object.
2. Have children project objects of different weight, size, texture, and surface area and compare the effects of gravity on each.
3. Have children drop objects from different heights or throw objects upward to different heights and observe the effects of the rebound. Discuss the reason for differences in rebound.

LAWS OF MOTION

Concepts about the laws of motion can be taught and reinforced through movement activities.

1. Provide opportunities for children to overcome the inertia of various kinds of objects and to compare the amount of force needed for different objects.
2. Have children test the principle of continuity of motion by comparing continuous and interrupted activity. For example, children may compare chinning executed without interruption with chinning executed with a pause between "chins."
3. Provide opportunities to test the principle of transfer of momentum by having children compare performance in jumping with arms swung with jumping with little or no movement of the arms.
4. Have children attempt to change direction while running at full speed and then at half speed. Ask children to compare and account for differences in their ability to change directions at different speeds.
5. Provide opportunities for children to compare the distance a ball rolls as a function of friction.
6. Have children compare throwing or kicking objects into and with the wind.
7. Provide opportunities for children to strike objects at different angles and discuss the effects of different angles of application.
8. Provide opportunities for children to apply force at, under, over, and to the side of the center of gravity of a ball. Discuss the effects of applying force at different points.
9. Have children compare and analyze the effects of walking on different surfaces and in different types of footwear.
10. Have children strike objects by holding striking implements firmly and loosely. Ask children to compare and analyze performance.
11. Ask children to compare performance in swimming, jumping for height, and starting from track starting blocks as a function of applying force in different directions.
12. Ask children to run past a large container and drop a ball into it. Children will realize that the task is more difficult because the ball is affected by the inertia it has developed while they are running.

TYPES OF MOTION

Types of motion can be explored through movement activities.

1. As children perform movement activities, ask them to identify the type of motion being exhibited.
2. Ask children to demonstrate translatory and rotary movements. Ask them to demonstrate a linear movement made possible by rotary movements or movements that combine linear and rotary motions.

LEVERS

Movement activities offer opportunities to learn about levers.

1. After first class levers are explained, children may be taken to a seesaw. The parts of a lever may be identified and opportunities

may be provided for children to manipulate force, resistance, effort arm, and resistance arm, reinforcing and understanding of the principles of leverage.

2. Explain a second class lever to children. Provide opportunities for them to execute wheelbarrow walks. Ask children to vary the point of application of force and explain the effect of such manipulation on the muscular effort required to lift and move the "wheelbarrow."

3. Explain third class levers to children. Provide opportunities for them to lift weights held at various distances from the body. Have children test the effect of holding striking implements at different positions and of resistance at varying points in attempting to hold the body or parts of the body of a partner to the floor or ground.

PROJECTILES

An understanding of projectiles can be reinforced through motor activities.

1. Provide opportunities for children to throw or kick objects for distance and speed. Encourage them to test various angles of projection and to explain the effects of altering the angle.

2. Provide opportunities for children to drop or thrust objects of varying qualities. Encourage them to analyze and explain the effects of varying qualities on the speed and distance attained by projectiles.

3. Have children jump for distance, speed, and height. Encourage them to analyze and explain the effects of varying angles of projection.

4. Provide opportunities for children to throw objects against walls at different angles and magnitudes. Encourage them to analyze and explain the effects of altering angle and magnitude.

5. Ask children to strike objects of varying coefficients of elasticity. Ask children to analyze and explain why certain objects may be projected for greater distance as force remains constant.

6. Ask children to apply spin and thrust to table tennis balls. Encourage children to analyze and explain the effect of spin on the path of the ball.

ABSORPTION OF FORCE

Principles regarding the absorption of force may be explored through the MALM.

1. Provide opportunities for children to catch or trap balls. Encourage experimentation and ask children to identify principles that may be applied in absorbing force as safely as possible.

2. Ask children to jump from various heights and to compare and analyze landing techniques in terms of the receipt of impact.

EQUILIBRIUM

Activities involving balance are presented in Chapter 3. The principles of stability may be applied as children participate in a wide variety of balance activities.

PHYSIOLOGICAL CONCEPTS

Motor activities provide many opportunities to learn physiological concepts.

1. As children perform exercises, ask them to observe changes in the structure of muscles.
2. Identify the major joints of the body and ask children to describe the movements possible at the various joints.
3. Provide opportunities for children to listen to the heart and feel the pulse before and after activity.
4. Provide opportunities for children to feel the chest and count the breaths taken in one minute before and after activity.
5. Have children perform various types of exercise. Ask them to rank the vigorousness of each and to analyze and identify the factors that make some exercises or activities more strenuous than others.
6. As children perform exercises, ask others to feel the action of muscles involved.
7. After children exercise, ask them to enumerate the changes that they see or feel on or within their bodies. In response, they may indicate that they are sweating, flushed, sore, tired. Ask them to explain the cause of such conditions.
8. Provide opportunities for children to test their strength, endurance, flexibility, speed, and agility. After such situations, they frequently wonder why they are not as proficient as others, why they may be more proficient, or how they may improve performance. In such instances, the "teachable moment" occurs, during which methods of training and the justification for such methods may be discussed.

COGNITIVE
DEVELOPMENT

It is certainly not surprising that intelligence is a vital concern of all educators. In fact, some educators feel that the primary purpose of education is to develop the intellect. Others hold different purposes to be paramount; however, even they recognize the importance of intellect in learning. But what is intelligence? Can it be developed? How is intellect developed? What are the contributions of physical and motor experiences to cognitive development? There have been many pages written and words spoken to consider and answer these questions. And yet, today there still exist many different answers.

This chapter is separated into six major sections. In the first section, the concept of intelligence is discussed. Since the chapter is concerned with the development of intelligence, a brief description of Piaget's theory of cognitive development is then presented. In the third, fourth, and fifth sections, implications of the theory for content and methods based on it are considered. In the last section, specific activities for the stimulation of cognitive development are presented. Since the measurement of intelligence or cognitive development has traditionally not been the province of educators, it is not treated in this chapter.

The Concept of Intelligence

The concept of intelligence has been studied by psychologists for many years. Approaches and results of study have varied, creating much variation in the meaning of intelligence. Some writers have been concerned with distinguishing the bright and the dull and have directed their efforts to measuring or determining individual differences in intelligence. Others have been interested in determining the nature and structure of intelligence. Finally, researchers have attempted to understand the developmental aspect of intelligence (how intelligence develops from age to age).

The intelligence test as we know it today was first developed by Alfred Binet (1857–1911). Since that time, his test has been revised, and many other tests have been developed to determine the intelligence of the human. Ironically, intelligence tests have had such a strong influence that intelligence sometimes is simply defined as the score one attains on an intelligence test. However, intelligence tests differ according to the author's concept of intelligence. It is appropriate at this point to consider some of the major differences in notions of intelligence.

A view widely accepted by American psychologists in the early part of the twentieth century was that intelligence is general. In other words, intelligence was thought to be a single ability factor pervading all mental activities such as learning, thinking, and adapting. This view was represented by the writings of Stern (1914) and by the intelligence tests of Binet (although Binet did appear to recognize specific abilities). It was also supported, to some extent, by Spearman (1927), who identified a general intelligence as well as specific factors.

E. L. Thorndike (1914) proposed that intelligence consisted of many factors. With the advent of factor analysis studies, his view was supported by the writings of Thurstone (1934), Thurstone and Thurstone (1941), Cattell (1957), Guilford (1959, 1967), and Guilford and Hoepfner (1971).

The work of Bruner has received a great deal of attention and has had considerable impact on education during the past two decades. Bruner (1964) takes the view that the development of intellectual functioning is shaped by the mastery of techniques of the use of the mind. These techniques (language being the primary example) are skills transmitted by the culture upon which cognitive growth depends. Thus, cognitive growth occurs from the "outside in" as well as from the "inside out." The first group of techniques involves or includes three vehicles of representation, or systems of processing information, that are utilized to structure regularities in the environment: action (*enactive representation*), imagery (*iconic representation*), and language (*symbolic representation*). Oversimplified, these systems involve moving, perceiving, and thinking. *Enactive representation* is the representation of past events through motor response. It involves the identification of objects by actions directed on them. *Iconic representation* "summarizes events by the selective organization of precepts and of images, by the spatial, temporal, and qualitative structures of the perceptual field and their transformed images." For Bruner (1964), a symbol system "represents things by design features that include remoteness and arbitrariness." The second group of techniques relates to integration. *Integration* "is the means whereby acts are organized in higher order ensembles, making possible the use of larger and larger units of information for the selection of particular problems." Integration is what separates "higher" from "lower" skills, or those performed by an adult from those performed by a child. Integration involves combining simple components into a composite or integrated sequence.

Bruner (1966) presents the following "benchmarks" of intellectual growth:

1. Growth is characterized by increasing independence of response from the immediate nature of the stimulus.
2. Growth depends upon internalizing events into a "storage system" that corresponds to the environment.
3. Intellectual growth involves an increasing capacity to say to oneself and others, by means of words or symbols, what one has done or what one will do.
4. Intellectual development depends upon a systematic and contingent interaction between a tutor and a learner, the tutor already being equipped with a wide range of previously invented techniques that he teaches the child.
5. Teaching is vastly facilitated by the medium of language, which ends by being not only the medium for exchange but the instrument that the learner can then use himself in bringing order into the environment.
6. Intellectual development is marked by increasing capacity to deal with several alternatives simultaneously, to tend to several sequences during the same period of time, and to allocate time and attention in a manner appropriate to these multiple demands. (Bruner, 1966, p. 546.)

Thus, Bruner views intellectual growth as taking place over a period of time, as dependent upon the environment, and as vastly facilitated by the medium of language. It is characterized by the ability to deal with more than one alternative simultaneously. Bruner recognizes the importance of these factors in stimulating intellectual development, and he also provides guidelines that may aid in the maximizing of the tutorial process.

Perhaps the major reason for the great impact that Bruner has had on education is that he attempts to link theories of development, knowledge, and instruction. For Bruner, lack of such linkage reduces the study of cognitive development to triviality. Thus, Bruner (1966) offers theoretical guidelines for instruction or for curriculum development relative to the structure and the form of knowledge, sequencing, reinforcement and feedback, and predispositions to learn.

Guilford (1967) constructs a three-dimensional theoretical structure-of-intelligence model (SI Model), which is presented in Figure 6–1. The first dimension is identified as *mental operations* and encompasses the major kinds of intellectual activities engaged in by the organism. They are the mental operations characteristic of the intellect and are what the organism does mentally in the processing of information. The five mental operations consist of *cognition* (the knowing of information), *memory* (fixation of newly gained information in storage), *divergent production* (generation of logical alternatives from given information), *convergent production* (generation of logical conclusions from given information), and *evaluation* (making

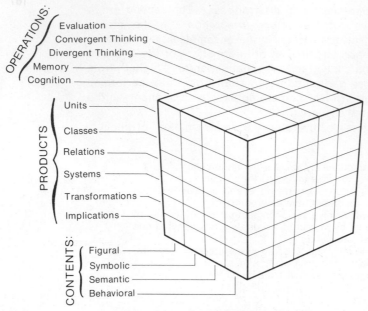

Figure 6–1. The structure of intellect model. From: Guilford, J. P. *The Nature of Human Intelligence.* New York: McGraw-Hill Book Co., 1967, p. 63.

judgements about that which is known or produced). The second dimension is identified as *contents*; it is grouped in four categories: *figural* (information in concrete form or as it is perceived), *symbolic* (information in the form of signs or codes such as letters, numbers, or musical notations), *semantic* (information in the form of conceptions or mental constructs to which words are often applied, such as in verbal thinking and verbal communication), and *behavioral* (information involved in human interactions). *Contents* represent materials that are used in testing or in gaining information and may include concrete objects, numbers, letters, verbal meanings, and interpersonal relationships. The third dimension, identified as *products,* comprises the basic forms that information takes in the organism's processing of it. Information may take the form of *units* (segregated chunks), *classes* (grouped by virtue of common properties within sets), *relations* (meaningful connections), *systems* (organized patterns), *transformations* (existing information), and *implications* (connections between information suggested by other information).

Guilford and Hoepfner (1971) indicate that the model is not hierarchial but is a cross-classification of abilities. Although the model theoretically identified 120 unique abilities (5×4×6), an even greater number of separate abilities is expected since certain cells represent more than one ability. On the other hand, although separate abilities are identified, two or more are ordinarily involved in the solving of any problem and thus do not function in isolation.

Guilford (1959) indicates that the implications of the SI Model for education are numerous. He suggests that education may play a greater role in the development of the intellect, although he recognizes that the extent to which each factor is determined by learning (as opposed to heredity) is not known. He suggests that each intellectual factor provides a particular goal at which to aim. A curriculum could be established to provide opportunity for practice to achieve improvement. According to Guilford (1959), "we need a better balance of training in the divergent thinking area as compared with training in convergent thinking and in critical thinking or evaluation."

The first theory with primary emphasis on intellectual development or on the nature of developmental change was developed by Piaget (1963). In his vast writing, Piaget proposes that children move through states in cognitive development. From the sensorimotor stage (ages 0–2), the child moves to the preoperational stage (ages 2–7), the stage of concrete operations (ages 7–11), and the stage of formal operations (age 11 or 12 to adulthood). Since development is the focus of this book, Piaget's theory is presented in more detail in the next section. Prior to discussing it, it appears useful to consider further the nature of intelligence, individual differences in intelligence, and the roles of environment and heredity in intelligence. For this, we turn to the work of Hebb.

Hebb (1949) theorizes that there are two kinds of intelligence distinguished by two types of brain tissue. The first kind is innate potential, or the capacity for development, and is called *intelligence A.* It makes use of sensorimotor brain tissue and amounts to the possession of a "good brain" and a "good neural metabolism." Sensorimotor tissue functions to manage impulses associated with sensory input and motor output and then governs the potential or capacity for intellectual development. Sensorimotor tissue is known as "committed tissue" because it presumably cannot acquire functions that were not present at birth.

The second type of intelligence, known as *intelligence B,* makes use of associative tissue. The functions of this tissue are not "committed." Instead, the functions need to be acquired or established, and thus the functioning of associative tissue is influenced by experience. It is the functioning of a brain in which development has gone on. Hebb feels that the ratio between associative and sensorimotor tissue (A/S ratio) determines the limits of intelligence. The larger the proportion of associative tissue to sensorimotor tissue, the greater the potential for intelligence. Therefore, humans possess greater proportions of associative tissue than animals lower on the phylogenetic scale.

In regard to humans, Hebb theorizes that two factors account for differences in intelligence. The first is simply that the inherited A/S ratio differs. The second is that the associative tissue, or intelligence B, is more developed in one human than in another. The first we can do little about. The second, however, is very important, since the environment of the individual can be manipulated.

During the first two years, the activity of the organism is primarily sensorimotor. During this time, functions of associative tissue (intelligence B) are established. This sensorimotor activity provides time for associative tissue to be developed. After associative tissue establishes its function, it is nurtured and affected by experiences throughout the developmental years.

It is important to recognize, as Hebb points out, that experience is essential to the development of intelligence. The focus of this chapter is on the experience that nurtures the development of intelligence. In order to gain insight into the nature of these experiences, it would be of benefit to understand cognitive development. For this, we draw on the work of Piaget.

Piaget's Theory of Cognitive Development

Before educators may rationally contribute to or gain insights from intellectual or cognitive development, they need to know more about how it occurs. In this section, a brief description of Piaget's theory of cognitive development is presented. Since Piaget's work in this area is vast, the description here has drawn heavily on secondary sources that have served to condense Piaget's work as well as on this author's review of primary sources.

In his description of intellectual development, Piaget (1963) identifies four developmental stages. The first stage, the *sensorimotor*, extends from birth to approximately 2 years of age and is further differentiated into six developmental substages. The second stage, the *pre-operational stage*, extends from age 2 to approximately age 7. The *stage of concrete operations,* the third stage, extends from approximately 7 to 11 or 12. The final stage, *the stage of formal operations,* begins at age 11 or 12 and continues through adulthood. Although Piaget has established developmental stages, it is important at the outset to understand that he feels that development is not an additive process but a continual reconstruction process of existing cognitive structures. Piaget feels that although there is an absolute continuity of all developmental processes, each new phase entails repetition of processes of the previous level in a different form or organization.

Before presenting a description of the sensorimotor stage, the basic concept of a schema will be introduced. From this introduction, the function of a schema in the sensorimotor stage will be presented. For Piaget, a *schema* is a form of a knowing activity that will change, expand, and adapt. It may be a simple response to a stimulus, an overt action, a means to an end, an end in itself, an internalized thought process, or a combination of overt actions and internalized thought processes. Examples of schemata include grasping, sucking, and tossing a ball. During the *sensorimotor* stage, the child develops the schema of grasping, which is internally controlled and can be utilized in grasping the mother's finger, picking up different objects, or picking up an object from varying angles. A schema often will function in combination or in sequence with other schemata, as when the child throws a ball. For example, in this activity the child combines the schemata of grasping and releasing.

When a schema is developed it may be incorporated into the environment or it may be altered or modified according to the demands of the environment. When children deal with the environment in terms of their current structures or schemata, they exhibit the process of *assimilation.* For example, assimilation occurs if grasping becomes a developed schema and the infant subsequently grasps an object such as a rattle. In this instance the infant deals with a novel object in the environment by calling upon an available schema (grasping). On the other hand, *accommodation* occurs if the child modifies basic structure or schema to the demands of the environment. In grasping objects, the infant may need to reach out for the rattle or modify grip according to the shape of the rattle. In this case, the infant changes his response to environmental demands and exhibits accommodation.

For Piaget (1963), intelligence is an adaptation, and adaptation is an equilibrium between assimilation and accommodation. He states that "intelligence is assimilation to the extent that it incorporates all the given data of experience within its framework," but that assimilation can never be pure "because by incorporating new elements into its earlier schemata the intelligence constantly modifies the latter in order to adjust them to new elements." Therefore, intelligence also depends upon accommodation to the environment.

> In short, intellectual adaptation, like every other kind, consists of putting an assimilatory mechanism and a complementary accommodation into progressive equilibrium. The mind can only be adapted to a reality if perfect accommodation exists, that is to say, if nothing, in that reality, intervenes to modify the subject's schemata. But, inversely, adaptation does not exist if the new reality has imposed motor or mental attitudes contrary to those which were adopted on contact with other earlier given data: adaptation only exists if there is coherence, hence assimilation. Of course, on the motor level, coherence presents quite a different structure than on the reflective or organic level, and every systematization is possible. But always and everywhere adaptation is only accomplished when it results in a stable system, that is to say, when there is equilibrium between accommodation and assimilation. (Piaget, 1963, p. 7.)

The Sensorimotor Stage

THE SENSORIMOTOR SUBSTAGES

The first substage of the sensorimotor stage is characterized by the use of reflexes and extends from birth to approximately 1 month. During this substage, the major behavior of the infant is to exhibit reflexes (*unlearned responses*). The stage is necessary to the maturation of such unlearned responses as crying, looking, listening, sucking, and grasping, enabling them to eventually become stabilized, generalized, and discriminative. These reflexes may be considered schemata that are used to adapt. In the first substage, schemata consisting of innate reflexes are developed.

The second substage involves the first acquired adaptations or conditioned reflexes in behavior and extends from approximately 1 month to 4 months. These first acquired adaptations are known as *primary circular reactions,* in which the child adapts and modifies basic innate schemata. The schemata are characterized by repetitive, deliberate, and prolonged responses to recognized stimulation. New behaviors come about by "groping," i.e., by chance rather than intention. For example, adaptation of the sucking reflex includes playing with the tongue or systematic thumb sucking. A child may hold the finger of the mother or grasp an object and put it to the mouth in adapting the grasping reflex. These examples demonstrate the prolonging of reflex use (primarily assimilation) and adding an acquired element of accommodation. Although the response of the infant is deliberate, the infant is not interested in the effect that behavior has on the environment. The child, in essence, provides an opportunity for the adaptation and modification of innate reflexes.

The third substage, that of *secondary circular reactions,* is characterized by intentional activity and learning of new schemata. It consists of the beginning of intentional adaptations of previous schemata and the rapid proliferation of new schemata and extends from approximately 4 to 8 months. The child engages in acts with the intention of "seeing" their effect on the environment. For example, the child may pull a chain in order to put in motion a mobile suspended over the crib. According to Piaget, the child discovers that certain acts produce changes in the external environment, and the child repeats such acts intentionally to produce interesting effects. Whereas in the second substage the child may deliberately respond to a stimulus and grasp for the sake of grasping, in the third substage the child has the intention of producing an effect. In this substage, the rewarding event is something external (a mobile in motion), and means and ends are gradually differentiated. There is also most certainly a rapid expansion of schemata. The child in this stage begins to realize, although at a rudimentary level, that there are objects in the external world that maintain their identity. However, the child fails to realize that the object has permanence, as evidenced by his apparent assumption that objects out of sight are out of existence.

The fourth substage extends from approximately 8 to 12 months and involves the coordination of secondary schemata. In other words, schemata are intentionally combined to attain a particular goal. For example, a child may combine the schemata of grasping and letting go in playing with objects. This substage is characterized by the acquisition of instrumental behavior and by an active search for a vanished object. The child combines learned responses as a means to an end, i.e., learned responses are used as a means to obtain a desired goal. The child develops a new ability to use familiar schemata in new situations (accommodation). Schemata are freed from their originating situations. They become part of a child's repertoire and can be used in the imitation of a model. Here, the response is not an end in itself but is used to help the child solve simple problems. The child is able to distinguish situations and begins to be able to select behavior appropriate to situations. When a child can recognize and perceive a situation and formulate a particular response to it, a form of *intellectual reasoning* is evidenced. In this substage, a child moves a pillow in order to obtain an object underneath it, as a separate act in advance of reaching a desired object. The child is able to conceive of an object as being behind a pillow and thus to think of it in its relation to other objects. In the previous substage, the infant is able only to prolong accommodations that were in progress when an object disappeared. For example, in the third substage (secondary circular reaction), the child is able to recapture an object visually if the child actually follows the object with the eyes (prolonged accommodation).

The next substage is that of *tertiary circular reactions,* and extends from approximately 12 to 18 months of age. This stage is characterized by trial-and-error experimentation, the formation and discovery of new schemata, and the appearance of a higher type of coordination of schemata in the search for new means. In this substage, the child tries different responses to obtain the same goal. Schemata are expanded and varied to make them improved tools for solving problems. In this substage, there is accommodation for the sake of accommodation, i.e., a search for new reactions to adapt to unfamiliar situations. It involves the application of secondary circular reactions to new reactions. Instead of limiting attempts to pick up a toy beyond reach with the hand, the child uses other means such as pulling the string attached to the toy or reaching with a stick to get the toy. At this substage, means and ends are clearly differentiated. The child attempts to develop new means of attaining goals and to discover new ways of solving problems.

The ability to deliberately vary schemata or actions facilitates imitation. Children become able, at this stage, to imitate actions that they have never performed, rather than simply to imitate actions that were part of their repertoire (as was true in previous substages). During this stage, children make advances in their *object concept*. Baldwin (1967) identifies this advance.

> Stage 5 marks progress also in the development of the object concept. During stage 4, the child's search for a hidden object included the removal of obstacles to finding it, but by the end of the stage he was still unable to decipher a successful sequence of hidings of the object. If the ball were put under one pillow and then removed and put under a second pillow, the child looked for it under the first pillow. By Stage 5 the child looks for the ball where he last saw it go, but Stage 5 still lacks an important kind of inference about the location of a vanished object, namely, the possibility of invisible movements. Thus in this stage if an object is put into one's hand, which is put behind a pillow, leaving the object there, and the closed hand is then brought out for the child to examine, he will search the hand vigorously; he will not try the hypothesis that the object may have been left behind the pillow while the hand was there, however, because that movement was invisible to him and requires an inference about a possible movement of the object. As we shall see, in Stage 6 the child copes with invisible movements. (Baldwin, 1967, p. 216.)

The final substage in the sensorimotor stage involves the invention of new means through deduction or internal mental combinations. This substage is achieved at approximately 18 months and is characterized by the development of a primitive form of representation. When children at this substage wish to attain an end for which they have no available means, they invent a means. This kind of invention requires symbolic images for the manipulation of reality. Thus, the child is capable of imagined representation. It is important to realize that the child does not develop means by trial and error, as in the previous substage. In this substage, actions or events are planned before they are acted out. During this substage the child has the ability to defer imitation, i.e., to reproduce behavior of an absent model from memory. For example, a child may view another child moving a pillow with a stick on a particular day. The child has the capability of deferring imitation and is able to imitate the actions of the other child and move the pillow with a stick at a later time.

PLAY

Piaget (1962) feels that play is essentially assimilation or the primacy of assimilation over accommodation. Behaviors related to play are *ludic behaviors,* engaged in to amuse or excite the individual. Although the age at which the individual begins to play is difficult to determine, Piaget indicates that behaviors become play when they are repeated for functional pleasure (mere assimilation). Activity conducted for functional pleasure appears as early as the second substage and becomes clearly discernible at the third substage of the sensorimotor period. This is evidenced by children's looking for the sake of looking, or handling objects for the sake of handling them. The most primitive type of play is known as *practice play* or *exercise play.* Play occurs when assimilation is freed or becomes disassociated from accommodation. Play is distinguished from intellectual assimilation by this disassociation from accommodation and by the conduct of activity for pleasure. Play occurs when the child engages in behavior for its own sake. It is at the third substage that there is a clear differentiation between play and intellectual assimilation.

At the fourth and fifth substages, the play patterns in which the child engages are called *ritualization* by Piaget. At the fourth substage, the mobility of schemata allows for the formation of real ludic combinations for use in new situations. Play is used as a happy display of mastered activities. Gestures are repeated and combined as a ritual, and the child makes a motor game of them. In the fourth substage, ludic combinations are borrowed from adapted schemata, whereas in the fifth substage, ludic combinations are new and have the immediate character of play. Ritualization leads the child to symbolic play.

At the sixth substage, the *ludic symbol* is disassociated from ritual and the mere following of habitual movements. The child develops symbolic schemata and mental associations. The symbolic schemata enable the child to defer imitation (to view a situation and repeat it at a later time) and to "pretend," or "make believe." Thus, the ludic symbol emerges as opposed to simple motor activity. At this substage, the child uses schemata that have been ritualized in make-believe situations. Deferred imitation has the effect of stimulating representation, which is the basis for symbolic play appearing around the age of two.

Throughout the sensorimotor stage, play is individual or egocentric. Rules are not a part of play.

PERCEPTUAL SPACE AND PERCEPTION

During the sensorimotor stage, the foundation for the construction of space is constituted. According to Piaget and Inhelder (1967b), the foundation is based on topological space involving the spatial relationships of proximity or nearness, separation or disassociation, order or spatial succession, enclosure or surrounding, and continuity. Piaget and Inhelder (1967b) state that the first two substages of the sensorimotor stage are characterized by rudimentary development of these spatial relationships, by lack of coordination between the various sensory spaces, and in particular by lack of coordination between vision and grasping. The next two substages are characterized by the coordination of vision and grasping, the perception and recognition of certain perceptual forms (lines, circles, angles), development of perceptual constancy of shape and size, the search for objects that disappear, and the ability to distinguish activity of the subject from that of objects. The last two substages (in the child's second year) are marked by systematic observation and enquiry, internal coordination among elements, and mental images leading to delayed imitation. By the sixth stage, perceptual space becomes a part of representational space.

The sensorimotor stage is characterized by perception and perceptual activity. For Piaget and Inhelder (1967b), *perception* is the knowledge of objects that results from direct contact with them. In perception, the totality of relations is given immediately and simultaneously with each "centering." Perception is like a still picture — a momentary view. *Perceptual activity,* on the other hand, is characterized by a number of consecutive fixations, as, for example, when the child views parts of a form that are integrated into a single perception of the stimulus. Perceptual activity may be involved in perceiving a single object or in making comparisons between objects. Perceptual activity, thus, is characterized by the occurrence of decentralization. According to Piaget and Inhelder (1967b), movement is active from the very beginning of perception and is even more important in perceptual activity. These authors indicate that movements mark the transition from one perception to another, and thus every movement may be regarded as a transformation of the perceptual field and every perceptual field as a group of relationships determined by movements. In addition, movement allows the child to view objects from different perspectives, and perceptions stimulate body movements. Thus, perceptual activity and motor activity are considered as one rather than as separate.

SUMMARY

Thus, between birth and the ages of 1½ to 2 years the child moves through six substages of sensorimotor intelligence. In the first substage, that of reflexes, the child uses and develops innate reflexes — the first schemata. In the second substage, that of primary circular reactions, acquired adaptations and modifications of these basic reflexes are developed to form new schemata, which by chance rather than by intention have new end results. In the second substage, the child provides an opportunity for the basic schemata to mature. In the substage of secondary circular reactions, the child intentionally or accidentally acquires new or secondary behavior patterns (schemata) and utilizes them to intentionally reproduce or prolong an interesting effect. During this stage, the child gradually develops the ability to differentiate means and ends. The fourth substage involves the coordination of secondary schemata. The child intentionally combines schemata to attain a particular goal. Schemata are freed for new ends and for imitation. The child is able to coordinate familiar schemata for use in new situations for the purpose of solving problems. The fifth substage, that of tertiary circular reactions, is characterized by trial-and-error experimentation, the formation and discovery of new responses, and the appearance of a higher type of coordination of schemata in the search for new means. In this stage, then, the child is able to intentionally vary behavior to obtain the same goals. In the final substage, the child invents new means

through internal mental combinations. The child is able to symbolically represent actions or events before acting them out in reality.
New means are utilized for problem-solving purposes. This kind of
invention requires the use of symbolic images, or imagined representation, for the manipulation of reality. In this substage, the child develops schemata that are the first signs of conceptual thinking.

The Preoperational Stage

The preoperational stage extends from approximately 1½ or 2 years
to approximately 6 or 7 years of age. The stage includes a preconceptual substage, which lasts until about the age of 4 and the substage of intuitive thought, which lasts from approximately age 4 to
age 7.

REPRESENTATION AND SYMBOLISM

During the final sensorimotor substage, the child develops the
ability to symbolically represent actions before acting them out. However, it must be recalled that this form of representation is primitive.
Representation is limited to schemata associated with one's own actions. In the preconceptual substage, the representation is further developed. Eventually, the child will be able to represent objects
through language. At the stage of concrete operations, the child will
be able to mentally manipulate representation of the concrete and at
the stage of formal operations to mentally manipulate the abstract.

One of the primary activities occurring during the preconceptual
substage is the development of representation, i.e., of linking meaning to objects. This is accomplished by distinguishing signifiers from
the signified, or significants from the significates. The distinction of
these progresses from indices to signals, to symbols, and to signs.
When the child is able to represent objects by signs, the most "distant" form of representation of objects has been mastered. The notions that children attach to the first verbal signs they learn to use
are known as *preconcepts*. Thus, the development of preconcepts
occurs during the preconceptual substage of the preoperational
stage. This process will be discussed following the clarification of
terms.

> In fact, we should distinguish between symbols and signs on the
> one hand and indices or signals on the other. Not only all thought,
> but all cognitive and motor activity, from perception and habit to
> conceptual and reflective thought, consists in linking meanings, and
> all meaning implies a relation between a significant and a signified
> reality. But in the case of an index the significant constitutes a part
> or an objective aspect of the significate, or else it is linked to it by a
> causal relation; for the hunter tracks in the snow are an index of
> game, and for the infant the visible end of an almost completely
> hidden object is an index of its presence. Similarly, the signal, even
> when artificially produced by the experimenter, constitutes for the
> subject simply a partial aspect of the event that it heralds (in a con-
> ditioned response the signal is perceived as an objective anteced-
> ent). The symbol and the sign, on the other hand, imply a differentia-
> tion, from the point of view of the subject himself, between the
> significant and the significate; for a child playing at eating, a pebble

representing a sweet is consciously recognized as that which sym-
bolizes and the sweet as that which is symbolized; and when the
same child, by "adherence to the sign," regards a name as inherent
in the thing named, he nevertheless regards this name as a significant, as though he sees it as a label attached in substance to the
designated object. (Piaget, 1967a, p. 124.)

Thus, at the index level, the child links the visible end of a partly
covered object (*significant* or *signifier*) with an object (*significate* or
the signified). A child may see a part of a football and realize that it is
a football although it is not totally visible. The smell of food is a link
with or a signal of food itself. At the symbol level, representation is
differentiated from the object. For example, the child may use the
body to represent objects (imitate an animal), use a box to represent
an elephant, make a duck from clay, draw pictures of things, or utter
the sounds made by animals. Finally, the child uses signs to represent objects. One of the signs of obvious importance is language.
When children verbalize, they are, in effect, associating a sign with
an object or event. Important to language development is the opportunity for children to explore their environment and to associate language with objects. Piaget indicates the importance of this process.

To sum up, the beginnings of thought, while carrying on the
work of sensorimotor intelligence, spring from a capacity for distinguishing significants and significates, and consequently rely both on
the invention of symbols and on the discovery of signs. . . .
   Pre-concepts are the notions which the child attaches to the
first verbal signs he learns to use. The distinguishing characteristic
of these schemata is that they remain midway between the generali-
ty of the concept and the individuality of the elements composing it,
without arriving either at the one or at the other. (Piaget, 1967a, pp.
126–127.)

The child's speech is in a sense egocentric, and little effort is
made to adapt it to the needs or interests of listeners. The child
does, however, develop the ability to distinguish words or images
and perceptually absent events. The child is able to think about objects and activities and manipulate them verbally and symbolically.

According to Piaget, the thinking of the child at the preconceptual substage is static: it focuses on one feature at a time. Thought is
"centered" as the child attends primarily to one aspect of a problem
and neglects other important parts of the problem. Children are unable to think about their own thinking or to look for possible con-
tradictions in it. Their thinking at this substage is egocentric, without
genuine concept, concrete rather than abstract, and incoherently organized.

At the intuitive substage of the preoperational stage, there is a
significant advance on the preconceptual or symbolic thought that is
developed in the preconceptual stage. The child engages in a rudimentary form of logic. However, complete intellectual construction is
limited by various factors. Piaget states:

In fact, from 4 to 7 years we see a gradual co-ordination of representative relations and thus a growing conceptualization, which
leads the child from the symbolic or preconceptual phase to the beginnings of the operation. But the remarkable thing is that this intelligence, whose progress may be observed and is often rapid, still
remains pre-logical even when it attains its maximum degree of ad-

aptation; up to the time when this series of successive equilibrations culminates in the "groupings," it continues to supplement incomplete operations with a semi-symbolic form of thought, i.e., intuitive reasoning, and it controls judgements solely by means of intuitive "regulations," which are analogous on a representative level to perceptual adjustments on the sensorimotor plane. (Piaget, 1967a, p. 129.)

CLASSIFICATION

Piaget analyzes the formation of classes (classification) to distinguish preoperational and operational thinking. *Classification* is the ability to group things that have certain common characteristics. When children are able to group similar things together according to their similarities and differences but to do so without the cognitive structure of class inclusion, they are said to be functioning in the preoperational period of "non-graphic collections." At this level, children are able to concentrate on the qualitative aspects of classification but not on its quantitative aspects. At this level, children proceed from the ability to dichotomize objects that are identical to the ability to group things that are similar. Piaget (1963) found that children at age 4 can usually dichotomize or trichotomize wooden beads that are identical in every way except for color. However, when presented with six wooden brown beads and two wooden white ones and asked whether there are more brown beads than wooden beads, the child at the non-graphic collection level will typically reply that there are more brown beads. This is because the child can compare this group but he is unable to include both brown and white beads in a single class of beads. The child "centers" on the brown beads and thus is unable to recognize the conservation of the whole. When children become capable of class inclusion, they attain the ability to classify. This is associated with the period of concrete operations.

SERIATION

Seriation is another element included under the rubric of logical operations. *Seriation* is the ability to arrange things according to a dimension along which they differ. For example, a child may be asked to order ten sticks of different lengths in an ascending or descending order. In developing seriation, the child proceeds from dichotomies and trichotomies to greater orders. Children at the intuitive stage will usually be able to determine who is the taller of two people, or which of two sticks is longer, and even to order a series of elements by grouping. According to Piaget,

> not until the operational level is seriation achieved straight away, by such a method as, for example, finding the smallest of all the forms and then the next smallest, etc. It is at this level, similarly, that the inference $(A<B) + (B<C) = (A<C)$ becomes possible, whereas at intuitive levels the subject declines to derive from the two perceptually verified inequalities $A<B$ and $B<C$, the conclusion $A<C$. (Piaget, 1967a, p. 134.)

NUMBERS

The structure of numbers is another important element of logical operations. Development proceeds from an intuition about groups of objects to reversibility. As was true with classification and seriation, the child is able to dichotomize quantities during the preoperational period. The child develops an intuition about groups of objects as containing "a lot" or "a little bit." The 4-year-old child usually bases the judgment on spatial consideration. There is no difficulty in choosing a line of ten balls over a line of three balls, but considerable difficulty in choosing between a line of ten balls and a line of nine balls because the space occupied is nearly the same. If two lines containing ten balls were arranged in rows of equal lengths, the child would have no difficulty indicating that both lines had the same number of balls. However, if one line was lengthened, the child at the intuitive level would indicate that the longer line had the greater number of balls. This is because optical correspondence has changed. The space occupied is different. Therefore, the number is different. The child "centers" on one dimension, the space occupied. Object permanence is not accepted. This is an example of a quasi-perceptual error resulting in incomplete intellectual construction.

CONSERVATION

Related to the structure of numbers is the concept of *conservation,* the invariance of quantity. It may include the number, shape, length, or position of things. Conservation also includes reversibility. One of the many experiments Piaget has designed involves filling two identical glasses with water to equal heights. In the experiment, children agree that the amounts are equal in the two glasses. However, when the liquid of one is poured into another container which is narrower and longer, children at the preoperational level will generally respond that the narrower and longer container has the greater amount of water. Since they fail to realize that the liquid could be poured back to the original glass and that the amount of water is the same, they lack *reversibility.* Again, children center on one dimension (length of the glass), fail to accept the permanence of objects, and commit a quasi-perceptual error that results in an inaccurate deduction.

SPATIAL–TEMPORAL RELATIONS

Piaget also analyzes spatial–temporal operations to demonstrate differences between preoperational and operational abilities. During the preconceptual period, the child progresses from the ability to recognize objects to the ability to recognize and draw topological relations such as openness or closure, proximity, and separation. Since Euclidean shapes are not recognized, circles and squares cannot be distinguished. At the intuitive level, the representational space of the child develops through increased perceptual activity and exploration. The child begins to recognize Euclidean shapes on the basis of differentiation of rectilinear and curved shapes, differentiation of angles, recognition of parallels, and relations between equal and unequal sides of a figure.

Children at the preoperational stage are still dominated by their point of view. Piaget (1967a) presents an example of a doll moving around a mountain while a child is asked to pick out pictures that depict the view of the doll at various points. Children have difficulty selecting the correct pictures even though they themselves have "moved" around the mountain previous to watching the movement of the doll. Piaget points out that children have particular difficulty with front-behind and left-right reversals up to 7 or 8 years of age.

Children at the preoperational level also have difficulty reversing the order of objects presented to them or determining the order of objects when the containers in which they are placed are turned in different positions. Piaget presents similar data in regard to temporal relations. At 4 and 5 years, the child's notions of time are rudimentary and are based on spatial distances and perceptual data. *Before* and *after* are conceived of in terms of spatial succession rather than temporal succession. Eventually, sequence or order grows out of causal relationships.

Time durations are also rudimentary at this level. The lack of homogeneity in the duration of time is evidenced when children conceive of 15 minutes as different when they enjoy activity from when they dislike activity. In addition, the child is unable to accept the notion of a time common to various movements at different velocities. Piaget (1967a) illustrates this with an example.

> When two moving objects leave the same point A and arrive at two different places, B and B', the 4–5 year old child acknowledges the simultaneity of the departure but usually contests that of the arrivals, although this is easily perceptible. He recognizes that one of the objects ceased to move when the other stopped, but he refuses to grant that the movements ceased "at the same time," because there simply is as yet no time common to different speeds. (Piaget, 1967a, p. 136.)

Piaget (1967a) also illustrates temporal relations at the intuitive level.

> Two equal quantities of water flowing, at the same rate through the two branches of a tube into differently shaped bottles, give rise, for example, to the following judgements: the 6–7 year old child recognizes the simultaneity of starts and stops but denies that water has been flowing into one bottle for as long as it has flowed into the other. Ideas concerning age give rise to similar statements; if A was born before B, that does not mean that he is older and, if he is older, that does not exclude the possibility that B might catch up with him or even overtake him! (Piaget, 1967a, p. 137.)

PERCEPTUAL ACTIVITY

A critical difference between the preconceptual and conceptual stages is that during the preconceptual stage the child's abilities depend markedly on perception. Children typically center on perceiving rather than "knowing" as a basis for thought processes. Since perception is subject to many distorting factors, children may often be inaccurate in their judgments.

The difference between perceptual and conceptual judgments has often been illustrated by using the Muller-Lyer illusion (Figure 6–2). Children looking at the figure perceive the lines in the figure as being of different lengths. However, if they measure lines, they would find that the lines are of the same length. The children's conclusions

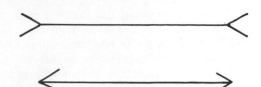

Figure 6–2.   The Muller-Lyer illusion.

about line length differs from their perceptual judgments when they add a broader body of knowledge. This indicates that conceptual thought is different from perception. Thus, although perception and perceptual activity are functional and important, knowledge based on perception alone may not be totally accurate.

During the intuitive period, perceptual activity become quite apparent. The perceptual activity of the child increases, enhancing exploration and also enchancing progression from perception, per se, to operations. Such activity contributes to increased knowledge of objects and eventually reversibility and operations. Perceptual activity, which is characterized by decentralization, provides coherence and progressive synthesis of perception and takes the individual to the threshold of operations. Perceptual activity enhances perception beyond immediate contact, beyond the perceptual field itself and at increased distances in time and space (representational space). This liberation allows for complete perceptual mobility and enhances the attainment of reversibility, which is associated with operations in later stages.

PLAY

The preconceptual period marks the transition between practice play and symbolic play. In understanding the transition, it is important to recall that the child practices ludic symbolism at the sixth substage of the sensorimotor stage. However, at the sixth substage, such symbols are related to the child's own actions (the child pretends to be doing one of his or her usual actions). For example, the child pretends to sleep or to eat. In the preconceptual period, new ludic symbols appear, which, for example, will enable children to pretend that objects or people other than themselves sleep or eat.

In discussing symbolic play, Piaget (1962) describes three stages. The first stage is associated with the preconceptual substage. In the first stage, Piaget presents three types of symbolic play, each of which has parts to it. The first part of the first type involves the projection of symbolic schemata to new objects. For example, after pretending to eat or sleep, the child "makes" a pet eat or sleep. The second part of the first type of symbolic play involves projection of imitative schemata to new objects. Here the schemata projected are not one's own but are acquired by imitation. For example, a child may watch an adult using the telephone. The child imitates this schema and projects it to an object representing a telephone. For example, the object may be a spoon, leaf, or stone.

The second type of symbolic play involves (1) simple identification of one object with another and (2) identification of the child's body with that of other people or with things. For the first, Piaget presents the example of a child seeing an egg shell and calling it a cup. The child then may drink or pretend to drink out of the egg shell. In the case where the child identifies the body with that of another person or with an object, the person or object is absent. For example, a child may pretend that he/she is a cat and may imitate the activities of the cat.

The third type of symbolic play involves (1) *simple* combinations in which whole scenes rather than isolated imitations or single assimilated objects are constructed, (2) *compensatory* combinations in which reality is corrected through play rather than reproduced for pleasure, (3) *liquidating* combinations in which the child compensates for or accepts difficult or unpleasant situations in symbolic play (make-believe), and (4) *anticipatory symbolic* combinations in which the consequences of disobedience or the rejection of advice is symbolized.

It must be emphasized that play is critical at the substage of preconceptual development. It occupies most of the child's waking hours and serves as the primary means of adaptation. It is an opportunity to perform real life tasks and, although egocentric, leads to gradual socialization.

At ages 4 through 7 (intuitive thought stage), there is an advance in the symbolic play of the child. First, there is an increased orderliness of ludic constructions. For example, the child can convey a story in correct order. Second, the child is capable of a more exact and accurate imitation of reality. Third, although in its infancy, collective symbolism emerges. A child begins to play with one or more companions but also continues to display parallel play. In play, the child can think in terms of others, and social rules begin to replace individual ludic symbols. For example, games of tag replace spontaneous games, and games related to the hiding of a moving object appear.

The Stage of Concrete Operations

The stage of concrete operations extends from approximately age 7 to age 11 or 12. During this stage, children achieve *operational thought,* which enables them to develop mental representations of the physical world and manipulate these in their mind (*operations*). Operational thought enables the child to order and relate to organized whole experiences that are related to action. The fact that such operations are limited to those of action, to the "concrete," or to those that depend on perception distinguishes this stage from the stage of formal operations. The fact that the child is able to develop and manipulate mental representations of the physical world distinguishes this stage from earlier stages. Thus, the child is able to mentally carry through a logical idea. The physical actions that predominated in earlier stages can now be internalized and manipulated as mental actions.

In the stage of concrete operations, reversibility is demonstrated as a certainty in thought. The child functioning at this level gradually understands that liquids and solids change shape without changing substance, weight, and volume. Thus, there is a *conversion* of thought instead of a centering of thought. In early stages, attention was centered to one part of an object or a particular point of view. Thus, for example, the child was unable to admit to conservation of quantity when a certain number of beads or a certain amount of water was transferred from a short wide container to a narrow long one. Attention was centered on length and did not consider length and width. The child functioning at the level of concrete operations, however, realizes that if the number of objects in two rows is equal, they are equal in quantity regardless of the shape of the rows. The child responds to or centers on not just the perceptual aspect of the quantity but also the conceptual aspect of quantity itself.

Piaget further describes the mental actions taking place during this period as the establishment of a hierarchy of classifications. This hierarchy is founded upon recognition of the aspect of equality. A child sees objects as being equal according to one property when objects being considered have the same properties. A child recognizing the aspect of equality would be able to choose players of equal height for a team. Children are able to determine who can run the fastest or who else can run as fast as they can. This equivalence may be represented by considering three individuals, represented by A, B, C. If A is the same height as B and B is the same height as C, then C is the same height as A. From this base of equivalence, the child moves upward in the hierarchical system of classification. Since this hierarchy does not appear to contribute significantly to the purposes of this book, it will not be presented here. However, the hierarchy is presented and can be studied in Piaget's writings.

Children in the stage of concrete operations are able to arrange objects according to some quantified dimension operationally, i.e., by mentally arranging them rather than by physically comparing them in succession, which is characteristic of the intuitive period in the preoperational stage. This enables them to function rapidly without having to measure. Thus, they need not manipulate physically (as children do at the preoperational stage), but they are unable to manipulate abstractions (as children can who are at the stage of formal operations).

During this period, concepts of time and space become much more sophisticated but are still tied to physical action and object manipulation. Up to now, the child had rudimentary notions of temporal order (before-after) and differences in time were dependent upon spatial distances and perceptual data. At the phase of concrete operations, the child's temporal continuum expands (past-present-future). Temporal order is coordinated with duration as the child is able to understand concepts of shorter-longer or faster-slower. The child is able to accept the notion of a time common to various movements at different velocities; two objects can be moved for the same period of time at different velocities. The child can understand that the duration of an hour remains constant even though the activity performed during different hours is different.

During the period of concrete operations, concepts of space further develop. There is a conservation of length and area, progressing from the perceptual estimations associated with the preoperational phase. By the time the child reaches the stage of concrete operations, understanding of topological concepts is complete. Since the stage of concrete operations covers an extensive period, the abilities of chidren within the stage will differ. However, during this period and after, children will begin to use some basic Euclidean concepts. For example, children are able to measure length, area, and angles, to identify and count the number of sides or angles in a figure, and to identify the parallel sides of a figure. Consistent with this stage, children are able to apply such operations to objects or figures that are visible, finite, or tangible. They are still limited, however, in their understanding of abstractions and in the number of relationships they can deal with. There is limitation in generalizing beyond the case at hand and difficulty solving verbal problems dealing with spatial concepts.

From ages 7 or 8 to 11 or 12 (stage of concrete operations), play is characterized by expanded socialization, a decline in symbolic play, and a rise in games with rules. Games with rules may be "handed down" or may be developed spontaneously. However, there is a necessity for and great attention to rules. Although games with rules continue to be played after this stage, play diminishes as imitation finds its equilibrium and curiosity finds its expression in intellectual experimentation.

During the period of concrete operations, children become increasingly sophisticated in the use of language and other signs in representational schemata. During the preoperational phase, children develop word meaning without a full understanding of what words mean. In the stage of concrete operations, language becomes a vehicle for the thinking process as well as a tool for verbal exchange. There is an internalization of words and thoughts. This internalization is combined with an internalization of actions, and communicated language correlates with the individual's conceptual activity.

At the beginning of this stage, children are able to analyze situations from perspectives other than their own. They become less egocentric, and they are able, for example, to cooperate in play rather than to simply "co-act" in play situations. This decentering enables thinking to become more logical and the conception of the environment to be more coherently organized. During the period of concrete operations, children's thinking becomes consistent, stabilized, and organized. Although children are able to perform the operations described in this section, they are generally incapable of them when they cease to manipulate objects or when such operations are not tied to physical action.

The Stage of Formal Operations

The stage of formal operations (the adult stage of cognitive development) usually begins at age 11 or 12. Children functioning at this level are not confined to concrete objects and events in their operations but are able to think in terms of the hypothetical and to use abstractions to solve problems. They enter into the world of ideas. They can rely on pure symbolism instead of operating solely on physical reallty. Children are capable of considering all the possible ways a particular problem may be solved and of assuming and understanding the effect of a particular variable upon a problem. Individuals at this stage have the ability to isolate the elements of a problem and to systematically explore possible solutions. Whereas children at the stage of concrete operations tend to deal largely with the present, children functioning at the stage of formal operations are able to be concerned with the future, the remote, and the hypothetical. They can establish assumptions and hypotheses, test hypotheses, and formulate principles, theories, and laws. They are able not only to think but to think about what they are thinking and why they are thinking it.

Piaget expresses thinking ability at this level by means of algebraic notations representing various levels of formal logic. Since the implications for development are not clear at this time, no attempt will be made to present the equations here. Suffice it to say that individuals at this level of cognitive development are able to review choices systematically and sequentially and are thus capable of combinational thinking, and of using systems of formal logic in their thinking. Hypothetical-deductive reasoning serves as a major criterion for denoting attainment of this phase of development. Logical verification predominates.

At this stage, individuals can design situations that will allow them to study possible relationships. This differs from the period of concrete operations, since children are able to advance beyond understanding the relationships presented to them. They design situations that will provide them with the opportunity of studying relationships. This requires the ability to think of all kinds of relationships that can exist among events rather than simply to understand the relationships that occur and that are presented.

Children at the stage of formal operations are able to understand concepts of equilibrium, including the effects of double inverses. For example, the velocity of an object is equal to the distance it covers over a period of time. If the distance covered is increased while the time remains the same, the velocity increases. If one wished to bring the object back to its original velocity one could either decrease distance covered or increase the time it takes. Either of these changes restores the original velocity. This kind of equilibrium problem arises whenever there is a simple law of proportions in which one variable equals the quotient of two other variables.

Play, as such, diminishes during this period. Children engage in games with rules. The games are conducted in structured social situations.

Finally, in regard to spatial concepts, children are capable of understanding more than the tangible and the finite. They are able to deal with infinity and the intangible and to develop the sophistication required to solve verbal problems dealing with spatial concepts.

Again, the rate and degree of completion of formal operations will vary with each individual. It is also possible to achieve an intellectual maturity in one area and at the same time have an incompletely developed maturity in other areas. Thus, the process of developing formal operational maturity may extend beyond the age period designated by Piaget.

Program Components and Movement Experiences*

Most educators drawing implications from cognitive theory agree that the most suitable environment for cognitive nurturing is one that is rich, stimulating, and natural. However, for day-to-day applicability, it is necessary to delineate more specifically the nature of such an environment in a movement setting. Traditionally, physical educators have asserted that intellectual abilities are involved and, thus, enhanced by activities such as learning the rules and strategies of games and sports, studying the history of dance and sport, or learning physiological and biomechanical principles involved in physical activities. More recently, the problem-solving approach has been advanced by those desirous of making thinking a goal in movement programs. Unfortunately, these approaches have provided little direction for programs designed to enhance development. In many of his works, Cratty (1972, 1973a, 1974b) has identified intellectual abilities and has presented specific motor activities to enhance their development. Furth and Wachs (1975) have developed a program of thinking games for the stimulation of cognitive development based on Piagetian concepts.

In this section, program components and early movement experiences are suggested for the stimulation of cognitive development on the basis of cognitive theory. They derive from the writings of Guilford (1959, 1967) and Bruner (1964, 1966) and from the numerous works of Piaget. The experiences suggested relate most closely to the fields of physical education and recreation. They are fun and motivating, and they involve the natural movements of children. Their concrete nature provides an observable physical or motor expression of cognitive functioning. They are not presented for the teaching of cognitive concepts per se. They are presented as examples of experiences that may serve to stimulate the cognitive development of children at appropriate levels of functioning. They are types of activities or situations in which a child may engage to nurture cognitive abilities. They are primarily designed to stimulate thinking and are most suitable for children functioning at beginning levels of development. If employed in physical education or physical recreation settings, these activities should be conducted in conjunction with or in addition to activities designed for physical and motor development.

Many of the activities and some of the program components presented here have been suggested by other authors. However, the overall categorization of these activities is unique. The organization of experiences as well as specific activities is recommended on the basis of logic rather than research data. The effectiveness of these experiences for cognitive development must await further research.

Play

Play has been recognized as a key activity for the cognitive development of the child. Bruner (1973) indicates that play serves to mature

*Parts of this section have been excerpted from: Joseph P. Winnick, "Early Movement Experiences and Program Components for the Stimulation of Cognitive Development," Proceedings of *The Seventh Annual Interdisciplinary International Conference on Piagetian Theory and the Helping Professions.* Los Angeles: University of Southern California, 1978.

modular routines for the child's later use. For Piaget (1962), play is essentially assimilation over accommodation. Behaviors related to play are ludic behaviors, i.e., behaviors engaged in to amuse or excite the individual. For Piaget, the most primitive type of play is known as *practice* or *exercise play*. The child repeats activities for the joy and satisfaction of repeating them. At later stages, play is characterized by ritualization. There is mobility of schemata, allowing for the formation of new ludic combinations for use in new situations. Gestures are repeated and combined as a ritual, and the child makes a motor game of them. According to Piaget (1962), the child needs opportunities to practice mastered schemata for the sheer pleasure and satisfaction of it. He also places great importance on sensory and motor experiences during this period. This suggests that the environment should be arranged to enhance the formation of new ludic combinations from acquired schemata. In addition, the movement environment should be rich but unstructured to allow for independent exploration and discovery, during the first two years of life in normally developing youngsters and for longer periods in children retarded in cognitive development.

At the preconceptual substage (ages 2 to 4), symbolic play becomes the primary tool of adaptation for the child, according to Piaget (1962). The child engages in play for most of his waking hours. Although play is still egocentric, opportunities for parallel play stimulate socialization. Play at this level serves an expressive function. It provides opportunities not only for imitation and identification but also for projection of these schemata to new objects. Play should be encouraged, since it is through play that the child learns to perform real life tasks. In addition, opportunity is provided to correct reality and to compensate for its unpleasantness. Symbolic play (make-believe and pretending) is the child's way of developing and dealing with the environment. At this level, play is characterized by greater order and organization, imitation, and role playing. Opportunities should be provided for free, unstructured, and spontaneous play. Children at this level are not positively responsive to group games with sophisticated rules.

Piaget (1962) indicates that, as the child moves through the substage of intuitive thought (ages 4 to 7), he or she advances from egocentricity to reciprocity. Therefore, opportunities for cooperative play become appropriate. However, it should be remembered that this collective symbolism is at its beginning during this period. Guessing games, games characterized by looking for missing objects, games of make-believe, and spontaneous games are stimulating for children in this period. The fact that the child is responsive to tag games, for example, indicates that the child is beginning to play with others and to think of others in his play. It is conceivable that trainable mentally retarded youngsters should be provided with such activities until 14 years of age.

At the stage of concrete operations, Piaget (1962) states, there is a rise of games with rules in the play of the child. Such rules may be "handed down," as in cultural games, or developed spontaneously by children. In addition, there is an expansion of socialization and a consolidation of social rules. Thus, the playing and construction of group games with rules become very attractive to children. As the child enters and moves through this period, play becomes less concerned with make-believe and pretending and more concerned with "real" games.

At this stage, play may be structured, social, and bound by rules. Although some youngsters may be ready for such games at their seventh birthday, children retarded in cognitive development may not be ready until after adolescence.

According to Piaget (1962), games with rules continue to be played through the stage of formal operations. Games engaged in by adults are "real" and structured and may be conducted in social settings. Since Piaget views play as the primacy of assimilation over accommodation, and since such primacy diminishes during this period, the role of play in adulthood is not clear. There appears to be a lack of clarity concerning the existence of ludic behavior in adults functioning at the level of formal operations.

Self-Awareness and Movement Mastery

According to Piaget (1963), knowing is bound to personal external action during the sensorimotor stage of development. Children functioning at this level adapt and modify basic reflexes, extend basic reflex patterns to form new schemata, and utilize acquired behavior patterns to produce effects on the environment. During the latter period of the sensorimotor stage, children distinguish means and ends, utilize familiar schemata for problem-solving purposes, engage in trial-and-error experimentation, and finally, symbolically plan actions or events before carrying them out externally.

From Piaget's description of sensorimotor intelligence, it appears that the separation of self from external objects is basic to successful sensorimotor development. Unless extremely deviant, children will be able to make such distinctions by the time they come in contact with professional recreation personnel or physical educators. If necessary, their distinctions between self and the external environment can be enhanced by having children reach for, push, pull, feel, smell, taste, hear, and follow objects in the environment. At other times, the immediate environment may be manipulated to produce effects on the individual. Examples include washing the child, placing the child in a wading pool, rubbing the heel of the child with materials of different texture, and stimulating the child in warm interpersonal interactions.

Separation of self from the environment enhances exploration of and learning from it. Barsch (1967) indicates, however, that before a child may fully explore and learn from the environment, the child needs to possess the ability to move and to move efficiently. Furth and Wachs (1975) hold that the ability to move frees the child to focus on more abstract movement problems. The ability to move requires static and dynamic balance, static and dynamic strength, agility, and flexibility. The ability to move efficiently for optimal environmental learning requires controlled, flexible, and rhythmic movement. It requires the ability to orient the body in space and to plan movements. Since movement ability and movement efficiency enhance exploration and discovery, and since exploration and discovery are important for cognitive stimulation, the benefit of movement is readily apparent.

On the basis of the writing of Piaget (1962), it appears to this author that mastered movement may be considered a schema. If movement is a schema and if schemata are forms of knowing, it logically follows that mastered movement can be viewed as "knowledge." Thus, movement abilities may be viewed as "ends" to be attained as well as means for environmental exploration. Further, when actions are performed for some goal, "thinking" is involved. There is a need to know the body movements required to accomplish the goal, the location of body parts, the relationship of parts of the body, how to counteract and make use of gravity, how to sequence movements, and how to judge space. In addition, the child must develop the ability to innervate appropriate muscle groups, to exhibit gross motor control, and to move as efficiently as possible. Of course, when movements are mastered, the individual need not "think" consciously of each detail. However, thinking is evidenced when one is attempting to learn or to master a motor ability.

Activities that develop basic physical abilities, balance, body awareness, gross motor control, movement flexibility, and rhythmic movement should be employed for the development of mastered movement. Since such activities may be easily found in the literature on the subject, specific activities are not presented here.

Perceptual Activity

As the child develops basic abilities to explore the environment, perceptual abilities are further developed in order that valuable information from the environment can be gained through the senses. As Furth and Wachs (1975) point out, "the organic impairment or inadequate functioning of any of these information systems could cause 'noise of the circuit' and confuse the other thinking systems — thus handicapping the learning process in academic and preacademic situations." Piaget and Inhelder (1967b) identify the role of perceptual activity in development and portray a close relationship between perception and movement. Piaget points out that the child's understanding of the environment depends to a great extent upon perception in the early years. However, he adds that, from the standpoint of cognitive development, accurate understanding of the environment occurs when perception is combined with "knowing" or conceptual activity. During the preconceptual stage, for example, perceptual abilities continue to develop, but they are not yet fully combined with conceptual development. Thus judgments made are frequently inaccurate or distorted.

Although it is important that all perceptions be appropriately and maximally developed, visual, auditory, kinesthetic, and tactual perceptions are particularly important for movement in and learning from the environment. Although perceptions may be developed without association with observable movement, motor activities may be arranged to enhance visual, auditory, kinesthetic, and tactual development. Movement activities for perceptual development may be easily found in the literature.

Logico-Mathematical Thinking

Activities related to logico-mathematical thinking, i.e., classification and seriation, are used to describe intellectual development and are included in many programs to stimulate thinking. Piaget studies these abilities in children in order to understand thinking processes. Guilford's (1971) "product" dimension, which pertains to ways of knowing or understanding, includes units, classes, and relations. Cratty (1970b), Furth and Wachs (1975), Lavatelli (1970), and Kamii and Radin (1970) have suggested activities to stimulate logico-mathematical thinking in their programs related to cognitive development. These programs have totally or in part depended on Piaget for their theoretical basis.

It must be stressed that the activities suggested here are not recommended in order that logico-mathematical abilities be taught. Instead, they are offered in the spirit conveyed by Furth and Wachs, who indicate that logical thinking games "are played for the thinking that the child must do and not for the learning of specific subject matter or the rules for solving problems" (Furth and Wachs, 1975, p. 209). In other words, the activities stimulate and focus on thinking and enable one to understand the thinking ability of the child.

Classification is the ability to group things that have common characteristics. There is agreement in the literature that classification experiences emphasizing qualitative aspects without class inclusion are appropriate for children functioning within the preoperational level. Suitable activities for this level include those in which the child dichotomizes and trichotomizes objects according to their similarities and differences. Such opportunities in physical education include arranging or selecting games where balls of different colors, sizes, shapes, and textures are grouped; arranging games or movement experiences in which movements such as walking, running, hopping, and jumping are involved and distinguished; selecting games and movement experiences in which squares, triangles, circles, or other geometric forms are utilized and distinguished; arranging obstacles or confidence courses that provide an opportunity for children to perceive similar and varying qualities in objects (slanted, moveable, suspended, rolling) and that stimulate varied movement responses such as climbing, jumping, creeping, balancing; selecting games and rhythmic activities that stimulate auditory discrimination; and including mimetic activities in which children learn to identify, imitate, and distinguish various animals.

Seriation is the ability to arrange things according to a dimension along which they differ. It focuses on the recognition of sequences and includes awareness of quantitative differences. As was true with classification, it is recommended in the literature that early experiences begin with dichotomizing and trichotomizing things in proper order. Opportunities for such activity are unlimited in the physical education or recreational environment. Children may be asked to order each other in terms of height, weight, and girth. They have many opportunities to order balls, bats, tires, balance beams, targets, and distances. Through movement exploration, children may be guided to seriate forms they create with their own bodies or with others. Examples include forming progressively larger geometric shapes and progressively larger or smaller letters or numbers with their bodies, or with other children. More demanding activities involve those in which the number of items to be ordered is increased and sequencing is conducted according to more than one variable.

Spatial–Temporal Thinking

Piaget (1967a) also analyzes spatial-temporal relations to demonstrate differences between preoperational and operational abilities. As was true with classification and seriation, it appears to this author that spatial-temporal activities may be utilized to encourage thinking and to stimulate the expression of the child's cognitive abilities. In addition, spatial-temporal experiences may be employed to further the child's understanding of the environment.

According to Piaget and Inhelder (1967b) the child *begins* to develop primitive topological relations in the sensorimotor stage, and these relations undergird spatial concepts that will be further developed in later years. Movement experiences that provide an opportunity for the child to experience near and far (proximity), to realize that objects and movements in the environment may be separated from each other as well as from the self (separation), and to experience the sequencing of activity (order) appear to this author to be appropriate for the nurturing of topological relations.

One of the very direct contributions of physical education or movement activities is in the area of spatial reasoning. The development of spatial concepts begins in infancy as children reach for and move toward and away from objects. As such movements occur, muscular tensions and exertions kinesthetically provide information to the child about the location and distance of objects. Movement also enhances the opportunity to group objects in space and to view objects from different points of view. For example, a child learns size constancy of a football as the image reflected on the eyes varies in accordance with distance from the object. Through countless movement experiences, children develop egocentric localization and an awareness of their bodies in space. As the child moves through the preoperational period, the ability to "decenter" develops as the child gains the ability to locate objects in relation to one another.

At the preconceptual level, the child further develops basic spatial concepts and learns to recognize spatial shapes such as circles, squares, triangles, and rectangles. The ability to recognize spatial shapes is dependent upon figure-ground perception skills. The recognition of major shapes and figure-ground abilities may be nurtured by activities in which children move through, around, over, under, inside, outside, on, and off shapes made by the teacher from cardboard or made by children out of rope, by perception box activities, by mimetic activities, or by activities in which children match movements to geometric forms, numbers, and letters of the alphabet.

Activities designed to stimulate the distinction, distance, and location of objects in space and the position of the self in space may also be employed for the development of spatial reasoning. Games or activities conducted with balls, balance beams, barrels, perception boxes, ropes, hoops, tires, and vaulting boxes may be selected to provide such stimulation. Obstacle courses or follow-the-leader games may be employed to develop basic spatial concepts at the level of the child's ability. Other favorite activities for the development of basic spatial concepts are trampolining (or bed jumping), tumbling, and swimming. The environment should be stimulating and include objects of different sizes, shapes, colors, and sounds.

Temporal reasoning may be enhanced by allowing children to create and conduct locomotor or other movement activities involving temporal sequence, temporal duration, speed, and cause-and-effect relationships. Examples include having children reproduce one or a series of movements demonstrated by the teacher or pupils. Activities may be made more demanding by increasing the number performed in a series and the complexity of patterns. To add enjoyment, games may be selected that require temporal sequencing or memory. Children may be motivated to move through an obstacle course in a particular way or to perform routines on a tumbling mat or trampoline. Distinctions in speed and duration are, of course, beautifully demonstrated in rhythmic and dance activities. Finally, causal activities in which children are asked to predict the consequences of actions are recommended for the development of temporal reasoning. For example, children may be asked to predict what occurs when balls are rolled against the wall with varying degrees of force or when balls are dropped from varying heights.

Representation and Social Interaction

The importance of language or verbal ability has been recognized in almost every notable theory of intelligence. Guilford (1967) recognizes semantic information in his "contents" dimension. Bruner (1966) indicates "intellectual growth involves an increasing capacity to say to oneself and others, by means of words or symbols, what one has done or what one will do." For Bruner (1964), language facilitates intellectual growth and provides a means for transferring as well as presenting experience. Cratty (1973a) includes language communication as a part of his program to tax the intellectual abilities of children.

For Piaget (1963), language is useful in communication, but it is not a principal factor in cognitive development. What is important to Piaget are the mental operations that occur in cognitive development. As these mental operations are developed, language may be used to communicate thinking. Once what a child knows is linked to language or other signs, the child may use them in his thinking and in communicating with others. The ability to represent objects in the environment, or that which is known, progresses from indices to symbols to signs. Kamii and Radin summarize these three types of external representation as presented by Piaget:

    a. Indices
        (1) Part of the object (e.g., the bottom of the bottle).
        (2) Marks causally related to the object (e.g., foot marks in the snow).
    b. Symbols
        (1) Imitation (the use of the body to represent objects, e.g., walking like a duck).
        (2) Make-believe (the use of the body to represent other objects, e.g., using a box to represent a duck).
        (3) Onomatopoeia (e.g., uttering "quack, quack").
        (4) Three dimensional models (e.g., making clay ducks).
        (5) Pictures (e.g., drawing ducks).
    c. Signs
        (1) Words and other signs (e.g., algebraic signs). (Kamii and Radin, 1970, p. 98.)

The activities suggested here are presented for the purpose of helping the child to eventually link that which he knows to signs —specifically language. The progression leads from knowing an object from index (some indication of it) to the association of an object with language. Following these activities, movement activities designed to use language are presented. Such activities are presented not only to stimulate verbalizing but also to stimulate communicating one's viewpoint to others (decentering) and to stimulate "social" thinking. Social thinking activities are presented on the assumption that intelligence is involved in the social as well as the physical world. Language enhances social communication and therefore enhances social thinking.

Representation at the index level is enhanced by providing opportunities for children to manipulate objects and to view them from various perspectives. Children may be encouraged to move over, under, around, through, and between objects in their environment.

At the symbol level, experiences can be arranged in which the child uses his body to represent objects. Examples include having children imitate cartoon characters, animals, airplanes, trains, cars, toys, or positions formed by dolls. Children may also be encouraged to represent objects with other objects. For example, the bed of a trampoline may represent the surface of the moon, a balance beam may represent a bridge, a ball may represent a bomb, a scooter board may represent a fire truck, or a series of scooters bound together may represent a train. As the child engages in games and activities in which he imitates and represents objects, he may reproduce sounds associated with them. Subsequently, games may be selected in which children need to guess objects being represented on the basis of gestures or sound. Story plays in which children are stimulated to pretend that they are objects or animals and to act out or dramatize these representations are appropriate. Also helpful are activities in which children are asked to produce movements demonstrated in pictures.

At the sign level, opportunities may be provided for communication through language, movement, and gestures. Such opportunity would be found in games that enable children to enlarge their vocabulary and increase their comprehension of language. Possible movement experiences include games and activities in which children describe movements to other children, games and activities in which children recite rhymes or chants (Charlie Over the Water and rope jumping), games and activities in which motor activity is initiated (Run Rabbit Run, Hill Dill, Brownies and Fairies), changed (Streets and Alleys), or ended (Red Light) by language cues, and games and activities in which letter, word, symbol, or pattern recognition is required. Imitation of acceptable verbal communication as well as the opportunity for such communication in small groups or play settings is vitally important. The presentation of positive language models, the opportunity to speak, and the motivation to speak are also important.

Physical Knowledge

In his theory of cognitive development, Piaget (1962) gives a great deal of attention to exploring, manipulating, and acting on objects and on observing the effects of such action. In essence, the child is stimulated by things in the environment and observes how objects react to his or her actions. Obviously then, the greater the variety of things in the environment, the greater the possibility for unique observations. Further, the child learns about the nature of matter by acting on objects and is stimulated to apply cognitive abilities in understanding their nature. Thus, physical knowledge is not an isolated cognitive ability to be developed but is identified as an important programming implication for the stimulation of various thinking abilities.

Physical knowledge provides raw materials for exploration, discovery, and problem solving. The child makes contact with objects by moving in and exploring his environment. Through exploration and manipulation, the child gains information about the properties of objects such as texture, size, weight, and resiliency. In physical education or recreation programs, children have opportunities to drop, thrust, pull, push, bend, twist, punch, squeeze, or lift objects possessing various properties. They can compare the effects of their actions on similar and dissimilar objects and can begin to analyze and systematize the effects of their actions. They have an opportunity to predict the results of various actions. For example, children may be asked what would happen if a ball is thrown against a wall or is deflated. At higher levels, children may be asked to explain the cause of an action. Children are intrigued by new things. They want to touch, pick up, throw, kick, squeeze, push, pull, and manipulate. The implication is to have as diverse, enriched, and stimulating an environment as is possible and to promote freedom for the children to act on things in it.

Evaluation

Guilford (1967) has defined evaluation as "a process of comparing a product of information with known information according to logical criteria, reaching a decision concerning criterion satisfaction." He includes evaluation as a category in his model for the structure of intelligence. Cratty (1972) includes evaluation as a category of intellectual functioning in his attempt to correspond movement tasks with selected categories of intellectual functioning. Since evaluation involves making a judgment based on comparison of two or more phenomena, it is not mutually exclusive in its relationship with the other cognitive abilities previously identified. For example, the individual may evaluate classes to determine the common properties of the members that comprise it or may evaluate mathematical relations.

Evaluation is often an inherent aspect of games, exercises, and sports. Children evaluate their own performances and the performance of a partner, team, or opponent. In games, they are able not only to determine who wins but also frequently to analyze the reason for the outcome. Children compare the success of different techniques of performing a task. For example, they may compare and evaluate the results of pitching a softball with various wind-ups, different techniques of high jumping or broad jumping, different arm movements in walking a balance beam, different techniques in performing a chin-up, or different techniques in moving over an obstacle. They are able to evaluate their success in completing a hopscotch course, running a mile, or performing a headstand. Children distinguish those who are fastest, strongest, heaviest, tallest, or most skilled. Self-testing activities provide opportunity for children to determine their best abilities and their limitations. Since performances in games, exercises, and sports are frequently associated with "objective" and rather concrete criteria, they are conducive to evaluation on basic as well as more advanced levels.

Exploration, Discovery, and Problem Solving

Problem solving has been recognized as an indicator of cognitive functioning by various theorists, and opportunities for children to explore, discover, and solve problems have been advocated by nearly all educators drawing implications from cognitive theory. Bruner (1966) refers to problem solving when he speaks of the ability to deal with several alternatives simultaneously as a mark of intellectual development. Guilford (1967) speaks of the generation of logical alternatives from given information *(divergent production)* and the generation of logical conclusions from given information *(convergent production)*. In citing implications for education, Guilford (1959) advocates that more emphasis be given to divergent thinking. In an application of the Guilford model, Cratty (1972) places movement activities on a continuum at whose extremes lie convergent and divergent thinking. The task of composing a dance routine would be an example of extreme divergent thinking. Tasks in which a single response is required or sought characterizes extreme convergent thinking.

In his description of cognitive development, Piaget continually refers to the child's ability to solve problems. During the sensorimotor period, the child develops schemata and uses them to reproduce or prolong an interesting effect, to attain a particular goal, and to solve problems. He refers to the invention of new means and ends. For higher levels, Piaget speaks of the mental manipulation of concrete objects and the ability to use abstractions to solve problems. Relative to education, Piaget (1970b) discusses the importance of spontaneous work based on personal needs and interests.

Exploration, discovery, and problem solving appear to be most appropriate for the stimulation of cognitive development, particularly in the early stages. In essence, the child is provided with opportunity to "play" with the environment. The child learns by touching, manipulating, and acting on interesting objects selected by the teacher. The child develops an awareness of the properties of such objects and the use of them for the attainment of a particular goal. In the language of Piagetian theory, the child develops schemata relating to objects that serve, in later stages, as a basis for the formation of thought. Physical manipulation serves as a basis for mental and verbal manipulations in later stages. Mental and verbal manipulation is enhanced by prior manipulation of concrete objects. In these approaches, the child is encouraged to learn by doing rather than by passively receiving information. As the child develops cognitively, teachers may stimulate progress by posing questions and presenting problems for the child to solve. In addition, the teacher may confront the child with alternatives to his thinking and cognitively confront the child when his thinking is illogical. At higher stages, problem solving serves to clearly differentiate means and ends and can be arranged to stimulate logico-mathematical and spatial-temporal thinking. The pedagogical approach of problem solving is compatible with cognitive development because it is in this approach that thinking is maximized.

In physical education, this approach has been associated primarily with movement exploration and movement education. The child is encouraged to explore and discover the movement capabilities of his own body in the environment. Such exploration is enhanced when teachers arrange a stimulating environment, encourage exploration, pose alternatives, and cognitively confront children. From such exploration, a broad base of movement is developed that the individual may apply in movement activities or in the solution of movement problems. In this approach, attention is given to the why as well as the how of movement. Used in this way, movement exploration serves as a stimulus or vehicle for thinking. Although exploration, discovery, and problem solving are traditionally associated with movement education, they may be applied to the teaching of game, sport, aquatic, rhythmic and gymnastic activities. When they are, the opportunity for cognitive involvement increases. There is little question that exploration, discovery, and problem solving are the favored approaches when "thinking" is the objective.

Other Pedagogical Considerations

Cognitive Confrontation

In addition to providing opportunities for thinking, there is a need for intervention, which should be encouraged and supplied by the teacher. Sigel (1969) refers to this intervention as a type of *cognitive confrontation.* As has already been pointed out, Piaget feels that intelligence is an adaptation and adaptation is an equilibrium between assimilation and accommodation. The interaction of assimilation (current cognitive structure), or the state of the child's mind, and accommodation (new experiences of the thing to be known) presents incongruities and conflicts to the child. In this situation, a state of cognitive disequilibrium exists within the child, creating interest and motivating the child to modify cognitive structure in a constructive way.

Although cognitive confrontation often occurs naturally, Sigel (1969) encourages the inducement of disequilibrium at appropriate periods. For example, children should be confronted by one or more methods when their point of view is illogical. The teacher may ask questions, provide demonstrations, or otherwise manipulate the environment to convince children of an illogical conclusion. Assume, for example, that there are two rows of balls of equal length. In one row there are ten balls and in the other row there are nine balls. If the child answers that the number of balls is the same in both rows because the space occupied is the same, the teacher confronts the child by further reducing the row with nine balls to eight, seven, six, and so on. At some point, the child will more than likely realize that the quantity has changed even though the space occupied (equal length) is the same. In this situation, a disequilibrium is stimulated by a confrontation arranged by the teacher. This disequilibrium stimulates cognitive analysis and, hopefully, cognitive development. It is critical that such confrontation be applied appropriately. It must be remembered that cognitive development is a progressive process and that new processes evolve from pre-existing structures. If pre-existing structures have not been developed to the point where new experiences can be absorbed, the new experiences will not be assimilated. It would be inappropriate, for example, to confront a child at the sensorimotor stage with the idea of conservation of volume. Novel experiences should build progressively on presently existing structures. If this does not occur, development is discontinuous. New experiences built on existing structures can be explained by existing structures, and motivation and interest will be maintained. New cognitive structures should not be forced. Instead, teachers should provide an atmosphere in which optimal development can be nurtured.

Motivation and Forgetting

Most authors drawing inferences from Piaget agree that motivation for cognitive development is and should be intrinsic. Intrinsic motivation derives from the inherent need to maintain equilibrium between assimilation and accommodation. Furth holds that "parents and educators need not frantically look for contrived situations or rewards that will make intelligence grow. Intelligence grows from within. Thus, the task becomes one of furthering and nourishing this growth by providing suitable opportunities, not by explicit teaching of what to do or what to know" (Furth, 1970, p. 74).

Educators must, however, be careful not to equate motivation for cognitive development or thinking with motivation for learning or academic achievement. Nothing presented here should suggest to educators that motivation, be it intrinsic or extrinsic, for learning or academic achievement is not necessary or beneficial. What is being suggested is that motivation for thinking or cognitive development is intrinsic to a state of disequilibrium, and it can be heightened for development by appropriate cognitive confrontation and by guiding children in activities appropriate to their level of development.

Focus on Thinking

A discussion of motivation and forgetting prompts an analysis of the relationship and the distinction between learning or academic achievement, on the one hand, and cognitive development, on the other hand. The distinction frequently is not made in the literature on Piagetian theory, causing confusion in drawing implications based on Piaget. Cognitive development is essentially the development of thinking. Thinking or cognition, of course, is important and thus is related to academic achievement. However, intellectual development may occur without academic achievement. The ability to read or to master geometry are examples of academic achievement that depend on cognitive development. Thus, if an objective for education is to teach children to read, then it will be necessary to develop their reading abilities. If the goal of education includes cognitive development, then experiences to develop thinking are appropriate. If the only goal or primary goal of education is cognitive development, then the curriculum in our schools needs drastic revision. This position is advocated by Ginsberg and

Opper (1969). If the only goal or the primary goal of education is academic achievement or other learnings, then the necessary change in traditional curricula is not as vast. Since it is beyond the purposes of this book to discuss or recommend the aims and objectives of education, it is sufficient to say that when cognitive development is the goal, thinking activities should be incorporated as experiences in the school curriculum. It is important, however, to realize that thinking or operational concepts cannot be taught. They have to be experienced by the individual.

Interaction

There is general agreement among writers drawing implications from Piaget's theory that interaction between teacher and student and among students is vital for the nurturing of cognitive development. It is necessary to recall that the child at the sensorimotor and preoperational stages is egocentric in behavior. This does not mean that children are selfish but that they center attention on one aspect of a problem and that they view things from their own perspective and experiences only. Thus, children in early stages viewing the pouring of liquid from a glass to a narrower and longer container focus their attention on the length only rather than on length and width. Also, children fail to understand why people do not know their names when all they have to do is look and see and they will know their names.

Social interaction serves as a stimulus for thinking. Children are stimulated to convey their views and to relinquish their egocentricity. They are challenged to accept different viewpoints when their views are confronted. Children begin to realize that the words that they use may not be understood in the same way or may not mean the same thing when used by others. Interaction also provides an opportunity for the teacher to learn from children, to understand them, and thus to identify their level of functioning.

Since language is the usual method of communication, the development of language for communication is critical. Language is the vehicle for the transmission of information and thus serves as a basis for interaction. However, there are instances in which the development of language is delayed or impossible. In such instances, communication may take different forms (as the sign language of the deaf). The critical aspect for cognitive development is interaction and communication. Although those who are able to develop language have a clear advantage, communication by other means is, of course, suitable and acceptable. Furth and Wachs (1975), who subscribe to Piagetian theory, indicate that the lack of language does not lead to incomplete cognitive development.

Individuality

It must be recalled that Piaget presents a theory of cognitive development, based on stages, in which he assumes an order of cognitive development that is applied to the species. It is also clear from his writing, however, that individuals may operate at one stage in one area and at another stage in another area or at different substages within stages. It is, thus, inappropriate to label children as "preoperational" or "concrete operational." Also, although he correlates various stages with chronological age, he emphasizes that the time spent by children at various stages in various areas varies with different children. Since different children of the same age operate at various levels of cognitive development, and since the same child operates at different levels in different areas, individual differences must be taken into account in the consideration of enhancing cognitive development and in understanding the cognitive abilities of children. In regard to the role of the teacher in encouraging and developing individual differences, Athey and Rubadeau remind us that:

> Piaget's theory places firmly on the shoulders of the teacher the responsibility for knowing the experiential background which has brought each child to the particular level of functioning he has reached, and the areas in which he has lagged or forged ahead. At the same time, the theory enables her to compare each aspect of the child's thinking against the general developmental schedule. (Athey and Rubadeau, 1970, p. xvii.)

Related to the concept of individual differences but often overlooked is the fact that the thought and language of children are qualitatively different from that of adults. Children have different experiences and express them primarily through their own viewpoint (eogcentricity). One must understand these differences to effectively understand and teach the child.

> The implication of this very general proposition — that the young child's thoughts and language are qualitatively different from the adult's — is also very general. It must follow that the educator must make a special effort to understand the unique properties of the child's experience and ways of thinking. The educator cannot assume that what is valid for him is necessarily valid for the child. For example, while the educator himself may learn a great deal by reading a book or listening to a lecture, similar experiences may be far less useful for the young child. While the educator may profit from an orderly arranged sequence of material, perhaps the child does not. While the educator may feel that a given idea is simple and indeed self-evident, perhaps the child finds it difficult. It short, it is not safe to generalize from the adult's experience to the child's. What the educator needs to do is to try to improve his own capacity to watch and listen, and to place himself in the distinctive perspective of the child. Since the meaning expressed by the child's language is often idiosyncratic, the adult must try to understand the child's world by observing his actions closely. (Ginsberg and Opper, 1969, p. 220.)

Matching Intelligence and Instruction

The material presented in this section has primarily attended to teaching implications associated with nurturing cognitive development. However, educators have also drawn on Piagetian theory for the sequencing of subject matter. For example, Adler (1970) states that the child should be permitted multiple and varied opportunities in the early grades for directly acting on concrete objects and that the curriculum should move gradually from the concrete to the symbolic and formal.

Adler (1970) and Ginsberg and Opper (1969) present some interesting ideas for educators in the area of mathematics and science.

The concept of matching intelligence and instruction has implications for physical educators, too. As in other subject areas, in physical education classes children should be provided opportunities to apply direct action to concrete objects. A broad base of movement abilities should be developed in early childhood for use in movement activities or in the solution of movement problems. As children develop cognitively, they should be gradually stimulated to explain the why of movement. In such an analysis, time, space, and force are analyzed as variables of movement. At early stages, games involving simple rules and strategy should be presented. From this beginning, children may be able to develop games with their own rules. Activities involving complex rules and strategy should be presented later in the curriculum.

The Role of the Teacher

From the analysis of teaching styles presented above, it is possible to derive a description of the role of the teacher when the development of thinking is the goal. The teacher becomes a guide for development by creating a rich educational environment in which development can take place. Such guidance is planned rather than haphazard. If appropriate experiences are selected, children not only will be stimulated but will respond enthusiastically, thus eliminating the need for extrinsic motivation. In addition to the guiding function, the teacher cognitively confronts the child in appropriate situations, provides activities that focus on thinking, constantly interacts with the child, and encourages others to do so. Although the teacher provides group activities, individual differences are recognized and accommodated. When the goal of the curriculum is subject-centered, the teacher analyzes activities for their cognitive demand and presents material in sequences that are within the grasp of pupils. The goal of the program is not to force the development of new cognitive structures but rather to provide an environment that nurtures cognitive development.

Specific Activities

On the basis of cognitive theory and the implications drawn from it, specific activities to nurture cognitive development are presented in this section. It should be noted that these are only examples of activities that may be selected. Teachers may develop their own activities once the principles upon which selection is based are understood. It must be stressed that the activities must be suited to the abilities of each child in order to provide challenging and successful experiences for children.

The activities suggested here are arranged into five groups. In the first group, two kinds of logico-mathematical thinking activities are presented. In the first, activities are suggested to stimulate basic classification of movements, stunts, locomotor activities, children, the abilities of children, shapes, objects, activities in which children give impetus, and activities in which children receive impetus. In the second part, activities characterized by seriation and order are presented.

In the second group, activities to stimulate spatial-temporal thinking are separated into two kinds. In the first part, activities to develop spatial relations are presented. They are designed to stimulate the distinction, distance, and location of objects in space and the position of the self in space. The second kind of activities is designed to stimulate temporal thinking. Activities stimulating temporal sequencing, spatial-temporal translation, cause and effect, and temporal relations (involving speed and duration) are presented.

The third group includes activities to stimulate representation and social interaction. The first kind is activities to stimulate representation at the index and symbol levels. The second kind stimulates the development of signs (with emphasis on language), communication, and social interaction.

In the fourth group, examples of activities for evaluation are presented. The activities suggested involve self-evaluation, the comparison and evaluation of the performances of individuals or teams, the comparison and evaluation of techniques of performance, and the comparison and evaluation of movements and activities.

Although the possibilities are unlimited, a brief list of problem-solving activities is presented in the final section. Motor activities that stimulate physical (motor) knowing and perceptual activity are presented in other portions of this book. Since play is such a comprehensive concept, the author feels no need to present activities for it. Play activities depend on the schemata available to each individual child. It is felt that the information presented in the previous section pertaining to physical knowledge amply directs the reader in terms of specific activities.

Logico-Mathematical Thinking Activities

CLASSIFICATION

The following activities may be arranged to differentiate and classify movements, stunts, locomotor activities, other children, the abilities of children, shapes, objects, activities in which children give impetus, and activities in which children receive impetus.

1. Games that may be used for classification include: Back to Back, Add One, Angels in the Snow, Do This, Do That, Simon Says, Hot Potato, Wood Tag, Posture Tag, and Red Rover. In many cases, the games will need to be modified. For example, in the game of Red Rover, instead of simply calling a name or names, the game may be modified so that redheads, boys, girls, or people with blue eyes "come over."
2. Relays that involve classification include those that involve matching or sorting objects or performing animal walks or other locomotor activities.
3. Rhythms and dances that involve classification include those in which children differentiate body parts (Looby Loo or Hokey Pokey), those that involve various locomotor movements, and those that utilize various combinations of dance steps.
4. Trampolining may be utilized to stimulate the classification of movements, stunts, and activities in which participants give and receive impetus.

5. Scooter board activities may be used to stimulate the classification of movements, stunts, locomotor activities, and activities in which children give impetus.
6. Perception box activities may be used to distinguish and classify shapes.
7. Mimetics may be arranged to stimulate the classification of movements, stunts, locomotor activities, shapes, and objects.
8. Swimming and other water activities may be arranged to stimulate the classification of movements, stunts, locomotor activities, and the giving and receiving of impetus.
9. In movement exploration, classification can be enhanced and stimulated by asking questions such as:
   a. How many different ways can you show me to move from here to there?
   b. How many different-sized circles can you make with your body?
   c. Can you match your body to these shapes?
10. Other activities suggested for classification include hula hoop activities, movement imitation, and grouping children by various characteristics.

SERIATION AND ORDERING

1. Rhythms and dances characterized by movement patterns conducted in a sequence involve seriation.
2. Many rope-jumping games are characterized by performance of activities in sequence.
3. Stunts and movements imitated on mats, trampolines, balance beams, tires, or scooters stimulate sequencing.
4. Obstacle courses by their nature involve performing activities in order.
5. Activities in which children order each other in terms of height, weight, girth are helpful in stimulating ordering.
6. Movement exploration activities can be used to develop seriation and ordering.

Spatial-Temporal Thinking Activities

SPATIAL RELATIONS

1. Games that involve locating objects in relation to each other or that stimulate a recognition of one's position in space include Dodge Ball, Hill Dill, Huntsman, Tag Games, Follow the Leader, Jump the Shot, Cat and Rat, Hide and Seek, and Steal the Bacon.
2. Other activities suggested for the development of spatial discrimination include rope jumping, playground activities, scooter board activities, trampolining, stunts and tumbling, movement exploration, obstacle courses, and mazes.
3. Activities where children move under, over, and through tunnels, barrels, boxes, hoops, chairs, tires, cargo nets, ropes, or other objects.

TEMPORAL RELATIONS

Activities involving temporal relations include those that distinguish speed, duration of time, temporal sequence, cause and effect, and spatial-temporal translation.

1. Games that may be arranged to enhance temporal relations of speed, direction, order, or cause and effect include Simple Tag, Wood Tag, Hill Dill, Cowboys and Indians, Crows and Cranes, Fox and Geese, Red Light, Basketball Shooting, Three-Pin Bowling, Shuffleboard, Follow the Leader, Hopscotch, Twister, Add One, Wall Ball, Darts, and Tether Ball.
2. Races conducted between individuals and teams (relays) involve temporal relations.
3. Speed (tempo), duration, and order are essential elements in rhythms and dances and, therefore, involve temporal relations.
4. Since imitation of movement involves reproducing an activity perceived in space and time, such activities are recommended for spatial-temporal translation.
5. Executing a series of movements on the trampoline, balance beam, tires, mats, and scooters enhances temporal awareness.
6. Movement exploration can be used to enhance spatial-temporal relations. For example, children may be asked the following questions:

   What will happen if you throw the ball hard against the wall? Softly? High? Low?
   How fast (or slow) can you move?
   How fast can you throw the ball?
   How far can you throw the ball?
   How far you can jump?
   How long you can stand on one foot?
7. Other activities that may be arranged to stimulate temporal thinking include obstacle courses, rope jumping activities, punching bag activities, throwing objects for distance and speed, jumping for speed and distance, throwing and catching objects of different weight, size, texture, and form, swimming activities, kicking objects of different weight, size, texture, and form, and balance beam and balance board activities.

Representation and Communication

INDEX AND SYMBOL

1. Games that can be arranged to enhance representation at the index and symbol level include Duck Duck Goose, Midnight, Cowboys and Indians, Crows and Cranes, Squirrel in the Trees, Cat and Rat, Dog and Bone, and games conducted with objects.
2. Story Plays, mimetics, and animal walks help to develop representation at the index and symbol level.
3. Other activities may include having children depict objects presented in pictures; imitate objects formed by dolls; represent vehicles such as trains, airplanes, and trucks; use playground objects for boats, wagons, and bridges; guess what things are represented by gesture or sound.

SIGNS AND COMMUNICATION

1. Games that enhance language and social communication include Red Light, Red Rover, Run for Your Supper, Simon Says, Do This, Do That, Back to Back, Steal the Bacon, Call Ball, Charlie Over the Water, and Have You Seen My Sheep. In such games, activity is begun, conducted, changed, or ended by signs.
2. Rhythms and dances include Looby Loo, Dry Bones, Ring Around the Rosy, London Bridge, and Farmer in the Dell.

3. Other activities that enhance representation and communication abilities on the sign level include:
   a. Reciting or acting out nursery rhymes.
   b. Reciting rope jumping chants.
   c. Performing activities in which movement is initiated, changed, or ended by language or signs.
   d. Moving through obstacle courses in which activity is directed by pictures.
   e. Guessing what objects are being represented by gestures or sounds.
   f. Describing movements made by other children.
   g. Performing movements suggested by listening to records.
   h. Developing games, explaining them to other children, and then playing them.

Evaluation

SELF–EVALUATION

1. Ask children to indicate how far or how high they can jump. Ask them to jump and compare their predictions and their performance.
2. Ask children to indicate how far they can run, hop, or skip and to compare their predictions and performances.
3. Have children view demonstrations of various movements and ask them to reproduce the movements and evaluate their performance.
4. Ask children to set goals for running obstacle courses and performing physical conditioning activities. Subsequently, ask children to evaluate their performance.

COMPARING PERFORMANCES

In order to develop a sensitivity for self-concept, children may be asked to compare their performances with others'. They may be asked such questions as:

1. Why did your team win (or lose) the game?
2. Who is the tallest? The fastest? The strongest?
3. Who can jump the highest? Jump the farthest? Run around the track? Catch the ball? Walk the beam? Do a chin-up? Jump over a brook? Stand on one foot?
4. Who are the good sports? Why?

COMPARING TECHNIQUES OF PERFORMANCE

1. Ask children to balance on one foot with eyes open and then with eyes closed. Ask them to compare the two techniques.
2. Ask children to walk a balance beam with arms folded and then with arms free. Ask them to compare the techniques.
3. Ask children to throw objects for distance and to vary heights. Ask them to determine which height is most effective.
4. Ask children to perform locomotor activities as fast as possible. Ask them to rank techniques that enable one to move from one point to the other in the shortest possible time.

COMPARING MOVEMENTS AND ACTIVITIES

1. Have children form groups of three, and give a ball, stick, and a hoop to each group. Ask children in each group to plan a game with these materials. Subsequently, ask them to explain the game to the class and have the class play the game. Evaluate the games according to criteria such as: the most fun, the most active, the safest, the most difficult.
2. Demonstrate four movements to the child. An example is hopping forward, jumping forward, walking forward, and walking backward. Ask children which movement doesn't "belong." Ask them to explain why — there may be no correct answer. Ask children to develop their own series of movements of stunts and have them ask others which doesn't "belong."
3. Perform a series of movements, skills, and stunts. Ask children to group them in ways such as: those that give impetus or receive impetus, those conducted while stationary or while moving, those with objects or without objects, and so on.
4. At the end of a class, ask children to determine the parts of the session that were most strenuous, the most fun, the easiest, or the most difficult. Ask children to explain their answers.

Problem Solving

Problem solving is, of course, a method of learning and a method of teaching. In physical education, the problem-solving approach is associated with movement education but may be applied in the teaching of skills and activities or to encourage the child to be involved in a variety of activities. The activities presented below are examples of problems that may be posed to stimulate thinking in movement or physical education activities. The list, of course, should be considered endless. Emphasis is placed on the generation of divergent thinking.

MOVING

Ask children to move from one end of a mat or room to the other end. Then ask questions such as:

1. How many other ways can you move?
2. Can you move with only one part of your body touching the floor? Two parts? Three parts?
3. Can you move slowly? Quickly?
4. Which way is the fastest? Slowest? Easiest?

CARRYING OBJECTS

Ask children to carry objects between two points, and ask them the following questions:

1. How many different ways can you carry an object?
2. Which is the fastest way to carry an object? Slowest?
3. Which is the easiest way to carry an object?

JUMPING

Ask children the following questions about jumping.

1. How many ways can you jump over the rope?
2. Which way of jumping enables you to jump farthest? Highest? Why?
3. How many different ways can you jump in and out of a hoop?
4. What happens when you don't use your arms in jumping?

MOVING OBJECTS

Have children move objects and ask them the following questions.

1. How many ways can you move this ball?
2. How can you make the ball move farther?
3. What happens when you kick under the ball?
4. How many different ways can you throw the ball? Which way makes the ball go fastest? Farthest?

TRAVERSING OBSTACLES

Have children move across a balance beam and ask them the following questions.

1. Which is the easiest way of moving along a balance beam?
2. How many different ways can you move on the balance beam? How can you make it easier? Why is it easier?
3. What stunts can you do on the balance beam?

OTHER ACTIVITIES

1. Ask children to demonstrate the number of safe ways a ball, rope, hoop, or tire can be used in a game.
2. Ask children to demonstrate the number of ways they can move through, around, over, on, and off various objects.
3. Ask children to demonstrate how different letters, numbers, geometric designs, animals, or vehicles can be formed with a partner.
4. Ask children to design games with rules.

7

VISUAL AND AUDITORY HANDICAPS

Visual and auditory handicaps are among those that most severely affect the development of the child. Children with sensory impairments are at an obvious disadvantage in development. However, with proper nurturing, they are able to develop the necessary abilities to learn, live a happy and wholesome life, and contribute significantly to society. For convenience, visual and auditory handicaps will be discussed separately in the following pages. However, it should be recognized that many children have not only both visual and auditory handicaps but other types of impairments as well. The first part of this chapter includes information pertaining to definitions, classifications, incidence, etiology, assessment, and general characteristics of the visually handicapped. The second section includes information pertaining to definitions, classifications, incidence, types of defects, causes, assessment, and general educational needs of the deaf and the hard-of-hearing.

Visual Handicaps

Definition, Classification, and Incidence

Although at first the definition of *blindness* may be considered simply the absence of sight, the fact that there are many degrees of blindness makes definition much more complex. Certainly, when no visual ability exists, or when blindness is complete and total, it is not difficult to understand or define. However, most visually handicapped individuals have some residual vision. In some cases, there is little residual vision, and in other cases, the ability to perceive distance and motion exists. The National Society for the Prevention of Blindness (1966) defines *blindness* as visual acuity for distance vision of 20/200 or less in the better eye with best correction, or visual acuity of more than 20/200 if the width diameter of field vision subtends an angle no greater than 20 degrees. The Society classifies as *partially seeing* those persons with a visual acuity greater than 20/200 but not greater than 20/70 with correction. A vision of 20/200 means that a person sees at 20 feet what a normally sighted person sees at 200 feet. The latter aspect of the definition refers to a person who may have better than 20/200 visual acuity but whose vision is constricted to a limited area at a particular time, i.e., to whom a small area of usable vision is available. The Society's definition has served as a legal definition of blindness in the United States.

Although the legal definition of blindness still is commonly applied, it is not completely acceptable, and many service and professional organizations are beginning to modify legal standards. In addition, professionals are developing definitions that have greater relevance for their field. In regard to education, for example, Kirk (1972) refers to those who can learn to read print as *visually impaired* and to those who cannot read print and need instruction in Braille as *blind.* Kirk prefers this definition to the legal one because it determines the mode of education the child is capable of using. Other educators refer to those who must be educated through other than visual media as *blind* and to those able to be educated through the medium of vision with special aids as *partially sighted.*

Regardless of the terms or classifications utilized, it must be stressed that there are different degrees and kinds of blindness. The functional abilities of each person must be considered individually. In addition, the concept of blindness is not absolute, and it varies according to the purposes it is intended to serve. For the purpose of this book, the terms *blind* and *partially sighted* will be used as legally defined. The designation *visually handicapped* will be used to encompass both conditions.

Because of problems of definition, failure to report blindness, and other sources of error, estimates of the incidence of visual handicaps have been difficult to make and have varied considerably. The American Foundation for the Blind (1963) reported that the number of blind persons in the United States in 1963 was estimated to be at least 400,000, or an average of 2.14 blind persons in each 1000 of the general population. This organization further reported that 10 per cent of blind persons are under 21 years of age and at least 50 per cent are over 65. Hatfield (1973) estimated the rate per 100,000 population in the United States to be 225.1. The lowest rate was reported for the state of Hawaii (139.3), and the highest rate was reported for the District of Columbia (370.1). The National Society for the Prevention of Blindness (1966) estimated that 13.5 per cent of the blind are 20 to 39 years of age and 29.5 per cent are 40 to 64 years of age. Authorities agree that a low percentage of total blindness occurs during the developmental years. Also encouraging is the fact that the incidence of blindness among pre-school children has considerably decreased with the prevention of retrolental fibroplasia (RLF). Hatfield found that the rate of blindness for children under 7 years of age was 12.9 per 100,000 population in 1967. She indicates that this represents a decrease of 50 per cent from the rate of 25.7 obtained in a 1950 study of the same age group. The high rate in 1950 was owing to the high incidence of RLF. Kirk (1972) points out that over half of all blindness in pre-school children during the period 1945 to 1955 was caused by RLF. Based on his review of the literature, Kirk (1972) reported "approximately one-third of visually handicapped children enrolled in local day care residential schools have multiple handicaps (deaf, blind, blind—mentally retarded, and so forth)."

Causes of Blindness

Blindness may occur as a result of many factors. The most frequently observed causes of blindness are diseases (including scarlet fever, syphilis, meningitis, mumps, and German measles), accidents and injuries, poisoning, tumors, prenatal influences, and hereditary factors. A disease of the retina, retrolental fibroplasia (RLF), characterized by a mass of scar tissue behind the lens of the eye, ran rampant in the late 1940s and early 1950s. In the early 1950s, it was discovered that the major cause of RLF was the administration of high concentrations of oxygen to permaturely born infants over an extended period of time. Since this discovery, blindness caused by this practice has been significantly reduced. Another cause of blindness that may now be controlled is rubella (German measles). Blindness as well as other deviant conditions results when the rubella virus has been contracted by women during the first trimester of pregnancy. With the availability of a rubella vaccine, it is now possible to control this cause of blindness as well. In her study of 3115 legally blind children under 7 years of age, Hatfield (1973) reported the following statistics on the causes of blindness: infectious diseases, 10.2 per cent; injuries and poisoning, 5.8 per cent; neoplasms, 4.9 per cent; diseases not classified elsewhere, 3.2 per cent; prenatal influences, 60.8 per cent; causes unknown to science, 0.4 per cent; and causes not determined or not specified, 14.7 per cent.

Types of Visual Defects

Although they are not mutually exclusive, refractive errors, structural defects, impaired muscle functioning, and lens abnormalities are among the most common types of visual impairment. Errors in refraction result from deviations in the curvature of the cornea or lens. Variations in lens curvature are caused by the action of the internal ciliary muscles of accommodation, which are activated as objects are viewed from varying distances. When the curvature of the eyeball results in an elongated anterior-posterior axis, rays of light focus in front of the retina when objects are viewed from a distance of 20 feet or more. The images of such objects are unclear, resulting in a condition known as *nearsightedness,* or *myopia.* Conversely, *farsightedness*, or *hyperopia*, occurs because the anterior-posterior axis of the eyeball is shortened or because the corneal surface is flattened. Instead of an excess of refractive power, which is associated with myopia, there is an insufficiency, as the rays of light fall behind the retina. For the nearsighted individual, vision beyond 20 feet is characteristically blurred. Kirk (1972) points out that farsightedness implies only that distant objects can be seen with less strain on the muscles of lens accommodation and does not mean, as is often thought, that the hyperope can see farther or more clearly at a given distance than can the *emmetrope* (normally sighted). Correction of myopia is made with a concave lens, and of hyperopia with a convex lens. A third type of refractive error is *astigmatism*, a condition characterized by blurring owing to irregularity in the curvature of the cornea or the lens. Instead of converging on the same point on the retina, light rays from objects are spread over a diffuse area. Words and letters may blur together and are easily confused. Although the eye attempts to compensate for irregularities, it is unable to fully do so, and external correction is necessary. In most cases, astigmatism is correctable.

A second group of visual impairments is associated with defects in the functioning of external ocular muscles. Of these defects, *strabismus* (cross-eyes) and *heterophoria* are the most common. Strabismus is a condition in which the eyes fail to simultaneously focus on the object because of a lack of coordination of external ocular muscles. *Internal strabismus* occurs when one eye focuses on an object and the other turns inward, medially, and *external strabismus* occurs when the deviating eye turns outward, or laterally. The term *alternating strabismus* is used in cases in which the deviating eye alternately turns inward or outward. When the properly focused eye sees the true image and the deviating eye views a displaced image, double vision may occur. If the condition is not corrected, the individual learns to attend to the "true" image and to ignore the displaced image. However, such a practice may result in impaired visual acuity. *Heterophoria,* as described by the National Society for the Prevention of Blindness (1960), is a defect in the muscular balance of the eyes, resulting in a constant tendency of the eyes to deviate from a normal position for binocular fixation, counterbalanced by simultaneous fixation forces through muscular effort (prompted by the desire for single binocular vision). The deviation is said to be latent since it is not usually apparent. The lack of coordination of the eyes tends to inhibit the ability to coordinate or fuse the two images into a single image. In this condition, the eyes may pull medially toward the nose (*esophoria*), laterally away from the nose (*exophoria*), or upward or downward (*hyperphoria*).

A third type of visual defect involves abnormalities of the lens. Cataracts and dislocation or displacement of the lens are among the conditions associated with lens abnormalities. A *cataract* is a disorder in which the lens of the eye, its capsule, or both become opaque, causing loss of visual acuity. Distance vision, the ability to view objects clearly, and color discrimination may be impaired. Barraga (1973) points out that children with congenital cataracts often appear unable to see at all and that they need to make an effort to view objects closely; opportunities are made for such children to develop muscular control and motility in order to be able to fixate and attend to objects. Although cataracts occur in children, senile cataracts occur most commonly in persons over 50 years of age. Senile cataracts result in a gradual loss of vision as the lens becomes milky and cloudy. Regardless of the age of the person or the type of cataract, passage of light through the affected eye is inhibited, and the stimulation of retinal cells is reduced. Current treatment for the condition involves surgical removal of the affected lens. A second abnormality of the lens is dislocation or displacement. Such displacement is caused by trauma or accident. Although the lens may be returned to its normal position in certain cases, permanent displacement and corresponding loss of visual functioning may occur. Visual functioning is, of course, relative to the extent of displacement.

Structural anomalies are a fourth type of visual defect. Hatfield (1963) reported that structural anomalies of the eyeball accounted for 23.4 per cent of the defects of 7757 legally blind children aged 5 to 20 who were attending local and residential schools in 36 states from 1955 to 1959. In the same study, retrolential fibroplasia accounted for 33 per cent of the defects. Since the incidence of blindness due to retrolential fibroplasia has decreased sharply, the present percentage of blindness owing to structural anomalies may be expected to be greater than the percentage reported by Hatfield. In her later study of 3115 legally blind children under 7 years of age, Hatfield (1973) reported that 24.8 per cent of the cases were caused by structural anomalies and 9.0 per cent were caused by RLF. Structural anomalies identified by Hatfield include multiple anomalies, myopia, glaucoma (infantile), albinism, coloboma, anophthalmos, microphthalmos, and aniridia. Of these conditions, myopia has already been discussed. The National Society for the Prevention of Blindness (1960) has defined the other conditions as follows:

1. *Glaucoma* — increased pressure inside the eye; "hardening" of the eyeball, caused by accumulation of aqueous fluid in the front portion.
2. *Albinism* — a hereditary loss of pigment in the iris, skin, and hair usually associated with lowered visual acuity, nystagmus, and photophobia and often accompanied by refractive errors.
3. *Coloboma* — congenital cleft due to the failure of the affected part of eye to grow completely.
4. *Anophthalmos* — absence of a true eyeball.
5. *Microphthalmos* — an abnormally small eyeball.
6. *Aniridia* — absence of the iris, either congenital or caused by an accident.

In addition to the conditions already discussed, visual impairments may be associated with choroid, retina, and optic nerve involvement. Such conditions are associated with a variety of etiologies and various degrees of visual handicap. Retinal defects include retrolental fibroplasia, retinal and muscular dysfunction, and retinoblastoma. Damage to or atrophy of the optic nerve, impairment of the pathways, or damage to visual centers of the brain are factors that impede the transmission of visual sensations and result in a variety of atypical visual conditions. Hatfield (1963) reported that 40.4 per cent of anomalies of the eye were retinal. Over 75 per cent of the retinal irregularities (33 per cent of total) were associated with retrolental fibroplasia. It must be stressed however, that this figure was based on data pertaining to the period from 1958 to 1959. In a later study of legally blind children under 7 years of age, Hatfield (1972)

reported that 17.0 per cent of the cases were caused by retinal irregularities. Only 9 per cent (or slightly over one half of retinal causes)
were caused by RLF. Thus, the discovery of the cause of RLF has
reduced the percentage of RLF-caused blindness. On the other hand,
Hatfield's finding of 9.5 per cent incidence for blindness associated
with disorders of the optic nerve would be considered underestimat-
ed today. In fact, Hatfield (1972) later found that 22.4 per cent of the
causes of blindness of preschool blind were associated with disorders of the optic nerves and pathways.

Diseases That Primarily Affect the Eye

In addition to the causes of blindness that have been discussed previously, there are infectious diseases that primarily affect the eyes
and frequently cause loss of sight. (These are distinguished from infectious diseases that secondarily affect the eyes.) Two of the more
common of these diseases are trachoma and ophthalmia. According
to the National Society for the Prevention of Blindness (1960), *trachoma* is a form of infectious keratoconjunctivitis caused by a specific
virus that in the chronic form produces severe scarring of the eyelids
and cornea. *Ophthalmia* is inflammation of the eye or of the conjunc-
tiva.

Assessment

Just as total blindness is easy to define, it is relatively easy to recognize. When it occurs in infants, total blindness is almost always detected within the first years. The diagnosis is, of course, immediate
when it occurs later in the life of the individual. The greatest problems of detection of visual impairments occur in pre-school or early
school-aged youngsters: Very often, the children are unable to recognize visual handicaps and thus do not communicate difficulties. Their
concept of normal vision is based on their own experience rather than
on an external criterion. Since they do not realize what others see, their
reference of normality is based on their own abilities and thus they
do not report visual problems.

The screening tests most commonly used to assess vision are
the Snellen Eye Charts. These tests contain letters of the alphabet
(*E's*) of different sizes and positions. The tests may be quickly administered by professionals or nonprofessionals and can be used with
young children as well as adults. Although considered a measure of
visual ability, the test primarily assesses visual acuity (refractive
errors) and thus may not be useful in detection of other visual defects such as nearpoint vision, peripheral vision, convergence, disorders of binocular fusion, or muscular imbalance. Kirk (1972) therefore recommends that the following indications of possible visual
difficulty be observed and noted:

1. Strabismus; nystagmus.
2. How the child uses his eyes: tilting his head, holding objects
   close to his eyes, rubbing his eyes, squinting, displaying sensitivity to bright lights, and rolling his eyes.

3. Inattention to visual objects or visual tasks such as looking at pictures or reading.
4. Awkwardness in games requiring eye-hand coordination.
5. Avoidance of tasks that require close eye work.
6. Affinity to tasks that require distance vision.
7. Any complaints about inability to see.
8. Lack of normal curiosity in regard to visually appealing objects. (Kirk, 1972, p. 295.)

If screening tests or observations suggest a defect, referral to an oculist or ophthalmologist is indicated. These professionals are responsible for identifying visual defects, ascertaining the degree and kind of visual handicap present, and treating the condition. Treatment may include the use of optic aids, muscle exercises for the eye, or surgery. If necessary, these specialists will indicate to the educational agency that the child needs a special education program.

Some Characteristics of the Visually Handicapped

In a discussion of the characteristics of the visually handicapped, the first point to be stressed is that the only major characteristic that the visually handicapped have in common is the absence of normal sight. Furthermore, as has been discussed earlier, there is great variation in the useful vision of those considered visually handicapped. Thus, the abilities, interests, and needs of the visually handicapped vary, and each person must be considered individually. Since the following discussion deals with the visually handicapped as a group, one must be careful not to assume that such characteristics appear in every case.

Movement mannerisms known as *blindisms* are among the characteristics that may be exhibited by blind persons. Movement forms may include rocking back and forth, waving the hands in front of the face, twitching, thrusting the fingers into the eyes, nose, or mouth, manipulating ears, nose, lips or locks of hair, turning the head back and forth or bending it forward and backward, and jerking the limbs. Since these mannerisms are peculiar to blind people, their expression tends to draw attention to their blindness, thus hindering social acceptability. Many authorities recommend that blindisms be reduced or eliminated so that blind people are less likely to be set apart from their normally sighted peers. Others, however, feel that undue attention to the inhibition of such mannerisms may be counterproductive, since the repression of one type of movement pattern or physical response may lead to the substitution of another. In dealing with such mannerisms, it is important to determine their causes. Attention should be focused on eliminating the cause as well as the symptom. Unfortunately, the exact cause of mannerisms may not be known in a particular instance. Many authors speculate that blindisms are a symptom of the lack of physical activity. Fait (1972) holds that blindisms are physical movements through which the blind seek to fulfill the need for muscular movement without moving about through space. It has been frequently suggested that blindisms result from the lack of external stimulation and that the blind, thus, turn toward their own bodies for stimulation. This lack of stimulation may be visual or physical. Hanninen (1975) suggests that mannerisms that include such activities as putting the fingers in the eyes and holding the head forward may have their origin in ocular irritation. Children develop the habit of putting the hands to the eyes when the eyes hurt, and the behavior persists even after the irritation has ceased.

Cratty (1971b) has observed that the rocking movements of an individual child seem consistent for that child. He has presented a wide range of possibilities for various blindisms. He states that a child exhibits blindisms while engaged in a task as well as while unoccupied. He reports that some clinicians have had reasonable success in the modification of blindisms through helping the child gain an understanding of appropriate movements, using behavior modification, and supplying the opportunity for activity in a rich sensory environment. For a child whose blindisms result from lack of physical stimulation, the obvious implication is to increase involvement of the child in physical activity. In such cases, the urge for movement is satisfied in a more acceptable movement pattern.

Because of their visual impairment, the visually handicapped strive to develop their other senses to the highest possible degree. Unfortunately, the notion that the blind have a "sixth sense" that enables them to compensate for their lack of sight is scientifically unsupported. The lack of vision limits the blind individual to the senses of hearing, touch, taste, and smell. The blind individual is dependent on these senses and acutely attends to the input provided by each. For example, while the normally sighted person may attend little to auditory stimuli available in the environment, the blind individual attends maximally to such stimuli in order that orientation in space may be maintained. However, differences between blind and sighted persons in attention to, interpretation of, and use of auditory stimuli do not mean that blind persons have better hearing. If differences exist, they result from the better use that the blind make of their hearing abilities.

A second important point relevant to a discussion of the characteristics of the visually handicapped is that functioning is affected by the age of onset and the suddenness of blindness. Blindness at birth is generally more handicapping than blindness occurring later in life. Establishing visual concepts is impossible or more difficult when afflictions occur at birth or early in life. On the basis of his review of research, Lowenfeld (1973) indicated that children who have lost their sight before ages 5 to 7 do not retain a useful visual imagery and are unlikely to know color ideas. Since they have not experienced sight, those afflicted at birth may adjust to blindness with fewer psychological problems than those afflicted later in life. Sudden loss of sight requires attention to psychological adjustment. As Lowenfeld (1973) points out, the sudden onset of blindness may result in shock and possible withdrawal with adverse psychological effects that lessen in time. Gradual onset may disturb a child profoundly for a longer time period since his future seems uncertain. Regardless of the age of onset or the suddenness of the affliction, it is clear that the reactions of those afflicted vary, and care must be taken to relate to the visually handicapped on an individual basis.

Over the years, considerable research has been conducted to examine the intelligence, educational achievement, and emotional stability of the visually handicapped. Very often, such research has been conducted without sufficient attention to the causes of blindness, the setting in which children are educated, and the quality of programs to which they are exposed. In addition, instruments that have been standardized on the basis of the results of the normally sighted have been indiscriminately applied to the visually handicapped. On reviewing this research, Kirk (1972) found that the "intelligence and educational achievement of visually handicapped children do not deviate substantially from that of the seeing child." He indicates that the distribution of scores in intellectual tasks of the visually handicapped approximates that of the normally sighted when tests like auditory-vocal or haptic-motor channels of communication are used. Kirk recognizes that, as is true of some members of any group, some blind children have emotional problems. However, he holds that "broad generalizations about the personality of blind children or their social adjustment are not warranted." He has also found negative attitudes regarding the blind but suggests that the social acceptability of blindness is enhanced when the normally sighted are provided opportunities for association with the visually handicapped.

Auditory Handicaps

Definition and Classification

Since it so significantly affects communication and the social and educational development of the individual, deafness is among the most severe of handicapping conditions. Over the years, many terms and definitions have been used in connection with auditory handicaps, causing considerable confusion in understanding these conditions.

In order to clarify terminology related to auditory handicaps, the Committee on Nomenclature of the Conference of Executives of American Schools for the Deaf (1938) developed some commonly used classifications and definitions. The Committee defines *deaf* persons as those in whom the sense of hearing is nonfunctional for the ordinary purposes of life. This group is made up of two classes, and the division is based on the time the loss of hearing occurred. The *congenitally deaf* have been born deaf. The *adventitiously deaf* are persons who were born with normal hearing but whose sense of hearing has become nonfunctional later through illness or accident. The committee defines the *hard of hearing* as those people in whom the sense of hearing, although defective, is functional with or without a hearing aid. In addition to the clarity it provides, the preceding description explicitly recognizes (1) that *auditory handicapped* describes those with total functional hearing loss (the deaf) as well as those with functional but subnormal hearing (hard of hearing), and (2) that the auditory handicapped may be born with their hearing defect or may acquire it. Both the amount of functional hearing and the time of onset of hearing loss are important in the education of the individual.

The amount of hearing loss, measured in decibels (dB), has also been used as a basis for classifying the hard of hearing. In this system, the hearing ability of each individual is measured by an audiometer and is compared with agreed standards. A decibel value of 0 (zero) is established as the basic reference of sound intensity. A decibel loss of 50, for example, means that the person can hear sounds at 50 decibels that the normally hearing person can detect at 0 decibels. Hearing loss is commonly classified as slight when decibel (dB) loss is 27 to 40 dB, mild when loss is 41 to 55 dB, marked when loss is 56 to 70 dB, severe when loss is 71 to 90 dB, and extreme when loss is 91 dB or greater.

Incidence

Since definitions, methods of testing, and a variety of other factors influencing estimates of impaired hearing have differed over the years, the task of determining incidence has not been an easy one. In terms of overall incidence, most reliable estimates are in relatively close agreement that about 5 per cent of school-aged children have some type of hearing impairment. Based on his review of studies dealing with incidence, Berg and Fletcher (1970) estimated that as many as 150,000 hard-of-hearing children in the United States are potentially in need of considerable language, communication, academic, and counseling assistance and that another 950,000 hard-of-hearing children typically require less extensive assistance. They also present data to support the generally accepted notion that incidence decreases as severity of auditory impairment increases. In regard to comparison of sexes, Myklebust (1964) reports that 8 per cent more male than female children were enrolled in schools and classes for the deaf between 1850 and 1964.

There is some evidence indicating that the incidence of hearing impairments is increasing. The causes of such an increase are believed to be lengthened life span (leading to the development of hearing impairment with increased age), improved medical knowledge that has saved the lives of handicapped infants who would have died in previous years, and noise pollution. The latter cause includes listening to loud rock music and exposure to noise associated with certain industrial and military work.

Types of Defects

Although hearing defects may occur in a variety of forms, the two major types of defects are the *conductive* and the *sensorineural*, or *perceptive*, types.* A *conductive* hearing loss is one in which vibrations of sounds are prevented from fully and appropriately reaching the auditory nerve in the inner ear because of some dysfunction in the outer or middle ear. Most acquired hearing disabilities are of the conductive type. In a normal ear, sound waves pass from the external

---

*Other types that have been identified include *psychogenic* or *functional* deafness, *central* deafness, and *mixed* deafness.

canal of the outer ear to the eardrum (tympanic membrane), where vibrations are picked up by a series of bonelike structures in the middle ear and passed on to the inner ear. Conductive hearing loss occurs when sound vibrations are blocked or are affected at any point in this pathway. Inflammation, wax accumulation, or malformations may cause blockage in the external ear. Rupture or distention due to infection may affect vibration by the eardrum. Infections and inflammations may obstruct bone movement in the middle ear and prevent normal transmission of sound waves. In all conductive hearing losses, the intensity of sound reaching the inner ear is reduced. Thus, the main problem associated with this type is amplification (loudness) of sound. Kirk (1972) indicates that this type of defect seldom causes complete hearing loss, since some bone conduction is usually present.

The *sensorineural* or *perceptive* type of hearing loss is much more serious. Hearing losses of this type may be partial or total, and hearing aids generally have not adequately compensated for them. As the name implies, this type of defect is caused by damage to the cells or nerve fibers that normally function to transmit auditory impulses to the brain. Sensorineural defects are known to affect hearing at some frequencies more than at others. In fact, profound hearing loss at high frequencies is an indicator of sensorineural deafness. Discrimination of sounds is a greater problem than amplification in cases of sensorineural hearing losses. Audiograms of individuals with sensorineural hearing losses show bone conduction losses particularly at high frequencies. The most common sensorineural hearing loss is *presbycusis* (progressive hearing loss associated with the natural aging process).

Causes of Deafness

Throughout the years, many causes of deafness have been identified, and they have been classified in a number of ways. One of the more common methods classifies deafness according to the time at which damage to the hearing mechanism actually takes place and includes damage occurring before birth (*prenatal*), damage occurring at or near birth (*perinatal*), and damage occurring after birth (*postnatal*). Prenatal causes may be hereditary or nonhereditary. They include maternal infections or toxic conditions that affect the child, such as rubella, influenza, mumps, and glandular fever; maternal nutritional deficiencies such as beriberi or diabetes; drugs and chemicals such as streptomycin, salicylates, quinine, and thalidomide; certain diseases affecting the auditory mechanism in utero; and deformity, absence, or arrested development of parts of the ear or auditory mechanism.

Damage occurring during the perinatal period may be caused by prematurity; by damage to the nervous system resulting from trauma during delivery; by lack of oxygen due to prolonged labor, heavy sedation, and infant respiratory difficulties; and by blood incompatibility.

Postnatal damage to the hearing mechanism may be caused by diseases such as scarlet fever, mumps, measles, meningitis, diphtheria, whooping cough, typhoid fever, pneumonia, and influenza. With the possible exception of meningitis, the frequency with which these infectious diseases cause deafness has decreased because of medical advances in their prevention and control.

A very important postnatal condition that may result in hearing loss is *otitis media*, an infection or inflammation of the middle ear. It may be caused by many diseases but is most commonly associated with upper respiratory diseases and infection of tonsils, adenoids, and sinuses. If not cured or controlled, otitis media may become chronic (chronic otitis media). Chronic inflammation may cause adhesions to form between the tympanic membrane and the bony structures in the middle ear, destroying these structures and preventing normal sound wave transmission. Although rare, it is possible for infection to spread to the mastoid process of the temporal bone, resulting in mastoiditis. Such a spread may call for a mastoidectomy and may result in hearing loss. Further, spreading may affect meninges of the brain, causing meningitis.

A cause of deafness that is believed to be hereditary in origin but that appears in later life is *otosclerosis*. Otosclerosis is a bony disease in which the normal hard mature capsule bone of the ear is replaced with soft spongy immature bone. As the disease progresses, it encroaches upon the stapedial foot plate. Fixation of the stapes reduces the transmission of sound and causes progressive deafness.

Most authorities agree that the natural process of aging is the most common cause of deafness. Progressive deterioration of hearing owing to old age is known as *presbycusis* and is often accompanied by a deterioration in balance. Presbycusis is associated with sensorineural hearing loss and diminished sensitivity for sounds at higher frequencies.

Other postnatal causes of loss of hearing include concussion, prolonged exposure to high frequency sounds, and auditory nerve damage caused by intracranial tumors, cerebral hemorrhage, and drug toxins. Finally, it is possible for hearing loss to have psychological or emotional causes. Auditory defects due to psychological or emotional causes are known as *psychogenic* types. Some authorities identify psychogenic deafness as a third type of deafness.

Assessment

The determination of hearing ability is vitally important and should be made as early as possible. Thorough evaluation provides helpful information relative to the cause and treatment of defects and also provides information upon which educational implications may be based. Although severe or total deafness is relatively easy to ascertain, the determination of hearing loss in less severe cases is much more complicated. Audiometry as well as informal methods have been employed to obtain crude measures of hearing ability. Informal methods are generally used for detection or screening purposes. Audiometry is designed to determine exact hearing ability and requires professional competence for testing and interpretation.

The watch tick test, the conversational test, and the whisper test are among the informal tests used to assess hearing loss. In the watch tick test, the examiner observes the distance at which children are able to acknowledge the sound of a ticking watch. In the conversational test, the examiner simply speaks at a conversational tone to a child placed 20 feet away. As necessary, the child moves toward the examiner until speech is heard. With the exception that whispers rather than spoken words are used, the whisper and conversational tests are administered in the same way. Techniques in which children are asked to identify and locate a variety of sounds, including speech sounds, have also been employed in informal assessment. These techniques are particularly relevant for use with infants and preschool youngsters.

Although there are a variety of audiometers, the most accurate instrument is a pure-tone audiometer. A pure-tone audiometer is used to present sounds of known intensity and frequency to subjects. *Intensity* is the amplitude, or loudness, of sound and *frequency* is pitch (the number of vibrations or cycles per second of a given sound wave). As mentioned previously, the unit of measurement to express the intensity of sound is a *decibel* (dB). Frequency is expressed in hertz (Hz). In audiometry, subjects are asked to respond when tones are heard, and their responses are compared with normal hearing, i.e., a 0 (zero) level decibel loss. The degree of hearing loss is plotted on an audiogram for each ear for both air and bone conduction receivers.

The assessment of hearing generally begins with screening. Children are generally screened by a school nurse, audiologist, or hearing specialist. Screening may be accomplished by administering one of several informal tests, very commonly the sweep-check audiometric test. In this test, subjects are asked to respond to a given intensity of sound at six different pitches. If the subject fails to hear a predetermined number of tones, referral is made for further formal testing under a qualified examiner.

Hearing loss may often be noticed prior to testing by observing common behaviors exhibited by hard-of-hearing youngsters. Since their behavior may affect learning, it is important that educators be aware of this. Gearheart and Weishahn (1976) list the following behaviors and medical symptoms that may indicate hearing loss: lack of attention; turning or cocking of the head; difficulty in following directions; acting out, stubborn, shy, or withdrawn; reluctance to participate in oral activities; dependence on classmate for instructions; achievement best in small groups; disparity between expected and actual achievement; frequent earaches; fluid running from the ears; frequent colds and sore throats; and recurring tonsillitis.

Characteristics

The one common characteristic of the auditory handicapped is, of course, total or partial loss of hearing. However, it is the lack of the ability to communicate rather than loss of hearing per se that causes social, psychological, and educational difficulties for the deaf. When the ability to communicate is reduced, social interaction diminishes, and the deaf become frustrated in their attempts at communication. The tendency is to withdraw and to become introverted. In essence, they live in a "dead" world in which they tend to be more introverted and less dominant than their hearing peers. In view of such characteristics, it is not surprising that a great deal of attention must be placed upon the social development of the deaf. They need to be provided with social contacts and to gain social acceptance. In view of their tendency to withdraw, a great deal of encouragement must be provided by parents, teachers, peers, and other professionals.

There is little question that the lack of language and communication abilities inhibits the education of the deaf and that the development of these abilities must be a major concern. There are three approaches for the development of communication skills: *oralism, manualism,* and the *combined approach.* There is still considerable controversy regarding the preferred approach. In the *oral* method, communication is developed through speech and speechreading. The oral method, sometimes referred to as the *oral-aural* approach, emphasizes the use of residual hearing and discourages the use of signs or finger spelling. The *manual* method employs movements of the hands and arms as signals and finger spelling for purposes of communication. Two forms of the *combined* approach are the *simultaneous* approach, in which signs, finger spelling, and the oral method are combined, and the *Rochester method,* in which the oral approach is combined with finger spelling. Since communication with normal hearing individuals is accommodated by it, the oral method is preferred and thus is recommended for those able to use it. However, the oral method is rather difficult to learn and requires many years of training for the attainment of proficiency. Not all individuals, especially the very young, are able to master the oral method and therefore they must rely on the manual method or must attempt to combine methods for communication. The method selected and utilized will vary according to the philosophy of the individuals who come in contact with the deaf and according to the needs and abilities of the deaf individual.

Since they possess residual hearing, educational provisions for the hard of hearing are different from those for the deaf. In educational programs for the hard of hearing, emphasis is placed on speech reading (lip reading), auditory training (sound discrimination), speech training, and appropriate use of hearing aids. Kirk (1972) compares the educational implications of auditory handicaps as a function of severity:

> Because hard-of-hearing children have the ability to acquire speech and language through hearing, the problem in teaching them is mainly one of making it possible for them to learn through the methods and techniques used with hearing children. With hearing aids, some individual help in speech, speechreading, auditory training, and a few special arrangements, most of these children can acquire an education in classes with hearing children.
> The deaf child faces quite a different problem. Because he never hears speech, he does not normally acquire language or the subtleties of meaning which are more readily acquired through the sense of hearing. The important factor to remember in educating deaf children is that their major deficiency is not so much lack of hearing as inability to develop speech and language through the sense of hearing. Their education, therefore, is probably the most technical area in the whole field of special education. (Kirk, 1972, p. 257.)

8

MENTAL RETARDATION, SPECIFIC LEARNING DISABILITIES, AND EMOTIONAL-BEHAVIORAL DISABILITIES

The three groups of children to be discussed in this chapter are the mentally retarded, the specific learning-disabled, and the emotionally-behaviorally disturbed. They have handicapping conditions that strongly influence their educational development and that are often considered educational handicaps. These disabilities are discussed together in one chapter to emphasize their interrelationship. In some cases, it is impossible to separate these handicapping conditions for either medical or educational purposes. In other cases, differences are easily discernible.

Mental Retardation

Mental retardation is one of the most prevalent handicapping conditions. It has received a great deal of attention in the past decade in relation to physical education and recreation. Although many forces have created this attention, a major reason is the recognition that the mentally retarded enjoy and may be successful in movement experiences. Successful experiences are of extreme importance since they are directly and indirectly associated with effects that influence total growth and development.

Although many definitions of mental retardation have been presented in the past, one that is widely used in educational circles was developed by the American Association on Mental Deficiency (1973). According to this group, "mental retardation refers to significantly subaverage general intellectual functioning existing concurrently with deficits in adaptive behavior, and manifested during the developmental period." It is clear that this definition emphasizes the function of the individual rather than medical or other causes of mental retardation.

In the AAMD definition, "significantly subaverage general intellectual functioning" is performance two or more standard deviations below the mean on a standardized intelligence test. For example, if the mean score on the Wechsler Intelligence Scale for Children (WISC) is 100 and the standard deviation is 15, then all individuals scoring below 69 would meet the criterion of significantly subaverage intellectual functioning for mental retardation. A score of 80, although subaverage, is not "significantly" subaverage and would not meet the criterion for mental retardation. It should be recognized that the "subaverage" concept associated with this definition makes the definition a relative as well as statistical concept. This means that retardation is defined in terms of the performance of an entire population. In addition, according to this definition, 2½ per cent of the population will always meet the theoretical criterion for mental retardation, since 2½ per cent of the population scores two standard deviations below the mean. Interestingly, this would be true regardless of the medical progress toward "curing" mental retardation. When retardation is regarded as a relative concept, the concept of a cure becomes ambiguous. Medical advances could serve to raise the mean score on a test but would not change the percentage of individuals labeled *retarded*.

In considering intellectual functioning, the concept of intelligence quotient (IQ) should be understood. IQ is determined by the formula $IQ = MA/CA \times 100$, where MA is mental age and CA is chronological age. For example, if the mental age of the child is 3 years and the chronological age is 6 years, then the IQ is 50. This means that the child performs tasks expected of a 3-year-old but is unable to perform tasks normally expected of older children. In determining IQ, standard psychometric intellectual tests are administered. Intelligence then, is essentially defined as a score on a test. Brain functioning per se is not determined. In essence, the performance of a child at a given age is compared to the performance of other children. Such performance may be affected by the prior experiences of the individual as well as by the organic functioning of the brain.

A second important element in the AAMD definition that should be noted is the association of the developmental period with mental retardation. In essence, mental retardation is the term applied to retarded functioning manifested in the first 18 years of life.

The fact that attention is given to adaptive behavior in the AAMD definition is important. Significantly subaverage general intellectual functioning is a necessary but not a sufficient criterion for determining mental retardation. A child must demonstrate a deficit in general intellectual functioning and adaptive behavior in order to be identified as mentally retarded. The term *adaptive behavior* refers to the degree of effectiveness with which the individual meets age and cultural group standards of personal independence and social responsibility. Maturation, learning, and social adjustment are considered in determining the level of adaptive behavior, since they are reflections of it. Assessment of the maturation of a child at an early age includes judgment of communication and sensory-motor abilities as well as self-help skills such as crawling, creeping, sitting, standing, walking, and bowel and bladder control. The facility with which children learn the basic academic achievment skills is considered in assessing learning. The abilities of the child to interact with others and participate in group activities are among factors that influence the assessment of social adjustment throughout the developmental period.

There are some other important issues relevant to the definition of mental retardation. First, mental retardation is not synonymous with brain damage. An individual may be brain-damaged but may or may not be retarded. An individual may be retarded but may or may not be brain-damaged. Second, the present concept of mental retardation is a dynamic one. This means that intellectual functioning may vary. It may be changed by experience. It is not something that is stamped on the individual and remains static.

Over the years, the mentally retarded have been classified according to behavioral characteristics, etiology, learning ability, and social adjustment. Systems of classification vary according to their purpose. With the exception of classification according to cause, levels of this system are usually associated with intelligence scores. These scores, however, vary to some extent with different intelligence tests. Since educational capabilities have been developed in association with them, two classifications are most widely used in educational circles: the AAMD and educational systems. These two systems are presented in Table 8–1.

Although systems of classification enhance communication and perhaps serve other useful purposes, they sometimes help to create problems. It must be recognized that classifications are labels that sometimes trigger strong emotional reactions. For example, in the

Table 8–1. Classification of the Mentally Retarded.

Classification	Descriptors	Intelligence Quotient
Educational	Slow learners	70 to 90 or 75 to 90
	Educable mentally retarded (EMR)	50 to 69 or 50 to 74
	Trainable mentally retarded (TMR)	25 to 49
	Totally dependent or custodial	00 to 24
AAMD	Mild	52 to 68 Stanford-Binet (Cattell)
		55 to 69 Wechsler Scales
	Moderate	36 to 51 Stanford-Binet (Cattell)
		40 to 54 Wechsler Scales
	Severe	20 to 35 Stanford-Binet (Cattell)
		25 to 39 Wechsler Scales
	Profound	00 to 19 Stanford-Binet (Cattell)
		00 to 24 Wechsler Scales

Table 8–2. Estimates of Retardation by Age and Degree—1970.

1970 Census	All Ages	Under 21 Years	21 Years and above
General Population	203.2 million	80.5 million	122.7 million
Retarded Population			
(3% general population)	6.1 million	2.4 million	3.7 million
Profound (IQ 0–20)	92 thousand	36 thousand	56 thousand
(about 1½%)			
Severe (IQ 20–35)	214 thousand	84 thousand	130 thousand
(about 3½%)			
Moderate (IQ 36–51)	366 thousand	144 thousand	222 thousand
(about 6%)			
Mild (IQ 52–67)	5.4 million+	2.1 million+	3.3 million+
(about 89%)			

National Association for Retarded Citizens. *Facts on Mental Retardation,* Arlington, Texas: National Association for Retarded Citizens, 1973, p. 6.

past, the retarded were classified as *imbeciles, idiots,* and *morons.* It is obvious that such terms would be unacceptable today because of their emotional overtones. It is possible that the terms used at present will carry similar overtones in the future. Another problem in using these terms is the tendency to associate absolute maturational, learning, and social characteristics with them. When this happens, preconceived notions about abilities and disabilities of individuals are formed. When an individual is described in terms of disabilities, a negative self-fulfilling prophecy is enhanced that retards development.

Several investigations have been conducted to determine the prevalence of mental retardation in the United States. They have helped in estimations of the total number of individuals considered retarded, the number at each level of retardation, and the relationships between socioeconomic status and incidence of mental retardation. Total estimates of retardation have been based on both theoretical and empirical prevalence estimates. The percentage of persons with scores under two standard deviations below the mean on a normal distribution curve is 2.14 per cent. By multiplying this percentage (2.14) by the total population (220 million), the total number (4.7 million) of retarded can be determined. Studies of prevalence generally estimate an incidence rate of between 2 and 3 per cent. Thus, the theoretical and empirical prevalence estimates are in general agreement.

The prevalence decreases with more severe forms of retardation. On the basis of the 1970 census, the President's Committee on Mental Retardation (1970) issued estimates of the number of mentally retarded in this country (Table 8–2).

Table 8–3. Estimated number of children with low IQs per 1000 school-age children.

Level of Community	Totally Dependent	Trainable	Educable
Low	1	4	50
Middle	1	4	25
High	1	4	10

Kirk, Samuel A., *Educating Exceptional Children,* Boston: Houghton Mifflin Co., 1972, p. 186.

Studies dealing with the relationship between socioeconomic status and the prevalence of mental retardation have yielded interesting results. They agree that the incidence of retardation at the educable and slow learner levels increases as socioeconomic level decreases. However, the incidence at the trainable and custodial level is unrelated to socioeonomic level. Based on his review of the literature, Kirk (1972) summarizes the relationship of socioeconomic status and incidence of retardation at various levels (Table 8–3).

Conditions Commonly Associated with Mental Retardation

Of a large number of diseases and clinical conditions associated with mental retardation, phenylketonuria (PKU), microcephaly, hydrocephaly, and Down's syndrome are among the most prevalent, most obvious, and best known.

PHENYLKETONURIA (PKU)

Phenylketonuria (PKU) is a well-known inherited disease, transmitted as a recessive trait, that affects proper growth of the brain because of the presence of phenylpyruvic acid. It is a metabolic disorder in which a deficiency of phenylalanine hydroxylase (an enzyme) inhibits proper metabolism of phenylalanine (an amino acid In protein foods). As a result, abnormal amounts of phenylpyruvic acid accumulate. Although the disease is genetic in origin and present in the prenatal period, it does not manifest its toxicity until the postnatal period.

At the present time, most states have programs for the detection and treatment of the condition. Detection involves the taking of a blood test soon after birth. The condition may also be signified by high levels of phenylpyruvic acid in the urine. Early detection is critical, since normal development may be attained if proper treatment is given early. If treatment is delayed just a few weeks beyond birth, intellectual impairment may be irreversible. A diet that involves controlling phenylalanine intake while meeting all nutritional needs of the child is the treatment for PKU. The diet administered must provide some phenylalanine, since it is necessary to normal intellectual and physical development.

Johnson and Magrab (1976) indicate that children with PKU are typically blond and blue-eyed, that a number have increased muscle tone and hyperactive reflexes, and that about 70 per cent of PKU victims are also microcephalic. Irritability, restlessness, slow development of motor skills, difficulties in communication, and convulsions are also associated with PKU.

MICROCEPHALY

A high correlation exists between mental retardation and the clinical condition *microcephaly*. As the name implies, *microcephaly* is a "small skull." Generally, a small skull is one that measures less than 17 inches in circumference or as one whose circumference is

Figure 8–1. A microcephalic youngster.

two standard deviations below the normal mean. The head of the microcephalic is sometimes described as "cone-shaped." Retardation may be caused by a small, deformed, or partially missing brain.

There are two forms of microcephaly. The primary form is an inherited condition associated with autosomal recessive characteristics. This is sometimes called "true" microcephaly. The secondary form is caused by extrinsic factors such as metabolic disturbances, congenital infections, chromosomal abnormalities, and irradiation.

The characteristics displayed by the microcephalic vary with the form and severity of the condition. Common characteristics include an alert vivacious temperament, a sense of well-being (*euphoria*), the ability to imitate actions of others (*echopraxia*), and mimicry of sounds (*echolalia*). Although the level of retardation is related to the severity of the condition, most microcephalics function at trainable levels.

HYDROCEPHALY

Hydrocephalus (water-on-the-brain), or hydrocephaly, is a condition characterized by the accumulation of excessive amounts of cerebrospinal fluid within the skull and generally (but not always) by a large head. External hydrocephaly is associated with excessive cerebrospinal fluid and an abnormally large head, and internal hydrocephaly occurs with excessive cerebrospinal fluid and normal head

Figure 8–2.   Hydrocephalic boy enjoys swimming.

size. Cerebrospinal fluid accumulates to excess when it is not absorbed as rapidly as necessary or when it is restricted by obstructed passageways. Obstruction may be caused by tumors, meningeal inflammation, infections, and injuries. The build-up of cerebrospinal fluid increases brain size, but brain tissue is "thinned" and destroyed, causing damage and subsequent retardation. The degree of retardation depends on the severity of brain damage.

Several characteristics are associated with hydrocephaly. In infants, the head may be so heavy that the neck is unable to support it, and lifting the head is prohibited. Defective hearing and vision, delayed walking, and convulsions are also associated with the condition. Walking and other balance activities are affected by the upward shift of the center of gravity. Strabismus of one or both eyes and paralysis of the legs are commonly associated with hydrocephaly.

Hydrocephalus is treated through surgical intervention. Obstructions may, at times, be removed through surgery. More commonly, blocked ventricles are drained. Shunts consisting of plastic tubes leading from the ventricle to the heart or abdomen have been devised as a more permanent drainage system.

DOWN'S SYNDROME

Down's syndrome affects approximately 5 per cent of the retarded population. It is named for Dr. Langdon Down, who first described the condition in 1866. Although it is not a term used in professional circles today, children with Down's syndrome have been referred to as *mongoloid* in the past, since a chief characteristic of the condition is almond-shaped slanting eyes. There is a close resemblance in the facial features and overall body structure among those with Down's syndrome.

Figure 8–3. Typical features of the Down's syndrome child.

The cause of Down's syndrome is a chromosomal abnormality. Of the different possible chromosomal anomalies causing Down's Syndrome, trisomy 21 occurs in about 95 per cent of cases. The normal individual has 23 pairs of chromosomes, a total of 46. In Down's syndrome, owing to trisomy, all cells contain 47 rather than 46 chromosomes, because pair number 21 has a third member. A second type of chromosomal abnormality that causes 3 per cent of the cases of Down's syndrome is translocation. In this disorder, the child has 46 chromosomes but a part of one is broken and is attached to another chromosome.

The cause of chromosomal aberrations is unknown. However, the probability of occurrence increases when parents themselves carry chromosomal defects, when parents' chromosomes are exposed to irradiation or to some chemicals, and as the age of the mother increases. An incidence rate of 1 in 600 or 700 births for women between 25 and 30 years progressively increases to about 1 in 50 for women up to age 45.

Although no cure for Down's syndrome exists, genetic counseling and prenatal screening may considerably reduce its occurrence. The presence of chromosomal abnormality may be demonstrated by analyzing the free-floating fetal cells in the amniotic fluid of a pregnant woman. The removal of such fluid for study is called *amniocentesis*. It is possible for pregnancy to be terminated if chromosomal abnormality is detected.

Chromosomal abnormalities significantly affect the total growth and development of the individual. Intellectual functioning is generally at the moderately retarded level (40–55 IQ). Socially, Down's children are generally quite mature. They are usually affectionate, relaxed, friendly, cheerful, cooperative, and concerned for others.

Table 8–4. Characteristics of the Child with Down's Syndrome.

Characteristic	Implications for Movement Experiences
Lag in physical growth. (Growth ceases at an earlier than normal age and generally results in shorter height and smaller overall stature.) Lag is evident in motor development.	The child may need to participate in activities geared for younger age groups.
The circulatory system is less well developed. Arteries are often narrow and thinner than normal, and less vascular proliferation is evidenced. Many children (especially boys) exhibit congenital heart disorders, heart murmurs and septum defects being the most common.	Although there is a need for the development of endurance, youngsters will have difficulty in endurance activities. It is necessary for all children to have a medical examination and for the instructor to develop a program with medical consultation.
Poor respiration and susceptibility to respiratory infections. (Underdeveloped jaw causes mouth to be too small for normal-sized tongue, inducing mouth breathing.)	Poor respiration may impede participation in endurance activities.
Perceptual handicaps	Children may be clumsy and awkward. Activities to develop perceptual abilities should be emphasized.
Poor balance.	Since balance is important in most physical and motor activities, lack of balance will affect performance ability. Children need balance training.
Enjoyment of music and rhythmic activities.	The instructor should include rhythmic activities in the program to provide successful and enjoyable experiences and should use music as an aid in teaching.
Obesity.	General overall participation in activity as well as activities that enhance weight reduction are recommended.
Flabbiness. (Hypotonicity, particularly associated with newborn infants, develops with age.)	The instructor should provide opportunity for movement experiences at early ages and activities to increase strength at later ages.
Protruding abdomen, lack of muscle and ligament support around the joints, and pronated ankles.	Activities to enhance body alignment and to increase muscle and ligament support around the joints and abdominal exercises are recommended.
Ability to mimic.	Instructor should demonstrate activities and ask children to imitate them.

However, stubbornness and compulsiveness may be exhibited, in certain instances, to a greater extent than in normal children. Visual and hearing deficits are commonly associated with Down's syndrome, and speech is often poor, thick, and not clearly articulated. In addition to the characteristics already presented, there are several characteristics that have greater implication for the conduct of movement experiences. These characteristics and some general implications are presented in Table 8–4. Additional data related to these characteristics will be presented in subsequent sections.

Figure 8–4. Down's syndrome children enjoy catching balloons.

Causes of Mental Retardation

Over the years, literally hundreds of causes of mental retardation have been identified. These have been classified in a number of ways by many different writers. It is not possible to cover all the causes in detail here; in fact, not all causes of retardation will be discussed in this chapter. Those mentioned, however, are most important, most common, or best known. Although the causes are organized into three major groups, it will be apparent that the groups are not mutually exclusive.

DISEASES AND CONDITIONS
RUBELLA (GERMAN MEASLES)

One of the more common diseases that may cause mental retardation is rubella or German measles. The rubella virus infects the mother and, in about 50 per cent of cases, invades the fetus by passing through the mother's bloodstream to the placenta. Such invasion of the fetus is most serious if it occurs during the first trimester of pregnancy, since it is during this period that structural development of major organ systems occurs. The central nervous and cardiovascular systems are most likely to be affected. Effects may include microcephaly, general retardation in physical growth, heart defects, eye cataracts, glaucoma, and hearing loss. Although less severe, secondary effects may occur if the mother contracts the virus after the first trimester of pregnancy. Since the rubella virus has been isolated and a vaccine has been developed, it is now possible to eliminate the disease.

TOXINS

Poisoning by lead, carbon monoxide, and other toxins may lead to encephalopathy (brain inflammation). Encephalopathy may cause brain hemorrhage, accumulation of fluid, swelling or shrinking of the brain, and atrophy of certain parts of the brain. Lead poisoning may result from the ingestion of paint or from chewing objects that contain lead. Destruction of brain cells and degeneration of capillaries of the brain may result. Since interior paints are now usually lead-free, the incidence of the lead poisoning may be expected to decline. However, many exterior paints still contain lead. In addition to direct poisoning, ingestion of toxic agents by the mother during pregnancy may also result in brain damage for the child.

BLOOD INCOMPATIBILITY

Although there are a variety of blood incompatibilities that may lead to mental deficiencies, the most common is *Rh incompatibility.* This condition exists when the mother is Rh negative and the child is Rh positive and the Rh positive substance is introduced to the mother's bloodstream. The mother's bloodstream develops antibodies against the Rh positive substance that destory the red blood cells of the fetus (erythroblastosis fetalis). To compensate, additional red blood cells are developed by the fetus. However, because a large number are required, the cells developed are immature and carry no nuclei. Such cells are unable to carry oxygen adequately. They release hemoglobin, which changes to a chemical substance known as bilirubin as it is destroyed. Lack of oxygen and the failure of the liver to rid the body of bilirubin, allowing the substance to diffuse to the central nervous system, cause brain damage. First children are usually not affected since the mother's antibodies are not sufficiently developed. Third and succeeding fetuses, however, may be affected and may be aborted. Fortunately, mental retardation due to Rh incompatibility can be virtually eliminated through preventive procedures and counseling.

RADIATION

Although x-ray treatment may be necessary in certain situations, exposure of the mother to massive doses of radiation during the first six weeks of pregnancy will, in many instances, be lethal to or cause gross abnormalities in the fetus. Massive exposure after six weeks but still early in pregnancy may produce certain defects in fetal body function. The condition most frequently associated with excessive radiation is microcephaly. The effects of irradiation were demonstrated following the dropping of the atomic bomb on Hiroshima. A mother pregnant less than 20 weeks who was within one-half mile of the explosion was likely to give birth to a physically or mentally abnormal child. Fortunately, the effects of irradiation can be diminished today with the use of protective shields during x-ray.

INFECTIOUS DISEASES

Mental deficit may occur during infancy and childhood as a result of infectious diseases. These diseases may be associated with high fever or toxins. Viruses that attack cells of the central nervous system and brain, cause brain hemorrhage, reduce normal oxygen supply to the brain, and impede growth of the brain also cause mental deficit. The most common diseases are measles, scarlet fever, chickenpox, whooping cough, meningitis, pneumonia, and encephalitis. Encephalitis may be caused by one of several viruses or may occur after an attack of another infectious disease.

BIRTH INJURIES

Mechanical trauma, lack of oxygen, and hemorrhage can cause mental retardation. They may result from birth conditions such as premature birth, caesarean birth, prolonged pregnancy, and dry birth, from maternal conditions such as seizure, pelvic malformation, and hemorrhage, and from fetal conditions such as breech birth and twisting of the umbilical cord. Improper use of forceps and improper administration of anesthetic may also cause brain damage.

GENETIC FACTORS

As knowledge of the etiology of mental retardation has increased, more and more genetic causes have been identified. Those genetic syndromes are more often associated with severe or profound retardation than with mild retardation. Mutant genes and recessive traits that are transmitted cause metabolic disorders, chromosome abnormalities, faulty endocrine secretions, and abnormalities in skull formation. Genetically transmitted diseases or conditions include Down's syndrome, phenylketonuria, cretinism, (faulty biochemical functioning), microcephaly, galactosemia, and a large number of other less prevalent syndromes.

PSYCHOLOGICAL-SOCIOLOGICAL ENVIRONMENTAL FACTORS

There is little doubt that an individual's basic abilities, including cognitive abilities, are greatly influenced by experiences. Such experiences constitute, to a great extent, the environmental influences on mental functioning. Just as a seed needs soil, water, and sunlight for optimum growth, the endowed abilities of the individual need a rich environment for optimal development. The many individuals and groups with which a person interacts are a part of the environment and affect development. Social, racial, ethnic, religious, and neighborhood groups influence and are important in the development of intellectual abilities. They influence work habits, economic status, motivation, child-rearing practices, education, growth and maturation, family size, love, and aspiration — all of which potentially affect development. Of vital importance to optimal intellectual development are the teacher and the school. These are also a part of the child's environment. It is, indeed, important and rewarding to realize that a proper educational environment can make a difference.

Over the years, the relative importance of environment and heredity has been debated. There has been a great deal of research relevant to this question. It is sufficient for our purposes to assume that both are important. Each child is born with a certain potential — a hereditary influence. The degree to which this potential is developed is a function of the environment. It is not possible to determine the exact potential of an individual. Even if it were possible, the "proper" environment for a particular potential is not known. Therefore, it is important to simply strive to produce the most enriched environment possible so that optimal development may occur.

Specific Learning Disabilities

It has been stated that learning disabilities are to the educator what the virus is to the physician; when a lack of learning cannot be explained in another way, the child is often said to have a learning disability. Since the "cure" is not fully established, all kinds of remedies are concocted. Of the various types of handicapping conditions, learning disability is among the newest and the most difficult to define and is one that has attracted the interest of various professional groups. The newness of the field, the interest of various professions in the field, the heterogeneity of the group of children who are unable to learn, and an increase in knowledge have all contributed to confusion and change in terminology over the years. *Minimal brain dysfunction*, *central processing dysfunction*, *perceptual handicap*, *dyslexia,* and *brain injury* are among the labels that have been associated with various learning problems.

Most writers agree that the modern impetus of the field may be traced to Alfred A. Strauss and Laura Lehtinen (1947). Strauss used the term *brain-injured* to describe children who display disturbances in perception, thinking, and emotional behavior that prevent or impede normal learning. It was not long, however, before professionals began to object to the term, since it was thought to be of little or no help in regard to the methods of treatment and teaching. It was a medical term that was negative in implication and that presented a threat to both parents and youngsters. It was so broad in meaning that it could include conditions such as cerebral palsy, epilepsy, and schizophrenia — conditions that do not necessarily give rise to the characteristics identified by Strauss. Thus, the term *Strauss syndrome* was substituted by Stevens and Birch (1957) to describe children unable to learn whose problems could not be classified with other handicapping conditions. Stevens and Birch (1957) recommended that *Strauss Syndrome* be used to describe children who exhibited several of the following characteristics:

1. Erratic and inappropriate behavior on mild provocation.
2. Increased motor activity disproportionate to the stimulus.
3. Poor organization of behavior.

4. Distractibility of more than ordinary degree under ordinary conditions.
5. Persistent faulty perception.
6. Persistent hyperactivity.
7. Awkwardness and consistently poor motor development

In view of the observation that children displaying the Strauss syndrome are but one segment of the total number of children with learning disabilities, efforts to develop and classify terms continued. To emphasize differences in impairment and to maintain the concept of near average or above average intellectual functioning and the association with central nervous system etiology, Clements (1966) and others preferred using the term *minimal brain dysfunction syndrome.*

> Minimal brain dysfunction as a diagnostic and descriptive category refers to children of near average, average, or above average intellectual capacity and potential with learning and/or certain behavioral abnormalities ranging from mild to severe, which are associated with subtle deviant functioning of the central nervous system. These may be characterized by various combinations of deficits in perception, conceptualization, language, memory, and control of attention, impulse, or motor function. (Clements, 1966.)

Another term related to learning deficit was presented by Johnson and Myklebust (1967). These authors selected *psychoneurological learning disabilities* to describe the problems of children who are deficient in learning but possess adequate motor ability, average and above average intelligence, and adequate hearing, vision, and emotional adjustment. Johnson and Myklebust use the term *psychoneurological* to imply a neurological etiology for behavioral-educational disorders.

Because of the difficulties in identifying central nervous dysfunction or brain damage, in linking such neurological conditions with learning problems, and in explaining learning disabilities associated with non-neurological conditions, further definitions were advanced. Bateman (1965), for example, defined the learning disabled as those who

> manifest an educationally significant discrepancy between their estimated intellectual potential and actual level of performance related to basic disorders in the learning process, which may or may not be accomplished by demonstrable central nervous system dysfunction, and which are not secondary to generalized mental retardation, educational or cultural deprivation, severe emotional disturbance, or sensory loss. (Bateman, 1965, p. 220.)

It is quite obvious that definitions such as that proposed by Bateman require a definition of *discrepancy.* Bryan and Bryan (1975) state that discrepancy is often defined as academic performance six months below grade level as determined by academic achievement tests for children in the early years and performance one and a half years below grade level at grade three and above. In this view of discrepancy, potential is based upon the assumption of intelligence within normal ranges, and performance is indicated by results on an achievement test.

Certain professionals have noted and emphasized irregular growth patterns *within* children (intraindividual differences) with specific learning disabilities. Their profiles reveal uneven growth in abilities related to education. Kirk (1972) found that various theorists recognized intraindividual differences or discrepancies in growth to be characteristic of children with learning disabilities. Kirk focuses on these developmental discrepancies in abilities in his conception of learning disabilities. These discrepancies are the basis for adding the term *specific* to the term *learning disabilities*. According to Kirk (1968a), then, "a learning disability refers to a specific retardation or disorder in one or more of the processes of speech, language, perception, behavior, reading, spelling, writing, or arithmetic."

Perhaps the most widely used definition of *learning disability* was developed by the Office of Education of the United States Department of Health, Education, and Welfare.

> "Specific learning disability" means a disorder in one or more of the basic psychological processes involved in understanding or in using language, spoken or written, which may manifest itself in an imperfect ability to listen, think, speak, read, write, spell, or to do mathematical calculations. The term includes such conditions as perceptual handicaps, brain injury, minimal brain dysfunction, dyslexia, and developmental aphasia. The term does not include children who have learning problems which are primarily the result of visual, hearing, or motor handicaps, of mental retardation, or of environmental, cultural, or economic disadvantage. (United States Office of Education, 1977, p. 42478.)

Incidence

Since definitions have varied and diagnostic procedures and criteria have not been developed adequately, estimates of the prevalence of specific learning disabilities have varied considerably. Estimates have ranged from 1 to 30 per cent. Although determination of prevalence was not the major thrust of a study conducted by Myklebust and Boshes (1969), these authors screened nearly 2800 children in the third and fourth grades on the basis of an educational-discrepancy definition. It was determined that 7 to 8 per cent of this public school population exhibited learning disabilities. Since the children in the study generally were only one year retarded educationally, it is possible that the 7 to 8 per cent estimate includes minor as well as "hardcore" learning disabilities and thus is too high. One of the most widely accepted estimates of severe cases of specific learning disabilities was provided by the National Advisory Committee on Handicapped Children (1968). This group conservatively estimates that the number of severe cases requiring special remedial procedures comprises from 1 to 3 per cent of the school population. For the purpose of determining financial allocations to schools under the Education for All Handicapped Children Act of 1975, children with specific learning disabilities may not comprise more than one sixth of the total population of handicapped childred aged 5 to 17.

Characteristics

In considering the characteristics of children with specific learning disabilities, it becomes quite apparent that there is a core of characteristics that apply in most cases and a much greater number of characteristics that are not necessarily specific to the learning disabled and that may be exhibited by only a portion of all learning-disabled children. The heterogeneity of the group is one of its prime characteristics and may be demonstrated by the fact that "opposite" behaviors (hyperactive and hypoactive) are accepted as possible characteristics of the group of children labeled as learning-disabled. It should be noted that study in the area of learning disabilities is relatively new. The characteristics that have been associated with this group have been identified primarily on the basis of informal observation and clinical data. More precise identification of characteristics must await further research.

The characteristics all learning disabled children have in common are explicitly or implicitly associated with the definition of *special learning disabilities* developed by the National Advisory Committee on Handicapped Children (1968). First and foremost, a learning disorder must be exhibited. Such disorders may be manifested by abnormalities in listening, thinking, talking, reading, writing, spelling, or arithmetic. Second, such disorders must not be caused primarily by visual, auditory, or motor handicaps, or by mental retardation, emotional handicaps, or environmental disadvantage. Thus, the child identified as *learning disabled* must be near average, average, or above average in intelligence. Third, the learning-disabled child exhibits an educational discrepancy. The achievement of children is less than expected for their intelligence, age, and educational opportunity. Finally, learning-disabled children exhibit significant intraindividual differences, i.e., abnormal discrepancies in their abilities.

Although the previously mentioned characteristics are exhibited by learning-disabled children, many other characteristics associated with the learning disabled vary in kind and degree. Although not present in all children, the interrelated characteristics described in the following section are among those most frequently associated with learning disabilities.

PERCEPTUAL DISORDERS

Although the emphasis placed on the relationship between perceptual impairments and learning disabilities varies, most theorists include perceptual disorders in their lists of characteristics of learning-disabled children. Deficits in visual, auditory, and haptic perception are believed to result in problems with academic achievement. Although important, olfactory and gustatory perceptions are of less significance in academic learning. Deficits in visual perception are associated with inadequate skills in figure-ground perception, spatial relationships, perceptual constancy, visual discrimination, and the matching of visual and motor abilities. Similarly, deficits in auditory perception may be associated with inadequacies in auditory figure-ground perception, auditory discrimination, sound localization, and temporal auditory perception. Deficits in haptic perception are associated with inadequate body awareness, laterality, and tactual perception. Perceptual approaches to remediation of learning disabilities assume that perceptual development undergirds or influences academic development.

HYPERACTIVITY

Although hyperactivity is not always present in the learning-disabled child, its presence is relatively common and it is listed as a characteristic by virtually all major theorists. Hyperactive children usually exhibit greater than normal motor activity, which is disruptive to those in contact with them. Such children are often observed to be restless, fidgety, unable to sit still, or constantly shuffling or swinging their feet and legs. Their movements frequently cause conflict in the classroom and lead to behavioral as well as learning problems. Hyperactivity prohibits a child from attending to a task long enough for academic progress to take place. It should be noted that hypoactivity (listlessness or inactivity) has also been cited by some authors as a characteristic of the learning disabled. Its occurrence, however, is either much less common than hyperactivity or much less troublesome to the educator.

PERSEVERATION

Perseveration is repetition of a behavior or inability to change the focus of behavior or to shift easily from one behavior or idea to another. In essence, the spread and duration of a stimulus are increased. For example, a child is drawn to a particular letter or word while writing and copies or writes the letter or word over and over again. Or, a child will continue bouncing a ball or running in a play area long after a signal to stop such activity has been given. The stimulus to which a child may unduly attend can be either auditory or visual, and perseveration may be externally or internally triggered.

DISORDERS OF MEMORY

Disorders of memory involve failure to recall information or failure to recall it in proper sequence. They may involve the inability to recall spoken words (reauditorization), inability to carry out a series of instructions, inability to recall words previously read (revisualization), difficulty in remembering the sequence of letters or sounds within words, or difficulty in retaining the sequence of steps used in solving arithmetic problems.

DISTRACTIBILITY

Distractibility is a disorder of attention, characterized by the inability to block out irrelevant stimuli in order to give normal attention to surrounding events and circumstances. A distractible child gives fleeting attention to a stimulus that other children normally attend to for a more sustained period of time. The child is easily drawn from a task by the slightest awareness of usually extraneous visual, auditory, or olfactory stimuli in the environment. Although children may try to block out irrelevant stimuli, they are not always able to do so. This inability to concentrate inhibits learning.

DISSOCIATION

The tendency to respond to parts of a stimulus rather than to perceive it as a whole is called dissociation. For example, visual dissociation is evidenced when a child draws a square by reproducing four parallel lines. Auditory dissociation is evidenced when a child fails to combine syllables in a correct sequence when attempting to form a word or fails to grasp the meaning of an entire sentence even if individual words are understood. Thus, the child fails in attempts to integrate elements into a meaningful whole.

CLUMSINESS OR AWKWARDNESS

Overall or nonspecific awkwardness, clumsiness, and incoordination typify children with learning disabilities. It is not uncommon for learning-disabled children to display a lag in locomotor development. In addition, young children are often impaired in their ability to throw, catch, and kick and perform other motor skills. In some children, balance problems predominate, causing falling and stumbling in games and other playground activities. Because of a lack of gross and fine motor control, the learning-disabled child frequently displays greater than normal difficulty in cutting with scissors, coloring, tracing, writing, copying, buttoning clothes, tying shoes, and completing pegboard activities and puzzles. Since clumsiness or awkwardness in motor activities is readily noticeable, children become quickly embarrassed if their abilities are below those of their peers. In order to enhance self-concept as well as coordination abilities, it is important to help the child improve motor skills as quickly as possible.

IMMATURE BODY IMAGE

Kephart (1971), Frostig and Maslow (1970), and Ayres (1965) have observed that immature body image and deficits in visual perception and learning frequently occur together. Johnson and Myklebust (1967) recognize the inability to accurately perceive one's own body as a nonverbal learning disability. According to these authors, affected children find it difficult or impossible to identify parts of their own bodies (including the fingers), recognize their faces in a mirror, construct models of the human body, or accurately draw a human figure. Deficits in body image are believed to be associated with poor spatial orientation and thus to influence academic performance. The origin of deficits in body image has been under considerable discussion for many years. In certain instances such deficits have been traced to brain damage, whereas in other cases they have been attributed to the lack of or inadequacy of opportunities to develop body image. The meaning and analysis of body image are presented in greater detail in other portions of this book.

POOR SPATIAL ORIENTATION

Disturbances in spatial orientation affecting perception of the self in space and perception of the relationship of two or more objects in space have been associated with the learning-disabled child by many authors (Kephart, 1971; Frostig and Maslow, 1970; Johnson and Myklebust, 1967; and Barsch, 1967 and 1968). Spatial orientation has been closely allied with body image, since awareness of the parts of one's own body is believed to be a precursor of the awareness of one's position in space and the relationship of objects in space. Children exhibiting poor spatial orientation have difficulty judging their position in space, estimating distance, knowing the coordinates of space, and perceiving relationships between objects in space. As a result, they bump into each other and objects and have difficulty moving through narrow openings and under or over obstacles. In academic areas, poor spatial orientation may lead to deficits in laterality, directionality, and other perceptual abilities that affect academic achievement. The role and importance of spatial orientation to perceptual and academic achievement vary with different theorists. The reader is referred to Chapter 4 for an in-depth discussion of this relationship.

"SOFT" SOCIAL, EMOTIONAL, AND NEUROLOGICAL SIGNS

Several writers have noted the presence of other signs in association with learning disabilities. On the basis of their literature review, Bryan and Bryan (1975) include emotional outbursts that are not reasonably expected, impulsivity, and equivocal neurological signs in their list of characteristics. Johnson and Myklebust (1967) list social imperception as a nonverbal disorder of learning. Gearheart (1973) notes that lack of motivation is a characteristic that frequently appears in referral reports of learning-disabled children. Clements (1966) includes impulsivity, emotional lability, and electroencephalographic irregularities as equivocal or "soft" neurological signs in his list of major signs and symptoms of minimal brain dysfunctions. Clements also lists transient strabismus, poor hand-eye coordination, mixed laterality, confused laterality, mild speech impairment, a history of slow or irregular speech development, and general awkwardness.

Educational Approaches to Learning Disabilities

Although the term *specific learning disabilities* has come into common usage only since the early 1960s, the foundation for this study of exceptionality may be traced to the early 1800s. The work of Itard (1962), and Seguin (1907), published originally in the nineteenth century, laid the foundation for the sensory-motor approaches that emerged during the twentieth century. The foundation for today's neurological approaches may also be traced to theories of cerebral dominance developed in the early 1800s. An important milestone for the study of language disabilities was reached when Henry Head published his writings on language disorders based on his work with aphasic subjects. By the first third of the twentieth century, Samuel T. Orton (1937) had developed a theory of cerebral dominance to explain certain kinds of disabilities and had provided the background for an educational remediation program for certain disabilities that still is used today. Orton coined the word *strephosymbolia* (twisted symbols) to describe the disorder of children who had difficulty remembering the order of letters and sounds.

The modern thrust and interest in learning disabilities are generally attributed to the work of Strauss and Lehtinen (1947). In *Psychopathology and Education of the Brain-Injured Child,* these authors presented their research, theory, and educational methods pertaining to brain-injured children. Strauss collaborated with Hans Werner in the development of theory and the conduct of research and worked with Laura Lehtinen in the construction of appropriate educational methods and programs. To deal with the hyperactivity and inattentiveness associated with the brain-damaged child, Strauss and Lehtinen developed special methods to control the child's environment. The purpose of their program was to reduce distractions and hyperactive behavior. In addition, they designed instructional materials to correct or ameliorate perceptual, thinking, and academic problems. Strauss and Lehtinen were among the first to distinguish methods of teaching the brain-injured and the normal child.

The ideas of Strauss and Lehtinen were further expanded by William Cruickshank and his associates. On the basis of his work with brain-injured persons, Cruickshank (1967) identified their characteristics as sensory and motor hyperactivity, dissociation, figure-ground reversal, perseveration, and motor incoordination. In agreement with Strauss that the school environment for the brain-injured must be controlled, Cruickshank developed an educational plan that involves reducing to a minimum the environmental stimuli and the space for working, providing a structured environment, and enhancing the stimulus value of instructional materials. In addition, the Cruickshank program includes materials and objectives associated with the perceptual-motor programs of Barsch, Getman, and Kephart.

Beginning in the 1950's, programs employing movement as a basis as well as a modality for perceptual development and academic achievement were proposed by various theorists. Newell Kephart (1960, 1971), who worked with Strauss, designed a perceptual motor program that he felt served as a basis for successful academic achievement and attainment of intellectual abilities. Similarly, Barsch (1967, 1968) developed a "movigenic" curriculum to facilitate perceptual-motor development and academic achievement. Getman (1962) and Getman and Kane (1964) devised a theory and program to develop readiness skills for performance and learning. Like Kephart and Barsch, Getman contends that perceptual and academic abilities develop from a motor base.

Frostig and her associates (1964b, 1970, 1973a, 1973b) and Cratty (1970c) have also developed perceptual programs. The Frostig program is designed to enhance visual perceptual abilities and employs movement experiences as a modality to attain this goal. Cratty (1970c) has devised a model for the maturation of human abilities based on the assumption that perceptual abilities develop in association with movement experiences. He has published a series of books presenting specific activities to enhance academic and intellectual abilities. All the perceptual motor programs mentioned above are described in detail in Chapter 4.

A number of remedial reading approaches have been employed for children with learning disabilities. It is beyond the scope of this book to identify and analyze all the different approaches. However, the Fernald approach and the Gillingham and Stillman method will be discussed briefly since they are multi-sensory and relatively well-known. The approach developed by Grace Fernald (1943) has been called the kin-esthetic, tracing, or *VAKT* approach. It involves the use of visual, audito-ry, kinesthetic, and tactual sensory channels for teaching reading and spelling. A child following this approach begins by tracing a known word while vocalizing it. This process is repeated until the child can write the word from memory. As the child progresses, tracing is elimi-nated and the child looks at the word, says it, and attempts to write it from memory. Later in the sequence, the child writes words without needing to say them and is eventually encouraged to write stories. The ability to read type as well as cursive lettering is developed as words and stories are typed. At the final stage, the child develops the ability to recognize new words through their similarity to words or parts of words already learned.

A second multi-sensory approach is based on theoretical con-structs developed by Orton and further refined by Gillingham and Still-man (1965). Sometimes referred to as the *VAK* method, it is similar to the Fernald method. However, the method of Gillingham and Stillman is based on phonetics rather than whole words. Instead of copying words, children learn names and sounds of letters. They are asked to look at letters and phonemes, reproduce the sound associated with them, trace them, and write them from memory. After a sufficient number of phonemes are learned, the child is asked to blend sounds to form a word. Subsequently, words are made into sentences, paragraphs, and stories for the child to read. The approach employs a visual-auditory kinesthetic sequence and association.

The psycholinguistic diagnosis remediation system designed by Kirk (1962) and later refined by Kirk and Kirk (1971) is still another approach that has been employed to remediate learning deficits. In this approach, an educational program to remediate learning deficits is determined to a great degree by results obtained on a standardized test. On the basis of their research and clinical experience with the mentally retarded and other children with learning deficits, Kirk, McCarthy, and Kirk (1968b) developed the Illinois Test of Psycholin-guistic Abilities (ITPA) to evaluate communicative abilities of children. As Kirk (1972) points out, the twelve subtests comprising the test are designed to measure:

a. the ability to receive and understand what is seen and heard;
b. the abilities to make associations and understand interrelationships of what is seen and heard;
c. the ability to express oneself by verbal and motor responses;
d. the ability to grasp automatically the whole of a visual pattern or verbal expression when only part of it is presented; and
e. the ability to remember and repeat visual and auditory sequences of material. (Kirk, 1972, p. 55.)

In this approach, a profile is developed and areas of disabilities are noted after the ITPA test is administered to pupils. Largely on the basis of test results, an educational program is established to overcome deficits noted on the tests. Although the ITPA is a major tool in the psychoeducational diagnostic procedure, Kirk (1972) is careful to point out that the complete diagnostic procedure that leads to a program of remediation proceeds in five stages:

1. determining whether the child's learning problem is specific, general, or spurious;

2. analyzing the behavior manifestations which are descriptive of the specific problem;
3. discovering the physical, environmental, and psychological correlates of the disability;
4. evolving a diagnostic inference (hypothesis) on the basis of the behavior manifestations and the correlates; and
5. organizing a systematic remedial program based on the diagnostic inference. (Kirk, 1972, p. 62.)

Myklebust, a well-known researcher and writer in the area of the deaf and the learning disabled, developed a well-received educational remediation program for the amelioration of what he refers to as "psychoneurological learning disabilities." Although he views learning disabilities as behavioral, Myklebust (1968) presumes that such disabilities are caused by minor disturbances in the brain and uses the term *psychoneurological* to emphasize this concept. According to Johnson and Myklebust (1967), the learning-disabled child is one who displays adequate motor ability, average to high intelligence, adequate hearing and vision, and adequate emotional adjustment but a deficiency in learning. These authors indicate that the principal criterion for identifying the learning-disabled is that their intellectual, emotional, sensory, and motor abilities fall within a normal range but they exhibit behavioral or neurological evidence of dysfunction in the brain.

According to Johnson and Myklebust (1967), learning disabilities may include disorders of auditory language, reading, written language, mathematical abilities, and nonverbal learning. Nonverbal learning disorders include deficits in learning through pictures, gestural problems, nonverbal motor learning problems, inadequate body image, problems in spatial orientations, right-left orientation problems, social perception problems, distractibility, perseveration, and disinhibition.

In their book, Johnson and Myklebust (1967) present and discuss the theoretical constructs upon which their program is based and recommend educational experiences to remediate the learning deficits they have identified. Emphasis is placed on neurological, psychological, and educational assessment to determine the nature of the learning disability. Once the disability is identified, specific activities are recommended to alleviate the problem. In view of the emphasis given to auditory-vocal disabilities, this approach is often referred to as a *language development system.* However, the approach does recognize and suggest activities for the remediation of nonverbal disabilities.

Emotional-Behavioral Disabilities

Definitions and Classifications

Of the various human deviances considered in this book, those related to social or emotional aspects of the human are among those most difficult to define. Definitions that are developed vary according to perspective and purpose, so that the same individual may carry a number of labels. For example, a child labeled as *emotionally disturbed* by a psychiatrist may be labeled as *socially maladjusted* or *juvenile delinquent* by a social or legal professional and as *hard to teach* or *behaviorally disabled* by an educator. In the past few years, special educators have begun to use *behavioral disabilities* or *behavioral disorders* as comprehensive terms to describe the emotionally disturbed and the socially maladjusted. Grauhard (1973) defines behavioral disabilities as "a variety of excessive, chronic, deviant behaviors ranging from impulsive and aggressive to depressive and withdrawal acts (1) which violate the perceiver's expectation of appropriateness, and (2) which the perceiver wishes to see stopped." In regard to education, Grauhard points out that the perceivers are educators, teachers, and administrators who want the behavior of the pupil changed or, failing this, want to remove the child from the regular classroom. Kirk (1972) defines a behavior disorder as "a deviation from age/appropriate behavior which significantly interferes with (1) the child's own growth and development and/or (2) the lives of others." According to Kirk (1972), behavioral disorders in children are, in essence, "actions which retard social and emotional and sometimes educational growth, or they may be actions which are detrimental to other people." Kirk would include withdrawal, neurosis, autism, schizophrenia, delinquency, and social maladjustment in his conception of behavioral disorders.

Although considered by many to be of limited value for education and treatment, the classification of mental disorders developed by the American Psychiatric Association (1968) is one of the best known (Table 8–5). This system identifies a variety of psychoses, neuroses, and personality disorders. General characteristics associated with these disorders are presented in the next section. Behavioral disorders of childhood and adolescence constitute another area in the classification system. Since the descriptions associated with behavioral disorders perhaps best delineate behavior manifestations that may be useful in educational planning, they are presented in the next section, in Table 8–6.

Autism, although it is not included in the American Psychiatric Association (APA) classification, has received a great deal of attention in the literature on learning disabilities written during the past few years. The term *early infantile autism* was introduced by Kanner in 1943 to describe a type of schizophrenia associated with childhood. An *autistic child* (or a child with autistic characteristics) is one who exhibits extreme withdrawal and is unable to adequately attend or relate to the environment. Autistic children function within themselves and are considered "loners." They are generally unable to communicate through speech or are retarded in language development. They often exhibit peculiar manners and responses. Their inability to relate to objects in the environment results in retarded intellectual development. The autistic child appears to be happiest when left alone and allowed to "close out" the outside world.

Educators and other professionals have been gradually moving away from psychiatric or psychological definitions and classifications for children and adolescents exhibiting deviations in behavior and toward those more relevant to education. It is clear that the terminology of many professional groups is in transition. Educators are increasingly using the terms *behavioral disability* or *behavioral disorder* to describe children formerly referred to as *emotionally disturbed.* However, they are only beginning to develop a body of knowledge consistent with this terminology. In view of this transition, it is important to identify and understand how terms will be used in this section. The term *emotional*

Table 8–5. List of DSM-II Diagnosis and Code Numbers.***

I. Mental Retardation

310.	Borderline
311.	Mild
312.	Moderate
313.	Severe
314.	Profound
315.	Unspecified

II. Organic Brain Syndromes (OBS)

A. Psychoses

Senile and pre-senile dementia

290.0	Senile dementia
290.1	Pre-senile dementia

Alcoholic psychosis

**291.0	Delirium tremens
**291.1	Korsakov's psychosis
**291.2	Other alcoholic hallucinosis
**291.3	Alcohol paranoid state
**291.4*	Acute alcohol intoxication*
**291.5*	Alcoholic deterioration*
**291.6*	Pathological intoxication*
291.9	Other alcoholic psychosis

Psychosis associated with intracranial infection

292.0	General paralysis
292.1	Syphilis of CNS
292.2	Epidemic encephalitis
292.3	Other and unspecified encephalitis

With each: following or associated with

.0	Infection or intoxication
.1	Trauma or physical agent
.2	Disorders of metabolism, growth, or nutrition
.3	Gross brain disease (postnatal)
.4	Unknown prenatal influence
.5	Chromosomal abnormality
.6	Prematurity
**.7	Major psychiatric disorder
**.8	Psycho-social (environmental) deprivation
.9	Other condition

Psychosis associated with other physical condition

294.0	Endocrine disorder
294.1	Metabolic and nutritional disorder
294.2	Systemic infection
294.3	Drug or poison intoxication (other than alcohol)
**294.4	Childbirth
294.8	Other and unspecified physical condition

B. Non-Psychotic OBS

309.0	Intracranial infection
**309.13*	Alcohol* (simple drunkenness)
**309.14*	Other drug, poison or systemic intoxication*
309.2	Brain trauma
309.3	Circulatory disturbance
309.4	Epilepsy
309.5	Disturbance of metabolism, growth, or nutrition
309.6	Senile or pre-senile brain disease
309.7	Intracranial neoplasm

292.9 Other intracranial infection

Psychosis associated with other cerebral condition

293.0 Cerebral arteriosclerosis
293.1 Other cerebrovascular disturbance
293.2 Epilepsy
293.3 Intracranial neoplasm
293.4 Degenerative disease of the CNS
293.5 Brain trauma
293.9 Other cerebral condition

III. Psychoses Not Attributed to Physical Conditions Listed Previously

Schizophrenia

295.0 Simple
295.1 Hebephrenic
295.2 Catatonic
**295.23* Catatonic type, excited*
**295.24* Catatonic type, withdrawn*
295.3 Paranoid
**295.4 Acute schizophrenic episode
295.5 Latent
295.6 Residual
295.7 Schizo-affective
**295.73* Schizo-affective, excited*
**295.74* Schizo-affective, depressed*
295.8* Childhood*
295.90* Chronic undifferentiated*
295.99* Other schizophrenia*

IV. Neuroses

300.0 Anxiety
300.1 Hysterical
**300.13* Hysterical, conversion type*
**300.14* Hysterical, dissociative type*
300.2 Phobic
300.3 Obsessive compulsive

309.8 Degenerative disease of the CNS
309.9 Other physical condition

Major affective disorders

296.0 Involutional melancholia
296.1 Manic-depressive illness, manic
296.2 Manic-depressive illness, depressed
296.3 Manic-depressive illness, circular
**296.33* Manic-depressive, circular, manic*
**296.34* Manic-depressive, circular, depressed
296.8 Other major affective disorder

Paranoid states

297.0 Paranoia
**297.1 Involutional paranoid state
297.9 Other paranoid state

Other psychoses

298.0 Psychotic depressive reaction

300.4 Depressive
**300.5 Neurasthenic
**300.6 Depersonalization
**300.7 Hypochondriacal
300.8 Other neurosis

Table continued on following page.

Table 8-5. List of DSM-II Diagnosis and Code Numbers*** *Continued*

V. Personality Disorders and Certain
Other Non-Psychotic Mental Disorders

Personality disorders

301.0	Paranoid
301.1	Cyclothymic
301.2	Schizoid
**301.3	Explosive
301.4	Obsessive compulsive
**301.5	Hysterical
**301.6	Asthenic
301.7	Antisocial
301.81*	Passive-aggressive*
301.82*	Inadequate*
301.89*	Other specified types*

Sexual deviation

**302.0	Homosexuality
**302.1	Fetishism
**302.2	Pedophilia
**302.3	Transvestitism
**302.4	Exhibitionism
**302.5*	Voyeurism*
**302.6*	Sadism*
**302.7*	Masochism*
302.8	Other sexual deviation

Alcoholism

**303.0	Episodic excessive drinking
**303.1	Habitual excessive drinking
**303.2	Alcohol addiction
303.9	Other alcoholism

Drug dependence

**304.0	Opium, opium alkaloids and their derivatives
**304.1	Synthetic analgesics with morphine-like effects
**304.2	Barbiturates
**304.3	Other hypnotics and sedatives or "tranquilizers"
**304.4	Cocaine
**304.5	Cannabis sativa (hashish, marihuana)
**304.6	Other psycho-stimulants
**304.7	Hallucinogens
304.8	Other drug dependence

VI. Psychophysiologic Disorders

305.0	Skin
305.1	Musculoskeletal
305.2	Respiratory
305.3	Cardiovascular
305.4	Hemic and lymphatic
305.5	Gastro-intestinal
305.6	Genito-urinary
305.7	Endocrine
305.8	Organ of special sense
305.9	Other type

VII. Special Symptoms

306.0	Speech disturbance
306.6	Enuresis

306.1 Specific learning disturbance
**306.2 Tic
**306.3 Other psychomotor disorder
**306.4 Disorders of sleep

VIII. Transient Situational Disturbances

307.0* Adjustment reaction of infancy*
307.1* Adjustment reaction of childhood*
307.2* Adjustment reaction of adolescence*

IX. Behavior Disorder of Childhood and Adolescence

**308.0* Hyperkinetic reaction*
**308.1* Withdrawing reaction*
**308.2* Overanxious reaction*
**308.3* Runaway reaction*

X. Conditions without Manifest Psychiatric Disorder and Non-Specific Conditions

Social maladjustment without manifest psychiatric disorder

**316.0* Marital maladjustment*
**316.1* Social maladjustment*
**316.2* Occupational maladjustment*
**316.3* Dyssocial behavior*
**316.9* Other social maladjustment*

XI. Non-Diagnostic Terms for Administrative Use

319.0* Diagnosis deferred*
319.1* Boarder*

**306.7 Encopresis
**306.8 Cephalalgia
306.9 Other special symptom

307.3* Adjustment reaction of adult life*
307.4* Adjustment reaction of late life*

**308.4* Unsocialized aggressive reaction*
**308.5* Group delinquent reaction*
**308.9* Other reaction*

Non-specific conditions

**317* Non-specific conditions*

No Mental Disorder

**318* No mental disorder*

319.2* Experiment only*
319.3* Other*

*These diagnoses are for use in the U.S. only and do not appear in ICD-8.
**These are new diagnoses, that do not appear in DSM-I.
***Many of the titles here are listed in abbreviated form.

Modified from American Psychiatric Association, Diagnostic and Statistical Manual of Mental Disorders, Washington, D. C.: American Psychiatric Association, 1968, pp. 126–127.

disability or *disturbance* refers to the psychiatrically-based conditions of psychoses, neuroses, and personality disorders. *Behavioral disability* refers to hyperkinetic, withdrawing, overanxious, runaway, unsocialized aggressive, and group delinquent reactions of childhood or adolescence. These are conditions associated with the APA category of behavior disorders and are consistent with definitions provided by Grauhard (1973) and Kirk (1972). It must be stressed, however, that the conditions are not mutually exclusive; the same child may be appropriately regarded as emotionally and behaviorally disabled. In the following discussion, these terms will be used separately or jointly, as appropriate.

General Characteristics of the Emotionally Disturbed

Characteristics associated with functional psychoses, psychoneuroses, and personality disorders are presented below, and characteristics associated with behavior disorders appear in Table 8–6. More specific characteristics associated with performance in physical and motor activities are discussed in Chapter 12.

Functional psychoses are characterized by loss of contact with or inability to recognize reality, failure to attend and relate adequately to people and objects in the environment, tendency to withdraw or to live in a "shell" or "dream world" and deficits in perception, language, and memory.

Psychoneuroses are characterized by anxiety and by distortion in some aspects of reality with the ability to function adequately in other aspects. People with psychoneuroses generally exhibit symptom formation (phobia, anxiety).

Personality disorders are characterized by chronic maladaptive behavior that does not cause anxiety in the individual exhibiting such behavior.

Incidence

Differences in defining and classifying emotional disturbances have made it extremely difficult to determine their prevalence. Although some estimates have been as high as 22 per cent, most studies report an incidence within the 5 to 15 per cent range.

Causes

The view that a change in behavior may be enhanced by an understanding of its cause is held by many — particularly by proponents of psychodynamic theory. Few would disagree that a knowledge of cause sometimes enhances treatment and education. However, the limitations of cause as a basis for educational planning and programming must also be recognized. Where the cause of deviant behavior may be determined and explained, the knowledge may be of great value to educators or therapists in some cases and of little value in other cases. Sometimes, however, it may not be possible to discover the cause of

Table 8—6. Behavior Disorders of Childhood and Adolescence.

Hyperkinetic reaction of childhood (or adolescence)

> This disorder is characterized by overactivity, restlessness, distractibility, and short attention span, especially in young children; the behavior usually diminishes in adolescence.

Withdrawing reaction of childhood (or adolescence)

> The disorder is characterized by seclusiveness, detachment, sensitivity, shyness, timidity, and general inability to form close interpersonal relationships.

Overanxious reaction of childhood (or adolescence)

> This disorder is characterized by chronic anxiety, excessive and unrealistic fears, sleeplessness, nightmares, and exaggerated autonomic responses.

Runaway reaction of childhood (or adolescence)

> Individuals with this disorder characteristically escape from threatening situations by running away from home for a day or more without permission. Typically they are immature and timid and feel rejected at home, inadequate, and friendless. They often steal furtively.

Unsocialized aggressive reaction of childhood (or adolescence)

> This disorder is characterized by overt or covert hostile disobedience, quarrelsomeness, physical and verbal aggressiveness, vengefulness, and destructiveness. Temper tantrums, solitary stealing, lying and hostile teasing of other children are common. These patients usually have no consistent parental acceptance and discipline.

Group delinquent reaction of childhood (or adolescence)

> Individuals with this disorder have acquired the values, behavior and skills of a delinquent peer group or gang to whom they are loyal and with whom they characteristically steal, skip school, and stay out late at night. The condition is more common in boys than girls. When group delinquency occurs with girls it usually involves sexual delinquency, although shoplifting is also common.

Other reaction of childhood (or adolescence)

> Here are to be classified children and adolescents having disorders not described in this group but which are nevertheless more serious than transient situational disturbances and less serious than psychoses, neuroses, and personality disorders. The particular disorder should be specified.

Excerpted from American Psychiatric Association, *Diagnostic and Statistical Manual of Mental Disorders.* Washington, D. C.: American Psychiatric Association, 1968, pp. 49–51.

deviant behavior, since such determination is complicated and time-consuming, requires qualified personnel, and is expensive. Unfortunately, there is often a lack of agreement among professionals in regard to the underlying causes for deviations in behavior.

Over the years, many explanations for deviations in behavior have been offered. These have filled countless pages and often have been based on detailed and complicated theoretical constructs. In this book, etiological factors related to emotional-behavioral problems will be discussed only in general terms. The causes of deviations in behavior considered here include those that are hereditary, organic, and functional in nature.

Although heredity is believed to play a role in psychiatric disorders, there is a lack of agreement concerning its exact role. Psychiatrists have long believed that hereditary factors do affect certain mental illnesses. However, the importance attributed to heredity has diminished as knowledge concerning emotional problems has accumulated. A direct association between heredity and mental illness is considered to be relatively infrequent. Perhaps heredity is more often an indirect cause. It is known that heredity plays some role in mental and physical conditions of the organism and that such conditions, in turn, affect the emotional or behavioral functioning of the individual. For example, heredity may contribute to a certain body type or to obesity, which in turn affects the behavior of the individual. Most professionals are careful not to overemphasize heredity as an explanation for deviations in behavior. The reasons for being cautious in this regard are that (1) some therapists, teachers, and parents tend to be less optimistic about improving a condition believed to be caused by hereditary factors, and (2) exact causes are difficult to isolate.

The second category of causes of deviation in behavior is organic. Although for sake of discussion we have separated the causes of deviation into categories, they are not mutually exclusive. Organic factors include glandular and other chemical imbalances that affect personality and behavior, illness and injury, and various neurological conditions. Many of the conditions occur at or near the time of birth. The birth process itself is traumatic, and physical damage may occur during it. A variety of conditions may deprive the child of oxygen and cause damage to the central nervous system during the birth process; infections and injury during the first year of life may also result in permanent damage to the central nervous system. Such damage may, of course, seriously affect personality functioning.

Deviations in behavior owing to functional factors compose the third category. Included in this category are deviations in behavior due to psychological factors. As may be expected, this category is very broad in nature and perhaps accounts for most emotional-behavioral problems.

A major source of functional emotional-behavioral disability is frustration. Frustration occurs when the individual is unable to attain desired goals or to satisfy needs. For example, in a school situation a child may become frustrated when a discrepancy exists between the capability to behave and the requirements imposed by teachers, parents, or peers. Frustration may also be caused when an individual is unable to choose between two courses of action. For example, children may be placed in a situation in which they must choose between requirements imposed by peers and those imposed by teachers or parents. Symptoms of frustration include hostility and aggression, regression in behavior, and withdrawal. Such symptoms are associated with a variety of other forms of deviant behavior.

Family influences are, of course, important in influencing behavior. Relationships with parents, siblings, and other family members (grandparents, in-laws) affect the emotional environment and thus influence behavior. There is little question that the behavior of the child reflects the attitudes, ideas, standards, and values of the family. Child-rearing practices may also explain certain behavior patterns of children. Emotional development is enhanced when children are accepted, their needs are met, and the climate of the home is filled with love. On the other hand, emotional development is impeded when the child is rejected or neglected or is given inconsistent and inappropriate discipline.

Cultural and social factors also affect behavior to a great extent and thus become a source of deviant behavior. When an individual becomes part of a cultural or social group, the standards of behavior are established for the individual within the group, and these standards are used as a reference for behavior as the individual moves to other groups. Behavioral problems emerge as the behavior of the individual comes into conflict with expectations of the cultural or social group or when the individual moves to other groups with different behavior standards. For example, racial, ethnic, religious, and socioeconomic groups have different behavioral expectations. It is not uncommon for individuals to exhibit behavioral conflicts as they come into contact with other groups. Similarly, conflict often arises between the behavioral expectations of a child's peer group and those of the family group.

Educational Approaches

PSYCHODYNAMIC APPROACH

One of the best-known approaches in the education of emotionally disturbed children is the *psychodynamic approach.* Although it is used in association with educational programming and in educational settings, the major thrust of this approach is therapeutic in nature, placing education in a role secondary to that of therapy and making the teacher an auxillary of the therapist. The approach is designed to improve emotional functioning by helping the child to relieve underlying interpsychic conflicts. As unconscious conflicts are treated, causes of undesirable behavior are, it is hoped, eliminated, enabling the child to learn. The psychodynamic educator assumes that undesirable symptoms exhibited by the child are caused by psychic conflicts that must be resolved. These conflicts emerge from abnormal characteristics of the id, ego, and superego or from abnormal relationships among them. The psychodynamic approach assumes that removal of symptoms without removal of underlying causes simply changes the nature of symptoms.

The classroom or school employing this approach exhibits several identifiable characteristics. Teachers focus on the "why" rather than the "what" in terms of behavior. They attempt to understand the child by attending to the cause of behavior. Every effort is made to develop close and positive relationships with the student. A rather permissive environment is considered necessary to encourage the child to vent feelings and to display behavior. An atmosphere of acceptance regardless of the behavior manifested is encouraged, i.e., the child is accepted but undesirable behavior is not. Every effort is made for the child to develop self-understanding and for the teacher to understand the child.

Although many of the principles of the psychodynamic approach are undoubtedly applied by most teachers in some form, the approach in its purest form has generally been limited to psychiatric hospitals, residential schools, and day treatment centers. There are at least five reasons for this limited application. First, the success of the approach with children has been questioned. Second, there has been a lack of funds to employ trained personnel to implement the approach. A relatively long treatment effort in a special setting is a third factor inhibiting use. Fourth, educators have questioned their role and their preparation for goals that are primarily psychological. Finally, many educators have selected approaches that they believe to be more effective in educating the emotionally disturbed child.

BEHAVIOR MODIFICATION

Behavior modification is a second major approach that has been employed in the education of emotionally-behaviorally disabled children. Whereas the psychodynamic approach focuses on the cause or "why" of behavior, the behavior modification approach focuses on the "what" of behavior. The behavior modification approach is based on the assumption that behavior is learned and can be changed without the need to determine its cause. Further, proponents of behavior modification are quick to point out that symptoms exhibited by the individual may, indeed, be the cause of behavioral problems.

In the implementation of behavior modification programs, behavior is changed by the manipulation of stimuli that precede a response (respondent or classical conditioning) or by manipulation of the stimuli that follow responses (operant conditioning). A child fearful of the water because of unpleasant or painful events associated with it may serve as an example for the first type. In this case, the teacher attempts to change behavior by providing repeated pairings of pleasant stimuli with the water. Learning through operant conditioning is demonstrated when a teacher holds a picture of an exercise for the child to see and do (stimulus), the child is expected to do it (contingency), the child looks at it and does the exercise (response), and the teacher praises performance (positive reinforcement). The key to learning through operant conditioning is contingency; positive or negative reinforcement is employed contingent upon pupil behavior.

The purpose of the behavior modification strategy is to change unacceptable behavior and to maintain the behavior that is considered acceptable. To change behavior, it is necessary for the teacher to delineate the behavior to be modified, to determine what is reinforcing to the child, and to arrange experiences in the environment to systematically change behavior. In planning to change behavior of children with behavioral disabilities, it is particularly important to delineate fine progressions toward the desired behavior. Progress is enhanced by success and positive reinforcement, and success is more often possible when steps in the progression are small and attainable. It is vital that the complexity of tasks be increased gradually.

A broad range of consequences have been employed in the behavior modification strategy. Tangible rewards such as candy, gold stars, green stamps, and balloons have been used by many teachers. Others establish a "token economy" in which tokens (in various forms) may be exchanged for a back-up reinforcer. For example, two poker chips may be exchanged for a small balloon, and five poker chips may be exchanged for a large balloon or another item of greater value to the child. When properly employed, group incentives have been effective in changing academic and social behavior. Another effective approach is based on the Premack (1959) principle — behavior normally occurring at a low rate may increase in frequency when it is followed by behavior that occurs at a high rate (activities the child enjoys and desires). For example, a child is told that he or she can play basketball if conditioning exercises are executed properly beforehand. Finally, attention and praise by the teacher have been and will continue to be used as reinforcers — perhaps the most powerful of positive reinforcers.

Since not all behavior is positive, not all consequences that are utilized should or can be positive. Although it is recommended that they be avoided to the greatest extent possible, negative consequences may be employed when the child fails to respond appropriately. Such consequences must be carefully used, since they may lead to a break in communication and may have other undesirable and disruptive effects on learning. Whelan and Haring (1966) reported that removal of the child from the classroom for inappropriate behavior to a "time out" room for a specified period was found to be a useful negative reinforcer if the "time out" room was less attractive to the child than the actual classroom. Other negative reinforcers include denying children certain privileges, such as participation in activities they enjoy and desire. Some teachers view the lack of positive reinforcement in and of itself or the ignoring of behavior as negative. Although the ignoring and punishment of inappropriate behavior are less desirable techniques than positive reinforcement, they have been effectively employed by good teachers to change behavior. Since it is rare that negative reinforcement is not used, new teachers need not feel guilty about employing it. However, the undesirable effects of negative reinforcement must be weighed against the effects of positively changed behavior.

Although positive results have been attained with the behavioral modification strategy, it is not a panacea. Behavior modification is a system to develop behavior, but it does not specify which behaviors to develop. A great deal of attention is given to selecting and employing reinforcers; relatively little is known, however, about phasing out reinforcement and about the long-term effects of this particular approach. The teacher using behavior modification is not immediately concerned about suppressing behavior or shifting behavior to satisfy some need, but it may not be advisable to ignore these concerns over the long run. Finally, conditioning appears to some to be a dehumanizing and therefore an undesirable approach.

DEVELOPMENTAL STRATEGY

An approach that was originally devised for the education of children with emotional disturbances but that has relevance to the problems of all exceptional children is the *developmental strategy* of Hewett (1968). In the developmental approach, learning and the readiness for learning rather than the causes of emotional problems are the primary concerns. Hewett considers this approach to be more relevant to education and teachers, since it focuses on learning rather than on psychology or psychiatry.   Developmental strategy assumes that essential behaviors and competencies must be met if children are to successfully learn in school. These are structured by Hewett in a developmental sequence of seven educational goals (Fig. 8–5). The first five of these (attention, response, order, exploratory, social) prepare the child to pay attention, respond, follow directions, freely and accurately explore the environment, and function effectively as a member of a reacting social group. The goal of mastery (sixth goal) is concerned with acquiring

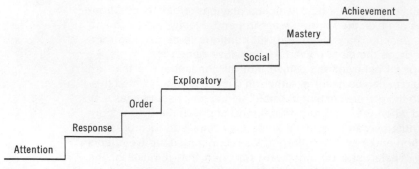

Figure 8–5. A developmental sequence of educational goals. *From* Frank M. Hewett, *The Emotionally Disturbed Child in the Classroom.* Copyright © 1968 by Allyn and Bacon, Inc., Boston. Reprinted with permission.

basic intellectual and adaptive skills and environmental information to enhance independent and successful functioning. The goal of achievement (seventh goal) occupies the enrichment level, which focuses on the attainment of self-motivation and the pursuit of intellectual and adaptive skills in depth.

Following the establishment of his developmental sequence of educational goals as the "somethings" needed, Hewett (1968) turns to methodology. In essence, he asserts that if the teacher can provide the child with the appropriate task under the appropriate condition and can reinforce appropriately, the learning process is under way. This is the approach that Hewett uses to move the child up the developmental sequence of educational goals and that he has implemented in his "engineered classroom."

Hewett (1968) compared the effectiveness of the engineered classroom with traditional designs in teaching emotionally disturbed children. The traditional classroom design consisted of any approach the teacher chose to follow that did not include the use of check marks, tokens, or any other tangible rewards. On the basis of his research, Hewett (1968) states:

> The engineered classroom design appears basically a launching technique for initiating learning with children who often fail to "get off the ground" in school. It does not appear to be essential in its present form for more than one semester with many children, and indeed as additional work is done it may be found that children profit from it primarily the first few weeks of the program after which they are ready to move on to a more traditional learning environment. (Hewett, 1968, p. 333.)

LEARNING DISABILITY STRATEGY

Learning disability or *behavioral deficit strategies* are undoubtedly present in many forms and are widely used in educational programs for children with emotional-behavioral disabilities. Kirk (1972) points out that the learning disability strategy involves remediation of specific disabilities in language, reading, writing, spelling, thinking, and perceiving. Graubard (1973) indicates that behavioral deficit strategies involve the determination and remediation of social behavioral deficits as well as academic deficits. The object of these approaches is to enhance the development of proper behaviors by correcting social and academic deficits. The approach is based on the hypothesis that appropriate behavior will be developed as the child experiences success and gains a feeling of self-worth. Contrarily, it is proposed that failure and frustration lead to poor self-concept and aberrant behavior.

In discussing the learning disability strategy, Kirk (1972) alludes to the relationship of learning disabilities and emotional problems. He points out that in many cases it is difficult to determine how much a learning disability may contribute to emotional disturbance and how much an emotional disturbance may be ascribed to a learning disability. He feels that failure and a feeling of frustration occur (1) when a discrepancy exists between school and other social requirements and the capability of the individual to meet those requirements or (2) when a discrepancy exists between the level of a child's ability in one area and the level of abilities in another area. If Kirk's view is accepted, then the approaches presented in the section on learning disabilities may also be employed as strategies in the educational treatment of the emotionally disturbed child or of the child with behavioral disabilities.

PSYCHOEDUCATIONAL STRATEGY

An eclectic approach that has received a great deal of attention in the past few years has been called the *psychoeducational strategy.* In the psychoeducational strategy, the goal is to develop in the child those social and academic readiness skills necessary for successful experiences in the school, the home, and society. If a child is not so prepared or is experiencing difficulty, psychiatric and educational personnel jointly plan an intervention program to help the child. The goal of this strategy is not mutually exclusive of that of some of the other approaches; this helps to explain the eclectic nature of the approach. Since the psychoeducational strategy is concerned with the "why" of child behavior and attempts to explain it in psychodynamic terms, it is aligned with the psychodynamic approach. Since behavior is explained in psychiatric terms, there is a need for psychological or psychiatric input on the psychoeducational team. The *life-space* interviewing technique is a basic approach associated with the strategy. In *life-space examination,* "first aid treatment" of behavior is administered on the basis of an analysis of the cause of the behavior. Although it is concerned with the "why" of behavior, it is also concerned with the behavior itself. In this sense, the psychoeducational approach draws from behavior modification theory and practice. Since the psychoeducational strategy attempts to correct or remediate readiness and academic abilities, it is also associated with the learning disability strategy. Since the plan to change behavior may involve cultural bearers as well as cultural violation, the ecological strategy may be subsumed by the psychoeducational strategy (see the following discussion on ecological strategy).

In essence, the psychoeducational strategy is concerned with psychology or psychiatry and education. There is a greater balance between psychiatry and education in this approach, and correspondingly, a more balanced and cooperative planning than would exist in the psychodynamic strategy. As its name implies, the psychoeducational approach gives the teacher and school a larger role in the educational development of the child. Although educational goals are important to this approach, there is an emphasis on acceptance of the child and on positive interpersonal adult-child relationships. Acceptance of the child, however, does not mean acceptance of inappropriate behavior.

Maladaptive behavior precipitates the implementation of the psychoeducational strategy. When such maladaptive behavior occurs, a process of study and planning is implemented. The demands placed on the child, the ability of the child to meet those demands, the child's self-concept, the child's motivation, and the student-student, student-teacher, and student-parent relationships are examined. After such an analysis, a program to remediate the situation is developed. Psychologists, psychiatrists, teachers, administrators, and other professional personnel all play an important role in implementing as well as planning appropriate programs.

ECOLOGICAL STRATEGY

All of the previously discussed strategies have focused on the child and on changing the child. The assumption in these approaches has been that the child exhibits some problem that can be remediated by changing the child. Proponents of the ecological strategy, on the other hand, feel that human problems occur as a result of agitation between the child *(cultural violater)* and the environment *(cultural bearer,* which may include family, sibling, peers, and teachers) and that the remediation of such problems should include consideration of this relationship and should not be limited to psychotherapy, behavior modification, or learning techniques. In a sense, ecological strategy recognizes an ecological discrepancy. Rhodes (1967) very distinctly sets the stage for an understanding of the ecological strategy

> In this alternative view of disturbance it is suggested that the nucleus of the problem lies in the content of behavioral prohibitions and sanctions in the culture. Any behavior which departs significantly from this lore upsets those who have carefully patterned their behavior according to cultural specifications. The subsequent agitated exchange between culture violater and culture bearer creates a disturbance in the environment. It is this reciprocal product which engages attention and leads to subsequent action. (Rhodes, 1967, p. 449)

It is clear that proponents of this view do not wish to limit intervention procedures to the child. The family, peers, teachers, and community at large may be a part of a program. Since they are as much a part of the disorder as the so-called "emotionally disturbed" child, it may be necessary to teach the community to be tolerant of "deviant" or "different" behavior.

One of the best known and most successful projects that has employed the ecological approach is Project Re-Ed for the re-education of emotionally disturbed children, which was developed by Hobbs (1969) and his colleagues. The project was designed to re-educate emotionally disturbed children for a short period of time (four to six months) while treatment was also directed at the family, school, and community. Although the child was removed from the family for approximately six months, the goal was to successfully return the child to his former ecosystem as soon as possible. Project Re-Ed was designed to present experiences that could restore to the child some trust in adults, help the child with academic work, help the child to extinguish behavior that causes rejection and develop behavior that encourages acceptance, arrange successful experiences for the child to enhance confidence and self-respect, develop a sense of responsibility in the child, help the child develop an awareness of the body, promote the child's growth through physical activities, and help the child "have fun." The children in the project established their own goals and a variety of techniques were employed to reach the goals. There is presently some evidence that this approach has been effective in maintaining improved behavior.

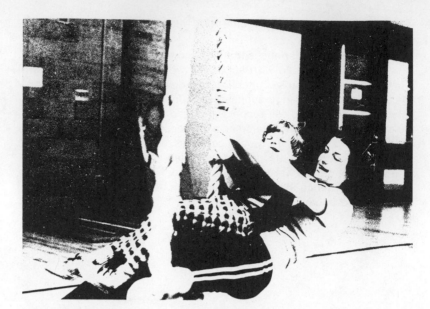

9

ORTHOPEDIC, NEUROLOGICAL AND NEUROMUSCULAR, AND OTHER HANDICAPS

In this chapter orthopedic, neurological and neuromuscular, and other handicapping conditions are described. Amputations, disorders of the hip, spina bifida, talipes, Osgood-Schlatter's disease, torticollis, and spondylolisthesis are discussed in the orthopedic section. Neurological and neuromuscular disorders include muscular dystrophy, epilepsy, cerebral palsy, poliomyelitis, and multiple sclerosis. Other conditions discussed are bronchial asthma, cystic fibrosis (mucoviscidosis), diabetes mellitus, and cardiovascular disorders.

Orthopedic Conditions

Amputations

An *amputation* is the removal or absence of part or all of an extremity. Amputations may be congenital or acquired. In congenital amputation, fetal maldevelopment causes absence of part or all of an extremity that is evidenced at birth. Acquired amputations are generally caused by trauma, tumor, infection, or vascular impairment. Specific causes associated with acquired amputation include car and farm accidents, malignant tumors, diabetes, and arteriosclerosis. Acquired

Figure 9–1. *Left,* terms used to describe deficiencies of limbs from birth defects. *Right,* terms used to describe amputation levels. From: Bleck, Eugene E., "Amputations in Children," in *Physically Handicapped Children — A Medical Atlas for Teachers,* edited by Eugene E. Bleck and Donald A. Nagel. New York: Grune & Stratton, Inc., 1975, p. 17. By permission.

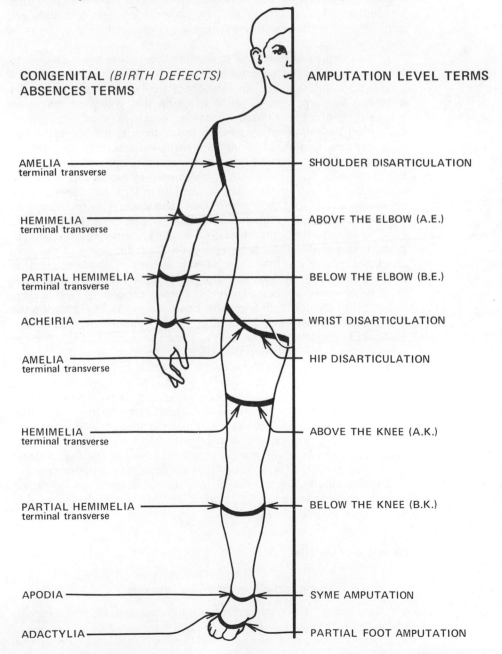

CONGENITAL *(BIRTH DEFECTS)* ABSENCES TERMS

AMELIA
terminal transverse

HEMIMELIA
terminal transverse

PARTIAL HEMIMELIA
terminal transverse

ACHEIRIA

AMELIA
terminal transverse

HEMIMELIA
terminal transverse

PARTIAL HEMIMELIA
terminal transverse

APODIA

ADACTYLIA

AMPUTATION LEVEL TERMS

SHOULDER DISARTICULATION

ABOVE THE ELBOW (A.E.)

BELOW THE ELBOW (B.E.)

WRIST DISARTICULATION

HIP DISARTICULATION

ABOVE THE KNEE (A.K.)

BELOW THE KNEE (B.K.)

SYME AMPUTATION

PARTIAL FOOT AMPUTATION

and congenital amputations are often classified according to the site and level of absence. Further, when an amputation is performed through a joint, it is referred to as a *disarticulation*. Terms used to describe limb deficiencies due to congenital or acquired amputation are presented in Figure 9–1.

According to Adams, Daniel, and Rullman (1972), it has been estimated that there are 311,000 amputees in the United States, of which 32 per cent have lost part or all of the upper extremity and 68 per cent the lower extremity. These authors also report data indicating that 7 per cent of the amputees are under 21 years of age, that the congenital-to-acquired ratio in children is 2:1, and that there are generally more upper-extremity than lower-extremity amputations in the juvenile population.

Treatment of amputations is designed to enable the individual to function as normally as possible, generally through the use of a prosthetic appliance. The application of a prosthetic device may be preceded by surgery to produce a stump that will yield maximum efficiency and comfort. Where possible, a general conditioning program may be employed to prepare the individual for surgical treatment. Adams, Daniel, and Rullman (1972) indicate that the first important phase in treatment occurs after surgery and before fitting of the prosthesis. Such treatment involves care of the stump, including a massaging to aid in the reduction of stump size; bandaging to aid shrinkage and hold dressings in place; and exercising to strengthen muscles and mobilize joints after the stump heals sufficiently.

The selection of a prosthesis is a major undertaking and generally requires a professional team approach. Occupational and personal characteristics of the individual as well as medical realities must be considered in the decision-making. After application, the prosthesis must be checked periodically for fit. Such a procedure is especially important in children, since growth can change the fit. Following the fitting of the prosthesis, the stump must be continually cared for. Particularly important is the need to keep the stump clean to prevent infection, abrasion, and skin disorders.

Once a prosthesis is applied, the individual must develop skill to use and adjust to it. A professional interdisciplinary team consisting of orthopedists, pediatricians, social workers, prosthetists, engineers, physical therapists, occupational therapists, psychiatrists, and psychologists is generally involved in attaining this goal. Important in training is the development of daily living skills for eating, drinking, and dressing. In addition, attention must be given to the development of skills pertaining to play, household activity, and schoolroom activity. Physical therapy is employed to enhance ambulation, to inhibit atrophy and contractures, to improve or maintain body mechanics, and to promote the general physical conditioning of the amputee.

Disorders of the Hip

COXA PLANA (LEGG–CALVE–PERTHES DISEASE)

Coxa plana is a condition of the hip characterized by necrosis (local death of tissue), degeneration, and fragmentation of the epiphysis (growing end of a bone) of the femoral head with regeneration and replacement. Necrosis is caused by a vascular disturbance (lack of blood supply). Although the cause of the condition is unknown, trauma and infection are among the causes more frequently hypothesized. Radiological examinations are used to diagnose the condition and to indicate the nature and severity of degeneration. In some cases involvement is partial, and in other cases there is complete destruction. Coxa plana may affect either hip, most frequently occurs between ages four to ten, predominately affects males, and is bilateral in about 15 per cent of cases (Turek, 1967).

One of the earliest symptoms of the condition is a limp that becomes more gradually pronounced. In addition, patients may complain of stiffness and of an ache in the groin and the inner side of the thigh and knee. Adduction and internal rotation of the hip may be limited, and movement may cause pain (especially toward extremes). Muscle spasm, some muscle atrophy, and tenderness over the anterior aspect of the joint may be exhibited (Turek, 1967).

Coxa plana develops in stages. The early or acute stage is characterized by necrosis and degeneration of the femoral head. As the condition develops, the femoral head becomes flattened and deformed, producing an incongruous joint. The head increases in density, and the forward neck becomes broadened and shortened. During the regenerative stage, newly formed bone replaces necrotic bone. At the chronic stage, when healing is complete, the individual may experience restricted motion and a slight limp but no pain. The cause of the condition is not known but strain and trauma are thought to be most likely.

Treatment for coxa plana varies according to the orthopedist's approach and the specific nature of the situation. In the acute stage, bed rest is often presented. In addition, braces and casts are applied in certain situations. Surgery may be performed to expedite the repair process and enhance the security of the femoral condyle and acetabulum. Complete replacement of the femoral head takes about two or three years (Turek, 1967). During this period of regeneration, emphasis is placed on removing stress on the femoral head by prohibiting weight bearing. Crutches, braces, special casts, and slings are among the devices used to prevent the joint from bearing weight. In the sling-and-crutch method, a sling holding the foot is strapped

Figure 9–2. Legg-Perthes disease. Destruction of the growth center may be partial or complete (as illustrated here) before the reparative process begins. From: Nagel, Donald A., "Temporary Orthopaedic Disabilities in Children," in *Physically Handicapped Children — A Medical Atlas for Teachers,* edited by Eurgene E. Bleck and Donald A. Nagel. New York: Grune & Stratton, Inc., 1975, p. 196. By permission.

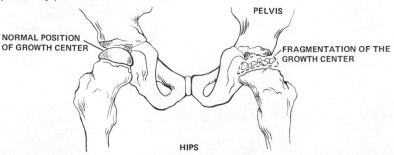

over the shoulder to keep the foot off the ground as the knee and hip are kept in a flexed position. Adams and Puthoff (1975), in suggesting physical activity guidelines for children with developmental hip disorders, indicate that the traditional treatment for children with Legg-Calve-Perthes disease is to prevent weight bearing but report that many orthopedic specialists no longer feel that allowing the affected limb to bear weight is dangerous as long as the leg is abducted so that the femoral shock is reduced. Unfortunately, these authors have cited no research data to justify such a practice. As is true with most diseases, the earlier the treatment procedures are instituted, the greater the possibility of return to normality. Since the effects of congenital hip disorders on participation in physical activity will vary from case to case, program development must be individualized.

ADOLESCENT COXA VARA (SLIPPED FEMORAL EPIPHYSIS)

Coxa vara is a deformity of the hip in which the angle between the neck of the femur and its shaft becomes abnormally decreased. The reduction in angle may have congenital or acquired causes. Coxa vara due to a slipped femoral epiphysis is the most prevalent type, generally occurs between the ages of 11 and 16, and is sometimes referred to as *adolescent coxa vara.* In adolescent coxa vara, the femoral epiphysis usually slips both inferiorly and posteriorly in relation to the neck of the femur. The condition may begin as a slight slip which can later become complete owing to injury. In addition, slips may be partial (in which case the treatment is more effective). Estimates of bilateral hip involvement generally range from 20 to 40 per cent.

The exact cause of the condition is not known. In some cases, it apparently occurs in response to trauma. In explaining the occurrence in other cases, some orthopedists hypothesize that coxa vara is associated with growth hormones. In discussing various explanations, Nagel (1975) states that during adolescence, slippage is easier

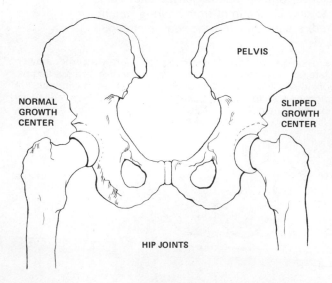

Figure 9–3. Slipped epiphysis. The growth center usually slips inferiorly and posteriorly. From: Nagel, Donald A. "Temporary Orthopaedic Disabilities in Children," in *Physically Handicapped Children — A Medical Atlas for Teachers,* edited by Eugene E. Bleck and Donald A. Nagel. New York: Grune & Stratton, Inc., 1975, p. 198. By permission.

because the relationship of the growth center to the rest of the thigh bone changes from a horizontal to a more vertical plane. He also indicates that an increase of growth hormones in prepuberty is normally followed by an increase in sexual hormones during adolescence that brings about fusion of the growth center with the remainder of the bone. The fact that the disorder generally occurs during rapid growth, in sexually immature individuals, and in girls before boys lends credibility to the hormonal theory. In addition, individuals who develop adolescent coxa vara tend to be obese or extremely tall.

Early symptoms of coxa vara are similar to those associated with coxa plana. The individual may exhibit a limp, some pain in the thigh and knee, a limit in range of motion, and pain on weight bearing. As the condition progresses, shortening of the affected leg leads to increased limping, and external rotation and abduction may be observed during movement. As slippage progresses, greater pain is experienced, and commonly, in the Trendelenburg test, the pelvis tilts downward to the non-affected side as the victim stands on the affected leg.

Treatment for coxa vara may involve arresting slippage by means of bed rest, leg traction, casting, the prevention of weight bearing, and surgical intervention. When appropriate, an operation is performed to affix the epiphysis to the femoral neck by pins or bone grafts. In addition, the epiphysis may be brought to the acetabulum for a more normal and secure articulation. Since the bone is cut in such a procedure, healing time is long. The postoperative period generally lasts from three to six months.

During the postoperative period, weight bearing is contraindicated, and the patient needs crutches for ambulation. Physical therapy during this period involves strengthening the quadriceps and hamstring muscles. Although the child may participate in games, the games should not be strenuous and should not require the affected leg to bear weight.

CONGENITAL HIP DISLOCATION

The term *congenital* or *developmental hip dislocation* refers to conditions in which the femoral head may be partially displaced upward (subluxated) or completely displaced from the acetabulum. Although the actual cause is not known, hereditary trends are apparent. The condition may be caused by faulty prenatal development and abnormal birth conditions. According to Turek (1967), females are more commonly affected than males (the ratio is 9:1). The condition is more prevalent in the left hip than the right, and involvement is generally unilateral. Since the disorder is congenital, treatment generally will be instituted before school age. Thus, professionals in education will usually deal with children with a history of congenital hip dislocation rather than with children in the acute stages of the disorder.

Certain characteristics, although not present in every case, are associated with congenital hip dislocation. Displacement may be caused by a shallowness, smallness, or improper formation of the acetabular fossa, which fails to provide adequate bone support or resistance to upward muscular pull or weight bearing. Defective development of the acetabulum is called *dysplasia*. As the condition develops, the fossa may fill with fibrofatty tissue. In complete dislocation, the femoral head is displaced upward and backward and characteristically pushes the joint capsule against the ilium to form a "false" acetabulum. Muscle and ligament deviations occur in response to displacement. The rectus femoris, hamstrings, and adductors may become hypershortened, and the gluteus medius and gluteus minimus may exhibit weakness. Tension of the iliopsoas in response to displacement of the femoral head may lead to lordotic and scoliotic vertebral deviations.

Symptoms vary according to the nature of the involvement. According to Turek (1967), folds in the groin area, below the buttocks, and along the thighs display asymmetry on the affected side in infants. A click may be heard if the femoral head slips over the acetabular rim in cases of partial dislocation. In cases of complete dislocation, the femoral head can be felt, the affected extremity is shortened, and the limb can be displaced by pressure. Limping, of course, would be evidenced if the child were old enough to walk. The trochanter of the affected side is prominent. A waddling gait is evidenced as a response to bilateral involvement. Unilateral involvement is associated with a "positive" Trendelenburg test and, according to Turek (1967), may be demonstrated by the Allis sign (the knee of the affected limb lies at a lower level when the infant lies on the back, flexes the knees, and rests the feet on the supporting surface). Initially, the child may exhibit little or no discomfort or pain. As range of motion is reduced and deformities develop, greater pain and discomfort may be expected. Radiological examination is, of course, employed to determine the specific nature of the condition.

Treatment for this disorder depends on the child's age and whether it is partial displacement or complete dislocation. The earlier the treatment is administered, the greater the possibility of developing normal locomotion. For infants, treatment for displacement typically involves abducting the hip to place the femoral head in the acetabulum and splinting for a period of three months to a year (Turek, 1967). When dislocation is complete, closed reduction and casting may be employed. In older individuals, treatment is more likely to consist of open reduction and surgical procedures designed to remold the socket. As the age of the child increases, placing the head in its normal position is more difficult, and muscles, ligaments, and other tissues resist reduction and may need altering. Treatment at later stages generally involves traction, casting, and surgery. Physical therapy is given as soon as possible. Although all muscles involved in hip movement need development, particular attention is given to the development of the hip adductors and extensors.

Spina Bifida

Spina bifida is an open defect (or a lack of closure) of one or more neural arches of the spinal vertebrae, through which contents of the spinal column may protrude. Such defects result from abnormal de-

Figure 9–4. Spina bifida occulta. From: Deaver, G. C., Buck, D., and McCarthy, J.: Spina Bifida, in Krusen, F. H., Elkins, E. C., and Deaver, G. C. (eds.): 1951 YEAR BOOK OF PHYSICAL MEDICINE AND REHABILITATION. Copyright © 1952 by Year Book Medical Publishers, Inc., Chicago. Used by permission.

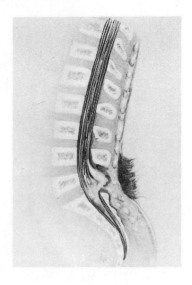

velopment of the fetus, and the incidence of occurrence is between 0.1 and 4.13 per 1000 live births (Bleck, 1975b). The condition does not appear to be associated with definite genetic patterns. Although the cause of spina bifida is not known, Bleck (1975b) indicates that the neural tube fails to develop completely and to close in the first 30 days of pregnancy, and he speculates that the cause may be a virus or some other unidentified noxious agent. Although defects generally occur in the lumbar region, thoracic and sacral segments of the spine may also be affected. How the disorder affects motor and other functioning depends on the location and severity of involvement.

Three types that have been differentiated are *spina bifida occulta, meningocele,* and *myelomeningocele. Spina bifida occulta,* the mildest type, involves a defect in the fusion of the posterior neural arch. There is no protrusion by the meninges or spinal cord. The

Figure 9–5. Spina bifida with meningocele. From: Deaver, G. C., Buck, D., and McCarthy, J.: Spina Bifida, in Krusen, F. H., Elkins, E. C., and Deaver, G. C. (eds.): 1951 YEAR BOOK OF PHYSICAL MEDICINE AND REHABILITATION. Copyright © 1952 by Year Book Medical Publishers, Inc., Chicago. Used by permission.

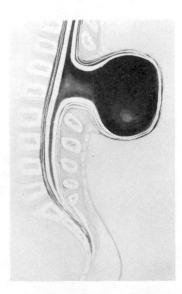

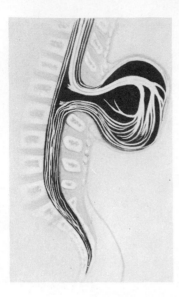

Figure 9–6. Spina bifida with meningomyelocele. From: Deaver, G. C., Buck, D., and McCarthy, J.: Spina Bifida, in Krusen, F. H., Elkins, E. C., and Deaver, G. C. (eds.): 1951 YEAR BOOK OF PHYSICAL MEDICINE AND REHABILITA- TION. Copyright © 1952 by Year Book Medical Publishers, Inc., Chicago. Used by permission.

defect is covered with skin and perhaps a growth of hair. Although there may be some sensitivity to touch in the area involved, the con- dition is generally otherwise asymptomatic.

In the *meningocele* type, the coverings of the spinal cord (men- inges) protrude, forming a sac that is externally observable. The dural sac lies beneath the skin and subcutaneous covering and con- tains spinal fluid. Care must be taken to protect the sac, since infec- tion of the spinal fluid (leading to meningitis) may occur if the sac is ruptured or if spinal fluid leaks through the sac coverings. The sac does not contain neural elements. This condition, like spina bifida occulta, is rarely associated with neurological disabilities.

The most common and most severe type is *myelomeningocele.* In this condition, the protruding sac contains the meninges, portions of the spinal cord, and nerve roots. This condition is always associated with neurological defect and generally associated with hydrocephaly. Because herniation involves the spinal cord and nerve roots, flaccid paralysis of the lower limbs and trunk occurs. The exact location and extent of paralysis depends on the area of spinal cord involvement. Partial paralysis leads to muscular imbalance, which contributes to bone deformities such as equinovarus (club foot), calcaneal valgus, hip dislocation, scoliosis, kyphosis, and lordosis. Again, depending on the location of spinal cord involvement, loss of skin sensitivity to pain, temperature, and touch may occur, leading to skin problems. Bowel and bladder paralysis are commonly associated with the con- dition. Since infections may be caused by the child's inability to empty the bladder, care must be taken to manage bowel and bladder control.

Treatment includes surgical closure in cases of the meningocele and myelomeningocele types. Hydrocephaly is treated as early as possible by the drainage of cerebral spinal fluid. Orthopedic surgery is employed to reduce bone deformities. Depending on the severity of the condition, braces, crutches, or a wheelchair may be employed to increase support and enhance ambulation. Physical activity is beneficial to strengthen weak muscles and to maintain maximum use of unaffected parts of the body. Attention is given to preventing obesity, preventing and treating infections, and providing a proper diet. Bladder and bowel training plays an important role in treatment. Because of the possibility of urine stagnation and subsequent infection, periodic medical evaluations are indicated. Drainage systems vary but generally include collecting bags or catheters. Bladder and bowel training is critical for normal development and well-being and should be supervised by a urologist and a pediatrician.

Talipes (Clubfoot)

Talipes, commonly called clubfoot, is a gross foot deformity. Although the condition may be acquired as a result of or in association with various neuromuscular diseases, it is most commonly congenital. Since neuromuscular diseases are discussed in other sections, the discussion in this section will emphasize the congenital type. Although the cause of congenital talipes is not known, possible causes that have been advanced include inheritance, abnormal tendon insertion, arrest in fetal development, intra-uterine pressure, and muscular imbalance.

Whether acquired or congenital, the following terms serve as the basis for describing the direction of deformities:

1. Equinus — a plantar flexed forefoot in which the toes are lower than the heels.
2. Calcaneus — a dorsiflexed forefoot in which the heels are lower than the toes.
3. Varus — an inverted (turned in) heel and forefoot causing the plantar surface of the foot to face medially.
4. Valgus — an everted (turned out) heel and forefoot causing the plantar surface of the foot to face laterally.
5. Equinovarus — combination of equinus and varus.
6. Equinovalgus — combination of equinus and valgus.
7. Calcaneovarus — combination of calcaneus and varus.
8. Calcaneovalgus — combination of calcaneus and valgus.

Turek (1967) reports that equinovarus is the most common type of talipes, accounting for 95 per cent of cases. In this condition, inversion and plantar flexion are created and maintained by shortening of tendons and contraction of muscles and liagments. In response to these pressures, bone deformities occur, and bone growth may be inhibited. If the deformity is allowed to continue, the individual begins to walk on the outside of the foot and ankle.

Conservative treatment is employed in cases diagnosed early. Such treatment involves manipulation to stretch contracted tissue and subsequent casting, splinting, or special shoes to maintain the position. In older individuals, and for cases failing to respond to conservative treatment, surgery may be performed. Manipulation or exercise for the purpose of correcting clubfoot must be implemented under direct medical supervision.

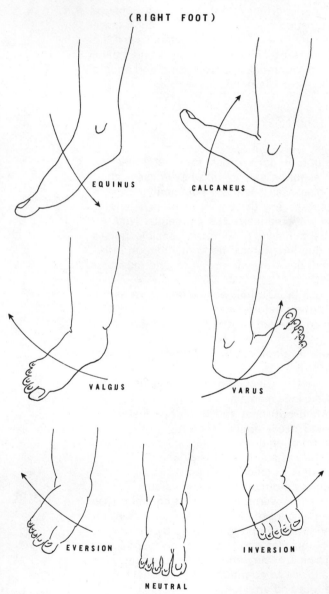

Figure 9–7. Terminology of foot abnormalities or positions. From: Caillet, Rene. *Foot and Ankle Pain.* Philadelphia: F. A. Davis Co., 1976, p. 58.

Figure 9–8. Talipes equinovarus: "club-foot." Talipes equinovarus or clubfoot has an inflexible adducted forefoot and a varus heel. The toes are usually flexed. The medial tissues of the foot and ankle are contracted, the Achilles tendon is shortened, and there is usually some internal tibial torsion. These deformities resist passive stretching. From: Caillet, Rene. *Foot and Ankle Pain.* Philadelphia: F. A. Davis Co., 1976, p. 76.

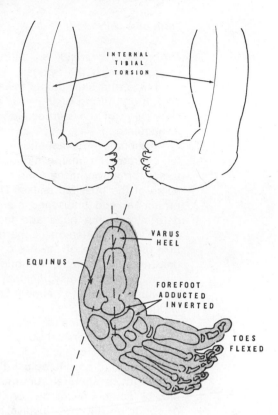

Osgood-Schlatter's Disease

Osgood-Schlatter's disease is a painful swelling about the tibial tubercle associated with enlargement and partial or complete separation of the tubercle from the tibia. Since the quadriceps tendon is attached to the tubercle of the tibia, one of the primary causes for the condition is believed to be strain resulting from the pulling and stretching of this tendon during movement. Other causes include direct injury and abnormal alignment of the legs. It is a condition most frequently observed in boys between the ages of 11 and 15.

Although it tends to recur, Osgood-Schlatter's disease may have a sudden onset and a short duration. In many cases, the condition ceases before age 18, if fusion of the tubercle with the tibia takes place without medical treatment. In more severe cases, treatment may involve casting to maintain the knee in complete extension. In cases of prolonged disability, an operation may be performed to enhance fusion and to remove detached fragments.

Because the quadriceps tendon is involved, pain during contraction of the quadriceps may be expected. Further, continued activity tends to aggravate and further inflame the condition. Thus, exercise of the affected extremity is contraindicated during the acute stage. In fact, immobilization of the knee through casting may be expected if the condition persists. It is not uncommon for vigorous use of the affected leg to be prohibited for six months or longer.

Torticollis (Wryneck)

Torticollis or *wryneck* is a tilting of the head toward one side with a rotation toward the opposite side. Thus, if the head is tilted to the right side, the chin points toward the left side. It is characterized by flexion and tilting of the head and often is associated with a hyper-shortening of the sternocleidomastoid muscle. It may be congenital or acquired.

Although the exact etiology of congenital torticollis is not known, fetal intrauterine malposition, circulation difficulties during labor, and tumor formation in the child's sternocleidomastoid are believed to be some of the possible causes (Turek, 1967). Characteristics include a prominent and shortened sternocleidomastoid and, at later stages, deformity of the head and face. Other common characteristics include hypershortening of the musculature and the soft tissue structure on one side of the neck, paralysis on one side, and congenital deformity of the spine. Although it varies with the nature of the condition, treatment may include passive movement and surgery. It is recommended that treatment begin as early in the life of the infant as is possible.

Acquired torticollis may be caused by a sprain, dislocation, or fracture of the cervical spine; neuritis of the spinal accessory nerve; infection of the cervical spine; and poliomyelitis (Turek, 1967). Hearing, sight, and psychological disturbances may lead to habit patterns that produce postural abnormalities. The acquired type of torticollis may be acute, spasmodic, or chronic. Treatment varies with the type of condition and may involve traction, heat, a soft collar, rest, sedation, surgery, correction of faulty habits, massage, and physical therapy. In certain cases, exercises may be employed to stretch the affected muscle and to strengthen and shorten the contralateral muscle. Corrective exercises are often a part of physical therapy and are conducted under medical supervision.

Spondylolisthesis

Spondylolisthesis is a condition of the spine characterized by a forward vertebral displacement generally owing to defects in the posterior arch. If posterior arch defects are present but forward displacement has not occurred, the condition is referred to as *spondylolysis* or *prespondylolisthesis* (Turek, 1967). The fifth lumbar vertebra is the usual site of involvement. The exact cause of neural arch defects is not known; however, congenital, developmental, and traumatic causes have been proposed. Some researchers distinguish types of spondylolisthesis according to origin, i.e., traumatic and congenital (true) spondylolisthesis.

In certain cases, the condition is mild, and the patient may exhibit no symptoms and may feel little or no pain. If the condition progresses, however, the individual may experience pain and discomfort when moving, when straightening the back from a bent position, or when extending or hyperextending the trunk. In spondylolisthesis resulting from injury, pain and other symptoms may be evidenced immediately. Other associated signs or symptoms include lower back pain, a lordotic condition, and pain in the thighs and legs.

In many cases, pain may be relieved by bed rest. Discomfort may be reduced or prevented by developing or maintaining a proper functional posture, by emphasizing the use of the legs rather than the back in lifting, and by avoiding extension or hyperextension of the back. Stress may also be reduced by the maintenance of proper body weight and mechanics, particularly during pregnancy. In severe cases, surgical intervention may be required.

Neurological and Neuromuscular Conditions

Muscular Dystrophy

The Muscular Dystrophy Association of America defines *muscular dystrophy* as "a general designation for a group of chronic diseases whose most prominent characteristic is the progressive degeneration of the skeletal or voluntary musculature." Muscular dystrophy is further characterized by muscular weakness and atrophy. Although most victims come from families with a history of muscular dystrophy, spontaneous mutation causes the condition to appear in people without family history of the disease. The hereditary pattern of transmission varies with the different types of muscular dystrophy. With the most common type (pseudohypertrophic or Duchenne), the tendency is carried as a recessive trait by an unaffected female, and with other types the hereditary defect may be transmitted by either or both parents.

Although some research progress is being made, the exact cause of muscular dystrophy is not yet known. It appears to be a metabolic disorder resulting in the inability to properly metabolize foodstuffs for use by the body, particularly vitamin E. Although the site of the primary lesion is not known, the disorder evidently causes a progressively defective state of nutrition in the muscles, leading to weakness and atrophy. Striated muscle degenerates and is replaced by fat and fibrous tissue.

The diagnosis of muscular dystrophy includes the identification of female carriers and the analysis of enzymes, biopsy samples, and electromyographic readings. An analysis of family medical history helps to trace hereditary patterns. In addition, symptoms of the victim play an important role in distinguishing muscular dystrophy from other diseases of the muscular system.

No effective treatment has been found for muscular dystrophy. Medical efforts attempt to relieve symptoms and counteract complications. Treatment is provided to combat respiratory infections, cardiac failure, and obesity. Physical activity and preventive bracing are also part of treatment programs. None of the forms of treatment has a curative effect on the disease, but all of them serve to enhance the quality and length of the patient's life.

Although the disease is generally classified according to the age of onset and the location of involved musculature, classifications of muscular dystrophy have changed and will probably continue to change as more is known about its etiology. The characteristics of three major and relatively well-defined types are presented below. Distal, congenital, ocular, and ocular-pharyngeal types are less common, generally less well-defined, and more specialized and thus will not be considered further here.

PSEUDOHYPERTROPHIC (DUCHENNE)

Pseudohypertrophic muscular dystrophy is the most prevalent, most progressive, and most serious type. It is much more prevalent in males than in females, since it is transmitted through the female and predominantly affects male offspring. The disease occasionally appears soon after birth, but it generally begins between the ages of 2 and 6. The disease may be detected before classical symptoms appear. Although antibiotics have prolonged survival beyond this time in some patients, death generally occurs within ten years of onset. Since the victim becomes progressively weakened and unable to combat infections, death usually results from chest infection with respiratory failure and sometimes is precipitated by cardiac failure.

Initial muscle involvement occurs in the proximal muscles of the pelvic girdle. Weakness gradually spreads to the muscles of the trunk and shoulder girdle. Involvement of the muscles of the pelvic area results in lordosis and a waddling gait. During early stages, the child exhibits difficulty in rising from the floor and in ascending stairs. As weakness spreads to the shoulder girdle, asymmetrical involvement may result in scoliosis. Clumsy walking with a tendency to fall, delayed and awkward walking, and inability to run are other symptoms of the disease. A common sign (known as Gower's sign) of this condition is the tendency of a child to "walk up" the lower limbs with the hands when asked to get up from a sitting position on the floor.

The predominant characteristic of this type of muscular dystrophy is enlargement of calf and mastication muscles. Pseudohypertrophy occurs occasionally but less often in the deltoid, quadricep, and other muscles. The pseudohypertrophic state is caused by increased deposits of fat that replace wasting muscle tissue. It is rare for victims to show no enlargement of muscles during any phase of the disease. It must be pointed out that growth may temporarily exceed the deteriorating effects caused by the disease, giving the appearance of improvement. However, this is a false impression, since deterioration is progressive.

The nature of the condition reduces participation in physical activity, because strength and endurance are poor. Muscular weakness makes rising from the floor, walking, running, and even sitting erect difficult as the disease progresses. Unevenness of muscle involvement causes imbalance of muscular strength in different parts of the body. Walton and Gardner-Medwin (1974) report that at later stages there is almost invariably severe scoliosis, widespread decalcification, and early gross distortions and disorganization of the skeletal system. These authors feel that such changes make bones very susceptible to fracture and that bone changes are the result of disease, absence of normal muscular stresses and strains, and abnormal postures of the body and extremities as the disease progresses. Cardiac involvement is quite common in later stages. In addition, intellectual retardation is common in this type of muscular dystrophy (Walton and Gardner-Medwin, 1974).

Figure 9–9. Increased lumbar lordosis— trunk extension to maintain balance. Photograph courtesy of Irwin M. Siegel, M.D.

As weakness and contracture progress, various observable phenomena occur. These overlap in occurrence and many take place concurrently in response to muscle weakness. In studying the "pathomechanics" of stance in Duchenne muscular dystrophy, Siegel (1972) identified the following phenomena: (1) lumbar lordosis and hip flexion in an attempt to maintain torso balance as hip extensors and shoulder stabilizers weaken (Fig. 9–9), (2) toe walking in response to weight shifts and hip abduction to widen the base of support as equilibrium becomes more precarious (Fig. 9–10), (3) broad base stance and a waddling gait as the tensor fascia lata continue to contract and ankle varus as the child attempts to align the axes of the ankle and knee joints (Fig. 9–11), (4) a true hypertrophy of the triceps surae (Fig. 9–12), (5) equinocavovarus as the tensor fascia lata continues to contract and the base of support widens further (Fig. 9–13), and (6) the myopathic stance (Fig. 9–14) characterized by pseudohypertrophy, lumbar lordosis, hip flexion and abduction, ankle equinus, and calcaneocavovarus of the feet. In later stages, braces are applied to aid the child in sitting and maintaining an upright position. Although braces may delay the progress to wheelchair and bed, the latter are inevitable as the muscle wasting process continues.

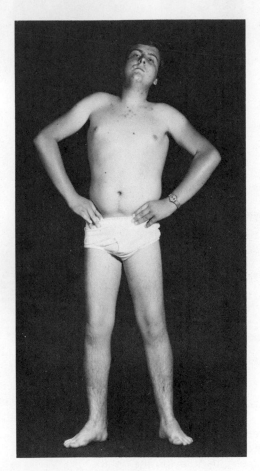

Figure 9-10. Hip abduction—increases base of support. Photograph courtesy of Irwin M. Siegel, M.D.

Figure 9-11. Ankle varus—an attempt to align the axes of ankle and knee joints. From: Siegel, Irwin M., "Pathomechanics of Stance in Duchenne Muscular Dystrophy," *Arch. Phys. Med. and Rehab.* 50: 403–406, 1972, p. 404.

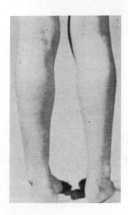

Figure 9–12.   Exercise hypertrophy of triceps surae. From: Siegel, Irwin M., "Pathomechanics of Stance in Duchenne Muscular Dystrophy," *Arch. Phys. Med. and Rehab.* 50:403–406, 1972, p. 404.

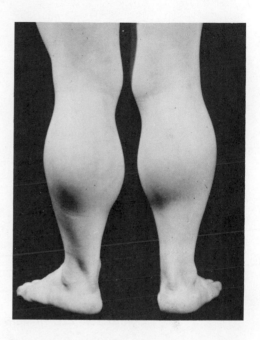

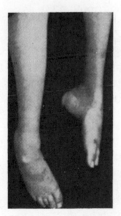

Figure 9–13.   Equinocavovarus foot deformity. From: Siegel, Irwin M., "Pathomechanics of Stance in Duchenne Muscular Dystrophy," *Arch. Phys. Med. and Rehab.* 50:403–406, 1972, p. 404.

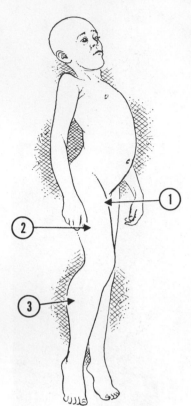

Figure 9–14. Contracted musculature contributing to myopathic stance and gait. (1) Hip flexors; (2) tensor fascia lata; (3) triceps surae. From: Siegel, Irwin M., "Pathomechanics of Stance in Duchenne Muscular Dystrophy," *Arch. Phys. Med. and Rehab.* 50:403–406, 1972, p. 405.

FACIO–SCAPULO–HUMERAL (LANDOUZY–DEJERINE)

The *facio-scapulo-humeral* type of muscular dystrophy is the second most common type, occurring as often in girls as in boys, and appearing generally in early adolescence but occasionally as late as the middle twenties. It is transmitted usually as an autosomal dominant trait by either parent with 50 per cent probability of incidence among offspring. Although life span is rarely shortened by this type of muscular dystrophy, considerable disability may be suffered, and death from respiratory infection may occur in middle life in more rapidly progressive cases. Although severity is variable, this type is progressive. Generally, progress is relatively slow and "plateaus" occur.

First symptoms are usually seen in early adolescence. Initially, the muscles of the face are involved, inhibiting facial mobility and the ability to elevate the angle of the mouth, to whistle, or to drink through a straw. Early symptoms also appear in the shoulder girdle, causing difficulty in raising the arms over the head and a characteristic forward sloping of the shoulders. Other symptoms may include inability to close the eyes completely, even during sleep. Hypertrophy is rare but may occur at the calves and deltoids. Since the course of the disease is progressive, eventual involvement of most voluntary muscles is characteristic. However, involvement is mild when compared with that in the pseudohypertrophic form. Involvement of musculature produces a "winging" of the scapulae, elevation of the scapulae when the arms are abducted, and lordosis. The asymmetry of muscle weakness may result in the development of scoliosis. On the other hand, muscle contractures and skeletal deformities are rare, and the range of intelligence of people with facio-scapulo-humeral muscular dystrophy is normal.

LIMB–GIRDLE (INCLUDING JUVENILE TYPE)

The hereditary pattern of the *limb-girdle* type of muscular dystrophy is usually autosomal recessive. Thus, both parents must carry the defective gene for the disease to become manifest, and boys and girls are equally affected. The probability of carrying but normal offspring is 50 per cent, of clinically affected offspring is 25 per cent, and of offspring completely free of the defect is 25 per cent. Onset is generally in the middle teens or early twenties. The major difference between this type and the facio-scapulo-humeral type is that generally no facial involvement occurs in the limb-girdle type. Initial involvement usually occurs in the proximal muscles of the pelvic or shoulder girdle. The rate of muscle wasting varies, but it is never as rapid as in the Duchenne type, and patients may have a normal life span. Pseudohypertrophy may occur, and girdle wasting, the typical lordotic condition, and waddling gait are seen. If they occur at all, muscular contractions and skeletal deformity develop later in the disease.

Epilepsy

Epilepsy is a general term used to label a condition in which a disturbance in the brain becomes outwardly manifested. It is not a disease per se but a symptom or clinical syndrome characterized by recurrent seizures and convulsions that may result in disturbances in consciousness. Two broad types of epilepsy, classified according to cause, are *idiopathic* and *symptomatic*. In the *idiopathic* type, sometimes referred to as "true" epilepsy, structural damage or disease of the nervous system is absent but liability of recurrent attacks resulting in seizures and convulsions is present. These symptoms are believed to be caused by transient disturbances in the electrochemical activity of the brain. In essence, electrical impulses of the brain become overactive in their discharge. The brain of the epileptic is otherwise normal. *Symptomatic* epilepsy, on the other hand, may result from a variety of factors, including infections, head injuries, abnormality of prenatal conditions, malnutrition, birth injuries, and brain tumors.

Epilepsy is not disfiguring or painful, and the personality, intelligence, and abilities of epileptics are as varied as those of the general population. The notion that epilepsy causes retardation or psychological peculiarities is erroneous. Although it is generally associated with childhood and adolescence, epilepsy may occur at any age. The cause of the idiopathic type is not known, but there is some tendency for it to be inherited.

TYPES

The central feature of epilepsy is seizure, and the types of epilepsy have been classified by the kinds of seizures exhibited. Four types commonly identified include *grand mal* (great illness), *petit mal* (little illness), focal, and psychomotor seizures.

The grand mal type is most common. Grand mal seizures are characterized by convulsions and complete unconsciousness. In about one half of cases, grand mal seizures are signaled by an *aura.* During the aura, the patient may experience feelings of nausea or trembling, a flash of light, dizziness, numbness, tingling in the hands, a strange smell, or pain in the extremities or stomach. The aura is the beginning of the attack itself, and may provide the epileptic with enough time to lie down and perhaps remove false teeth. When the warning that precedes the attack lasts for several hours, the name *prodrome* is applied to it (Scott, 1973). This much less common warning is described by Scott (1973) as including a feeling of tension, depression, excitement, or elation. After the aura, the epileptic may cry out, indicating that the seizure itself has begun. The arms and legs may become stiff and there may be a rigid contraction of the muscles of the chest and other parts of the body. There may be a momentary cessation of breathing, during which time the face may turn to a blue-grey color. The eyes may roll up, but the heart continues to beat. As the seizure continues, other characteristics evidenced include loss of consciousness; violent jerking of the head, arms, and legs; excessive saliva flow; vomiting; loss of bladder and bowel control; biting of the tongue or cheek; and profuse sweating. After the seizure, which usually lasts only a few minutes, the epileptic generally falls into a deep sleep. The individual may be confused and exhausted but usually has no memory of the episode.

Petit mal seizures are characterized by sudden but brief losses of consciousness. This type of seizure is often seen in children and generally disappears after adolescence. The victim may appear to daydream, stare, or show a blank look for a few minutes. Rhythmic blinking of the eyes, flickering movements of the face, and jerking movements of the arms (*myoclonic jerks*) are associated with seizures. Difficult to diagnose, petit mal seizures may be unnoticed or easily thought to be inattentive behavior. There is no recovery stage in this type of seizure. Although not characteristic of petit mal seizures, loss of balance and falling may occur if the attack becomes more generalized. It is not uncommon for an individual to have petit mal seizures several times a day. Children experiencing such seizures are subject to the convulsive type as well.

In the focal seizure, the subject generally remains alert and is thus able to give an account of the experience. As the name suggests, focal seizures begin in and may be limited to a particular area of the body. There may, however, be a spreading to other parts of the body (*Jacksonian seizure*). Seizures may consist of jerking or stiffening of muscles, or they may produce numbness, tingling, or heaviness in a part of the body. For example, a focal seizure may begin as twitching, tingling, or numbness in the distal portions of the hand or foot or as an involuntary movement of the thumb. With a Jacksonian seizure, the entire extremity may be affected. Sometimes, this type of seizure may precede convulsive seizures. Although there are different types of focal seizures, they generally last for only a few minutes, leaving a feeling of weakness in the affected area.

A fourth type of seizure, often mistaken as a psychiatric disorder, is known as *psychomotor seizure*. Although the exact location varies with individuals, this type of seizure begins in one small part of the brain and results in a variety of behaviors. The patient often exhibits a blank look and then begins some kind of repetitive and "automatic" behavior. The activity of the individual is often relatively complex and may appear to be purposeful. Examples include chewing, stroking the hair, rubbing the leg, repeating various phrases, or wandering aimlessly. At times, temper tantrums, hyperactivity, inactivity, confusion, or other nonsocial behaviors may be exhibited. Psychomotor seizures are characterized by a clouding of consciousness and a partial loss of contact with reality. As Scott (1973) explains, the patient is not unconscious but in a kind of dream, and thus able to remember little, if anything, of what happened during the seizure. Attacks are generally over after a few minutes. Psychomotor seizures are the only type exhibited by some patients, but they can occur in patients who also experience grand mal and petit mal seizures.

DIAGNOSIS AND TREATMENT

The diagnosis of epilepsy has become much more sophisticated in recent years. Basic to examination is a complete medical history. From the patient's medical history, it is possible to obtain information about the nature and severity of seizures, the state of consciousness during seizures, behavior during recovery, circumstances of birth, and health history of the family. In addition to a general physical examination, a neurological examination is performed to obtain further information about the causes and nature of the seizures. Electroencephalogram recordings are taken in order to determine the nature and location of brain overactivity, and x-rays are administered to ascertain skull and brain abnormalities. Spinal fluid, blood, and urine analyses are also included in diagnostic examination.

If the patient has symptomatic epilepsy, it can be cured through elimination of the cause. The treatment of idiopathic epilepsy, however, involves control rather than cure. Anticonvulsant drugs such as phenobarbital, Dilantin, Mysoline, Tridione, and Zarontin are employed to control and reduce seizures. The drug or combination of drugs selected varies according to the type of seizure and the effect of the drug on the patient. The plan of medication has to be developed by a physician, since there is no one drug treatment applicable for every epileptic. It is especially important that the patient report any reactions to the therapy and cooperate fully with the physician. Drowsiness, dizziness, irritability, skin rash, and lack of coordination are not uncommon side effects of drugs. The importance of these side effects must be weighed, of course, with the benefits of the therapy. In addition to the administration of anti-convulsant drugs, it is not uncommon for electroencephalograms and blood tests to be taken at regular intervals. It is generally thought that most patients given anticonvulsants can have their seizures fully controlled or can have the frequency of their seizures reduced to the extent that they may lead relatively normal lives.

Since emotional stress, idleness, fatigue, lack of sleep, constipation, illness, alcoholic beverages, irregular use of medication, and menstruation tend to make seizures occur more frequently, care must be taken to avoid or reduce the effect of these conditions. Since these factors may influence the effectiveness of medication, epileptics should discuss methods of dealing with them with their physicians.

In addition to physical treatment, attention must be given to the social and psychological adjustment of the epileptic. Various misconceptions about epilepsy have frequently led to reactions of misunderstanding, rejection, fear, and prejudice. To combat such misconceptions, it is important for the general public to understand epilepsy, to lay aside ignorance and learn about the condition. Teachers and other professionals in contact with the child during the developmental years must be aware of the epilepsy and must help the child deal with the social and psychological problems that arise. With this help, children can be integrated into their school environment and will be allowed to engage in normal play and recreational activities. As they become adults, epileptics can generally work, marry, have children, drive a car, and engage in everyday activities. Although the disorder creates certain limitations, they are generally not so severe that the epileptic cannot lead a full, happy, and nearly normal life. It must be stressed that for the majority of epileptics, control or reduction of the frequency of seizures is possible so that they do not significantly interfere with education, play, or employment. Methods of dealing with social and psychological adjustment problems should be constantly discussed with qualified professionals.

Cerebral Palsy

Although the precise definition of cerebral palsy varies among authoritative individuals and groups, there is general agreement about the central features of the condition. It is a disorder characterized by disturbances in voluntary motor functioning resulting from lesions in the brain that affect the motor control centers. Cerebral palsy is a nonprogressive condition rather than a disease arising out of malfunction of or damage to the brain. The condition may be characterized by mental, sensory, and psychological disturbances as well as motor dysfunction. As Perlstein and Hood (1964) point out, "cerebral palsy is not a single disease entity, but comprises a group of syndromes with the common denominator of a chronic motor disability due to involvement of the motor control center of the brain." After reviewing and analyzing various definitions, Keats (1965) indicates that *cerebral palsy* is a general term designating any paralyzing weakness, incoordination, or functional deviation of the motor system resulting from intracranial lesion. Since the brain is the center not only of muscle control but of intelligence, behavior control, and personality, many human functions may be affected. Depending on the location of the lesion and the degree of involvement, brain injury may result in convulsion, motor paralysis of the extremities, mental deficiencies, personality problems, or sensory disturbances such as hearing loss and visual defects. Cerebral palsy, then, is a nonprogressive complex clinical entity that gives rise to a multitude of handicaps. It is particularly important to note that although mental retardation, sensory disturbances, and personality problems can result from intracranial lesion, such conditions may not necessarily occur. It is clear that the syndromes associated with cerebral palsy vary in type and degree.

It is well known that cerebral palsy usually occurs before, during, or shortly after birth. In a study of 4546 cases, Perlstein and Hood (1964) found that cerebral palsy was acquired in 14 per cent of cases and congenital in 86 per cent of cases. The condition was considered acquired if it occurred at some time after the first two weeks of life and congenital if it occurred before that time. Prenatal causative factors of cerebral palsy that have been cited include irradiation during the first trimester of pregnancy; maternal infections (such as rubella and syphilis); prenatal anoxia (caused by placental abnormalities, maternal anoxia, or cord anomalies); cerebral hemorrhage; blood incompatibility (Rh factor); premature birth; maternal metabolic disturbances (particularly diabetes mellitus); and other functional disturbances of the mother (such as high blood pressure).

The most common paranatal causes may be separated into two groups. The first group consists of the conditions that produce anoxia. Examples are excessive premedication of the mother, inappropriate drug administration during labor, prolonged labor, rapid delivery, excessive forcep pressure, cyanosis, atelectasis, and congenital pneumonia. These conditions often cause respiratory suppression or obstruction leading to inadequate oxygen supply to the brain. The second group of paranatal conditions are those that produce cerebral hemorrhage. They include prolonged labor, birth trauma, excessive forcep pressure, breech birth (feet first), caesarean section, and spontaneous delivery.

The chief postnatal or acquired causes of cerebral palsy are encephalopathy, skull injury due to accidents, meningitis, and vascular accidents. Cerebral palsy is most frequently caused by paranatal conditions and least frequently by postnatal or acquired conditions.

TYPES

The Nomenclature and Classification Committee of the American Academy of Cerebral Palsy has developed generally acceptable classifications of cerebral palsy. The following classification is based on limb involvement and is referred to as a *topographical classification.*

1. *Monoplegia* is a rare condition that involves one limb.
2. *Paraplegia* generally includes the spastic type or rigid type and involves only lower limbs.
3. *Hemiplegia* usually includes the spastic type but athetoid and rigid types are seen; it involves upper and lower limbs on the same side.
4. *Triplegia* generally includes the spastic type and involves three extremities, usually two legs and an arm.
5. *Quadriplegia* is involvement of all four extremities.
6. *Diplegia* is major involvement in lower limbs and minor involvement in upper limbs.
7. *Double hemiplegia* involves upper limbs more than the lower limbs; this term is seldom used.

A second classification developed by the American Academy for Cerebral Palsy in 1956 was a physiological classification derived from observable symptoms. The most common of these types are spasticity, athetosis, ataxia, tremor, and rigidity; they will be discussed in the following pages. Those that will not be further discussed are the atonic type, which is extremely rare and usually develops into athetosis, and the mixed type, which involves some combination of the other types. It is

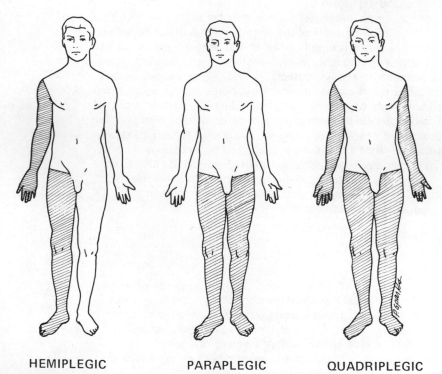

HEMIPLEGIC   PARAPLEGIC   QUADRIPLEGIC

Figure 9–15. Terminology according to limb involvement in cerebral palsy. From: Bleck, Eugene E., "Cerebral Palsy," in *Physically Handicapped Children — A Medical Atlas for Teachers,* edited by Eugene E. Bleck and Donald A. Nagel. New York: Grune & Stratton, Inc., 1975, p. 38. By permission.

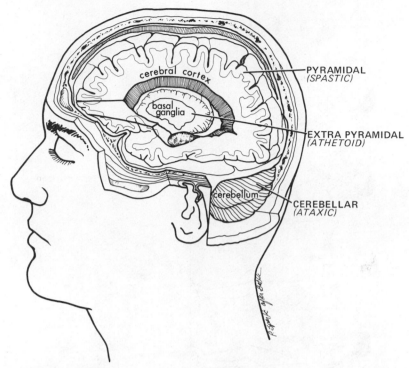

Figure 9-16. Representation of the major portions of the brain involved in cerebral palsy of three major types. From: Bleck, Eugene E., "Cerebral Palsy," in *Physically Handicapped Children — A Medical Atlas for Teachers,* edited by Eugene E. Bleck and Donald A. Nagel. New York: Grune & Stratton, Inc., 1975, p. 44. By permission.

important to realize that there are cases in which the types of cerebral palsy are mixed.

SPASTICITY

Spasticity is the most prevalent kind of cerebral palsy and is frequently associated with mental retardation. It is characterized by stiff and contracted muscles, which inhibit normal movement. Spasticity is caused by damage to the motor cells and nerve fibers located in the pyramidal areas of the cerebral cortex. Such damage results in a disturbance in the functioning of the stretch tendon reflex and thus inhibits proper stimulation of the muscles. Exaggerated stretch reflexes cause the individual to respond to muscle stimulation with vigorous contraction. Excessive contractility by the antagonist leaves the stimulated muscle in a state of contraction instead of relaxation. The pull of the spastic muscles causes movements to be slowed and inaccurately performed. For example, stimulation of the Achilles tendon results in a plantar flexion. Not only is the movement exaggerated, but the muscle continues to contract repetitively (*clonus*), keeping the foot in the same position. If contractures continue, muscles eventually become shortened, and bone deformities occur.

Spasticity is most commonly associated with the antigravity mus-

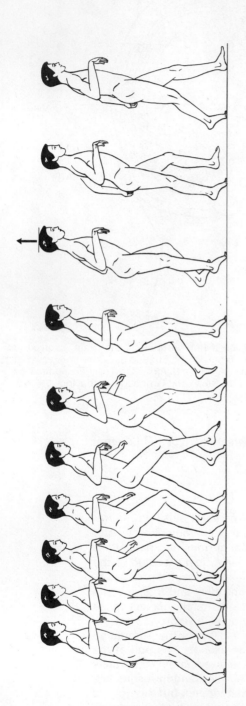

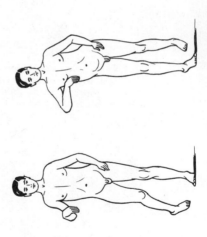

Figure 9–17. From: Ducroquet, Robert, Jean Ducroquet, and Pierre Ducroquet. *Walking and Limping: A Study of Normal and Pathological Walking.* Philadelphia: J. B. Lippincott Co., 1968, p. 223.

cles. Lower limb involvement is frequently characterized by contracture of the gastrocnemius (resulting in a plantar flexed foot); flexion and inward rotation of the hip, and adduction of the knees. When the heel is drawn up, the victim walks on the toe or on the outer part of the ball of the foot. Upper limb involvement is characterized by flexion of the elbow, wrist, and fingers and pronation of the forearm. These conditions contribute to the "scissor gait" characteristic of the spastic cerebral palsied child.

RIGIDITY

The condition of *rigidity* is often thought of as a severe form of spasticity. In rigidity, both contracting and contralateral muscles are affected, thus further inhibiting motion. Whereas spasticity is associated with localized brain involvement, rigidity is believed to be caused by diffuse brain involvement. It is further characterized by the lack of stretch reflex, lack of involuntary motion, hypertonicity, lack of muscle elasticity, and greater resistance to slow rather than rapid motion. When the degree of rigidity varies, the condition is described as *intermittent.* Children with rigidity are often quadraplegic and mentally retarded.

TREMOR

Whereas spasticity and rigidity are characterized by lack of movement, tremor is characterized by uncontrolled, involuntary, rhythmic, alternating, and pendular movement. Tremor is caused by a lesion in the basal ganglia. In certain cases, tremor is continuous (*nonintention*), and in other cases it occurs only when movement is attempted (*intention*). In children, continuous tremor is not common. Movements are caused by alternating contractions of agonist and antagonist muscles.

The stereotyped postures generally associated with cerebral palsy are not characteristic of the tremor type. Greater strength can be expected of those with the tremor type. As would be expected, those with the tremor type of cerebral palsy have greater success with gross motor tasks than with fine motor tasks.

ATAXIA

Ataxia is a type of cerebral palsy associated with lesions in the cerebellum. Its chief features include poor kinesthesia (sense of position in space) and incoordination (due to disturbance in the sense of balance). Victims exhibit difficulty in walking and standing. Walking is characterized by a weaving, staggering, and stumbling gait. Falling down and spreading the feet while walking are common. In attempting to lift or move objects, the cerebral palsied person frequently overreaches or underreaches. Muscle tone is poor, and speech may be drawling and slow. In some cases, nystagmus, and deficits in stereognosis and depth perception are evident.

ATHETOSIS

Athetosis results from a lesion in the extrapyramidal system of the brain. It specially involves the globus pallidus of the basal ganglia. Under normal conditions, this part of the brain provides a system of coordinated muscular control and automatic movement as a result of influence from the basal ganglia. When the functioning of the globus pallidus is impaired, as it is in the athetoid, various uncontrolled and involuntary movements are exhibited. The person is unable to produce the movement desired. An overflow of muscle stimulation causes excessive movement. Movement in one part of the body is accompanied by extraneous movement in another part. The normal ability to coordinate muscular impulses is impaired in the athetoid because of inadequate cerebral functioning. When movements are attempted or when emotionality increases, the overflow of stimulation increases and extraneous movements become intensified.

The second most prevalent type of cerebral palsy, athetosis is associated with a variety of symptoms. Some of these symptoms are present in some cases and absent in other cases. The condition is sometimes characterized by contorted movements. They may include rotation and twisting of the limbs; distorted positioning of the limbs, neck and trunk; thrashing of the limbs; or spontaneous jerking of the fingers and toes. For some athetoids, the distorted position of the neck, trunk, arms, and legs may be held involuntarily for a few seconds or even for a few minutes. For others, contorted movements are not characteristic. However, repetitive movement of a tensed limb is almost always evidenced. Lack of muscular control sometimes affects swallowing and speech. Walking may be characterized by stumbling. Movements frequently described are writhing and twisting, which cause grimacing when they occur in the facial muscles.

Mental retardation, perceptual impairment, and seizures are not as prevalent in athetosis as in some other types of cerebral palsy. However, hearing loss, speech disorders, and certain visual disorders are not uncommon in the athetoid.

SUMMARY

In reviewing the types of cerebral palsy, it becomes apparent that cerebral palsy is a multifaceted condition. In certain cases, mental retardation is associated with motor disability, but mental retardation does not always accompany cerebral palsy. In fact, it is well known that the cerebral palsied may have superior intelligence. Perceptual handicaps, particularly in spastics, are also frequently exhibited. Hearing loss is more common in people with cerebral palsy, particularly those with athetosis, than in the normal population. In certain cases, visual defects are evident. The common denominator in the condition is a lesion in the motor area of the brain with consequent motor dysfunction.

DIAGNOSIS

The diagnosis of cerebral palsy depends to a great degree upon the patient's medical history and symptoms of motor dysfunction. A knowledge of conditions at birth as well as of motor progress of the child yields valuable information for diagnostic purposes. Neurological examinations, skull x-rays, electroencephalograms, pneumoencephalograms, brain scans, cerebral arteriograms, and blood and urine examinations are used to more specifically delineate the nature of the condition.

TREATMENT

Treatment of cerebral palsy is, of course, related to the type of cerebral palsy exhibited and the symptoms of the disorder. Physical therapy is invariably an important part of therapy. Stress is generally placed on increasing flexibility and on improving body alignment, ability to perform purposeful movement, balance, and kinesthesia to the fullest extent possible. Orthopedic surgery is often employed to avoid or reduce bone deformity by relieving stretch reflexes and muscle contractures. Drug therapy is used to control seizures and to reduce excitability. Hearing, speech, and occupational therapy are also utilized as appropriate.

In addition to treatment of the more obvious types of symptomatology, attention must generally be given to psychological and social adjustment. The deformities, drooling, facial grimaces, poor speech, incoordination, and generally unpleasant appearance of a cerebral palsied person often cause abnormal reactions in other people. In some cases, the person is pampered, overprotected, and pitied. In other cases, fear, ridicule, or repulsion may result in the person's social isolation. The inability to move efficiently or to carry out tasks in a normal way is frustrating to the victim and leads to fear, anger, anxiety, and a tendency to withdraw. In addition, certain emotional behaviors are believed to be associated with various types of cerebral palsy. When mental retardation, hearing loss, visual defects, perceptual problems, and seizures occur, the problem is further complicated. A vicious circle exists: the effect of motor dysfunction creates emotionality, and emotionality heightens motor dysfunction. In view of such circumstances, it is certainly understandable that adjustment problems exist.

Parents as well as children often need professional guidance in coping with the adjustment problems associated with cerebral palsy. People with this disease need to deal with the situation as objectively as possible. They must be motivated to improve their condition and to develop their abilities to the maximum. Hopefully, they will be convinced that they are able to develop many self-care skills and to improve their appearance. They should be given the incentive to develop skills that will enable them to successfully participate in normal settings and should be encouraged to participate in such settings to the greatest extent possible. As they do so, other people will learn to accept them and include them in their activities. Psychological and social adjustment may be as difficult as or more difficult than coping with the motor dysfunctions themselves. However, with help, the cerebral palsied can make progress in dealing with such problems. They must realize that there are many people afflicted with cerebral palsy who have overcome seemingly impossible obstacles to lead full and productive lives.

It becomes readily apparent that treatment for cerebral palsy primarily aims to control the condition and to develop functional ability to the fullest extent possible. Since damaged nervous tissue cannot be repaired, there is no cure for the condition per se. It is also apparent that treatment requires a team approach. Although the process is long and depends very much on the attitude of the individual, progress can be

made and many people with cerebral palsy are able to live very productive lives.

Poliomyelitis

Poliomyelitis is a disease that could be eliminated by the Salk and other,
similar vaccines. In the 1950s, people dreaded poliomyelitis because it
attacked many thousands of children, but today the disease is quite rare.
Now, only people who have not used immunization develop poliomyelitis. Although it has been traditionally associated with youngsters, the
disease may also occur in adults. It is indeed fortunate that few cases of
poliomyelitis will be seen in schools today. Since the disease may be
prevented, however, it is sad to see even one case.

Poliomyelitis is an acute infectious disease caused by a filterable
virus. Although the virus may cause inflammation of various parts of the
central nervous system, it most characteristically attacks the motor cells
of the anterior horn of the spinal cord. When these nerve cells are
destroyed, impulses to associated muscles are not discharged. The
result is a lack of movement (*flaccid paralysis*). Muscles lose their tone
and become atrophied. If the nerve cells are damaged but not destroyed,
the result may be temporary loss of muscle function, movement, and
strength. In this case, recovery is possible and is enhanced by passive,
active-assistive, active, and progressive-resistance exercises administered at appropriate times. Most authorities agree that 18 to 24 months
should elapse before a decision is made as to the permanence of paralysis.

TYPES

Three commonly described forms of poliomyelitis are *abortive,
nonparalytic,* and *paralytic.* In the *abortive* form, symptoms may include
nausea, headache, fever, vomiting, and sore throat. Such signs, however, may not be evident. This form is minor and possibly may not be
recognized as poliomyelitis.

In the *nonparalytic* form, motor cells are affected but are not destroyed. In addition to the symptoms noted for the abortive form, nonparalytic poliomyelitis also causes pain and shortening in one muscle
group or a combination of muscle groups of the neck, back, calves,
thighs, and upper extremities.

As the name implies, paralysis due to the destruction of motor cells
is the central feature of the *paralytic* form of poliomyelitis. The nature
and severity of this form are, of course, directly related to the number
and location of motor cells involved. The paralytic form is, thus, further
classified into the *spinal* type, the *bulbar* type, and the *spinal-bulbar* type.
In the *spinal* type, which is the most common type, destruction occurs
predominantly in the spinal cord. The outstanding symptom is paralysis
of muscles of the lower or upper extremities, of the trunk, or both. In
some cases, the muscles of respiration are affected. Involvement of the
cranial nerves and the respiratory center of the medulla are associated
with the *bulbar* type. This form involves paralysis of muscles of the nose,
throat, and face and creates difficulty in eating, drinking, and breathing.
Mortality is particularly high in the early stages of this type of the disease.

The *spinal-bulbar* type, of course, is a combination of spinal and bulbar and is the most serious type of poliomyelitis.

TREATMENT

Depending on the nature and severity of the case, treatment during the early stages of poliomyelitis may include bed rest, therapy for muscle spasm, passive movement of paralyzed extremities, limb splinting or other techniques to prevent deformity, and mechanical respiration. During convalescence, treatment is continued under medical supervision.

Physical therapy is employed for the functional restoration of affected musculature for patients whose motor cells have not been destroyed. Stretching exercises may be used to restore the proper length of muscles and to prevent or reduce contractures. Passive, active-assistive, active, and progressive-resistance exercises are progressively employed to develop muscular strength. Corrective or preventive exercises may be used to counteract muscular imbalance and subsequent bone deformity. In cases of motor cell destruction, therapy is prescribed to help patients develop self-care skills. As appropriate, the therapist may teach patients to move with braces, crutches, or wheelchairs. Attention is given to other self-help skills such as climbing, feeding, elimination, and grooming. Orthopedic surgery may be appropriate as deformities develop. Treatment during acute and convalescent periods is generally conducted for a considerable period of time under direct medical supervision. Educational implications are generally associated with the chronic phase of poliomyelitis.

Multiple Sclerosis

Multiple sclerosis is a chronic and degenerative neurological disease whose symptoms rarely appear before the teen-age years. The disease, the cause of which is not known, generally appears in persons between 20 and 40 years of age. It is characterized by a destruction of the myelin sheath (covering of the nerve cells) along the central nervous system. This demyelination causes "patches" or sclerotic plaques along various locations in the central nervous system as the myelin in affected areas is replaced by scar tissue (sclerosis). Multiple sclerosis may involve the brain and the brain stem as well as the spinal cord. Caillet (1968) indicates that the three principle characteristics of multiple sclerosis are neural dysfunction caused by multiple lesions in segmental patches of the white matter of the cord and brain, complete or partial reversibility of many of the lesions at different stages of the disease, and permanent damage leading to permanent dysfunction when the myelin is replaced by scar tissue.

The symptoms of the disease vary according to the type and severity of involvement. Symptoms commonly identified include numbness, extreme weakness, stiffness, bladder dysfunction, lack of coordination, ataxia, vertigo, nystagmus, intention tremor, slurred speech, staggering gait, and urinary incontinence. It must be stressed that individuals are affected differently and these symptoms may or may not appear. In addition, symptoms other than those mentioned here may be expected.

Sometimes, the disease is progressive, and at other times it is episodic, with exacerbations and remissions (Caillet, 1968, and Soden, 1949). The onset and progress may be slow or rapid. The age of onset apparently affects the course of the disease and the effectiveness of the treatment.

Unfortunately, there is no cure for multiple sclerosis. In view of this, Caillet (1968) asserts that "management of the multiple sclerosis patient" appears to be the most appropriate concept. He contends that the goal of treatment is to maintain general condition, retain as much function as possible, and prevent psychological and physiological deterioration. Treatment, as appropriate, involves medication for relief of symptoms and infections; care to avoid extreme exhaustion and emotional stress, building of morale, rest in response to an initial attack or an acute exacerbation, bracing and splinting, surgical intervention for certain complications, and physical therapy under medical guidance. Physical treatments generally aim to prevent or contain spasticity, muscle weakness, contractures, and loss of equilibrium. Isometric, isotonic, active, and passive exercises have been used to increase range of motion, muscular strength, and endurance. Ambulation and self-care activities are constantly encouraged for the maintenance of muscle tonus, and muscle stretching exercises are recommended to prevent or reduce the effects of contractures. Physical activity encourages change of position, which is particularly important to patients confined to beds or wheelchairs. Such change helps to prevent decubitus ulceration. Although daily activity is generally advocated, care must be taken to avoid prolonged exertion and exposure to sudden and marked changes in temperature.

Other Conditions

Bronchial Asthma

DEFINITION AND TYPES

The word *asthma* is derived from the Greek word for "panting" or "gasping." Although the disease has been identified and described for centuries, differences in definition still occur. As it is used here, the term *bronchial asthma* refers to a chronic disease characterized by wheezing and breathing difficulty caused by interference with the normal flow of air in and out of the lungs because of involvement in the bronchial tree. The bronchial tube becomes narrowed from tightening of muscles (spasm), increase in fluid, and distention of blood vessels. In addition, the lumen of the bronchus is narrowed as a result of increased mucus production. Narrowing leads to bronchial obstruction, inadequate ventilation of the lungs, and difficulty in inhaling and exhaling. The asthmatic person has difficulty in inhaling sufficient oxygen to meet bodily needs and exhaling the carbon dioxide produced by the blood. Although physiologically there is increased resistance during both inhalation and exhalation, exhalation is generally more difficult and more prolonged than inhalation. If exhalation is obstructed, it occurs more slowly through a more narrowed tube. Accessory muscles of the chest are called upon to assist breathing. As the condition progresses, abdominal muscles may be brought into play to enhance diaphragmatic breathing.

The Joint Committee of the Allergy Foundation of America and the American Thoracic Society (1973) defines three categories of asthma: *allergic, idiopathic,* and *nonspecific.* Allergic asthma is characterized by bronchospasm induced by inhaled antigen. This type has been designated by various authors as *extrinsic, exogenous, immunologic,* and *noninfectious.* Attacks of this type of asthma are triggered by pollen, molds, dust, or other substances to which the patient is allergic. It generally occurs before the age of 45 and is associated with a family history of allergy and "positive" skin tests.

The idiopathic type of asthma, often referred to as the *intrinsic* type, is characterized by the absence of clearly defined initiating or precipitating factors. It is not associated with allergy. There may be no family history of allergy, and skin tests may be "negative."

The nonspecific type (classified by some authors with the intrinsic type) includes cases in which diverse triggering effects stimulate undefined pathogenic mechanisms leading to asthma. It includes but is not limited to asthma following viral infection of the respiratory tissues; exercise-induced asthma (exacerbation due to exercise); and emotion-induced asthma (asthmatic symptoms precipitated by changes in the central and autonomic nervous systems owing to stress). The classifications of asthma used in this system are related not only to the cause of the disease but also to the treatment.

Asthma attacks may be precipitated by emotional stress, excessive physical activity, drugs, organic chemicals, cold air, smoke, allergic exposures, and respiratory infection. In an asthmatic attack, thick mucus blocks the terminal bronchioles, causing shortness of breath. The lack of ventilation makes individuals feel that they are suffocating, and thus they give all their attention to breathing. Coughing becomes more evident

Figure 9–18. Working with the child provides security.

and produces a great amount of clear, white sputum. Sputum is associated with infection if it is yellowish in color. Wheezing and a high whistling sound are heard during the attack and may be heard between attacks. Although more common during exhalation, these sounds may be heard during inhalation. Occasionally the asthmatic person may exhibit blueness of the lips, fingernails, and face. The normal breathing pattern may be altered, and accessory muscles become involved in respiration. Attacks may last for a few minutes to several days. They may be intermittent in the early stages of the disease but can be rather constant in the chronic phase. If the asthmatic person is unable to expel the mucus produced, it accumulates and stagnates and becomes a source of further respiratory difficulties. Although some individuals may not have any symptoms after an acute attack, wheezing and shortness of breath following attacks is not uncommon. In certain cases, symptoms of the disease may become progressive. In some children, asthmatic symptoms appear within the first three years of life and are associated with acute respiratory infections but may not appear after age ten. When asthma reaches the condition of sustained shortness of breath, is intractable to ordinary treatment, and lasts for long periods of time, it is known as *status asthmaticus.*

INCIDENCE

Statistics on the actual incidence of asthma vary; they do, however, provide valuable information about age and sex differences and the effects of the condition on school and work attendance. The American Lung Association (1973) estimates that about 10 in every 1000 persons in the general population have asthma and that the prevalence among children age 15 or younger is between 5 and 15 per cent. The Association states that asthma occurs more frequently in males under 14 and over 45 and in females between 15 and 45. In agreement with other authorities, they report that the allergic type usually begins in the first four decades and the idiopathic type most commonly begins after age 40. After reviewing the research, Harvey (1975a) noted that asthma is the chronic condition causing the highest percentage of days lost from school. The Joint Committee of the Allergy Foundation of America and the American Thoracic Society (1973) also recognizes asthma as a leading cause of time lost from work and school and identifies a death rate from asthma at less than 1 per 100,000 for people under 35 and of 10 per 100,000 for people over 60.

CAUSE

The exact cause of bronchial asthma is unknown, but several factors have been identified. Although the specific role of genetic factors is unknown, bronchial asthma is more likely to occur in persons with a family history of the disorder. As the American Lung Association (1973) indicates, "underlying allergic asthma is an inherited tendency — atopy — to develop hypersensitivity resulting in the antigen-antibody type reaction." In a person with this constitutional predisposition, asthmatic attacks occur when the individual comes in contact with allergens to which the body reacts. Idiopathic asthma, as mentioned previously, may be caused by reactions to viral infection of respiratory tissues, to exercise, to emotion, and to exposure to cold. Asthma may also be induced by aspirin in a person with nasal polyps. More specifically, attacks may be precipitated by ingestants such as milk, eggs, chocolate, citrus fruits, nuts, and drugs; inhalants such as grass, trees, pollens, house dust, wool, feathers, and animal dander; smog; smoke; hair sprays; perfume; emotional stress; exertion, and exposure to cold. Bottomley (1968) hypothesizes that the effects of exertion increase the depth of respiration, thus stirring mucus secretions that were undisturbed during rest; increased breathing leads to ever greater trapping of air in the lungs. The Joint Committee of the Allergy Foundation of America and the American Thoracic Society (1973) postulates that "activation of subepithelial receptors in the airways stimulates efferent cholinergic discharge with resultant bronchospasm." Since exercise-provoked asthma may be prevented, however, it should be mentioned at this point that this group feels that a program to improve physical fitness is a valuable part of the rehabilitation of chronic asthma.

TREATMENT

The most obvious and most important aspect of treatment is to remove or to avoid to the greatest extent possible those factors that cause asthmatic attacks. This, of course, is not always possible, and other treatment procedures need to be implemented. Although not a cure, hyposensitization injections may be employed for some people over a long period of time to help them develop antibodies against various substances. Some drugs provide relief of distress due to bronchospasm and other symptoms. Fluids may be recommended to combat dehydration, and oxygen inhalation may be employed during severe attacks. Bronchial aspiration may be used to clear pulmonary passageways. Respiratory infections are specifically treated, and measures are taken to prevent respiratory reoccurrences. In some cases, the patient may be advised to move to a warm, dry, smog-free, fog-free climate. Treatment may also include attention to the removal of emotional stresses that precipitate attacks. In other cases, surgery may be indicated. The Joint Committee of the Allergy Foundation of America and the American Thoracic Society states that a program designed to improve physical fitness is a valuable part of the rehabilitation of the chronic asthmatic but indicates that the value of specific breathing exercises is controversial. The Committee also reports that physiotherapy techniques of chest wall vibration often help in mobilizing bronchial mucus. Benack (1967) advocates the use of breathing exercises, under medical supervision, to increase proper and maximum use of the lungs. He feels that such exercises aid diaphragmatic breathing. More on the role of exercise in treatment of asthma is presented in later sections of this book.

Cystic Fibrosis

DEFINITION

Cystic fibrosis is a childhood disease transmitted as a simple recessive hereditary disorder. Appearing predominantly in Caucasians, it is a rare disease occurring in approximately one of every 1500 babies born and carried by one of every 25 Caucasians (Harvey, 1975). The name *cystic fibrosis* was first associated with the disease when it was recognized to cause cysts and fibrous scarring in the pancreas. The name *mucoviscidosis* has also been used since the discovery that other organs and exocrine glands such as those producing sweat, mucus, saliva, and other digestive juices may also be involved in the disorder.

In cystic fibrosis, the secretions of the exocrine glands are abnormal in composition. Instead of normal thin secretions, the glands produce a viscid (thick and sticky) substance that clogs and obstructs the lungs, pancreas, and liver. Such obstruction may lead to the development of cysts and fibrous scarring of the organs. As blockage prohibits pancreatic secretions from reaching the intestine, there is less breakdown of food, resulting in more symptoms of the disease and a loss of calories through elimination. In the lung, mucus is not properly cleared, thus trapping air in the organ's periphery. Proper expiration is inhibited, possibly resulting in atelectasis (collapse of the lung) and infection. In addition, other respiratory complications may occur. Although beyond the scope of this discussion, similar problems may occur in the liver. Finally, sweat and saliva contain abnormal amounts of salt — an important finding in regard to the diagnosis of the disease.

SYMPTOMS

The symptoms of the disease as well as the appearance of a child with cystic fibrosis vary with the nature and severity of the disease. Early indications of pulmonary involvement include excessive mucus, wheezing, chronic and progressively more severe coughing, and difficult and rapid breathing. Respiratory infections are more frequent and prolonged. Intestinal involvement, caused by a lack of normal pancreatic secretions, may be evidenced by bulky, fatty, foul stools and frequent elimination. Incomplete digestion and resultant loss of calories may result in a great appetite but failure to gain weight. The sweat of victims of cystic fibrosis is characterized by high salt content. The analysis of sweat for salt content is, in fact, an important aspect in the diagnosis of the disease. In order to counteract heavy salt loss and possible heat prostration, it may be necessary to provide supplemental amounts of salt. Other characteristics may include big rounded chest, distended and protruding abdomen, thin extremities, and clubbing of the fingers.

CONTROL

The National Cystic Fibrosis Research Foundation indicates that for each year since 1960, one year of life has been added to the life span of persons with cystic fibrosis and that the average age of death has risen from 2 years to 12 or 14, with many patients living into their teens, twenties, and beyond. Although present methods of treatment are not able to cure the disease, progress has been made in the past few years in controlling it. Treatment of pancreatic or gastrointestinal aspects of the disease is enhanced by the administration of pancreatic extract in tablet or powder form and by doses of water-soluble vitamins. Dietary control involves decreasing fat intake and increasing caloric and protein intake. To counteract heat prostration and salt depletion, salt supplements are recommended; this is particularly important in hot weather and in periods of activity during which children perspire quite freely. The use of antibiotics to counter infection, particularly in the lungs, has been very effective in altering the course of the disease. In addition, a great deal of attention is given to keeping the lungs as clear of mucus as possible. Techniques employed for this purpose include postural drainage (child is placed in various positions to enhance drainage of the lungs as different parts of the chest are shaken and tapped vigorously in an attempt to dislodge and move mucus), breathing exercises, and inhalation therapy. Finally, it is highly recommended that children with cystic fibrosis be given the usual childhood immunization.

DIAGNOSIS

In addition to considering other symptomatology, diagnosis of the disease is made by analyzing the salt content of the sweat. Chest x-rays, tests of pulmonary functioning, and other laboratory techniques are used to determine the nature and severity of involvement. As is generally the case with any disease, early diagnosis enhances treatment. Although the condition is progressive and relentless, treatment can slow the rate of progression. The earlier the diagnosis, the better the response to treatment and the greater the chances that children with cystic fibrosis will lead prolonged and useful lives. Most deaths associated with the disease are caused by pulmonary complications. Other less frequent causes have included heart failure, liver failure, and shock from rapid salt loss.

Diabetes Mellitus*

DEFINITION

Diabetes mellitus is a hereditary metabolic disorder in which the ability of the body to properly metabolize or utilize food is impaired. Inadequate functioning is caused by an insufficient amount of insulin or by the interference with the action of insulin in tissues. Insufficient amounts of insulin result from disturbance in the functioning of the islets of Langerhans of the pancreas, where it is produced. The hormone insulin is necessary for the conversion of glucose to glycogen for storage in the liver and other body tissues and for the conversion of glycogen to glucose for use by the body tissues. Without a sufficient supply of insulin, glycogen cannot be properly stored in the body, and thus it accumulates in the blood stream in the form of glucose. Blood sugar levels rise above normal (*hyperglycemia*) and some of the glucose spills into the urine (*glycosuria*). When the primary source of energy (sugar and starches) is lost, the diabetic compensates by increasing the utilization of protein and fat. Overuse of fat as a source of energy produces acidosis, which leads to diabetic coma.

SYMPTOMS

The most common symptoms of diabetes include excessive urination, thirst, hunger, and fatigue. Less common symptoms include cuts,

---

*Parts of this section are based on an earlier article by the author: Winnick, Joseph P. "Planning Physical Activity for the Diabetic," *Physical Educator* 27:15–16, 1970.

bruises or infections that are slow to heal; changes in vision, itching; pain in fingers and toes, drowsiness; and skin infection in the form of boils, carbuncles, or gangrene sores. In addition to symptomatology, urine, blood, and glucose tolerance tests are used for diagnostic purposes. Diagnosis may be made accurately with little difficulty.

Two conditions associated with diabetes are diabetic coma and insulin reaction or insulin shock. It is important to be able to distinguish between them in order to give proper treatment. Diabetic coma may be caused by failure to take insulin, an insufficient amount of insulin, resistance to insulin, too much food, infection, vomiting, diarrhea, injury, surgery, shock, pregnancy, anesthesia, or emotional stress (Schmitt, 1973). In this condition, blood sugar exceeds normal levels (hyperglycemia), and the body is deprived of its primary source of energy. Overuse of fat produces acidosis and subsequently diabetic coma. A person in diabetic coma should receive immediate medical attention. Insulin reaction or insulin shock may occur if the individual receives too much insulin, ingests too little food, or exercises to excess. Blood sugar levels become abnormally low (*hypoglycemia*), creating a need for a quick source of energy such as candy, ice cream, or soda. Insulin reaction occurs more rapidly than diabetic coma. In comparing insulin shock to diabetic coma, Schmitt (1973) indicates that in insulin reaction, the diabetic is nervous and hungry, the face is pale, the skin is moist, blood pressure and pulse are normal, and convulsions may appear. Abnormal thirst, abdominal pain, leg cramps, and odor on the breath are not characteristic of insulin reaction. Symptoms and signs of diabetic coma include extreme thirst, loss of appetite, abdominal pain, leg cramps, a flushing of the face, dry skin, a fruity odor on the breath, lowered blood pressure, and rapid pulse. Nervousness, convulsion, and trembling are not characteristic symptoms of diabetic coma. Nausea, vomiting, and blurred vision may appear with both conditions (Schmitt, 1973, p. 193).

There is no doubt that diabetes is more prevalent in middle-aged and older people than in children. In fact, diabetes is relatively rare in children. It is also clear that the incidence is greater is women and in people who are overweight.

TREATMENT

A cure for diabetes has not yet been found. Treatment is therefore designed to control the disease and includes drugs with insulin properties, dieting, and exercise. Since the purpose of treatment is to bring blood sugar levels within recommended levels, the patient's insulin intake, diet, and exercise must be coordinated. Drugs are taken orally or by injection. The specific dosage depends on the severity of the condition and the lifestyle of the patient. A proper diet is of extreme importance and must be regulated. It is particularly important that normal weight be maintained.

Exercise, considered by medical authorities to be an integral part of treatment, helps maintain normal body weight (excess weight places a strain on the heart, blood vessels, liver, and pancreas), maintain or increase muscular strength, and improve circulation to extremities. Evidence is available indicating that less insulin is required to reduce blood sugar levels when patients are active than when they are sedentary

(Engerbretson, 1963; Engerbretson, 1970; Sindoni, 1959). Schmitt (1973) suggests that one reason for this is that contracting muscles produce a chemical that acts like insulin. Bleck and Nagel (1975) indicate that exercise works like insulin in that it burns glucose so less insulin is needed to convert it to glycogen for storage. A hypothesis that has received some support holds that exercise increases the pancreatic production of insulin. Although exercise is a part of treatment, there are guidelines that should be followed in programs of physical activity. These are presented in detail in Chapter 12.

Cardiovascular Disorders

Cardiovascular disorders are among the childhood conditions of most concern to children, parents, and teachers. The category of cardiovascular disorders includes all diseases and defects of the heart and blood vessels. Cardiovascular disorder is the primary cause of death in adults over 30 years of age. Owing to a lack of understanding, children with

Figure 9–19. The normal heart. American Heart Association. *Heart Disease in Children.* New York, 1963. © American Heart Association. Reprinted with permission.

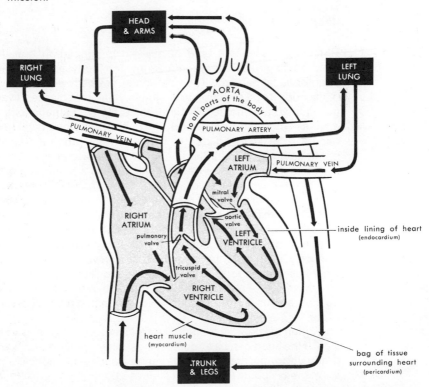

The right atrium receives blood from the veins of the body; and the right ventricle pumps this blood through the pulmonary artery to the lungs where it picks up fresh oxygen.

The left atrium receives oxygenated blood from the lungs, and the left ventricle pumps it through the aorta to the body.

cardiovascular disorders are often restricted from physical activity when activity would be beneficial to them or are allowed to participate in certain activities when activity is contraindicated. To properly plan activity, it is helpful to have a basic understanding of cardiovascular disorders.

According to the American Heart Association (1966), rheumatic fever and congenital heart defects are the cause of most cardiac disorders in children. These two conditions are therefore the focus of this section. The American Heart Association estimates that in the United States, about 500,000 children aged 5 to 19 and about 500,000 adults have had rheumatic fever. The Association estimates that 30,000 to 40,000 children are born with heart defects in this country each year. This number is less than 1 per cent of all children born in the United States each year. Although rheumatic fever may result in heart disorder, it should be noted that a great many rheumatic fever patients recover without permanent damage to the heart valves. Medical authorities generally agree that about two thirds of rheumatic fever victims exhibit some indication of cardiac damage. Ross and O'Rourke (1976) estimate that rheumatic valvular heart disease is responsible for about 15,000 deaths each year in the United States in people under 65 years of age.

Rheumatic Fever

Rheumatic fever is a type of allergic inflammation that develops in reaction to antibodies produced by the body as a defense against streptococcal bacteria. The reaction abnormally affects certain tissues of the body. Most commonly, the joints, heart muscle, heart valves, brain, and kidneys are affected. With the exception of damage to the heart, the effects in most parts of the body are temporary. Rheumatic heart disease occurs from scarring of the heart valves. Although the disorder is precipitated by acute inflammation, the major damage associated with rheumatic heart disease generally occurs as a result of a gradual scarring of the heart over several years. Rheumatic fever follows a streptococcal infection that is not directly caused by bacterial infection. As Ross and O'Rourke (1976) point out, acute rheumatic fever occurs in less than 1 per cent of individuals who have a streptococcal infection, and less than half of these subsequently develop chronic rheumatic valvular disease. Once patients have rheumatic fever, however, they become most susceptible to repeated attacks, and recurrent episodes increase the possibility of permanent heart damage. Although rheumatic fever is not contagious, the streptococcal infection that precedes it is communicable.

When the heart is permanently injured, one or both valves on the left side of the heart can be affected. In response to inflammation, scar tissue gradually forms, preventing the valves from opening or closing properly. Valves may become narrowed (*stenotic*) or leaky (*regurgitant*) and thus interfere with the work of the heart in pumping blood throughout the body. In many cases, scarring of the heart is gradual, occurring in response to recurrent episodes. Symptoms may not appear until late childhood or adulthood.

Since rheumatic fever may take several forms, it is frequently difficult to recognize. Signs or symptoms of acute rheumatic fever may serve as a basis for referral to a physician. The American Heart Association (1971) lists the signs and symptoms for parents and teachers.

> Poor appetite and failure to gain weight; pallor and fatigue; unusual restlessness, irritability, twitching or jerky motions (St. Vitus dance); behavior and personality changes; decreasing accomplishment in schoolwork by a child who had been doing well previously. (American Heart Association, 1971, p. 4.)

Since the exact cause of rheumatic fever is not known, there is no cure for the disease. However, many advances have been made in treatment. The foremost treatment is to prevent hemolytic streptococcal infections and to provide immediate and proper therapy when they occur. Upon diagnosis of a "strep" infection, physicians will generally prescribe penicillin or other antibiotics to control infection before rheumatic fever sets in. Long-term prevention may involve daily use of sulfonamide or antibiotics such as penicillin over a period of years. Other preventive methods include low-salt diet, weight reduction, and avoidance of irregular and overly strenuous exertion. Because of susceptibility to infection, patients may also be advised to take antibiotics before and after dental work.

During the acute phase of rheumatic fever, bed rest and drugs to suppress symptoms are prescribed. In many cases, convalescence may last for several months, requiring both hospital and home care. As the acute phase of the disease is passed, physical activity may be gradually increased. If the condition of the heart valves warrant it, an operation may be performed to replace or repair them. Following convalescence, some children will need to be restricted in physical activities and others will not. Since unwarranted restriction of activity and failure to restrict activity may have serious consequences, it is important to follow medical advice in determining the extent of a child's participation in physical activity.

Congenital Heart Defects

A congenital heart defect is an abnormality existing at birth in which the heart or the major blood vessels near the heart fail to mature properly. Defects may occur singly or in combination and may be so slight that the person is barely affected over a lifetime or so severe that life may be prolonged for only a short period. With advances in surgery, it is now possible for heart defects to be completely or partially corrected.

There are many types of congenital defects and differences in the incidence of each. The American Heart Association (1963b and 1970) describes those that may be completely or partly repaired by surgery as follows.

1. *Coarctation of the aorta* — a narrowing or constriction of the aorta.
2. *Patent ductus arteriosus* — an open passageway between the pulmonary artery and aorta.
3. *Septal defect* — an opening in the wall of tissue (septum) that divides the heart into left and right sides.
   a. *Ventricular septal defect* — defect in the thick muscular portion of the wall between the ventricles (two lower chambers).

      b. *Atrial septal defect* – defect between the left and right atria (upper chambers).

4. *Tetralogy of Fallot* — a defect that causes poor oxygenation of blood, resulting in cyanotic or "blue" babies. The tetralogy of Fallot is a combination of four defects:
      a. *Ventricular septal defect* — abnormal opening between the two ventricles causing unoxygenated blood to mix with oxygenated blood.
      b. *Overriding aorta* — the aorta straddles both ventricles instead of rising solely from the left ventricle. This causes both oxygenated and unoxygenated blood to be transported throughout the body.
      c. *Pulmonary stenosis* — narrowing of the pulmonary valve resulting in obstruction of blood flow through the pulmonary artery to the lungs.
      d. *Enlarged right ventricle* — overwork of right ventricle caused by the strain of pumping blood through a narrowed pulmonary valve.

5. *Transposition of the great vessels* — a defect in which the pulmonary artery is attached to the left rather than the right ventricle and the aorta is attached to the right rather than the left ventricle.

6. *Truncus arteriosus* — a defect in which a single artery from the heart gives rise to the aorta and the lung arteries.

7. *Abnormalities of valves* — valves without opening or a narrow valve opening of the heart causing obstruction. Stenosis in the valve may cause valve leaflets which normally move freely to become stiff or to be stuck together. Stenosis near the valve causes a "bottleneck" of muscle fibers that obstructs blood flow.
      a. *Aortic stenosis* — stenosis of the aortic valve.
      b. *Pulmonary stenosis* — stenosis of the pulmonary valve.
      c. *Tricuspid atresia* — abnormal development of the tricuspid valve through which blood in the right atrium can flow into the right ventricle. This defect is combined with an abnormal opening in the wall between the ventricles.

Sherrill (1976) points out that one half of all congenital heart defects are caused by the following conditions: ventricular septal defects (22 per cent), patent ductus arteriosus (17 per cent), and tetralogy of Fallot (11 per cent). Of the remaining half, 32 per cent are caused by the following conditions: transposition of the great vessels (8 per cent), atrial septal defect (7 per cent), pulmonary stenosis (7 per cent), coarctation of the aorta (6 per cent), and aortic and subaortic stenosis (4 per cent). The remaining 18 per cent are caused by a number of rare conditions.

Although all the causes are not known, Selzer (1969) indicates that congenital heart defects are either genetically determined, caused by injury during pregnancy, or the result of some disease that affects the mother and fetus during pregnancy after the heart is fully formed. Baum (1975) reports that congenital heart defects caused by a single mutant gene syndrome comprise less than 1 per cent of cases and those resulting from a gross chromosomal abnormality less than 5 per cent. He points out that about 40 per cent of mongoloid children have some type of heart defect. German measles is one of the most common causes of injury to the fetus.

Treatment of congenital heart defects may involve surgery or medical treatment. Surgery is performed to repair or correct conditions of the heart or blood vessels. It may be closed or open heart surgery. In some cases, surgery brings about a complete cure, while in other cases, the defects may be only partially corrected. The kind of operation and the age at which the child undergoes it vary with the type of defect. It is generally recommended that surgery be performed before the child reaches the age of 6. According to the American Heart Association (1963b), medical treatment is designed to prevent complications, relieve the patient of symptoms until surgery is performed, or relieve symptoms throughout the patient's lifetime.

The period of convalescence after surgery may range from a few weeks to a few months. During this time, the child may perform breathing exercises if so advised by the physician. When the child completes the period of convalescence, medical supervision of activity is again necessary. The American Heart Association (1970) indicates that a child can usually take part in all normal activity if the defect is completely corrected. If, however, the defect is only partially corrected, the child's activity may be limited. After convalescence, it is of vital importance that the physician prescribe activities that the child may do as well as those the child may not do. Children with congenital heart defects will rarely be totally restricted from physical activity.

10

THE RELATIONSHIP OF VISUAL AND AUDITORY HANDICAPS TO PHYSICAL AND MOTOR PERFORMANCE

It is well-known that individuals with visual and auditory handicaps need and are able to participate very successfully in physical and motor experiences. Given the opportunity and inclination to participate, persons with these impairments not uncommonly excel in movement and sport activities. In this chapter, information is presented about the abilities, limitations, and needs of groups of children with visual and auditory handicaps. The point that needs most emphasis, however, is that each child is an individual. Generalizations emanating from group data should not be indiscriminately applied to a particular individual. Over-generalizations from the normative data presented herein are unwarranted. Data presented in this chapter concerning performance were gathered at a particular time, at a particular place, with a particular group, and under specific conditions. They should in no way be considered to represent the potential of individuals or groups or be used to restrict the pursuit of maximum development.

Visual Handicaps

The need for the visually handicapped to participate in physical and motor activities is widely accepted. Although certain activities must be modified for successful participation, many others need little or no modification and provide opportunities for the visually handicapped to participate with the normally sighted in wholesome educational and recreational activities. Their participation in movement activities is important not only for its expected physical and motor values but also because it provides the children with opportunity to socialize, to develop a knowledge of sports activities, to enhance their understanding of the extent to which blindness becomes a limiting factor in activity, and to gain experience in orientation and mobility training.

In implementation of programs, it is important to understand that blindness does not inherently cause physical and motor deficits or limit physical activity for physiological reasons. However, lack of vision tends to inhibit the stimulation to move. For example, a child seeing a toy or some other attractive object is stimulated to move toward it. The blind individual, however, does not have the advantage of visual input, and the stimulation to move is reduced. This lack of visual stimulation must be compensated for by the use of other avenues for sensory input. In addition to reduced stimulation, the blind lack the primary steering mechanism (vision) for movement. Without this steering mechanism, physical activity tends to be restricted. In many cases, movement is restricted because the blind instinctively fear injury. In other cases, the fear of injury is transmitted to the visually handicapped by overprotective teachers, parents, or peers. Thus, it is not uncommon for blind children to be sedentary, discouraged from participation, or inhibited in taking opportunity for movement experiences. The net result of these various factors is deficiency or lag in physical and motor development and performance. The importance of opportunity for movement or mobility was supported by a study by Norris and her associates (1957). The authors noted that "in every case where the rating on mobility was below average, the child had been extremely limited in motor experience and had not been allowed on the floor or permitted freedom to explore objects." Buell (1950b) reported that motor performance of the visually handicapped was affected by the physical education they received in school and elsewhere.

Although this discussion concerns the visually handicapped as a group, it must be emphasized that these children vary greatly in ability. In addition to the lack of opportunities for movement and the attitudes of these children and their parents, factors affecting motor performance include the residual vision available and the age of onset and the duration of the visual handicap. Buell (1950a) found that partially sighted youngsters often exceeded the performance of totally blind youngsters in physical and motor tasks. Normative data compiled by Buell (1966, 1973) indicates that the motor and physical proficiency of partially sighted boys and girls generally exceeds that of their totally blind peers. In regard to the onset and duration of blindness, Buell (1950a, 1950b) reported that children who lose their vision after 6 years of age do not have as much difficulty in adjusting to physical activities as do children blind from early childhood. He

Figure 10-6. Visually handicapped youngsters enjoy physical activity.

Figure 10-2. The visually handicapped child must be motivated to keep his head up.

found that recently blinded girls performed better in running, throwing, and jumping than those afflicted earlier. He also found that boys losing their vision after 6 years of age threw a basketball farther than their blind peers, who had never seen a throw.

In view of the material presented in the preceding paragraphs, it becomes apparent that opportunity for participation in physical and motor activities is basic to programming for the visually handicapped. In addition, children must be stimulated and encouraged to move. Parents and teachers must be careful not to overprotect the blind child. Physical activity is rarely contraindicated, since such activity for the visually handicapped is generally of no greater risk for them than for the normally sighted. In the past, it has been contended that participation in rough or contact sports should not be allowed for those with myopic conditions. However, Rachun (1968) has reported that no instance of retinal detachment due to sports injury has been recorded at Cornell and thus has indicated that myopia does not lead to loss of vision as a result of contact sports except possibly in the extreme progressive form. However, he recommends that an athlete blind in one eye not engage in contact or collision sports. He feels that such participation does not justify the risk of total blindness. If there is doubt as to the extent and nature of a blind child's participation in movement experiences, medical consultation should be obtained.

Limitations

Although movement experiences for the visually handicapped child should be encouraged, certain limitations in participation should be recognized. First, the lack of visual stimulation will reduce the child's motivation to move. As Scholl (1973) points out, the blind infant at 16 weeks of age has little motivation for holding up the head. It is necessary to compensate for this lack by providing stimulation through the remaining sensory modalities. Second, the blind child is obviously deficient in the ability to learn by imitation or to view demonstrations. This requires that kinesthetic teaching, during which the child's body is moved or during which the child perceives the correctness of movements by feeling others, be employed. Third, the visually handicapped child is limited in the ability to move about and explore the environment. This limitation often results in an attempt to satisfy the basic desire for movement within oneself rather than in the environment. The visually handicapped child is more encouraged to move about in a familiar environment. The child should be taught where objects are located and where unobstructed pathways exist. Care must be taken to keep the environment structured and consistent. Fourth, the blind child is limited in certain activities, which must be modified for successful participation. Rowing, calisthenics, wrestling, bowling, and hiking require little modification. However, games such as basketball, softball, volleyball, and football must generally be modified considerably. Methods of modifying these and other activities may be found in a number of texts and articles in professional literature.

Physical and Motor Proficiency

Although there is a paucity of research comparing the performances of visually handicapped and normally sighted children, it has been generally found and there is agreement among writers that the visually handicapped are poorer in physical fitness measures than their normally sighted peers and that the scores of partially sighted children exceed those of totally blind youngsters. Median norm comparisons on the 50-yard dash, the 600-yard run-walk, and the standing broad jump of normal youngsters (AAHPER, 1975) and visually handicapped youngsters (Buell, 1966, 1973) indicate that the performance of normally sighted boys exceeds that of blind and partially sighted boys and that the performance of normally sighted girls exceeds that of blind and partially sighted girls. These data also support the belief that the partially sighted exceed the performance of the totally blind. Norms prepared for visually handicapped girls (Buell, 1966, 1973) reflect an expected improvement in these measures of physical proficiency between the ages of 6 and 13 or 14. However, little difference in the performance of visually handicapped girls on these measures is expected between the ages of 13 or 14 and 17. Visually handicapped boys on the other hand, show a constant improvement in performance between the ages of 6 and 17 (Buell, 1966, 1973).

Although the performance of the normally sighted exceeds that of the visually handicapped, comparison of the data mentioned above reveals that differences between these groups decrease as age increases. In the broad jump, for example, differences are less than 5 inches for boys at age 17 and less than 10 inches for girls at age 17. At ages 6 to 7, differences are about 16 inches for boys and about 15 inches for girls. Normally sighted 10-year-old boys run the 50-yard dash about 2.9 seconds faster than blind boys and about 1 second faster than partially sighted boys of the same age. At age 17, normally sighted boys run only 1.4 seconds faster than blind boys and .4 second faster than partially sighted boys. Normally sighted 10-year-old girls run the 50-yard dash about 4.8 seconds faster than blind girls and about 2.5 seconds faster than partially sighted girls of the same age. At age 17, the differences decrease to 3.0 seconds and 1.8 seconds, respectively. Normal 10-year-old boys perform the 600-yard run-walk about 47 seconds faster than blind 10-year-old boys and about 28 seconds faster than partially sighted 10-year-old boys. At age 17, these differences decrease to 33 and 16 seconds for the totally blind and partially sighted, respectively. Normal 10-year-old girls perform the 600-yard run-walk about 87 seconds faster than blind 10-year-old girls and about 57 seconds faster than partially sighted 10-year-old girls. At age 17, the differences decrease to 69 seconds and 39 seconds, respectively.

Buell (1950a) conducted a rather comprehensive study in which visually handicapped and seeing subjects were compared in selected track and field events (running, throwing, and jumping). He found that the mean scores of visually handicapped children in most events and at most levels (elementary, junior high, and senior high school) fell far below those of seeing pupils. The visually handicapped were found to score lowest in the basketball throw and highest in the standing broad jump. The only event and level in which blind and partially sighted youngsters performed better than seeing subjects was in the standing broad jump for high school boys. Buell feels that this superiority is probably a result of familiarity and training. Visually handicapped boys were more familiar with the task since seeing subjects performed running broad jumps more often than the standing broad jump. Since the visually handicapped generally perform the standing rather than the running broad jump, they have more training in it. Buell found in this study that mean scores in running and jumping for visually handicapped boys more nearly approached the norms for the seeing than did the average score for girls with defective vision. In throwing, the mean scores for visually handicapped girls more nearly approached the norms for the seeing. He also found that the mean scores in running and jumping for older boys in schools for the blind more nearly approached the norm for the seeing than did scores for younger visually handicapped youngsters. In comparing the blind and partially sighted, Buell (1950a) found that the partially sighted excelled the blind in running and throwing and in the girls' broad jump. The performance of older blind subjects in the standing broad jump was equal to that of the partially seeing.

On the basis of the research presented and on clinical evidence, it is clear that the performance of the visually handicapped in measures of physical proficiency varies with the type of activity performed. Blind youngsters have particular difficulty in activities that involve throwing. Since they have not seen the activity performed correctly, a great deal of effort must be made in learning and in teaching the activity. Differences in throwing fitness items may owe more to coordination and learning than to real differences in physical fitness. Since running involves movement from place to place, high scores in that activity are difficult for blind youngsters to attain. Performance is restricted by having to maintain contact with guide wires, performing with a partner, or being guided by auditory or tactual cues. Such problems result in poor scores in dashes, long distance runs, or shuttle runs. The blind come nearer to the norms of the normally sighted in uncomplicated activities performed in place. Examples include the flexed arm hang, sit-ups, pull-ups, and the standing broad jump. When the visually handicapped perform below normal standards in these events, real differences in physical fitness are more likely to exist, and these differences are invariably influenced by their former participation in physical activity. In regard to physical fitness testing, Buell (1973) states that squat-thrusts and push-ups or his achievement scales in the basketball throw create adequate substitute items for the shuttle run and softball throw.

As was true with physical proficiency, there is a paucity of research about the motor development of the blind. The evidence available indicates that the blind follow an orderly progression in motor development, that there is a wide variation in development, that the blind tend to be retarded in motor development, and that such retardation is due to inadequate space perception and a lack of movement experiences. Gesell and his associates (1950) followed the development of a visually handicapped child from infancy through the age of 4 and found that developmental sequences progressed normally in posture, manipulation, locomotion, exploration, social behavior, and language. Noting that the subject in the Gesell study possessed some vision of practical value, Wilson and Halverson (1947) conducted another study in which they observed the development of a boy whose vision was far below normal during his second year of life. These investigators found that retardation was greatest in the motor and adaptive fields of behavior and least in that of language. The subject was about 4 to 5 months retarded in creeping, 4 to more than 9 months retarded in standing, 6 to more than 9 months retarded in walking, and 6 to 18 months retarded in prehension. At 24 months, the child was never observed to stand or walk independently. Although seeing children are able to construct a tower of six to seven cubes at 24 months, the subject in this study showed no ability in tower building with cubes at that age. Investigators also noted lack of spontaneity in the subject's movements and a disinclination to initiate movements involving alteration of position or extension of his arms. The investigators attributed retardation to inadequate space perception. The tests the child failed required the use of movements that depended upon the appreciation of space beyond the body.

Norris and her associates (1957) conducted a normative study in which the majority of their blind subjects had retrolental fibroplasia. In comparing results of this study with data for normally sighted youngsters, it was evident that the blind children in their study were, as a group, retarded in standing alone, walking alone, and jumping with both feet. These investigators reported that fine motor coordination and success in grasping spatial relationships were found to develop spontaneously, though usually at a later age than for sighted children, in blind children who had had adequate opportunities for gross motor activity and who had been permitted to explore their environment. These investigators further reported that children who received high ratings on a mobility scale were those who had been permitted to explore their environments freely rather than those who had been limited in early motor development. Scholl (1973) indicates that retardation in learning to control fingers and to use hands efficiently is not uncommon in young blind children. Since jumping and skipping are not seen by the blind, Scholl also emphasizes that these activities must be specifically taught to them.

In his doctoral dissertation, Buell (1950) administered the Iowa Brace Test to visually handicapped youngsters and compared the results to those for seeing children. The Iowa Brace Test includes items that measure coordination, agility, control, and balance. He reported that (1) the scores of visually handicapped children fall below those of seeing pupils on all levels, (2) visually handicapped boys more closely approached norms for the seeing than did girls with defective vision, (3) the lag of children with defective vision is general rather than isolated in specific areas, (4) partially sighted elementary school children scored significantly higher than blind elementary school children, partially sighted junior high school girls scored significantly over blind girls, partially sighted junior high school boys did not score significantly better than blind junior high school boys, and there was little difference between performances of blind and partially sighted youngsters at the senior high school level, and (5) the visually handicapped compared more favorably with the seeing in static balance than in any of the other factors measured by the Iowa Brace Test.

Figure 10-3. Visually handicapped girl successfully walking a balance beam.

Myler (1936) administered the Brace Motor Ability Test in her study of the motor ability of the blind. Subjects in her study included 118 males and 78 females between the ages of 7 and 26 at the Texas School for the Blind. Myler found that (1) blind males performed better than blind females on the Brace test, (2) motor abilities of the blind increased throughout the adolescent period (ages 13–18) but decreased after this period, (3) seeing girls scored higher on the Brace test than blind girls, (4) the motor ability of blind boys approximated that of normal boys, (5) different test items were not of equal difficulty for blind and seeing children, and (6) failure to maintain balance was the most common cause of failure of blind youngsters on various items of the test.

It is evident that the visually handicapped lag in motor development. Seeing and partially sighted youngsters appear to make more rapid progress than the blind in the early years, and differences between these groups decrease with age. The results of the few studies that have been conducted suggest that differences result from the inactivity of blind children rather than from factors associated with blindness per se. The blind also apparently perform best in tasks that they understand and that do not require visual orientation or balance.

Cratty (1971b) has suggested tasks that he feels can be accomplished by blind children who do not have difficulties in motor abilities (Table 10–1). He indicates that if a child is unable to perform a majority of these tasks well, some motor problems may be present that may call for special remediation or further neurological evaluation.

Table 10–1. A Schedule of Motor Tasks for Blind Children.

At 4 years of age, a child without vision should be able to do the following:

1. Walk with a normal gait pattern including correct and free arm-swing coordinated with his stride.
2. Run properly, evidencing correct arm-leg coordination.
3. Balance while standing, feet parallel and in line with each other, legs at shoulder width apart, not evidencing pronounced body sway or the need to "catch" himself by suddenly spreading the feet wider.
4. Walk forward about 10 feet in a heel-to-toe manner.
5. Throw a ball with some weight shift.
6. Move arms or legs, separately or together, while in a back-lying position in response to a tactual cue (i.e., when touched).
7. Get up to a stand from a back-lying position in about 2 seconds or less.
8. Walk backwards, feet apart, and move laterally in a coordinated manner, using a step-close-step pattern. Movement to one side should be equally proficient as movement to the other side.

At 5 years of age, the blind child should also be able to do the following:

1. Hop three times on a preferred foot without losing balance.
2. Jump forward with two-footed take-offs, using his arms to some degree.
3. Balance with feet together and parallel for 6 to 8 seconds.
4. Balance in a standing position with the feet in a heel-to-toe position, in line with each other, for 6 to 8 seconds.
5. Jump up about 10 inches in the air from a two-footed take-off.
6. Jump backward a short distance.
7. Throw a ball with a weight shift forward as the ball is released.
8. Arise from a back-lying position to a stand in about 1.5 seconds.

By 6 to 6½, a blind child may be expected to do the following:

1. Skip reasonably well.
2. Throw a ball with a weight shift, accompanied by a step by the leg under the throwing arm.
3. Arise from a back-lying position in about 1 second.
4. Perform a kneel and then a stand with accuracy, one foot at a time, not placing hands on the knees or touching the hands to the mat.
5. React properly to simultaneous touches on the same side arm and leg by moving the other two limbs while in a back-lying position.
6. Move laterally with reasonable speed, using a step-close-step movement and with equal speed and accuracy either side.

By 7½, the blind child should also be able to do the following:

1. Move quickly and accurately in a lateral step-close-step movement to either side.
2. Run rapidly and accurately for a short distance.
3. Jump backward and hop forward on either foot three times in a row.
4. Arise from a back-lying position (when asked to do so as rapidly as possible) in about 1 second or less.
5. When asked to move the limbs touched, react reasonably quickly and accurately to touches occurring at the same time on opposite arms and legs, without evidencing extraneous movement in the other arms.

The child from 8 to 12 years of age should accomplish the tasks outlined above but in addition will, if given the opportunity, participate in various games and evidence an ability to utilize rules of increasing complexity.

From: Cratty, Bryant J. *Movement and Spatial Awareness in Blind Children and Youth*, 1971. Courtesy of Charles C Thomas, Publisher, Springfield, Illinois.

Perceptual Ability and Body Awareness

There is, of course, no question that visual handicaps affect visual perceptual abilities and create a need for the blind to optimally develop their other senses. Contrary to popular misconception, blind people do not have a "sixth sense" but rely on optimal development and use of remaining senses to compensate for the lack of visual input. Although the blind obviously depend on other senses to a greater degree, there is not complete agreement among researchers that these senses are better developed in the blind than in the normally sighted. Seashore and Ling (1918) found that although blind people are skillful in the use of touch, muscle sense, and hearing, they are not more sensitive or keen in sensory discrimination than seeing persons when fundamental capacities are tested. Hanninen (1975) points out that both normally sighted and visually handicapped children born prematurely or deprived of physical activity may exhibit poor kinesthetic awareness. As a result of their observations, Cratty and Sams (1968) reported that concepts of laterality (the ability to distinguish left from right) are extremely poor in congenitally blind children. These authors recommend early training of these children to heighten awareness of body parts, concepts of left and right, and location of objects in relation to themselves.

In a later work, Cratty (1971b) summarized data regarding blind children's verbal responses to various requests to identify components of their bodies. Among his findings he noted (1) that there are blind children who have normal intelligence quotients (IQs) and are free from emotional and motor problems who are as proficient as sighted youngsters of the same age in the verbal identification of body parts, the left-right dimensions of their bodies, and similar judgments, (2) that the deficiencies in body image of blind children with below normal IQs are similar to those that would be expected in populations of sighted youngsters with comparable IQs, (3) that there are no significant differences in the responses of blind girls and boys, and (4) that the verbal identification of body parts may be significantly improved in both sighted and blind children. Cratty (1971b) also identified the following four stages through which children pass in their comprehension of various aspects of body image:

1. *Phase I* — Awareness of the parts of the face, the limbs, some of the less accurate bodily movements, the planes of the body (front, back, sides), and the placement of objects relative to these planes.
2. *Phase II* — Left-right discriminations of body parts and of the body's relationship to objects.
3. *Phase III* — Complex judgments of the body and of body-object relationships; identification of portions of the limbs.
4. *Phase IV* — Identification of body parts and body movements of another person. (Cratty, 1971b, p. 25.)

It is obvious that sight enhances orientation in space and, correspondingly, that blind children will have more difficulty in developing basic spatial judgments than their normally sighted peers. Because they lack sight, it is particularly important for the blind to use auditory cues in making spatial judgments, and early auditory training for this and other purposes is routinely advocated. Cratty (1971b) has studied basic spatial orientations of the blind as represented in rotary movements, perception of pathway linearity and distance while walking, and position relocation. He has found that these abilities can usually be improved through training and has provided useful suggestions for program implemenation.

Posture

The observation that the posture of visually handicapped children is below normal expectations has been made by numerous writers (Hanninen 1975, Cratty 1971b, Oliver 1970, Sherrill 1976). It is not uncommon for the visually handicapped to have kyphosis, lordosis, or scoliosis. In addition, many blind youngsters exhibit a rigid posture while sitting and a habitual flexing of the head on the chest. One of the chief causes of poor posture is lack of physical activity. However, the lack of sight also appears to contribute to postural problems because it inhibits the development of a visual concept of correct posture and the ability to see one's own posture during sitting, standing, and moving. Proper body alignment and balance are also affected by the lack of visual reference points. The normally sighted have the advantage of visual cues to orient themselves and move upright through space.

A number of techniques should be employed to remediate postural deviations with functional causes. One of the most important is

Figure   10–4. Visually   handicapped youngster displaying posture.

participation in a variety of physical and motor activities. Such participation enhances muscle strengthening in all the major muscle groups. Further, where muscular imbalance exists, exercises may be performed to strengthen and stretch appropriate muscles, i.e., to shorten those muscles that are stretched and lengthen those that are hypershortened. In addition to corrective exercises, activities that enhance proper body alignment may be performed. Swimming and gymnastic activities are particularly beneficial for this purpose. It is also important to place the individual in proper postures. Unless the blind person understands and feels what good posture is, he is unlikely to make it a habit. Cratty (1971b) recommends the use of a posture profile consisting of a number of moveable wooden dowels projecting through a vertical board which may be placed along the spine to give the blind child further tactual evidence as to what an upright posture means. In addition to experimenting with various postures and placing oneself in proper posture, the blind child can increase awareness of proper posture by feeling other persons or manipulating dolls. As postural training is given, the values of a good posture should be communicated and understood. In this regard, there is little question that the primary value of a good posture is the enhancement of appearance. The blind may be pursuaded to develop positive postural habits if they understand that a proper posture will enhance their appearance and their social acceptance.

Needs

Although the visually handicapped have the same basic needs for movement experiences as other children, there appear to be certain activities that generally need emphasis in programs for the blind. Since the lack of vision affects the motivation and ability to move, attention must be given to simply encouraging movement and providing opportunity for it. Lack of movement leads to a lag in physical and motor development and thus creates a need to emphasize physical and motor development in programs. Such programs should develop the physical proficiency, fundamental movements and skills, body awareness, and spatial awareness of visually handicapped youngsters. Greater than normal attention must be given to the development of proper body mechanics, fine motor coordination, and balance. Opportunities to learn about spectator sports must be provided so that the blind can gain the knowledge necessary to discuss sports and sport telecasts during early as well as adult years. Activities for the development of auditory discriminations are particularly important since they serve as a basis for orientation and mobility training. A variety of activities should be employed to help the blind understand their disabilities and overcome their fears of participation and movement. It is particularly important that visually handicapped youngsters develop proficiency in sports they can play during their adult years. It is also particularly important that skills be developed in activities that lend themselves to recreational participation.

Although certain activities require extensive modification for successful participation, many others require little or no modification. Activities requiring little or no modification include rowing, hiking, trampolining, bowling, dancing, shuffleboard, swimming, wrestling, weightlifting, snowshoeing, tobogganing, some gymnastic events, and some track and field events. Activities requiring a great deal of modification are generally team sports or sports that involve following a moving object. Examples are softball, baseball, volleyball, and basketball. Football, archery, and golf need some modification. However, these sports have been played with considerable success by many blind individuals.

It is recommended that visually handicapped children participate with normally sighted youngsters to the fullest possible extent. For such participation to be successful, teachers and leaders must carefully select games and plan experiences. Buell (1966) advises that one should look for games having the following characteristics:

1. Blindfolding of one or two players.
2. Sound enabling a sightless child to know exactly what is happening.
3. Different duties for the blind and the seeing.
4. Running to a goal that can be easily found by sightless players.
5. Limited playing area, such as a gymnasium or tennis court.
6. Direct contact, as in wrestling.
7. Line or chain formations.
8. The possibility of players' pairing up.

In teaching of the blind or partially sighted, certain methods should be stressed. Visual demonstrations must be replaced by "kinesthetic teaching." Teachers must move the parts of the body of the child so the child will "feel" the correctness of movement. The child may also better understand an activity by feeling the movement as it is executed by others. Visually handicapped children must also be informed of changes in game situations since they cannot visually follow the events. Teachers must make use of tactual and auditory stimuli in implementing activities. Play areas must be made familiar to participants and care must be taken not to change the location of objects in the play area without explaining the changes. Play areas should be large, uncluttered, and bounded safely (by hedges or different surface areas rather than fences or walls). Balls, boundaries, and equipment should be painted with bright colors (orange and yellow). Although certain special supplies and equipment (such as audible goal locators, audible balls, and guide wires) enhance teaching, most items used in physical activities for visually handicapped children are the same as those used in regular programming. Information pertaining to special supplies and equipment and their use may be found in several texts on adapted physical education.

Auditory Handicaps

Educators of the deaf generally agree that the most critical problem for deaf people is communication and that difficulties in communication strongly affect educational progress and social development. Play, physical education, and recreational experiences are important for the total development of the deaf and hard of hearing since they provide a unique opportunity for socialization. In addition, the auditory handicapped need to participate in such experiences to receive

Table 10–2. Results for Mentally Retarded Deaf Children
on the Heath Railwalking Test.

	N	Mean	SD	r with M. A.	r with M. A.*
Males	41	55.55	40.98		
Females	40	43.00	30.84		
Endogenous	21	64.38	41.08	.59 ± .13	.78 ± .09
Exogenous	22	34.14	23.71	.32 ± .19	−.09 ± .22

*C. A. held constant

Frisina, Dominic R. "A Psychological Study of the Mentally Retarded Child," Doctoral dissertation, Northwestern University, Evanston, Illinois, 1955. As abridged by Helmer R. Myklebust in *The Psychology of Deafness*. New York: Grune & Stratton, Inc., 1964, p. 189. By permission.

the physical and motor benefits derived therefrom. In this section, the relationship of deafness to physical and motor variables, the physical and motor needs of the deaf, the limitations of the deaf in movement activities, and considerations for implementing programs for the deaf will be discussed.

Physical and Motor Performance

The ability to balance has received the most attention of researchers studying the physical and motor status of the deaf. In one of the earliest studies evaluating the motor abilities of deaf children, Long (1932) found that the performance of hearing subjects in walking a balance beam was significantly superior to that of deaf subjects aged 8 to 17. In another study, Morsh (1936) found that, when blindfolded, deaf subjects showed balancing performances inferior to that of blindfolded hearing subjects. He found no difference in balancing performance between bright and dull deaf subjects, although bright hearing subjects were superior to dull hearing subjects. In regard to speed of eye movement, the performance of deaf subjects was inferior to that of hearing subjects. Without blindfolds, both deaf and hearing boys exceeded the balancing performances of deaf and hearing girls.

In another study, dealing with balance and etiology, Frisina (1955) administered the Heath Railwalking test to mentally retarded

Table 10–3. Comparison of Performances of Deaf and Hearing Children
on the Heath Railwalking Test by Age.

Age	Deaf		Hearing	
	N	Mean	N	Mean
7	8	40	72	53
9	10	44	45	77
11	16	63	60	82
13	20	70	51	96
15	21	79	47	118

Myklebust, Helmer R. *The Psychology of Deafness*. New York: Grune & Stratton, Inc., 1964, p. 190. By permission.

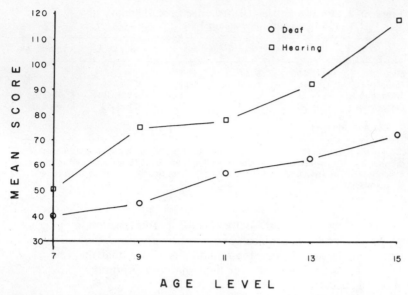

Figure 10-5. Comparison of deaf and hearing on railwalking ability. From: Myklebust, Helmer R., *The Psychology of Deafness.* New York: Grune & Stratton, Inc., 1964, p. 191. By permission.

deaf boys (mean chronological age of 13.5) and girls (mean chronological age of 13.8). He found that the endogenous group was significantly superior on the task to the exogenous group. (Table 10–2). Myklebust (1964) compared the results obtained by Frisina with results he obtained in testing normally hearing subjects of similar ages. He found that mean performances of 106.01 for males and 93.0 for females were significantly higher than the scores for mentally retarded deaf subjects obtained by Frisina.

In a more comprehensive study, Myklebust (1964) tested and compared the performance of deaf and hearing subjects on the Heath Railwalking test and again found that deaf children were inferior to hearing children (Table 10–3 and Figure 10–5). In addition, the deaf were found to progress in ability with age but the hearing were found to maintain their superiority throughout the age ranges studied. In the same study, Myklebust evaluated railwalking performance as a function of the etiology of deafness and found no significant differences between children with acquired, congenital, and undetermined causes of deafness (Table 10–4). However, children whose deafness resulted from meningitis were significantly inferior to each of the other three groups. Myklebust found that the poor performance of this group could be explained by malfunctioning of the semicircular canals — a condition frequently associated with this disease.

In another study, Myklebust (1964) tested the performance of 30 deaf boys and 20 deaf girls on the Oseretsky Test (Table 10–5). The mean chronological age of subjects was 11.1 and the range in chronological age was 8 to 14. The findings indicate that the total group earned a motor age of 9.50, which was about 1½ years behind hearing children. He also found that the deaf fell within the normal range in Dynamic Manual (manual dexterity) and Synkinesia (voluntary-

Table 10–4.   Comparison of Performances of Deaf Children on the
Heath Railwalking Test by Age of Onset and Etiology of Deafness.

Group	N	Mean C.A.	Mean Score	SD
Acquired	41	11.0	74.5	20.0
Undetermined	48	13.5	68.3	17.7
Congenital	86	11.9	71.6	18.4
Meningitis	23	13.3	30.0	7.4

Myklebust, Helmer R. *The Psychology of Deafness.* New York: Grune & Stratton, Inc., 1964, p. 190. By permission.

involuntary movement relationships) tests and showed some motor retardation in tests for General Dynamic (movements of the total body), Simultaneous Movement (movements in two parts of the body), General Static, and Speed. The scores for deaf children on the General Static test, an indicator of the ability to use and maintain balance, show that the children were about 2½ years behind the norm. The deaf were found to be most deficient in the Speed test, which on the Oseretsky Test measures the rate at which complex motor behaviors may be executed.

Myklebust (1964) pursued the factor of speed in a study in which the short form of the Minnesota Spatial Relations Test was administered to 80 deaf males ranging in age from 12 to 20. In this test, the time needed and errors made in placing pieces in proper recesses were determined. It was found that the time scores fell at the 50th percentile, but that scores in errors made for the deaf were at the 15th percentile. Thus, the deaf were inferior not in speed of performance but in quality of performance. Myklebust attributed the difference to the observation that the deaf subjects used primarily a manual trial-and-error approach, trying to fit each block in a recess, whereas the hearing used a "mental" trial-and-error approach that resulted in fewer errors. On the basis of this study, Myklebust hypothesizes that differences in the performances of deaf and hearing children may be related more closely to quality of performance than to speed of performance.

Table 10–5.   Motor Age Scores for Deaf Children on the Oseretsky Test of Motor Proficiency.

	Males N-30 Mean	SD	Females N-20 Mean	SD	Totals N-50 Mean	SD
Chronological Age	11.30	1.20	10.11	1.40	11.10	1.30
Motor Age	9.50	1.60	9.50	1.70	9.50	1.70
General Static	8.11	2.90	8.40	2.10	8.70	2.11
Dynamic Manual	10.11	1.70	10.90	2.10	10.10	2.30
General Dynamic	9.80	2.30	9.90	2.40	9.80	2.30
Speed	6.11	1.11	7.10	2.00	7.50	2.00
Simultaneous Movement	8.90	1.70	9.40	1.90	9.00	1.80
Synkinesia	10.40	1.50	10.40	1.11	10.50	1.70

Myklebust, Helmer R. *The Psychology of Deafness.* New York: Grune & Stratton, Inc., 1964, p. 194. By permission.

As was mentioned previously, Long (1932) found that the hearing were superior to the deaf on balance beam walking. In the same study, Long compared the performances of deaf and hearing subjects in spool packing, serial discrimination (speed of response to visual stimuli), pursuit rotor performance (ability to follow a target), tapping, motility rotor (turning the crank of a drill), and grip strength. Subjects in the study were between 8 and 17 years of age and were paired with hearing subjects by age, sex, and race. For the most part, deaf boys proved superior to hearing boys and deaf girls inferior to hearing girls. When sexes were combined, the scores for deaf and hearing groups were about equal. Of all the test items, the only significant difference between the deaf and hearing was on the balance item. Deaf girls were inferior to deaf boys to a greater degree than hearing girls were to hearing boys.

As was true with other physical and motor areas, relatively little research has been conducted concerning the motor maturation or the development of locomotor abilities of the deaf. Myklebust (1964) conducted a study in which the sitting and walking ages for normal, aphasic, emotionally disturbed, mentally retarded, and deaf subjects were compared. Differences between deaf and hearing children were not significant. The mean age for the normal child to sit unsupported was 6.41 months and for the deaf child 7.03 months. The mean age, in months, to begin to walk was 13.50 months for normal subjects and 14.09 months for those with peripheral deafness. Myklebust concluded that neither sitting unsupported nor beginning to walk was significantly slower for deaf children than for normal children. Frisina (1955) found that mentally retarded deaf children were significantly inferior to normal deaf children in beginning to sit and walk. In view of Mykelbust's finding of no difference between the deaf and the hearing, Frisina's finding suggests that in any group comparison of the motor maturation of deaf and hearing children, the mental age must be a controlled factor.

It seems fair to conclude on the basis of completed research that the deaf, as a group, are inferior to the hearing on static and dynamic balance and motor speed. However, there appears to be little or no difference between hearing and deaf children in motor maturation as reflected by sitting and walking ages and other indicators of motor proficiency. Differences between the deaf and hearing are probably the result of malfunctioning of the semicircular canals.

Clinical data and other observations of the performance of the deaf have led professionals to attribute other physical and motor characteristics to them. Although convincing empirical evidence is lacking, some writers have indicated that deaf children may be underdeveloped physically because of their tendency to withdraw from play activities, games, and sports requiring communication with others. As was mentioned previously, such withdrawal is caused by problems of communication. Mykelbust (1964) states that persons with severe hearing losses tend to walk with a shuffling gait. Since this characteristic is not limited to those with semicircular dysfunctioning, Myklebust assumes it results from the inability of the deaf child to hear movement sounds, i.e., to hear the shuffling noise. Morsh (1936) states that many deaf people with semicircular canal involvement walk with a staggering gait or "walk wide" with their legs apart at night when visual cues are absent. He further states that some excellent deaf swimmers with semicircular canal dysfunctioning never dive for fear they will lose their sense of direction under water. Arnheim, Auxter, and Crowe (1969) state that deaf children have poor body mechanics and poor patterns of locomotion. Fait (1972) asserts that the movements of deaf children may be poorly coordinated, purposeless, vague, and distorted because of the loss of background sounds for orientation and accuracy in the recognition of space and motion.

Limitations

Fortunately, there are few restrictions on the participation of deaf children in games, sports, rhythms, or other movement activities. Perhaps the most important limitation is associated with semicircular canal malfunctioning. If such malfunctioning exists, balance may be impaired. If balance is impaired, high climbing, participation in certain stunts and tumbling activities, and other activities dependent on balance may be contraindicated. When difficulties in balance are caused by semicircular canal dysfunction, improvement in balance as a result of training may not always occur. Training in balance may help the individual to maximize visual and kinesthetic cues for maintaining balance and thereby improve performance in balance activities. However, such training will not alter semicircular canal functioning.

A second major restriction relates to ear operations and infections. It is not uncommon for physicians to curtail swimming, participation in cold weather sports, and climbing for children who have ear infections or who are recovering from ear operations. Since infections may spread and cause more serious damage, such restrictions should be strictly adhered to. In most cases, the wearing of ear plugs serves to completely protect the child in water or in cold weather activities. Participation in such cases should follow medical advice.

Needs

Several techniques should be employed in implementing movement programs for the deaf. Most of these may be traced to the difficulties in communication inherent in deafness. The most basic need is to find a means of communication. As was mentioned previously, communication may take the form of oralism, manualism, or some combination of these techniques. For those who lip-read, the instructor must take care to speak at a moderate rate without exaggerating mouthing sounds. Whenever possible, the deaf should be spoken to at face level rather than from below or above. The instructor should not have deaf people face the sun as they are spoken to out of doors. Whenever possible, the deaf should be allowed to place themselves in the best situation to receive information; this will generally be near the speaker. Care must be taken not to raise the voice to abnormally high levels when speaking to children who wear hearing aids. When physical activity is quite vigorous, it may be advisable to have them remove their hearing aids.

When game and sport activities are implemented, it is particularly important to develop a system of communication to start, stop, or adjust play. Such a system is necessary for safety as well as to control activity. Some of the techniques that have been employed include hand manipulation, switching lights on and off, waving colored flags, and striking percussion instruments. A technique that holds promise for indoor use is a system in which a bright light is activated in response to a whistle.

When teaching the deaf, it is necessary for the group to be small. Group size should not generally exceed seven to ten pupils if groups consist only of deaf pupils. If children have multiple handicaps or are very young, it may be necessary to reduce class size even further. With older and more capable pupils, the class size may be increased. (It should be remembered that sports such as baseball require 18 players for a full team.) When the deaf are integrated with the hearing, class size may be increased. However, exact enrollment will always vary with the type and level of activity and the nature and needs of pupils involved.

In view of their disadvantage, it is particularly important that children with auditory handicaps develop and use their remaining sensory abilities and that teachers and others involved in education and development maximize the use of other senses in educating the deaf. Visual aids can be employed to compensate for the lack of verbal communication. Films, slides, and chalkboards are particularly useful in games and sports. In addition, deaf or hard-of-hearing pupils may be provided with written descriptions of games, rules, and strategy.

Deafness will obviously affect the methods of teaching and learning dances and other rhythmic activities dependent on music. In conducting dance and rhythmic activities, it must be recognized that many children who are unable to hear melodic sounds are able to perceive vibrations. For this reason percussion instruments and other instruments with a low bass sound are employed to enhance the "hearing" of the beat. The deaf may also use their vision to recognize tempo. They may watch the rhythmic movements of the hearing, a rhythmic blinking light, a metronome, or simply the rhythmic beating of a drum. As children learn the beat, they may learn the movements that accompany music. Success in the development of rhythmic and dance skills is important for the deaf because such skills may be applied in social situations; they may serve to draw the deaf toward the mainstream of society. In addition, such activities may be used to enhance auditory perception for those with residual hearing.

As is true with the hearing, the deaf and hard of hearing need a broad, well-rounded program of movement experiences. Program emphasis will vary according to the needs of each individual. For those who are physically underdeveloped, specific exercises and activities to improve cardiovascular endurance, dynamic strength, static strength, flexibility, agility, and power need to be stressed. Analysis of the physical and motor characteristics of the deaf as a group points to a need for activities to improve body mechanics, spatial concepts, and coordination. Many deaf and hard-of-hearing individuals need specific training in balance activities. Training should be designed to enhance balance by developing the ability to utilize and coordinate visual and kinesthetic cues. Such cues are helpful to all children but may be particularly useful for those who need to compensate for semicircular canal dysfunctioning. Where balance deficits and the lack of sound cues lead to shuffling gait, attention should be placed on proper body mechanics, particularly in developing proper walking abilities. In view of the data which indicates that deaf children are inferior in speed of complex motor acts, Myklebust (1964) suggests that programs include a series of motor functions progressing from simple manual acts to complex body integrations.

In programs for the hard of hearing, attention must be given to auditory training, i.e., learning to optimally use what hearing is available. Dance and rhythmic activities are particularly helpful in the development of listening abilities. Activities designed to develop other auditory perceptual abilities are recommended. For the deaf, training of the other senses to compensate for the loss of hearing must be stressed.

In planning activity programs for the deaf, there is nothing more important than involving them in activities that promote social interaction. The deaf tend to withdraw because of lack of communication skills, and withdrawal obviously affects social development. Lifetime sports, group games, rhythm and dance activities, informal play, and other play and leisure activities need to be stressed to draw the deaf into wholesome social situations. Sports such as fencing, archery, golf, badminton, bowling, and tennis are excellent for lifetime interaction in leisure settings. Aquatics are also of value. Not only are such activities important for their physical and motor values but also for the social interaction they may stimulate. Few things are more important for deaf persons than the opportunity for social interaction.

11

MENTAL RETARDATION, EMOTIONAL-BEHAVIORAL DISABILITIES, AND SPECIFIC LEARNING DISABILITIES AND PHYSICAL AND MOTOR PERFORMANCE

This chapter deals with the relationship of physical and motor performance to the most prevalent special populations: the mentally retarded, children with specific learning disabilities, and the emotionally-behaviorally disabled. The physical and motor abilities, interests, limitations, and needs of these populations are discussed. In addition, the effect of these deviances on implementation of movement programs is analyzed, and practical hints for teaching are presented.

Throughout this chapter, the physical and motor performances of children with these three handicapping conditions are identified and are compared with those of normal children. The identifications and comparisons made are generally based on data collected in relevant research. Before reading the material, however, it is important to realize that the data presented indicate status and not potential. Although the present status of handicapped children is generally below that of normal children of the same sex and age on measures of physical and motor performances, this information is not meant to imply that this is as it *should* be or *can* be. The data only reflect what *is* or what *has been*.

Mental Retardation

G. Lawrence Rarick and his associates have conducted much of the research regarding the physical and motor abilities of the mentally retarded. Since repeated reference will be made to these studies, it may be helpful to briefly describe and distinguish them. Francis and Rarick (1959) designed the first major project to obtain information on the gross motor abilities of mentally retarded, using children attending the public schools of Madison and Milwaukee, Wisconsin. The IQs of these children were between 50 and 90 and their chronological age ranged from 7.5 to 14.5 years. The subjects included 181 boys and 103 girls. Scores of the mentally retarded on a battery of 11 motor performance tests were compared with the achievements of normal children.

Subsequently, Rarick, Widdop, and Broadhead (1970) studied the motor performance of a national sample of educable mentally retarded (EMR) children and compared their performance by age and sex with national standards. Usable sample data were collected from 4235 EMR children from ages 8 to 18 with an IQ range of 50 to 80. The subjects attended public schools during the 1966 calendar year. A modification of the AAHPER Youth Physical Fitness test was administered to the subjects, and the results served as the basis for norms for the mildly retarded (AAHPER, 1976) and the Special Fitness Test Manual for the Mentally Retarded (AAHPER, 1968).

Rarick and Dobbins (1972) later conducted an investigation (1) to identify the factor structure of motor abilities of mentally retarded boys and girls in two age ranges 6 to 9 years and 10 to 13 years and to ascertain the extent to which the factor structure differed with chronological age and sex, (2) to determine if the factor structure of motor abilities of EMR children differed from that of intellectually normal children of the same age and sex, (3) to provide baseline data by which the motor performances of EMR children and normal children could be compared by age and sex, and (4) to prepare appropriate guidelines for curricular development based on the findings of the investigation. The 406 subjects in the study included 135 young retardates (ages 6 to 9), 126 older retardates (ages 10 to 13), and 145 intellectually normal youngsters. All subjects were from the San Francisco Bay Area and were tested in 1970 and 1971. IQs ranged from 44 to 81 (Stanford-Binet Scale) and 44 to 95 (WISC Scale). Different tests were used to assess the intellectual abilities of students, and except for a few isolated cases, the IQs were well within what is generally accepted to be the IQ range of the EMR. A total of 61 tests were administered and grouped into the following 14 categories: static muscular strength, explosive muscular strength, muscular strength endurance, gross body coordination, cardiorespiratory endurance, limb-eye coordination, manual dexterity, static balance, dynamic balance, kinesthesis, flexibility, speed and coordination of gross limb movements, body fat, and body size. This study was originally reported by Rarick and Dobbins (1972) and later was published by Rarick, Dobbins, and Broadhead (1976); in subsequent discussion in this chapter, the latter reference will generally be used. However, in some instances, material discussed here is available only in the first report (Rarick and Dobbins, 1972) and will be so designated.

Rarick and McQuillan (1977) conducted a study to determine the factor structure of motor abilities of trainable mentally retarded (TMR) boys and girls, to utilize the results of the factor analysis in developing diagnostic tests appropriate for the assessment of the perceptual-motor and gross motor abilities of TMR children, and to prepare guidelines for the development of curricular materials based on the results of the factor analysis. Actual data collection began late in August of 1973 and lasted until early March of 1975. Subjects included both institutionalized and home-reared TMR males and females in the age range 6 through 21. Approximately 20 per cent of the sample were from Sonoma State Hospital, and the remainder attended schools in the San Francisco East Bay Area. Subjects were grouped into the following four categories: youngest or late childhood (6 to 9 years), young or early adolescence (9 to 13 years of age), old or middle adolescence (14 to 17 years), and oldest or late adolescence (18 to 21 years). Usable data were obtained on 266 males and 194 females. Approximately one third of the subjects were Down's Syndrome children. A total of 54 tests and measures were used for data analysis. Performance was measured in the following hypothesized factors: static muscular strength, explosive muscular strength, muscular strength endurance, limb-eye coordination, manual dexterity, static balance, dynamic balance, flexibility, body fat, and body size. Comparisons within age groups and by sex were made between the TMR subjects in this study and the EMR children studied earlier by Rarick and Dobbins (1972).

Physical Proficiency

In this section, the physical performances of retarded and normal subjects will be identified and compared. The areas of physical performance to be analyzed are static strength, dynamic strength, explosive strength, flexibility, speed, cardiovascular endurance, and agility.

STATIC STRENGTH

Results obtained by Rarick, Dobbins, and Broadhead (1976) and those reported by Francis and Rarick (1959) clearly demonstrate that intellectually normal subjects of both sexes exceed the performance levels of EMR children, that the slopes of the performance scores of the normal and the retarded are similar, and that significant sex differences favoring boys exist on measures of grip strength (Tables 11–1 and 11–2). Rarick, Dobbins, and Broadhead (1976) reported that the rank order of normal boys (NB), normal girls (NG), educable mentally retarded boys (EMR-B), and educable mentally retarded girls (EMR-G) was invariable for children aged 6 through 9. The percentage of mentally retarded boys and girls equal to or above normal median points of performance was relatively small (range from 6.3 per cent to 11.3 per cent). Howe (1959) found that the grip strength of normal boys significantly exceeded that of retarded boys but that the grip strength of normal girls was not significantly different from that of retarded girls. Results reported by Rarick, Dobbins, and Broadhead (1976) and by Francis and Rarick (1959) reveal improvement in performance with age (Fig. 11–1). Results on measures of elbow and knee flexion and extension strength reported by Rarick, Dobbins, and Broadhead (1976) generally are in agreement with results reported on grip strength. These indicate that normal children are substantially stronger than EMR children of the same age and sex.

The flexed-arm hang has also been utilized as a measure of static strength for intellectually normal girls and retarded boys and girls. Comparison of the data on the performances of normal girls (AAHPER, 1975) with those on the performances of mildly retarded boys and girls (AAHPER, 1976) indicates that the performance of mildly retarded boys exceeds that of intellectually normal and mildly retarded girls (Table 11–3). Little difference exists between the performances of mildly retarded girls and normal girls between the ages of 10 and 17. Throughout this age span, mildly retarded boys show consistent improvement, while normal and retarded girls show little change.

Rarick and McQuillan (1977) measured the elbow strength, knee strength, and grip strength of TMR subjects and compared their performance with that of EMR subjects measured in the earlier study of Rarick, Dobbins, and Broadhead (1976). They reported that the elbow strength, knee strength, and grip strength performance of EMR subjects exceeds that of TMR subjects of the same sex and age (ages ranged from 6 to 13). They further reported that the performance of TMR boys exceeds that of TMR girls on measures of static strength and that TMR boys show continued improvement between the ages of 6 and 21. Although TMR boys were found to improve in knee strength, their rate of improvement declined after the 14 to 17.9 year period. TMR girls showed a decline in elbow and knee strength but an improvement in right grip strength in the same period.

DYNAMIC STRENGTH

A measure of dynamic strength that has been used frequently in assessing the physical proficiency of intellectually retarded and normal pupils is the number of sit-ups performed in one minute. Comparison of norms of the mildly retarded (AAHPER, 1976) with those of normal boys and girls (AAHPER, 1975) shows clearly that the performances of normal boys and girls exceed those of mildly retarded boys and girls (Table 11–4). These same data indicate a superiority in sit-up performance of boys over girls between the ages of 10 and 17 with a wider gap as age increases. Rarick, Dobbins, and Broadhead (1976) reported that between the ages of 6 and 8, the gap in performance between normal boys and girls is negligible. These authors

Text continued on page 331

Table 11–1. Comparisons of EMR and Normal Boys and Girls on Selected Measures of Physical Fitness.

Components of Physical Fitness	Group Mean Comparisons	Sex Comparisons at Different Ages	Normal and EMR Comparisons	Percentage of EMR Subjects Equal to or Above Normal Median (%)
Static Strength Right grip strength (kg.)	NB 19.04 NG 17.92 EMR-B 14.86 EMR-G 12.73	Rank order at ages 6–9 is NB, NG, EMR-B, EMR-G. Significant sex differences favoring boys.	Both EMR and N increase with age. Slopes of curves are similar. N significantly exceed EMR.	Boys 11.3 Girls 6.3
Left grip strength (kg.)	NB 18.66 NG 17.06 EMR-B 14.25 EMR-G 12.12	With the exception of comparable performance at age 7 by NB and NG, rank order is: NB, NG, EMR-B, and EMR-G. Overall significant sex differences favoring boys.	Both EMR and N increase with age. Slopes of curves are similar. N significantly exceed EMR.	Boys 7.0 Girls 7.8
Dynamic Strength Sit-ups (No. in 1 min.)	NB 22.59 NG 21.24 EMR-B 16.76 EMR-G 11.72	At ages 6–8, the gap between the performance levels of retarded boys and girls is substantial, whereas that between normal boys and girls is negligible.	EMR-B about 2 years behind NB. EMR-G do not reach the performance of 6-year-old NG until age 11.	Boys 19.7 Girls 17.2
Explosive Strength Vertical jump	NB 8.65 NG 7.94 EMR-B 6.61 EMR-G 5.68	At ages 6–9, performance of boys significantly exceeds that of girls.	N significantly superior to EMR. Slopes of curves are similar.	Boys 19.7 Girls 0

Test	Group	Value		
Standing broad jump (in.)	NB NG EMR-B EMR-G	52.35 50.86 44.41 37.98	At ages 6–9, the gap between EMR boys and girls is substantial. Gap between normal boys and girls is small.	At ages 6–9, EMR significantly below N. Slopes of curves are similar.	Boys 19.7 Girls 0
Flexibility Toe touch (cm.)	NB NG EMR-B EMR-G	20.49 21.90 16.91 15.27	Between ages 6–9, NG exceed NB at 3 of 4 ages; EMR-B exceed EMR-G at 3 of 4 ages.	EMR are less flexible than N. EMR show little improvement with age.	Boys 33.8 Girls 7.8
Speed 5–35-yard dash	NB NG EMR-B EMR-G	5.31 5.42 5.73 6.23	All groups increase with age; rank order at all ages: NB, NG, EMR-B, EMR-G. Performance of boys is significantly better than that of girls, but gap is greater between EMR than between N.	EMR are about 2 years behind N of the same sex and age, and gap increases with age. Difference is significant.	Boys 25.0 Girls 15.6
Cardiovascular Endurance Physical work capacity (kpm/min.)	NB NG EMR-B EMR-G	347.30 269.20 306.70 266.80	NB exceed NG, and curves diverge, EMR-B exceed EMR-G, but curves tend to remain parallel. Overall sex differences favor boys.	EMR-B superior to NG, NB superior to EMR-B. At age 8, EMR-G slightly better than NG. Overall difference between EMR and N not significant.	Boys 39.4 Girls 35.9
150-yard dash	NB NG EMR-B EMR-G	28.87 29.32 32.18 35.83	Performance of boys significantly exceeds that of girls. EMR-G particularly poor on this test.	Significant differences favoring N were found. EMR are about 4 years behind N. The performance of all subjects improves with age, and the gap between N and EMR increases with age.	Boys 19.7 Girls 7.8

Table continued on following page

Table 11–1.   Comparisons of EMR and Normal Boys and Girls on Selected Measures of Physical Fitness (*Continued*)

Components of Physical Fitness	Group Mean Comparisons		Sex Comparisons at Different Ages	Normal and EMR Comparisons	Percentage of EMR Subjects Equal to or Above Normal Median (%)
Agility Scramble (sec.)	NB NG EMR-B EMR-G	5.21 5.31 5.75 6.37	Performance of boys significantly exceeds that of girls. Gap between EMR-B and EMR-G is much greater than that between NB and NG.	Performance of N significantly exceeds that of EMR. Curves are parallel.	Boys 25.4 Girls 14.1
Skinfold Abdominal (mm.)	NB NG EMR-B EMR-G	4.95 7.03 8.33 12.12	Skinfold of EMR-B less than that of EMR-G and curves are generally parallel. Skinfold of NB less than that of NG at age 6 and 8; skinfolds are similar.	Skinfold of N significantly less than that of the EMR.	Boys 80.3 Girls 78.2

N = Normal; EMR = Educable Mentally Retarded; B = Boys; G = Girls.

Abridged from G. Lawrence Rarick, D. Alan Dobbins, and Geoffrey D. Broadhead. *The Motor Domain and Its Correlates in Educationally Handicapped Children,* Englewood Cliffs, N.J.: Prentice-Hall, Inc., 1976, pp. 38–39.

Table 11-2. Measures of Central Tendency of Selected Populations on the Grip Strength Test (pounds).*

			Populations							
	Normal Boys (Fleishman 1964a)	Normal Girls (Fleishman 1965a)	Normal Boys (Keogh 1965)		Normal Girls (Keogh 1965)		Retarded Boys† (Francis and Rarick, 1959)‡		Retarded Girls† (Francis and Rarick, 1959)‡	
Age			RH	LH	RH	LH	RH	LH	RH	LH
5			18.3	18.1	16.1	15.8				
6			23.5	21.8	19.3	18.4				
7			26.8	83.6	22.9	22.2				
8			31.3	29.6	28.0	27.1	13.4	12.1	7.8	7.6
9			37.3	35.2	30.8	29.4	14.4	13.0	12.3	12.0
10			40.1	38.7	35.3	34.0	15.6	14.1	12.3	12.5
11			45.2	44.3	45.8	42.4	17.7	16.7	17.1	15.7
12							18.6	17.5	17.9	16.9
13	65	42					24.0	23.7	18.9	18.6
14	78	43					26.4	24.8	22.2	22.9
15	93	55								
16	106	59								
17	109	63								
18	114	67								

RH = Right Hand; LH = Left Hand.

*All scores reported are median points unless noted otherwise.
†Mental retardation defined as IQ of 50–90.
‡Mean scores.

Figure 11-1. Means of normal and educable mentally retarded children on tests of grip strength by chronological age and sex. From: Rarick, G. Lawrence, and D. Alan Dobbins. *Basic Components in the Motor Performance of Educable Mentally Retarded Children: Implications for Curriculum Development.* Berkeley: Department of Physical Education, University of California, 1972, p. 68.

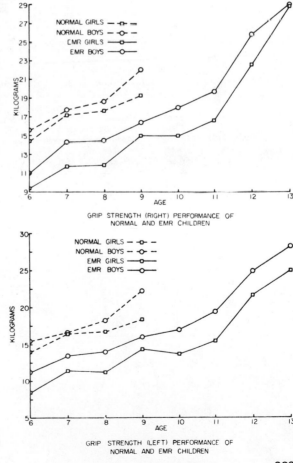

GRIP STRENGTH (RIGHT) PERFORMANCE OF NORMAL AND EMR CHILDREN

GRIP STRENGTH (LEFT) PERFORMANCE OF NORMAL AND EMR CHILDREN

329

Table 11–3. Median Points of Selected Populations on the Flexed Arm Hang (seconds).

Age	Normal Girls (AAHPER 1975)	Populations		
		Mildly Retarded Boys (AAHPER 1976)	Mildly Retarded Girls (AAHPER 1976)	Moderately Retarded Boys (Johnson and Londeree 1976)
5				
6				
7				
8		7	5	
9		8	6	
10	7	8	8	
11	8	11	7	
12	6	12	5	
13	7	10	5	
14	7	13	6	1.0
15	8	12	5	
16	7	17	5	1.2
17	8	17	4	
18		25	7	

Table 11–4. Median Points of Selected Populations on the Sit-up Test.

Age	Normal Boys (AAHPER 1975) (60 sec.)	Normal Girls (AAHPER 1975) (60 sec.)	Mildly Retarded Boys (AAHPER 1976) (60 sec.)	Populations Mildly Retarded Girls (AAHPER 1976) (60 sec.)	Moderately Retarded Boys (Johnson and Londeree 1976) (30 sec.)	Moderately Retarded Girls (Johnson and Londeree 1976) (30 sec.)
5						
6					0	
7						0
8			16	13	4	
9			17	15		
10	24	22	20	18	6	
11	28	23	22	18	7	4
12	37	29	24	19	8	
13	42	31	25	18		
14	45	32	26	20	10	7
15	47	31	31	20	12	6
16	49	31	29	21	10	8
17	49	32	30	20	10	
18	49	32	31	20	9	7

also found that 19.7 per cent of mildly retarded boys and 17.2 per cent of mildly retarded girls scored above the normal median for their sex. Data provided by Rarick, Dobbins, and Broadhead (1976) and by Rarick, Widdop and Broadhead (1970) indicate that the performance of retarded boys exceeds that of retarded girls, that the gap between the two is substantial, and that the gap increases with age. It is also evident that the performance of normal boys consistently increases to age 17, whereas little improvement is noted in the scores of retarded boys after age 15, retarded girls after age 14, and normal girls after age 14. Results in a 30-second sit-up test administered to moderately retarded children by Johnson and Londeree (1976) suggest that this group would perform significantly below the mildly retarded if the tests were of the same length (Table 11–4). Rarick, Dobbins, and Broadhead (1976) employed bicycle ergometer performance and trunk and leg raises for time as other measures of muscular strength endurance, and they report results similar to those found for sit-up tests in regard to disability, age, and sex comparisons.

Rarick and McQuillan (1977) administered four tests of muscular strength endurance to TMR subjects: sit-ups, leg raises for time, trunk raises for time, and bicycle ergometer with resistance. These investigators subsequently compared the results with those of normal and EMR boys and girls and reported that the performances of normal and EMR subjects exceeded those of TMR boys and girls of the same sex and age.

EXPLOSIVE STRENGTH

Although not included in the AAHPER Youth Fitness Test, the vertical jump has been used extensively as a measure of explosive strength. Howe (1959) found that the performance of normal boys and girls significantly exceeds that of retarded subjects of the same sex on the Sargent jump. Results reported by Rarick and Dobbins (1972) indicate that normal boys and girls are significantly superior to EMR boys and girls and that the slopes of the curves are similar throughout ages 6 to 9 (Fig. 11–2). In addition, the performance of boys signifi-

Figure 11–2. Vertical jump performance of normal and EMR children. From: Rarick, G. Lawrence, and D. Alan Dobbins. *Basic Components in the Motor Performance of Educable Mentally Retarded Children: Implications for Curriculum Development.* Berkeley: Department of Physical Education. University of California, 1972, p. 56.

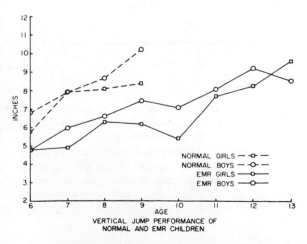

VERTICAL JUMP PERFORMANCE OF
NORMAL AND EMR CHILDREN

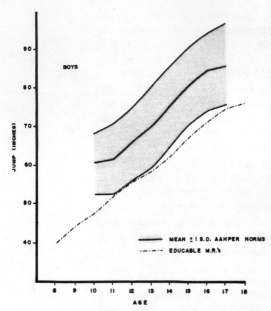

Figure 11–3. Mean performance of educable mentally retarded boys and girls on the standing broad jump in comparison to standards on normal boys and girls (AAHPER norms). From: Rarick, G. Lawrence, James H. Widdop, and Geoffrey D. Broadhead. "The Physical Fitness and Motor Performance of Educable Mentally Retarded Children." *Except. Child.* 36: 509–519, 1970, p. 513.

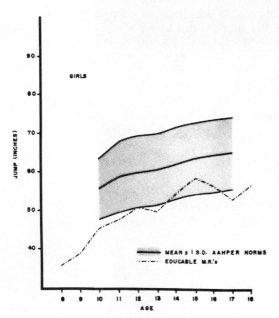

cantly exceeds that of girls. The percentage of mentally retarded subjects equal to or above normal median points is 19.7 per cent for boys and 0 per cent for girls.

A very frequently used measure of muscular power has been the standing broad jump. A comparison of median points of selected populations on the standing broad jump is presented in Table 11–5, in which the results of several studies are compared. The data indicate the superiority of normal boys over retarded boys and of normal girls over retarded girls on the standing broad jump. Interestingly, the performance of normal girls exceeds or is equal to that of retarded boys up to age 14, after which the performance of retarded boys is superior. Both normal and retarded boys show improvement from ages 10 to 17, and both normal and retarded girls show little change in performance after age 14. Rarick, Widdop, and Broadhead (1970) frequently found that the scores of the mentally retarded are often one standard deviation below the normal mean for subjects of the same sex (Fig. 11–3).

In comparing standing broad jump performances of intellectually normal and retarded youngsters between the ages of 6 and 9, Rarick, Dobbins, and Broadhead (1976) found that the retarded groups perform significantly below normal and that the gap between sexes in the EMR group is substantial in this age range (Fig. 11–4). The gap between normal boys and girls is negligible at those ages. However, the gap between normal boys and girls also increases with age. That the gap between normal and EMR girls is greater than that between normal and EMR boys is supported by the fact that the performances of 19.0 per cent of EMR boys and 0 per cent of EMR girls are equal to or above normal median points. Data in Table 11–5 clearly indicate that moderately retarded boys and girls perform below levels attained by both normal and mildly retarded subjects. Sengstock (1966) found that normal boys significantly exceed EMR boys on the standing broad jump.

Rarick and McQuillan (1977) investigated the standing broad jump ability of TMR subjects aged 6 to 21 (Fig. 11–5). They report that the performance of TMR boys exceeds that of TMR girls at all age levels. Although the performances of TMR boys and girls increase up to age 17, the researchers noted a decline in the performance of both sexes in the 18 to 21 age range. In comparing the performance of TMR children with that of EMR subjects aged 6 to 13, these investigators found that the performance of EMR subjects exceeds that of TMR subjects of the same sex and age.

Figure 11–4. Standing broad jump performance of normal and EMR children. From: Rarick, G. Lawrence, and D. Alan Dobbins. *Basic Components in the Motor Performance of Educable Mentally Retarded Children: Implications for Curriculum Development.* Berkeley: Department of Physical Education, University of California, 1972, p. 56.

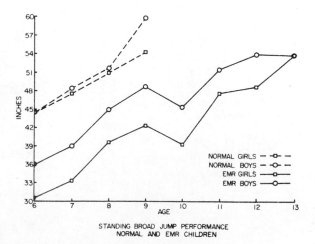

STANDING BROAD JUMP PERFORMANCE
NORMAL AND EMR CHILDREN

Table 11–5. Median Points of Selected Populations on the Standing Broad Jump (inches).

	Populations									
Age	Normal Boys (Keogh 1973)	Normal Girls (Keogh 1973)	Normal Boys (Espenshade 1968)	Normal Girls (Espenshade 1968)	Normal Boys (AAHPER 1975)	Normal Girls (AAHPER 1975)	Mildly Retarded Boys (AAHPER 1976)	Mildly Retarded Girls (AAHPER 1976)	Moderately Retarded Boys (Johnson and Londeree 1976)	Moderately Retarded Girls (Johnson and Londeree 1976)
5			33.7	31.6					10	12
6	46	43	37.4	36.2					14	11
7	50	46	41.6	40.0						13
8	53	49	46.7	45.9			40	37	25	17
9	56	52	50.4	51.3			46	40		22
10	61	56	54.7		60	55	47	46	26	24
11	66	63	61.0	52.0	62	58	54	48	34	24
12	70	62	64.9		66	60	58	51	32	26
13	76	63	69.3	62.1	70	60	60	51	38	27
14	82	63	73.2	62.7	76	63	63	54	45	27
15	84	64	79.5	63.2	81	64	69	54	39	28
16	86	64	88.0	63.0	85	64	73	56	39	27
17			88.4		87	65	74	57	37	34
18							78	57		

Figure 11–5. Mean standing broad jump scores by age and sex of TMR and EMR subjects. From: Rarick, G. Lawrence, and James P. McQuillan. *The Factor Structure of Motor Abilities of Trainable Mentally Retarded Children: Implications for Curriculum Development.* Final Report, Project No. H23–2544. Grant No. OEG-0-73-5170 (607). Department of Health, Education and Welfare, U.S. Office of Education. Bureau of Education for the Handicapped. Berkeley: Department of Physical Education, University of California, 1977, p. 99.

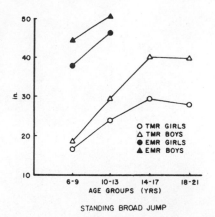

STANDING BROAD JUMP

FLEXIBILITY

Although it has often been asserted that the mentally retarded are quite flexible, relatively little research has been conducted on flexibility. Rarick, Dobbins, and Broadhead (1976) compared the toe touching, spinal rotation, spinal extension, and lateral spinal extension performances of EMR and normal youngsters between the ages of 6 and 9 and found that normal children are significantly superior to EMR children on all four measures of flexibility and that the EMR boys are superior to EMR girls on each of the four tests. Except for spinal rotation, the performance of normal girls exceeds that of normal boys. However, EMR boys excel EMR girls on all four measures of flexibility. Interestingly, the performances of 33.8 per cent of retarded boys and 7.8 per cent of retarded girls equal or exceed normal median points in toe touching.

Rarick and McQuillan (1977) administered tests for toe touching, spinal extension, and lateral spinal extension to TMR boys and girls between the ages of 6 and 21. These investigators found differences between sexes were mixed and that the scores of TMR children on flexibility measures declined with age. However, when age comparisons were made with scores of EMR subjects (ages 6 to 13), it was noted that TMR subjects showed greater flexibility.

SPEED

In one of the earliest studies in which the speed of retarded children was compared to that of normal youngsters, Francis and Rarick (1959) reported that the superiority of the normal child is so great that at no age between 8 and 14 did the mean scores of the mentally retarded approximate those of normal children of the same sex. Howe (1959) also found that the mean 50-yard dash performances of normal boys and girls were significantly better than those of retarded boys and girls, respectively. Sengstock (1966) found that normal boys significantly exceeded EMR boys on the 50-yard dash.

An analysis of data on 50-yard dash performance obtained in a number of studies leads to several interesting observations (Table 11–6). Of the groups considered, normal boys perform the best and continue to improve from age 10 to age 17. Normal girls perform

Table 11-6. Median Points of Selected Populations on the 50-Yard Dash (seconds).

					Population					
Age	Normal Boys (AAHPER 1975)	Normal Girls (AAHPER 1976)	Mildly Retarded Boys (AAHPER 1976)	Mildly Retarded Girls (AAHPER 1976)	Moderately Retarded Boys (Johnson and Londeree 1976)	Moderately Retarded Girls (Johnson and Londeree 1976)	Blind Boys (Buell 1973)	Blind Girls (Buell 1973)	Partially Sighted Boys (Buell 1973)	Partially Sighted Girls (Buell 1973)
5										
6					16.6	18.2				
7					17.1	17.8				
8			10.5	11.3	14.3	17.8				
9			9.9	10.5	13.1	15.6				
10	8.2	8.5	9.2	9.3	13.1	14.8	11.1	13.3	9.2	11.0
11	8.0	8.4	8.9	9.1	13.0	13.4	10.3	12.7	8.8	10.6
12	7.8	8.2	8.3	8.8	11.0	14.0	9.8	12.0	8.7	10.3
13	7.5	8.1	8.2	8.9	12.1	13.0	9.3	11.2	8.5	10.0
14	7.1	8.0	8.0	8.7	10.7	13.0	9.0	11.2	8.1	9.6
15	6.9	8.1	7.5	8.6	10.0	12.2	8.6	11.2	7.6	9.6
16	6.7	8.3	7.3	9.0	10.1		8.3	11.0	7.3	10.0
17	6.6	8.2	6.9	9.0	10.4	12.4	8.0	11.2	7.0	10.0
18			7.1	9.0	10.3	12.8				

Figure 11-6. Mean performance of educable mentally retarded boys and girls on the 50-yard dash in comparison to standards on normal boys and girls (AAHPER norms). From: Rarick, G. Lawrence, James H. Widdop, and Geoffrey D. Broadhead. "The Physical Fitness and Motor Performance of Educable Mentally Retarded Children," *Except. Child.* 36:509–519, 1970, p. 514.

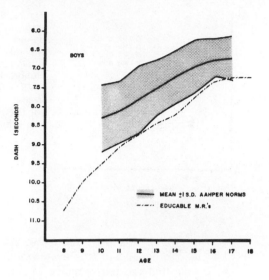

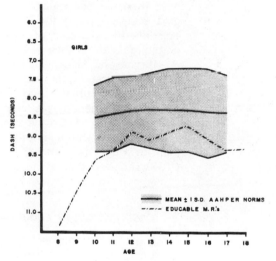

more slowly than normal boys but exceed the performance of retarded boys up to age 13. After that age, the performance of mildly retarded boys exceeds that of normal girls. Mildly retarded boys improve in ability from age 8 to age 17 and invariably surpass mildly retarded girls. Mildly retarded girls and moderately retarded boys and girls are slowest in performance. These groups show improvement up to about age 15. After age 15, performance either decreases or remains stable. A graphic view of the data indicates that the gap between normal and retarded girls tends to decrease as age increases but remains stable for boys (Figure 11–6).

In their study, Rarick, Dobbins, and Broadhead (1976) measured performance on the 5-to-35-yard dash — which they consider a measure of explosive muscular strength. In this event, the subject's score is the time required to negotiate a 5 to 35 yard distance. These investigators found that the performance of normal children was superior to that of retarded children, that the performances of retarded boys

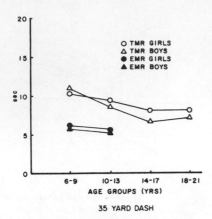

Figure 11–7. Mean 35-yard dash scores of TMR and EMR subjects. From: Rarick, G. Lawrence, and James P. McQuillan. *The Factor Structure of Motor Abilities of Trainable Mentally Retarded Children: Implications for Curriculum Development.* Final Report, Project No. H23–2544. Grant No. OEG-0-73-5170 (607). Department of Health, Education, and Welfare. U.S. Office of Education. Bureau of Education for the Handicapped. Berkeley: Department of Physical Education, University of California, 1977, p. 99.

and girls were about two years behind normal, and that the gap increased with age even though all groups improved with age. The fact that the performance of retarded boys was closer to that of normal boys than the performance of retarded girls was to that of normal girls is supported by the finding that 25.0 per cent of retarded boys but only 15.6 per cent of retarded girls were equal to or above the normal median for their sex.

Rarick and McQuillan (1977) also investigated the performance of TMR boys and girls on the 35-yard dash and compared results to those of EMR subjects (Fig. 11–7). They found that the performance of TMR boys generally exceeded that of TMR girls throughout the age period 6 to 21. On the average, both groups improved in performance between the ages of 6 and 17 but showed either no improvement or a decline in the 18 to 21 year period. Rarick and McQuillan (1977) reported that at no age level was the performance of TMR subjects as good as that of 6- to 9-year-old EMR children.

CARDIOVASCULAR ENDURANCE

A very commonly used measure of cardiovascular endurance that has been employed with normal youngsters has been the 600-yard run-walk. Sengstock (1966) found that normal boys significantly exceeded EMR boys on the 600-yard run-walk. Since this distance has generally been found to be too long for retarded subjects, the 300-yard run-walk has been employed to measure their cardiovascular endurance. Data from several studies indicate that the mildly retarded exceed the moderately retarded on the 300-yard run-walk and that the performance of boys exceeds that of girls at the same intellectual level (Table 11–7). Mildly retarded boys show constant improvement between the ages of 8 and 18, whereas the performance of mildly retarded girls appears to level off at age 15. Moderately retarded youngsters improve from age 7 to age 10 or 11 but their performances appear to fluctuate beyond that point; this fluctuation may be due to inadequacy of the number of subjects used to develop norms.

Rarick, Dobbins, and Broadhead (1976) compared the performances of retarded and normal children on a physical work capacity test and a 150-yard dash (see Table 11–1). Results are somewhat dif-

Table 11-7. Median Points of Selected Populations on the 300-Yard Run-Walk (seconds).

Age	Mildly Retarded Boys (AAHPER 1976)	Mildly Retarded Girls (AAHPER 1976)	Moderately Retarded Boys (Johnson and Londeree 1976)	Moderately Retarded Girls (Johnson and Londeree 1976)
5				
6				188
7			151	144
8	93	94	144	
9	84	93	139	138
10	80	83	127	129
11	75	83		125
12	72	78	99	131
13	70	76	112	117
14	67	75	102	125
15	61	80	91	128
16	59	78	100	120
17	56	82	85	114
18	57	80		111
19				
20			242	153

ferent from those found in other tests of physical proficiency. They indicate that retarded boys are superior to normal girls between the ages of 6 and 9 and that at age 8 retarded girls perform slightly better than normal girls. These data account for the overall lack of significant difference between the performances of normal and retarded subjects. Overall sex differences, however, favor boys.

On the 150-yard dash, significant differences in favor of normal subjects were found for age 6 through age 9. Although the performance of all subjects improved with age, the gap between EMR and normal subjects also increased with age. Normal boys excelled normal girls, normal girls excelled retarded boys, and retarded boys surpassed retarded girls. Retarded girls performed very poorly in this test.

Rarick and McQuillan (1977) studied the 150-yard dash performances of TMR boys and girls between the ages of 6 and 21. They reported that the performance of TMR boys exceeded that of TMR girls and that the gap between the two groups increased with age. The scores of TMR boys and girls improved from age 6 to age 17. However, the performances of both groups declined in the 18 to 21 year period. In comparing these results with those of EMR subjects between the ages of 6 and 13, Rarick and McQuillan found that the performance of EMR subjects exceeded that of TMR subjects of the same sex and age.

AGILITY

Rarick, Dobbins, and Broadhead (1976) administered the scramble test as a measure of agility in their investigation of the motor performance of EMR youngsters. In the scramble test, the subject is asked to move as quickly as possible from the supine position to the vertical position and to retrieve a baton and return to the starting supine position. As summarized in Table 11-1, the performance of normal subjects significantly exceeds that of the retarded. The per-

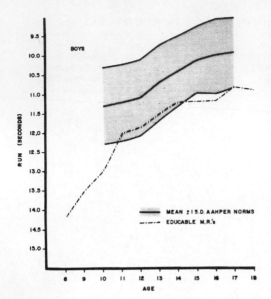

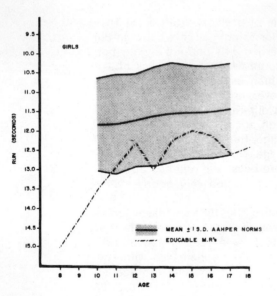

Figure 11–8. Mean performance of educable mentally retarded boys and girls on the shuttle run in comparison to standards on normal boys and girls (AAHPER norms). From: Rarick G. Lawrence, James H. Widdop, and Geoffrey D. Broadhead, "The Physical Fitness and Motor Performance of Educable Mentally Retarded Children," *Except. Child.* 36:509–514, 1970, p. 512.

centage of retarded boys and girls equal to or above the normal median for their age and sex was 25.4 per cent and 14.1 per cent, respectively. An inspection of the performance curves reveals a greater gap between retarded boys and girls than between normal boys and girls. In the scramble test, the performance of boys exceeded that of girls. Rarick, Dobbins, and Broadhead (1976) also administered a mat crawl and a tire run as measures of agility. Results similar to those found for the scramble test were reported. With the exception of one age level, the performance of normal girls exceeded that of normal boys in the tire run.

Rarick and McQuillan (1977) tested TMR boys and girls on the scramble test and the mat crawl and compared their performances with those of the EMR subjects aged 6 to 13 who were tested by

Rarick, Dobbins, and Broadhead (1976). Rarick and McQuillan found that the performance of EMR subjects exceeded that of TMR subjects on both items.

In other studies, Howe (1959) found that normal boys and girls performed a zigzag run significantly faster than retarded subjects of the same age and sex. Francis and Rarick (1959) reported that normal youngsters surpassed retarded subjects on the Burpee test. Sengstock (1966) found that normal boys significantly exceeded EMR boys on the shuttle run. Rarick, Widdop, and Broadhead (1970) compared the performance of EMR boys and girls on the shuttle run with 1965 standards of the AAHPER Youth Fitness Test. As illustrated in Figure 11–8, the performance curves of the retarded subjects of both sexes were well below those of intellectually normal children. The gap between girls was less than that between boys. There is some evidence to suggest that the slope of the performance curve at certain ages was a function of the complexity of the task rather than of the level of motor proficiency required.

Height, Weight, and Skinfold Measures

Rarick, Dobbins, and Broadhead (1976) found that the height of normal boys is superior to the height of EMR boys at three of four age levels beteen 6 and 9. They also noted that normal girls are taller than EMR girls at three of four age levels between 6 and 9. No significant sex differences in height were found.

Rarick and McQuillan (1977) measured the height of TMR subjects aged 6 to 21 and compared the results with those of normal and EMR subjects tested in a study by Rarick, Dobbins, and Broadhead (1976). Rarick and McQuillan reported that the pattern of growth of TMR subjects from 6 to 13 was similar to that of EMR subjects and that TMR subjects followed patterns seen in normal children. Little difference in height was found between TMR boys and girls at all levels up to age 13. The velocity of growth of females declined after 13, accounting for wide gaps favoring boys in this period. The velocity of growth declined in males after the 14 to 17 year period. The investigators reported that both normal subjects and EMR subjects are taller than TMR subjects of the same sex and age.

Rarick, Dobbins, and Broadhead (1976) found that the weights of normal and EMR boys and girls are quite similar at each age level from 6 to 9. No significant sex differences in weight were found. Rarick and McQuillan (1977) measured the weight of TMR subjects aged 6 to 21 and found TMR boys to be heavier. They reported that increases in weight with advancing age are greater on the average in the male TMR than in the female with a significant difference in the 18 to 21 year period. In a comparison of the weight of TMR subjects with that of EMR subjects measured by Rarick, Dobbins, and Broadhead (1976), it was found that EMR subjects are heavier in both the 6 to 9 and 10 to 13.9 year periods.

Rarick, Dobbins and Broadhead (1976) administered skinfold measurements at three sites (abdominal, subscapular, and triceps) in normal and EMR youngsters between the ages of 6 and 9 and in EMR youngsters to age 13. They found that skinfolds for the retarded were significantly greater at all three sites and that skinfold measurements were consistently greater for girls than for boys in both retarded and normal groups. These investigators also indicate that abdominal skinfolds of EMR boys exceeded those of EMR girls at ages 12 and 13, and that subscapular skinfolds were nearly equal for both sexes at ages 11, 12, and 13. The triceps fold of EMR boys was less than that of EMR girls throughout ages 7 through 13. Further data on abdominal skinfolds is presented in Table 11–1. The results of these tests generally show that EMR children possess a greater percentage of body fat than normal children of the same age and sex.

Rarick and McQuillan (1977) measured the triceps, subscapular, and abdominal skinfolds of TMR boys and girls and compared the data with those for EMR subjects tested by Rarick, Dobbins, and Broadhead (1976). Results indicated that the skinfolds of TMR girls not only exceeded those of TMR boys throughout ages 6 to 21 but that the gap between the two sexes increased with age. In comparing TMR and EMR children, Rarick and McQuillan (1977) noted that the skinfolds of TMR subjects exceeded those of EMR children of the same sex and age.

On the basis of the research previously presented, it is clear that normal children are taller than retarded children of the same age levels. It is also clear that retarded subjects possess a greater percentage of body fat than normal subjects of the same age. Since little or no difference exists between the weights of normal and retarded subjects, it is apparent that the retarded children are too heavy for their heights. The greater weight of the retarded child may be accounted for by a greater percentage of body fat.

Balance

Investigations of the static balance abilities of the mentally retarded indicate that their performance is generally below that of individuals of normal intellect of the same sex and age. Although a small sample size was employed in their study, Turnquist and Marzolf (1954) found that mentally normal individuals were significantly superior to the mentally retarded in balancing on tip toes with eyes closed, balancing on one leg with eyes closed, and balancing on tiptoes with right foot and with left foot. Howe (1959) found that normal children between the ages of 6½ and 12 were significantly superior to mentally retarded children of the same age and sex in balancing on one foot. In Howe's study, 2 of the 43 retarded and 28 of the 43 normal children were able to balance on one foot for one minute. Data collected by Cratty (1974b) indicate that the balance of normal subjects aged 5 to 11 exceeds that of EMR children of the same age and sex and that the balance performance of the EMR group exceeds that of TMR youngsters. Cratty also found that none of the 113 TMR subjects (mean age 10 years with age range of 5 to 24) in his study was able to balance on one foot without vision.

Rarick, Dobbins, and Broadhead (1976) compared the static balance of mentally normal and retarded subjects between the ages of 6 and 9. To assess static balance, these investigators measured stabilometer performance and administered the Bass test (in which the sub-

Figure 11–9. Balance beams may be differentiated in width and height to accommodate individual abilities.

ject balances for as long as possible on the preferred foot on the long axis of a 1 × 1 × 12 inch stick) and the Stork test (the subject balances on one leg for as long as possible under various conditions while standing with the support foot on a 12 × 3¼ × 3¼ inch footboard). Mean scores for the retarded and normal subjects appear in Table 11–8. The data indicate that retarded children are markedly inferior to normal children of the same sex and age on these tests.

Rarick and McQuillan (1977) also assessed the dynamic balance ability of TMR subjects aged 6 to 21 by administering the following three tests: railwalking forward, railwalking backward, and railwalking sideward (see Table 11–8). They reported that the performance of TMR boys exceeded that of TMR girls at all levels and in all tests

Table 11–8.   Mean Performance of EMR and Normal Children Aged 6–9 on Selected Measures of Balance.

	Populations			
	EMR		Normal	
Item	Boys	Girls	Boys	Girls
Static Balance				
Bass Test (sec.)	7.45	6.63	31.21	37.19
Stabilomotor (wk. add. units)	142.90	162.20	122.70	121.90
Stork Test (cm.)	17.36	15.59	23.72	28.80
Dynamic Balance				
Railwalking				
forward (ft.)	35.61	31.77	46.56	47.58
backward (ft.)	24.68	17.34	34.30	37.73
sideward (ft.)	30.39	23.69	35.89	37.36

Abridged from G. Lawrence Rarick, D. Alan Dobbins and Geoffrey D. Broadhead. *The Motor Domain and Its Correlates in Educationally Handicapped Children*, Englewood Cliffs, N. J. Prentice-Hall Inc., 1976, p. 45.

except at the 6- to 9-year-old level in walking forward and backward. The performance of TMR boys and girls increased between 6 and 17.9 years but declined after the 14 to 17.9 year period. In comparing the performance of TMR and EMR subjects aged 6 to 13, these investigators noted that the performance of EMR subjects exceeded that of TMR subjects of the same sex and age.

A comparison of normal and retarded youngsters for dynamic balance yields results similar to those found for static balance. In comparing normal and retarded youngsters aged 6 through 9 on forward, backward, and sideward railwalking, Rarick, Dobbins, and Broadhead (1976) found statistically significant differences favoring normal children (see Table 11–8).

Clear sexual differences in the performances of both normal and retarded children are generally found in investigations dealing with balance abilities. Distefano, Ellis, and Sloan (1958) reported that the railwalking performance of mentally defective males was significantly superior to that of mentally defective females. Howe (1959) found that retarded boys attained higher mean scores than retarded girls in balancing on one foot. Francis and Rarick (1959) found that the balance beam performance of mentally retarded boys generally exceeded that of mentally retarded girls (aged 8 to 14). Rarick, Dobbins, and Broadhead (1976) found no significant sex differences on the balance tests they administered; however, significant sex by disability interactions were found. Whereas the performance of normal girls surpassed that of normal boys, the performance of EMR boys exceeded that of EMR girls.

As a group, the mentally retarded generally improve in balance abilities between 6 and 13 years of age. Francis and Rarick (1959) found that the average balance beam performance of mentally retarded boys and girls generally increased between the ages 8 and 13 and showed a decline in performance at age 14. These results agree with those expected for normal youngsters. Rarick, Dobbins, and Broadhead (1976) found little improvement on the Bass test for retarded boys and girls between the ages of 6 and 9, whereas normal children showed substantial improvement on this test with age. On the other five balance tests included in their study, Rarick, Dobbins, and Broadhead (1976) generally found that both retarded and normal youngsters improved with age. It should be noted, however, that the investigators limited their analysis of performance to normal subjects between the ages of 6 and 9 and to retarded subjects in the 6 to 13 age range. Both of these investigations were cross-sectional in nature.

Although results are not yet conclusive, several investigators have compared balance performances of certain subgroups of retarded individuals. Heath (1942) reported a significant relationship between mental age and railwalking performance in a familial (endogenous) group of mentally retarded boys but no such relationship when a non-familial (exogenous) group was considered. Later, Heath (1953) again found a significant relationship between mental age and railwalking scores of familial retardates but no correlation for non-familial retardates. He also noted that familial retardates were superior to non-familial retardates in railwalking performance. Heath suggested that such results could have etiological as well as programming implications. LeBlanc (1975) found that the dynamic balance performance of Down's syndrome trainable subjects significantly exceeded that of non-Down's syndrome trainable retardates but that the static balance performances of the two groups were not significantly different. This finding differed from results reported by Cratty (1966), who indicated that the static and dynamic balance of Down's syndrome subjects was inferior to non-Down's syndrome retardates. In view of this discrepancy, further research is needed before programming implications based on subgroups of the retarded can be made.

Motor Development

Investigations designed to study and compare the motor development of mentally retarded and normal children have often employed the Oseretsky Scale or some adaptation of it. In one of the earliest and most often cited studies, Sloan (1951) compared the performance of 20 institutionalized retarded subjects with that of 20 nonretarded subjects of the same ages. The mean IQ for the retarded males was 54.2 and for retarded females was 56.2. The mean IQ for normal males was 105.8 and for normal females was 99.2. The mean chronological age (CA) for all subjects was 10 years. Sloan found a significant difference in favor of the nonretarded on all six subtest areas. A definite relationship between intelligence and motor proficiency was noted. No significant differences were found between boys and girls or between familial and undifferentiated retarded subjects.

The results reported by Fallers (1948) are in agreement with those reported by Sloan (1951). In her study, Fallers administered the Lincoln-Oseretsky Scale to 30 mildly and moderately retarded girls. She found that none of the subjects in her study attained a normal rating and that subjects with lower IQs generally scored lower on the Lincoln-Oseretsky Scale. She also found that the girls performed most poorly on speed items.

Turnquist and Marzolf (1954) also administered the Oseretsky test in comparing the motor proficiency of retarded and non-retarded populations. In this study, the performance of an experimental group of all mentally retarded subjects was compared with the performance of 11 subjects of normal intelligence (each group contained six boys and five girls). The retarded group had a mean chronological age of 13 years 6 months, a mean IQ of 69, and an IQ range of 55 to 83. The group of nonretarded subjects had the same mean chronological age, a mean IQ of 102, and an IQ range of 93 to 113. The non-retarded subjects significantly surpassed the mentally retarded on 20 of 65 items on the test, and the retarded significantly surpassed the non-retarded group on 5 items. The investigators noted that the most clear-cut differences were found on test items classified as Synkinesia, Simultaneous Movement, and General Static (Balance). The groups differed least in Dynamic Manual, General Dynamic, and Speed test items. The retarded did significantly better on items dealing with throwing at a target, catching, and speed of executing certain tasks. The significance of the study is limited by the small number of subjects in each group.

In a study similar to that of Fallers (1948), Distefano, Ellis, and Sloan (1958) investigated the relationship between intelligence and motor proficiency. The Lincoln-Oseretsky Motor Development Scale, the Rail-walking test, the placing and turning subtests of the Minnesota Rate of Manipulation test, a Hand Steadiness test, and a Hand Dynamometer test were given to 76 mentally defective subjects. The mean chronological age and mental age of 40 male subjects was 19.73 and 9.90, respectively. The mean chronological age and mental age of 36 female subjects was 22.25 and 9.14, respectively. Performances on the Lincoln-Oseretsky Scale and the Minnesota placing and turning subtests were found to have the highest correlations with mental age. The Lincoln-Oseretsky was found to correlate most highly with mental age.

Malpass (1960) designed a study to determine whether comparable groups of institutionalized and non-institutionalized retarded children could be differentiated on the basis of motor proficiency and whether the motor ability of normal and retarded children could be distinguished. The three groups of subjects in the study included retarded subjects from an institution, educable mentally retarded children in public school classes, and children with normal intelligence. The mean chronological age of all subjects was between 11 and 12 years. The Lincoln revision of the Oseretsky Motor Development Scale was used as an indicator of motor proficiency. No significant differences were found between insti-tutionalized and non-institutionalized retarded children. The scores of normal children significantly exceeded the scores of the retarded chil-dren, thus supporting the claim that motor proficiency is related to intellectual ability. Malpass found that this relationship resulted from a significant relationship within the retarded population. The coefficients of correlation for normal groups clustered around zero.

In still another investigation on motor development, Langan (1965) found that mildly retarded children with chronological ages between 7 years 6 months and 10 years 5 months who were enrolled in public school classes scored significantly below a sample of youngsters of normal intelligence on the Lincoln-Oseretsky Motor Development Scale. A motor deficiency of $1\frac{1}{2}$ years at age 8 increased to 2 years at age 10. Although at a lower level, the developmental curve of retarded subjects was similar to that of normal subjects. No significant differences were found between middle and lower class retardates or between EMR boys and girls.

Rabin (1957) also employed the Lincoln-Oseretsky Development Scale to investigate the relationship of age, intelligence, and sex to motor proficiency. Subjects consisted of 60 children aged 10 to 14 with IQs between 40 and 69 from two public institutions for mental defectives. The subjects were diagnosed as familial or idiopathic. Rabin found a significant positive relationship between motor proficiency and age. However, motor proficiency was not found to vary as a function of sex or to be significantly related to intelligence. Rabin indicated that the lack of a significant relationship between motor proficiency and intelligence could have resulted from the effects of an insufficiently controlled vari-able.

Howe (1959) compared the performance of mentally retarded and normal children on a variety of motor skill tasks. Subjects in the study consisted of 43 retarded and 43 nonretarded pupils ranging in age from $6\frac{1}{2}$ to 12 years. Howe found that normal boys significantly exceeded retarded boys in a ball throw for accuracy. The difference between normal and retarded girls on this task was not significant.

In their study, Rarick, Dobbins, and Broadhead (1976) compared the performances of retarded and nonretarded children aged 6 to 9 in the speed and accuracy of throwing. These investigators found a large and significant difference in the throwing velocity of boys and girls in favor of boys. Retarded boys performed the velocity throw better than normal girls. Unlike the differences in most other measures of physical and motor performance, the gap between retarded and normal subjects in this study was less at age 9 than at age 6. In the test for throwing accuracy, the performance of normal subjects was significantly superior to that of retarded subjects of the same sex and age.

Cratty (1974b) tested 172 normal boys, 183 normal girls, 38 educable retardates, and 113 trainable retardates on his six-category gross motor test. The six categories measure body perception, gross agility, balance, locomotor agility, throwing, and tracking. Results clearly indicate that normal subjects surpassed educable retardates and the latter exceeded trainable retardates of comparable age.

The claim that the performance of non-retarded populations exceeds that of retarded populations in tests for motor proficiency is supported by Sloan (1951), Fallers (1948), Turnquist and Marzolf (1954), Langan (1965), Howe (1959), Rarick, Dobbins, and Broadhead (1976), and Cratty (1974b). A positive relationship between intelligence and motor proficiency within retarded populations was reported by Sloan (1951), Fallers (1948), and Malpass (1960) but was not found by Rabin (1957). Both Sloan (1951) and Rabin (1957) found no significant difference in motor proficiency between retarded males and retarded females on the Oseretsky scales. However, significant differences in favor of boys were usually found by Rarick, Dobbins, and Broadhead (1976). A positive relationship between mental age and motor proficiency was reported by Distefano, Ellis, and Sloan (1958) and between chronological age and motor proficiency by Rabin (1957). The claim for relationships between both mental and chronological age and motor proficiency is generally supported by Rarick, Dobbins, and Broadhead (1976).

Other Physical and Motor Characteristics

Although learning-disabled children may be distinguished from them, mentally retarded children often possess learning disabilities or perceptual handicaps. Many retarded children exhibit poor body mechanics and body alignment and walk with a shuffling gait and a wide stance. The legs of the Down's syndrome youngster frequently are disproportionately small in relation to other parts of the body. Retardates with large skulls (hydrocephalic) have particular difficulty in maintaining equilibrium. Many Down's syndrome retardates (especially boys) are cardiopathic, and many have respiratory difficulties that increase susceptibility to respiratory infections. Flabbiness and hypotonic musculature are additional characteristics associated with the retarded child.

Non-Physical and Non-Motor Characteristics

Many characteristics associated with mentally retarded children indirectly affect the nature and quality of their performance in movement activities. Their difficulty with abstractions suggests that they will respond most positively to concrete demonstrations of concepts rather than to verbalization. Also, retarded youngsters will have more difficulty than the nonretarded in understanding rules and strategies of games. In activities of a complicated nature, differences in performance between retarded and nonretarded populations owe more to difficulties in understanding than to real differences in motor abilities. Fait and Kupferer (1956) suggested that differences between scores of retarded and nonretarded children in the Burpee Squat-Thrust resulted from the complexity of the task rather than basic differences in motor ability. Studies by Heath (1943 and 1944) support the claim that the awkwardness exhibited by certain types of retardates was caused more by intellectual factors than by motor factors.

The lack of normal intellectual abilities affects the day-to-day implementation of movement activities. Retarded children often have difficulty following directions. They often fail to completely understand a task. They have difficulty performing movements in a sequence. Their inability to concentrate for prolonged periods requires that activities be frequently changed and not be overly demanding for prolonged periods.

There is little doubt that social skills may be taught to the retarded, and many such children are as socially mature as or more socially mature than non-retarded children the same age. However, as a group, the retarded do tend to be socially immature. Deficits in intellectual ability may cause retarded children to be ridiculed and to withdraw from social settings. Withdrawal from social activities may lead to withdrawal from play and movement activities as well, reducing opportunity for normal physical and motor development.

One of the most often described characteristics of the mentally

Figure 11–10. Learning to hit a ball by first striking a stationary object.

retarded child is a short attention span, which has often been cited as one of the major reasons why retarded children lag in development and learning. Some writers, however, note that the retarded have been observed to engage in tasks over prolonged periods provided that they are interested in the tasks and are successful in performing them. These writers indicate that greater attention should be focused on selecting appropriate tasks for the retarded. Regardless of its cause, lack of attention accompanies and causes problems in learning.

Cratty (1974b) has made an analysis of arousal level and the improvement of attention of retardates. He notes in his review of literature that gross motor training has been found to heighten attention and self-control in retarded children, an effect that transfers to different kinds of problem-solving behavior requiring their attention. Recognizing that medication may be the only answer for controlling behavior in certain hyperactive children, he offers relaxation training, prolongation of the task, and impulse control as three additional strategies. Relaxation techniques emphasize tensing and relaxing parts of the body. Self-control through prolongation of the task involves encouraging the child to perform a task for a longer period than previously. Impulse control involves seeing how slowly a child can move. Tasks selected for this purpose include both those that involve specific limbs and those that involve the whole body.

Teaching Hints

Many of the hints for teaching the mentally retarded overlap with those that apply to the teaching of children with emotional-behavioral disabilities or specific learning disabilities. Techniques for teaching children who exhibit hyperactivity, perseveration, and distractibility will be discussed in the section on specific learning disabilities. Since many retarded children possess these characteristics, the same hints apply to them. Subsequent suggestions for teaching and conducting movement experiences for the emotionally-behaviorally disabled also apply to the mentally retarded. These include (1) arranging and building upon successful experiences, (2) developing and following progressions, (3) creating a structured and routinized environment, (4) establishing control, (5) stressing positive reinforcement, (6) repeating and reviewing often, (7) using well-liked activities as rewards, (8) providing individual attention, (9) being calm, (10) heightening relevant stimuli and reducing distractions, (11) using a variety of sensory modalities in teaching, (12) placing compatible groups of children together when arranging groups, (13) providing a "home base" for each child, (14) using students to demonstrate skills, (15) applying physical restraint to assure safety, (16) being prepared and knowing the subject matter, (17) being "yourself" and assuming "your" role as an adult and teacher, and (18) allowing children and teacher to "save face" in the resolution of conflicts. In addition, it is particularly important to provide slow instruction and to be as concrete as possible when communicating to the retarded. Verbal directions are of limited value. New or complex activities should be given special emphasis. Imitation should be employed often, since this is a major asset of many retarded children.

Figure 11–11. Each student has a "home."

·Activities

As is true with most populations of special pupils, the retarded are a heterogeneous group exhibiting a wide variety of abilities and interests. Thus, the concept of "a program for the mentally retarded" is misleading and tends to contribute to the development of preconceived notions about what people can or cannot accomplish. Although comments about activities for the mentally retarded, as a group, will be presented in this section, it must be remembered that programs should be individualized. It is important to recognize that mentally retarded individuals may exceed or may fail to attain the ability levels associated with activity recommendations presented here. Further, differences between programs for normal and retarded populations may be negligible — especially for children whose retardation is mild. Grouping children in movement activities on the basis of intellectual abilities is not generally recommended; grouping should be based on abilities related to movement experience.

A guide that has been used for the selection of activities for the mentally retarded is to pitch the activities to the mental age of the class. Retarded children are generally able to learn activities and to progress in physical and motor proficiency, but they do so at a slower rate than the non-retarded. As the retarded increase in age, however, they become more and more sensitive to social aspects of activity participation. For example, games such as "Duck, Duck, Goose" are viewed as "baby" games and therefore hold limited interest for older retardates. Thus, the use of mental age as a guide must be tempered by the social implications of the activities.

Certain kinds of activities are generally more effective for the retarded than others. Retarded pupils respond more positively to activities requiring little or no memorization of playing rules or strategy. They enjoy activities involving music, dancing, and rhythms if they have learned the basic abilities for participation in these activities. As a group, the retarded appear to enjoy and to be most successful in individual rather than team activities: those dealing with nature, gross body activities, playground activities, water activities, co-recreational activities, and leisure-time activities engaged in by non-retarded peers of similar chronological age. Some of the favorite activities of retarded pupils include swimming, fishing, hunting, hiking, trampolining, cycling, tumbling, skating, dancing, rhythms, badminton, bowling, tennis, table tennis, racketball, paddleball, relays, weightlifting, and archery. Activities least popular involve fine coordination, reciprocity or cooperation in a large group or periods of waiting, or emphasize academic skills for successful participation. Activities associated with these characteristics include calisthenics, drills, marching, group games (at certain ages), shuffleboard, basketball (however, pupils enjoy shooting baskets), and playing certain positions in baseball and football.

Shotick and Thate (1960) studied the reaction of a small group (N of 7) of educable mentally handicapped children to a program of physical education. The activities more highly rated in regard to the enthusiasm of the subjects and their response to instruction included fundamental skill activities, trampolining, mat stunts and tumbling, certain rhythmic activities, and swimming. Those rated lowest included marching, calisthenics, hanging and handwalking on a suspended ladder, and creative

Figure 11–12.   Children enjoy shooting baskets.

Table 11–9. Responses of EMR Children to Games of Low Organization.

Activity	Enthusiasm	Response to Instruction
Stealing Sticks	3.00	2.00
Fox and Geese	3.00	3.00
Nose Tag	3.00	2.60
Freeze	3.00	2.33
Dodgeball	2.96	2.84
Kickball	2.96	2.86
Swat Tag	2.88	3.00
Steal the Bacon	2.83	3.00
Newcomb	2.80	3.00
Modified Soccer	2.80	2.68
Tiger Hunt	2.69	2.50
Modified Baseball	2.66	3.00
Catch and Pull	2.60	2.80
Hide the Keys	2.50	3.00
Shuffleboard	2.00	2.85
Volleyball	2.00	1.58

Shotick, Andrew and Charles Thate. "Reactions of a Group of Educable Mentally Handicapped Children to a Program of Physical Education," *Except. Child.* 26, 1960, p. 249.

rhythms. Girls displayed more enthusiasm for rhythmic activities than boys, and an increase in enthusiasm for rhythmic activities was noted as the term of the study progressed. Responses of the subjects to games of low organization are rated in Table 11–9, and responses to rhythmic activities are rated in Table 11–10.

On the basis of their research with EMR youngsters aged 6 to 13, Rarick, Dobbins, and Broadhead (1976) attempted to determine the factor structure of motor abilities and to draw implications therefrom for curricular development. They found that in young normal youngsters aged 6 to 9 and EMR children aged 6 to 13 there were no clearly defined factors such as the static muscular strength, dynamic strength, or explosive muscular force that have been noted in older normal subjects. The sample studied revealed less specificity in motor skills than have been noted in older subjects of normal intelligence. The four factors that accounted for over half of the common variance of EMR subjects were strength-power-body size, body fat, fine visual-motor coordination, and gross limb-eye coordination. Based on this finding as

Table 11–10. Responses of EMR Children to Rhythmic Activities.

Activity	Enthusiasm			Response to Instruction		
	Boys	Girls	Group	Boys	Girls	Group
Changing Polka Step	3.00	3.00	3.00	1.50	3.00	1.83
Teaching Squares	2.89	3.00	2.94	2.56	2.75	2.62
Little Brown Jug Polka	2.80	3.00	2.85	2.60	2.50	2.50
La Raspa	2.70	3.00	2.83	1.70	2.50	1.80
Children's Polka	2.66	3.00	2.72	2.33	2.50	2.27
Chimes of Dunkirk	2.55	3.00	2.66	1.88	2.83	2.10
Galloping to Music	2.50	3.00	2.66	2.25	3.00	2.50
Schottische	2.40	3.00	2.50	1.50	2.00	1.50
Creative Rhythms	2.20	2.50	2.33	2.20	2.50	2.30
Performance Test	1.80	3.00	2.10	2.72	3.00	2.80

Shotick, Andrew and Charles Thate, "Reactions of a Group of Educable Mentally Handicapped Children to a Program of Physical Education," *Except. Child.* 26, 1960, p. 250.

well as on other research, these investigators recommend that approximately 30 per cent of any program in physical education be devoted to activities designed to develop muscular strength and power, 20 per cent to activities to develop gross coordination of limb and body movements, 5 to 10 per cent to activities to develop balance abilities, and 5 to 10 per cent to activities to improve flexibility. In addition, Rarick, Dobbins, and Broadhead (1976) recommend that the educational program provide opportunities for children to develop fine visual-motor coordination and include activities that increase energy expenditure.

In their study, Rarick and McQuillan (1977) investigated the factor structure of motor abilities of TMR youngsters and compared the results with those obtained by Rarick, Dobbins and Broadhead (1976) for EMR subjects. Although the performance of TMR subjects was generally below that of EMR subjects, the factor structure of abilities was similar. Thus, the investigators recommend that the types of activities stressed for EMR pupils should also be stressed for TMR pupils. Specifically, the investigators emphasized the need for the development of such basic components as lower and upper body strength, leg power, balance, limb-eye coordination, flexibility, and fine motor control. In addition, activities that place demands on the cardiovascular and respiratory systems, those of an aerobic nature, and those that require the utilization of energy (to reduce adipose tissue) were strongly recommended.

In view of the definite relationship of physical and motor proficiency to intelligence in the retarded population, an analysis of programming by degree of retardation appears warranted. Activities for the mildly retarded may closely approximate those for the non-retarded. Generally, mildly retarded pupils may be integrated with non-retarded individuals. Many (about 10 to 25 per cent of EMR children) match or exceed the average performance levels of normal subjects, and most EMR children perform close to or within one standard deviation of the mean performance of normal individuals. The mildly retarded generally lag in performance and need more time to learn activities, but they can approximate normal performance levels. More than normal emphasis will generally need to be given to the development of basic motor abilities, physical fitness, and perceptual-motor abilities — particularly for young retarded pupils.

Activities for the moderately retarded will often differ from regular programs in terms of level and emphasis. Moderately retarded youngsters below the chronological age of 9 will function at pre-school levels in many human attributes. Because they are still egocentric, they are ready for individual and nonstructured play activities. Although they enjoy parallel play, they are not generally ready for the reciprocity and cooperation that characterize most group games. For their chronological age, greater than normal emphasis needs to be placed on physical conditioning, motor development, and perceptual development. Rhythmic activities, stunts and tumbling, self-testing activities, and creative activities should be less demanding in nature. As the moderately retarded increase in age and approach adolescence, they will be much more responsive to group and team games. However, they will retain their interest in individual activities. As moderately retarded students reach the chronological age of the normal high school student (14 or 15 years), they will become responsive to and successful in individual and dual sport activities. In view of their value for life-time sports, the skills for

Figure 11–13. Climbing stairs is a basic ability that must be learned.

Figure 11–14. Bowling is an important leisure activity for all.

Figure 11–15. Older boys enjoy weightlifting.

Individual and dual activities should be stressed in programs for these students. Although the moderately retarded may participate in sport activities with self-satisfaction, they generally will not achieve high skill levels.

Persons severely and profoundly retarded in intellectual abilities are usually also retarded in movement activities. The need for locomotor, basic skill, balance, physical conditioning, and sensory-motor activities will continually exist. The severely retarded will generally respond positively to swimming, unstructured play activities, conceptually simple activities performed within a group (parallel play), and conceptually simple group games. They are able to perform many of the skills used in team sports but generally are not successful as participants in such activities. Activities that hold a great deal of promise for success include bowling, swimming, fishing, weightlifting, dancing, rhythms, and certain self-testing activities.

Emotional-Behavioral Disabilities

The Importance of Play and Physical Activity

The importance of play for emotionally-behaviorally disabled children and youth has long been recognized. Play has served as a tool for both diagnosis and therapy. It provides an opportunity for the development of a variety of social, emotional, physical, motor, and cognitive abilities, for individual expression, and for the learning and practice of "real life" skills in a relatively non-threatening environment. As the child progresses in the ability to play, games with rules are played. The child learns the importance of and develops the ability to follow rules. Opportunities to develop social skills are provided as the individual moves from egocentric play to parallel play, small group play, and finally, team play.

Although most children learn to play without formal teaching, many emotionally-behaviorally disabled children need to learn to play. In many instances, constructive play skills need to be developed. The first step in such development is to recognize the importance of play so that opportunities for play are provided.

Physical activity is invariably advocated for the emotionally-behaviorally disabled. Although participation in physical activity per se does not resolve underlying causes of emotional or behavioral problems, unless such problems are associated with physical activity, participation in such activities enhances therapeutic and educational efforts. In addition to the usual physical and motor values of participation in physical activity, there are a number of social and emotional values. The theoretical basis for these values depends heavily upon Freudian theory. Some of the most important of these are:

1. Games, sports, exercise, and play provide an opportunity to express hostility and release tension in socially acceptable ways.
2. Group physical activities serve as an attraction for children with withdrawal characteristics to participate in social activities.
3. Play and physical activity are fun and provide a zest for living. Since children as well as adults look forward to participation in enjoyable play and physical activity, such participation provides a desired goal to attain which may be anticipated.
4. Physical activity improves body appearance which tends to improve body image and self-concept.
5. Participation in physical activities provides an opportunity for skill development and success in an area. Such success is often of vital importance to the self-esteem and self-confidence of the individual.
6. Physical activities provide a unique setting for social and emotional-behavioral development. With appropriate leadership, unsocialized behavior is curbed and socialized behavior is encouraged.
7. Participation in physical activities helps to change the focus of attention of the individual. Such a change helps the individual to "take the mind off" bothersome thoughts and gain a different perspective on a situation.
8. Physical activities provide a unique setting for reality testing.

Physical and Motor Performance

Although the relationship of emotional disturbance to physical and motor performance is often discussed, there is a need for objective research in this area. Available research is generally unable to adequately isolate or differentiate emotional-behavioral, mental, physical, or other factors that could possibly influence results. Some researchers do not attempt such distinctions and combine the mentally retarded with the emotionally disturbed or the emotionally disturbed with the learning disabled in their investigations. Differences in criteria and in diagnostic procedures contribute to the inability to attain comparable and conclusive data. In addition, the emotionally disturbed are individuals with a wide variation in physical and motor abilities at a particular age level. Their abilities range from extremely low to highly gifted.

Although it is necessary to determine abilities on an individual basis, evidence presently available tends to support the contention that, as a group, emotionally disturbed youngsters fall below their normal peers in measures of physical proficiency. Fait (1972) and Sherrill (1976) agree that the physical fitness of mental patients is frequently very low. Webb (1972), on the other hand, contends that the emotionally disturbed child is not retarded physically. Dewey (1972) points out that in regard to coordination, there appears to be a great variation among autistic children. In one of the few published studies, Poindexter (1969a) reports that emotionally disturbed youngsters seemed to score less well than their normal peers on measures of strength, power, agility, speed, coordination, and balance. In her study, Poindexter measured grip, knee, and shoulder strength. Power was evaluated by performance in the standing broad jump and abdominal strength by performance on the Kraus-Weber test and in bent knee sit-ups. Speed was reflected by performance in the 30-yard dash and agility determined by a shuttle run task and a walking beam. Assessments of locomotor ability, trampoline performance, and static and dynamic balance ability were also included.

Clinical observations and some research evidence indicate that the perceptual-motor abilities of emotionally disturbed children are below normal. Arnheim, Auxter, and Crowe (1973) as well as Moran and Kalakian (1977) state that the emotionally disturbed often have difficulty in making space and time assessments. Poindexter (1969a) found that the performance scores of emotionally disturbed children on the Kephart Perceptual-Motor Survey were less than those of a comparable group of normal youngsters. The Kephart survey includes items to assess balance and postural adjustment, body image and differentiation, perceptual-motor matching, ocular control, and form perception. Perceptual-motor difficulties may cause children to have difficulties in games and activities involving balance, gross motor coordination, and the tracking of moving objects. They are also inhibited in activities in which successful participation is heavily dependent on body awareness.

In addition to comparison of the physical and motor performances of normal youngsters with those of children exhibiting deviances in behavior, the relationship of deviant behavior to physical and motor performance may be studied by analysis of indirect factors. Indirect factors include those characteristics that influence and thereby help to explain physical and motor status. They may be associated with one or more deviances in behavior.

A common characteristic of emotionally-behaviorally disabled children that influences physical and motor status is uncooperative and aggressive behavior. Children chronically exhibiting aggressive behavior will have difficulties in interpersonal relationships involving peers, teachers, or leaders. Although the children may wish to conform to group standards, they cannot and therefore are often left to play alone. A great deal of difficulty is exhibited in team games and group activities. Aggressive children who "act out" may be a safety threat to others and thus need careful supervision during group activities. Chronic aggressive behavior directed toward teachers or leaders impedes learning and practice of physical and motor activities.

Many emotionally disturbed children have difficulty attending and relating to the environment. The child with autistic-like tendencies, for example, fails to relate to the environment and thus has neither desire nor skill to move through it and learn from it. Such a child is not attracted to people and things in the environment and does not interact with them. The autistic-like child lives in a "shell" and has little need to relate to the environment. Similarly, many emotionally-behaviorally disabled children withdraw from social situations. This leads to less participation in physical activity, since many such activities are conducted in social settings. In still other instances, the emotionally-behaviorally disabled child is preoccupied with problems that prohibit normal attention to physical activity.

Some children associate failure and ridicule with physical and motor activities and develop an aversion for physical activity. They are not interested in movement activities and do not want to participate in them. They are not motivated to learn and practice skills and therefore are not successful in them. Others enjoy activity but do not have or are denied the opportunity to participate. Lack of success and lack of participation lead to low performance level in physical and motor activities.

Finally, characteristics inherently associated with emotional problems themselves often lead to reactions or conditions that make successful participation difficult. For example, the child who deals with anxiety by eating may become so obese that movement is difficult and probability of success in movement activities is small. Also, a psychological disturbance may cause a phobia that affects the nature and quality of performance.

It should be pointed out, however, that many emotionally-behaviorally disabled children excel in physical and motor performance. Many youngsters have their major success in such activities and tend to spend more than average time participating in them. If success in movement activities is considered important by the individual and peers, participation and performance levels are increased.

Movement Activities

Children exhibiting emotional-behavioral problems are especially heterogeneous in physical and motor performance. Some exceed normal performance levels, but many others will function far below normal expectations. Some children enjoy and look forward to participation in movement experiences while others dislike and avoid it. As a group, the emotionally disturbed will lag one to two years behind the norms in physical and motor abilities. Thus, they often participate most successfully in activities geared for younger children. In addition, the nature of a particular disturbance dictates individual needs and variation in program emphasis. For example, children who are withdrawn need social activities to draw them into the mainstream of a group. On the other hand, relaxation activities should be emphasized and competitive activities should be avoided for children who are hyperactive or who have high anxiety levels. Variation in needs, interests, and abilities of children with emotional problems means that programs must be individualized to the greatest possible extent.

Since many emotionally disturbed children lag in physical and motor abilities, it is often necessary to emphasize developmental activities in programs for them. Physical conditioning, balance, and basic movement activities must often be stressed to overcome this lag and provide a basis for successful participation in movement activities. Attention must be given to the development of fundamental locomotor and non-locomotor movements and of basic coordination and skill abilities. In addition, it may be necessary to emphasize perceptual activities, since the emotionally disturbed frequently exhibit inadequate perceptual abilities. It is most desirable that basic physical and motor abilities be developed through games, sports, aquatics, self-testing, rhythms, and play activities. Although remedial exercises are also beneficial, children are generally better motivated to participate in games and other activities they enjoy.

Relaxation activities and warm water swimming are usually of particular importance in programs for hyperactive, overanxious, and aggressive individuals. Children who are depressed or who exhibit autistic-like characteristics, on the other hand, may be stimulated through swimming activities. Many children find success in swimming activities, and consequent enhancement of self-concept may transfer to other endeavors.

Activities that provide an opportunity for the release of aggression are recommended for emotionally-behaviorally disabled children, provided that the activities are not characterized by aggression against others. Such activities include those in which children strike, kick, punch, push, pull, twist, or throw objects. They may hit a punching bag, kick a soccer ball, or strike a softball. The support for such activities is derived from psychodynamic theory. Such activities are recommended to give the child an opportunity to release aggression in socially acceptable ways.

Vigorous activities that provide an opportunity to "let off steam" or to reduce energy have also been recommended for hyperactive children. It is felt by some educators that such activities will fatigue and quiet the children for instruction. Although such a result may occur in isolated cases, this author has found that such activities generally further stimulate and excite the children, making it difficult to calm them. Although vigorous activities are recommended for physiological benefits, they are not recommended for the purpose of calming pupils. Relaxation activities are recommended for such a purpose.

Activities that encourage socialization generally need to be stressed in movement programs for emotionally-behaviorally disabled children. Children who tend to withdraw need activities that gradually induce them to social interaction. Activities requiring interaction, teamwork, and cooperation for success may serve as a stimulus and setting for the development of positive social abilities. Coeducational and co-recreational activities may be employed to nurture proper relationships with members of the opposite sex. In implementation of programs, social activities should be gradually developed. The size of groups, the amount of time spent in group settings, and the "sociability" of group members are all factors to manipulate in gradually developing social abilities.

Play and leisure-time activities should also be stressed in programs for children exhibiting emotional-behavioral problems. Pre-school and early school-aged children should be provided with opportunities to develop basic abilities in order that they may play successfully with their peers. Success in activities regarded highly by peer groups will enhance

Figure 11–16.   Learning childhood leisure activities is important.

the self-esteem of the child. As children increase in age, opportunities should be provided for the development of skills necessary to success in leisure-time activities as well as for participation in the activities themselves. Wholesome leisure-time activities provide a zest for living and enable individuals to use their time in constructive rather than destructive ways.

Since the self-expression of children is sometimes otherwise thwarted, opportunities should be provided for self-expression and interpretation in physical and motor activities. Interpretive dance, mimetics, play, problem solving, and other creative experiences are among those activities that may provide those opportunities. In order for the experiences to be successful, basic abilities needed in creative experiences must first be developed.

Few activities are contraindicated for the emotionally-behaviorally disabled child unless the child is extremely deviant. Children with autistic characteristics will have difficulty in group activities and team sports. Highly competitive activities or those requiring fine motor coordination may frustrate certain children and thus are inappropriate for them. Until children become independent and are capable of self-direction, they may not engage successfully in non-directed or unstructured activities. Participation in group activities may need to be planned so that the child progresses from egocentric play to parallel play and small group activities.

Suggestions for Teaching and Conducting Movement Experiences

In the implementation of recreation, physical education, or other movement-oriented programs for children exhibiting deviant behavior, the methods employed are as important as or even more important than the activities selected. Although methodology is critical, no one list of methods can be developed and applied to all children with equal results. Children are different, and their responses to different approaches will vary. Further, teachers and leaders are different, and the methods that are successful for one individual in teaching and conducting movement experiences may not work for another individual. Finally, every method will be affected by the prevailing philosophy of the institution, the administration, and the teachers or leaders responsible for program implementation. General as well as specific methodology will vary in kind and degree, to some extent, according to whether one or more of the following strategies are employed: psychodynamic, behavior modification, developmental, learning disability, psychoeducational, or ecological. In view of the many factors that influence specific methodology, it appears to be most appropriate to discuss suggestions rather than principles for conducting movement experiences. Some of those considered most important by this author are presented briefly.

1. Arrange and build upon successful experiences. Emotionally-behaviorally disabled children generally have a history filled with failure. They need successful experiences to enhance self-concept and self-confidence, making them better adjusted and increasing the likelihood of success in learning.

2. Develop and follow progressions in implementing programs. The key to arranging successful experience is in developing and following suitable progressions for learning. Physical and motor variables should be emphasized in developing progressions related to games, sports, exercise, and play. In addition, cognitive, social, and emotional variables should also be considered in developing progressions and should be given most emphasis when they are most important in influencing learning and participation.

3. Create a structured and "routinized" learning environment. A structured learning environment is made more predictable and provides needed security for emotionally-behaviorally disabled children. When children are better able to adjust, structure may be reduced and routine may be altered.

4. Establish control. In implementing programs, it is necessary that teachers or leaders be in control at all times. Teachers or leaders are inhibited in teaching if they are unable to control behavior, and children are impeded in learning and security when the teacher or leader fails to control behavior. Discipline should be firm and consistent and should be administered humanely. Although authoritarian methods may be effective in certain instances, less directive approaches may have greater effect in other situations. Control of the environment is essential regardless of the approach employed, and it can be attained through various approaches.

5. Stress positive reinforcement. Although negative reinforcement may be applied in certain instances and does result in behavioral change, undesirable side effects associated with it such as distrust, withdrawal, hostility, and a breakdown in communication make it less desirable than positive reinforcement in teaching. Praise, in particular, is preferred, since it enhances positive human interactions.

6. Repeat and review often. Learning and retention of information appears to be enhanced by repetition and review. Learning by emotionally disturbed children appears to be more efficient when activities are conducted often but with short duration than when they are presented or conducted less often for longer periods of time.

7. Use well-liked activities as rewards. Reward children with participation in activities they enjoy and desire if they participate in other necessary activities that they like less. Participation in preferred activities may be made contingent upon participation in activities that are important to the individual but which are not as well-liked.

8. Provide individual attention. Small pupil-teacher ratios enable greater individual attention and should be employed to the greatest possible extent. When the pupil-teacher ratio is too large, teacher aides and volunteers may be employed to provide greater individual attention to the child.

9. Be calm. Panic and anxiety displayed by the teacher may unduly excite pupils and cause feelings of insecurity. The perception of teacher calmness and control contributes to an uncharged, secure, and more relaxed emotional environment. Periods of quietness may be employed to gain control.

10. Heighten relevant stimulation and reduce distractions. Make tasks as stimulating as possible and reduce distraction to the fullest possible extent. Environmental stimuli for hyperactive emotionally disturbed children should be kept to an absolute minimum, since overstimulation heightens hyperactivity.

11. Use a variety of sensory modalities in teaching. Teaching and learning may be enhanced by appropriately employing a variety of sensory modalities.

Figure 11–17. Small teacher-pupil ratio enhances learning.

12. Consider interpersonal relationships when grouping children. When arranging groups of children, place compatible children together.

13. Provide a "home base" for children in a movement environment. All children should be given spots or home positions in a movement environment to help make them feel more secure and to enhance organization for teaching. The spot may be an "X" taped on the floor, a picture painted on the floor, or some other designation. The home base may serve as a point from which to start a class or receive instruction, or to which to move during emergency situations.

14. Use students to demonstrate skills. When children demonstrate skills, they are meeting their need for attention in a socially acceptable manner, are demonstrating the correct way to execute a skill, and are showing the class that the skill may be mastered by a member of their peer group.

15. Apply physical restraint to assure safety. When the safety of children is threatened, it may be necessary to judiciously apply physical restraint. Such situations are most common with aggressive children and youth. It must be emphasized that physical restraint is not equated with corporal punishment.

16. Children and teachers must "save face" in the resolution of conflicts. Confrontations between aggressive children or youth and teachers are relatively common and require resolution. In order to preserve acceptability to the rest of the group, the resolution should enable both teachers and pupils to "save face." In accordance with this concept, discipline problems should be dealt with privately and on a one-to-one basis whenever possible.

17. Be prepared; know the subject matter. Children exhibiting behavioral disorders are more receptive to instruction when they are convinced that the teacher knows the subject matter and is prepared. An unprepared teacher often exhibits insecurity and a general lack of confidence that, if perceived by pupils, will impede teaching and learning.

18. Be yourself and assume your role. Children with emotional and behavioral disorders appear to respond most positively to and to respect teachers and leaders who display behavior that is comfortable and characteristic. For example, teachers who use the language of children when they are uncomfortable doing so sound "funny" to the students and therefore are ridiculed by them. Teachers and leaders are expected to assume and not to abdicate their roles; they are teachers or leaders, not pupils. In assuming their roles, teachers or leaders should make every effort to develop and enhance positive human relationships.

Specific Learning Disabilities

Since the area of specific learning disabilities is still to a great extent an enigma to educators, any discourse on the relationship of learning disabilities to physical and motor performance must be tentative. Many questions are unanswered and will remain so until further research provides the basis for a better understanding of learning disabilities. As has already been mentioned, one aspect upon which there is consider-able agreement is that children labeled as learning disabled are a heterogeneous group. The major characteristic of the group is the presence of learning disability. The fact that the learning disabled are so different from each other obviously points to a need for individualized attention in methodology and programming. There is no *one* method or program for the learning-disabled child.

In a discussion of the relationship of learning disabilities to physical and motor performance, certain questions appear to be relevant. How do learning disabilities affect performance in physical and motor activities? Do physical and motor experiences affect learning disabilities (or abili-ties)? If physical and motor experiences do affect the abilities of the learner, what kind of disabilities may be remediated through movement? What kind of movement experiences are most useful for the remediation of learning disabilities? This section is designed to deal with these questions by focusing on the characteristics of the learning-disabled population.

Physical and Motor Performance

There is little doubt that most characteristics associated with the learning-disabled child potentially affect performance in physical and motor activities. In regard to specific academic learning disabilities, a child with receptive or expressive language disorders will display such disorders in movement as well as in other settings. For example, children with language disorders may exhibit difficulties in following directions or in playing games involving vocalization. A child with reading or writing disorders will exhibit those disorders when such skills are called upon in movement settings. Disorders in arithmetic will become known when children are called upon to count, add, subtract, divide, or multiply in game situations. Children with problems in visual perception may exhibit difficulties in throwing and catching, body awareness, eye-hand and eye-foot coordination, gross and fine motor abilities, awareness of position in space, spatial relationships, and balance. Deficits in auditory perception may result in difficulty in following directions, participating in rhythms and dances, and playing games and activities involving communication. Deficits in haptic perception may affect body aware-ness, laterality, gross and fine motor abilities, and balance. With such learning and perceptual problems, it is not surprising that awkwardness and clumsiness are characteristics associated with the learning-disabled child.

Although the learning and perceptual disabilities mentioned above are those most commonly associated with learning-disabled children, other characteristics associated with this group of children may also be expected to affect performance in physical and motor experiences. The hyperactive child may continue to exhibit abnormal movement, restless-ness, and inattention even though the setting is movement-oriented. In fact, movement may trigger even greater hyperactivity. The child who perseverates in reading or writing may be expected to do likewise in movement settings. That dissociation and disorders of memory affect performance in movement experiences may be evidenced when children fail to carry out a series of instructions, dance patterns, or movement routines. Distractibility may affect attention and concentration in movement settings just as it could in classroom settings. Finally, the "soft" social, emotional, and neurological signs that have been identified as characteristic of the learning disabled may be demonstrated in movement settings in the form of emotional outbursts, impulsive behavior, inadequate social relationships, and chronic lack of motivation.

Activities and Methods

Although the characteristics of children with specific learning disabilities will affect the type and quality of physical and motor performance, movement experiences may be employed to remediate learning deficits and to improve many of these characteristics. Since these characteristics are not unique to the learning disabled, the contributions of movement experiences to their improvement has already been covered in other sections of this book. The most common association of movement with learning disabilities has occurred in the perceptual motor approaches of Kephart (1971), Barsch (1967, 1968), Cratty (1970c), Getman and Kane (1964), and Frostig and Horne (1964b, 1973b). In addition to activities that enhance visual and auditory perception, these programs offer activities to remediate dissociation and disorders of memory, body image, spatial orientation, balance, gross motor skills, and coordination. Components of perceptual motor programs as well as specific activities for perceptual development are discussed in Chapter 4 and will not be repeated here. Participation in perceptual-motor activities may often be the appropriate prescription in the educational program for children with learning disabilities.

Movement experiences may be employed at times to develop academic concepts. Children who have difficulty understanding academic concepts in the traditional way may respond favorably to the motor activity learning medium (MALM). Programs in which motor activities are used directly as a medium for academic achievement have been developed by Cratty (1969d, 1970d, 1971a, 1973a), Humphrey (1965a), and Humphrey and Sullivan (1970a) as well as by other writers in the area of elementary physical education. In this book, specific activities to develop selected academic concepts are presented in Chapter 5.

The relationship of physical and motor activities with the characteristics of perseveration, distractibility, and hyperactivity have not been discussed in other sections of this book and thus will be briefly dealt with here. As was mentioned previously, perseveration is characterized by the repetition of a behavior or the inability to change the focus of or to shift easily from one behavior or idea to another. In physical and motor activity, perseveration is evidenced when a child continues bouncing a ball or running after the signal to stop has been given. A child may persist in playing with a particular toy or object in a particular way. Auditory perseverations are displayed when a child continues repeating the same word over and over or hums the same tune for long periods of time. To help remediate perseverations, it is recommended that children be provided activities characterized by change or interruption. Games so characterized include Follow the Leader, Streets and Alleys, Red Light, Freeze, and Simon Says. Since they involve single non-repetitive responses, obstacle courses are also recommended. Dance and movement routines involving a sequence of different activities may also be beneficial to counter perseveration.

Whereas perseveration involves the inability to shift attention, distractibility is the inability to focus attention on a particular stimulus for a sufficient time. The distractible child fails to block out and instead is distracted by the slightest irrelevant stimulus. Although the distractible child must eventually learn to filter out and attend to relevant stimuli from a background of irrelevant stimuli, it is recommended that this ability be gradually developed. The child is distracted less when the environment is made less stimulating. Instead of conducting a number of activities in a setting, it may be necessary to conduct one activity at a time. Instead of overstimulating a child by providing a variety of play materials, one or a small number of play materials are presented at once. Other techniques to reduce distraction include working in small areas, establishing and blocking off play and work areas, and conducting activities in areas as free as possible from auditory and visual distraction. Since children tend to be distracted less when they are active and involved, attention should be given to selecting enjoyable and active games.

One of the characteristics most often associated with the learning-disabled child is hyperactivity. Although different types of hyperactivity may be identified, the chief characteristic of the hyperactive child is greater than normal activity in a particular situation. Such activity impedes learning, since the child's ability to concentrate on and attend to a task is considerably reduced. The hyperactive child is unable to sit still long enough to listen. The short attention span associated with hyperactivity is one of the most difficult pupil characteristics with which teachers have to deal. Although medication is used to control hyperactivity, it is a "last resort" in dealing with the hyperactive child.

The educational techniques most often employed for hyperactive children are based on the concepts developed by Strauss and Lehtinen (1947) and expanded and modified by Cruickshank (1967). In introducing his approach, Cruickshank (1967) indicates that "usually the best classroom in your community for normal children is the worst classroom for brain injured children." The approach advocated by Cruickshank consists of four major elements. He recommends first that the environmental stimuli to which the child is exposed be reduced to a minimum. Second, the space in which the child works should be reduced to a minimum. Third, the program should be highly structured. Fourth, the stimulus value of relevant stimuli should be maximally enhanced. In regard to control of environmental stimuli, Cruickshank feels that overstimulation contributes to hyperactivity. Balls, bats, and other supplies and equipment should not be placed in the child's view unless they are being used in the present activity. It may be necessary to prohibit visitors from watching children perform and to reduce the type and number of activities being conducted at any one time. In a stimulus-free environment, there are no bulletin boards, chalkboards, or photographs.

The application of the concept of space reduction, which implies that the child should be taught in relatively small and limited areas, will be inhibited in movement settings to a great extent. In classrooms, learning cubicles are constructed to inhibit distraction. Cubicles for play, game, and sport settings are generally not recommended, since they defeat the primary purpose of movement activities. In extreme cases, however, swimming pools and other play areas may be divided into sections.

The concept of structure has a great implication for teachers and recreation leaders. In a structured situation, a child comes to a class in a particular way and moves to a specifically assigned location or spot at the start of a class. This location or spot is designated as the child's "home" or reference point. To add enjoyment and to motivate the child, spots may consist of paintings of animals or cartoon characters. The order of class activities follows a particular routine. At the beginning of class, the children may play a warm-up game or move through an obstacle course. Following this, they may learn a new activity, play a vigorous game, and end the class by playing a quiet game. Equipment is handed out in a particular way. Children always move to a prescribed spot to obtain instructions. Major pieces of equipment are always placed in the same position. Rules for classroom procedures such as obtaining and putting away equipment or making formations are established and closely followed. In essence, the children have the security of knowing what to expect because the environment has been made predictable. Students are not given an opportunity to make choices because such opportunities can be threatening to them. The uncertainty and over-stimulation associated with a less structured environment are reduced in this environment. Although the environment is structured, it should be filled with love, kindness, warmth, and concern for human welfare. A close physical relationship between the teacher and child enhances the structural environment.

Finally, it is important to maximize or heighten the recognition of relevant stimuli, i.e., those pertinent to the learning experience. For example, targets for accuracy throws may consist of faces of clowns or cartoon characters. Such targets or other objects are painted with bright

Figure 11–18. Exercising on one's own "home."

Figure 11-19. Learning accuracy by throwing at a stimulating target.

colors. Records for rhythmic activities must be clear and of sufficient loudness. Verbal directions provided by the teacher are given loudly and in a silent background. Pictures are used to help explain movements. In essence, every effort is made to draw the child to the appropriate stimulus.

It is not unusual for learning disabilities to affect the self-esteem or self-concept of the child. Learning deficits in one area may make the child feel inadequate in other areas. Children so affected may withdraw from social relationships, resulting in inadequate interaction with peers. Older youngsters with learning disabilities may prefer to relate to younger children. The younger child with less mature skill development is less threatening to the self-concept of the learning-disabled child and may exert less peer pressure. As with most handicapped children, the learning-disabled child must be provided with an opportunity to experience success. Undue emphasis on competition is contraindicated, since the learning-disabled child needs to succeed rather than fail. Too often, the child's past is filled with failure. One of the most unfortunate aspects of learning disabilities is that relatively minor inadequacies in learning may lead to troublesome emotional disturbances. For this reason, diagnosis and remediation should take place as early as possible.

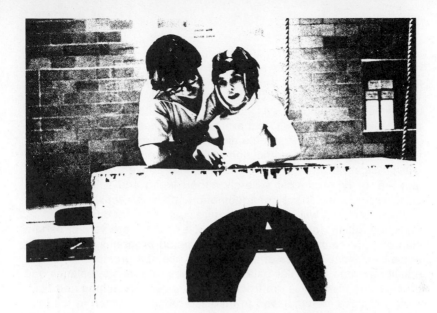

THE RELATIONSHIP OF MOVEMENT TO ORTHOPEDIC, NEUROLOGICAL AND NEUROMUSCULAR, AND OTHER HANDICAPS

In this chapter, the abilities, limitations, and needs of children with orthopedic, neurological and neuromuscular, and other handicapping conditions are considered. Although the chapter is arranged according to deviances, it must be stressed that there are wide variations in the abilities of individuals with the same handicapping condition. Therefore, it is necessary to plan individualized programs stressing the abilities rather than the handicaps.

Orthopedic Conditions

Amputation

The functional capacities of the individual and the effects of amputation on participation in physical activity will, of course, vary with the site and level of amputation and the function provided by the prosthetic appliance. People with above-the-elbow amputations, for example, are less functional than those with below-the-elbow amputations. People with unilateral above-the-knee amputations can become quite proficient in walking but are limited in competitive sports and in activities requiring speed of movement. Individuals with unilateral below-the-knee amputations exhibit almost normal walking with prostheses and are able to participate successfully in competitive sports. Bilateral below-the-knee amputation makes a person less proficient, and generally modification and restriction are required in certain physical activities. People with bilateral above-the-knee amputation are, of course, most severely handicapped and will often need crutches or wheelchairs for locomotion; physical activity programs for these children will invariably require significant modification.

Although the needs and abilities of amputees are varied, certain elements are common in physical rehabilation programs designed for amputees. Since the loss of a limb or the use of a prosthesis disrupts equilibrium and muscular balance, activities to enhance balance and proper body mechanics are frequently indicated. Stretching and flexibility exercises are employed to increase range of motion in the joint and to inhibit contractures. Muscle strengthening activities are employed to prevent atrophy of affected as well as unaffected limbs. Exercise and activities to develop dynamic balance and ambulatory abilities are employed for children with lower extremity amputations. General exercises are employed to promote stump circulation and general fitness of the amputee. Although the responsibility for implementing physical rehabilitation lies with physical therapists, movement activities to supplement physical therapy may be provided by physical educators, classroom teachers, recreators, or others involved in organizing movement experiences.

Because of the relative difficulty of moving and successfully participating in movement experiences, the amputee may tend to lead a sedentary existence. This is particularly true of children with above-the-knee amputations. In view of this, it is not uncommon for them to become overweight and thus to further aggravate their movement disabilities. Children must therefore be constantly encouraged and motivated to participate in physical activities, especially those that enhance weight control.

Although all children need opportunities to develop gross and fine motor abilities, the amputee is particularly in need of such opportunities. Grasp and release patterns and the ability to throw, catch, and strike are particularly important for children with upper-extremity amputation. Children with lower-extremity amputation must be provided with opportunities to develop or improve the ability to shift weight, to balance, to walk forward, backward, and sideward, to turn, to climb, to get up from the floor, to protect themselves during a fall, and to negotiate ramps. Corresponding abilities are necessary when crutches or wheelchairs are employed.

In many cases, games and sports need to be modified if amputees are to successfully participate in them. There are many sports, however, in which amputees may participate with little or no modification. Sports or activities requiring little or no modification for people with single arm amputation include badminton, bicycling, bowling, dancing, diving, fencing, fishing, racquetball, shuffleboard, skating, skiing, soccer, squash, swimming, track, and volleyball.

Figure 12–1. A cart that can be propelled by upper-body movement only.

Sports requiring little or no modification for children with single leg amputation include archery, fishing, bowling, canoeing, diving, golf, gymnastics, horseback riding, and swimming. Skating, skiing, soccer, and swimming may be performed with little or no modification by children with double arm amputation and archery, fishing, canoeing, diving, certain gymnastic stunts, horseback riding, shuffleboard, and swimming are among the activities requiring little or no modification for children with double leg amputaton. Although they are beyond the scope of this book, many sports and activities have been ingeniously modified for participation by amputees and youngsters confined to wheelchairs. Although children are encouraged to try as many activities as possible, it is also recommended that they concentrate on two or three sports so that they will develop the skill necessary for successful participation during their adult years.

Disorders of the Hip

The relationship of coxa plana, adolescent coxa vara, and congenital hip dislocation to participation in physical activity will be discussed in this section. Although these conditions vary to some extent, many generalizations can be made about physical activity possible with hip disorders. Since weight-bearing activities are commonly contraindicated for certain periods and children with hip disorders often use braces, casts, or crutches for ambulation, it is necessary to modify activities for safe and successful participation. Hip conditioning activities will often be prescribed to overcome muscle weakness, atrophy, and loss of range of motion. Activities to improve ambulation skills and posture are invariably warranted during convalescent or chronic phases. Swimming activities are of particular benefit for children with disorders of the hip. Since motor development may be delayed or inhibited, activities to enhance motor development are advocated in most instances. Participation in physical activities should be gradual and progressive, and care must be taken not to allow a child to exercise to fatigue. Throughout the period of convalescence, emotional support and encouragement must be constantly provided. Within the limitations imposed by their conditions, every effort should be made to involve children with hip disorders in physical activities to the fullest possible extent. Since the effects of different conditions vary, programs must be individually developed with medical consultation.

The effects of coxa plana on participation in physical activity vary according to the stage of the condition, the nature and severity of the condition, and the medical treatment employed. Since the condition generally occurs between the age of 4 and 10, effects on physical, perceptual, and motor development may be expected. There is no reason to expect deviations in development prior to the onset of coxa plana. However, early symptoms such as limping, stiffness, and an ache in the groin and the inner side of the thigh and knee will obviously affect movement ability. In the acute stage, the individual may be confined to bed braces and casts may be applied, and surgical treatment may be administered. During the regenerative phase, weight-bearing activities are generally prohibited. Since the period of regeneration may last for two to three years, however, it is important not to totally prohibit participation in movement experiences. To do so not only may contribute to a lag in physical and motor development but also may affect normal perceptual and psychological development. If the child is prohibited from engaging in weight-bearing activities, adaptations may be made. For example, the child may engage in physical and motor activities while seated, and games requiring locomotion may be limited. Activities such as bag punching, ring tossing, tether ball, fishing, archery, ball throwing and catching, swimming, and certain conditioning exercises are among those that may be easily arranged to avoid weight bearing. It should be noted that prolonged inactivity may lead not only to muscle atrophy but to contractures.

During the chronic phase, muscles of the hip joint may be affected by weakness, atrophy, and poor range of motion. Although they are to be conducted with medical guidance, progressive-resistance and flexibility exercises to develop hip abductors and extensors may be employed. Gradually, the individual will be able to engage in weight-bearing activities. As involvement increases, every effort should be made to avoid fatigue and pain. The individual should be "phased into" complete involvement through systematic and progressive programming. Throughout the various stages of the disorder, the child needs and should be given emotional support.

Strenuous exercise and weight bearing during the three- to six-month postoperative period is also contraindicated in cases of adolescent coxa vara. While the child is using crutches, movement experiences need to be modified. Activities to supplement physical therapy programs designed to strengthen quadricep and hamstring muscles may be provided under medical management. Even during the chronic phase, attention to participation may need to be continued. For some children, activities characterized by violent hip exertion, twisting, or absorption may be contraindicated for prolonged periods. Since patients with coxa vara are frequently obese, a program of weight control may be necessary.

Treatment for congenital hip dislocation may involve traction, casting, and surgery. As with coxa plana and adolescent coxa vara, weight bearing may be contraindicated for various periods. Physical therapy, with emphasis on the development of the hip abductors and extensors, may be prescribed. Involvement in exercise should be gradual and progressive and should include, as appropriate, stretching as well as active and resistance exercises. As is true with all the hip disorders discussed here, attention is given to the development of ambulatory skills. In view of the likelihood of postural deviations, activities for the improvement of spinal posture and general body mechanics are usually needed. Even as the chronic stage of dislocation is reached, it is likely that these activities will be prescribed.

Spina Bifida

The effects of spina bifida on participation in physical activity will vary with the type and severity of the condition. In spina bifida occulta, for example, there may be no effect on the movement abilities of the child. On the other hand, children with the myelomeningocele type may be confined to wheelchairs or may depend on braces or crutches for support and ambulation. Paralysis, muscle weakness, obesity, bone deformities, perceptual handicaps, retardation, and loss of skin sensation are frequently associated with the myelomeningocele type.

Since the types and severity of spina bifida vary, no single program of activities may be prescribed. Wheelchair activity may be indicated for those whose movement is otherwise restricted by paralysis or weakness. Physical activity programs in combination with dietary programs designed to reduce weight are indicated for the obese child. In severe cases, exercises and activity should be employed to prevent contractures associated with bone deformities such as hip dislocation, equinovarus (clubfoot), calcaneovalgus, scoliosis, kyphosis, and lordosis. In addition, physical activity is important to maintain or increase the strength and endurance of unaffected parts of the body. In view of the loss of skin sensations of pain, temperature, and touch, children must constantly inspect their skin for signs of pressure to prevent gradual death of the tissue. The child is susceptible to burns and ulcers caused by pressure (decubitus ulcers) as a result of lack of skin sensitivity to pain. With medical consultation, the child should be assisted in dealing with collecting bags and catheters during movement experiences. Activity should be provided at a regular time so that it becomes part of a routine. Such a procedure helps children to master bowel and bladder control. Teaching and curricular implications of mental retardation and perceptual handicaps found elsewhere in this book should also be applied for children with these complications.

Talipes

The effects of talipes (clubfoot) on participation in physical activity will vary according to the nature and severity of the condition and its residual effects. In certain cases, deformity will be slight, enabling the individual to participate in activities with little or no modification. In severe cases, inability to run, jump, and perform other locomotor activities will require that activities be modified for successful participation. If appropriate, manipulation or exercises designed to correct clubfoot will be prescribed by a physician. Unless they are prescribed, these exercises should not be employed. The physical activity program should be designed to promote motor and physical development, improve ambulatory abilities, enhance body mechanics, and provide opportunities for children to attain the usual benefits of movement experiences. Every effort should be made to integrate the child into normal activities to the fullest extent possible.

Osgood-Schlatter's Disease

Osgood-Schlatter's disease is a painful swelling about the tibial tuberosity associated with enlargement and partial or complete separation of the tubercle from the tibia. Since the quadriceps tendon is attached to the tubercle of the tibia, pain during contraction of the quadriceps may be expected. Continued activity tends to aggravate and inflame the condition. Therefore, the affected extremity must be rested during acute stages. Activities involving weight bearing, straining of the quadriceps, or absorption of shock are also contraindicated during this period. Walking, running, and other locomotor activities, particularly on hard surface, will generally be prohibited. If the condition is mild and asymptomatic, participation in movement activities may be possible. Decisions on participation, however, should be made with the benefit of qualified medical consultation.

Although activity involving the affected extremity will be limited, activities involving unaffected parts of the body should be continued. Following onset of the disorder, a conditioning program designed to restore normal functioning of the affected extremity should be established. Arnheim and associates (1969) have developed a sample six-week program designed for such purposes that progresses from passive and active-assistive exercises to an active program of physical activities. These authors suggest that children with Osgood-Schlatter's be returned to regular physical education only when they have attained normal range of movement of the knee, the strength of the affected quadriceps is equal to that of the unaffected leg, they display the ability to move freely, and they exhibit no symptoms of the disease.

Torticollis

Generally, chronic torticollis does not limit participation in physical activities. It is possible that the individual with torticollis will exhibit an abnormal appearance which may induce a negative reaction by peers. This may be the most important factor affecting performance, and it may be necessary to give attention to helping the class accept the child and encourage the child to perform to the maximum potential. In certain cases, the individual may be receiving physical therapy designed to stretch affected muscles and to strengthen contralateral muscles. In such cases, the individual may be given movement experiences to supplement such therapy.

Spondylolisthesis

Spondylolisthesis is a condition of the spine characterized by a forward vertebral displacement that is generally caused by defects in the posterior arch. Although little pain or discomfort may be experienced in some cases, the condition may restrict participation in physical activity in other cases. Vigorous activity, activities involving twisting and bending of the back, contact sports, and weightlifting may be contraindicated for children in more advanced stages of the disorder.

Although limitation in physical activity may be warranted, specific activities may be prescribed to prevent further aggravation and enhance improvement. Postural exercises may be employed to remediate functional lordosis. In order to reduce stress caused by excessive body weight, activities to aid weight reduction may be prescribed. Individuals should be taught proper weightlifting procedures so that the muscles of the legs rather than those of the back are used.

Neurological and Neuromuscular Conditions

Muscular Dystrophy

Any child with muscular dystrophy has similar physical restrictions, but it must be remembered that there are different types of muscular dystrophy. Since the pseudohypertrophic type is the most common in children, this section is written primarily with this type in mind. Walton and Gardner-Medwin (1974) as well as many other authorities indicate not only that physical activity is beneficial but that inactivity is detrimental for all people with this disease. Activity must not exhaust the individual and should be conducted under the supervision of qualified physicians. Ziter and Allsup (1975) believe that active exercises should be encouraged, and they prescribe range-of-motion exercises to be conducted twice a day for about ten minutes per session. Abramson and Rugoff (1952) found that muscle strength and contracture in their subjects improved as a result of their exercise program. Vignos and Watkins (1966) report that increases in muscular strength, especially in people with the limb-girdle and facio-scapulo-humeral types, may be developed through organized programs of maximum resistance exercise. In their research with 27 patients, Vignos, Spencer, and Archibald (1963) found that the duration of ambulation from onset of symptoms could be increased from an average of 4.4 years to 8.7 years for people who participated in a program utilizing early diagnosis, close supervision of patients, a physical therapy program, and bracing for ambulation when independent walking was no longer possible. Bleck and Nagel (1975a) recommend that group games be employed when appropriate to help children maintain range of motion and breathing capacity. Walton and Gardner-Medwin (1974) indicate that contractures are to some extent preventable and reversible but that none of the physical methods halt the progress of the disease. This role of physical activity is generally accepted.

The most critical aspects of muscular dystrophy are the degeneration of muscle tissue, muscular weakness and wasting, and contracture. Movement and activity become difficult for the child. Although physical activity is important to them, children with muscular dystrophy thus tend to become less active. As muscular weakness progresses, the child may exhibit difficulty in rising from the floor, ascending stairs or curbs, walking, and running. The child may walk with a waddling gait, with the feet wide apart, or on tiptoe. Imbalanced weakness of the shoulder girdle and spinal muscles causes scoliosis, and weakness and contracture of muscles in other parts of the body contribute to severe cases of lordosis. Continued degeneration eventually leads to wheelchair and bed existence for people with certain types of muscular dystrophy. Excessive eating and immobility may result in obesity (although not all patients are overweight), and lack of activity contributes to skeletal changes that make bones susceptible to fracture. Cardiac problems are also exhibited by many people with muscular dystrophy. In the pseudohypertrophic type, intellectual retardation sometimes occurs. It is also not unusual and is of course understandable for the child to exhibit psychological difficulties in coping with the condition. Respiratory infections are common at later stages owing to general weakness of the body.

It is important that children with muscular dystrophy participate in physical activity to the fullest extent possible. Activities conducted under medical supervision may be designed to help children stretch muscles, delay the onset of contractures, maintain and develop strength, maintain breathing capacity, enhance coordination and balance, aid cardiovascular functioning, maintain the health of the skeletal structure, and improve or maintain walking abilities. Physical activity and proper diet may be employed to maintain body weight at proper level. Skills should be developed so that children are able to participate in childhood games. Children should be allowed and encouraged to participate in "fun" activities in order to counteract the boredom and loneliness to which they are susceptible. In developing a program, the professional should not hesitate to modify sports and games for successful participation by pupils with muscular dystrophy. Children should not be forced into activities. In working with children, it is important for the teacher or leader to exhibit restrained optimism and constant encouragement. The hope that research may lead to a discovery of treatment for muscular dystrophy should be communicated.

Epilepsy

Participation in physical activity by epileptics is not only accepted but encouraged. For cases in which good seizure control has been gained, participation is characterized by few restrictions. Goldenshon and Barrows (n.d.) indicate that restricted activity and idleness tend to make seizures occur more frequently. Scott (1973) also reports that seizures are caused more commonly by idleness than by exertion and concentration. Kemp (1963) feels that participation in games is not only more likely to discourage attacks than to encourage them but also is beneficial for psychological adjustment. Forche (1973), a research analyst for the Epilepsy Foundation of America, has stressed that the practice of prohibiting children with epilepsy from physical activity is outmoded. It is generally accepted that participation in games and physical activity is important for the normal development of the epileptic. Particularly beneficial in this regard are group games. Besides having the usual physical values such as increases in strength and stamina, participation in such activities helps to integrate the epileptic into the mainstream of society.

Although participation in physical activities is encouraged, certain restrictions and safeguards need to be considered in regard to seizures, anxiety, and head injury. The first and foremost problem is the possibility of seizure during participation. Unless their seizures are adequately controlled and medical approval is given, epileptics should not normally engage in activities that might result in injury if seizure occurred during participation. Thus, activities such as climbing, some gymnastics, bicycling, diving, horseback riding, archery, and rifle shooting are generally contraindicated. Swimming activities are recommended as long as the children are closely supervised. Since anxiety tends to increase the frequency of seizures, it may be necessary to prohibit or limit participation in highly competitive activities. For certain cases of epilepsy, the danger of head injury may

Figure 12–2. Children susceptible to seizures may wear a helmet to avoid injury from falling.

require a restriction of participation in contact sports. Sports such as boxing, wrestling, football, and ice hockey may be contraindicated. Since the nature and severity of epilepsy varies from child to child, decisions about participation should be made on an individual basis.

As a result of social ostracism or parental and social overprotection, it is not uncommon for epileptics to lead a sedentary existence. Thus, muscle weakness, lack of stamina, poor body mechanics, and generally low tolerance of exercise may be expected. As a side affect of drug therapy, a lack of coordination may be expected. It is recommended that the intensity of participation be gradually increased so that the child does not become unduly fatigued. Since fatigue tends to make seizures occur more frequently, gradual involvement in vigorous physical activity is particularly desirable for the epileptic.

It is important for teachers or leaders of movement programs to be aware of first aid measures to be taken in case of seizure. A summary of the standard procedure follows.

1. Be calm. The person having a seizure is not suffering pain and is not in danger of choking, swallowing the tongue, severe injury, or dying as a result.
2. If the epileptic has an aura, help the individual to a safe, quiet, and inconspicuous place where it is possible to lie on a bed, soft rug, or mat.
3. Cushion the epileptic's fall and place the person on the floor away from sharp objects, radiators, and furniture.
4. Loosen tight clothing, especially around the neck.
5. Wipe saliva and froth from the mouth so that it is not inhaled.
6. When the jaw is open, place a soft object too big to be swallowed between the teeth to prevent the person from biting the tongue and cheeks.

7. Do not attempt to open a clenched jaw or restrain movements during the seizure.
8. Be calm and reassuring during recovery.
9. If the seizure continues for more than 10 minutes, obtain medical help.
10. The epileptic who falls asleep after a seizure should be allowed to awaken naturally.

Cerebral Palsy

There is little question that participation in movement activities is extremely important for the normal development of the cerebral palsied child. It is also evident, however, that conditions associated with cerebral palsy affect participation. In addition, a great deal of variation may be expected in view of the variety in types and severity of affliction. As a group, cerebral palsied children exhibit a lag in motor and physical development, difficulty in controlling movement, lack of coordination, perceptual inadequacy, and poor body mechanics. Many victims are overweight and easily distracted, and have a short attention span. A disproportionately high number are mentally retarded (Cardwell, 1956) and have difficulty achieving social acceptance (Force, 1956). Many use splint braces and other assistive devices to compensate for physical and motor disabilities. Although only slight modification of activities is necessary for some children, a great deal of modification may be required for successful participation by severely afflicted children.

Since motor dysfunction is the central feature of cerebral palsy, physical therapy has become an important part of treatment. Such treatment generally is designed to develop and facilitate muscular functioning and voluntary muscular control, secure muscular relaxation, enhance motor development, and to help the child learn motor skills basic to recreation and daily activities. Although the responsibility for physical treatment lies with the physical therapist, it is important that recreators, physical educators, and others involved in conducting movement experiences help to supplement the treatment. In addition, these professionals may help the child develop motor abilities and skills for participation in play, games, sports, exercise, and dance.

Several systems have been developed for the purpose of physical therapy. Some of the more commonly used systems include the Bobath treatment, the Fay-Doman-Delacato method, the Kabat-Knott system, the Rood method, and the Phelps and Deaver methods. However, most therapists use an eclectic method. A sequence of muscle education that is often employed includes passive, active-assistive, active, and progressive-resistance exercises. In the beginning, movement of affected limbs is initiated by the therapist. As training progresses, the patient develops the ability to move with assistance, to move without assistance, and finally to move against resistance.

In addition to the restoration of muscular movement and the development of strength, physical activity is important to the cerebral palsied for other reasons. Stretching exercises are employed to increase flexibility (range of motion), to relieve muscular contractures, and thus to inhibit bone deformity. In cases where muscular imbalance occurs, exercise and activities may be used to counter spinal deviations and to enhance proper body alignment. Muscle reciprocation exercises are employed to facilitate the action of contralateral muscles. Muscle relaxation exercises aid in reducing muscular tension and thus encouraging controlled movement. Exercises that create and reduce tension in various parts of the body are used to promote body awareness or kinesthesia. Since the development of basic movement patterns and motor skills is necessary for play, locomotion, and self-care, exercises and activities that enhance these abilities are highly recommended for the cerebral palsied. For example, children may be helped to grasp and release, to extend and flex the limbs, to bend and extend the trunk, to stand, and to walk. If they are able to perform these actions, they are well on their way to developing the abilities essential for play and self-care. As physical activity is conducted, attention is continually placed on the development of conscious control of movement.

Although nearly any kind of movement experience is beneficial for the cerebral palsied, some are of particular benefit and are emphasized in programs developed for these children. An activity that is particularly important is swimming. If warm enough, water has a relaxing effect that facilitates the reduction of muscular tension and thus enhances controlled movement. During swimming, muscles not normally used may be activated and developed. Locomotor activities are important for all cerebral palsied victims, and balance activities are particularly emphasized for the ataxic. In the early years, games

Figure 12–3. The cerebral palsied enjoy the trampoline.
(Illustration continued on opposite page)

Figure 12–3. Continued.

involving basic movement patterns and skills are important, since these serve as a basis for participation in sports in the later years. Balance activities and other activities that encourage proper body alignment are also frequently recommended. Movement activities that emphasize visual-motor coordination and perceptual development are also important in movement programs for the cerebral palsied.

Several factors must be considered in implementing programs for the cerebral palsied. First and foremost, it is important to provide successful experiences. The establishment of progressive steps that are attainable is important. Undue attention to perfection and to winning may be counterproductive. Second, the environment should be one as free of anxiety as possible. This is particularly important to the cerebral palsied, since emotionality tends to inhibit controlled voluntary movements. Since excitement is usually a characteristic of athletics, participation in athletics by cerebral palsied children is advised only with medical approval. At times, it may be appropriate for the child to substitute participation in active team games with a less exciting activity. Third, it is important to intersperse activity with rest periods. Fatigue inhibits effective performance and may be a source of frustration for the child. Fourth, the environment should be as free of distraction as possible. Many children with cerebral palsy have short attention spans and may have difficulty concentrating on an activity. Distraction tends to interrupt concentration and thus makes program implementation more difficult.

There is little question that the cerebral palsied child has more problems in adjustment than normal youngsters. In his study of the social status of the physically handicapped, Force (1956) found that physically handicapped children in integrated classes were less accepted than normal children. He also found that cerebral palsied children were particularly low in choices as friends, playmates, and workmates. Deformities, drooling, facial grimaces, poor speech, incoordination, and possibly a generally poor cosmetic appearance of the cerebral palsied child may cause abnormal reactions in others. Inability to move efficiently, to be independent, or to perform tasks in a normal way causes frustration in the child and may lead to fear, anger, anxiety, and a tendency to withdraw. The situation is complicated by the possibility of inappropriate psychological behavior caused by organic lesions. Cerebral palsied children may be feared, ridiculed, pampered, overprotected, pitied, or repulsed. Lack of understanding makes it difficult for them to be accepted by members of a normal peer group. Whenever possible, professionals must help the child deal with such problems. Where participation may be safe and successful, they should be included in regular settings. Leaders should help others understand the condition, encourage the victim toward normal functioning, and set a positive example in working with the cerebral palsied child. Attention to adjustment is extremely important in programs for the cerebral palsied child.

Although the use of movement experiences as an adjunct to physical therapy and other rehabilitative purposes is certainly appropriate in programming for the cerebral palsied, attention must also be given to movement activities that contribute to the total normal development of the child. Experiences that prepare the cerebral palsied child to participate in integrated physical and motor experiences are appropriate. Psychological and sociological objectives are important in the normal development of any youngster and must be sought in program development. Play, games, rhythms, gymnastics, and aquatics should be advocated for fun and for their other recreational values.

Since the types of cerebral palsy are varied, it is important to consider the distinguishing features of each type in selecting movement experiences. Children with spasticity tend to be inactive and thus overweight. In addition, they have a tremendous fear of falling, and non-swimmers often exhibit abnormal fear of the water (Adams, Daniel, Rullman, 1972). Mental retardation often accompanies the spastic type of cerebral palsy, and Cruickshank and his associates (1965) report that genuine abnormalities of visual perception exist in many spastic cerebral palsied children. Although generally slow to anger, the spastic is usually introverted, concerned about his handicap, and filled with fears (Perkins, 1963). The unique features of spasticity, however, include muscle stiffness and contracture resulting from disturbance of the stretch reflex and the hyperactive tendon reflex. Movement for the child with the spastic type of cerebral palsy is thus very difficult. An important training goal is to lengthen spastic muscles and strengthen contralateral muscles. To attain this goal, the spastic muscles should be relaxed, slowly stretched, and held momentarily in this position. It is particularly important to perform such movements slowly in order to avoid stimulating the stretch reflex. It is also important to shorten and strengthen muscles contralateral to the spastic muscles. In addition to preventing contractures, such activities help the child develop and improve motor skills. In view of the scissors gait so characteristic of spastics, activities to improve balance and body alignment are advocated by many authorities.

With the rigid type of cerebral palsy, both agonist and antagonist muscles are affected, with the result being even greater difficulty in movement than with the spastic type. There is no stretch reflex, and the muscles lack elasticity. According to Keats (1965), the aim of treatment is to prevent contractures, to induce relaxation, and to develop and improve motor skills. Since both agonist and antagonist muscles are involved, both groups need to be stretched and strengthened. Keats (1965) indicates that for people with the rigid type, exercises and movements should be done more quickly.

Although the child with ataxia often displays visual and speech defects, the chief feature of this type is incoordination due to poor kinesthesia and a disturbance in the sense of balance. In walking, victims often exhibit a weaving, staggering, and stumbling gait. In planning activities for the ataxic, emphasis is placed on activities to promote balance, to develop kinesthetic perception, and to improve motor coordination and motor skill. In addition, resistance exercises are often provided to stimulate the proprioceptors. Many authorities recommend that the ataxic child perform movements while watching them in a mirror in order to compensate for the lack of kinesthesia. Kinesthetic teaching (touching body parts) is also advocated, since the ataxic child has difficulty in body awareness.

The athetoid exhibits uncontrolled and involuntary movements owing to an overflow of muscle stimulation and a lack of coordination of muscle impulses. Extraneous movements are characteristic of the athetoid's attempts at purposeful movement. When movements are attempted or when emotionality increases, overflow increases and extraneous movement intensifies. Although hearing and speech disorders are not uncommon in the athetoid, perceptual impairment and mental retardation are not as common in athetosis as in other types of cerebral palsy. Athetoids are often affectionate, easily aroused, and extroverted (Perkins, 1963). Although there are many types of athetosis, training generally is designed to help athetoids perform purposeful movement and to relax. Balance and relaxation activities are highly recommended. In addition, activities to enhance motor development and motor coordination are indicated. Whereas in spasticity and rigidity the goal is to increase voluntary movement capabilities, the goal of training in athetosis is to reduce involuntary movements.

Like athetosis, the tremor type of cerebral palsy is associated with too much movement. Movement in the tremor type is distinguished from that of athetosis in that it is rhythmic, alternating, and pendular. As Keats (1965) points out, the goal of physical training for children with the tremor type of cerebral palsy is the same as that for athetoids.

Poliomyelitis

Educators and regular recreators generally come into contact with pupils in the chronic phase of poliomyelitis. Since the severity and type of poliomyelitis and its effects on the individual may vary, no specific movement program can be recommended. A program must be based on the individual needs of youngsters. In general, children in the chronic phase of this disease will exhibit muscular weakness, lack of stamina, and poor motor coordination. In certain cases, scoliosis will be evidenced. For many children, movement is dependent on the use of crutches and braces, and some children may need to use wheelchairs. In some cases, the restoration of certain muscles is not possible, and in other cases, muscular restoration may be enhanced or maintained by movement experiences, which serve as an adjunct to physical therapy. It is therefore important that medical guidance be obtained in planning appropriate movement experience for the "post-polio" child.

Although no specific program can be recommended for all post-polio children, any program should meet some general criteria. Since muscular weakness and lack of endurance are common consequences of the disease, exercises and activities to increase these components of physical fitness are generally important. It is, of course, absolutely necessary that the intensity of activity progress gradually. Measurement of physical proficiency should be taken at the outset of a program and periodically as the program is implemented. The antigravity muscle groups of the hips, back, abdomen, and legs are generally in greatest need of development.

It is not uncommon for the post-polio child to exhibit muscular imbalance and contracture in certain muscle groups. These conditions may lead to paralytic scoliosis, pathological dislocation of the hip, dropping of the foot, deformities of the elbow, wrist, and hand, and generally poor body mechanics. To the greatest extent possible, exercises and activities that contribute to body alignment should be employed. Stretching activities may be employed to inhibit contractures and to maintain or increase the range of movement in a joint. In addition, care must be taken not to further contribute to muscular imbalance by inappropriately developing contralateral muscles at different rates.

Water activities are highly recommended for children who have had poliomyelitis. Properly implemented, water activities serve to relax the muscles and to enhance reciprocal innervation of muscle groups. In addition, water activities provide opportunities for the activation of muscle groups not generally used. It is not uncommon for post-polio patients to succeed in water activities. Water activities provide immediate physical, social, and psychological benefits and excellent recreational activity which can be pursued during adult years.

Since paralysis is permanent for some children, there may be a need to modify activities for successful participation. Such modification follows the principles of adapting activities for other physical handicaps. Although they are important, these modified activities should be complemented by the attainment of success in activities requiring little or no modification. It is rare that the individual is not able to participate in certain recreational activities in a normal or nearly normal manner. Participating in activities requiring little or no modification, of course, enhances inclusion in the mainstream of society. The educator or recreator must always remember that children as well as adults like to be treated as normally as possible. This implies that the program developed for the child should be as normal as possible, and whenever possible the post-polio child should be integrated into regular movement programs.

Multiple Sclerosis

Fortunately, the symptoms of multiple sclerosis do not normally appear prior to the teen years. Onset in childhood or during the elementary school years is unlikely. People with the disease, however, often do exhibit symptoms that affect their involvement in physical activity. Spasticity, contractures, lack of muscular strength and endurance, lack of coordination, and ataxic characteristics inhibit movement effectiveness. For pupils with braces, there may be a need for modification in activity. Intolerance to external temperature change may affect motivation for participation in activity and may require alteration in the conduct of physical activity programs. Since prolonged exertion may cause exacerbations, intensity of participation must be controlled.

Although the effects of multiple sclerosis influence participation in physical activity, such participation is recommended for the management of the disease as well as for general movement objectives. Physical activity may be used as physical therapy or as an adjunct to physical therapy. Activities particularly appropriate include those in which participants move through the maximum range of motion, those that serve to develop and maintain strength and endurance, those that enhance coordination and balance abilities, and those that prevent and contain spasticity and contractures. Activities and exercises that involve ambulation and stretching are also widely recommended. For people confined to bed or a wheelchair, it may be necessary to modify activity. However, participation in such activity is considered valuable because even movements involving changes in body position help to prevent pressure sores and possible ulcerations.

It must be stressed, however, that participation in physical activity should not be restricted to "therapeutic" objectives per se. Although physical activity may contribute to therapy, activities are important for their psychological, sociological, and educational benefits as well.

It must be recognized that the symptoms and causes of multiple sclerosis vary. Thus, the abilities, limitations, and needs of the participants in physical activity will also vary. Physical activity does not cure multiple sclerosis, but it is effective in managing the disease and helping victims to live as normally as possible. Physical activity should be provided for people with multiple sclerosis and should be conducted with medical guidance.

Other Handicaps

Bronchial Asthma*

It has long been known that asthmatic attacks may be precipitated by exercise, emotion, and fatigue. Since these factors are associated with play and movement experiences, youngsters have often been restricted in such activities. As the effects of these activities have been further studied, there has emerged a change in attitude regarding participation. The Committee on Children with Handicaps and the Joint Committee on Physical Fitness, Recreation, and Sports Medicine of the American Academy of Pediatrics (1970) have approved participation in physical education, under medical supervision, for the majority of asthmatic children. It is also agreed that decisions on participation should be made on an individualized basis. The committee also has made various recommendations on the nature of such a program; their recommendations will be discussed later in this section. Harvey (1975a) advocates participation in physical education so that asthmatic children do not feel different from their peers. The Joint Committee of the Allergy Foundation of America and the American Thoracic Society (1973) indicates that an exercise program designed to improve physical fitness is a valuable part of rehabilitation of the chronic asthmatic. The Joint Committee indicates that exercise-provoked asthma can be prevented by use of an aerosol of epinephrine or isoproterenol or by administration of an ephedrine capsule so that the patient need not keep from exercising.

Although participation in physical activity is generally advocated,

---

*This section was originally published by Joseph P. Winnick, as "Physical Activity and the Asthmatic Child," *Amer. Corr. Ther. J.* 31:148–151, 1977.

direct or associated effects of asthma may limit the intensity and nature of participation. Children may be fearful of participation because of the possibility of asthmatic attack. Although characteristics of asthmatic children are certain to be variable, general muscular weakness and poor endurance may be expected because of a sedentary history. Owing in part to inactivity and in part to the nature of the condition, vital capacity and aerobic capacity may be poor, resulting in poor cardiovascular endurance. Previous inactivity often causes a low psychological as well as physiological tolerance for physical activity. The Committee on Children with Handicaps of the American Academy of Pediatrics (1970) indicates that participation in contact sports by severe asthmatics is contraindicated unless it is medically approved. Because emotionality may induce an attack in certain cases, decisions on a child's participation in athletics or highly competitive activities should be made with medical consultation. However, every effort should be made to minimize restrictions.

PROGRAM EMPHASIS

Although a well rounded program with little restriction or modification may be quite appropriate, certain activities are generally needed and should be emphasized for asthmatics. Because most asthmatics have relatively poor motor and physical proficiency, individually prescribed activities for physical and motor development are appropriate. In view of respiratory obstruction, many authorities recommend that particular attention be devoted to increasing the strength of abdominal, trunk, and shoulder muscles; the development of these muscles is particularly important since they aid in diaphragmatic breathing. Activities for the improvement of vital capacity and aerobic capacity are also particularly valuable. Daniels and Davies (1975) recommend activities to stimulate conscious relaxation for preventing and reducing reactions to stress. It is felt that such activities may be helpful in preventing emotion-induced asthmatic attacks. Seligman, Randel, and Stevens (1970) have employed conscious relaxation exercises in their program with some success. Activities that contribute to proper body alignment are also recommended for enhancement of respiration as well as for other values. Blowing and breathing games designed to enhance breathing have been employed in programs for asthmatics with some success. Franklin (1971) found an improvement in the aerobic capacity of asthmatic subjects as a result of a one-month physical condition program that included blowing games. In her program, children played games in which they attempted to keep small squares of tissue paper from falling to the floor by blowing them upward, relay games in which they blew ping pong balls for a particular distance, balloon relays in which players ran to a designated point, inflated a balloon, and then sat on it until it broke, candle blowing from certain distances, and ping pong "croquet," in which players blew ping pong balls through a series of hoops placed on a floor.

The Committee on Children with Handicaps of the American Academy of Pediatrics (1970) recommends non-contact sports and gymnastic activities but indicates that participation in such activities be evaluated on an individual basis for each asthmatic child. Hayden (1971), Hyde and Swarts (1968), Peterson and McElhenney (1965), Scherr and

Frankel (1958), and McElhenney and Peterson (1963) have successfully employed stunts or gymnastic activities in their programs. Another important and well received activity is swimming and water play. It is important, however, that the water temperature be between 85 and 90 degrees. Blumenthal and Pederson (1967), McElhenney and Peterson (1963), Scherr and Frankel (1958), and Seligman, Randel, and Stevens (1970) have successfully employed swimming activities in their programs for asthmatics. Although the development of endurance is an important objective, Harvey (1975) suggests that "short burst" activities such as baseball may be preferred to those that require continual activity such as soccer and running. Inherent in such "short burst" activities are opportunities to sit and rest. This recommendation would be in agreement with the Joint Committee of the Allergy Foundation of America and the American Thoracic Society (1973), which indicates that "too vigorous an exercise program, such as forced participation in endurance sports such as track, can be extremely hazardous." Hayden (1971) and Scherr and Frankel (1958) have successfully employed judo and other self-defense skills in programs for asthmatic children.

PRECAUTIONS

Certain precautions should be employed in the implementation of movement programs for asthmatic children to enhance safe and successful participation. Care must be taken to avoid or reduce exposure to cold and to sudden changes in temperature, since these conditions may trigger asthmatic attacks. Since attacks may be caused by over-exertion, the intensity of activity must be suited to the physical tolerance of the individual. Frequent rest periods and gradual involvement in activity are of particular importance for inhibiting or preventing attacks caused by over-exertion. Exposure to substances to which the participant may be allergic must be avoided or reduced to the greatest possible extent; examples include mat or chalk dust, grass, trees, and pollens. Since the prevalence of such causative agents may vary on a day-to-day basis, flexibility in the type and intensity of participation is recommended.

BREATHING EXERCISES

Breathing exercises are often recommended in rehabilitation programs for the asthmatic. Although generally administered by physical therapists, and under medical supervision, breathing exercises are frequently combined with exercise or movement programs administered by other professionals. In such cases, an understanding of breathing exercises is helpful. According to Wood, Kravis, and Lecks (1970), most rehabilitation centers follow the program established by the Asthma Research Council (1962). The purpose of breathing exercises is to improve ventilation by enhancing expiration. Since the diaphragm becomes less active in the asthmatic, exercises are intended to enhance ventilation by effectively employing the diaphragm in breathing (diaphragmatic breathing). According to Zohman (1968), breathing exercises "will result in improved alveolar ventilation, a decrease in the work of breathing, and will lessen the patient's natural desire to relieve his shortness of breath by hurried, gasping inspiration which overinflates the lungs and traps still more air." During diaphragmatic exercises, the abdomen is protruded during inhalation and moved in during exhalation. As the individual exhales, the abdominals are used to assist the diaphragm in squeezing air from the lungs. Thus, the diaphragm is put in a better position to enlarge the chest during inspiration and to create intrathoracic pressure to help squeeze the lungs during expiration. Zohman (1968) indicates that the diaphragm can be trained through breathing against resistances such as the hands of a therapist, sandbags with graduated weights up to ten pounds, or a hot water bottle filled with water. Other assistance techniques suggested by Zohman (1968) and other researchers include loosening a band of cloth encircling the patient during inspiration and tightening it during expiration, compressing the lower chest and abdomen with the hands during exhalation, and compressing the abdomen and lower part of the chest with the arms during expiration. Benack (1967) recommends that initially such exercises be done two or three times daily and then less often. Dorinson (1954) indicates that they should be practiced for 10–20 minutes twice a day.

In addition to diaphragmatic breathing exercises, pursed-lip breathing, trunk bending, and leg raising exercises are sometimes employed to enhance ventilation. During pursed-lip breathing, the lips are partially closed during expiration. This results in a hissing or whistling sound. Patients may be asked to produce "s," "v," or "f" sounds or to bend the flame of a candle in order to help them experience proper pursed-lip breathing. The purpose of pursed-lip breathing is to maintain an air passage within the lungs. By pursing the lips, resistance to air flow is created, thus placing the individual in a more normal mid-expiratory position. In this way, intra-airway pressure is maintained at a higher level than that at which premature collapse of the airways occur.

The Joint Committee of the Allergy Foundation of America and the American Thoracic Society (1973) indicates that the value of systematic breathing or diaphragmatic exercise is controversial. In a review of the research, this author has identified a number of studies that have not demonstrated any significant benefit from such exercises. In view of this finding, breathing exercises should be administered only under medical supervision.

THE VALUE OF PHYSICAL ACTIVITY

The value of exercise and general physical activity programs in reducing medicinal requirements and frequency of attacks and in improving school attendance, coughing, and adjustment has been noted by several investigators. Blumenthal and Pederson (1967) and McElhenney and Peterson (1963) reported that less medication was needed by subjects during periods in which their programs of physical activity were implemented. In regard to the frequency of attacks, McElhenney and Peterson (1963) reported a 30 per cent reduction in the number and severity of asthmatic attacks in response to their physical fitness program. Dorinson (1954) found that subjects were able to abort or minimize attacks by doing simple breathing exercises gently. Peterson and McElhenney (1965) reported that parents of children in their study noted a marked reduction in number and severity of asthmatic attacks in their children in response to a physical fitness program. Scherr and Frankel (1958) found a reduction in the frequency and severity of asthmatic attacks in their subjects in response to their program of general physical conditioning. The lack of attendance at school and work because of asthmatic attacks has been widely documented. Blumenthal and Pederson (1967) and Peterson and McElhenney (1965) noted an increase in the school attendance of test subjects as a result of participation in a general physical conditioning program. Blumenthal and Pederson (1967) also noted that their program resulted in less coughing and excitability in participants. Peterson and McElhenney (1965) found that the emotional upsets of asthmatic children, as determined by parental observation, decreased in response to their program of physical fitness. These authors also reported that 80 per cent of classroom teachers said children had improved in acceptance by other children and participated more fully in playground activities in response to their program. Scherr and Frankel (1958) noted a loss of fear about asthmatic attacks as a result of a physical conditioning program consisting of respiration exercises, general physical exercises, and confidence-building activities. On the basis of subjective observation, Dorinson (1954) also noted reduction in participants' fear during attacks.

The effects of physical activity program on physiological variables have also been investigated. Franklin (1971), Hirt (1964), Itkin and Nacman (1966), McElhenney and Peterson (1963), Peterson and McElhenney (1965), Scherr and Frankel (1958), and Seligman, Randel, and Stevens (1970) are among the investigators who have reported positive effects of physical participation on pulmonary efficiency, aerobic capacity, workload, and other measures of physical fitness.

It is evident that participation to the greatest possible extent in physical activity is recommended for asthmatic children. It is also evident that the nature and intensity of activity will vary from case to case. Programs, therefore, need to be developed after the needs and abilities of each child are determined. In severe cases, it is necessary for professionals implementing such programs to work closely with physicians.

Cystic Fibrosis

The effects of cystic fibrosis, or mucoviscidosis, on individuals varies according to the nature and severity of involvement. Children with the disease should be treated as normally as possible and should be allowed to participate in movement activities to the greatest extent possible. Because involvement varies, it is necessary to ascertain the effects of the disease on an individual basis. It is not uncommon, however, for the physical stamina of the child to be less than normal owing to lung involvement and loss of energy through elimination. In view of abnormal salt loss, children need to be carefully observed during activity; this is especially important in hot weather and during strenuous activity. In these situations, the child may sweat profusely, with subsequent salt depletion and heat exhaustion. It is necessary to develop procedures for the ingestion of salt and to discuss the intensity of participation in consultation with the child's physician. Finally, care must be taken to practice good respiratory hygiene to prevent respiratory infection. For example, water for swimming should be warm and children should dry thoroughly after swimming. Drying should be done with clean towels.

As the child with cystic fibrosis participates in physical activity, certain other rather common behaviors or characteristics may be evident. It may be necessary for the child to take medicine during class hours and to be excused frequently to eliminate stools. A hearty appetite is characteristic, as is supplementary salt intake during activity that causes perspiration. Frequent coughing is also characteristic and necessary to help the child to move mucus out of the lungs. It must be recognized that all such behaviors and characteristics are associated with cystic fibrosis and that the child must be helped to deal with them as unobtrusively as possible. It is important to minimize attention to differences between the child and others. Children generally prefer to be and thus should be treated as normally as possible.

Although the child may have some limitations, participation in physical activities should be as normal as possible. Breathing exercises are recommended and may be administered under medical supervision. Certain activities are thought to help loosen mucus. Schleichkorn (1977) states that active play and running, swimming, and skipping are often more effective than other forms of therapy for raising sputum. He also stresses that children with cystic fibrosis should be encouraged to take part in any form of exercise of which they are capable. Also recommended are activities that help to maintain or improve posture and those that increase physical proficiency and provide the child with the motor abilities necessary for successful participation in physical activities. Very important, however, is the objective of providing experiences that help the child engage in play and movement as normally as possible.

Diabetes Mellitus*

The benefits of exercise for the diabetic are widely recognized, and it is well known that many "champion" athletes have been diabetics. The diabetic child should be encouraged to participate in games, sports, exercise, and rhythmic activities. Certain guidelines, the implementation of which relates to the severity of the condition, are helpful in planning and conducting safe and successful movement experiences.

First, it is important that physical activity tolerance levels be established and be known to professionals implementing programs and to the children themselves. This not only helps to provide safe experiences but also helps the child understand and adjust to the disease. Professionals responsible for implementing movement programs should have access to and be familiar with the medical records of the child. Physical activity tolerance levels should be established on the basis of such records and under medical supervision.

In view of the close relationship among them, physical acitivity must be coordinated with insulin and food intake. Too much exercise may result in insulin reaction. In view of this possibility, it is not uncom-

---

*Parts of this section are based on an earlier article by the author: Winnick, Joseph P. "Planning Physical Activity for the Diabetic," *Phys. Educ.* 27:15–16, 1970.

mon for diabetics to carry a lump of sugar with them during activity. Some physicians recommend that diabetics have immediate access to quick energy such as candy, orange juice, ice cream, or a soft drink. To the greatest extent possible, exercise should be uniform in amount and should be taken regularly at a planned time each day. Activity should progress from short, mild sessions to longer, more strenuous sessions, preferably scheduled after a small meal or snack. Because of the possibility of insulin shock during muscular work, it is particularly important that children be supervised closely during swimming activities.

Infections should be prevented to the fullest extent possible because infections may increase the need for insulin by increasing metabolism generally, interfering with the utilization of insulin, limiting the output of insulin by the pancreas, or increasing the "poison" or toxins absorbed by the blood stream and thus bringing about acidosis. It is not uncommon for an infectious disease to precipitate the onset of diabetes. Thus, contact sports such as boxing and wrestling that make the body vulnerable to injury and infection should be engaged in only after medical consultation. Cuts, abrasions, and blisters should be treated immediately. It is advisable for the diabetic to avoid walking with bare feet in locker rooms and to treat "athlete's foot" immediately. For diabetics whose skin is quite sensitive, rubbing with a towel should be avoided (gentle blotting is preferred). Clean towels must be available for drying after showers.

Care must be taken to avoid circulatory restrictions during physical activity, because there is a strong tendency for the arteries and blood vessels of diabetics to become hardened and thickened. This may cause narrowing of passageways to such an extent that circulation is reduced in larger vessels and is prevented in smaller vessels. In severe cases, inadequate circulation reduces nourishment to tissues and, "death" of the tissue (known as gangrene) results. Tight-fitting garments, sneakers, and socks should be prohibited. Garters and tight or adhesive bandages should not be used. One benefit of physical activity for the diabetic is that it enhances circulation, and every effort should be made to encourage rather than reduce circulation during physical activity.

Psychic stress may influence metabolism, resulting in changes in blood sugar levels, ketone production, and urinary excretion. Thus, participation in competitive activities may affect the diabetic. If participation affects the child adversely, methods of curbing stress and the question of continued participation should be discussed with a physician. Every effort should, of couse, be made not to suppress the child's play.

The maintenance of proper body weight is stressed in the treatment of diabetes. Excess fat is "dead weight" that places undue strain on the heart, blood vessels, liver, and pancreas. Such strain obviously hinders rather than aids the control of diabetes. Physical activity along with proper diet is of paramount importance to the diabetic. Professionals implementing physical activity programs may help the diabetic child by offering motivation to participate in and by arranging suitable physical activity.

Although no comprehensive studies have been conducted regarding the physical and motor proficiency of diabetics, those that have been conducted with small groups have produced interesting results. On the basis of their research and a review of literature, Cunningham and Etkind (1975) report that juvenile diabetics are below norms in height and weight (particularly in the 14–15 year age range) and have a later puberty than their normal peers. Also, diabetic boys aged 14–15 compare favorably with non-diabetic boys in maximal oxygen uptake. In their study, the mean predicted maximal oxygen consumption of diabetic and non-diabetic boys was 45.6 ml/kg/min and 44.4 ml/kg/min, respectively; the difference was not significant. In another study, Etkind and Cunningham (1971) reported that, with the exception of the 600-yard run-walk, the performance of 175 diabetic boys aged 10 through 15 was significantly below the mean performance of non-diabetic boys on items of the AAHPER Youth Fitness Test. These data indicate that diabetics are able to participate in endurance activities with success. The diabetics performed fairly well in the sit-up and the shuttle run and most poorly in the softball throw and the standing broad jump.

Sterky (1963) compared the physical work capacity (PWC) of diabetic and non-diabetic Swedish children. A total of 129 diabetic and 123 non-diabetic children aged 7 through 20 served as subjects for his study. The investigator measured height, weight, blood pressure after exercise and heart rate responses to standard loads on a bicycle ergometer. It was found that diabetic boys were shorter and weighed less than non-diabetic boys. Teenage diabetic girls, however, were heavier than their non-diabetic peers. Although the heart rate response to the standard exercise tests of prepubertal diabetics and non-diabelics did not differ, postpubertal diabetic boys and girls had significantly higher heart rates during the standardized exercises (Table 12–1). The investigators also gathered data regarding the frequency of physical education classes at school and time estimates of daily physical activity and concluded that the inferior physical work capacity may possibly be explained by inadequate training of diabetics.

This author knows no reason why diabetics cannot improve their physical and motor proficiency. This view is commonly held by medical authorities, and research is available to support it. Zankle (1957) found that hospitalized diabetic patients were able to improve their physical proficiency after 23 days of physical activity. Larsson and associates (1962) found that a majority of adolescent girls improved their physical work capacity after long-term and short-term training sessions. These investigators indicated that the favorable effect of exercise was especially conspicuous in patients with high blood sugar levels. In another study Larsson and associates (1964) found that maximal oxygen intake and heart volume increased significantly in adolescent diabetic boys after a five-month training program, with no untoward effects of exhaustion. However, insufficient caloric supply and the concomitant risk of hypoglycemia appeared to be a limiting factor in prolonged heavy work. Engerbretson (1970) found that after a program of physical activity, diabetic subjects aged 17 through 21 receiving insulin therapy increased their maximum oxygen uptake and work capability and improved their performance on a mile run. He also reported that on the average, daily insulin dosage and concentration of glucose in the fasting blood sample was reduced as a result of this conditioning program.

Table 12–1. Heart Rate of Boys and Girls at Different Workloads.*

Age Group	150 kpm/min D	150 kpm/min N	300 kpm/min D	300 kpm/min N	450 kpm/min D	450 kpm/min N	600 kpm/min D	600 kpm/min N	900 kpm/min D	900 kpm/min N
Boys										
7–10	128.1 ± 4.9 (13)	123.0 ± 2.7 (13)	149.3 ± 2.0 (12)	149.7 ± 3.4 (11)		151.0 (1)				
11–12			137.9 ± 2.6 (9)	128.6 ± 4.6 (10)	166.1 ± 3.4 (10)	150.2 ± 5.5 (9)		157.0 (3)		
13–14			129.3 ± 2.7 (16)	122.6 ± 4.1 (16)	149.6 ± 3.0 (17)	139.9 ± 4.3 (16)	155.6 ± 3.1 (5)	145.3 ± 3.2 (9)		
15–16			124.7 ± 2.2 (10)	118.3 ± 4.1 (7)			151.5 ± 4.6 (8)	144.5 ± 6.9 (9)	171.0 (2)	159.5 (2)
17–20			117.4 ± 1.0 (8)	114.6 ± 4.4 (11)			140.8 ± 4.7 (8)	127.4 ± 2.6 (7)	159.5 (2)	150.8 ± 3.1 (5)
Girls										
7–10	136.4 ± 2.8 (16)	135.0 ± 3.6 (12)	163.8 ± 1.9 (13)	164.1 ± 2.3 (8)						
11–12			147.0 ± 8.8 (5)	144.4 ± 1.9 (11)	164.4 ± 6.6 (5)	173.5 ± 2.7 (13)				
13–14			143.5 ± 2.9 (15)	141.8 ± 5.3 (11)	166.9 ± 3.0 (14)	165.2 ± 5.5 (10)		190 (1)		
15–16			144.5 ± 3.9 (16)	132.4 ± 3.0 (17)			187.8 ± 2.4 (15)	174.7 ± 3.3 (11)		
17–20			133.9 ± 5.0 (7)	130.2 ± 2.7 (9)			172.7 ± 3.0 (6)	172.4 ± 4.6 (7)		

*Mean values ± standard errors of the means are given. Figures in parentheses denote number of cases. D = Diabetic; N = Non-diabetic.
From: Sterky, Goran. "Physical Work Capacity in Diabetic Schoolchildren." *Acta Paed.* 52:1–10, 1963. p. 3.

Cardiovascular Disorders

In the past few years, a great deal of attention has been given to the importance of exercise in the prevention and treatment of cardiac conditions in adults. Few researchers disagree with the belief that appropriately administered exercise programs are beneficial for preventive and rehabilitative purposes. Although this area is perhaps receiving less attention, it is also quite evident that physical activity is important for children who have experienced cardiovascular disorders. In some cases, little or no restriction on participation is necessary. For some children, however, activity may need to be curtailed, restricted, or modified according to the nature, severity and stage of the condition. It must also be emphasized that the manner in which a program is administered is just as important as the type of activities it includes.

Most childhood cardiovascular disorders are caused by rheumatic heart disease and congenital heart defects. During the acute phase of rheumatic fever, bed rest and drugs to suppress symptoms are prescribed. As the acute phase of the disease passes and the child convalesces, physical activity may be prescribed and gradually increased. Following convalescence, participation in physical activity is generally recommended.

Children with congenital heart defects who are recovering from surgery are also restricted in physical activity. As they recuperate, breathing exercises may be prescribed by a physician. Once the period of convalescence is completed, children generally are able to become gradually involved in physical activity. Eventually, many will need little or no restriction in physical activity, but others will be allowed participation with some safeguards applied to activity selection and program implementation.

Participation in physical activities by pupils with cardiac disorders must be approved by a physician. It is the responsibility of the physician to periodically administer a medical exam, indicate the types of activities that are suitable, and specify safeguards to follow in program implementation. In addition, the duration of any restriction should be clearly identified. This information should be discussed with the child, the parents and the teacher and should become a part of the child's permanent records.

The reaction of children to participation in physical activities will vary widely. Some children will have little or no desire to participate, and others will be fearful. It may be necessary to encourage participation. Some children will "feel fine" and will want to engage in all activities without restriction. It is not uncommon for children with cardiac disorders to feel "left out" or "different" because of restrictions placed on their physical activity. In view of these reactions, it is necessary that the child and the parents receive counseling. The exercise tolerance of the child should be explained to and should be understood by the child and the parents. The child must understand what to do when exercise limits are approved, to which type of activities to give particular attention, and how to determine when cardiac stress is approaching. The importance of sleep, rest periods, proper diet, and other protective measures should be stressed. Youngsters need to be counseled on proper ways to react to peer pressure, which may coax them beyond safe limits. Finally, the importance of proper exercise should be explained to the child, the parents, and the teachers.

LIMITATIONS

Although children who have or have had cardiovascular disorders will generally be able to participate in some form of physical activity, they may have to be limited or restricted in certain activities. Some may need little or no restriction. Except possibly for the most mildly affected children, heavy weight lifting is contraindicated for children with cardiovascular disorders. If youngsters do lift weights, they must be instructed to breathe normally while lifting. Holding the breath causes Valsalva's phenomenon, which results in greater strain on the heart and blood vessels.

In implementing programs for the child with a cardiac disorder, it is best to provide short periods of activity interspersed with rest or quiet activities. Participation in endurance activities must be gradual. It is possible that many children with cardiac disorders will be unable to participate in sustained activity, and for some, exercise may be limited to walking and relaxation exercises or their equivalent in physical demand.

Although physical exercise is generally recommended for these children, there may be instances in which exercise is contraindicated. This is generally true during the acute phase of rheumatic fever and very often true during convalescence from surgery. In addition, there are children whose cardiovascular systems simply are not able to tolerate the demands required by exercise. In cases where such conditions are short in duration, it is advisable not to involve the child in physical activity. When the situation is prolonged, however, efforts may be made to interest and include youngsters in leisure time activities requiring minimal physical exertion.

Children who are restricted in physical activities must be closely supervised. Activity should be stopped if they exhibit shortness of breath, blueness, dizziness, faintness, fatigue, or cardiac stress. Such children may be taught to rest when their heart rate becomes rapid. Sherrill (1976) indicates that if the pulse rate of a child does not return to normal within three minutes after the cessation of movement, the exercise is too strenuous and should be modified. Fait (1972) believes that if cardiac patients can perform an activity without breathing through the mouth or without forced breathing through the nose, they are not overexerting. He feels that this guide helps participants know their tolerance levels.

ACTIVITIES

In view of the great differences in cardiac conditions and their implications for physical activity, the American Heart Association has developed a classification that may be used as a basis for selecting activities for children with cardiac conditions and as a guide for their general involvement in physical activities. Four classes are included in this classification.

Class I: Patients with cardiac disease but without resulting limitation of physical activity. Ordinary physical activity does not cause undue fatigue, palpitation, dyspnea, or anginal pain.

Class II: Patients with cardiac disease resulting in slight limitation of physical activity. They are comfortable at rest. Ordinary physical activity results in fatigue, palpitation, dyspnea, or anginal pain.

Class III: Patients with cardiac disease resulting in marked limitation of physical activity. They are comfortable at rest. Less than ordinary activity causes fatigue, palpitation, dyspnea, or anginal pain.

Class IV: Patients with cardiac disease resulting in inability to carry on any physical activity without discomfort. Symptoms of cardiac insufficiency or of the anginal syndrome are present even at rest. If any physical activity is undertaken, discomfort is increased.

Individuals in Class I (mild) require no restriction in ordinary physical activity but need to avoid highly competitive play, highly strenuous activity, or activity conducted over prolonged periods of time. Individuals in Class II need moderate restriction in physical activity, and individuals in Class III need great restriction in physical activities. Both groups should carefully follow the guidelines for program implementation that are presented later in this section. For individuals in Class IV (severe), participation in physical activity other than that which may be conducted while lying in bed is ordinarily not prescribed. Examples of activities that normally may be employed with little or no modification for Class II and Class III individuals appear below. Final selection of appropriate activities should, however, receive the approval of a medical doctor.

CLASS II (MODERATE RESTRICTION)

Sports	Games	Other Activities
Softball	Dodge Ball	Hiking
Table Tennis	Busy Bee	Swimming
Tennis	Run Rabbit Run	Backpacking
Badminton	Brownies and Fairies	Bicycling
Fencing		Canoeing
Handball		Skating
Racketball		Stunts and Tumbling
Squash		Relays

CLASS III (MARKED RESTRICTION)

Sports	Games	Other Activities
Archery	Croquet	Walking
Horseshoes	Hopscotch	Fishing
Shuffleboard	Steal the Bacon	Social Dancing (slow)
Bowling	Duck Duck Goose	Square Dancing (walk)
Golf	Red Rover	Sailing (little effort)
	Red Light	
	Drop the Handkerchief	

The American College of Sports Medicine (1975) has developed a list, primarily for adults, of activities and their approximate ranges of energy cost; the list may be a useful guide for selecting appropriate activities for youngsters with cardiac problems (Table 12–2). Energy cost in these activities is expressed in *METS.* One MET is equivalent to a resting oxygen consumption, which is approximately 3.5 ml/kg–min.,

Table 12–2. Leisure Activities: Sports, Exercise Classes, Games, Dancing — Approximate Range in Energy Cost (METS)

Activity	METS	Activity	METS
Archery (target or field)	3–4	Horseshoe pitching	2–3
Back Packing	5–11	Hunting (bow or gun)	3–7
Badminton	4–9	Small game (walking, carrying light load)	3–7
Basketball			
Non-game	3–9	Big game (dragging carcass, walking)	3–14
Game Play	7–12		
Bed Exercise (arm movement supine or sitting)	1–2	Jogging (running)	7–15
		Mountain climbing	5–10
Bicycling (pleasure or to work)	3–8	Paddleball (or racquet-ball)	8–12
Bowling	2–4	Sailing	2–5
Canoeing, rowing and kayaking	3–8	Scuba diving	5–10
Conditioning exercises (calisthenics)	3–8	Shuffleboard	2–3
		Skating, ice and roller	5–8
Dancing (social and square)	3–7	Skiing, snow	
Fencing	6–10	Downhill	5–8
Fishing		Cross-country	6–12
From bank, boat or ice	2–4	Skiing, water	5–7
Stream (wading)	5–6	Sledding (and tobogganing)	4–8
Football, touch	6–10	Snowshoeing	7–14
Golf		Squash	8–12
Using power cart	2–3	Soccer	5–12
Walking (carrying bag or pulling cart)	4–7	Softball	3–6
		Stair-climbing	4–8
Handball	8–12	Swimming	4–8
Hiking, cross-country	3–7	Table Tennis	3–5
Horseback riding	3–8	Tennis	4–9
		Volleyball	3–6

American College of Sports Medicine. *Guidelines for Graded Exercise Testing and Exercise Prescription.* Philadelphia: Lea & Febiger, 1975, p. 31.

and METS used in exercise are the result dividing the working metabolic rate by the resting metabolic rate. The American College of Sports Medicine indicates that initial work load should not exceed two to three METS for high risk or poorly conditioned participants.

FIRST AID

Although it is not common, a cardiac crisis may occur in movement settings. When a crisis occurs, Fait (1972) recommends that the following first aid steps be taken:

1. Let the person assume the most comfortable position — this will usually be a sitting position.
2. Loosen tight clothing.
3. Give him plenty of air but avoid drafts.
4. Call the doctor immediately. Reassure the patient. The teacher's manner will affect the entire class as well as the patient, so he should strive to remain calm and unemotional. (Fait, 1972, pp. 117–118.)

GUIDELINES FOR PROGRAM IMPLEMENTATION

1. Begin physical activity with at least five minutes of warm-up activities and gradually taper off exercise toward the end of activity sessions.

2. Employ a "buddy system" when children are performing water activities or activities in which the onset of cardiac distress may cause immediate danger to the participant.
3. Intersperse vigorous activities with frequent rest and quiet activities.
4. Be sure children are adequately protected for or are excused from activity during rainy, cold, hot, and damp weather.
5. Appropriately reassure children about the state of their health.
6. Encourage children to keep their weight within acceptable limits and suggest activities that enhance weight reduction.
7. Be prepared to modify activities to reduce their vigorousness. For example, court size may be reduced for volleyball, badminton, dodge ball, or basketball.
8. Develop physical activity on the basis of the child's medical status and in accordance with medical advice.
9. Insure gradual and progressive involvement in physical activity.
10. Provide a well-balanced program of activities.
11. To reduce the effects of competition against others, encourage children to stress improving their own performances rather than comparing their performances against others'.
12. When they first begin to participate, have children perform exercises that may be executed in the lying position and perform only a few repetitions at a slow cadence.

13

ASSESSMENT

Assessment is designed to determine and evaluate the status of an individual or group. The purposes of assessment include screening individuals from a group, diagnosing problems for educational habilitation and remediation, identifying the level of entry into programs, determining the advisability and safety of program participation, judging progress, motivating program participants, grouping participants, evaluating teaching, justifying programs, and evaluating programs.

With the advent of multidisciplinary and psychoeducational approaches to development, the question of responsibility and authority for assessment may become confused or blurred. For example, it is well known that physicians administer medical exams and that psychologists administer intelligence tests. But is it always clear who is responsible for seeing that these tests are administered? Who decides whether a child is to be placed in a special education class or a special physical education class? Which member of the psychoeducational team should administer the motor aspect of a screening test? These and many other questions must be considered, and it is recommended that all pre-schools, schools, agencies, and institutions develop policies regarding responsibility and authority for assessment, testing, and placement.

For the purposes of this chapter, it is assumed that responsibility and authority will be determined by the established policy of an institution. It is further assumed that those concerned with the development of movement should be expected to take responsibility in assessing variables dealing with movement and that they have knowledge about movement experiences that contribute to other aspects of development, even though it is not their responsibility to assess those aspects. Therefore, discussion in this chapter is limited to those tests that totally or in part deal with physical fitness, basic motor development, motor skills, and perceptual-motor development.

Assessment is frequently based on results obtained from instructor-devised scales, inventories, or other tests used in specific situations or locations. Although eclectically developed or selected, they should be based on accepted objectives and on an understanding of underlying theory. Some professionals rely completely or primarily on assessment tools that are standardized or that have been developed by other professionals and may be therefore generally applied. Quality standardized tests have the advantage of yielding normative data, which serve as a basis for comparisons and which attest to the test's validity, reliability, and objectivity.

Whatever the approach, there is a need to draw upon various tools of assessment. In this chapter, the first and most basic assessment tool to be considered is the medical examination. Its placement in this chapter is appropriate, since it is the basis for determining the advisability, safety, and nature of a child's participation in a program. In the second section, the importance and the methods of determining nutritional status are discussed. The criteria for developing or selecting tests, scales, or inventories will be briefly considered in the third section. In the final section, standardized and other scales, inventories, and tests will be identified and analyzed

The Medical Examination

The most basic and most important assessment for developmental purposes comes, of course, from a comprehensive medical examination administered by a physician. The medical examination provides a basis for determining the level of a student's entry into active participation, offers an opportunity for professionals to detect defects that may limit activity, and serves as a means to discover and diagnose problems that may be reduced or eliminated through developmental programs. The pre-school child should have a comprehensive medical examination before taking part in developmental programs. Fait (1972) recommends medical examinations four times during the school career of a student, the first at the time of entry, the second in the intermediate grades, the third at the beginning of adolescence, and the fourth at the end of school.

It is critical that professionals responsible for program implementation work as closely as possible with physicians. Communication is enhanced when professionals make physicians aware of the philosophy and nature of their programs. Policies for program modification and medical exemption should be clearly developed and communicated — preferably with the help of a physician.

One of the major difficulties that physicians and educators encounter is that of a student's medical exemption from activity. Educators frequently receive notes from physicians proscribing activity for illegibly scribbled reasons. This problem can be reduced if educators

FORM 1

ANY CITY PUBLIC SCHOOLS
SCHOOL HEALTH DEPARTMENT
PHYSICAL EDUCATION DIVISION

Physical Education Medical Referral Form
ASAW #1313-1975ˑ

Dear Dr. _____:

(This space can be used for information about state/local physical education
requirements, rationale of adapted physical education, objectives and
benefits of local programs, organization and administration of local classes,
purposes and uses of this form and related areas to improve understanding
and communication among physicians, physical educators, parents, and others
concerned with and involved in the education, health, and welfare of the
student. Procedures for returning the form can be included in this section
or at the end of the form.)

John J. Jones, M.D.   George T. Smith, Supervisor
Director, School Health Department   Division of Health, Physical
                                        Education and Athletics

STUDENT INFORMATION

Name_____School_____

Home
Address_____ City_____ State_____ Zip____

Home
Telephone ( )_____Grade & Section_____

CONDITION

Brief description of condition

Condition is   ☐ permanent ☐ temporary

Comments_____

If Appropriate:
   Comments about student's medication and its effects on participation in physical
activities

Student may return to unrestricted activity_____ , 19 ____

Student should return for examination_____ , 19 ____

FUNCTIONAL CAPACITY

☐ Unrestricted - no restrictions relative to vigorousness or types of activities

☐ Restricted - Condition is such that intensity and types of activities need
                to be limited (check one category below)

   ☐ Mild - ordinary physical activities need not be restricted but usually
            vigorous efforts need to be avoided

   ☐ Moderate - ordinary physical activities need to be moderately restricted
               and sustained strenuous efforts avoided

   ☐ Limited - ordinary physical activities need to be markedly restricted

Activity Recommendations

Indicated body areas in which physical activities should be minimized, eliminated, or maximized.

	Maximized	Minimized	Eliminated	Both	Left	Right	Comments Including Any Medical Contraindications to Physical Activities
Neck							
Shoulder Girdle							
Arms							
Elbows							
Hands & Wrists							
Abdomen							
Back							
Pelvic Girdle							
Legs							
Knees							
Feet & Ankles							
Toes							
Fingers							
Other (specify)							

Remedial

☐ Condition is such that defects or deviations can be improved or prevented from becoming worse through use of carefully selected exercises and/or activities. The following are remedial exercises and/or activities recommended for this student. (Please be specific)

_____

_____

_____

_____

_____

_____

_____

_____

Signed _____ M.D.

Address _____

_____ Zip _____

Telephone No. ( ) _____

Date _____ 19 ____

Figure 13–1. Example of medical referral form for physical education. Adapted from: Physical Education and Recreation for the Handicapped: Information and Research Utilization Center, *Adapted Physical Education Guidelines: Theory and Practice for the Seventies and Eighties.* Washington, D.C.: American Alliance for Health, Physical Education, and Recreation, 1976, pp. 47–48.

develop concise medical forms stating the aims, objectives, and nature of their programs and requesting that the physician inform them of the nature of the medical condition and the duration of exemption and supplying a checklist of physical activity tolerance (vigorous, moderate, mild, quiet) or of prescribed or restricted activities. The completion of such a form should be an established policy of a school, agency, or organization. The referral form developed by the Information and Research Utilization Center (IRUC) is presented here as an example of an appropriate form that may be either adapted or employed in a particular school setting (Fig. 13–1). Further information about the form may be found in "Referral Forms for Adapted Physical Education" *Journal of Health, Physical Education and Recreation,* Volume 40, pages 71–73, 1969.

In the best interests of the patient, the physician has a responsibility to complete such forms in a professional manner. The educator, on the other hand, has a responsibility to follow medical advice in order to assure the child's safety.

Nutritional Status

Although height and weight determinations are included in medical exams, it is advisable for professionals to periodically measure children to discover those who are malnourished. Such tests not only may help to determine the cause of behavior but also may indicate implications for developing programs. Several age, height, and weight tables are available for use by professionals. It is recommended that the tables adopted consider physique as well as height and weight determinations.

In addition to height and weight determinations, increased attention is being given to measurement of adipose tissue. Research studies clearly indicate that height and weight tables are limited in their usefulness in the determination of leanness or fatness or the percentage of body fat. Ideally, body composition measurements are obtained by underwater weighing techniques using specific gravity. However, this method is rather elaborate and expensive. A very inexpensive and reasonably precise technique for estimating leanness or fatness is by skinfold tests. The examiner grasps the skinfold at various parts of the body between the thumb and index finger and measures thickness with a caliper.

Brozek (1956) indicates that leanness or fatness may be determined directly from adipose tissue measurements. He recommends, at minimum, taking skinfolds on the back of the upper arm over the triceps and over the inferior angle of the scapula. Other recommendations on the number of skinfolds to be taken for the estimation of body fat range from 1 to more than 50. Using the single skinfold measurement taken over the triceps, Seltzer and Mayer (1965) provide norms for persons ages 5 through 50 (Table 13–1). The triceps fold is taken in the middle of the back of the upper arm, which is flexed at 90 degrees. Sloan, Burt, and Blythe (1962) provide a simple method for predicting body density from two skinfold measurements, over the iliac crest and on the back of the arm. They report an error of ±3 per cent in estimating body density. Calipers for skinfold meas-

Table 13-1. Skinfold Measurements (Triceps) for Caucasian Americans *

Age (years)	Skinfold Measurements Males	Females
5	12	14
6	12	15
7	13	16
8	14	17
9	15	18
10	16	20
11	17	21
12	18	22
13	18	23
14	17	23
15	16	24
16	15	25
17	14	26
18	15	27
19	15	27
20	16	28
21	17	28
22	18	28
23	18	28
24	19	28
25	20	29
26	20	29
27	21	29
28	22	29
29	23	29
30-50	23	30

*Minimum triceps skinfold thickness in millimeters indicating obesity. *Adapted from:* Seltzer, Carl C. and Jean Mayer, "A Simple Criterion of Obesity," *Postgrad. Med.* 38: 101-107, 1965, p. 105.

urement may be purchased commercially. It is recommended that calipers used for skinfolds exert a pressure of 10 grams per square millimeter on a contact area from 20 to 40 square millimeters.

Criteria for the Development and Selection of Tests

To intelligently develop or select a "good" physical and motor test, it is important to establish criteria on which to make judgments. The establishment and study of such criteria is not easy and has been the topic of volumes of professional materials. Simply stated, a test is generally considered "good" if it is valid, reliable and economical and provides standards for comparative purposes. In this section, such criteria are briefly considered to serve as a review, to reduce problems of semantics, and to provide a basis for later analysis of assessment tools.

Validity

A test is considered valid when it measures what it is designed to measure. Although, at first glance, this appears to be an obvious and simple standard, it is difficult to attain and often violated. Validity in physical and motor tests is generally established by demonstrating content validity, criterion-related validity, construct validity, or any combination of the three.

Content validity is relevant to achievement measures in written tests and therefore is important to educators. It is used when one wishes to estimate how an individual performs in the universe of situations the test is intended to represent (American Psychological Association, et al., 1974). For example, an instructor may wish to develop a test to measure knowledge of basketball rules. In developing the test, the "universe" of rules may be categorized in a particular way and test questions selected to represent these various categories. If the instructor logically demonstrates that the developed test appropriately samples the universe of possible rules, the test possesses content validity.

It should be noted that content validity is not limited to tests of knowledge. It can also be applied to the establishment and measurement of those aspects of a child's ability that are considered indicators of good physical and motor performance. For example, an instructor may wish to develop a test to measure physical fitness. A definition of physical fitness is established that includes several components. Test items are then selected and administered to measure the established components. The test is valid if it measures those components of physical fitness that are most important. Terms that have been associated with this aspect of validity include *descriptive validity, face validity,* or *logical validity.* However, a joint committee of the American Psychological Association, the National Council for Measurement in Education, and The American Educational Research Association indicates that content validity is quite different from face validity. Face validity involves a judgment that the test *appears* to be relevant. Content validity is determined by a set of operations.

Logic is important in demonstrating content validity. Logical descriptions include data relevant to the definition or identification of the universe, the sampling techniques utilized, the relationship between test items and the universe, and an internal analysis of the test. Internal analysis is frequently accomplished through factor analysis.

Criterion-related validity refers to the relationship between a test and external criteria. This kind of validity generally emphasizes prediction. Examples of external criteria include an established test, appropriate items on different tests, teacher evaluations, job success, and success in school. Criterion-related validity is demonstrated by coefficients of correlation between the predictor and criterion variable, by multiple correlations between the criterion and one or more predictors, and by canonical correlations between a composite predictor and a composite criterion.

Construct validity is used, according to Cronback and Meehl (1966), "whenever no criterion or universe of content is accepted as entirely adequate to define the quality to be measured." Although no criterion or universe is accepted, a hypothesized construct is assumed to be present in the performance of a test. Following the identification of the construct, individuals reflecting different levels of the construct are tested. Subsequently, characteristics are associated with individuals reflecting different levels of the construct. There is, thus, the matching of construct and characteristics which leads to hypotheses that are then tested. For example, a particular test is assumed to reflect the construct of physical fitness. Individuals considered "high" or "low" in physical fitness on the basis of the test are studied, and characteristics associated with both groups are established. A characteristic that may be identified is that strength is associated with persons high in physical fitness. This characteristic may be stated in the form of a hypothesis, which may then be verified or refuted. From the results of such a process, complete theories surrounding the construct are developed.

Common techniques for determining construct validity include correlations with other tests, factor analysis, manipulation of variables in experimental studies, and demonstration of differences in groups. For example, the construct of physical fitness may be correlated with other tests (criterion-related validity). In factor analysis, a large number of traits are studied and reduced to a minimum number of traits. An excellent example is the work of Fleishman (1964a). Changes in strength may be measured in training programs to determine whether the gains reflect changes in physical fitness. Other examples include determining whether results of tests for physical fitness change because of age, time, or sickness.

In regard to size of coefficients of correlation, Guilford (1965) feels that one must be a relativist when dealing with problems of test validity and expects coefficients of correlation for validity to be in the lower brackets, usually .00 to .80. Since the percentage of predictability over chance increases as the coefficient increases, it is obviously desirable to have coefficients as high as possible. However, low coefficients of correlation are acceptable when alternative tests are less precise and when fine precision of prediction is not necessary.

Reliability

The second criterion for the development and selection of tests is reliability. For the purpose of this book, *reliability* is the consistency or repeatability of the test. In other words, it is an indicator of the consistency with which a test measures what it is supposed to measure. Several factors contribute to the lack of reliability of or to the variability in test results. In physical and motor tests, an individual is often biologically unable to perform a motor skill or physical fitness test consistently from trial to trial or from day to day. For example, warm-up and fatigue are factors in motor and physical fitness tests that typically influence results. In addition, variability of results is caused by the mood and motivation of the individual being tested, differences in test content, equipment error, differences in test administration, or environmental factors such as heat, cold, and noise.

Although there are several methods of determining reliability, the techniques most common to education and psychology involve retesting the subject on the same test (*test-retest*), presenting alternate forms of the same test on two different occasions (*alternate forms*), and splitting a test into parts and administering the whole test on one occasion (*split-halfs*). Of these, the test-retest method is most frequently used in physical and motor performance tests and thus will be briefly considered further.

In regard to physical and motor performance tests, the test-retest technique may involve administering the same test on two different days (between-days source of variation) or administering repeated trials of the test on the same day (within-day source of variation). When two scores are involved in the test-retest technique, investigators frequently employ correlational techniques and report reliability coefficients. In motor performance tests, it is not uncommon to have three or more trials of a particular item in the same test. Rather than reducing trials to some representative score, Safrit (1973) recommends the use of the intraclass correlation coefficient or "R," obtained through the use of analysis of variance techniques as an expression of reliability. Another technique, which is employed as a statistical expression of reliability and in which the same test is utilized, is the standard error of measurement.

Objectivity has been used to describe the consistency of test scores recorded by the same administrator on two different occasions or by two or more different administrators. This, of course, is a source of variation that should be considered in the development and selection of tests. Statistical methods for expressing this source of variation are available in many tests on measurement. Generally speaking, however, the techniques parallel those used in determining other sources of variation.

As was true in the case of validity, higher coefficients of correlation mean greater reliability. Factors that tend to increase reliability include lengthening the test (to a point), administering the test to a heterogeneous group, providing items on the test that discriminate ability levels, and administering tests to individuals rather than groups. According to Guilford (1965), coefficients of correlation for reliability should be in the upper brackets, usually .70 to .98. However, one must be a relativist when dealing with reliability. Factors that must be considered are the importance of the test in decision-making, the precision required, and the availability of alternate tests.

Economy

Economy of time and money must also be considered in developing and selecting tests. Tests that involve a great deal of time generally are preceded by a screening examination of some kind. Screening tests may be arranged so that they can be administered to groups rather than individuals. When necessary, however, professionals have the responsibility to provide complete and individual attention.

Many tests require very expensive equipment such as is found in laboratories. Most educational tests, however, are relatively inexpensive and declining to administer them because of cost is generally inexcusable. All of the tests described in this chapter involve minimal expenditure.

Standards

Tests yield measurements of performance that are employed in evaluation. When measurements are compared to a standard, they have more meaning. Three commonly used types of standards are *norm-referenced, content-referenced,* and *criterion-referenced.* Norm-referenced standards, generally called "norms," are most directly associated with standardized tests. They serve as the basis for comparing an individual performance with the performances of members of a particularly defined group. They may be used to place individuals into ability groups. Usually associated with summative evaluation, norm-referenced standards tend to deal with broad categories of behavior.

A Joint Committee of the American Psychological Association, the American Educational Research Association, and the National Council on Measurement in Education (1974) defines content-referenced and criterion-referenced standards as follows:

> Content-referenced interpretations are those where the score is directly interpreted in terms of performance at each point on the achievement continuum being measured. Criterion-referenced interpretations are those where the score is directly interpreted in terms of performance at any given point on the continuum of an external variable. An external criterion variable might be grade averages or levels of job performance. (Joint Committee of the American Psychological Association, the American Educational Research Association, and the National Council on Measurement in Education, 1974, p. 19).

Content-referenced standards are used to determine the degree to which a student achieves a standard that nearly all children should be able to achieve in a content area. These standards specify expected levels of performance in relation to explicitly defined instructional objectives. Although they are group-related to the extent that the standards selected may be gained from analysis of the performance of groups, content-referenced standards lend themselves to an analysis of individualized progress toward instructional objectives. Content-referenced standards focus on individual competence at points along a continuum. They are useful for analyzing very specific areas of performance rather than broad categories of behavior. Content-referenced standards have greater day-to-day applicability in the process of improving performance in curricular areas. Therefore, they are associated with formative rather than summative evaluation. Criterion-referenced standards use an external variable in assessment rather than an achievement continuum inherent in a curricular area.

Differences and relationships between norm-referenced, content-referenced, and criterion-referenced standards may be illustrated in an example involving the development of physical fitness. If an instructional unit on physical fitness is selected, the teacher may wish to administer a standardized test of physical fitness. The result is a score that, though broad in meaning, may be compared with others using standardized norms. In such an instance, norm-referenced standards are being applied. The teacher may then establish a broad goal to improve the physical fitness of the child. This rather broad goal may be evaluated periodically. On the other hand, the teacher

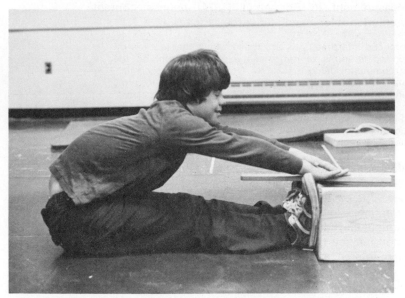

Figure 13–2.   Content-referenced measure of flexibility: sitting.

Figure 13–3. Content-referenced measure of flexibility: standing.

may break the concept of physical fitness into more specific parts, for example, improving cardiovascular endurance by running a mile in a particular time. This instructional objective may be evaluated by asking the child to run one mile in 10 minutes. Thus, a standard has been established for measuring the attainment of the objective. It is a content-referenced standard, since performance at each point on the achievement continuum can be measured and it is a measurement within a content area. The standard selected may be based on the child's present level of performance, the opinion of the teacher, an analysis of scores on standardized tests, research, the performance of others, or other information. Criterion-referenced standards would be evidenced if performance is translated to the student's grade on the unit.

Although norm-referenced, content-referenced, and criterion-referenced standards all play a role in improving performance, content-referenced standards are most applicable in the day-to-day implementation of programs. They are particularly important in the development of individualized education programs for the handicapped. Content-referenced standards may be employed in measuring progress toward the attainment of short-term objectives and long-term goals. To reach goals and objectives, specific areas of the curriculum may be arranged in a hierarchy of skills according to the child's needs. Each child may then follow the progression, and subsequent progress may be determined. The emphasis is on the improvement made by the child in the content area rather than on comparisons with other children.

Tests, Scales, and Inventories

In this section, a number of tests, scales, and inventories for measuring basic motor development, perceptual-motor development, motor skills, and physical fitness are presented in alphabetical order. Information is given pertaining to the source of the instrument and the population for which it may be used. The components of development that it measures and data on the test's validity and reliability are presented along with some general comments. Where space permits, the test's specific test items are also listed. Information about validity and reliability is generally based on original data reported. Readers are encouraged to review the literature for additional analysis.

AAHPER YOUTH FITNESS TEST

Source: Hunsicker, Paul, and Guy G. Reiff. *AAHPER Youth Fitness Test Manual* (revised 1976 edition). Washington, D.C.: American Alliance for Health, Physical Education and Recreation, 1976. The manual may be purchased from AAHPER Publication-Sales, 1201 16th St. N.W., Washington, DC 20036.

Population: Boys and girls aged 9–17.

Components of Development and Test Items:

COMPONENTS	TEST ITEMS
Arm and shoulder girdle strength	Flexed-arm hang (girls) Pull-ups (boys)
Efficiency of abdominal and hip flexor muscles	Sit-ups (flexed leg)
Speed and agility	Shuttle run
Explosive muscular power	Standing long jump
Speed	50-yard dash
Cardiovascular efficiency	600-yard run-walk (Options include a 1-mile or 9-minute run (ages 10–12) or 1 1/2-mile or 12-minute run (ages 13 and above) when extensive running has been a continuing part of the physical education program.

Comments: Initial test norms of 1958 were based on test results of 8500 boys and girls in grades 5–12 involved in a national survey. In 1960, norms were developed for college men and women and are presently available. In 1965, new norms were developed based on test administration to 9200 boys and girls and are available for boys and girls, ages 10–17. In 1975, the national norms were again updated for boys and girls aged 9–17 and items in the test were modified. In a summary of research on the reliability of the 1965 AAHPER Youth fitness test items, Safrit (1973) reports reliability coefficients ranging from .57 to .99 for the various items. Generally, reliability coefficients were at least .80. The highest coefficients of reliability appear to be in the long jump and the 50-yard dash and the lowest appear to be in the sit-up and the shuttle run.* A detailed analysis of the validity of the test is also presented by Safrit (1973). She states that a difficulty in constructing any test of physical fitness is that the many components cannot be measured by a single test. The test may be administered in approximately two physical education periods with a minimum amount of equipment. Awards are available for various levels of achievement.

---

*The sit-up test was revised in the 1975 edition.

AAHPER SPECIAL FITNESS TEST FOR MILDLY MENTALLY RETARDED PERSONS

Source: American Alliance for Health, Physical Education, and Recreation. *Special Fitness Test Manual for Mildly Mentally Retarded Persons.* Washington, D.C.: American Alliance for Health, Physical Education, and Recreation, 1976. This test may be purchased from AAHPER Publications-Sales, 1201 16th Street N.W., Washington, DC 20036.

Population: Mildly mentally retarded aged 8–18.

Components of Development and Test Items:

COMPONENTS	TEST ITEMS
Arm and shoulder girdle strength	Flexed-arm hang
Efficiency of abdominal and hip flexor muscles	Sit-ups
Speed and agility	Shuttle run
Explosive muscular power	Standing broad jump
Speed	50-yard dash
Skill and coordination	Softball throw for distance
Cardiovascular efficiency	300-yard run-walk

Comments: Norms based on a random sample of some 4200 educable mentally retarded boys and girls in the public schools of the continental United States are available for mildly mentally retarded boys and girls aged 8–18. Test administration takes about two physical education classes with a minimum amount of equipment. Awards are available for various levels of achievement.

AMMP (AWARENESS, MOVEMENT, MANIPULATION OF ENVIRONMENT, POSTURE AND LOCOMOTION) INDEX

Source: Webb, Ruth C. "Sensory-Motor Training of the Profoundly Retarded," *Amer. J. Ment. Def.* 74:283–295, 1969.*

Population: Profoundly retarded aged 2 1/2–17 1/2.

Components of Development and Test Items:

COMPONENTS	TEST ITEMS
Level of awareness	Awareness items are separated into 3 groups. In the first group, 7 items are provided to assess approach-avoidance reactions. In the second group, 4 additional items are provided to assess avoidance-approach reactions. In the third group, 7 items are provided to assess discriminatory reactions.
Manipulation of environment	Ten items are provided to assess manipulation of the environment. Scale items involve reaching for, grasping, holding, manipulating, and combining objects. Other items involve removing a towel from the head, patting a mirror image, communicating, and the ability to relate to persons.
Movement	The test contains 10 items to assess movement. Movements involve rolling, rocking, bouncing, and swinging. In addition, the subject's ability to give active assistance when limbs are moved in rhythm is assessed.
Posture and locomotion	The test contains 12 items to assess posture and locomotion. Items involve holding up the head, sitting, moving on the back, moving on the seat, creeping, crawling, standing, walking, riding a tricycle, and climbing stairs.

Comments: This scale is presently in its experimental stages. Normative data, measures of reliability, and measures of validity are not provided by the author. It is recommended that the test be administered by trained teachers.

---

*Ruth Webb and the staff of the Department of Developmental Therapy, Glenwood State Hospital School, Glenwood, Iowa, are in the process of developing the Glenwood Awareness, Manipulation, and Posture Index (AMP) to measure sensory motor integration of children with multiple handicaps and profoundly retarded children.

BODY-IMAGE SCREENING TEST FOR BLIND CHILDREN

Source: Cratty, Bryant J. *Movement and Spatial Awareness in Blind Children and Youth.* Springfield, Ill.: Charles C Thomas, Publisher, 1971b, Cratty, Bryant J., *Some Educational Implications of Movement.* Seattle, Wash.: Special Child Publications, Inc., 1970b, and Cratty, Bryant J., and Theressa A. Sams. *The Body-Image of Blind Children.* New York: The American Foundation for the Blind, Inc., 1968. This test is available from the Foundation at 15 West 16th Street, New York, NY 10011.

Population: Designed for blind youngsters; with a few modifications, the test can be used with sighted, retarded, and deaf children.

Components of Development and Test Items:

COMPONENTS	TEST ITEMS
Body planes	This part of the test is separated into 3 groups. The first group tests identification of body planes and includes touching the top of the head, the bottom of the foot, the side of the body, the front of the body, and the back. The second group involves placing body planes in relation to external, horizontal, and vertical surfaces. Children are asked to touch the side, stomach, and back to a mat and to touch the hand, side, and back to a wall. The third group involves placing objects in relation to body planes from a seated position. Children are asked to place a box so that it touches the side, stomach, back, top of the head, and bottom of the foot.
Body parts	This part of the test includes 4 groups. In the first group, on body part identification, the child is asked to touch the arm, hand, leg, elbow, and knee. The second group, called *parts of the face,* tests the ability of the child to touch the ear, nose, mouth, eye, and cheek. The third group, called *parts of the body: complex (limb parts),* tests the child's ability to touch the wrist, thigh, forearm, upper arm, and shoulder. The last group tests the ability of the child to separately hold up the thumb and each finger.
Body movements	This part of the test includes 15 items separated into 3 groups. The first group consists of 5 activities involving trunk movement. The second group includes 5 gross movements in relation to body planes: walking forward, walking backward, jumping up, and sidestepping in two directions. The third group, designated *limb movement,* asks children to bend one arm at the elbow, lift one arm while in a back-lying position, bend one knee, bend one arm, and straighten the arm.

COMPONENTS	TEST ITEMS
Laterality	This part of the test involves 15 items separated into 3 groups of 5 items each. The first group consists of items to assess body laterality (simple). The child is asked to touch the right knee, left arm, right leg, left foot, and left ear. The second group includes items to assess laterality in relation to objects. Items include placing a box so that it touches the right side, the right knee, and the right foot and holding the box in the left and then the right hand. The third group includes items to assess laterality of the body (complex). While seated, the child is asked to touch left hand to right hand, right hand to left knee, left hand to right ear, right hand to left elbow, and left hand to right wrist.
Directionality	This part of the test involves 15 items separated into 3 groups of 5 items each. The first group includes items to assess directionality relative to other people. The child is asked to tap the examiner's left shoulder, left hand, right side, right ear, and left side of the neck. The second group includes items to assess directionality of objects and includes touching the right side of a box, the left side of the box, the right side of a box with the left hand, the left side of a box with the right hand, and the left side of a box with the left hand. The third group of items involves laterality of others' movements. The tester bends right and then left while seated and facing the child, while seated with the back to the child, and while standing and facing the child and asks the child which way the tester is bending.

Comments: The items selected for the test were based on a survey of the literature and on practice with similar forms administered to retarded, neurologically handicapped, and blind children. The test was administered to 91 blind children with a mean age of 10.06 and a mean IQ of 88.32. A test-retest reliability coefficient of .81 was found following the testing of 18 blind children.

BUELL ADAPTATION OF THE AAHPER YOUTH FITNESS TEST

Source: Buell, Charles E. *Physical Education and Recreation for the Visually Handicapped.* Washington, D.C.: American Association for Health, Physical Education and Recreation, 1973, and Buell, Charles. *Physical Education for Blind Children.* Springfield, Ill.: Charles C Thomas, Publisher, 1966. The manual may be purchased from AAHPER Publication-Sales, 1201 16th St. N. W., Washington, DC 20036.

Population: Visually handicapped youngsters aged 10–17.

Components of Development and Test Items

COMPONENTS	TEST ITEMS
Speed	50-yard dash
Arm and shoulder girdle strength	Pull-ups (boys) Flexed arm hang (girls)
Efficiency of abdominal and hip flexor muscles	Sit-ups
Explosive muscular power	Standing broad jump
Cardiovascular endurance	600-yard run-walk
Agility or arm and shoulder girdle strength, respectively	Squat-thrusts or push-ups
Strength, power, and coordination	Basketball throw

Comments: The test is a modification of the 1965 AAHPER Youth Fitness test. Buell recommends that regular AAHPER norms for pull-ups, flexed-arm hang, sit-ups, and standing broad jump be used for testing the visually handicapped. Separate norms, however, are available for 50-yard dash. The 600-yard run-walk and the shuttle run for visually handicapped boys and girls are separately scored for the blind and the partially sighted. If the throwing event is used, Buell recommends using the basketball throw with his achievement scales. Since the shuttle run must be modified to a great extent, some professionals may not wish to use this item. In that case, Buell suggests substituting squat-thrusts or pull-ups with his regular achievement scales. Buell's achievement scales are based on the performance of a representative sample of about 3000 visually impaired boys and girls.

CABLE–TENSION STRENGTH TESTS

Source: Clarke, H. Harrison, and David H. Clarke. *Developmental and Adapted Physical Education.* Englewood Cliffs, N.J.: Prentice-Hall, Inc., 1963.

Population: General

Components of Development and Test Items:
The cable-tension tests were designed to measure static strength. Clarke and Clarke (1963) have developed and provided procedures for 38 cable-tension tests involving various parts of the body.

Comments: Using non-disabled subjects at the U.S. Naval Hospital in Chelsea, Massachusetts, Clarke (1948) originally developed 28 cable-strength tests and found that objectivity coefficients ranged between .92 and .97. Clarke (1948) reported that test results coincided with medical opinions of present status. From the original 28 items, 22 remained as part of the tests until further studies by Clarke (1950) and Clarke, Bailey, and Shea (1952) resulted in the selection of 38 test items with objectivity coefficients of at least .90. Reliable test administration requires training. Tests depend upon the availability of an appropriate testing table, a cable tensiometer, and appropriate accessories.

CRATTY SIX-CATEGORY GROSS MOTOR TEST

Source: Cratty, Bryant J. *Motor Activity and the Education of Retardates.* Philadelphia: Lea & Febiger, 1969a, and Cratty, Bryant J. *Perceptual-Motor Behavior and Educational Processes.* Springfield, Ill.: Charles C Thomas, Publisher, 1969b.

Population: Normal children aged 4–11, educable mentally retarded subjects aged 5–20, and trainable mentally retarded subjects aged 5–24.

Components of Development and Test Items:

COMPONENTS	TEST ITEMS
Body perception	Level I: execute lying movements. Level II: raise or touch body parts.
Gross agility	Level I: rise from lying position. Level II: from standing position, kneel on one knee, then stand.
Balance	Level I: Part I — Balance on one foot. Part II — Balance on one foot with arms folded. Level II: Balance on one foot for time with and without the use of sight or arms.
Locomotor agility	Level I: Crawl, walk, jump forward, jump backward, and hop. Level II: Jump forward, forward and sideward, and backward; hop forward, and forward and sideward.
Ball throwing	Level I: Ball throw 15 feet. Level II: Ball throw for accuracy.
Ball tracking	Level I: Catch a bounced throw from 10 feet. Level II: Touch a swinging ball.

Comments: This instrument was designed as a screening test for perceptual-motor functioning. Cratty (1969b) identified it as a *Screening Test for Evaluating the Perceptual-Motor Attributes of Neurologically Handicapped and Retarded Children.* The content of the tests was arrived at empirically, through a survey of the literature, and through an analysis of the opinions of developmental experts on the basic attributes considered important to children with perceptual-motor impairments. On the basis of testing over 200 children in the summer of 1966, Cratty (1969b) presents decile rankings for Down's syndrome children aged 5–22, trainable retarded aged 5–24, educable retarded, aged 5–20, and educationally handicapped aged 5–16. He reports a reliability coefficient of .91 based on test-retest scores of 83 children. In another book, Cratty (1969a) presents average scores for normal boys (N=172) and girls (N=183), aged 4–11, average scores for 38 educable retardates aged 5–20, and average scores for 113 trainable retardates aged 5–24. In addition, Cratty reports that the coefficients of correlation between separate items and the whole test ranged from .48 to .84. On the basis of 650 children's scores, he presents a factor analysis of the six categories. In comparing pre-test and post-test means of 65 normal children after a five-month program of motor training to remediate motor problems, Cratty (1969a) found no significant differences in the body image category, significant differences of .01 for the gross ability, locomotor ability, throwing, tracking, and total score areas, and significant differences of .05 for the balance category. In a similar study with 15 retarded children, he found no significant differences in the body image, balance, and throwing categories, and significant differences of .05 for the gross ability, locomotor ability and tracking categories; for the total score, significant difference was .01.

DENVER DEVELOPMENT SCREENING TEST (DDST)

Source: Frankenburg, William K., and Josiah B. Dodds. "The Denver Developmental Screening Test," *J. of Ped.* 71:181, 1967. Test kits, manuals, and forms may be purchased from LADOCA Project and Publishing Foundation, Inc., East 51st Avenue and Lincoln Street, Denver. CO 80216.

Population: The test is a method of screening for evidences of slow development in infants and pre-school children.

Components of Development and Test Items:

COMPONENTS	TEST ITEMS
Gross motor functions	This part includes 31 items that assess abilities to lift the head, lift the chest from the prone position, sit, roll, stand, walk, kick, throw, balance, jump, pedal, hop, and catch.
Language	The 21 items included in this part assess the following abilities: responding to sound, laughing, squealing, imitating speech sounds, vocabulary, comprehension, recognition of colors, naming objects, opposite analogies, definitions, and composition of materials.
Fine Motor-adaptive	The 30 items in this part assess abilities regarding following objects, prehension, eye-hand coordination, copying figures, drawing, searching for objects, lifting and transferring objects, scribbling, and imitation.
Personal-social	The 23 items in this part assess abilities relevant to regarding the face, smiling, pulling toys, playing peek-a-boo, playing pat-a-cake, playing ball, performing basic tasks, and playing interactive games.

Comments: Data on norms, reliability, and validity may be found in the work of Frankenburg and Dodds (1967). The sample on which the 105 items were standardized consisted of 1036 Denver children between the ages of 2 and 6.8 years. Reliability was determined by test-retest procedures using 20 children ranging in age from 2 months to 5 1/2 years. Subjects were tested twice by the same examiner with an interval of one week. For each child, the percentage of items performed the same way one week later ranged from 90 to 100 per cent. For all items for all 20 children the agreement over the one week-interval was 95.8 per cent, according to Frankenburg and Dodds (1967). Validity was determined by comparing results with the Revised Yale Developmental Schedule. No child with a Yale Developmental Quotient less than or equal to .89 was judged normal by the DDST. The test may be administered by individuals with no special training. Although some materials are needed for test administration, they are very easy to procure. The entire test is never administered — items are selected according to test purposes and performance. When sections of the DDST were compared with sections of the Yale Developmental Schedule, the closest correspondence was in the gross motor area and the poorest in the personal-social area, but all comparisons were significant (P<.01).

FAIT PHYSICAL FITNESS BATTERY FOR MENTALLY RETARDED CHILDREN

Source: Fait, Hollis, F. *Special Physical Education: Adapted, Corrective, Developmental.* Philadelphia: W. B. Saunders Co., 1972.

Population: Educable and medium and high trainable mentally retarded youngsters.

Components of Development and Test Items:

COMPONENTS	TEST ITEMS
Speed	25-yard run
Static muscular endurance	Bent-arm hang
Dynamic muscular	Leg lift
Balance–static	Balance
Agility	Thrusts
Cardiorespiratory endurance	300-yard run-walk

Comments: According to Fait, the items selected are widely accepted as tests that measure some factor of physical fitness. Modifications were made to reduce the complexity of movements and the need for memorizing difficult movement patterns. Items that had high correlation with intelligence quotients (IQ) and with each other were eliminated. Fait reported that all items on the test have a high reliability. The test may generally be administered in one period, or single items may be administered in different testing days. Very little equipment is necessary for administration. Norms have been established for trainable and educable retardates within the 9–12, 13–16, and 17–20 year age groups.

FLEISHMAN BASIC FITNESS TEST

Source: Fleishman, Edwin A. *Structure and Measurement of Physical Fitness.* Englewood Cliffs, N.J.: Prentice-Hall, Inc., 1964a, and Fleishman, Edwin A. *Examiner's Manual for the Basic Fitness Tests.* Englewood Cliffs, N.J.: Prentice-Hall, Inc., 1964b.

Population: Children of all ages.

Components of Development and Test Items:

COMPONENTS	TEST ITEMS
Extent flexibility	Trunk twist and touch
Dynamic flexibility	Bend, twist, and floor touch
Explosive strength	Shuttle run Softball throw
Static strength	Hand grip
Dynamic strength	Pull-ups Leg lifts
Gross body coordination	Cable jump test
Gross body equilibrium	Balance
Stamina	600-yard run-walk

Comments: From 100 physical fitness items and 11 primary factors relating to physical fitness originally identified, 10 tests were finally selected through factor analysis and were administered to 20,000 students in 45 cities throughout the United States. Norms based on this sample are available for boys and girls aged 12–18. Test-retest correlations ranged from .70 to .93 with 5 items above .90, 4 items between .80 and .89 and 1 item at .70 (cable-jump test). Primary factor loadings ranged from .47 to .81. Correlations between test items ranged from .02 to .52, with a majority below .20. The test may be administered in two regular classes and with minimal equipment.

FROSTIG DEVELOPMENTAL TEST OF VISUAL PERCEPTION

Source: Frostig, Marianne, Welty Lefever, and John R. B. Whittlesey. *The Marianne Frostig Developmental Test of Visual Perception.* Revised ed. Palo Alto, Cal.: Consulting Psychologists Press, Inc., 1966. The test is available from Consulting Psychologists Press, 577 College Avenue, Palo Alto, CA 94306.

Population: The test can be used as a screening device for nursery school, kindergarten, and first grade children or as a clinical evaluative instrument for older children who exhibit learning disabilities.

Components of Development and Test Items:

COMPONENTS	TEST ITEMS
Eye-motor coordination	Items require the drawing of continuous straight, curved, or angled lines between boundaries or from point to point.
Figure-ground	Items involve shifts in perception of figures against increasingly complex backgrounds.

COMPONENTS	TEST ITEMS
Constancy of shape	Items test the recognition of selected geometric figures presented in a variety of sizes, shadings, textures, and positions in space.
Position in space	Items involve the discrimination of reversals and rotations.
Spatial relationships	Items involve the analysis of simple forms and patterns.

Comments: The test may generally be administered to groups. However, where appropriate, individual testing may be conducted. The test does not include gross motor items. Normative data, based on a 1963 standardization sample of 2100 nursery school and public school children aged 3–9 is available in Frostig, et al. (1964a). In the same work, the authors report a test-retest reliability coefficient of .98 based on Perceptual Quotient (PQ) and testing of 50 children with learning disabilities, of .80 based on PQ and testing of 35 first graders and 37 second graders, and of .42 to .80 based on subtest scale scores of the same group of first and second graders. Split-half reliability was based on test scores of all children 5 years old or older in the standardization sample. Based on total scores, Pearson product-moment correlations corrected by the Spearman-Brown formula ranged from .78 in the 8–9-year-old group to .89 in the 5–6-year-old group. Frostig and associates (1964a) report that validity coefficients between the Frostig test and teacher ratings of classroom adjustment, motor coordination, and intellectual functioning range from .44 to .50. Validity coefficients between the Frostig test and the Goodenough test range from .24 to .46. The reader is asked to consult Frostig, et al. (1964a) for additional information on validity. Data is presented regarding the criterion of reading, the effects of training, and the relationship to neurological handicaps. The test may be administered in a single class period.

FROSTIG MOVEMENT SKILLS TEST BATTERY

Source: Orpet, R. E. *Frostig Movement Skills Test Battery (Experimental Edition).* Palo Alto, California: Consulting Psychologists Press, Inc., 1972. This test is available from Consulting Psychologists Press, 577 College Avenue, Palo Alto, CA 94306.

Population: Children aged 6–12.

Components of Development and Test Items:

COMPONENTS	TEST ITEMS
Bilateral eye-hand coordination and dexterity	Bead stringing
Unilateral coordination involving motor sequencing	Fist/Edge/Palm
Eye-hand and fine motor coordination	Block transfer
Visual-motor coordination involving aiming and accuracy	Bean bag target throw

COMPONENTS	TEST ITEMS
Ability to flex the spine	Sitting, bending, reaching
Leg strength	Standing broad jump
Running speed and ability to make quick stops, changes of direction, and changes of body position	Shuttle run
Speed and agility in changing body position from a lying to a standing position	Changing body position
Abdominal muscle strength	Sit-ups
Dynamic balance	Walking board
Static balance	Balancing on one foot with eyes open and with eyes closed
Arm and shoulder girdle strength	Chair push-ups

Comments: Factor analysis, reliability, and normative data are available in the test manual. Factor analysis results indicate that the 12 test items are saturated by 5 factors. These are: hand-eye coordination (items 1, 2, 3, 7); balance (items 10, 11a, 11b); strength (items 6, 7, 8, 9, 12); flexibility (item 5); and visually guided movement (item 4). The standardization sample consisted of 744 Caucasian elementary school children (K–6) in the Buena Park Elementary School District, California. Lower-bound estimates of reliability based on communalities from factor analysis for each of the 7 age groups ranged from .44 to .88, with only 14 of the 91 communalities being less than .60. The test requires minimal equipment and may be administered in approximately two physical education periods.

GODFREY-KEPHART MOVEMENT PATTERN CHECKLIST-SHORT FORM

Source: Godfrey, Barbara B., and Newell C. Kephart. *Movement Patterns and Motor Education.* New York: Appleton-Century-Crofts, 1969.

Population: Typical and atypical children.

Components of Development and Checklist Items:

COMPONENTS	CHECKLIST ITEMS
Movement patterns	The following movement patterns are evaluated using the Movement Pattern Checklist Short Form: walk, run, crawl, jump, hop, skip, climb, roll, slide, stand, sit, throw, catch, hit, kick, push, pull, carry. These movements are evaluated according to particular criteria, and abilities as well as deviations are noted.

Comments: This checklist may be used as a screening device. The authors do not present data relevant to reliability, validity, or norms. The checklist may also be used as a supplement to the Godfrey-Kephart Movement Pattern Checklist.

HAYDEN PHYSICAL FITNESS TEST FOR THE MENTALLY RETARDED

Source: Hayden, Frank. *Physical Fitness for the Mentally Retarded.* Toronto, Canada: Metropolitan Toronto Association for Retarded Children, 1964. This test is available from the Association at 186 Beverly Street, Toronto, Ontario Canada.

Population: Severely mentally retarded.

Components of Development and Test Items:

COMPONENTS	TEST ITEMS
Strength and endurance	Hang for time
Power, strength, and coordination	Medicine ball throw
Flexibility and strength	Back extension flexibility
Flexibility, strength, and endurance	Speed back lifts
Power	Vertical jump
Flexibility	Floor touch
Organic fitness	300-yard run

Comments: Norms are available for mentally retarded boys and girls aged 8–17. Statistical data on reliability and validity are not presented. Test can be administered in two physical education periods with minimal equipment requirements.

KRAUS-WEBER MINIMUM MUSCULAR FITNESS TESTS

Source: Kraus, Hans, and Ruth P. Hirschland. "Minimum Muscular Fitness Tests in School Children," *Res. Quart.* 25:178–188, 1954.

Population: Children aged 6–19.

Components of Development and Test Items:

COMPONENTS	TEST ITEMS
Strength of the abdominal muscles with psoas muscles	The subject must perform one sit-up from the supine position with hands behind the neck and feet held by the examiner.

COMPONENTS	TEST ITEMS
Strength of the abdominal muscles without psoas muscles	Same as the previous item with knees bent.
Strength of the psoas muscles and lower abdominal muscles	From the supine position with hands held behind the neck, the subject holds the legs fully extended with the heels 10 inches off the table for 10 seconds.
Strength of the upper back muscles	From the prone position with a pillow under the hips and lower abdomen and the hands behind the neck, the subject must raise the chest, head, and shoulders for 10 seconds. Feet are held down by the examiner.
Strength of the lower back muscles	From the same position as the previous test item, the subject must raise the legs with knees straight for 10 seconds. The examiner holds the subject's chest down.
Length of the back and hamstring muscles	From a standing position, the subject touches the floor with the fingertips for 3 seconds.

Comments: Since this test has received much attention, a great deal of analysis of it appears in the literature. It is recommended that potential users consult Safrit (1973) or other texts on tests and measurements. Many professionals score this test on a pass-fail basis. Kraus and Hirschland compare test results of American and European children. Data on reliability and validity are not presented.

LEIGHTON MEASURES OF FLEXIBILITY

Source: Leighton, Jack R. "A Simple Objective and Reliable Measure of Flexibility." *Res. Quart.* 13:205–216, 1945.

Population: General.

Components of Development and Test Items:

COMPONENTS	ITEMS
Flexibility	Elbow flexion and extension, shoulder flexion and extension, ankle flexion and extension, trunk and hip flexion and extension, sideward trunk and hip flexion and extension, hip flexion and extension, leg abduction, leg flexion and extension, thigh flexion, head rotation, head flexion and extension, wrist flexion and extension, arm flexion on the back.

Comments: Leighton developed a flexometer to measure range of movement or flexibility. Procedures for test administration are provided. The measurement of the 13 items may be completed in approximately 20 minutes. Reliability coefficients, based on the administration of two trials to 56 college students, were generally above .950 and ranged from .889 to .997. Means and standard deviations of the original sample are provided. The method may be used with most age groups.

LINCOLN-OSERETSKY MOTOR DEVELOPMENT SCALE

Source: Sloan, William. "The Lincoln-Oseretsky Motor Development Scale." *Genet. Psych. Monogr.* 51:183–252, 1955. The scale is published by C. H. Stoelting Co., 424 N. Homan Avenue, Chicago, IL 60624.

Population: Children aged 6–14.

Components of Development and Test Items:

COMPONENTS	TEST ITEMS
Motor development (includes finger dexterity, eye-hand coordination, and gross motor activity of the hands, arms, legs, and trunk).	The scale includes 36 items: walking backward, crouching on tiptoe, standing on one foot, touching nose, touching fingertips, tapping rhythmically with feet and fingers, jumping over a rope, moving fingers, standing heel to toe, closing and opening the hands alternately, making dots, catching a ball, making a ball, winding thread, balancing a rod crosswise on the index finger, describing circles in the air, tapping coins and matchsticks, putting matchsticks in a box, winding thread while walking, throwing a ball, sorting matchsticks, drawing lines, cutting a circle, putting coins in a box, tracking mazes, balancing on tiptoe, tapping with feet and fingers, jumping and touching heels, tapping feet and describing circles with fingers, standing on one foot with eyes closed, jumping and clapping, balancing on tiptoe, opening and closing hands, and balancing a rod vertically.

Comments: The Lincoln-Oseretsky scale excludes 49 of the original 85 items in the Oseretsky Scale. Scores on the Lincoln-Oseretsky are reported to increase with age except at the 13 and 14 year age levels. The coefficients of correlation between scale results and age are .87 with males and .88 with females. Standardization data are based on the testing of 380 males and 369 females aged 6–14. Norms based on standardization data are provided. Split-half reliability coefficients by age, corrected by the Spearman-Brown formula, ranged from .72 to .94 for males and .82 to .93 for females except for a .59 reported for females aged 14. Overall split-half reliability coefficients were .96 for males and .97 for females. Standard error of measurement was relatively constant from age to age.

MOTOR FITNESS TEST FOR THE MODERATELY MENTALLY RETARDED

Source: Johnson, Leon, and Ben Londeree. *Motor Fitness Testing Manual For the Moderately Mentally Retarded.* Washington, D.C.: American Alliance for Health, Physical Education, and Recreation, 1976. This test may be purchased from AAHPER Publication-Sales, 1201 16th Street N.W., Washington, DC 20036.

Population: Moderately mentally retarded aged 6–20.

Components of Development and Test Items:

COMPONENTS	TEST ITEMS
Arm and shoulder girdle strength	Flexed-arm hang
Efficiency of abdominal and hip flexor muscles	Sit-ups in 30 seconds
Muscular power	Standing long jump
Muscular power and coordination	Softball throw for distance
Speed	50-yard dash
Height	Height
Weight	Weight
Flexibility	Sitting bob-and-reach
Developmental skill	Hopping Skipping Tumbling progression Target throw

Comments: The norms were developed on the basis of tests administered to 1097 moderately retarded persons aged 6–21 throughout Missouri. Reliability per se was not measured. However, correlations between 1972 and 1973 administrations of the test to the same population were R=.80 or above on 8 of 12 items. A retest was not administered on the 300-yard run-walk. Of the exceptions, the flexed-arm hang and bob-and-reach tests have been reported to have test-retest reliabilities as high as r = .90. The 1972–73 correlations in the target throw were r = .60, and for skipping and tumbling were r = .70. In implementing the test, it is recommended that items be selected from the battery as needed. Administration of the whole test is relatively long. Awards are available for various levels of achievement. Relatively little equipment is necessary for test administration.

MOVE–GROW–LEARN MOVEMENT SKILLS SURVEY

Source: Orpet, R. E., and T. L. Heustis. *Move-Grow-Learn Movement Skills Survey.* Chicago: Follett Publishing Co., 1971.

Population: Children. (Do not rate children under 8 years old on the endurance item.)

Components of Development and Types of Activities:

COMPONENTS	TYPES OF ACTIVITIES
Coordination and rhythm	
gross motor	Tumbling, running, skipping, hopping, rope jumping, throwing.
fine motor	Drawing, coloring, writing, cutting.
eye-motor	Bead stringing, beanbag catching, ball catching and kicking, ball bouncing games, tetherball.
Agility	Dodge ball, shuttle runs, sitting-to-standing exercises
Flexibility	Toe-touches, back bends.
Strength	Trunk and shoulder girdle: sit-ups, leg lifts, push-ups. Limb (hands, arms, legs): pull-ups, jungle gym activities, broad jumps, rope climbing.
Speed	Running.
Balance	
static	Standing on tiptoe, standing on one foot (eyes open and eyes closed).
dynamic	Walking on a balance beam.
object	Carrying beanbag on head.
Endurance	Distance running, basketball, soccer.
Body awareness	Relaxing, discriminating right and left.

Comments: The survey was developed to assist classroom teachers, movement education supervisors, school psychologists, and other professional school personnel in evaluating selected aspects of a child's motor development. Assessment is based on observations of the child in classroom, playground, and movement activities. Since activities may vary, developmental norms are not provided by age level. Children are rated as severely impaired, mildly impaired, adequate, good, or excellent.

PURDUE PERCEPTUAL-MOTOR SURVEY

Source: Roach, Eugene G., and Newell C. Kephart. *The Purdue Perceptual-Motor Survey.* Columbus, Ohio: Charles E. Merrill Publishing Co., 1966.

Population: Children aged 6–10 and older children who are retarded. Not recommended for children who have specific defects, such as blindness, paralysis, and known motor disorders.

Components of Development and Test Items

COMPONENTS	TEST ITEMS
Balance and posture	Items include walking board forward, walking board backward, walking board sideward, and jumping.
Body image and differentiation	Items include identification of body parts, imitation of movement, obstacle course, 2 items from the Kraus-Weber test, and Angels in the Snow.
Perceptual-motor match	This part includes 7 items. The first 4 involve the chalkboard and require the child to make a circle, double circles, and lateral and vertical lines. The next 3 items survey rhythm, reproduction, and orientation in writing.
Ocular control	This part consists of 4 items involving convergence and ocular pursuits by both eyes, the right eye, and the left eye.
Form perception	Subjects are scored on the items of form and organization in reproducing visual forms.

Comments: Means and standard deviations are available for children in grades 1 through 4. The survey should be administered individually or in small groups. Although the survey requires a minimum amount of equipment, complete administration of the survey to a large group is quite time-consuming. Chi-squares computed on each item for comparison between achievers and non-achievers were statistically significant at the .05 level in all but one case. The sub-test of organization in the Visual Achievement form probably needs revision for non-retarded children, according to Roach and Kephart (1966). A Pearson correlation coefficient of .654 was obtained between total scores on the survey and teacher ratings. On a test-retest of 30 children, a stability coefficient of .946 was obtained. Since no examiner tested the same children in both the test and retest, the coefficient represents reliability and objectivity.

SOUTHERN CALIFORNIA PERCEPTUAL-MOTOR TESTS

Source: Ayres, Jean A. *Southern California Perceptual-Motor Tests.* Los Angeles, Cal.: Western Psychological Services, 1969. This test is available from Western Psychological Services, 12031 Wilshire Boulevard, Los Angeles, CA 90025.

Population: This test is designed to evaluate dimensions of perceptual-motor function in children ranging in age from 4 through 8 years.

Components of Development and Test Items:

COMPONENTS	TEST ITEMS
Imitation of postures	Subjects assume a series of positions or postures demonstrated by the examiner. Total score is based on 12 items.
Crossing mid-line of the body	Subjects perform a series of hand movements to the ear and eye. The score is based on 8 items.
Bilateral motor coordination	The 8 items of this test involve touching the palms of the hands to the thigh in various patterns. The tasks require smoothly executed interaction between the upper extremities. Total score is based on the 8 items.
Right-left discrimination	Subjects perform a series of 10 items designed to discriminate right from left on self, on another person, and in location of an object. A total score based on the 10 items is recorded. This test is not appropriate for 4-year-old or 5-year-old subjects.
Standing balance (eyes open)	With arms folded, subjects are asked to balance on one foot and then the other foot with eyes open.
Standing balance (eyes closed)	With arms folded, subjects are asked to balance on one foot and then the other foot with eyes closed.

Comments: All tests are individually administered. Administration of the battery requires approximately 20 minutes. The 6 tests were standardized on 1004 children ranging from 4 to 8 years of age. In some instances, the test appears to be truncated at the 4 and 8 year age levels. Normative data for ages 4 to 8 are available. Test-retest reliability coefficients range from .12 to .78.

TEACHING RESEARCH MOTOR DEVELOPMENT SCALE
FOR MODERATELY AND SEVERELY RETARDED
CHILDREN

Source: Fredericks, H. D. Bud, et al. The Teaching Research Motor-
Development Scale for Moderately and Severely Retarded Children.
Springfield, Ill.: Charles C Thomas, Publisher, 1972.

Population: Moderately and Severely Retarded Children, pre-school to
high school.

Components of Development and Test Items:

COMPONENTS	TEST ITEMS
The scale was designed to measure motor proficiency	The scale includes 51 items: standing on tiptoe with eyes open and eyes closed, crouching on tiptoe, standing heel to toe with eyes open and eyes closed; standing on one foot with eyes open and eyes closed, jumping a bar, jumping on toes rapidly, walking forward on a straight line of mats, on staggered mats, on a six-foot radius semicircle, and along a six-foot line heel to toe, walking backwards, imitating movements, touching nose and fingertips, closing and opening hands alternately, tapping rhythmically with feet and fingers, stepping over and ducking under an obstacle, passing between an obstacle and a wall, placing matchsticks and coins in boxes, winding thread, tapping, drawing lines, tracing mazes, cutting paper in straight lines and in a circle, bouncing, catching, and throwing a ball, hanging from a bar, doing pull-ups, lifting head and shoulders off the floor, performing sit-ups and push-ups, and running 50 feet, 100 yards, and 220 yards.

Comments: The scale was designed on the basis of concepts of testing
developed elsewhere — primarily the Lincoln-Oseretsky Motor Development Scale and physical fitness tests. Although 500 children have
been tested, no norms are assigned. The test may be administered
either in one sitting or over several days. The test requires a minimum
amount of equipment.

VALETT PSYCHOEDUCATIONAL INVENTORY OF BASIC LEARNING ABILITIES

Source: Valett, Robert E. *A Psychoeducational Inventory of Basic Learning Abilities.* Belmont, Cal.: Fearon Publishers, 1968. The kit may be purchased from Fearon Publishers at 6 Davis Dr., Belmont, CA 94002.

Population: Elementary and junior high pupils aged 5–12 with suspected learning disabilities.

Components of Development and Test Items:

COMPONENTS	TEST ITEMS
Gross motor development	Test includes 14 items to survey rolling, sitting, crawling, walking, running, throwing, jumping, skipping, dancing, self-identification, body localization, body abstraction, muscular strength, and general physical health.
Sensory-motor integration	Test includes 7 items to survey balance and rhythm, body spatial organization, reaction-speed dexterity, tactile discrimination, directionality, laterality, and time orientation.
Perceptual-motor skills	Test includes 15 items to survey auditory acuity, auditory decoding, auditory-vocal association, auditory memory, auditory sequencing, visual acuity, visual coordination and pursuit, visual-form discrimination, visual figure-ground differentiation, visual memory, visual-motor memory, visual-motor fine muscle coordination, visual-motor spatial form manipulation, visual-motor speed of learning, and visual-motor integration.
Language development	Test includes 7 items to survey vocabulary fluency and encoding, articulation, word attack skills, reading, comprehension, writing, and spelling.
Conceptual skills	Test includes 6 items to survey number concepts, arithmetic processes, arithmetic reasoning, general information, classification, and comprehension.
Social skills	Test includes 4 items to survey social acceptance, anticipatory response, value judgments, and social maturity.

Comments: As Valett states, the inventory is not standardized and relies entirely on the examiner's judgment and experience regarding the rating to be employed and the nature of the remedial program required. It is recommended that the inventory be individually administered. An examiner's kit provides necessary test materials.

VINELAND ADAPTATION OF THE OSERETSKY TESTS

Source: Cassel, Robert H. "The Vineland Adaptation of the Oseretsky Tests," *Trng. Sch Bull. Suppl.* 46:1–32, 1949.

Population: Mentally deficient children.

Components of Development and Test Items.

COMPONENTS	TEST ITEMS
General static coordination	The 10 items in this part include assessing the ability to balance on one foot or on the toes with eyes open or closed or with different body positions.
General dynamic coordination	The 10 items in this part involve jumping up and down on the toes, hopping on one foot, jumping over a rope, walking forward and backward on a line, jumping in the air while striking the heels, jumping in the air while clapping, and jumping, turning, and holding balance.
Dynamic manual coordination	The 10 items in this part involve touching the nose, rolling a piece of cigarette paper, throwing and catching a tennis ball, catching a ball, performing finger and thumb movements, screwing nuts, balancing a stick, and alternately opening and closing the hands.
Speed	The 5 items in this part involve putting nuts in a box, making dots, distributing playing cards, punching holes in a piece of paper as fast as possible, and standing up from a chair, running around it, and sitting on it again.
Simultaneous voluntary movement	The 9 items in this part involve winding thread while walking, putting nuts in a box, tapping the foot rhythmically, making circles with the fingers, performing rhythmic and coordinated foot and finger tapping, punching holes, and rhythmically patting the head with one hand while rubbing the abdomen with the other.

Comments: Modifications and changes of the Oseretsky tests were made empirically on the basis of performances of about 100 subjects. The Vineland adaptation was administered by Cassel (1949) to 27 exogenous (MA=7.1, CA=15.5) and 27 endogenous (MA=6.9, CA=16.0) mentally deficient subjects. Results indicated a general endogenous superiority in the test. Item analysis revealed that 4 test items were too hard and 2 were too easy. Cassel concluded that the Vineland adaptation reduces administration time (individual administration of the test requires about 45 minutes), minimizes the amount of equipment needed, eliminates tests that appear to be impractical, and standardizes testing procedures.

YALE OR GESELL DEVELOPMENTAL SCHEDULE (REVISED)

Source: Gesell, Arnold, et al. *The First Five Years of Life.* London: Methuen & Co., Ltd., 1950, and Gesell, Arnold, and Catherine S. Amatruda. *Developmental Diagnosis: Normal and Abnormal Child Development.* New York: Paul B. Hoeber, Inc., Medical Book Department of Harper & Brothers, 1948. Materials may be purchased from the Psychological Corporation, 522 Fifth Avenue, New York, NY 10036.

Population: Children aged 4 weeks to 5 years.

Components of Development and Test Items:

COMPONENTS	TEST ITEMS
Motor behavior	The examinations consider postural reactions, head balance, prehension, locomotion, object manipulation, general bodily coordination, and specific motor skills.
Adaptive behavior	The examinations consider the coordination of eyes and hands in reaching and manipulation, the ability to utilize motor equipment appropriately in the solution of practical problems, and the capacity to initiate new adjustments in the presence of simple problem situations set before the child.
Language behavior	Items included examine visual and audible forms of communication (including facial expression, gesture, postural movements, vocalization, words, phrases, and sentences), mimicry, and comprehension.
Personal-social behavior	Items included examine the child's feeding abilities, sense of property, self-dependence in play, cooperativeness, responsiveness to training and social conventions, and personal attitude to other persons.

Comments: This developmental examination of behavior provides test materials, examination sequences, test procedures, record forms, methods of scoring and appraisal, a behavior inventory, data on temporary behavior patterns, and normative data for children 4 weeks to 22 months of age. In basic texts, a background for interpreting both typical and atypical manifestations of growth is presented. In addition, adaptations for administering the inventory to atypical children are presented. Examiners using the developmental studies for children aged 4 weeks to 3 years should consult Gesell and Amatruda (1948), and those using the schedules for children aged 15 months to 72 months should consult Gesell, et al. (1950).

14

RESEARCH: THE
EFFECTS OF TRAINING

In this chapter, research pertaining to the effects of physical and motor experiences on selected developmental variables is reviewed and summarized. In the first section, research related to the effects of early stimulation and deprivation and the role of maturation and learning on motor development and skill acquisition is presented. Research pertaining to the effectiveness of training programs for the enhancement of physical and motor development of special populations is discussed in the second section. In the third section, research regarding the use of perceptual-motor programs for the development of perceptual and academic abilities of regular and special populations is reviewed and summarized. In the final section, research pertaining to the use of movement activities for the enhancement of academic abilities is presented and summarized. Although the use of movement experiences for the stimulation of cognitive development is advocated in this book, research on the effectiveness of the approach is only beginning (Leithwood, 1971 and Kershner, 1974). Therefore, this aspect of development must await further study.

Effects of Selected Environmental Influences on Motor Development and Skill Acquisition

The effects of early stimulation and deprivation and of instruction on the development and learning of youngsters are concerns of many professions. In this section, therefore, research related to the effects of these conditions on selected developmental areas will be briefly reviewed. Because of the obvious limitations on using human subjects, selected studies of infrahuman subjects will also be discussed. Following this, research regarding the effects of special practice or training and of instruction on early motor development and skill acquisition will be presented. Since the focus of this book is on the early developmental years, research on the effects of instruction on skill acquisition in later years will not be covered. There is little disagreement that such instruction is beneficial when implemented properly, although maturation must be considered whenever instruction occurs within the developmental years.

Stimulation and Deprivation in Infrahuman Subjects

The effects of stimulation and deprivation on the behavior of animals has been a topic of a number of investigations. For example, Kuo (1930) found that more than half the kittens kept in isolation with no opportunity to observe older cats in the presence of rats failed to demonstrate rat-killing behavior. Spalding (1902) reported that chicks kept in isolation for ten days after hatching did not follow the hen's call. Mowrer (1936) found that if the eyelids of pigeons were sewn closed until they were six weeks old, optokinetic nystagmus did not appear immediately. However, the birds did develop normal optokinetic nystagmus and normal fear and avoidance reactions within three days after the removal of stitches from the eyelids. In a study using animals less removed from man on the phylogenetic scale, Riesen (1947) reared two chimpanzees in darkness until they were 16 months of age. When they were finally exposed to light, the chimpanzees were "blind" except for certain reflexes to light. The chimps did not blink as a result of objects brought rapidly toward the eyes, fixation of still or moving objects was not evidenced, early reaching responses were grossly inaccurate, and visual recognition of a feeding bottle did not appear in one subject until the subject had been in light for 11 days. The latter finding occurred even though the subject was tactually and kinesthetically familiar with the feeding bottle. The eye blink response was exhibited in one subject only after 48 days of exposure to light. The findings of Riesen lend support to the contention that visual learning is associated with and thus not independent of visual experience.

Many studies show the effect of deprivation not only on immediate performance but on long-term performance as well. In a study with Scottie puppies, Thompson and Melzack (1956) found that puppies kept in isolation cages for seven to ten months showed highly inappropriate emotional responses and were significantly lower in problem-solving ability than their control group litter mates, who were normally reared. In addition, the puppies showed effects of environmental restriction for several years.

Nissen, Chow, and Semmes (1951) studied the effects of restricted opportunity for tactual, kinesthetic, and manipulative experience on the behavior of a chimpanzee. These investigators placed a chimp's limbs in cardboard cylinders and observed his discriminatory and motor responses. During the period of restriction (from 1 to 31 months of age), the chimpanzee failed to try many motor tasks. Observations made during and four months after encasement of its limbs revealed that the chimp's general behavior was very similar to that of control animals except in tasks involving motor coordination and tactual discrimination. The chimpanzee found motor coordination and tactual discriminations to be difficult and often refused to try such activities. In sitting, for example, the chimp exhibited a highly atypical posture. The subject did not bring the fingers to a stimulated region on the dorsal trunk or head. The chimp did not grasp or cling to the attendant who carried it and did not groom. After removal of the cardboard cylinders, the chimpanzee showed steady improvement in manipulative and climbing activities. The subject did bring the fingers to a given place with improved speed and accuracy but never brought the hand to the back of the trunk and rarely to the head. The tendency to cling to the attendant developed slowly, but grooming did not appear, and the atypical sitting posture continued.

Deprivation and Stimulation in Human Subjects

Dennis (1935, 1938, 1941) investigated the effects of restricted practice and minimum social stimulation on the development of fraternal twins. The twins were kept on their backs for 9 months and received a minimum of social stimulation for a period of 14 months. Although they received good physical care, social stimulation was kept at a minimum. The twins were restricted in the ability to use their arms for reaching, their hands were restrained during eating, and they were given freedom to practice sitting or standing. Dennis found that the motor development of these infants deviated only slightly from that of normally reared youngsters at 9 months. The restrictions apparently accounted for a slight retardation in sitting and walking. On the basis of these studies, Dennis concluded that prior to the second year of life, the behavioral development of the youngsters will proceed normally and without intervention from that of others, providing that the infant's well-being is assured. The contention that sitting, standing, and walking occur normally without teaching was supported by Sherman, Sherman, and Flory (1936).

Dennis and Dennis (1940) studied the effect of cradling on the walking ability of Hopi Indian infants. Children of Hopi Indians who are cradled are bound to a cradling board on the first day of life. This restricts the movement of the child but allows the mother to carry the child on her back and to lean the cradling board at various places while she engages in work or other activities. The infant is kept cradled almost continuously for three months, after which the time spent on the cradling board is decreased gradually until it is eliminated between the ages of 4 and 14 months. Since the practice has been eliminated in certain Hopi groups, comparisons with other Hopi children as well as with white children could be made. Dennis and Dennis reported that Hopi children who are cradled walk just as early as those who have not been cradled, but the walking age of Hopi infants is one to two months after that of white children. The cause of the difference could not be identified on the basis of this study.

In another study, Dennis (1960) compared the motor development of 174 children aged 1 to 4 years in three Iranian institutions. One institution provided its children with opportunities to sit and to play in the prone position, whereas the other institutions restricted such freedom. Dennis found that children in the enriched environment were less retarded in beginning to walk. Dennis indicated that the results of this study challenge the widely held view that motor development consists of the emergence of a behavioral sequence based primarily on maturation. He states that these facts seem to indicate clearly that experience affects not only the age at which a motor item appears but also its form.

Williams and Scott (1953) studied the relationship of child-rearing practices to motor development in two groups of Negro infants. Subjects were 104 Negro babies ranging in age from 4 to 18 months and living in the Washington, D.C., area. One group came from a low socioeconomic background and the other from a high socioeconomic background. The Gesell Developmental Schedules were used for the assessment of motor development. The investigators found that the group from the low socioeconomic background showed significant acceleration in motor activities. The results were attributed to the absence of cribs, play pens, high chairs, and similar equipment that serves to restrict overall movement. It was noted that specific practices as well as the overall home atmosphere were more permissive and less exacting among families in the low socioeconomic group.

Effects of Special Practice, Training, and Instruction on Motor Development and Skill Acquisition

The relative effects of learning and maturation in humans were examined in a study conducted by Gesell and Thompson (1929). Subjects included identical twin girls 46 weeks of age. One twin (T) was given special exercises in stair climbing and cube building for ten minutes a day over a period of six weeks. Control twin (C) was given no such training but was given exercise in the same activities for a period of two weeks following the six-week period during which twin T was practicing the exercises. Since twin C performed as well as twin T after the two-week period, it was concluded that practice did not hasten performance in stair climbing and cube building. This study shows not only that maturation is important but also that training does not transcend maturation in experiences such as climbing and building.

In a study conducted with twin boys, McGraw (1935) exercised the experimental twin (Johnny) from the age of 21 days to the age of 22 months in motor activities in which he showed capability. The control twin, Jimmy, although tested periodically, was given no such practice. Johnny was advanced in certain motor activities, but there were several in which he showed no superiority. McGraw concluded that phylogenetic activities (those that one must acquire to be considered normal in a culture) were least affected by practice and that ontogenetic activities (those that an individual may or may not develop) were accelerated by practice. In a follow-up study four years later, McGraw (1939) tested Johnny and Jimmy again. She reported a superiority of general muscular coordination for Johnny, who had received the longer and more intensive practice in motor activities. Johnny generally displayed greater motor coordination and more daring in physical performance.

Mirenva (1935) also investigated the effects of training on the performance of selected motor abilities of pre-school youngsters. One of each pair of 4-year-old twins was trained over a four-month period in jumping into the air, rolling a ball at a target, and hitting a target with a thrown ball. Results showed that both the trained and untrained groups improved, but the amount of change in the trained group was greater than that of the untrained group. The investigator noted that elementary functions were relatively independent of training, although training did accelerate their rate. More complex functions appeared to depend less on maturation.

Hilgard (1932) investigated the effects of training on the acquisition of skills including cutting with scissors, buttoning, and climbing a ladder. An experimental group received special training during a three-month period, and a control group received intensive practice for only the last week of the experiment. Subjects included two groups of ten children aged 24 to 36 months. Hilgard found that the performance of the experimental group on these activities exceeded that of the control group after 12 weeks of practice, but that one week of practice by the control group was sufficient to bring their scores to levels similar to those of the experimental group. The rapid gains of the control group were interpreted to mean that factors other than specific training contributed to the development of these skills. These findings support the contention that maturation is a very important factor in the skill acquisition of nursery school youngsters. In a later study, Hilgard (1933) compared the performance of an experimental twin receiving practice on walking board activities, cutting, digit memorizing, ring tossing, and object memorizing with that of a control twin receiving no special practice on these tasks. At the end of the eight-week training period, the 4½-year-old experimental twin was superior on all test measures except for walking time score on the largest walking board. However, after three months and six months, performance was similar.

Hicks (1930a) investigated the acquisition of motor skill as a result of practice in youngsters between the ages of 2½ and 6. One of two comparable groups of children practiced throwing at a moving target once a week for eight weeks. Hicks found that both groups improved but that the experimental group did not improve significantly more than the control group. Hicks suggested that the results were due to structural maturation and to general practice on activities related to the skill rather than to specific practice. Hicks (1930b) reported similar results on strength, a perforation test, and a tracing path test in a parallel study. In another study, Hicks and Ralph (1931) found that children with more practice in tracing the Porteus Diamond Maze did not gain significantly over a control group having less practice, although both groups improved. The subjects consisted of 24 children aged 24 to 40 months. Results were again attributed to structural maturation and general practice.

Ketterlinus (1931) conducted a study to determine whether children 2, 3, and 4 years of age could learn skills in tasks requiring new hand and eye coordinations and whether the new coordinations were learned more rapidly by older children. In this study, children were asked to pick up objects and put them into a cup, push discs with the foot, and push a toy cannon along a path. In each case, mirror reversals of the goals were employed. Ketterlinus found that children as young as 2 were able to acquire skill in such tasks and that younger children learned new habits more slowly than older children.

Dusenberry (1952) investigated the effects of practice and instruction on the ball-throwing ability of children aged 3 to 7. Two groups of children were matched on the basis of age, sex, race, and average distance of five throws. One group received practice and instruction in throwing twice a week over a period of three weeks, and the control group received no instruction. Dusenberrry reported that differences in favor of the experimental group were significant at the .07 level, that children aged 3 and 4 showed little improvement, and that children aged 5 and 6 showed improvement. She indicated that learning to throw for distance occurred over and above the effects of maturation.

Wild (1938), using cinematographic records, studied the throwing patterns of children aged 2 to 7 years. On the basis of her research, Wild indentified four types of throwing patterns. She indicated that maturational factors are most important in developing proper throwing patterns until the age of 6, at which time learning becomes critically important in performance.

The effects of practice, instruction, and participation in physical education on the skill acquisition of subjects in elementary school, junior high school, senior high school, and college has been the topic several investigations. On the basis of her review of research on this topic, Mohr (1960) reported that skill learning occurs as a result of practice and instruction. She also presents research to support the claim that participation in regular physical education programs enhances skill learning.

Summary

Research conducted with infrahuman subjects (Kuo 1930, Spalding 1902, and Riesen 1947) supports the contention that environmental stimulation in the form of practice is a factor in the development of certain behaviors and abilities in animals. Research with higher order animals (Thompson and Melzack 1951 and Nissen, Chow, and Semmes 1951) supports the contention that environmental deprivation not not only inhibits certain types of behaviors but also inhibits normal performance after restriction has been lifted.

In regard to the effects of environmental restriction on infant development, Dennis (1935, 1938, 1941) reported little difference in motor variables as a result of such restriction in his study of twins.

However, in his study of motor development of children in three Iranian institutions, Dennis (1960) found motor development less retarded in those institutions that provided children with more freedom. In their study of cradling by Hopi Indians, Dennis and Dennis (1940) were unable to determine the cause of differences in walking age between Hopi infants and white infants but found that Hopi infants who were cradled developed walking abilities at the same age as Hopi infants who were not cradled. Williams and Scott (1953) reported that Negro infants reared in homes where movement was less retricted were accelerated in motor development.

Gesell and Thompson (1929) found little benefit in encouraging practice of stair climbing and cube building, and McGraw (1935, 1939) found that practice of ontogenetic activities but not of phylogenetic activities benefitted youngsters at early age levels. Mirenva (1935) reported training was of benefit in the development of selected motor abilities of 4-year-olds. In one study, Hilgard (1932) found training to be of little value in the skill acquisition of youngsters. In another study, comparing trained and untrained twins, Hilgard (1933) found significant short-term gains but similar performance after three-month and six-month periods. Hicks (1930a, 1930b) in two studies and Hicks and Ralph (1931) in a third found that specific practice of motor skills yielded no significant improvement over gains attributed to maturation and general practice. Ketterlinus (1931) found that youngsters were able to learn unique motor tasks at early ages but could learn them faster at later ages. Dusenberry (1952) and Wild (1938) reported benefits of instruction on the acquisition of skills at early ages.

The research presented in this section appears to support the following generalizations regarding the effects of early environmental influences on motor development and skill acquisition:

1. The role of maturation is important, particularly in the early years, in motor development and skill acquisition. Training rarely transcends maturation. Maturation enables efficient learning to take place.
2. Extreme deprivation may result in temporary retardation. Long-term retardation of motor abilities as a result of extreme deprivation needs to be explored further.
3. It is important to provide opportunity for practice on those behaviors a child is ready to practice.
4. Instruction enhances the development of motor abilities providing that the individual is mature enough to benefit from such instruction.

These generalizations agree with those of McGraw (1943). On the basis of her work, she presents the following principles regarding the education of children from the developmental standpoint:

1. Training in any particular activity before the neural mechanisms have reached a certain state of readiness is futile.
2. Exercise of a newly developing function is inherent in the process of growth, and if ample opportunity is afforded at the proper time, specific achievements can be advanced beyond the stage normally expected.
3. Periods of transition from one type of neuromuscular organization to another are an inherent part of development and are often characterized by disorganization and confusion.

4. Spurts, regressions, frustrations, and inhibitions are an integral part of organic growth, and there is reason to believe that they also function in the development of complex behavior activities.
5. Maturation and learning are not different processes, merely different facets of the fundamental process of growth.
6. Evidence that a child is ready for a particular educational subject is to be found in certain behavior "signals" or behavior "syndromes," which reflect the maturity of neural mechanisms. (McGraw, 1943, pp. 130–131.)

Physical and Motor Development in Special Populations

The importance of movement experience for youngsters of preschool age is widely accepted. In addition, there is little controversy over the assertion that programs of physical and motor activity bring about improvement in attributes such as static strength, dynamic strength, explosive strength, cardiovascular efficiency, agility, flexibility, and motor abilities. It is also known that improvements in physical proficiency are transitory, i.e., when youngsters discontinue vigorous activity their proficiency decreases. Since formal calisthenics or other exercise programs are generally not implemented before the fourth grade or before age 10, there has been relatively little research on the effects of such programs on younger children. Unless special conditions indicate otherwise, the development of physical fitness before the fourth grade should be an outgrowth of normal play and physical activity. Operating on the documented belief that physical and motor abilities can be increased through movement experience, researchers studying older children have been concerned with comparing the effects of various approaches on improvement of abilities rather than with determining whether or not gains can be made. Since it is known that increases in physical and motor abilities can be realized with normal youngsters, it would be academic to pursue this matter here. However, the effects of movement experiences on special populations has not been as well established or is not as well known or as widely accepted. This section will therefore be limited to research pertaining to the effects of organized movement experiences on the physical and motor development of special populations during the developmental years.

Mentally Retarded Children

Corder (1966) investigated the effects of physical education activities on the intellectual, physical, and social development of educable mentally retarded (EMR) boys. An experimental group consisting of eight boys was given an intensive and progressive program of physical education for one hour per day for a 20-day period. A "Hawthorne" group met each day with the experimental group and carried on record-keeping and other responsibilities but did not engage in the program of activity. A control group was given pre-tests and post-tests but received the usual classroom instruction during the study. Subjects in the study, equated on CA and IQ, were between the ages of 12 years and 16 years 7 months and scored between 50 and 80 on the WISC. The effects of the program were measured by mean gain scores on the WISC, the AAHPER Fitness Test, and the Cowell Personal Distance Scale. The training group made gains over the "Hawthorne" and control groups on all seven physical fitness tests. All boys in the training group showed improvement in every subtest of the Youth Fitness Test. There were no differences among the three groups in mean gain scores on the Cowell Personal Distance Scale. The training group made significant gains on Full Scale mean IQ scores over the control group but there were no significant differences between scores of the training and "Hawthorne" groups. There were no significant differences between the "Hawthorne" and control groups on Full Scale mean IQ. Analysis of results in the verbal scale and performance scale indicated significant differences among the three groups on the verbal scale but not on the performance scale. Corder speculated that the factors that may have accounted for improved IQ scores were related to experiences of success, the desire to perform well, improved listening abilities, and improved ability to concentrate.

In another study, Corder (1969) examined the effects of a physical education program on the psycho-physical development of EMR girls aged 11 to 16 years. An experimental group of 15 subjects participated in a training program that met one hour a day, five days a week, for 30 days, while 15 control subjects participated in quiet activities. Measurements of cardiorespiratory efficiency, skinfold, weight, and performance on the AAHPER Youth Fitness Test were taken. Corder reported that significant improvement by EMR girls was made in loss of subcutaneous fat and in performance of sit-ups, shuttle run, 50-year dash, the softball throw, and 600-yard run-walk.

Oliver (1958) investigated the effect of physical conditioning exercises and activities on the mental characteristics of educationally subnormal boys. Two matched groups of educationally subnormal boys (age range 12 to 15 years, IQ range 57 to 86) were used as experimental and control groups. The experimental group was given a systematic and progressive ten-week program of physical conditioning activities and the control group continued with their normal physical education program. Tests given to both groups included the Terman Merrill IQ test, the Goodenough Draw-a-Man, Raven's matrices, the Porteus Diamond Maze, Goddard's form board, tests of motor educability (items from the Iowa Revision of the Brace test and the Metheny modification of the Johnson test), athletic achievement items (50-yard dash, standing broad jump, throwing a cricket ball for distance), and a physical fitness test (Indiana Motor Fitness Test). Analysis of gain scores revealed a significant improvement of the experimental group over the control group in athletic achievement, in physical fitness, in strength, on one of two tests of motor educability, and on the Terman Merrill IQ test. In addition, significant gains of the experimental group over the control group were found in the mental age determined by the Goodenough and Porteus tests but not by the Raven and the Form Board tests. Oliver attributed positive results in IQ to success and improved confidence, improved adjustment and the happier atmosphere that arises from it, and improved general fitness and the feeling of well-being that goes with it.

Solomon and Pangle (1967) conducted an investigation of the

effect of a structured physical education program on changes in physical development of mentally retarded boys. The 42 EMR boys serving as subjects (CA range 13 years 5 months to 17 years 3 months, MA range 7 years 2 months to 12 years 2 months) were placed in an experimental group (N of 24) and a control group (N of 18). The experimental group received eight weeks of structured physical education experiences, while the control group continued in a regular classroom schedule. Physical fitness was assessed by measures of three items on the AAHPER Youth Fitness Test (chins, sit-ups, and 50-yard dash). From these measures, a total fitness score was predicted. Measures of physical fitness were obtained before and after the eight-week program and again six weeks after the program had ended. Subjects in the experimental group received a 45-minute period of physical education daily. Results were compared with AAHPER normative data for normal populations. The authors concluded that levels of fitness can be significantly improved to the extent that favorable comparisons can be made with non-retarded peer groups and that such improvement can be demonstrated following a six-week post-experiment interval.

Wright (1968) conducted a study to determine whether a program of physical education would improve the motor fitness and motor ability of EMR children. Subjects (CA range 8 to 11 years and IQ range 55 to 79) were placed in an experimental group (N of 18) or a control group (N of 15). Each group was pretested and post-tested on the Brace Test for motor ability and on five tasks (shuttle run, standing broad jump, push-ups, trunk flexion, and squat-thrusts) for motor fitness. The experimental group participated in a physical education program for six weeks with three 30-minute sessions per week, while the control group received their regular class program. The treatment consisted of free play, body movement activities, apparatus activities, and games and relays. The experimental group showed significantly greater improvement than the control group in both motor fitness and motor ability at the conclusion of the experiment.

Rarick, Dobbins, and Broadhead (1976) investigated the role of educational physical activity in the modification of motor, strength, intellectual, social, and emotional development of educable mentally retarded (EMR) and minimally brain-injured children of elementary school age. Subjects included 49 classes of children in special education programs in California and Texas. A total of 275 EMR children and 206 children diagnosed as minimally brain-injured were involved. The investigators employed four treatments in the study. The first two included two different types of physical activity programs: one individually oriented and the other group-oriented. The third treatment was an art education program. The fourth group, a control group, received the usual classroom instruction. Tests involving five parameters were administered prior to and after the treatments, which were administered for approximately 35 minutes each school day for 20 weeks. Tests included a modified version of the AAHPER test battery (motor performance), the grip and push-pull tests with dynamometers (strength), the Peabody Picture Vocabulary Test and the Bender Motor Gestalt Test (intellectual development), the Cowell Social Behavior Trend Index (social development), and items from the Bender

Test and a Catell personality questionnaire (emotional development). Data were analyzed using multivariable analysis of covariance. The investigators summarized data results regarding motor performance as follows:

1. Improved motor performance was, on the average, characteristic of those classes involved in all the special experimental programs but was not so typical of the performance of the groups of children who were denied the special programs.
2. The improvements in motor performance favored those in classes involved in physical education rather than art, but the performance changes of those in the art groups exceeded the changes of those who were not involved in a special program. This finding was more characteristic of the older children.
3. Individualized physical education elicited greater gains in performance on the average than did group oriented physical education.
4. Relative motor performance improvements were generally more apparent in the brain-injured children than in the retarded children. (Rarick, Dobbins, and Broadhead, 1976, pp. 171, 176.)

Adams (1970) studied the effects of a one-semester adapted physical education program on the motor proficiency and social adjustment of EMR junior high school girls. An experimental group, consisting of 21 EMR subjects, was placed in adapted physical education classes for one semester, and a control group of 20 EMR girls was placed in regular physical education classes. A second control group, consisting of 23 intellectually normal girls, remained in their regular physical education classes. Subjects were tested prior to and at the completion of treatments on the K-D-K–Oseretsky Tests of Motor Development, the Cowell Social Adjustment Index, and the Cowell Personal Distance Scale. Although the motor performance of EMR subjects improved, Adams (1970) found the adapted program to be no more effective than the regular program in promoting motor development of EMR girls. Further, gains by the retarded were significantly greater than those made by intellectually normal youngsters regardless of program placement. The investigator also concluded that social adjustment among EMR girls appeared to be achieved better through participation in adapted physical education programs than through participation In regular physical education classes.

Chavez (1970) conducted a study to compare the effects of three types of physical education programs on the agility, balance, power, speed, and strength of 43 EMR boys. The performance of the subjects on the selected components of physical fitness was measured prior to and at the completion of six-week treatment programs conducted five days a week for 30 minutes a day. One group of subjects participated in activities related to the tested components of physical fitness, a second participated in activities related to the physical fitness components and game activities, and a third group participated in game activities. Chavez found no significant difference among the three types of programs in terms of changes in the components of physical fitness.

Nunley (1965) studied the effects of a 15-month physical activity program consisting of neuromuscular activities and modified exercises on the performance of 11 trainable mentally retarded (TMR) youngsters. The chronological ages of the subjects ranged from 9 to

11, and the mental age ranged from 4 to 6 years. The motor ability of the subjects was determined by a test developed by the author, which included items to measure basic developmental abilities, gross motor activities, fine motor function, coordination, and strength. The program included a variety of basic neuromuscular activities and modified exercises. After 15 months, gains were noted in strength, endurance, adjustment, and socialization. Unfortunately, as the author recognized, the study lacked controls, used a small sample, and lacked objective and scientific testing methods. The results of the study were very positive, however, and may serve as a basis for future investigations.

Funk (1971) studied the effect of a physical education program on the physical fitness and motor development of a group of children classified as trainable mentally retarded (TMR). The experimental group (N of 18) had a daily 30-minute planned physical education program for 58 consecutive school days. The control group (N of 18) had free play or teacher-directed recreational activity during this time. The program for the experimental group included balancing activities, running, jumping, crawling, throwing, catching, calisthenics, agility games, relays, and other similar activities. Tests included items of physical fitness from the Hayden Physical Fitness Test for the Mentally Retarded, the Special Fitness Test for the Mentally Retarded (straight arm hang, sit-up, shuttle run, standing long jump, and medicine ball throw) and the K-D-K–Oseretsky Tests of Motor Development. Significant improvement was found on the sit-up and the shuttle run. The author attributed failure to attain significant differences on other items to the types of activities that were included in the experimental program.

Goodwin (1970) designed a study to compare the effects of an individualized movement exploration program with the effects of a group-oriented physical education program on the physical fitness, IQ, and social maturity of TMR children aged 10 to 15. Subjects were tested prior to and upon completion of the treatments with the Hayden Physical Fitness Test and the Peabody Picture Vocabulary Test, and teachers provided information for the Vineland Social Maturity Scale on each of the 33 subjects. Three groups of 11 subjects were equated on the basis of chronological age, sex, and results of pretests. For ten weeks, Group I was exposed to a traditional physical education program, Group II was exposed to a movement exploration program, and Group III served as a control. Goodwin (1970) found that level of fitness of both experimental groups improved over that of the control group and that there was a significant difference in the physical fitness of the experimental subjects in favor of the traditional physical education program.

In addition to the studies previously discussed, several other studies that have been conducted to determine the effects of physical activities on the physical and motor performance of mentally retarded subjects deserve brief mention. Courtney (1972) found improvement in the dynamic balance and agility performance of EMR boys and girls after exposure to two types of training programs but found no improvement in static balance. Britt (1968) reported that a planned program of physical activities had significant effects on the balance and coordination of TMR boys and girls. Greenfell (1965) found that a structured physical education program had positive effects on the motor educability, physical fitness, and skill development of EMR boys and girls. Cavanaugh (1968) reported that EMR and minimally brain-damaged children showed significant improvement in selected components of motor development and physical fitness following participation in an organized physical education program.

SUMMARY

Research results indicate that both educable and trainable mentally retarded children are able to improve in physical fitness and motor ability as a result of organized and progressive programs of physical activity. Corder (1966), Corder (1969), Oliver (1958), Solomon and Pangle (1967), Rarick, Dobbins, and Broadhead (1976), Courtney (1972), Greenfell (1965), and Cavanaugh (1968) are among the investigators reporting positive changes in the physical proficiency of EMR subjects. Nunley (1965), Britt (1968), Goodwin (1970), and Funk (1971) found positive changes in the physical proficiency TMR subjects. Oliver (1958), Wright (1968), Adams (1970), Courtney (1972), Greenfell (1965), and Cavanaugh (1968) reported positive changes in the motor ability of EMR subjects. Nunley (1965) and Britt (1968) found positive changes on selected measures of motor ability of TMR subjects.

Children With Neurological and Neuromuscular Conditions

Healy (1957) conducted a study to compare the strength and range of motion developed by concentric and static programs of weight training for five boys afflicted with the spastic type of cerebral palsy. Exercises were administered over a period of eight weeks. Although no significant differences were found between the two techniques, the subjects improved significantly in strength and range of motion as a result of the exercises. In a similar study, Meditch (1961) found that athetoids improved significantly in forearm strength as a result of either a static or a concentric exercise program conducted for ten weeks but found no significant difference between the two techniques.

As part of her study, Wight (1937) investigated the effects of rhythmic training on the rhythmization of children identified as crippled and ranging from 57 to 143 months in age. Subjects in the study were receiving care at a home for convalescent crippled children in Chicago, Illinois. Almost all subjects admitted to the Home exhibit some form of disturbance in the skeletal structure of the body. There were four groups in the study. Two groups, having 13 subjects each and having been matched for chronological age, IQ, and rhythmization, served as experimental and control groups. A third group of 18 subjects, including all the subjects in the original matched experimental group plus unmatched subjects, served as a second experimental group. A fourth group of 17 subjects, including all the subjects in the original matched control group plus unmatched subjects, served as a second control group. For two months, the experimental subjects were given a regular program of rhythmic activities (a total of 18 classes) and the control groups were left to their usual routine. Wight (1937) found that rhythmization, as measured by the tests selected, is subject to improvement through both specific and general training. She noted that the spastic subjects showed surprising improvement as a result of such training.

Abramson and Rogoff (1952) studied the effects of an exercise regimen on 27 patients with muscular dystrophy. Subjects ranged in age from 6 to 20 years and included 10 patients still walking and 17 confined to wheelchairs. Patients were treated for a period of seven months by trained therapists three sessions a week for an hour each session. Muscle strength improved in 13 cases, was unchanged in 13, and showed barely noticeable deterioration in one case. In regard to contracture, 18 subjects improved, 7 remained the same, and none became worse. Two of the subjects in the study had no contractures to start with. It was noted that improvement was most rapid during the first eight to ten weeks of treatment.

Hoberman (1955) undertook a study to test the value of selected physical medicine and rehabilitation techniques for children with progressive muscular dystrophy. Subjects in the study included ten children aged 7 to 14 years with progressive muscular dystrophy. During the first four months, the subjects received only physical medicine and rehabilitation tests, instruction, and training. The physical training during this period was comprised of (1) 45 to 60 minutes of daily physical therapy consisting of passive and active-assistance stretching of tight and contracted areas, muscle reeducation and strengthening exercises, and mass movement exercises, (2) functional activities, (3) physical rehabilitation for 30 to 60 minutes daily, including mat exercises, bed and wheelchair activities, parallel bar exercises, gait ambulation, and elevation training, and (4) breathing exercises. As a result of this program, definite improvements were noted in the performance of daily living activities, vital capacity, endurance (to a lesser extent), and joint motion (with varying gains). No significant increase in muscle strength per se was found. Following this program, experimental drugs were administered. No definite improvement in strength, endurance, range of motion, or performance of daily activities could be attributed to the drugs. Hoberman (1955) concluded that neither muscle reeducation, strengthening exercise, nor activity performance can increase actual muscle strength in progressive muscular dystrophy patients. However, if properly motivated and not too severely disabled, these patients can improve performance of daily living activities and vital capacity.

Vignos, Spencer, and Archibald (1963) studied 27 patients with progressive muscle dystrophy to determine whether a comprehensive rehabilitation program could increase their duration of ambulation. Of the patients, 12 were in wheelchairs and 15 walked independently with long leg braces. The program included early diagnosis, close supervision of patients, a physical therapy program, and bracing for ambulation when independent walking was no longer possible. The physical therapy program emphasized passive stretching of flexion contractures about joints. It was found that the duration of ambulation from onset of symptoms could be increased from an average of 4.4 years to at least 8.7 years through a comprehensive rehabilitation program.

Dowben (1963) conducted a study to determine the effect of administering selected drugs to 37 patients of various ages with muscular dystrophy for periods ranging from 5 to 19 months. Nineteen of the patients suffered from pseudohypertrophic muscular dystrophy, three from the limb-girdle type, eight from the facioscapulohumeral type, and seven from myotonic dystrophy. All of the patients received vigorous physical therapy in the pretreatment period and during the period of drug administration. An increase in muscle strength occurred in eight patients (some of these had the facio-scapulo-humeral type). Three patients (all of whom had the progressive type) exhibited continued deterioration of muscle strength. The condition of the remaining 26 patients was essentially unchanged.

In a subsequent study, Fowler and his associates (1965) reevaluated the results obtained by Dowben. They treated 12 muscular dystrophy patients with drug therapy and exercise for a 12-month period and gave 6 children placebos for 6 months. These investigators found no significant improvement in muscle strength or working capacity. Further, marked decreases in strength were found in most of the children with the Duchenne type of muscular dystrophy. The investigators concluded that the drugs, used either alone or in combination, do not have therapeutic usefulness in the treatment of any of the most common forms of muscular dystrophy.

Vignos and Watkins (1966) studied the effect of a one-year maximum resistance exercise program on the muscular strength and functional abilities of 24 patients with muscular dystrophy. The program consisted of the following exercises: hip abduction, hip extension, knee extension, forward flexion of the arms, and sit-ups. Weights were used to offer active-assistance or active-resistance exercise as appropriate. In addition to measures of strength, the abilities to climb seven standard stairs, rise from a standard chair, rise from the floor, and walk a distance of 23 feet were assessed each month. Patients in this study spent approximately one half hour a day performing ten repetitions of each exercise for the first six months and one half hour three to five times per week for the next six months. Improvement in muscle strength occurred in all patients throughout the first four months regardless of the type of dystrophy. Subsequently, a plateau was reached that was maintained throughout the period of observation. Improvement in functional abilities was less than that seen in muscle strength. Patients with the limb-girdle and facio-scapulo-humeral types of muscular dystrophy derived greatest physical and functional benefit. Patients with the Duchenne type showed a slight decline in the amount of weight lifted at the end of one year; however, the decline was not significant, and in every case the amount of weight lifted at one year was greater than the initial amount of weight lifted. The authors felt that programs could be most effective if instituted early in the course of the disease.

SUMMARY

This section was intended to review research pertaining to the effects of school or recreation-type physical activity programs on the physical and motor performance of children with neurological and neuromuscular conditions. Although some studies involving physical therapy and remediation have been included in the review, no attempt has been made to include all such studies. The purpose of this review is to stress the developmental rather than the rehabilitative and the educational rather than the medical. Further, since the emphasis herein is child-oriented, research pertaining to the effects of training on the performance of adults has not generally been included. No research has been found pertaining to the effect of physical activity programs on children with epilepsy, poliomyelitis, or multiple sclerosis.

Although few in number, studies that have been conducted with cerebral palsied children indicate that they exhibit positive physical and motor gains as a result of physical and motor activity. Healy (1957) and Meditch (1961) have reported strength gains as a result of programs of exercise, and Wight (1937) has found gains in rhythmization through specific and general training.

Studies conducted to determine the effects of physical activity on the physical performance of patients with muscular dystrophy have yielded varying results. Abramson and Rogoff (1952), Dowben (1963), and Vignos and Watkins (1966) have reported positive improvement in strength as a result of their exercise programs. However, Hoberman (1955) and Fowler and his associates (1965) found no such gains. Vignos, Spencer, and Archibald (1963) reported that the duration of ambulation from onset of symptoms could be increased in patients with progressive muscle dystrophy, and Hoberman (1955) found improvement in the performance of daily living activities, vital capacity, endurance, and joint motion as a result of his rehabilitative program. It appears, then, that the benefit of physical activity may vary with the type and intensity of muscular dystrophy and the age at which programs are initiated. It also appears that physical activity, at best, tends to prolong muscular usefulness. It is quite evident that additional research is needed to fully understand the role of physical activity in treatment.

Children With Other Handicapping Conditions

ASTHMATIC CHILDREN

Franklin (1971) conducted a study to determine the relationship between participation in a physical conditioning program and changes in the pulmonary efficiency and aerobic capacity of asthmatic subjects aged 6 to 15. An experimental group of 13 subjects participated five days a week for four weeks in a program of physical conditioning, while a control group of 13 subjects adhered to their normal routine of daily activities. The author found that participation in a one-month program of physical conditioning contributed to a significant increase in aerobic capacity but not in pulmonary efficiency.

Hirt (1964) studied the effects of physical conditioning on 63 hospitalized patients with chronic asthma. Subjects ranged in age from 15 to 28 years. The 63 patients were separated into two groups: one group (N of 40) participated in the usual hospital activities but avoided excessive physical exercise, and the other group (N of 23) received two hours of strenuous physical exercise five times each week for three months. One hour of exercise consisted of weight resistance and one hour consisted of sports activity. The two groups were compared on first-second forced expired volume, ventilation (during maximum exercise), maximum oxygen consumption, and external work load. The group who had received physical exercise showed statistically significant changes in ventilation, maximum oxygen intake, and work load after three months. The control subjects showed no significant change either in maximum oxygen intake or ventilation but did significantly increase work load. The latter finding was not accounted for by the author. The author concluded that exercise does not seem detrimental to patients with severe asthma and that such patients respond very similarly to normal subjects exposed to physical training. It was also reported that the subjects suffered no exacerbation of their disease because of the physical activity.

Itkin and Nacman (1966) investigated the effects of exercise for two three-month periods on 39 adolescent and young adult inpatients with allergic asthma. During one period the subjects engaged in no strenuous exercise, and during the other period they performed specific conditioning exercises and athletic activities. The treatment consisted of one hour of calisthenics and one hour of planned sports activity each day five days per week for three months. These investigators reported that two of three patients improved in athletic ability as measured by treadmill performance, that three of four patients showed an increase in maximum oxygen uptake, that improvement in these values was preserved for at least three months, and that the condition of no patient who was able to walk on the treadmill for seven minutes was made consistently worse by exercise. No differences were found in the amount of medication required in the responses of males and females. These authors concluded that physical conditioning may be indicated for a larger number of subjects with asthma in order to increase the usefulness of their lives.

McElhenney and Peterson (1963) conducted a pilot study to determine whether a physical fitness program would decrease the physical and emotional handicaps of asthmatic children and to obtain evidence of the children's response to physical activities more strenuous than they had previously experienced. Subjects consisted of 20 boys aged 8 to 12 who had moderate to severe bronchial asthma. The program was conducted two times a week for four months. Tests were administered to assess psychological changes and changes in vital capacity. The program consisted of calisthenics, games of simple organization, relays, lead-up games, tumbling, weight training, and swimming. Subjects were also given basic breathing exercises. The authors reported no significant difference in psychological tests, a significant increase in vital capacity of 18 per cent, a 30 per cent reduction in the number and severity of asthmatic attacks, and an equivalent diminution in the need for symptomatic drug therapy.

Peterson and McElhenney (1965) followed the pilot program with a study to determine the effects of a physical fitness program on 20 boys ranging in age from 8 to 13 years who had moderate to severe bronchial asthma. Most subjects were considered substandard in capacity for physical activity. A total of 18 boys completed the eight-month program, during which subjects met for one hour three times per week. The program consisted of calisthenics, relays and games of simple organization, skills and lead-up games to team sports, graded stunts, self-testing activities, and tumbling. Data were collected relevant to physical fitness (50-yard dash, standing broad jump, sit-ups, softball throw, agility run, pull-ups, grip strength, and rope climb), vital capacity, and school attendance. Parental evaluations were analyzed to ascertain if an increase or decrease in the number of severity of attacks occurred, to determine exercise tolerance, and to discover changes in emotional stability. Additional data included teacher evaluation of school progress, results of psychological tests, and an allergist's evaluation of the number and severity of asthmatic attacks. There was no control group. The investigators found significant improvement in physical fitness (all items), significant improvement in vital capacity, and a decrease in school absence. In 16 of 18 cases, parents indicated a marked reduction in number and severity of their sons' asthmatic attacks. From a total of 16 reporting, 15 mothers noted that emotional upsets decreased. A total of 80 per cent of the classroom teachers said that the children had improved in acceptance by other children, had participated more fully in playground activities, and had shown improvement in emotional stability. Parents of seven subjects indicated that overall improvement was excellent, and parents of nine indicated that overall improvement was good.

Scherr and Frankel (1958) developed a physical conditioning program consisting of respiration exercises, general physical exercises, and confidence-building activities for asthmatic children. Specific activities included apparatus workouts with Roman rings, horizontal bars, medicine balls, and climbing ropes, swimming, tumbling, boxing, judo and self-defense activities, and diaphragmatic-assistive breathing exercises. The program was implemented with 25 asthmatic children (boys and girls) between the ages of 6 and 14. Although the results were subjective, the investigators reported that there was a loss of fear concerning asthmatic attacks, that the frequency and severity of asthmatic attacks were reduced, and that pulmonary functions were improved.

Seligman, Randel, and Stevens (1970) conducted a pilot project to study the effects of two conditioning programs designed to teach conscious relaxation, develop controlled breathing, increase chest and trunk mobility, and develop endurance. Eleven boys and girls with asthma completed the first program, and seven completed the second program. Each program was conducted for one and one-half hours a week for eight weeks. A third of each session was devoted to conscious relaxation and breathing during activity, a third to group games and relays, and a third to swimming and water play. Emphasis was placed on exhalation and active contraction of the abdominal wall. Exercises were used for mobilization and strengthening of the trunk, shoulder girdle, and lower extremities. Pre-tests and post-tests included assessment of vital capacity, expiratory capacity, chest mobility, and pulse rate after treadmill walking. Many of the children showed improvement in the variables studied, indicating that further study would be useful. However, the lack of a control group, the small number of subjects, the need for further data analysis, and the need for more sophisticated measurement of functional capacity inhibit further generalization.

CHILDREN WITH DIABETES MELLITUS

Larsson and associates (1962) studied the physical working capacity (PWC) of a group of 22 Swedish adolescent diabetic girls and compared their performances with those of a control group of 27 non-diabetic girls of the same age. The ages of the subjects ranged from 10 to 18 years of age. The investigators found that the PWC was slightly lower in the diabetic group and that the difference between the two groups was most evident in the 15 to 18 year age range. The investigators also studied the effects of a two-month program of intense physical activity and a strenuous one-week program on PWC. They found that PWC increased in the majority of diabetic patients as a result of training and that increases were most pronounced in girls 13 to 14 years of age who took part in hard training. A regular decrease of blood sugar during work and a significant correlation between the initial blood sugar values and the extent of blood sugar decrease was noted. Larsson and associates (1962) emphasized that the favorable effect of exercise was especially conspicuous in patients with a high blood sugar level.

Zankle and his associates (1957) conducted a preliminary study of 30 diabetic patients and a later study of 19 patients to determine the effects of supervised exercise on their physical fitness index (PFI) as determined by the Rogers Physical Fitness Test. Subjects were patients hospitalized at the Crile Veterans Administration Hospital. The second study involved nine patients who were given 15 minutes of exercise twice daily and ten control subjects who participated in alternate activities. The number of days of treatment ranged from 5 to 30, with a mean of 23 days. The investigators found that all but one patient who received exercise showed an increase in PFI and that the average increase for the nine patients was 29 per cent. The ten patients not receiving exercise decreased in PFI by 3.7 per cent. In the preliminary study conducted with 30 diabetic patients, patients showed an average increase of 19 per cent in PFI

Larsson and associates (1964) investigated the effects of a five-month physical activity program with step-by-step increases in intensity on selected physiological variables of six diabetic and six non-diabetic boys aged 15 to 19 years. At the end of the training period, the subjects took part in a cross-country ski run on three consecutive dqys. During the five-month training period, the subjects were given a joint training program consisting of rigorous physical activity. Exercise tests of maximum oxygen intake at submaximal and maximal workloads were made at regular intervals. The investigators found that diabetic boys had lower functioning capacity than non-diabetic control subjects at the beginning of the study. During training, however, maximum oxygen consumption as well as heart volume increased similarly and significantly in both groups. The investigators noted no outward effects of exhaustion. In the diabetic group, insufficient calorie supply and resultant hypoglycemia seemed to be an important factor in performing prolonged heavy work.

Engerbretson (1962) studied the effects of interval training on selected physiological parameters, insulin dosage, and measures of physical performance. Three diabetic young men serving as subjects followed a training routine for a period of six weeks. Engerbretson reported that the subjects decreased their adipose tissue and increased their motor and cardiovascular fitness. Engerbretson (1970) conducted another study to determine the effect of physical conditioning on the regulation of diabetes mellitus. Five diabetic young men 17 to 21 years of age who were receiving insulin served as subjects and exercised for 14 weeks. The Workload–170 (WL–170), mile run, and maximum oxygen intake were selected as measures of physical fitness and were administered before and after the physical conditioning program. Engerbretson found minor changes in average body weight, body density, and sum of 10 skinfolds or percentage of body fat. Maximum oxygen intake and WL–170 increased and mile run time decreased following physical exercise.

SUMMARY

The purpose of this section was to review the effects of physical and motor training on the physical and motor performances of children with diabetes, asthma, cystic fibrosis, and cardiopathic handicaps. However, this author has found no studies pertaining to the effects of recreation or school-type physical activity programs on the performance of children with cystic fibrosis, rheumatic fever, or congenital heart defects. In regard to cardiopathic handicaps, many studies have been conducted with adult subjects and generally present data indicating the value of appropriately administered programs of physical activity. Larsson and associates (1962), Zankle and associates (1957), Larsson and associates (1964), and Engerbretson (1962, 1970) have demonstrated that programs of physical activity have yielded positive changes in physical and physiological performance of diabetic subjects. Studies by Franklin (1971), Hirt (1964), Itkin and Nacman (1966), McElhenney and Peterson (1963), Peterson and McElhenney (1965), Scherr and Frankel (1958), and Seligman, Randel, and Stevens (1970) indicate that fitness, vital capacity, and certain other pulmonary functions of asthmatic subjects may be improved through physical activity programs.

The Effects of Perceptual-Motor Training

Several studies have been conducted to examine the effects of perceptual-motor programming on perceptual-motor abilities and various measures of academic and intellectual ability. Painter (1966) investigated the effect of a rhythmic and sensory motor activity program on the perceptual-motor spatial abilities of kindergarten children. She divided the 20 lowest functioning children in a normal kindergarten class into an experimental group (N of 10) and a control group (N of 10). The experimental group was given a carefully sequenced program based on the theories of Barsch and Kephart for 20 half-hour training sessions extending over a period of seven weeks at a frequency of three times a week. Painter reported significant changes in measurements of perceptual-motor integration, body image, and psycholinguistic abilities. However, this was considered a pilot study, since the number of subjects involved was small and equal time was not spent with the control group.

Chansky (1963) explored the effectiveness of perceptual training on achievement levels and psychometrically measured intelligence of educable mentally retarded (EMR) children aged 8 to 11. Subjects were assigned three groups of 13 subjects each. The first experimental group received ten weekly perceptual training sessions on an individual basis for 45 minutes to an hour, and the second experimental group received essentially the same training in a group setting. The control group received no planned perceptual training. Tests administered included the Wechsler Intelligence Scale for Children (WISC), the Benton Visual Retention Test (BVR), and the California Achievement Test (CAT). Chansky reported that EMR children who were trained to make discriminations, to organize, to perform left and right orientation, and to make inferences improved in measured achievement and intelligence.

Talkington (1968) investigated the effects of three months of perceptual training with the Frostig-Horne materials (1964b) on the performance of children as measured by the Developmental Test of Visual Perception (Frostig, et al., 1964c). The study included 100 severely retarded subjects (age range 84 to 220 months, IQ range 17 to 48) equally divided into a control group and an experimental group. The experimental group received perceptual training for one hour daily five days a week for three months, and the control group participated in pre-school classroom activities. The experimental group evidenced significantly greater test-retest gains in all five areas of the DTVP. The effect that such training has on skills necessary for academic progress was not determined in this study.

Haring and Stables (1966) investigated the effects of gross motor development on the visual perception and eye-hand coordination of 24 EMR children aged 7 to 15. The subjects were divided into an experimental group (N of 13) and a control group (N of 11). The control group received the normal structured pattern of class work without special emphasis on motor development, and the experimental group received the same class work with special training in gross motor coordination and visual perception. Kephart's Perceptual Survey Rating Scale was used for testing, and Kephart-type activities were conducted to strengthen the subjects' weaknesses. The program was conducted for 30 minutes a day five days a week for seven months. Tests were given before treatment, after treatment, and again four months after treatment ended. Significant differences in the mean gain scores of the experimental group compared to the mean gain scores of the control group were found in the post-test, and the gains remained significant for the experimental group on the follow-up test.

Davis (1973) investigated the effects of a perceptually oriented physical education program on the perceptual-motor ability and academic ability of children in kindergarten and first grade. Three classes of kindergarten and first grade children were each randomly divided into four groups. Three of the groups received large amounts of perceptually oriented physical education training, and the fourth group served as a control and received no physical education. The training program was conducted for 15 weeks for both grade levels. The ABC Inventory and the Dayton Sensory Motor Awareness Survey were used to evaluate kindergarten children, and the Boehm Test of Basic Concepts and the Purdue Perceptual Motor Survey were used to evaluate first-grade children. Davis found correlation coefficients of $r = .61$ and $r = .09$ between academic ability and perceptual-motor ability of kindergarten and first-grade children, respectively. No significant difference in the results of the treatment was found in the academic or perceptual-motor abilities of kindergarten children. No significant difference was found among first-grade groups in academic ability following the perceptually oriented physical education program. A significant difference in perceptual-motor ability was found between the three first-grade experimental groups and the control group in favor of the experimental groups. The authors indicated that perceptually oriented physical education seems to be of some value in enhancing perceptual-motor ability at the first-grade level.

In his doctoral research, August (1969) examined the effect of a physical education program on reading readiness, visual perception, and perceptual-motor development in normal kindergarten children. The study consisted of six experimental groups and six control groups consisting of 20 subjects each. All subjects received 36 sessions of physical education; however, the program of the experimental group included laterality and directionality skills. Pre-tests and post-tests included Form A of the Metropolitan Readiness Test, the Developmental Test of Visual Perception, and the Purdue Perceptual Motor Survey. Although no significant improvement was found in reading readiness, the experimental subjects showed significant improvement in visual perception and perceptual-motor development. Changes in perceptual-motor performance did not correlate significantly with changes in reading readiness and visual perception.

In an experimental study, Bieger (1974) compared the reading achievements of an experimental group (N of 25) receiving perceptual training plus remedial reading instruction with a control group (N of 23) receiving only remedial reading instruction over a seven-month period. Subjects included second-grade and third-grade non-readers from poverty areas who were judged to have visual-perceptual deficiencies and assumed to have only a reading disability. Children in the program attended one-hour sessions, two times a week if they were bussed and four times a week sessions if they were not bussed. The control group followed a remedial program including activities in language and auditory perception as needed — researchers used whatever method seemed to work with the child, such as linguistic approach or phonics, programmed instruction, tapes, film strips, or records — but basal readers and visual-perceptual training materials were not used. The experimental subjects received visual-perceptual training activities for 30 minutes during each one-hour session. The rest of their session was the same as that for the control group. The programs were implemented by educational assistants under the direct supervision of a professional teacher. Although there was no significant difference between the groups in reading, both groups showed significant improvement in reading. Control subjects gained eight months in reading achievement, and experimental subjects gained six months. The experimental group improved significantly on the DTVP, and the control group did not.

Lipton (1970) conducted a program of perceptual-motor development and examined its effects on visual perception and reading readiness of first-grade children. Two groups were exposed to a perceptual-motor program for 12 weeks, and two other groups took part in a conventional physical education program. The four classes involved in the study were divided randomly into control and experimental groups. The 92 subjects were evaluated in perceptual-motor development (Purdue Perceptual Motor Survey), visual perception (Frostig Developmental Test of Visual Perception), and reading readiness (Metropolitan Readiness Test) prior to and immediately following the program. The experimental program included balance, locomotor, coordination, spatial awareness, tactual-dynamic, and rhythmic activities. Two-way ANOV, using difference scores (pre-test and post-test), was used to analyze gains among classes. Lipton found that the experimental physical education program, which emphasized directionality of movement, produced significantly greater (.01 level) gains in perceptual-motor development, visual perception, and reading readiness than the conventional curriculum, which did not have this emphasis.

DeGroat (1971) conducted a study to determine the effects of a perceptual-motor skills program based on Getman's theories on the reading ability of first-grade children. During the first semester of an academic year, two classes of first-grade students participated in a traditional physical education program. During the second semester, the experimental class was given perceptual-motor skills training, and the control group continued with the traditional physical education program. Pre-test and post-test scores of both groups on Scott Foresman and Company reading tests were compared. Using analysis of covariance, the researchers found a significant difference between the reading scores in favor of the experimental group.

McCormick and his associates (1968) conducted a study to determine whether slow-learning or otherwise underachieving children would improve in reading achievement as a result of perceptual-motor training. In this study, 42 underachieving first-grade children matched for age, sex, IQ, and Lee-Clark reading grade level were randomly assigned to three groups. One group participated in sequenced perceptual-motor activities (crawling, walking, balancing, rope jumping, gross motor activities, and activities to increase attention span). The second group, serving as a control group for extra attention and extra activity, performed exercises from the regular physical education curriculum (simple games, dodge ball, jump rope, throwing and catching, locomotor activities, rhythms, and relays). The third group served as a control group, receiving no extra training, activity, or attention. For seven weeks, the first two groups met for two 45-minute sessions per week prior to the beginning of the regular school day. The Lee-Clark Reading test, Primer, Form A was given prior to the commencement of training, and Form B was given at the conclusion of training. The experimental group was found to have made statistically significant gains, while the other two groups had made no such gains. However, an analysis of covariance employed to compare the groups did not yield significant results.

Thomas and associates (1975) completed a study to assess the effects of a specifically designed perceptual-motor training program on the level of perceptual-motor development, self-concept, and academic ability of kindergarten children. The 40 children were randomly assigned to an experimental group (N of 20) and a control group (N of 20). Each group received the same kindergarten program, except that the experimental group was exposed to a specifically designed perceptual-motor program for 30 minutes daily for five months, and the control group was permitted free play for 30 minutes daily. The treatment was administered in a "station" plan, with aides at each station. Subjects worked at all stations but were free to work repeatedly on tasks they enjoyed and were encouraged to work at stations where they experienced difficulty. Children were administered a Shape-O Ball Test, a stabilometer test for dynamic balance, an Otis-Lennon Mental Ability Test, and an adapted form of the Parker Scale (self-concept). In addition, teachers rated the academic abilities of the children. The investigators concluded that a program of perceptual-motor training was useful for developing perceptual-motor skills but that the results tended to negate any perceptual-motor theory that claimed transfer from perceptual-motor tasks to academic performance.

O'Connor (1968) designed a study for his doctoral degree to investigate the effects of physical activities on the development of motor ability, perceptual ability, and academic achievement of first-grade children. The subjects, 59 boys and 64 girls, were placed in either an experimental group or a control group. Measures of motor ability, the Perceptual Forms Test, the Metropolitan Reading and Achievement Tests, and the Harris test of Lateral Dominance were administered. In addition, teachers rated the reading and academic ability of the children. The control group received a regular physical education program, and the experimental group received a six-month training program of activities based on Kephart's theory. Significant differences were found on a number of motor abilities, and the experimental group significantly exceeded the control group on measures of internal awareness. No significant difference between the groups was found on the Metropolitan Achievement Test, in teacher ratings of reading ability, or in overall academic ability. O'Connor concluded that changes in gross motor ability do not necessarily affect the perceptual or academic ability of the average first-grade child. Slacks (1969), with a design similar to that employed by O'Connor, reported no significant difference on a Perceptual Forms Test and Metropolitan Tests between children exposed to a program based on Kephart's theory and those participating in a traditional physical education program. This program was conducted with first-grade pupils over a six-month training period.

Fretz, Johnson and Johnson (1969) designed a study to determine whether test scores of children enrolled in an eight-week physical development clinic program would show significantly greater improvement from pre-clinic to post-clinic testing than those of a control group of similar children not enrolled in the clinic. Subjects included 53 children enrolled in the program and 34 children on a "waiting list." All subjects were male, presumably slow in perceptual-motor development, and between the ages of 5 and 11. The dependent variables included intelligence (WISC), perceptual-motor development (Frostig Developmental Test of Visual Perception and Bender-Gestalt Test), and kinesthetic and tactual perception skills (Southern California Kinesthesia and Tactile Perception Test). The program was designed to develop body awareness, basic skills, and efficiency, stamina, and power of the body. It included gymnasium activities, conditioning and coordination exercises, games, and modified sports. The experimental group made significant improvements in all five parts of the Frostig and Bender Gestalt tests. The control groups showed no significant improvement in any of the Frostig subtests and actually showed a significant decrease in memory in the Figure-Ground subtest and the Bender-Gestalt test. The experimental group showed significant improvement in performance IQ, whereas the control group showed significant improvement on verbal IQ. No significant improvement was found in kinesthetic and tactile perception skills. In fact, both experimental and control groups showed significant decrease in some of these categories.

Fisher (1971) conducted a study with EMR children to test the effectiveness of a structured program of perceptual-motor training following

Kephart's principles. The 54 EMR children were randomly assigned to three groups. Group I received an individualized, structured program of perceptual-motor training twice a week for four and one half months. Group II met with the trainer but played table games. Group III maintained its normal classroom schedule. The Perceptual Motor Survey (PMS) and WISC were given directly before and after the treatment. The Wide Range Achievement Test (WRAT) and Stanford Achievement Test (SAT) were given directly prior to and two months following the treatment. Using analysis of covariance techniques, the researchers found no significant difference among the three groups on any of the tests of perceptual-motor status, intelligence, or achievement. However, for children under 10 years, there was a significant difference between the training group and the control group in favor of the training group on total score on the PMS. All three groups demonstrated significant improvement from pre-test to post-test scores on PMS and achievement tests. Fisher indicated that although there is some evidence that a short-term program of training in perceptual-motor abilities may be effective in improving the perceptual-motor performance of EMR children younger than 10, there is no evidence that such short-term training affects the intellectual functioning or the academic achievement of such children.

Buckland and Balow (1973) conducted a study to determine the effect of visual-perceptual training on the perceptual readiness and word recognition skills of first-grade children judged to have low readiness. An experimental group consisting of 88 subjects worked on Frostig worksheets, and a control group consisting of 78 subjects listened to stories for 15 minutes a day for 40 consecutive school days. All subjects were in the lower half of their classes in reading status. No significant difference was found between the groups. The authors noted that some children made particularly good gains; however, tests of significance applied in the study were based on mean scores. They indicated that the visual perception worksheets might be better used for selected pupils than for groups of pupils who are simply low in readiness.

Chasey and Wyrick (1970) investigated the effect of a gross motor development program on form perception skills of EMR children. Seven perceptual forms of the Winter Haven Perceptual Forms Test (PFT) were administered to 20 EMR children before and after they participated in a 15-week physical development program and to 12 EMR children not enrolled in the program. Subjects ranged in age from 73 months to 146 months and in IQ from 50 to 85 as measured by the Stanford-Binet Intelligence Scale, Form L-M. A university student studying physical education was assigned to three or four subjects for the entire 15-week program. The program, conducted five days a week for one hour a day, consisted of playground activities, conditioning and coordination exercises, gymnastics, games, and modified sports. Selection of activities was based on the needs of the individuals. The control subjects received no formal physical education instruction but did participate in free play during recreational periods. The investigators reported that a developmental program of gross motor activity appears to have no effect on a mentally retarded child's ability to perceive and copy geometric forms. The authors indicated that the results of the study lend support to the theory of the specificity of motor performance.

Alley and Carr (1968) investigated the effects of a two-month training program of sensory-motor activities on sensory-motor abilities (using total score on the Lincoln-Oseretsky Motor Development Scale and scores on the Purdue Perceptual-Motor Survey), visual perception (various measures including total raw scores on the Frostig DTVP), and concept formation tasks (total raw score on the Illinois Test for Psycholinguistic Abilities). A total of 56 EMR children were divided into two age-matched, sex-paired groups (N of 28). Both groups were involved in physical education, but the experimental group engaged in sensory-motor activities and the control group engaged in traditional special education classroom activities that did not involve gross motor activities. Sensory-motor activities based on Kephart's theory and additional activities designed by the investigators, graduated in difficulty, were utilized. The experimental group met for 30 minutes each day with proficient and certified instructors. No significant differences between the groups were found in the study.

Belmont, Flegenheimer, and Birch (1973) compared the effects of seven months of perceptual-motor training and remedial instruction on the reading ability of beginning poor readers. Matched groups of poor readers with 16 subjects in each were provided with supplementary perceptual-motor training or remedial instruction in addition to regular first-grade classroom instruction. The perceptual-motor group received a program based on Frostig and Kephart activities, and the remedial reading group received a wide variety of sequenced activities designed to reinforce attained reading skills. Tests administered included the Metropolitan Achievement Test, the Wide Range Achievement Test, the Gates-MacGinitie Reading Test, and the Gates-McKillop Reading Diagnostic Test. Both groups made equivalent advances in reading level; however, no significant difference was found between them.

McBeath (1966) studied the effects of a modified Frostig program and physical activities based on Kephart's theory on the reading readiness of kindergarten pupils who scored below the 25th percentile on the Frostig tests of visual perception. After 64 days, none of three experimental groups performed better than the control group.

Allan, Dickman and Haupt (1966) investigated the effects of one semester of training with Frostig-Horne materials for approximately one hour daily on skills evaluated by the Frostig Developmental Test of Visual Perception (Frostig, LeFever, and Whittlesey, 1966). An experimental group of EMR pupils (N of 10) received the training, and a control group of EMR pupils (N of 6) participated in their usual school activities. Since both groups improved in three subtests, the scores were combined into a single test score. Results showed that the improvement made by the experimental group was significantly greater than that made by the control group. Since this was a pilot study, the investigators simply stated that the results justified further research.

Rosen (1966) investigated the effects of perceptual training on the performance of first-grade children on selected measures of reading achievement. A total of 12 experimental classes were exposed to a 29-day adaptation of the Frostig program for 30 minutes per day, and 13 control classrooms added comparable time to regular reading instruction. Rosen did not find significant improvement in reading scores, but differences in reading achievement between experimental boys initially classified as "low perceivers" and comparable control subjects strongly suggest the need for follow-up research efforts with Frostig materials.

Pre-testing and post-testing of experimental and control groups revealed that the experimental first-grade classes had indeed improved in visual-perceptual skills as measured by the Frostig tests but that there was no concomitant influence on their reading skills.

Several investigations have been conducted to study the relationship among perceptual, reading, and intellectual abilities. In regard to reading achievement, Chang and Chang (1967) reported a significant but low-level relationship between visual-motor-perceptual scores and reading achievement of superior second-grade children but not of superior third-grade children. These authors suggest that superior pupils may have developed other skills to compensate for average visual-motor abilities. Cobb, Chissom, and Davis (1975) reported low-level positive relationships between perceptual-motor abilities and academic abilities of children in kindergarten and the first two grades. Greenberg and Alshan (1974) found that black children classified as low achievers made significantly more errors than black children classified as high achievers on the Bender motor-Gestalt test. Trussell (1969) found low or nonsignificant correlations between performance scores in reading achievement, the Frostig DTVP, the Lincoln-Oseretsky Motor Development Scale, and two perceptual-motor tasks. Correlations were not high enough for reliable prediction of one variable from another. Results of factor analysis tended to indicate that reading development, perceptual development, and motor development are more likely to exhibit independence than association with each other, according to Trussell. Olsen (1966) found some significant but low-level relationships between visual perception and academic achievement but generally reported nonsignificant relationships of little predictive value. He found that the correlation between poor word recognition and figure-ground perception was not significant, that form constancy has little predictive value, and that the correlation between scores on the Position in Space Subtest of the Frostig DTVP and the reversing of words was .386 (significant at the .01 level). The latter finding supports Frostig's notion that children who reverse letters or rotate words have difficulty in perceiving position in space. Davis (1973) found correlation coefficients of $r = .61$ for kindergarten children and $r = .09$ for first-grade children between academic ability and perceptual-motor ability.

In regard to the relationship of visual-perceptual abilities of children to intelligence, Allen, Haupt, and Jones (1965) reported that EMR "high perceivers" scored significantly better in the WISC than EMR "low perceivers." Chang and Chang (1967) found significant correlations (r ranged from .46 to .50) between Bender-Gestalt and WISC scores of pupils judged to have superior ability.

Argenti (1968) investigated the effects of systemic motor training on selected perceptual-motor attributes of mentally retarded children. The sample included 31 boys and 8 girls aged 8 through 14 with IQ ranging from 51 to 87. One group of retarded subjects received systemic motor training, the second participated in free play consisting of (gross motor) activities, and a third performed library and study activities. Tests were administered prior to and at the completion of a 15-week experimental period. Measures of body perception, gross agility, balance, locomotor agility, ball-throwing skill, and ball tracking were determined. Argenti reported that the perceptual-motor attributes studied significantly improved as a result of the systematic motor training program, that free play activities were as effective as the systematic motor training program in developing perceptual-motor attributes, and that limited activity compared unfavorably with the systematic motor training program in developing the perceptual-motor attributes of mentally retarded subjects. Argenti also noted a marked rise in the improvement of the motor training group, compared with a gradual rise in the improvement of the free play group.

Summary

It is clear that research conducted in applied settings has been quite diversified. One concern of the research has been whether perceptually oriented programs significantly increase perceptual abilities. Painter (1966), August (1969), Lipton (1970), Thomas and associates (1975), O'Connor (1967), Slacks (1969), Rosen (1966), and Davis (1973) found improvement with primary grade youngsters in their studies. Talkington (1968), Haring and Stables (1966), Bieger (1974), Fretz, Johnson, and Johnson (1969), Fisher (1971), Argenti (1968), and Allen, Dickman, and Haupt (1966) have reported success with EMR children, children from poverty areas, low achievers, perceptually handicapped youngsters, or children classified as low in reading readiness. Studies by Buckland and Balow (1973), Chasey and Wyrick (1970), and Alley and Carr (1968), however, found no significant improvement in perceptual abilities as a result of the training programs they implemented.

An analysis of the research indicates that improvement in perceptual-motor skills does not necessarily transfer to improvement in reading readiness, academic achievement, or intelligence test scores. In regard to reading readiness and academic achievement, Lipton (1970), Painter (1966), and DeGroat (1971) reported training success with normal youngsters, and Chansky (1963) and McCormick and associates (1968) found some success with young retardates and underachieving youngsters, respectively. In addition, Chang and Chang (1967), Davis (1973), Cobb, Chissom, and Davis (1975), and Greenberg and Alshan (1974) reported evidence supporting a relationship between perceptual and academic abilities. However, Thomas and associates (1975), O'Connor (1968), and Slacks (1969) found no evidence of such a relationship with normal youngsters; Fisher (1971), Buckland and Balow (1973), Rosen (1966), Belmont, Flegenheimer, and Birch (1973), and McBeath (1966) report the same results with children with low readiness scores, poor readers, or retarded youngsters. It should be noted that although Buckland and Balow (1973) did not report significant differences in group mean scores, they noted particularly good gains by some children and suggested that the visual-perceptual work sheets might be better used for selected individuals rather than for groups of pupils simply low in readiness. Also, Belmont, Flegenheimer, and Birch (1973) found significant improvement in reading by a group who had received perceptual training, but the improvement was not significantly better than that of a group receiving remedial reading instruction. Trussell (1969) and Olson (1966) report data indicating little or no relationship between perceptual-motor and academic abilities.

In regard to perceptual abilities and scores on intelligence tests,

Allen, Haupt, and Jones (1965) found a significant relationship between perceptual abilities and intelligence scores of EMR pupils. Fretz, Johnson, and Johnson (1969) reported that perceptually handicapped children made significant improvements in performance IQ as a result of a movement-oriented program, and Chansky (1963) found that EMR subjects made significant improvement in intelligence scores as a result of perceptual training. Fisher (1971), however, reported that a perceptual-motor training program with EMR pupils had no effect on intelligence scores. An analysis of these studies and others indicate that although gains in intelligence scores have occurred and relationships between perceptual training and improvement in IQ scores have been noted, the evidence does not conclusively establish that gains in intelligence scores are the result of perceptual-motor programs.

Various approaches have been taken to examine perceptual-motor theories and the effects of perceptual-motor development on academic and intellectual abilities. Of particular concern here is the success that has been attained in implementation of the principles of perceptual-motor development in applied settings. Although these investigations have limited value in supporting or refuting theories, they do shed light on the effectiveness of implementing these theories. After reviewing the research, the one thing that is most clear is that most investigations have been less than precise. The common problems noted include: (1) failure to employ control groups, (2) conducting studies with treatment periods for brief periods of time, (3) placing children in experimental groups without ascertaining if such pupils require special attention in perceptual areas or without regard to the cause of perceptual problems, (4) data analysis on the basis of mean scores, (5) the use of graduate students, aides, or other individuals with questionable expertise for test administration or program implementation, (6) giving little attention to the sequencing of treatment experiences, and (7) using too few subjects. In addition, studies presumably testing concepts emerging from Piagetian theory, which has a non-psychometric orientation, have employed psychometric tests of intelligence as criteria. Many of the studies have used perceptual-motor tests that fail to adequately discriminate abilities, such as the Purdue Perceptual Motor Survey.

In view of these problems, any implications drawn from the research must be tentative. However, on the basis of the research discussed above and other research not cited, the author feels that the following generalizations are warranted:

1. Perceptual-motor abilities, as measured by various perceptual-motor tests, may be enhanced by carefully sequenced programs.
2. Visual-perceptual activities are not the cause of all reading difficulties or all low scores in psychometric intelligence tests.
3. Improvement in perceptual abilities does not necessarily lead to improvement in academic success or in psychometric intelligence test scores.
4. Pupils low in perceptual-motor ability may be successful in academic pursuits.
5. The belief that sensory-motor or perceptual-motor experiences serve as the basis for academic and intellectual measures has not been conclusively demonstrated.

Movement Experiences and Academic Achievement

Although use of the motor activity learning medium (MALM) for the attainment of academic concepts has been advocated in various forms for many years, the majority of the research conducted to examine the effectiveness of the approach has been conducted only in the past two decades. Much of this research has been done by James Humphrey and his students or by Bryant J. Cratty and his associates. In the following pages, studies pertaining to the use of movement experiences for the attainment of academic concepts are described. They are presented in chronological order in the four academic areas of science, number concepts, language arts concepts, and reading. In the section following the description of studies, the research is summarized and generalizations are suggested.

Science Concepts

Ison (1961) compared the use of physical education activities as a learning medium with traditional methods in the development of selected fifth-grade level science concepts. In this study, one group of fifth-grade students was taught nine science concepts by the traditional method, and another group was taught nine other science concepts through the motor learning method. All 18 science concepts were matched and were taught by two fifth-grade teachers in separate schools. One period was used for each concept, and the two methods by which the concepts were developed were alternated. Post-test analysis revealed no significant difference between the two methods. However, it was observed that both classes of the motor learning group improved significantly in test scores, whereas only one of the two classes using the traditional method improved significantly. It was concluded that both methods can provide solid learning experiences for the selected science concepts.

Humphrey (1966) reported the results of two pilot studies designed to examine the effectiveness of the MALM on the attainment of science concepts. In one study, an analysis of pre-test and post-test data revealed that fourth-grade children answered a greater number of questions about science concepts after the concepts were developed through a motor activity learning medium. In the other study, Humphrey (1966) reported that post-test scores of 24 sixth-grade pupils on science concepts dealing with a unit on energy were significantly higher than pre-test scores. The treatment was the teaching of concepts through the motor activity learning medium. Although children did improve in these studies and Humphrey was encouraged by the results, the lack of a control group prohibits attributing the improvement to the treatment.

Werner (1971) investigated the effects of integrating physical education with selected science concepts on science knowledge and selected physical performance skills. Subjects in the study consisted of 180 boys and girls in the fourth, fifth, and sixth grades. The subjects were pretested and post-tested on nine criterion variables: the softball throw for distance, the soccer kick for distance, the playground ball wall pass, the McDonald Soccer Test, the standing long jump, the wall rebound test, the shuttle run test, the work test, and a written science knowledge test. The four science concepts integrated with physical education were Newton's first and third laws of motion, work, and levers. An experimental group participated in a seven-week classroom learning program three times a week for 40 minutes per session and a physical education program twice a week in which the physical education teacher integrated science concepts. The control group participated in the same program with the exception that no integration of science concepts was conducted by the physical education teacher. Significant differences were generally found between pre-test and post-test scores. In addition, significant differences were found favoring the experimental group after the treatment in all but the soccer kick for distance. The results of the study supported the contentions that it is advantageous to learn about science concepts through integration with physical education and that performance in physical skills may be enhanced by integrating science concepts with physical education.

Prager (1968) examined the use of physical education activities in the reinforcement of certain first-grade level science concepts. The 23 first-grade subjects were pre-tested on a science unit dealing with simple machines and were placed into matched experimental and control groups based on the results of the test. Using traditional procedures, the regular classroom teacher then taught eight science lessons to the entire class. After each lesson, the physical education teacher reinforced concepts through various kinds of physical education activities with the experimental group (N of 11). The control group (N of 12) engaged in enjoyable activities that were not science-related after each lesson with the classroom teacher. After a two-week period, the children were re-tested. The experimental group performed significantly better than the control group; the experimental group gained significantly, while the control group did not. Prager (1974) replicated his earlier study and obtained essentially the same results.

Humphrey (1972) conducted a study to compare the effect of using physical education activities with that of using traditional methods of developing science concepts in slow-learning fifth-grade children. Two groups of ten children each were equated on the basis of pre-test scores on ten science concepts. One group was designated as the physical education group (IQ range of 74 to 89, mean IQ of 85), and the second group was designated as the traditional group (IQ range of 72 to 90, mean IQ of 83). Both groups were taught by the same teacher, but the physical education group was taught through motor activity learning and the other through traditional procedures. Both groups were taught over a two-week period. Immediately after this period and again three months later, the children were tested. The results indicated a significant difference in favor of the physical education group in both the post-test and the extended interval test. On the basis of differences in test scores, Humphrey concluded that the children in the physical education group learned and retained significantly more than the traditional group.

Number Concepts

Humphrey (1966b) reported encouraging results in a pilot study in which the medium of active games was utilized for the learning of number concepts by first-grade boys and girls. From 35 first-grade children pre-tested on eight number concepts, 10 boys and 10 girls were matched and taught number concepts through the active game medium. Eight active games that involved number concepts and were appropriate for first-grade pupils were selected as the treatment. Comparisons of pre-test, and post-test scores were evaluated using the standard error of the mean difference and the t-ratio. There was a significant gain by the subjects and a tendency for boys to score higher than girls. Unfortunately, the lack of adequate experimental controls prohibited the unequivocal conclusion that results were attributable to the treatment.

Crist (1968) compared three methods of teaching time-telling concepts at the third-grade level. Treatment A consisted of instruction using a developmental-meaningful approach. Treatment B consisted of instruction using the drill approach. Treatment C consisted of instruction using the active game technique. In treatment C, motor activities were played on a 12-foot clock painted on the playground. All lessons were taught in ten teaching days, and all teachers were required to teach each lesson in 20-minute periods. Two parallel forms of a performance test in time-telling concepts were constructed and used as criterion measures in this study. Crist found no significant differences among the three techniques.

Although not all the games she used involved gross motor movements, Ross (1970) examined the use of games as a method of incidentally learning number concepts. An experimental group of 20 EMR children participated in a game program in which the intentional learning was general game skills and the incidental learning was basic number concepts. At the conclusion of a nine-month-period, the experimental group had improved more than the control group in knowledge of basic number concepts (Number Knowledge Test) and on general game skills (General Game Skills Test). Subjects in the study ranged in chronological age from 53 to 119 months, in IQ from 51 to 79, and in mental age from 37 to 87 months. Table reach, card, guessing, board, and active running games were included in the treatment for the experimental group. The investigator suggested that results were due to social facilitation, attention-directing variables, and consistent responding.

Language Arts Concepts

Humphrey conducted two studies on the use of motor activity learning medium in the development of language arts concepts. In a pilot study investigation, Humphrey (1962) explored the extent to which selected language arts concepts could be developed by third-grade children. The 23 subjects were pre-tested and post-tested on eight language arts concepts. Eight active games involving language arts concepts were taught to the children over a two-week period. In every case, there was a gain in raw scores between the first and second test, and the difference for the group was significant at the .01 level. The test-retest reliability coefficient was .73. On the basis of his research, Humphrey indicated that his approach facilitated teaching as well as learning. He noted that some concepts could be developed better through the physical education learning medium than through any other teaching procedure known to the teacher involved. He also noted better retention of concepts and a high positive reaction in the pupils. However, the lack of a control group prohibited attributing results to the treatment.

As a follow-up to the previous study, Humphrey (1965b) compared the use of active games and of language workbook exercises as learning media in the development of language and understandings. The 20 third-grade subjects were placed in two matched groups. One group was taught through active games and the other through language workbook exercises. Both groups were taught by the same teacher. All subjects were pre-tested and post-tested on 10 language and understanding concepts with 10 items for each concept for a total of 100 test items. An example of an active game that was modified to develop language arts concepts was Crows and Cranes. Instead of responding to the words "crows" and "cranes," the pupils had to appropriately react to and distinguish words spelled with a *c* or *s*. Both groups showed significant improvement from pre-test to post-test. The Wicoxen signed rank test of difference was applied to post-test scores of both groups and indicated significant improvement at the .05 level in favor of the active games group. Eight of the children in the active games group had a greater percentage of difference in gain than their counterparts, and two children in the language workbook group had a greater percentage of difference in gain. Humphrey concluded that either medium produced improvement but that the active games medium produced greater changes.

Penman, Christopher, and Wood (1977) compared the effectiveness of learning capitalization and punctuation skills through active games, passive games, and traditional methods. Two third-grade classes were taught these language arts skills using passive and active games over a four-week period. Their performance was compared to a third class (control) from the same district which was taught in the traditional manner for the same period. Pre-tests and post-tests utilized different forms and levels of the Iowa Test of Basic Skills, Language Arts. Post-test scores were analyzed using analysis of covariance with the pre-test scores as the covariates. The investigators found that, in regard to capitalization, the class taught through active games learned a significantly greater amount than either the class taught through passive games or the control class. No significant difference was found between the passive games class and the control class. In regard to punctuation, it was found that the active games class scored significantly better than the other two groups and that the passive games class performed significantly better than the control class. In a second post-test six months later, there was no significant difference in capitalization skills. For punctuation, there was a significant mean difference for the second post-test; the passive games class slightly increased their scores. It was found that retention was significantly better only for the passive games class. In analysis of the data from the second post-test, first post-test scores were used as the covariate. The investigators emphasized that the games employed were enjoyed by the experimental groups and that they continually asked to play the language arts games.

Reading

The results of a study by Hale (1940) provided some encouragement for the use of the motor activity learning medium as a motivating technique for teaching reading. In her study, Hale noted that a great degree of interest of children and teachers was developed and sustained in a project in which half the children in third-grade and fourth-grade classes wrote descriptions of games and the other half read the descriptions and then played the games. The second group also criticized the game descriptions and revised those that were not clear.

Humphrey and Moore (1958b) followed Hale's project by observing the interest of children 6 to 8 years old in reading material from the curricular area of physical education. In the project, children read stories describing games and then organized and played games based on their reading. Teacher ratings indicated that reading abilities improved. In addition, they observed that 46 per cent of the children showed "extreme interest," 24 per cent showed "some interest," 27 per cent showed "moderate interest," 2.7 per cent showed "some interest," and 0.3 per cent showed "little or no interest" in the material. Although the project did not adequately compare the effects of different types of reading material, the authors were encouraged by the results. They felt that the study supported the theory that children not only will read but will improve their reading when they are provided with reading material in which they are interested. They indicated that the urge to play provided the incentive to read about and learn new games.

Link (1958) examined the integration of physical education activities and reading vocabulary with third-grade children. Experimental and control subjects were equated according to their reading group level and their scores on the California Test of Mental Maturity–S Form and the "Reading Vocabulary Test" from the California Achievement Battery. Subjects were pre-tested and post-tested on a reading vocabulary test. The experimental group and the control group had the same reading lessons and the same physical education lessons, but with the experimental group, the teacher attempted to integrate reading words used as part of the physical education lessons in the experiment. No significant difference was found between the groups. However, 73.3 per cent of the experimental group improved on the vocabulary test, while only 46.6 per cent of the control group improved on the vocabulary test.

Humphrey (1967c) compared the use of active game learning with traditional procedures in the reinforcement of reading skills with fourth-grade children. From 73 children pre-tested on eight reading skills, 30 were chosen and separated into two groups of 15 each, an active games group and a traditional or conventional group. Reading skills were introduced and presented verbally to both groups and then were reinforced through one of the two techniques. Reading skills included word recognition, phonics, structural analysis, and vocabulary development. The traditional group used language workbooks, dictionary work, and ditto sheet work for reinforcement, while the active game group performed motor activities that reinforced reading skills. Treatments were administered for eight days. The results indicated that the active games group learned significantly more than the traditional group.

Cratty and Martin (1970e) studied the effectiveness of active learning games in the enhancement of certain academic operations with black and Mexican-American children in the central part of Los Angeles. The 127 subjects were first-grade to fourth-grade children with an average IQ of 85 who were identified by teachers and by standard test scores as evidencing academic achievement and potential one or more grade levels below normal. Subjects were exposed to one of four programs during an 18-week period. The first group received no extra class tutoring or special physical activity and served as a control. The second group received a special program of physical education for a half hour three times per week. The third group received small group tutoring in a classroom, and the fourth group was exposed to a variety of learning games for a half hour three times a week. The learning games were intended to promote self-control, verbal letter and pattern recognition, the ability to write and recite the alphabet, spelling, and serial memory, and to increase attention. These investigators found that the learning games group (1) improved more and achieved significantly higher final scores in tests of motor ability, (2) learned the letters of the alphabet earlier in the semester than the children in the other three groups, (3) exhibited significantly greater self-control by the twelfth week than the children in the other three groups, (4) earned significantly higher final scores in two serial memory tasks, and (5) earned significantly higher final scores in all grades in tests involving the ability to correctly recite the letters of the alphabet. Children in the tutorial group and the learning games group improved more and posted higher final scores in tests involving the verbal identification of six geometric shapes than children in the other two groups. Children in the learning games group had significantly higher final scores in spelling than children in the other three groups; however, they posted a higher initial mean in this test. As a result of these findings, the authors concluded that use of the active learning games approach can, if applied in the correct ways and to the right children, have a beneficial effect on selected academic operations.

Cratty and Szczepanik (1971c) investigated the effects of a program of learning games upon selected academic abilities in children with learning difficulties. In this study, 157 first-grade children in schools of the Catholic Archdiocese of Los Angeles were selected as subjects. The subjects in the study included pupils who scored low on the Metropolitan Reading Readiness test and who were considered by their teachers to have low learning potential. Group I was exposed to a program of learning games intended to improve academic operations for the first half of a school year for a half hour daily. During the same period, Group II remained in their regular classroom environment. During the second half of the year, the groups switched roles. A six-category test designed to evaluate the ability to verbally identify geometric patterns and letters, to write each letter of the alphabet after being shown it, to remember a series of letters and numbers, and to exercise self-control was administered. Significant improvement was noted in each group as a result of the enrichment program. The most marked improvement was seen on tests reflecting the ability to exercise self-control, to identify verbally selected geometric patterns, and to name letters of the alphabet when inspected. Little improvement was found in the tests of serial memory. The investigators concluded that the program of learning games had a significant effect on selected measures of academic achievement.

Summary and Generalization

In summarizing research regarding the contribution of the motor activity learning medium to the development of academic achievement, it appears that at least two generalizations are warranted. First, academic concepts generally can be developed or reinforced through the motor activity learning medium, which compares favorably with traditional approaches in the development and reinforcement of basic academic concepts. Second, the motor activity learning medium for the development and reinforcement of academic concepts is beneficial for use with children of average and below average intelligence. This use of the MALM has been investigated in studies dealing with science concepts, number concepts, language arts concepts, and reading skills.

Research into the contribution of the motor activity learning medium for the development of science concepts has generally been supportive of the approach. Although Ison (1961) found no significant difference between the traditional method and a motor learning method of teaching science concepts, he was encouraged by the observation that post-test scores of the motor learning group as well as those of the traditional group improved significantly over pre-test scores. Humphrey in two studies (1966a) found significant improvement when comparing scores in science concepts on tests given before and after the teaching of science concepts through the MALM. Unfortunately, the lack of control groups in these studies indicates that changes in scores could have had causes other than those associated with the motor activity learning medium. Werner (1971) found that a program in which physical education was integrated with science not only enhanced the learning of science concepts but improved performance in selected physical skills. Prager (1968, 1974) found that first-grade children for whom science concepts were reinforced using the motor activity learning medium performed significantly better than a control group for whom the MALM was not used. Additional positive results pertaining to the use of the motor activity learning medium were reported by Humphrey (1972) in which the performance of slow-learning fifth-grade children were studied. Humphrey found that children taught by the motor activity learning medium learned and retained science concepts significantly better than a group exposed to traditional procedures.

In regard to the learning of number concepts, Ross (1970) found that EMR children taught through small group games improved significantly more than a control group following traditional special-class programming on basic number concepts. Humphrey (1966b) found significant gains by first-grade children in the learning of number concepts as a result of the MALM. Crist (1968) found no significant difference between a drill approach, a developmental-meaningful approach, and the active game technique in teaching time-telling concepts at the third-grade level.

In regard to the learning of language arts concepts through the MALM, Humphrey (1962) found a significant difference between pre-test and post-test scores of third-grade pupils in language arts concepts taught through the motor activity learning medium. Humphrey commented that the MALM facilitated teaching as well as learning, that some concepts could be developed better through the physical education learning medium than any other teaching procedure known to the teacher involved, that better retention of concepts was noted, and that there was a high positive reaction from pupils. However, the research did not conclusively support these comments, and the lack of a control group prohibits attributing results conclusively to the motor activity learning medium. Humphrey (1965b), however, followed this initial investigation with a study in which an experimental group using the MALM was compared with a control group using traditional language workbook exercises for the development of language understanding. In this study, he found that both third-grade groups improved significantly but that the active games group improved significantly more than the traditional group. Penman, Christopher, and Wood (1977) reported that the learning of capitalization and punctuation skills by third-grade children was more enhanced when games were used in teaching than when traditional methods of teaching these skills were employed.

In regard to reading, Hale (1940) reported that the interest of both teachers and pupils was sustained in a project in which half the children in third-grade and fourth-grade classes wrote descriptions of games and the other half read the descriptions and played the games. Humphrey and Moore (1958b) reported that 70 per cent of children 6 to 8 years old who read stories describing games and then played the games showed considerable or extreme interest in reading. However, neither of these studies compared these reading methods with others. Link (1958), in an attempt to integrate vocabulary words and physical education, found no significance between a group receiving integrated experiences and a control group having regular physical education classes. However, on a second vocabulary test, 73.3 per cent of the experimental group improved, while only 46.6 per cent of the control group improved. Humphrey (1967c) compared active game learning with traditional procedures in the reinforcement of reading skills with fourth-grade children. Reading skills were introduced and presented verbally to two groups of children. For one group, reinforcement was supplied through the motor activity learning medium, and for the other, traditional methods were used. Results indicated that the motor activity learning group learned significantly more than the traditional group. Cratty and Szczepanik (1971c) found that children scoring low in a reading readiness test showed marked improvement in the ability to identify verbally selected geometric patterns and to name letters of the alphabet as a result of a program of learning games. Cratty and Martin (1970e) found that the games approach resulted in significant improvement in letter recognition, the identification of letter sounds, the naming of geometric figures, letter identification, and in certain kinds of serial memory tasks for black and Mexican-American children with below normal academic achievement and potential.

The second generalization discussed previously was that the motor activity learning medium is beneficial for the development and reinforcement of academic concepts with children who have average and below average intellectual and academic functioning. Although all the games in her study were not movement-oriented, Ross (1970) found that EMR children improved more in number concepts when they were taught through a games approach than through traditional procedures. Cratty and Szczepanik (1971c) and Cratty and Martin (1970e) reported that the active games approach could produce significant gains in selected academic operations of children with below normal academic achievement or potential. Humphrey (1972) found that slow-learning fifth-grade students included in a motor activity learning group gained and retained significantly more than those in a group following a traditional approach in learning science concepts. Although it is not yet substantiated by research, Humphrey (1975) suggests that for children with high-level intelligence it may be possible to introduce more advanced concepts at an earlier age through the motor activity learning medium.

BIBLIOGRAPHY

Abramson, Arthur S. *An Approach to the Rehabilitation of Children with Muscular Dystrophy.* New York: Muscular Dystrophy Association of America, Inc., 1953.

Abramson, Arthur S., and Joseph Rugoff. "Physical Treatment in Muscular Dystrophy: Abstract of Study." In *Proc. Second Med. Conf. Musc. Dys. Assoc. Amer.* New York: Muscular Dystrophy Association of America, Inc., 1952.

Abramson, Arthur S., and Edward F. Delagi. "The Contributions of Physical Activity to Rehabilitation," *Res. Quart.* 31 (Part II): 365–375, 1960.

Adams, Forrest H., Leonard M. Linde, and Hisazumi Miyake. "The Physical Working Capacity of Normal School Children. I: California," *Ped.* 28:55–64, 1961a.

Adams, Forrest H., et al. "The Physical Working Capacity of Normal School Children. II: Swedish City and Country," *Ped.* 28:243–257, 1961b.

Adams, Forrest H. "Factors Affecting the Working Capacity of Children and Adolescents." In *Physical Activity: Human Growth and Development,* edited by G. Lawrence Rarick. New York: Academic Press, 1973.

Adams, Kela Osbourn. "The Effects of Adapted Physical Education Upon the Adjustment and Motor Proficiency of Educable Mentally Retarded Girls," Doctoral dissertation, Indiana University, 1970.

Adams, Ronald C., Alfred Daniel, and Lee Rullman. *Games, Sports, and Exercises for the Physically Handicapped.* Philadelphia: Lea & Febiger, 1972.

Adams, Ronald C. and Eric Adamson. "Trampoline Tumbling for Children with Chronic Lung Disease," *J. Hea. Phys. Educ. and Rec.* 44:86–87, 1973.

Adams, Ronald C. and Martilu Puthoff. "Physical Activity Guidelines for Children with Developmental Hip Disorders," *J. Hea. Phys. Educ. and Rec.* 46:69–74, 1975.

Adler, Marilynne. "Jean Piaget, School Organization, and Instruction." In *Educational Implications of Piaget's Theory,* edited by Irene J. Athey and Duane O. Rubadeau, Waltham, Mass.: Xerox College Publishing, 1970.

Allen, Robert M., Thomas D. Haupt, and R. Wayne Jones. "Visual Perceptual Abilities and Intelligence in Mental Retardates," *J. Clin. Psychol.* 21:299–300, 1965.

Allen, Robert M., Isadore Dickman, and Thomas D. Haupt. "A Pilot Study of the Immediate Effectiveness of the Frostig-Horne Training Program with Educable Retardates," *Except. Child.* 33:41–43, 1966.

Allen, Robert M. "Factor Analysis of the Developmental Test of Visual Perception Performance of Educable Mental Retardates," *Percept. and Mot. Skills* 26:257–258, 1968.

Alley, Gordon ., and Donald L. Carr. "Effects of Systematic Sensory-Motor Tra...ing on Sensory-Motor, Visual Perception and Concept-Formation Performance of Mentally Retarded Children," *Percept. and Mot. Skills* 27:451–456, 1968.

American Academy of Pediatrics. Committee on Children with Handicaps. "The Asthmatic Child and His Participation in Sports and Physical Education," *Ped.* 45:150–151, 1970.

American Alliance for Health, Physical Education and Recreation. *AAHPER Youth Fitness Manual.* Washington, D.C.: American Alliance for Health, Physical Education and Recreation, 1975.

American Alliance for Health, Physical Education, and Recreation. *Special Fitness Test Manual for Mildly Mentally Retarded Persons.* Washington, D.C.: American Alliance for Health, Physical Education, and Recreation, 1976.

American Association for Health, Physical Education, and Recreation. *AAHPER Youth Fitness Manual.* Washington, D.C.: American Association for Health, Physical Education, and Recreation, 1965.

American Association for Health, Physical Education, and Recreation. *Special Fitness Tests Manual for the Mentally Retarded.* Washington, D.C.: American Association for Health, Physical Education, and Recreation, 1968.

American Association for Health, Physical Education, and Recreation. "Referral Forms for Adapted Physical Education," *J. Hea. Phys. Educ. and Rec.* 40:71–73, 1969.

American Association for Health, Physical Education, and Recreation. *Foundations and Practices in Perceptual Motor Learning—A Quest for Understanding.* Washington, D.C.: American Association for Health, Physical Education, and Recreation, 1971a.

American Association for Health, Physical Education, and Recreation. "A Clarification of Terms," *J. Hea. Phys. Educ. and Rec.* 42:63–68, 1971b.

American Association for Health, Physical Education, and Recreation. "Blowing Games for Asthmatic Children," *J. Hea. Phys. Educ. and Rec.* 43:77–78, 1972. (Games taken from "An Experimental Study of Physical Conditioning for Asthmatic Children," by Janice Carrie Franklin, master's thesis, Texas Women's University, May, 1971.)

American Association on Mental Deficiency. *Manual on Terminology and Classification In Mental Retardation.* Series No. 2. Baltimore: Garamond Pridemark Press, 1973.

American College of Sports Medicine. *Guidelines for Graded Exercise Testing and Exercise Prescription.* Philadelphia: Lea & Febiger, 1975.

American Diabetes Association, Inc. *Facts About Diabetes.* New York: American Diabetes Association, Inc., 1966.

American Foundation for the Blind. *Blindness: Some Facts and Figures.* New York: American Foundation for the Blind, 1963.

American Heart Association. *Heart Disease in Children.* New York: American Heart Association, 1963a.

American Heart Association. *If Your Child Has A Congenital Heart Defect.* New York: American Heart Association, 1963b.

American Heart Association. *Facts About Heart and Blood Diseases.* New York: American Heart Association, 1966.

American Heart Association. *If Your Child Has a Congenital Heart Defect.* New York: American Heart Association, 1970.

American Heart Association. *Children With Heart Disease.* New York: American Heart Association, 1971.

American Lung Association. *Introduction to Lung Diseases.* American Lung Association, 1973.

American National Red Cross. *Adapted Aquatics.* Garden City, New York: Doubleday & Company, Inc., 1977.

American Psychiatric Association. *Diagnostic and Statistical Manual of Mental Disorders.* Washington, D.C.: American Psychiatric Association, 1968.

American Psychological Association, et al. *Standards for Educational and Psychological Tests and Manuals.* Washington, D.C.: American Psychological Association, Inc., 1966.

Ames, Louise B. "The Sequential Patterns of Prone Progressions in the Human Infant," *Genet. Psychol. Monogr.* 19:411–460, 1937.

Argenti, Rudolph M. "The Effects of Systematic Motor Training on Selected Perceptual-Motor Attributes of Mentally Retarded Children," Doctoral dissertation, University of Tennessee, 1968.

Arnheim, Daniel D., David Auxter, and Walter C. Crowe, *Principles and Methods of Adapted Physical Education.* St. Louis: The C. V. Mosby Co., 1969.

Arnheim, Daniel D., David Auxter, and Walter C. Crowe. *Principles and Methods of Adapted Physical Education.* St. Louis: The C. V. Mosby Co., 1973.

Arnheim, Daniel D., David Auxter, and Walter C. Crowe. *Principles and Methods of Adapted Physical Education.* St. Louis: The C. V. Mosby Co., 1977.

Asmussen, Erling and K. Heeboll-Nielsen. "Physical Performances and Growth in Children: Influences of Sex, Age and Intelligence," *J. Appl. Physio.* 8:371–380, 1956.

Asmussen, Erling. "Growth In Muscular Strength and Power." In *Physical Activity: Human Growth and Development,* edited by G. Lawrence Rarick. New York: Academic Press, 1973.

Asthma Research Council. *Exercises for Asthma and Emphysema.* London: Asthma Research Council, 1962.

Astrand, Per-Olaf. "Human Physical Fitness with Special Reference to Sex and Age," *Physio. Rev.* 36:307–335, 1956.

Astrand, Per-Olaf, and Eric H. Christensen. "Aerobic Work Capacity." In *Oxygen in the Animal Organism,* edited by Frank Dickens and Eric Neil. Oxford, England; Pergamon Press, 1964.

Astrand, Per-Olaf, and Kaare Rodahl. *Textbook of Work Physiology.* New York: McGraw-Hill Book Co., 1970.

Athey, Irene J., and Duane O. Rubadeau., ed. *Educational Implications of Piaget's Theory.* Waltham, Mass.: Xerox College Publishing, 1970.

August, Irwin. "A Study of the Effect of a Physical Education Program on Reading Readiness, Visual Perception and Perceptual-Motor Development in Kindergarten Children," Doctoral dissertation, New York University (microfilm), 1969.

Auxter, David M. "Proprioception Among Intellectually Typical and Differentially Diagnosed Educable Mentally Retarded Boys," *Percept. and Mot. Skills* 21:751–756, 1965.

Auxter, David M., Edward Zahar, and Linda Ferrini. "Body Image Development of Emotionally Disturbed Children," *Amer. Corr. Ther. J.* 21:154–155, 1967.

Auxter, David. "Operant Conditioning of Motor Skills for the Emotionally Disturbed," *Amer. Corr. Ther. J.* 23:28–31, 1969.

Axline, Virginia M. "Play Therapy Procedures and Results," *Amer. J. Orthopsych.* 25:618–626, 1955.

Ayers, Jerry B., Michael E. Rohr, and Mary N. Ayers. "Perceptual-Motor Skills, Ability to Conserve, and School Readiness," *Percept. and Mot. Skills* 38:491–494, 1974.

Ayres, Jean A. "Patterns of Perceptual-Motor Dysfunction in Children," *Percept. and Mot. Skills* 20:335–368, 1965.

Ayres, Jean A. "Sensory Integrative Processes and Neuropsychological Learning Disabilities." In *Learning Disorders,* edited by Jerome Hellmuth, Vol. 3. Seattle, Wash. Special Child Publications, Inc., 1968.

Ayres, Jean A. *Southern California Perceptual-Motor Tests.* Los Angeles: Western Psychological Services, 1969.

Ayres, Jean A. *Sensory Integration and Learning Disorders.* Los Angeles: Western Psychological Services, 1972.

Bachman, John C. "Motor Learning and Performance as Related to Age and Sex in Two Measures of Balance Coordination," *Res. Quart.* 32:123–137, 1961.

Baldwin, Alfred L. *Theories of Child Development.* New York: John Wiley and Sons, Inc., 1967.

Ball, Thomas J. *Itard, Seguin, and Kephart: Sensory Education—A Learning Interpretation.* Columbus, Ohio: Charles E. Merrill Co., 1971.

Ballantyne, John. *Deafness.* London: J. & A. Churchill, 1970.

Balow, Bruce. "Perceptual-Motor Activities in the Treatment of Severe Reading Disability," *Read. Teach.* 24:513–525, 1971.

Bannatyne, Alex D. "Relationships Between Written Spelling, Motor Functioning and Sequencing Skills," *J. Learn. Dis.* 2:4–16, 1969.

Barr, David F. *Auditory Perceptual Disorders: An Introduction.* Springfield, Ill.: Charles C Thomas, Publisher, 1972.

Barraga, Natalie C. "Utilization of Sensory-Perceptual Abilities." In *The Visually Handicapped Child In School,* edited by Berthold Lowenfeld. New York: The John Day Co., 1973

Barsch, Ray H. *A Movigenic Curriculum.* Madison, Wis.: Wisconsin State Department of Public Instruction Bulletin No. 25, Wisconsin State Department of Public Instruction, 1965.

Barsch, Ray H. *Achieving Perceptual-Motor Efficiency: A Space Oriented Approach to Learning.* Vol. 1. Seattle, Wash.: Special Child Publications, Inc., 1967.

Barsch, Ray H. *Enriching Perception and Cognition: Techniques for Teachers.* Vol. 2. Seattle, Wash.: Special Child Publications, Inc., 1968.

Bateman, Barbara. "Learning Disabilities—Yesterday, Today, and Tomorrow," *Except. Child.* 31:167–177, 1964.

Bateman, Barbara. "An Educator's View of a Diagnostic Approach to Learning Disorders." In *Learning Disorders,* edited by Jerome Hellmuth, Vol. 3. Seattle, Wash.: Special Child Publications, Inc. 1965.

Baum, David. "Heart Disease in Children." In *Physically Handicapped Children: A Medical Atlas for Teachers,* edited by Eugene E. Bleck and Donald A. Nagel. New York: Grune & Stratton, Inc., 1975.

Baumgartner, Ted A., and Andrew S. Jackson. *Measurement for Evaluation in Physical Education.* Boston: Houghton Mifflin Co., 1975.

Bayley, Nancy. "The Development of Motor Abilities During the First Three Years," *Soc. Res. Child Develop. Monogr.* 1:1–26, 1935.

Beard, Ruth M. *An Outline of Piaget's Developmental Psychology for Students and Teachers.* New York: Basic Books, Inc., 1969.

Belenky, Robert. *A Swimming Program for Blind Children.* New York: American Foundation for the Blind, 1955.

Belmont, Ira, Hannah Flegenheimer, and Herbert G. Birch. "Comparison of Perceptual Training and Remedial Instruction for Poor Beginning Readers," *J. Learn. Dis.* 6:230–235, 1973.

Benack, Raymond T. *What is Allergy?* Springfield, Ill.: Charles C Thomas, Publisher, 1967.

Berg, Frederick S., and Samuel G. Fletcher, ed. *The Hard of Hearing Child.* New York: Grune & Stratton, Inc., 1970.

Berges, Shirley A. "Teaching Physical Education in Schools for the Deaf," *J. Hea. Phys. Educ. and Rec.* 43:81–83, 1972.

Beter, Thais R. "The Effects of a Concentrated Physical Education Program and an Auditory and Visual Perceptual Reading Program Upon Academic Achievement, Intelligence, and Motor Fitness of Educable Mentally Retarded Children," Doctoral dissertation, Louisiana State University, 1969.

Bieger, Elaine. "Effectiveness of Visual Perceptual Training on Reading Skills of Non-Readers, An Experimental Study," *Percept. and Mot. Skills* 38:1147–1153, 1974.

Binet, Alfred, and Theodore Simon. *The Development of Intelligence in Children.* Trans. by Elizabeth S. Kite. Baltimore: Williams & Wilkins, Co., 1916.

Blake, Kathryn A. *The Mentally Retarded—An Educational Psychology.* Englewood Cliffs, N. J.: Prentice-Hall, Inc., 1976.

Blakeslee, Berton, ed. *The Limb-Deficient Child.* Berkeley and Los Angeles: University of California Press, 1963.

Bleck, Eugene E., and Donald A. Nagel, ed. *Physically Handicapped Children: A Medical Atlas for Teachers.* New York: Grune & Stratton, Inc., 1975a.

Bleck, Eugene E. "Myelomeningocele. Meningocele, Spina Bifida." In *Physically Handicapped Children: A Medical Atlas for Teachers,* edited by Eugene E. Bleck and Donald A. Nagel. New York: Grune & Stratton, Inc., 1975b.

Bloom, Benjamin S., et al. *Taxonomy of Educational Objectives: The Classification of Educational Goals. Handbook I, Cognitive Domain.* New York: David McKay Co., Inc., 1956.

Blount, Walter P., and John H. Moe. *The Milwaukee Brace.* Baltimore: Williams & Wilkins Co., 1973.

Blumenthal, Malcolm N., and Earl Pederson. "Physical Conditioning Program for Asthmatic Children," *J. Assoc. Phys. Ment. Rehab.* 21:4–6, 1967.

Bobbitt, Eleanor W. "A Comparison of the Use of a Reading Readiness Workbook Approach and the Active Game Learning Medium in the Development of Selected Reading Skills and Concepts," Doctoral dissertation, University of Maryland, 1972.

Bottomley, H. W. *Allergy: Its Treatment and Care.* New York: Funk & Wagnalls, 1968.

Breckenridge, Marian E., and Margaret N. Murphy. *Growth and Development of the Young Child.* Philadelphia: W. B. Saunders Co., 1968.

Brest, Albert N. and John H. Moyer, ed. *Cardiovascular Disorders.* Vol. 1. Philadelphia: F. A. Davis Co., 1968.

Briney, Kenneth L. *Cardiovascular Disease: A Matter of Prevention.* Belmont, Ca.: Wadsworth Publishing Co., Inc., 1970.

Britt, Gladys G. "The Effects of a Physical Education Program on the Balance and Coordination of the Trainable Retarded in Hampton Virginia," Master's thesis, East Tennessee State University, 1968.

Broer, Marion. *Efficiency of Human Movement.* Philadelphia: W. B. Saunders Co., 1973.

Brown, B. J. "The Influence of A Physical Education Program on the Basic Motor Fitness of Disturbed Children," *Amer. Corr. Ther. J.* 30:15–20, 1976.

Brozek, Joseph, ed. *Body Measurements and Human Nutrition.* Detroit: Wayne University Press, 1956.

Bruner, Jerome S. *On Knowing: Essays for the Left Hand.* Cambridge, Mass.: The Belknap Press of Harvard University Press, 1962.

Bruner, Jerome S. "The Course of Cognitive Growth," *Amer. Psychol.* 19:1–15, 1964.

Bruner, Jerome S. *Toward A Theory of Instruction.* Cambridge, Mass.: The Belknap Press of Harvard University Press, 1966.

Bruner, Jerome S. *Processes of Cognitive Growth: Infancy.* Heinz Werner Lecture. Worcester: Clark University Press, 1968a.

Bruner, Jerome S., and David Kroch, ed. *Perception and Personality: A Symposium.* New York: Greenwood Press, Publishers, 1968b.

Bruner, Jerome S. *The Relevance of Education.* New York: W. W. Norton & Co., Inc., 1971.

Bruner, Jerome S. *Beyond the Information Given: Studies in the Psychology of Knowing.* New York: W. W. Norton and Co., Inc., 1973.

Bryan, Tanis H., and James H. Bryan. *Understanding Learning Disabilities.* Port Washington, N.Y.: Alfred Publishing Co., Inc., 1975.

Buckland, Pearl, and Bruce Balow. "Effect of Visual Perceptual Training on Reading Achievement," *Except. Child.* 39:299–304, 1973.

Buell, Charles E. "Motor Performance of Visually Handicapped Children," Doctoral dissertation, University of California at Berkeley, 1950a.

Buell, Charles E. "Motor Performance of Visually Handicapped Children," *Except. Child.* 17:69–72, 1950b.

Buell, Charles E. "Outdoor Education in a School for the Blind." *Except. Child.* 22:266–267, 1956.

Buell, Charles E. "Wrestling in the Life of a Blind Boy," *Int. J. for the Educ. of the Blind.* 7:93–96, 1958.

Buell, Charles E. "Developments in Physical Education for Blind Children," *The New Outlook for the Blind.* 58:202–206, 1964.

Buell, Charles E. *Physical Education for Blind Children.* Springfield, Ill.: Charles C Thomas, Publisher, 1966.

Buell, Charles E. "The Schools' Responsibility for Providing Physical Activities for Blind Students," *J. Hea. Phys. Educ. & Rec.* 41:41–42, 1970.

Buell, Charles E. *Physical Education and Recreation for the Visually Handicapped.* Washington, D.C.: American Association for Health, Physical Education, and Recreation, 1973.

Buxton, Doris. "Extension of the Kraus-Weber Test," *Res. Quart.* 28:210–217, 1957.

Cailliet, Rene. "Rehabilitation in Multiple Sclerosis." In *Rehabilitation and Medicine,* edited by Sidney Licht. New Haven, Conn. Elizabeth Licht, Publisher, 1968.

Cailliet, Rene. *Foot and Ankle Pain.* Philadelphia: F. A. Davis Co., 1976.

Cardwell, Viola E. *Cerebral Palsy: Advances in Understanding and Care.* New York: Association for the Aid of Crippled Children, 1956.

Cassel, Robert H. "The Vineland Adaptation of the Oseretsky Tests," *Trng. Sch. Bull. Suppl.* 46:1–32, 1949.

Cattell, Raymond B. *Personality and Motivation Structure and Measurement.* Yonkers-on-Hudson, N.Y.: World Book Co., 1957.

Cavanaugh, John R. "A Study to Determine the Effects of a Physical Education Program on Educable Mentally Retarded and Minimal Brain-Damaged Children," Master's thesis, Louisiana State University, 1968.

Cerasi, Erol, and Rolf Luft ed. *Pathogenesis of Diabetes Mellitus.* New York: Wiley-Interscience Division of John Wiley & Sons, Inc., 1970.

Chaney, Clara M., and Newell C. Kephart. *Motoric Aids to Perceptual Training.* Columbus, Ohio: Charles E. Merrill Co., 1968.

Chang, Thomas M. C., and A. C. Chang. "Relation of Visual-Motor Skills and Reading Achievement in Primary-Grade Pupils of Superior Ability," *Percept. and Mot. Skills* 24:51–53, 1967.

Chansky, Norman M. "Perceptual Training with Young Mental Retardates," *Amer. J. Ment. Def.* 68:460–468, 1953.

Chansky, Norman M. "Perceptual Training with Elementary School Underachievers," *J. Sch. Psych.* 1:33–41, 1963.

Chasey, William C., and Waneen Wyrick. "Effect of a Gross Motor Developmental Program on Form Perception Skills of Educable Mentally Retarded Children," *Res. Quart.* 41:345–352, 1970.

Chasey, William C. "Overlearning as a Variable in the Retention of Gross Motor Skills by the Mentally Retarded," *Res. Quart.* 42:145–149, 1971.

Chasey, William C. "Motor Skill Overlearning Effects on Retention and Relearning by Retarded Boys," *Res. Quart.* 48:41–46, 1977.

Chavez, Ricardo, "Effects of Three Physical Education Programs On Selected Physical Fitness Components of Educable Mental Retardates," Doctoral dissertation, University of Southern Mississippi, 1970.

Clarke, H. Harrison. "Objective Strength Tests of Affected Muscle Groups Involved in Orthopedic Disabilities," *Res. Quart.* 19:118–147, 1948.

Clarke, H. Harrison. "Improvement of Objective Strength Tests of Muscle Groups by Cable-Tension Methods," *Res. Quart.* 21:399–419, 1950.

Clarke, H. Harrison, Theodore L. Bailey, and Clayton T. Shay. "New Objective Strength Tests by Cable-Tension Methods," *Res. Quart.* 23:136–148, 1952.

Clarke, H. Harrison. *Application of Measurement to Health and Physical Education.* Englewood Cliffs, N.J.: Prentice-Hall, Inc., 1959.

Clarke, H. Harrison, and David H. Clarke. *Developmental and Adapted Physical Education.* Englewood Cliffs, N.J.: Prentice-Hall, Inc., 1963.

Clarke, H. Harrison. *Application of Measurement to Health and Physical Education.* Englewood Cliffs, N.J.: Prentice-Hall, Inc., 1967.

Clements, Sam D. *Some Aspects of the Characteristics, Management, and Education of the Child with Learning Disabilities (Minimal Brain Dysfunction).* Little Rock, Ark.: Arkansas Association for Children with Learning Disabilities, Inc., 1966.

Cobb, Patrick R., Brad S. Chissom, and Myron W. Davis. "Relationships Among Perceptual-Motor, Self-Concept, and Academic Measures for Children in Kindergarten, Grades One and Two." *Percept. and Mot. Skills* 41:539–546, 1975.

Cohen, Walter, Aaron Hershkowitz, and Marjorie Chodack. "Size Judgment at Different Distances as a Function of Age Level," *Child Dev.* 29:473–479, 1958.

Committee on Adapted Physical Education. "Guiding Principles for Adapted Physical Education," *J. Hea. Phys. Educ. and Rec.* 23:15 and 28, 1952.

Committee on Exercise of the American Heart Association. *Exercise Testing and Training of Apparently Healthy Individuals: A Handbook for Physicians.* Dallas: American Heart Association, 1972.

Committee on Nomenclature, Conference of Executives of American Schools for the Deaf. *Amer. Annals Deaf.* 83:1–3, 1938.

Cooper, Kenneth H. *Aerobics.* New York: Bantam Books, Inc., 1968.

Cooper, Kenneth H. *The New Aerobics.* New York: Bantam Books, Inc., 1970.

Cooper, Mildred, and Kenneth H. Cooper. *Aerobics for Women.* New York: Bantam Books, Inc., 1973.

Corbin, Charles B. *A Textbook of Motor Development.* Dubuque, Iowa: Wm. C. Brown Publishers, 1973.

Corder, W. Owen. "Effects of Physical Education on Intellectual, Physical, and Social Development in Educable Mentally Retarded Boys," *Except. Child.* 32:357–364, 1966.

Corder, W. Owen. "Effects of Physical Education on the Psycho-Physical Development of Educable Mentally Retarded Girls," Doctoral dissertation, University of Virginia, June, 1969.

Courtney, Louise. "Effects of Physical Activities on the Balance of Elementary Educable Mentally Retarded Children," Master's thesis, Pennsylvania State University, 1972.

Cratty, Bryant J. *The Perceptual and Motor Attributes of Mentally Retarded Children and Youth.* Los Angeles: Mental Retardation Service Board of Los Angeles County, 1966.

Cratty, Bryant J., and Theresa A. Sams. *The Body-Image of Blind Children.* New York: American Foundation for the Blind, Inc., 1968.

Cratty, Bryant J. *Motor Activity and the Education of Retardates.* Philadelphia: Lea & Febiger, 1969a.

Cratty, Bryant J. *Perceptual-Motor Behavior and Educational Processes.* Springfield, Ill.: Charles C Thomas, Publisher, 1969b.

Cratty, Bryant J. and Sister Margaret Mary Martin. *Perceptual-Motor Efficiency in Children.* Philadelphia: Lea & Febiger, 1969c.

Cratty, Bryant J. *Movement, Perception and Thought: The Use of Total Body Movement as a Learning Modality.* Palo Alto, Cal.: Peek Publications, 1969d.

Cratty, Bryant J., et al. *Movement Activities and the Education of Children.* Springfield, Ill.: Charles C Thomas, Publisher, 1970a.

Cratty, Bryant J. *Some Educational Implications of Movements.* Seattle, Wash.: Special Child Publications, 1970b.

Cratty, Bryant J. *Perceptual and Motor Development In Infants and Children.* New York: The Macmillan Co., 1970c.

Cratty, Bryant J. *Movement Activities, Motor Ability, and the Education of Children.* Springfield, Ill.: Charles C Thomas, Publisher, 1970d.

Cratty, Bryant J., and Sister Margaret Mary Martin. "The Effects of a Program of Learning Games upon Selected Academic Abilities in Children with Learning Difficulties." Washington, D.C.: U.S. Office of Education, Bureau of Education for the Handicapped, monograph printed at the University of California Los Angeles, 1970e.

Cratty, Bryant J. *Active Learning: Games to Enhance Academic Abilities.* Englewood Cliffs, N.J.: Prentice-Hall, Inc., 1971a.

Cratty, Bryant J. *Movement and Spatial Awareness in Blind Children and Youth.* Springfield, Ill.: Charles C Thomas, Publisher, 1971b.

Cratty, Bryant J., and Sister Mary Szczepanik. *The Effects of A Program of Learning Games Upon Selected Academic Abilities in Children with Learning Difficulties.* Washington, D.C.: U.S. Office of Education, Bureau of Education for the Handicapped. Monograph printed at the University of California, Los Angeles, 1971c.

Cratty, Bryant J. *Physical Expressions of Intelligence.* Englewood Cliffs, N.J.: Prentice-Hall, Inc., 1972.

Cratty, Bryant J. *Intelligence in Action: Physical Activities for Enhancing Intellectual Abilities.* Englewood Cliffs, N.J.: Prentice-Hall, Inc., 1973a.

Cratty, Bryant J. *Movement Through Action.* Anaheim, California: Skill Development Co., 1973b.

Cratty, Bryant J. *Psycho-Motor Behavior in Education and Sport.* Springfield, Ill.: Charles C Thomas, Publisher, 1974a.

Cratty, Bryant J. *Motor Activity and the Education of Retardates.* Philadelphia: Lea & Febiger, 1974b.

Crist, Thomas. "A Comparison of the Use of the Active Game Learning Medium with Developmental-Meaningful and Drill Procedures in Developing Concepts for Telling Time at the Third Grade Level," Doctoral dissertation, University of Maryland, 1968.

Cronbach, Lee J. *Essentials of Psychological Testing.* New York: Harper & Brothers, Publishers, 1960.

Cronbach, Lee J., and Paul E. Meehl. "Construct Validity in Psychological Tests." In *Readings in Educational and Psychological Measurement,* edited by Clinton I. Chase and H. Glenn Ludlow. Boston: Houghton Mifflin Co., 1966.

Crudden, Charles H. "Form Abstraction by Children," *J. Genet. Psych.* 58:113–129, 1941.

Cruickshank, William M., and George M. Raus, ed. *Cerebral Palsy: Its Individual and Community Problems.* Syracuse, N.Y.: Syracuse University Press, 1955.

Cruickshank, William M., et al. *A Teaching Method for Brain-Injured and Hyperactive Children: A Demonstration–Pilot Study.* Syracuse, N.Y.: Syracuse University Press, 1961.

Cruickshank, William M., et al. *Perception and Cerebral Palsy.* Syracuse, N.Y.: Syracuse University Press, 1965.

Cruickshank, William M., ed. *The Teacher of Brain-Injured Children.* Syracuse, N.Y.: Syracuse University Press, 1966.

Cruickshank, William M. *The Brain-Injured Child in Home, School, and Community.* Syracuse, N.Y.: Syracuse University Press, 1967.

Cruickshank, William M., and Daniel P. Hallahan. *Perceptual and Learning Disabilities in Children: Psychoeducational Practices.* Vol. 1. Syracuse, N.Y.: Syracuse University Press, 1975a.

Cruickshank, William M., and Daniel P. Hallahan. *Perceptual and Learning Disabilities in Children: Research and Theory.* Vol. 2. Syracuse, N.Y.: Syracuse University Press, 1975b.

Cruickshank, William M. *Cerebral Palsy: A Developmental Disability.* Syracuse, N.Y.: Syracuse University Press, 1976.

Cruikshank, Ruth M. "The Development of Visual Size Constancy in Early Infancy," *J. Genet. Psych.* 58:327–351, 1941.

Cunningham, Lee N., and Edward L. Etkind. "Let the Diabetic Play," *J. Phys. Educ. and Rec.* 46:40–42, 1975.

Cureton, Thomas Kirk. *The Physiological Effects of Exercise Programs on Adults.* Springfield, Ill.: Charles C Thomas, Publisher, 1969.

Daniels, Arthur S., and Evelyn A. Davies. *Adapted Physical Education.* New York: Harper & Row, Publishers, 1975.

Dauer, Victor P. *Dynamic Physical Education for Elementary School Children.* Minneapolis, Minn.: Burgess Publishing Co., 1971.

Davidson, Helen P. "A Study of the Confusing Letters B, D, P, and Q." *J. Genet. Psych.* 47:458–467, 1935.

Davis, Hallowell, and Fred W. Krantz. "The International Standard Reference Zero for Pure-Tone Audiometers and Its Relation to the Evaluation of Impairment of Hearing," *J. Speech and Hear. Res.* 7:7–16, 1964.

Davis, Robert. "Writing Behavioral Objectives," *J. Hea. Phys. Educ. and Rec.* 44:47–49, 1973.

Davis, Robert G. "The Effect of Perceptually Oriented Physical Education on Perceptual Motor Ability and Academic Ability of Kindergarten and First-Grade Children," Doctoral dissertation, University of Maryland, 1973.

Deaver, G. G., D. Buck, and J. McCarthy. "Spina Bifida." In *1951 Year Book of Physical Medicine and Rehabilitation.* Chicago: Year Book Medical Publishers, Inc., 1952.

DeGroat, Patricia D. "The Effect of Selected Perceptual-Motor Skills on Reading," Master's thesis, Central Missouri State College, 1971.

Delacato, Carl H. *The Diagnosis and Treatment of Speech and Reading Problems.* Springfield, Ill.: Charles C Thomas, Publisher, 1963.

De Lorme, Thomas L., and Arthur L. Watkins, *Progressive Resistance Exercise.* New York: Appleton-Century-Crofts, 1951.

Denhoff, E., and I. Robinault. *Cerebral Palsy and Related Disorders.* New York: McGraw-Hill Book Co., Inc., 1960.

Denhoff, Eric. *Cerebral Palsy—The Preschool Years.* Springfield Ill.: Charles C Thomas, Publisher, 1967.

Dennis, Wayne. "The Effect of Restricted Practice Upon the Reaching, Sitting, and Standing of Two Infants," *J. Genet. Psych.* 47:17–32, 1935.

Dennis, Wayne. "Infant Development Under Conditions of Restricted Practice and of Minimal Social Stimulation: A Preliminary Report," *J. Genet. Psych.* 53:149–157, 1938.

Dennis, Wayne, and Marsena Dennis. "The Effect of Cradling Practices Upon the Onset of Walking in Hopi Children," *J. Genet. Psych.* 56:77–86, 1940.

Dennis, Wayne. "Infant Development Under Conditions of Restricted Practice and of Minimum Social Stimulation," *Genet. Psych. Monogr.* 23:143–189, 1941.

Dennis, Wayne. "Causes of Retardation Among Institutional Children: Iran," *J. Genet. Psych.* 96:47–59, 1960.

DeVries, Herbert A. *Physiology of Exercise for Physical Education and Athletics.* Dubuque, Iowa: Wm. C. Brown Publishers, 1974.

Dewey, Margaret. "The Autistic Child in a Physical Education Class," *J. Hea. Phys. Educ. and Rec.* 43:79–80, 1972.

Dewey, Margaret. "Recreation and Exercise as Therapy for Autistic Children: The Historical Perspective," *J. Hea. Phys. Educ. and Rec.* 44:87–88, 1973.

Dibner, Susan Schmidt, and Andrew S. Dibner. *Integration or Segregation for the Physically Handicapped Child?* Springfield, Ill.: Charles C Thomas, Publisher, 1973.

DiCarlo, Louis M. *The Deaf.* Englewood Cliffs, N.J.: Prentice-Hall, Inc., 1964.

Distefano, Michael K., Jr., Norman R. Ellis, and William Sloan. "Motor Proficiency in Mental Defectives," *Percept. and Mot. Skills* 8:231–234, 1958.

Dobbins, D. Alan, and G. Lawrence Rarick. "Structural Similarity of the Motor Domain of Normal and Educable Retarded Boys," *Res. Quart.* 46:447–456, 1975.

Dobbins, D. Alan, and G. Lawrence Rarick. "Separation Potential of Educable Retarded and Intellectually Normal Boys as a Function of Motor Performance," *Res. Quart.* 47:346–356, 1976.

Dorinson, S. Malvern. "Breathing Exercises for Bronchial Asthma and Pulmonary Emphysema," *JAMA* 156:931–933, 1954.

Dowben, Robert M. "Treatment of Muscular Dystrophy with Steroids: A Preliminary Report," *New Eng. J. Med.* 268:912–916, 1963.

Drowatzky, John N. "Relationship of Size Constancy to Selected Measures of Motor Ability," *Res. Quart.* 38:375–379, 1967.

Druter, Robert J. "A Comparison of Active Games and Passive Games Used as Learning Media for the Development of Arithmetic Readiness Skills and Concepts with Kindergarten Children in An Attempt to Study Gross Motor Activity as a Learning Facilitator," Master's thesis, University of Maryland, 1972.

Ducroquet, Robert, Jean Ducroquet, and Pierre Ducroquet. *Walking and Limping: A Study of Normal and Pathological Walking.* Philadelphia: J. B. Lippincott Co., 1968.

Dunn, John M. "Behavior Modification with Emotionally Disturbed Children," *J. Phys. Educ. and Rec.* 46:67–70, 1975.

Dunn, Lloyd M., ed. *Exceptional Children In the Schools.* New York: Holt, Rinehart and Winston, Inc., 1973.

Dupont, Henry, ed. *Educating Emotionally Disturbed Children.* New York: Holt, Rinehart and Winston, Inc., 1975.

Dusenberry, Lois. "A Study of the Effects of Training in Ball Throwing by Children Ages Three to Seven," *Res. Quart.* 23:9–14, 1952.

Ebersole, Marylou, Newell C. Kephart, and James D. Ebersole. *Steps to Achievement for the Slow Learner.* Columbus, Ohio: Charles E. Merrill Co., 1968.

Eckert, Helen M. "Factorial Analysis of Perceptual Motor and Reading Skills," *Res. Quart.* 46:85–91, 1975.

Eckert, Helen M., and G. Lawrence Rarick. "Stabilometer Performance of Educable Mentally Retarded and Normal Children," *Res. Quart.* 47:619–623, 1976.

Elkind, David, Ronald R. Koegler, and Elsie Go. "Studies in Perceptual Development: II. Part-Whole Perception," *Child Dev.* 35:81–90, 1964.

Elkind, David, and John H. Flavell. *Studies in Cognitive Development.* New York: Oxford University Press, 1969.

Ellis, Norman R., and William Sloan. "Relationship Between Intelligence and Simple Reaction Time in Mental Defectives," *Percept. and Mot. Skills* 7:65–67, 1957.

Elrod, Joe M. "The Effects of Perceptual-Motor Training and Music on Perceptual-Motor Development and Behavior of Educable Mentally Retarded Children," Doctoral dissertation, Louisiana State University, 1972.

Emmons, Coralie A. "A Comparison of Selected Gross-Motor Activities of the Getman-Kane and the Kephart Perceptual-Motor Training Programs and Their Effects Upon Certain Readiness Skills of First-Grade Negro Children," Doctoral dissertation, Ohio State University, 1968.

Engen, Trygg, and Lewis P. Lipsitt. "Decrement and Recovery of Responses to Olfactory Stimuli in the Human Neonate," *J. Comp. Physiol. Psych.* 59:312–316, 1965.

Engerbretson, David L. "The Effects of Interval Training on Diabetes," Master's thesis, University of Illinois, 1962.

Engerbretson, David L. "The Effects of Interval Training on the Insulin Dosage, Sugar Levels and Other Indexes of Physical Fitness in Three Diabetic Subjects," Master's thesis, University of Illinois, 1962. Quoted in *Toward an Understanding of Health and Physical Education,* by Arthur H. Steinhaus. Dubuque, Iowa: Wm. C. Brown, Publishers, 1963.

Engerbretson, David L. "The Effect of Physical Conditioning Upon the Regulation of Diabetes Mellitus," Doctoral dissertation, The Pennsylvania State University, 1970.

Engerbretson, David L. "The Diabetic in Physical Education, Recreation, and Athletics," *J. Phys. Educ. and Rec.* 48:18–21, 1977.

Ersing, Walter F. "Current Directions of Professional Preparation in Adapted Physical Education," *J. Hea. Phys. Educ. and Rec.* 43:78–79, 1972.

Espenschade, Anna, Robert R. Dable, and Robert Schoendube. "Dynamic Balance in Adolescent Boys," *Res. Quart.* 24:270–275, 1953.

Espenschade, Anna. "Motor Development." In *Science and Medicine of Exercise and Sports,* edited by Warren R. Johnson. New York: Harper and Brothers, Publishers, 1960.

Etkes, Asher B. "Therapeutic Playgrounds," *J. Hea. Phys. Educ. and Rec.* 44:56–57, 1973.

Etkind, Edward, and Lee Cunningham. "Physical Activities in Diabetic Boys." Paper presented at the International Symposium Commemorating the 50th Anniversity of Insulin, Israel, October, 1971.

Ewing, Lady, and Sir Alexander Ewing. *New Opportunities for Deaf Children.* London: University of London Press Ltd., 1964.

Fait, Hollis F., and Harriet J. Kupferer. "A Study of Two Motor Achievement Tests and Its Implications in Planning Physical Education Activities for the Mentally Retarded," *Amer. J. Ment. Def.* 60:729–732, 1956.

Fait, Hollis F. *Special Physical Education: Adapted, Corrective, Developmental.* Philadelphia: W. B. Saunders Co., 1972.

Fallers, Jeanne Frances. "An Investigation of the Motor Ability of Thirty High Grade Mentally Defective Girls With the Oseretsky Tests of Motor Proficiency," Master's thesis, MacMurray College (Jacksonville, Illinois), 1948.

Fantz, Robert L. "Pattern Vision in Young Infants," *Psychol. Rec.* 8:43–47, 1958.

Fantz, Robert L. "The Origin of Form Perception," *Sci. Amer.* 204:66–72, 1961a.

Fantz, Robert L. "A Method for Studying Depth Perception in Infants Under Six Months of Age," *Psychol. Rec.* 11:27–32, 1961b.

Fein, Bernard T., and Leila H. Green. "Respiratory and Physical Exercise in the Treatment of Bronchial Asthma," *Annals of Aller.* 11:275–287, 1953.

Fein, Bernard T., and Eugenia P. Cox. "The Technique of Respiratory and Physical Exercise in the Treatment of Bronchial Asthma." *Annals of Aller.* 13:377–384, 1955.

Feingold, Ben F. *Introduction to Clinical Allergy.* Springfield, Ill.: Charles C Thomas, Publisher, 1973.

Ferguson, Albert B. *Orthopaedic Surgery in Infancy and Childhood.* Baltimore: Williams & Wilkins Co., 1968.

Fernald, Grace. *Remedial Techniques in Basic School Subjects.* New York: McGraw-Hill Book Co., Inc., 1943.

Fisher, Kirk L. "Effects of Perceptual-Motor Training on the Educable Mentally Retarded," *Except. Child.* 38:264–266, 1971.

Fisher, M. Bruce, and James E. Birren. "Age and Strength," *J. Appl. Psych.* 31:490–497, 1947.

Flavell, John H. *The Developmental Psychology of Jean Piaget.* New York: Van Nostrand Co., 1963.

Fleishman, Edwin A. *The Structure and Measurement of Physical Fitness.* Englewood Cliffs, N.J.: Prentice-Hall, Inc., 1964a.

Fleishman, Edwin A. *Examiner's Manual for the Basic Fitness Tests.* Englewood Cliffs, N.J.: Prentice-Hall, Inc., 1964b.

Fletcher, Gerald F., and John D. Cantwell. *Exercise and Coronary Heart Disease: Role in Prevention, Diagnosis, Treatment.* Springfield, Ill.: Charles C Thomas, Publisher, 1974.

Force, Dewey G. "Social Status of Physically Handicapped Children," *Except. Child.* 23:104–107, 1956.

Forche, Carolyn. "The Child with Epilepsy," *J. Hea. Phys. Educ. and Rec.* 44:83–86, 1973.

Ford, Frank R. *Diseases of the Nervous System: In Infancy, Childhood and Adolescence.* Springfield, Ill.: Charles C Thomas, Publisher, 1966.

Fowler, William M., Jr., et al. "Ineffective Treatment of Muscular Dystrophy with an Anabolic Steroid and Other Measures," *New Eng. J. Med.* 272:875–882, 1965.

Francis, Robert J., and G. Lawrence Rarick. "Motor Characteristics of the Mentally Retarded," *Amer. J. Ment. Def.* 63:792–811, 1959.

Frankenburg, William K., and Josiah B. Dodds. "The Denver Developmental Screening Test," *J. Ped.* 71:181–191, 1967.

Franklin, Janice C. "An Experimental Study of Physical Conditioning for Asthmatic Children," Master's thesis, Texas Women's University, 1971.

Fredericks, H. D. Bud, et al. *The Teaching Research Motor-Development Scale for Moderately and Severely Retarded Children.* Springfield, Ill.: Charles C Thomas, Publisher, 1972.

Fretz, Bruce R., Warren R. Johnson, and Julia A. Johnson. "Intellectual and Perceptual Motor Development as a Function of Therapeutic Play," *Res Quart.* 40:687–691, 1969.

Frisina, Dominic R. "A Psychological Study of the Mentally Retarded Child," Doctoral dissertation, Northwestern University, Evanston, 1955.

Frostig, Marianne, et al. *The Marianne Frostig Developmental Test of Visual Perception: 1963 Standardization.* Palo Alto, Cal.: Consulting Psychologists Press, 1964a.

Frostig, Marianne, and David Horne. *The Frostig Program for the Development of Visual Perception.* Chicago: Follett Educational Corp., 1964b.

Frostig, Marianne, et al. "The Marianne Frostig Developmental Test of Visual Perception, 1963 Standardization," *Percept. and Mot. Skills.* 19:463, 1964c.

Frostig, Marianne, Welty Lefever, and John R. B. Whittlesey. The Marianne Frostig Developmental Test of Visual Perception. Revised ed. Palo Alto, California: Consulting Psychologists Press, 1966.

Frostig, Marianne. "Testing as a Basis for Educational Therapy." *J. Spec. Educ.* 2:15–34, 1967.

Frostig, Marianne, and Phyllis Maslow. *Frostig MGL: Move, Grow, Learn (Teachers Guide).* Chicago: Follett Publishing Co., 1969.

Frostig, Marianne, and Phyllis Maslow. *Movement Education: Theory and Practice.* Chicago: Follett Publishing Co., 1970.

Frostig, Marianne. *Beginning Pictures and Patterns: Teachers Guide,* rev. ed. Chicago: Follett Publishing Co., 1972a.

Frostig, Marianne. "Visual Perception, Integrative Functions and Academic Learning," *J. Learn. Dis.* 5:1–15, 1972b.

Frostig, Marianne, and Phyllis Maslow. *Learning Problems in the Classroom.* New York: Grune & Stratton, Inc., 1973a.

Frostig, Marianne, and David Horne, in association with Phyllis Maslow. *Frostig Program for the Development of Visual Perception.* Chicago: Follett Publishing Co., 1973b.

Funk, Dean C. "Effects of Physical Education on Fitness and Motor Development of Trainable Mentally Retarded Children," *Res. Quart.* 42:30–34, 1971.

Furth, Hans G. *Piaget and Knowledge: Theoretical Foundations.* Englewood Cliffs, N.J.: Prentice-Hall, Inc., 1969.

Furth, Hans G. *Piaget for Teachers.* Englewood Cliffs, N.J.: Prentice-Hall, Inc., 1970.

Furth, Hans G., and Harry Wachs. *Thinking Goes to School: Piaget's Theory in Practice.* New York: Oxford University Press, 1975.

Gagné, Robert M. *The Conditions of Learning.* New York: Holt, Rinehart and Winston, Inc., 1965.

Gallahue, David L. "The Relationship Between Perceptual and Motor Abilities," *Res. Quart.* 39:948–952, 1968.

Gallahue, David L., Peter H. Werner, and George C. Leudke. *A Conceptual Approach to Moving and Learning.* New York: John Wiley and Sons, Inc., 1975.

Garton, Melinda Dean. *Teaching the Educable Mentally Retarded.* Springfield, Ill.: Charles C Thomas, Publisher, 1970.

Gastron, Sawnie R. "The Clubfoot," in *Foot Disorders: Medical and Surgical Management,* by Nicholas J. Giannestras. Philadelphia: Lea & Febiger, 1967.

Gearheart, Bill R. *Learning Disabilities: Educational Strategies.* St. Louis: The C. V. Mosby Co., 1973.

Gearheart, Bill R., and Mel W. Weishahn. *The Handicapped Child in the Regular Classroom.* St. Louis: The C. V. Mosby Co., 1976.

Gearheart, Bill R. *Learning Disabilities: Educational Strategies.* St. Louis: The C. V. Mosby Co., 1977.

George, Colleen, et al. "Development of an Aerobics Conditioning Program for the Visually Handicapped," *J. Phys. Educ. and Rec.* 46:39–40, 1975.

Gerber, Sanford E. "Cerebral Palsy and Hearing Loss," *Cereb. Pal. J.* 27:6–7, 1966.

Gesell, Arnold, and Helen Thompson. "Learning and Growth in Identical Infant Twins," *Genet. Psychol. Monogr.* 6:1–124, 1929.

Gesell, Arnold, et al. *The First Five Years of Life.* New York: Harper & Row, Publishers, 1940.

Gesell, Arnold, and Frances L. Ilg. *The Child from Five to Ten.* New York: Harper & Brothers, Publishers, 1946.

Gesell, Arnold, and Catherine S. Amatruda. *Developmental Diagnosis: Normal and Abnormal Child Development.* New York: Paul B. Hoeber, Inc., 1948.

Gesell, Arnold, et al. *The First Five Years of Life.* London: Methuen & Co. Ltd., 1950.

Gesell, Arnold, Frances L. Ilg, and Glenna E. Bullis. *Vision: Its Development in Infant and Child.* New York: Paul B. Hoeber, Inc., 1950.

Getman, G. N. *How to Develop Your Child's Intelligence.* A Research Publication. Luverne, Minnesota: G. N. Getman, 1962.

Getman, G. N., and Elmer R. Kane. *The Physiology of Readiness, An Action Program for the Development of Perception for Children.* Minneapolis: P.A.S.S. Inc., 1964.

Getman, Gerald N. "The Visuomotor Complex in the Acquisition of Learning Skills," in *Learning Disorders,* edited by Jerome Hellmuth. Vol. 1. Seattle, Wash.: Special Child Publications, 1965.

Getman, G. N., et al. *Developing Learning Readiness (Teacher's Manual).* St. Louis: McGraw-Hill Book Co., Inc., 1968.

Giangreco, C. Joseph, and Marianne Ranson Giangreco. *The Education of the Hearing Impaired.* Springfield, Ill.: Charles C Thomas, Publisher, 1970.

Giannestras, Nicholas J. *Foot Disorders: Medical and Surgical Management.* Philadelphia: Lea & Febiger, 1967.

Gibson, Eleanor J., and Richard Walk. "The Visual Cliff," *Sci. Amer.* 202:64–71, 1960.

Gibson, Eleanor J. "Development of Perception: Discrimination of Depth Compared with Discrimination of Graphic Symbols," *Monogr. Soc. Res. Child Dev.* 28:5–32, 1963.

Gibson, Eleanor J. "Learning to Read," *Science* 148:1066–1072, 1965.

Gillingham, Anna, and Bessie Stillman, ed. *Remedial Training for Children with Specific Disability in Reading, Spelling and Penmanship.* Cambridge, Mass.: Educators Publishing Service, Inc., 1965.

Ginsberg, Herbert, and Sylvia Opper. *Piaget's Theory of Intellectual Development: an Introduction.* Englewood Cliffs, N.J.: Prentice-Hall, Inc., 1969.

Godfrey, Barbara B., and Newell C. Kephart. *Movement Patterns and Motor Education.* New York: Appleton-Century-Crofts, 1969.

Goldenshon, Eli S. and Howard S. Barrows. *Handbook for Patients.* A pamphlet distributed by Ayerst Laboratories, New York, N.Y. (n.d.).

Goodwin, Lane A. "The Effects of Two Selected Physical Education Programs on Trainable Mentally Retarded Children," Doctoral dissertation, University of Utah, 1970.

Grandgenett, Richard. "Individualizing PE in the Primary Grades," *J. Phys. Educ. and Rec.,* 47:51, 1976.

Graubard, Paul J. "Children with Behavioral Disabilities," In *Exceptional Children in the Schools,* edited by Lloyd M. Dunn. New York: Holt, Rinehart and Winston, Inc., 1973.

Green, Donald Ross, Marguerite P. Furo, and George B. Flamer. *Measurement and Piaget.* New York: McGraw-Hill Book Co., Inc., 1971.

Greenberg, Judith W., and Leonard M. Alshan. "Perceptual-Motor Functioning and School Achievement in Lower Class Black Children." *Percept. and Mot. Skills* 38:60–62, 1974.

Greenfell, James E. "The Effect of a Structural Physical Education Program on the Physical Fitness and Motor Educability of the Mentally Retarded School Children in Whitman County, Washington," Master's thesis, Washington State University, 1965.

Gruber, Joseph H., and Melody Noland. "Perceptual-Motor and Scholastic Achievement Relationships in Emotionally Disturbed Elementary School Children," *Res. Quart.* 48:68–73, 1977.

Guilford, J. P. "The Structure of Intellect," *Psychol. Bull.* 53:267–293, 1956a.

Guilford, J. P. *Fundamental Statistics in Psychology and Education.* New York: McGraw-Hill Book Co., Inc., 1956b.

Guilford, J. P. "Three Faces of Intellect," *Amer. Psychol.* 14:469–479, 1959.

Guilford, J. P. *Fundamental Statistics in Psychology and Education.* New York: McGraw-Hill Book Co., Inc., 1965.

Guilford, J. P. *The Nature of Human Intelligence.* New York: McGraw-Hill Book Co., Inc., 1967.

Guilford, J. P., and Ralph Hoepfner. *The Analysis of Intelligence.* New York: McGraw-Hill Book Co., Inc., 1971.

Guilford, J. P., and Benjamin Fruchter. *Fundamental Statistics in Psychology and Education.* New York: McGraw-Hill Book Co., Inc., 1973.

Guttridge, Mary V. "A Study of Motor Achievements of Young Children," *Arch. Psychol.* No. 244:1–17, 1939.

Hale, Louise Kent. "Construction of Reading Material for Games," Master's thesis, State University of Iowa, 1940.

Halsey, Elizabeth, and Lorena Porter. *Physical Education for Children: A Developmental Program.* New York: Holt, Rinehart and Winston, Inc., 1963.

Halverson, H. M. "An Experimental Study of Prehension in Infants by Means of Systematic Cinema Records," *Genet. Psychol. Monogr.* 10:107–285, 1931.

Hamilton, Alicita, Pride Anderson, and Karol Merten. "Learning to Talk While Developing Motor Skills," *J. Hea. Phys. Educ. and Rec.* 43:80–81, 1972.

Hanninen, Kenneth A. *Teaching the Visually Handicapped.* Columbus, Ohio: Charles E. Merrill Co., 1975.

Haring, Norris G., and Jeanne Marie Stables. "The Effect of Gross

Motor Development on Visual Perception and Eye-Hand Coordination." *J. Amer. Phys. Ther. Assn.* 46:129–135, 1966.

Harvey, Birt. "Asthma," in *Physically Handicapped Children—A Medical Atlas for Teachers,* edited by Eugene E. Bleck and Donald A. Nagel. New York: Grune & Stratton, Inc., 1975a.

Harvey, Brit. "Cystic Fibrosis," in *Physically Handicapped Children—A Medical Atlas for Teachers,* edited by Eugene E. Bleck and Donald A. Nagel. New York: Grune & Stratton, Inc., 1975b.

Hatfield, Elizabeth M. "Causes of Blindness in School Children," *Sight-Saving Rev.* 33:218–233, 1963.

Hatfield, Elizabeth Macfarlane. "Blindness in Infants and Young Children," *Sight-Sav. Rev.* 42:69–89, 1972.

Hatfield, Elizabeth Macfarlane. "Estimates of Blindness in the United States," *Sight-Sav. Rev.* 43:69–80, 1973.

Hatlen, Philip H. "Physical Education for the Visually Handicapped," *Int. J. for the Educ. of the Blind* 17:17–21, 1967.

Hayden, Frank J. *Physical Fitness for the Mentally Retarded.* Toronto, Canada: Metropolitan Toronto Association for Retarded Children, 1964.

Hayden, Herbert. "B is for Breathing," *The Best of Challenge,* by the American Association for Health, Physical Education, and Recreation. Washington, D.C., 1971.

Haynes, Harold, Burton L. White, and Richard Held. "Visual Accommodation in Human Infants," *Science* 148:528–530, 1965.

Healy, Alfred. "A Comparison of Two Methods of Weight Training for Children with Spastic Type of Cerebral Palsy," Master's thesis, State University of Iowa, 1957.

Heath, S. Roy, Jr. "Rail-Walking Performance as Related to Mental Age and Etiological Type Among the Mentally Retarded," *Amer. J. Psych.* 55:240–247, 1942.

Heath, S. Roy, Jr. "The Military Use of the Rail-Walking Test as an Index of Locomotor Coordination," *Psych. Bull.* 40:282–284, 1943.

Heath, S. Roy, Jr. "Clinical Significance of Motor Defect with Military Implications," *Amer. J. Psych.* 57:482–499, 1944.

Heath, S. Roy, Jr. "The Relation of Rail-Walking and Other Motor Performances of Mental Defectives to Mental Age and Etiologic Type," *Trng. Sch. Bull.* 50:119–127, 1953.

Hebb, D. O. *The Organization of Behavior.* New York: John Wiley and Sons, Inc., 1949.

Hein, Fred V., and Allan J. Ryan. "The Contributions of Physical Activity to Physical Health," *Res. Quart.* 31 (Part II):263–285, 1960.

Herkowitz, Jacqueline. "A Perceptual-Motor Training Program to Improve the Gross Motor Abilities of Pre-Schoolers," *J. Hea. Phys. Educ. and Rec.* 41:38–42, 1970.

Hewett, Frank M. "A Hierarchy of Educational Tasks for Children with Learning Disorders," *Except. Child.* 31:207–214, 1964.

Hewett, Frank M. "Educational Engineering with Emotionally Disturbed Children," *Except. Child.* 33:459–467, 1967.

Hewett, Frank M. *The Emotionally Disturbed Child in the Classroom.* Boston: Allyn and Bacon, Inc., 1968.

Hicks, J. Allan. "The Acquisition of Motor Skill in Young Children: A Study of the Effects of Practice in Throwing at a Moving Target," *Child Dev.* 1:90–105, 1930a.

Hicks, J. Allan. "The Acquisition of Motor Skill in Young Children, II: The Influence of Specific and of General Practice on Motor Skill," *Child Dev.* 1:292–297, 1930b.

Hicks, J. Allan, and Dorothy W. Ralph. "The Effects of Practice in Training the Porteus Diamond Maze," *Child Dev.* 2:156–158, 1931.

Hilgard, Josephine R. "Learning and Maturation in Preschool Children," *J. Genet. Psych.* 41:36–56, 1932.

Hilgard, Josephine R. "The Effect of Early and Delayed Practice on Memory and Motor Performances Studied by the Method of Co-Twin Control." *Genet. Psychol. Monogr.* 14:493–567, 1933.

Hilsendager, Donald R., Harold K. Jack, and Lester Mann. "The Buttonwood Farms Project: A Physical Education-Recreation Program for Emotionally Disturbed and Mentally Retarded Children." *J. Hea. Phys. Educ. and Rec.* 39:46–48, 1968.

Hirschberg, Gerald G. *Rehabilitation.* Philadelphia: J. B. Lippincott Co., 1964.

Hirt, Michael. "Physical Conditioning in Asthma, I: Preliminary Results," *Annals of Aller.* 22:229–237, 1964.

Hobbs, Nicholas. "Helping Disturbed Children: Psychological and Ecological Strategies," in *Educating Emotionally Disturbed Children,* edited by Henry Dupont. New York: Holt, Rinehart and Winston, 1969.

Hoberman, Morton. "Physical Medicine and Rehabilitation: Its Value and Limitations in Progressive Muscular Dystrophy," *Amer. J. Phys. Med.* 34:109–115, 1955.

Holman, Portia. "The Relationship Between General Mental Development and Manual Dexterity," *Brit. J. Psych.* 23:279–283, 1933.

Horne, Betty and Will Justiss. "Comparison of Normal and Retardates on Three Perceptual and Motor Tasks," *Percept. and Mot. Skills* 26:539–544, 1968.

Howe, Clifford E. "A Comparison of Motor Skills of Mentally Retarded Children and Normal Children," *Except. Child.* 25:352–358, 1959.

Huckins, Ross. "Camping for Children Who Are Blind," *The New Outlook for the Blind* 57:91–94, 1963.

Humphrey, James H. *Elementary School Physical Education.* New York: Harper & Brothers, Publishers, 1958a.

Humphrey, James H., and Virginia D. Moore. "Some Observatories of Reading Interest and Motivation of 6–8 year old Children When the Reading Content is Oriented to Active Game Participation," Paper presented at the Research Section of the 60th convention of the American Association for Health, Physical Education, and Recreation, 1958b.

Humphrey, James H. "Reading and Physical Education," *J. Hea. Phys. Educ. and Rec.* 36:30–31, 1959.

Humphrey, James H., and Virginia D. Moore. "Improving Reading Through Physical Education," *Educ.* 80:559–561, 1960.

Humphrey, James H. "A Pilot Study of the Use of Physical Education as a Learning Medium in the Development of Language Arts in Third Grade Children," *Res. Quart.* 33:136–137, 1962.

Humphrey, James. *Child Learning Through Elementary School Physical Education.* Dubuque, Iowa: Wm. C. Brown Co., 1965a.

Humphrey, James H. "Comparison of the Use of Active Games and Language Workbook Exercise on Learning Media in the Development of Language Understandings with Third Grade Children," *Percept. and Mot. Skills* 21:23–26, 1965b.

Humphrey, James H. *Child Learning Through Elementary School Physical Education.* Dubuque, Iowa: Wm. C. Brown Co., 1966a.

Humphrey, James H. "An Exploratory Study of Active Games in Learning Number Concepts by First Grade Boys and Girls," *Percept. and Mot. Skills* 23:341–342, 1966b.

Humphrey, James H. "Academic Skill and Concept Development Through Motor Activity," mimeograph copy of a paper presented at the Second General Session of the American Academy of Physical Education, Las Vegas, Nevada, March 8, 1967a.

Humphrey, James H. "The Mathematics Motor Activity Story," *The Arith. Teach.* 14:14–16, 1967b.

Humphrey, James H. "Comparison of the Use of the Active Game Learning Medium with Tranditional Procedures in the Reinforcement of Reading Skills with Fourth Grade Children," *J. Spec. Educ.* 1:369–373, 1967c.

Humphrey, James H., and Dorothy D. Sullivan. *Teaching Slow Learners Through Active Games.* Springfield, Ill.: Charles C Thomas, Publisher, 1970a.

Humphrey, James H. "A Comparison of the Use of the Active Game Learning Medium and Traditional Media in the Development of Fifth Grade Science Concepts with Children with Below Normal Intelligence Quotients," *Res. Abs.* Washington, D.C.: American Association for Health, Physical Education, and Recreation, 1970b.

Humphrey, James. "The Use of Motor Activity Learning in the Development of Science Concepts with Slow Learning Fifth Grade Children," *J. Res. Sci. Teach.* 9:261–266, 1972.

Humphrey, James H. "The Use of Motor Activity in the Development of Science Concepts with Mentally Handicapped Children," Proceedings, National Convention of the National Science Teacher Association, Washington, D.C., 1973.

Humphrey, James H., and Joy M. Humphrey. *Child Learning Through Elementary School Physical Education.* Dubuque, Iowa: Wm. C. Brown, Publishers, 1974.

Humphrey, James H. *Teaching Elementary School Science Through Motor Learning.* Springfield, Ill.: Charles C Thomas, Publisher, 1975.

Hunsicker, Paul, and Guy G. Reiff. *AAHPER Youth Fitness Test Manual.* Revised 1976 ed. Washington, D.C.: American Alliance for Health, Physical Education, and Recreation, 1976.

Hunsicker, Paul, and Guy Reiff. "Youth Fitness Report: 1958–1965–1975," *J. Phys. Educ. and Rec.* 48:31–32, 1977.

Hyde, John S., and Charles L. Swarts. "Effect of an Exercise Program on the Perennially Asthmatic Child." *Amer. J. Dis. Child.* 116:383–396, 1968.

Inhelder, Bärbel. "Some Aspects of Piaget's Genetic Approach to Cognition," in *Cognitive Development in Children,* by the Society for Research in Child Development. Chicago: The University of Chicago Press, 1970.

Ison, Charles F. "An Experimental Study of a Comparison of the Use of Physical Education Activities as a Learning Medium with Traditional Procedures in the Development of Selected Fifth Grade Science Concepts," Master's thesis, University of Maryland, 1961.

Itard, Jean. *The Wild Boy of Avevron,* translated by G. and M. Humphrey. New York: Appleton-Century-Crofts, 1962.

Itkin, Irving H. "Exercise for the Asthmatic Patient: Physiological Changes in the Respiratory System and Effects of Conditioning Exercise Programs," *Phys. Ther.* 44:815–820, 1964.

Itkin, Irving H., and Martin Nacman. "The Effect of Exercise on the Hospitalized Asthmatic Patient," *J. Aller.* 37:253–263, 1966.

Johnson, Doris J., and Helmer R. Myklebust. *Learning Disabilities: Educational Principles and Practices.* New York: Grune & Stratton, Inc., 1967.

Johnson, Leon, and Ben Londeree. *Motor Fitness Testing Manual for the Moderately Mentally Retarded.* Washington, D.C.: American Alliance for Health, Physical Education and Recreation, 1976.

Johnson, Orval G., and James W. Bommarito. *Tests and Measurements in Child Development: A Handbook.* San Francisco: Jossey-Bass, Inc., Publisher, 1971.

Johnson, Philip R. "Physical Education for Blind Children in Public Elementary Schools," *The New Outlook for the Blind* 63:264–271, 1969.

Johnson, Robert D. "Measurements of Achievement in Fundamental Skills of Elementary School Children," *Res. Quart.* 33:94–103, 1962.

Johnson, Warren R., and E. R. Buskirk, ed. *Science and Medicine of Exercise and Sport.* New York: Harper & Row, Publishers, 1974.

Johnston, Robert B., and Phyllis R. Magrab, ed. *Developmental Disorders: Assessment, Treatment, Education.* Baltimore, Md.: University Park Press, 1976.

Joint Committee of the Allergy Foundation of America and the American Thoracic Society. *Asthma: A Practical Guide for Physicians.* New York: The National Tuberculosis and Respiratory Disease Association in cooperation with the Allergy Foundation of America, 1973.

Joint Committee of the American Psychological Association, the American Educational Research Association, and the National Council on Measurement in Education. *Standards for Educational and Psychological Tests.* Washington, D.C.: American Psychological Association, 1974.

Jokl, Ernst. *The Clinical Physiology of Physical Fitness and Rehabilitation.* Springfield, Ill.: Charles C Thomas, Publisher, 1958.

Jones, Jacquelyn B. "The Effect of a Physical Activity Program on Asthmatic Children," Master's thesis, Texas Tech. University, 1974.

Jones, Mary C., et al. *The Course of Human Development.* Waltham, Mass.: Xerox College Publishing, 1971.

Joslin, Elliott P., et al. *The Treatment of Diabetes Mellitus.* Philadelphia: Lea & Febiger, 1959.

Joslin, Elliott P. *Diabetic Manual.* Philadelphia: Lea & Febiger, 1974.

Kamii, Constance K., and Norma L. Radin. "A Framework for a Preschool Curriculum Based on Some Piagetian Concepts," in *Educational Implications of Piaget's Theory,* edited by Irene J. Athey and Daune O. Rubadeau. Waltham, Mass.: Xerox College Publishing, 1970.

Kanner, Leo. "Autistic Disturbances of Affective Contact," *Nervous Child.* 217–250, 1943.

Karmel, Louis J. *Measurement and Evaluation in the Schools.* Toronto, Canada: Collier-MacMillan Canada, Ltd., 1970.

Keats, Sidney. *Cerebral Palsy.* Springfield, Ill.: Charles C Thomas, Publisher, 1965.

Kemp, Robert. *Understanding Epilepsy.* London: Tavistock Publications Ltd., 1963.

Keogh, Barbara K., and Jack F. Keogh, "Pattern Copying and Pattern Walking Performance of Normal and Educationally Subnormal Boys," *Amer. J. Ment. Def.* 71:1009–1013, 1967.

Keogh, Jack. *Motor Performance of Elementary School Children,* Los Angeles: Physical Education Department, University of California at Los Angeles, 1965.

Keogh, Jack F. "Analysis of Individual Tasks in the Stott Test of Motor Impairment," Department of Physical Education, University of California at Los Angeles, Technical Report 2–68, 1968a.

Keogh, Jack F. "Developmental Evaluation of Limb Movement Tasks," Department of Physical Education, University of California at Los Angeles, Technical Report 1–68, December, 1968b.

Keogh, Jack. "Fundamental Motor Task," in *A Textbook of Motor De-*

velopment, edited by Charles B. Corbin. Dubuque, Iowa: Wm. C. Brown, Publishers, 1973.

Kephart, Newell C. *The Slow Learner in the Classroom.* Columbus, Ohio: C. E. Merrill Publishing Co., 1960.

Kephart, Newell C. "Perceptual-Motor Aspects of Learning Disabilities," in *Educating Children with Learning Disabilities,* edited by Edward C. Frierson and Walter B. Barbe. New York: Appleton-Century-Crofts, 1967.

Kephart, Newell C. *Learning Disability: An Educational Adventure.* West Lafayette, Ind.: Kappa Delta Pi Press, 1968.

Kephart, Newell C. *The Slow Learner in the Classroom.* Columbus, Ohio: Charles E. Merrill Publishing Co., 1971.

Kerby, C. Edith. "Causes of Blindness in Children of School Age," *Sight-Sav. Rev.* 28:10–21, 1958.

Kershner, John R. "Relationship of Motor Development to Visual-Spatial Cognitive Growth," *J. Spec. Educ.* 8:91–102, 1974.

Kershner, Keith M., Russell A. Dusewicz, and John R. Kershner. "The K-D-K-Oseretsky Tests of Motor Development," Harrisburg, Penn.: Bureau of Research, Administration and Coordination, Department of Public Instruction, Commonwealth of Pennsylvania, 1968.

Ketterlinus, Eugenia. "Learning of Children in Adaptation to Mirror Reversals," *Child Dev.* 2:200–223, 1931.

Kiphard, Ernst J. "Behavioral Interpretation of Problem Children Through Remedial Physical Education," *J. Hea. Phys. Educ. and Rec.* 41:4–45, 1970.

Kirchner, Glenn, and Don Glines. "Comparative Analysis of Eugene, Oregon, Elementary School Children Using the Kraus-Weber Test of Minimum Muscular Fitness," *Res. Quart.* 28:16–25, 1957.

Kirk, Samuel A. *Educating Exceptional Children.* Boston: Houghton-Mifflin Co., 1962.

Kirk, Samuel A. *The Diagnosis and Remediation of Psycholinguistic Disabilities.* Urbana, Ill.: University of Illinois Press, 1966.

Kirk, Samuel A. "The Illinois Test of Psycholinguistic Abilities: Its Origin and Implications," in *Learning Disorders,* edited by Jerome Hellmuth. Vol. 3. Seattle, Wash.: Special Child Publications, 1968a.

Kirk, Samuel A., James J. McCarthy, and Winifred D. Kirk. *Illinois Test of Psycholinguistic Abilities,* rev. ed. Urbana, Ill.: University of Illinois Press, 1968b.

Kirk, Samuel A., and Jeanne McRae McCarthy, ed. *Learning Disabilities: Selected ACLD Papers.* Boston: Houghton-Mifflin Co., 1970.

Kirk, Samuel A., and Winifred D. Kirk. *Psycholinguistic Learning Disabilities: Diagnosis and Remediation.* Urbana, Ill.: University of Illinois Press, 1971.

Kirk, Samuel A. *Educating Exceptional Children.* Boston: Houghton-Mifflin Co., 1972.

Knapczyk, Dennis R., and Wendell P. Liemohn. "A Factor Study of Cratty's Body Perception Test," *Res. Quart.* 47:678–682, 1976.

Knights, Robert M., Joseph A. Hyman, and Marius A. Wozny. "Psychomotor Abilities of Familial, Brain-Injured and Mongoloid Retarded Children," *Amer. J. Ment. Def.* 70:454–457, 1965.

Kraft, Robert E. "The Comparative Effects of a Perceptual-Motor Program and a Modified Traditional Program Upon the Gross Motor Development of Children with Learning Disabilities," in *Abstracts: Research Papers 1977 AAHPER Convention.* Washington, D.C.: American Alliance for Health, Physical Education, and Recreation, 1977.

Kral, Paul A. "Motor Characteristics and Development of Retarded Children," *Educ. and Train. of Ment. Ret.* 7:14–21, 1972.

Krathwohl, David R., Benjamin S. Bloom, and Bertram B. Maria. *Taxonomy of Educational Objectives: The Classification of Educational Goals. Handbook II: Affective Domain.* New York: David McKay Company, Inc., 1956.

Kraus, Hans, and Ruther P. Hirschland. "Minimum Muscular Fitness Tests in School Children," *Res. Quart.* 25:178–188, 1954.

Krug, Frank L. "The Use of Physical Education Activities in the Enrichment of Learning of Certain First Grade Mathematical Concepts," Master's thesis, University of Maryland, 1973.

Kulcinski, Louis E. "The Relation of Intelligence to the Learning of Fundamental Muscular Skills," *Res. Quart.* 16:266–276, 1945.

Kuo, Zin Yang. "The Genesis of the Cat's Responses to the Rat," *J. Comp. Psychol.* 11:1–36, 1930.

Lamport, Lance C. "The Effects of a Specific Perceptual-Motor Physical Education Program on the Self-Concept of Children with Learning Disabilities," in *Abstracts: Research Papers 1976 AAHPER Convention.* Washington, D.C.: American Alliance for Health, Physical Education, and Recreation, 1976.

Langan, James G. "A Comparison of Motor Proficiency in Middle and Lower Class Educable Mentally Retarded Children," Doctoral dissertation, Indiana University, 1965.

Langan, James Gregory. "A Comparison of Motor Proficiency in Middle and Lower Class Educable Mentally Retarded Children," Doctoral dissertation, Indiana University, Ann Arbor, Michigan: University Microfilms, Inc., 1966.

Langer, Jonas. *Theories of Development.* New York: Holt, Rinehart and Winston, Inc., 1969.

Larsson, Yngve A., et al. "Physical Fitness and the Influence of Training in Diabetic Adolescent Young Girls," *Diabetes* 11:109–117, 1962.

Larsson, Yngve, et al. "Functional Adaptation to Rigorous Training and exercise in Diabetic and Non-diabetic Adolescents," *J. Appl. Physio.* 19:629–635, 1964.

Laufman, Marjorie. "Blind Children in Integrated Recreation," *The New Outlook for the Blind* 56:81–84, 1962.

Lavatelli, Celia Stendler. *Piaget's Theory Applied to an Early Childhood Curriculum.* Boston: Center for Media Development, Inc., 1970.

LeBlanc, David G. "A Comparative Investigation of Performance on Static and Dynamic Balance Tasks by Down's Syndrome and Non-Down's Syndrome Trainable Mentally Retarded," Master's thesis, State University College, Brockport, New York, 1975.

Leighton, Jack R. "A Simple Objective and Reliable Measure of Flexibility," *Res. Quart.* 13:205–216, 1942.

Leithwood, Kenneth A. "Motor, Cognitive, and Affective Relationships Among Advantaged Preschool Children," *Res. Quart.* 42:47–53, 1971.

Lerner, Janet W. *Children with Learning Disabilities.* New York: Houghton-Mifflin Co., 1971.

Lewis, June E., and Irene C. Potter. *The Teaching of Science in the Elementary School.* Englewood Cliffs, N.J.: Prentice-Hall, Inc., 1970.

Licht, Sidney, ed. *Rehabilitation and Medicine.* New Haven, Conn.: Elizabeth Licht, Publisher, 1968.

Liemohn, Wendell, and Dennis R. Knapczyk. "Analysis of Cratty's Locomotor Ability Test," *Res. Quart.* 45:171–177, 1974.

Liemohn, Wendell P., and Dennis R. Knapczyk. "Factor Analysis of Gross and Fine Motor Ability in Developmentally Disabled Children," *Res. Quart.* 45:424–432, 1974.

Ling, Bing-Chung. "A Genetic Study of Sustained Visual Fixation and Associated Behavior in the Human Infant From Birth to Six Months," *J. Genet. Psychol.* 61:227–277, 1942.

Link, Ruth B. "An Exploratory Study of Integration of Physical Education Activities and Reading Vocabulary with Selected Third Grade Children," Master's thesis, University of Maryland, 1958.

Lipton, Edward D. "A Perceptual-Motor Development Program's Effect on Visual Perception and Reading Readiness of First-Grade Children," *Res. Quart.* 41:402–405, 1970.

Lloyd, Barbara B. *Perception and Cognition: A Cross-Cultural Perspective.* Baltimore: Penguin Books, Inc., 1972.

Long, John A. *Motor Abilities of Deaf Children.* 1932. Reprint. New York: AMS Press, Inc., 1972.

Lounsberry, James. "Weight Training: for the Mentally Retarded at the Primary Level," in *The Best of Challenge,* by the American Association for Health, Physical Education, and Recreation. Washington, D.C.: American Association for Health, Physical Education and Recreation, 1971.

Loveless, Myreen. "A Study of the Relationship Between Physical Fitness, Reading Achievement, and Perceptual-Motor Skills and Participation in a Concentrated Unit of Selected Physical Activities of Fifty Second and Third Grade Children," Master's thesis, Texas Women's University, 1967.

Lowenfeld, Berthold, ed. *The Visually Handicapped Child in School.* New York: The John Day Co., 1973.

McBeath, Pearl M. "The Effectiveness of Three Reading Preparedness Programs on Perceptually Handicapped Kindergarteners," Doctoral dissertation. Stanford University, 1966.

McCandless, Boyd R. *Children Behavior and Development.* New York: Holt, Rinehart and Winston, Inc., 1967.

McClure, K. L. "A Comparison of the Performance of Educable Mentally Retarded Girls and Intellectually Normal Girls in the American Association of Health, Physical Education and Recreation Youth Fitness Test Battery," Doctoral dissertation, University of Georgia, 1970.

McCormick, Clarence C., et al. "Improvement in Reading Achievement Through Perceptual-Motor Training," *Res. Quart.* 39:627–633, 1968.

McElhenny, Thomas R., and Kay H. Peterson. "Physical Fitness for Asthmatic Boys," *JAMA* 185:178–179, 1963.

McGraw, M. B. *Growth: A Study of Johnny and Jimmy.* New York: Appleton-Century-Crofts, 1935.

McGraw, Myrtle B. "Later Development of Children Specially Trained During Infancy: Johnny and Jimmy at School Age," *Child Dev.* 10:1–19, 1939.

McGraw, Myrtle B. *The Neuromuscular Motivation of the Human Infant.* New York: Columbia University Press, 1943.

McGraw, Myrtle B. "Maturation of Behavior," in *Manual of Child Psychology,* edited by L. Carmichael. New York: Wiley, 1946.

Maier, Henry W. *Three Theories of Child Development.* New York: Harper & Row, Publishers, 1969.

Malpass, Leslie F. "Motor Proficiency in Institutionalized and Non-Institutionalized Retarded Children and Normal Children," *Amer. J. Ment. Def.* 64:1012–1015, 1960.

Mann, Lester, and Donald W. Hilsendager. "The Four Phases: A New Conceptual Approach to Physical Education for Emotionally Disturbed Children," *Amer. Corr. Ther. J.* 22:43–45, 1968a.

Mann, Lester, and Donald W. Hilsendager. "Physical Recreation – An

Old-New Dimension in Helping the Emotionally Disturbed Child,"
Amer. Corr. Ther. J. 22:131–135, 1968b.

Markowitz, Milton, and Leon Gordis. *Rheumatic Fever.* Philadelphia:
W. B. Saunders Co., 1972.

Marks, Nancy C. *Cerebral Palsied and Learning Disabled Children.*
Springfield, Ill.: Charles C Thomas, Publisher, 1974.

Meagher, Mary E. "Balance Board Activities," *J. Hea. Phys. Educ. and
Rec.* 44:71–72, 1973.

Meditch, Carl. "Effectiveness of Two Methods of Weight Training for
Children with Athetoid Type of Cerebral Palsy," Master's thesis,
State University of Iowa, 1961.

Memmel, Rudolph L. "Arithmetic Through Play," *J. Hea. Phys. Educ.
and Rec.* 24:31 and 47, 1953.

Metheney, Eleanor. "The Present Status of Strength Testing for
Children of Elementary School and Pre-School Age," *Res. Quart.*
12:115–130, 1941.

Meyer, Edith. "Comprehension of Spatial Relations in Pre-School
Children," *J. Genet. Psychol.* 57:119–151, 1940.

Miller, James L. "Effect of Instruction on Development of Throwing for
Accuracy of First Grade Children," *Res. Quart.* 28:132–137, 1957.

Mirenva, A. N. "Psychomotor Education and the General Development
of Preschool Children: Experiments with Twin Controls," *J. Genet.
Psychol.* 46:443–454, 1935.

Mohr, Dorothy R. "The Contributions of Physical Activity to Skill
Learning," *Res. Quart.* 31 (Part II):321–350, 1960.

Montessori, Maria. *Spontaneous Activity in Education. The Advanced
Montessori Method.* Translated by Florence Simmonds. Cambridge, Mass.: Robert Bentley, Inc., 1964a.

Montessori, Maria. *The Montessori Method.* Translated by Anne E.
George. New York: Schocken Books, Inc., 1964b.

Montessori, Maria. *Spontaneous Activity in Education.* Translated by
Florence Simmonds. New York: Schocken Books, Inc., 1965.

Moran, Joan M., and Leonard H. Kalakian. *Movement Experiences for
the Mentally Retarded or Emotionally Disturbed Child.* Minneapolis: Burgess Publishing Co., 1974.

Morsh, Joseph E. "Motor Performance of the Deaf," *Comp. Psychol.
Monogr.* 13:1–51, 1936.

Mowrer, O. H. "'Maturation' vs. 'Learning' in the Development of
Vestibular and Optokinetic Nystagmus," *J. Genet. Psychol.*
48:383–404, 1936.

Muscular Dystrophy Association of America, Inc. *Muscular Dystrophy
Fact Sheet,* New York: Muscular Dystrophy Association of America,
Inc. (n.d.).

Mussen, Paul Henry, John Janeway Conger, and Jerome Kagan.
Child Development and Personality. New York: Harper & Row,
Publishers, 1974.

Myklebust, Helmer R. "Significance of Etiology in Motor Performance
of Deaf Children with Special Reference to Meningitis," *Amer. J.
Psych.* 59:249–258, 1946.

Myklebust, Helmer R. *Auditory Disorders in Children.* New York:
Grune & Stratton, Inc., 1954.

Myklebust, Helmer R. *The Psychology of Deafness.* New York: Grune
& Stratton, Inc., 1964.

Myklebust, Helmer, and Doris Johnson. *Learning Disabilities: Educational Principles and Practices.* New York: Grune & Stratton, Inc.,
1967.

Myklebust, Helmer R., ed. *Progress in Learning Disabilities.* Vol. 1.
New York: Grune & Stratton, Inc., 1968.

Myklebust, Helmer R., and Benjamin Boshes. *Minimal Brain Damage in Children*. Final Report, U.S. Public Health Service Contract 108-65-142. U.S. Department of Health, Education and Welfare. Evanston, Illinois: Northwestern University Publications, 1969.

Myler, Pauline V. "A Study of the Motor Ability of the Blind," Master's thesis, University of Texas, August, 1936.

Nagel, Donald A. "Temporary Orthopaedic Disabilities in Children," in *Physically Handicapped Children: A Medical Atlas for Teachers*, edited by Eugene E. Bleck and Donald A. Nagel. New York: Grune & Stratton, Inc., 1975.

Nash, John. *Developmental Psychology: A Psychobiological Approach*. Englewood Cliffs, N.J.: Prentice-Hall, Inc., 1970.

National Advisory Committee on Handicapped Children. *Special Education for Handicapped Children. First Annual Report*. Washington, D.C.: U.S. Department of Health, Education, and Welfare, 1968.

National Association for Retarded Citizens. *Facts on Mental Retardation*. Arlington, Texas: National Association for Retarded Citizens, 1973.

National Cystic Fibrosis Research Foundation. "Lung Diseases of Children . . . A Serious Health Problem in Every Community." New York: National Cystic Fibrosis Foundation (n.d.).

National Society for the Prevention of Blindness. *Vocabulary of Terms Relating to the Eye*. New York: National Society for the Prevention of Blindness, Inc., 1960.

National Society for the Prevention of Blindness. *NSPB Fact Book*. New York: National Society for the Prevention of Blindness, Inc., 1966.

Nelson, Pearl Astrid. *Elementary School Science Activities*. Englewood Cliffs, N.J.: Prentice-Hall, Inc., 1968.

Ness, Richard A. "Weight Training for Severely Mentally Retarded Persons," *J. Hea. Phys. Educ. and Rec.* 45:87–88, 1974.

Nissen, Henry W., Kao L. Chow, and Josephine Semmes. "Effects of Restricted Opportunity for Tactual, Kinesthetic, and Manipulative Experience on the Behavior of a Chimpanzee," *Amer. J. Psych.* 64:485–507, 1951.

Norris, Miriam, Patricia J. Spaulding, and Fern H. Brodie. *Blindness in Children*. Chicago: University of Chicago Press, 1957.

Nunley, Rachel L. "A Physical Fitness Program for the Mentally Retarded in the Public Schools," *J. Amer. Phys. Ther. Assn.* 45:946–954, 1965.

O'Connor, Colleen Mary. "The Effects of Physical Activities Upon Motor Ability, Perceptual Ability, and Academic Achievement of First-Graders," Doctoral dissertation, University of Texas at Austin, 1968.

Oliver, James N. "The Effect of Systematic Physical Conditioning on the Growth of Educationally Sub-Normal Boys," *Medical Officer* 97:19–22, 1957.

Oliver, James N. "The Effect of Physical Conditioning Exercises and Activities on the Mental Characteristics of Educationally Sub-normal Boys," *Brit. J. Educ. Psych.* 28:155–165, 1958.

Oliver, James N. "The Effects of Physical Conditioning on the Sociometric Status of Educationally Sub-Normal Boys," *Phys. Educ.* 156:38–46, 1966.

Oliver, James N. "Blindness and the Child's Sequence of Development," *J. Hea. Phys. Educ. and Rec.* 41:37–39, 1970.

Olson, Arthur V. "Relation of Achievement Test Scores and Specific Reading Abilities to the Frostig Developmental Test of Visual Perception," *Percept. and Mot. Skills* 22:179–184, 1966.

Olson, David M. "Motor Skill and Behavior Adjustment An Exploratory Study," *Res. Quart.* 39:321–326, 1968.

Orpet, R. E., and T. L. Heustis. *Move-Grow-Learn Movement Skills Survey.* Chicago: Follett Publishing Co., 1971.

Orpet, R. E. *Frostig Movement Skills Test Battery (Experimental Edition).* Palo Alto, California: Consulting Psychologists Press, Inc., 1972.

Orton, Samuel T. *Reading, Writing and Speech Disorders in Children.* New York: W. W. Norton and Co., 1937.

Painter, Genevieve. "The Effect of a Rhythmic and Sensory Motor Activity Program or Perceptual Motor Spatial Abilities of Kindergarten Children," *Except. Child.* 33:113–116, 1966.

Patterson, Marcia Drew. "Effectiveness of Perceptual Motor Therapy on Kindergarten Children," Master's thesis, University of California at Santa Barbara, 1974.

Penman, Kenneth A., Jon R. Christopher, and Geoffrey S. Wood. "Using Gross Motor Activity to Improve Language Arts Concepts by Third Grade Students," *Res. Quart.* 48:134–137, 1977.

Perkins, Fannie L. *Teaching Techniques for Cerebral Palsied Children.* New York: Vantage Press, Inc., 1963.

Perlstein, M. A., and Philip N. Hood. "Etiology of Postneonatally Acquired Cerebral Palsy," *JAMA* 188:850–854, 1964.

Perrigo, Roy. "Individualizing PE for Intermediate Grades," *J. Phys. Educ. and Rec.* 47:51–52, 1976.

Perry, Natalie. *Teaching the Mentally Retarded Child.* New York: Columbia University Press, 1974.

Peterson, Kay H., and Thomas R. McElhenney. "Effects of a Physical Fitness Program Upon Asthmatic Boys," *Ped.* 35:295–299, 1965.

Phillips, John L., Jr. *The Origins of Intellect: Piaget's Theory.* San Francisco: W. H. Freeman and Co., 1975.

Phillips, Marjorie, et. al. "Analysis of Results from the Kraus-Weber Test of Minimum Muscular Fitness in Children," *Res. Quart.* 26: 314–323, 1955.

Physical Education and Recreation for the Handicapped: Information and Research Utilization Center. *Adapted Physical Education Guidelines: Theory and Practice for the Seventies and Eighties.* Washington, D.C.: American Alliance for Health, Physical Education, and Recreation, 1976.

Piaget, Jean. *The Construction of Reality in the Child.* New York: Basic Books, 1954.

Piaget, Jean. *Play, Dreams and Imitation in Childhood.* New York: W. W. Norton and Co., Inc., 1962.

Piaget, Jean. *The Origins of Intelligence in Children.* Translated by M. Cook. New York: W. W. Norton and Co., Inc., 1963.

Piaget, Jean. "Response to Brain Sutton-Smith," *Psychol. Rev.* 73:111–112, 1966.

Piaget, Jean. *The Psychology of Intelligence.* London: Routledge and Kegan Paul Ltd., 1967a.

Piaget, Jean, and Barbel Inhelder. *The Child's Conception of Space.* Translated by F. J. Langdon and J. L. Lunzer. New York: W. W. Norton and Co., 1967b.

Piaget, Jean. *The Child's Conception of Movement and Speed.* New York: Basic Books, 1970a.

Piaget, Jean. *Science of Education and the Psychology of the Child.* Translated by D. Coltman. New York: Orion Press, 1970b.

Plack, Jeralyn J. "Relationship Between Achievement in Reading and Achievement in Selected Motor Skills in Elementary School Children," *Res. Quart.* 39:1063–1068, 1968.

Poindexter, Hally. "The Perceived and Actual Psycho-Motor Ability of Children: A Study of Normal and Emotionally Disturbed Children Ages 7–10." An unpublished study submitted to the United States Commissioner of Education, Washington, D.C.: Bureau of Education for the Handicapped, 1968.

Poindexter, Hally B. "Motor Development and Performance of Emotionally Disturbed Children," *J. Hea. Phys. Educ. and Rec.* 40:69–71, 1969a.

Poindexter, Hally. "The Status of Physical Education for the Emotionally Disturbed," *Physical Education and Recreation for Handicapped Children: A Study Conference on Research and Demonstration Needs.* Washington, D.C.: American Association for Health, Physical Education, and Recreation and the National Recreation and Park Association, 1969b.

Polak, Paul R., Robert N. Emde, and Rene A. Spitz. "The Smiling Response: II. Visual Discrimination and the Onset of Depth Perception," *J. Nerv. Ment. Dis.* 139:407–415, 1964.

Porter, Ruth, and Maeve O'Connor, ed. *Cystic Fibrosis.* Boston: Little, Brown and Co., 1968.

Prager, Iris J. "The Use of Physical Education Activities in the Reinforcement of Selected First Grade Science Concepts," Master's thesis, University of Maryland, 1968.

Prager, Iris J. "The Reinforcement of First Grade Science Concepts with the Use of Motor Activity Learning." *Research Abstracts.* Washington, D.C.: American Association for Health, Physical Education, and Recreation, 1974.

Pratt, Carl C. "The Effects of Repeated Visual Stimulation Upon the Activity of Newborn Infants," *J. Genet. Psychol.* 44:117–126, 1934.

Premack, David. "Toward Empirical Behavior Laws: I. Positive Reinforcement," *Psychol. Rev.* 66:219–233, 1959.

Pulaski, Mary Ann Spencer. *Understanding Piaget: An Introduction to Children's Cognitive Development.* New York: Harper & Row, Publishers, 1971.

Puthoff, Martilu. "New Dimensions in Physical Activity for Children with Asthma and Other Respiratory Conditions," *J. Hea. Phys. Educ. and Rec.* 43:73–77, 1973.

Quay, Herbert C., William C. Morse, and Richard L. Cutler. "Personality Patterns of Pupils in Special Classes for the Emotionally Disturbed," *Except. Child.* 32:297–301, 1966.

Rabin, Herbert M. "The Relationship of Age, Intelligence and Sex to Motor Proficiency in Mental Defectives," *Amer. J. Ment. Def.* 62:507–516, 1957.

Rachun, Alexius. "Vision and Sports," *Sight-Sav. Rev.* 38:224–226, 1968.

Radler, D. H., and Newell C. Kephart. *Success Through Play.* New York: Harper & Row, Publishers, 1960.

Rarick, G. Lawrence, V. D. Seefeldt, and Ionel F. Rapapurt. *Physical Growth and Development in Down's Syndrome. An Eight Year Longitudinal Study.* Madison, Wis.: Department of Physical Education, University of Wisconsin, 1966.

Rarick, G. Lawrence, James H. Widdop, and Geoffrey D. Broadhead. "The Physical Fitness and Motor Performance of Educable Mentally Retarded Children," *Except. Child.* 36:509–519, 1970.

Rarick, G. Lawrence, and D. Alan Dobbins. *Basic Components in the Motor Performance of Educable Mentally Retarded Children: Implications for Curriculum Development.* Berkeley, Cal.: Department of Physical Education, University of California, 1972.

Rarick, G. Lawrence, ed. *Physical Activity: Human Growth and Development.* New York: Academic Press, 1973.

Rarick, G. Lawrence, and D. Alan Dobbins. "A Motor Performance Typology of Boys and Girls in the Age Range 6 to 10 Years," *J. Motor Beh.* 7:37–43, 1975a.

Rarick, G. Lawrence, and D. Alan Dobbins. "Basic Components in the Motor Performance of Children Six to Nine Years of Age," *Med. Sci. Sports* 7:105–110, 1975b.

Rarick, G. Lawrence, D. Alan Dobbins, and Geoffrey D. Broadhead. *The Motor Domain and Its Correlates in Educationally Handicapped Children.* Englewood Cliffs, N.J.: Prentice-Hall, Inc., 1976.

Rarick, G. Lawrence, and James P. McQuillan. "The Factor Structure of Motor Abilities of Trainable Mentally Retarded Children: Implications for Curriculum Development." Final Report, Project No. H23–2544, for the Department of Health, Education, and Welfare, U.S. Office of Education, Bureau of Education for the Handicapped. Berkeley, Cal.: Department of Physical Education, University of California, 1977.

Redl, Fritz. "Why Life Space Interview?" in *Educating Emotionally Disturbed Children,* edited by Henry Dupont. New York: Holt, Rinehart and Winston, Inc., 1975.

Reinert, Henry R. *Children in Conflict: Educational Strategies for the Emotionally Disturbed and Behaviorally Disordered.* St. Louis: The C. V. Mosby Co., 1976.

Research Media, Inc. *Cardiovascular Diseases and Therapy Book 2: Hypertension and Antihypertensive Agents.* Hicksville, N.Y.: Research Media, Inc., 1975.

Rhodes, William C. "The Disturbing Child: A Problem of Ecological Management," *Except. Child.* 33:449–455, 1967.

Riesen, Austin H. "The Development of Visual Perception in Man and Chimpanzee, " *Sci.* 106:107–108, 1947.

Roach, Eugene G., and Newell C. Kephart. *The Purdue Perceptual-Motor Survey.* Columbus, Ohio: Charles E. Merrill Publishing Co., 1966.

Robinson, Halbert W., and Nancy M. Robinson. *The Mentally Retarded Child: A Psychological Approach.* New York: McGraw-Hill Book Co., 1965.

Robinson, Sid. "Experimental Studies of Physical Fitness in Relation to Age," *Arbeitsphysio.* 10:251–323, 1938.

Rodahl, Kaare, et al. "Physical Work Capacity," *Arch. Environ. Hea.* 2:499–510, 1961.

Rodin, Ernst. *The Prognosis of Patients with Epilepsy.* Springfield, Ill.: Charles C Thomas, Publisher, 1968.

Rosen, Carl L. "An Experimental Study of Visual Perceptual Training and Reading Achievement in First Grade," *Percept. and Mot. Skills* 22:979–986, 1966.

Rosentswieg, Joel, and Daisy Herndon. "Perceptual-Motor Ability of Kindergarten Age Children," *Percept. and Mot. Skills* 37:583–586, 1973.

Ross, Dorothea. "Incidental Learning of Motor Concepts in Small Group Games," *Amer. J. Ment. Def.* 74:718–725, 1970.

Ross, John, Jr. and Robert A. O'Rourke. *Understanding the Heart and Its Diseases.* New York: McGraw-Hill Book Co., 1976.

Rudel, Rita G., and Hans-Lukas Teuber. "Discrimination of Direction of Line in Children," *J. Comp. Physiol. Psych.* 56:892–898, 1963.

Rusalem, Herbert. *Coping with the Unseen Environment.* New York: Teachers College Press of Columbia University, 1972.

Russ, J. D., and H. R. Soboloff. *A Primer of Cerebral Palsy.* Springfield, Ill.: Charles C Thomas, Publisher, 1958.

Rutherford, William L. "The Effects of a Perceptual-Motor Training Program on Performance of Kindergarten Pupils on Metropolitan

Readiness Tests," Doctoral dissertation, North Texas State University, 1964.

Ryan, Allan J., ed. *Sports Medicine.* New York: Academic Press, 1974.

Safrit, Margaret J. *Evaluation in Physical Education.* Englewood Cliffs, N.J.: Prentice-Hall, Inc., 1973.

Scarnati, Richard A. "Recreation Therapy for Persons with Cystic Fibrosis—A Review," *Amer. Corr. Ther. J.* 23:7–13, 1969.

Scherr, Merle S., and Lawrence Frankel. "Physical Conditioning Program for Asthmatic Children," *JAMA* 168:1996–2000, 1958.

Schleichkorn, Jay. "Physical Activity for the Child with Cystic Fibrosis," *J. Phys. Educ. and Rec.* 48:50, 1977.

Schmitt, George F. *Diabetes for Diabetics: A Practical Guide.* Miami, Fla.: The Diabetes Press of America, Inc., 1973.

Scholl, Geraldine T. "Understanding and Meeting Development Needs," in *The Visually Handicapped Child in School,* edited by Berthold Lowenfield. New York: The John Day Co., 1973.

Schwebel, Milton, and Jane Raph, ed. *Piaget in the Classroom.* New York: Basic Books, Inc., 1973.

Scott, Donald. *About Epilepsy.* New York: International Universities Press, Inc., 1973.

Scott, M. Gladys. "The Contributions of Physical Activity to Psychological Development," *Res. Quart.* 31 (Part II):302–320, 1960.

Seashore, Carl E., and T. L. Ling. "The Comparative Sensitiveness of Blind and Seeing Persons," *Psych. Monogr.* 25:148–158, 1918.

Seashore, Harold G. "Some Relationships of Fine and Gross Motor Abilities," *Res. Quart.* 13:259–274, 1942.

Seashore, Harold G. "The Development of a Beam-Walking Test and its Use in Measuring Development of Balance in Children," *Res. Quart.* 18:246–259, 1947.

Seguin, Edward. *Idiocy and Its Treatment by the Physiological Method.* New York: Teachers College Press of Columbia University, 1907.

Seligman, Trude, H. O. Randel, and J. J. Stevens. "Conditioning Program for Children with Asthma," *Phys. Ther.* 50:641–648, 1970.

Seltzer, Carl C., and Jean Mayer. "A Simple Criterion of Obesity," *Postgrad. Med.* 38:101–107, 1965.

Selzer, Arthur. *The Heart—Its Function in Health and Disease.* Berkeley and Los Angeles: University of California Press, 1969.

Sengstock, Wayne L. "A Comparison of the Performance of EMR Boys with Performance of Intellectually Normal Boys in AAPHER Youth Fitness Test Battery," Doctoral dissertation, Syracuse University, 1963.

Sengstock, Wayne L. "Physical Fitness of Mentally Retarded Boys," *Res. Quart.* 37:113–120, 1966.

Sherman, Mandel, Irene Sherman, and Charles D. Flory. "Infant Behavior," *Comp. Psychol. Monogr.* 12:1–107, 1936.

Sherrill, Claudine. *Adapted Physical Education: A Multidisciplinary Approach.* Dubuque, Iowa: Wm. C. Brown, 1976.

Shick, Jacqueline, and Jeralyn J. Plack. "Kephart's Perceptual Motor Training Program," *J. Phys. Educ. and Rec.* 47:58–59, 1976.

Shirley, Mary M. *The First Two Years: A Study of Twenty-Five Babies. Volume I: Postural and Locomotor Development.* Westport, Conn.: Greenwood Press, Publishers, 1931.

Shirley, Mary M. *The First Two Years: A Study of Twenty-Five Babies. Volume II: Intellectual Development.* Westport, Conn.: Greenwood Press, Publishers, 1933.

Short, Francis X. "Team Teaching for Developmentally Disabled Children," *J. Phys. Educ. and Rec.* 46:45–46, 1975.

Shotick, Andrew, and Charles Thate. "Reactions of a Group of Educable Mentally Handicapped Children to a Program of Physical Education," *Except. Child.* 26:248–252, 1960.

Shyman, Bonnie. "Dance Therapy for the Emotionally Disturbed," *J. Hea. Phys. Educ. and Rec.* 44:61–62, 1973.

Siegel, Irwin M. "Pathomechanics of Stance in Duchenne Muscular Dystrophy," *Arch. Phys. Med. and Rehab.* 53:403–406, 1972.

Sigel, Irving E. "The Piagetian System and the World of Education," in *Studies in Cognitive Development,* by David Elkind and John H. Flavell. New York: Oxford University Press, 1969.

Sindoni, Anthony M. *The Diabetic's Handbook.* New York: The Ronald Press Co., 1959.

Singer, Robert N. "Interrelationship of Physical, Perceptual-Motor, and Academic Achievement Variables in Elementary School Children," *Percept. and Mot. Skills* 27:1323–1332, 1968.

Singer, Robert N. "Physical Characteristics, Perceptual-Motor, and Intelligence Differences Between Third and Sixth Grade Children," *Res. Quart.* 40:803–811, 1969.

Slacks, Rosemary, "The Effects of Physical Activities Upon Perceptual Ability, Reading Ability and Academic Achievement," Master's thesis, University of Texas at Austin, 1969.

Sloan, A. W., J. J. Burt, and C. J. Blyth. "Estimation of Body Fat in Young Women," *J. Appl. Physiol.* 17:967–970, 1962.

Sloan, William. "Motor Proficiency and Intelligence," *Amer. J. Ment. Def.* 55:394–406, 1951.

Sloan, William. "The Lincoln-Oseretsky Motor Development Scale," *Genet. Psychol. Monogr.* 51:183–252, 1955.

Smith, Bernard H. *Cervical Spondylosis and its Neurological Complications.* Springfield, Ill.: Charles C Thomas, Publisher, 1968.

Smith, Hope M. "Implications for Movement Education Experiences Drawn from Perceptual-Motor Research," *J. Hea. Phys. Educ. and Rec.* 41:30–33, 1970.

Smith, Paul. "Perceptual-Motor Skills and Reading Readiness of Kindergarten Children," *J. Hea. Phys. Educ. and Rec.* 41:43–44, 1970.

Soden, William H. *Rehabilitation of the Handicapped.* New York: The Ronald Press Co., 1949.

Solomon, Amiel H., and Roy Pangle. "The Effects of a Structural Physical Education Program on Physical, Intellectual and Self-Concept Development of Educable Retarded Boys," Behavioral Science Monograph No. 4. Nashville, Tenn. George Peabody College, Institute on Mental Retardation and Intellectual Development, 1966.

Solomon, Amiel, and Roy Pangle. "Demonstrating Physical Fitness Improvement in the EMR," *Except. Child.* 34:177–181, 1967.

Sonquist, Hanne, Constance Kamii, and Louise Derman. "A Piaget Derived Preschool Curriculum," in *Educational Implications of Piaget's Therapy,* edited by Irene J. Athey and Duane O. Rubadeau. Waltham, Mass.: Xerox College Publishing, 1970.

Southwood, A. R. *Heart Disease; Some Ways to Prevent It.* Springfield. Ill.: Charles C Thomas, Publisher, 1962.

Spalding, Douglas A. "Instinct: With Original Observations on Young Animals," *Pop. Sci. Mo.* 61:126–142, 1902.

Spearman, Charles E. *The Abilities of Man.* New York: The MacMillan Co., 1927.

Stark, Rachel E., ed. *Sensory Capabilities of Hearing-Impaired Children.* Baltimore, Md.: University Park Press, 1974.

Stein, Julian U. "Motor Function and Physical Fitness of the Mentally Retarded: A Critical Review," *Rehab. Lit.* 24:230–242, 1963.

Stein, Julian U., and Roy Pangle. "What Research Says About Psychomotor Functions of the Retarded," *J. Hea. Phys. Educ. and Rec.* 37:36–38, 1966.

Stein, Julian U. "What Research and Experience Tell us About Physical Activity, Perceptual-Motor, and Recreation Programs for Children with Learning Disabilities," *Amer. Corr. Ther. J.* 28:35–41, 1974.

Stein, Julian. "Sense and Nonsense about Mainstreaming," *J. Phys. Educ. and Rec.* 47:43, 1976.

Sterky, Göran. "Physical Work Capacity in Diabetic School Children," *Acta Paed.* 52:1–10, 1963.

Stern, William. *The Psychological Methods of Testing Intelligence.* Translated by G. M. Whipple. Baltimore, Md.: Warwick and York, Inc., 1914.

Stevens, Godfrey D., and Jack W. Birch. "A Proposal for Clarification of the Terminology Used to Describe Brain-Injured Children." *Except. Child.* 23:346–349, 1957.

Stevens, Godfrey D., and Jack W. Birch. "A Proposal for Clarification of the Terminology Used to Describe Brain-Injured Children," in *Educating Children with Learning Disabilities,* edited by Edward C. Frierson and Walter B. Barbe. New York: Appleton-Century-Crofts, 1967.

Stewart, Kerry, and Bernard Gutin. "Effects of Physical Training and Cardiorespiratory Fitness in Children," *Res. Quart.* 47:110–120, 1976.

Stollerman, Gene H. *Rheumatic Fever and Streptococcal Infection.* New York: Grune & Stratton, Inc., 1975.

Stott, Leland H. *Child Development: An Individual Longitudinal Approach.* New York: Holt, Rinehart and Winston, Inc., 1967.

Stott, D. H., F. A. Moyes, and S. E. Headridge. *Test of Motor Impairment.* 3rd revised edition. Guelph, Ontario, Canada: Department of Psychology, University of Guelph, 1968.

Strauss, Alfred A., and Laura E. Lehtinen. *Psychopathology and Education of the Brain-Injured Child.* New York: Grune & Stratton, Inc., 1947.

Strauss, Alfred A., and Newell C. Kephart. *Psychotherapy and Education of the Brain-Injured Child, Vol. II. Progress in Theory and Clinic.* New York: Grune & Stratton, Inc., 1955.

Streng, Alice, et al. *Hearing Therapy for Children.* New York: Grune & Stratton, Inc., 1958.

Sullivan, Dorothy D., and James H. Humphrey. *Teaching Reading Through Motor Learning.* Springfield, Ill.: Charles C Thomas, Publisher, 1973.

Suttie, Sandra J. "Piaget and Play," in *Piaget for Regular and Special Physical Educators and Recreators,* edited by Joseph P. Winnick and Ronald W. French. Brockport, N.Y.: State University College, 1975.

Sutton-Smith, Brian. "Piaget on Play: A Critique," in *Educational Implications of Piaget's Theory,* edited by Irene J. Athey and Duane O. Rubadeau. Waltham, Mass.: Xerox College Publishing, 1970.

Talkington, Larry W. "Frostig Visual Perceptual Training with Low Ability-Level Retarded," *Percept. and Mot. Skills* 27:505–506, 1968.

Thomas, Jerry R., et al. "Effects of Perceptual-Motor Training on Preschool Children: A Multivariate Approach," *Res. Quart.* 46:505–513, 1975.

Thompson, George G. *Child Psychology: Growth Trends in Psychological Adjustment.* Boston: Houghton Mifflin Co., 1952.

Thompson, William R., and Ronald Melzack. "Early Environment," *Sci. Amer.* 194:38–42, 1956.

Thorndike, Edward L. *Educational Psychology.* Vol. 3. New York: Columbia University Press, 1914.

Thurstone, L. L. *The Theory of Multiple Factors.* Ann Arbor, Mich.: Edwards Brothers, Inc., 1934.

Thurstone, L. L., and Thelma G. Thurstone. "Factorial Studies of Intelligence." *Psyc. Monogr.* No. 2. Chicago: University of Chicago Press, 1941.

Tidwell, Billy R. "The Effects of Gross-Motor and Fine Motor Skill Training on the Perceptual-Motor Skills and Intelligence Scores of Kindergarten Children," Doctoral dissertation, Texas A & M University, 1974.

Travis, Georgia. *Chronic Disease and Disability.* Berkeley: University of California Press, 1961.

Trevena, Thomas M. "Integration of the Sightless Student Into Regular Physical Activities," *J. Hea. Phys. Educ. and Rec.* 41:42–43, 1970.

Trout, Edwin. "A Comparative Study of Mathematical Concepts Developed Through Physical Education Activities Taught by the Physical Education Teacher and Traditional Techniques Taught by the Classroom Teacher," Master's thesis, University of Maryland, 1969.

Trussell, Ella M. "Relation of Performance of Selected Physical Skills to Perceptual Aspects of Reading Readiness in Elementary School Children," *Res. Quart.* 40:383–390, 1969.

Turek, Samuel L. *Orthopaedics: Principles and Their Application.* Philadelphia: J. B. Lippincott Co., 1967.

Turnquist, Donald A., and Stanley S. Marzolf. "Motor Abilities of Mentally Retarded Youth," *J. Hea. Phys. Educ. and Rec.* 25:43–44, 1954.

United States Office of Education. "Education of Handicapped Childres." *Federal Register* 42:42474–42518, 1977.

Upjohn Company. *Diabetes.* Kalamazoo, Michigan: Upjohn Co., 1960.

Valett, Robert E. *A Psychoeducational Inventory of Basic Learning Abilities.* Belmont, Cal.: Fearon Publishers, 1968.

Victor, Edward. *Science for the Elementary School.* New York: The MacMillan Co., 1975.

Vignos, Paul J., Jr., George E. Spencer, Jr., and Kenneth C. Archibald. "Management of Progressive Muscular Dystrophy of Childhood," *JAMA* 184:89–96, 1963.

Vignos, Paul J., Jr., and Mary D. Watkins. "The Effect of Exercise in Muscular Dystrophy.. *JAMA* 197:843–848, 1966.

Vinsant, Marielle O., Martha I. Spence, and Dianne C. Hagen. *A commonsense Approach to Coronary Care: A Program.* St. Louis: The C. V. Mosby Co., 1975.

Waggoner, Bernice E. "Motivation in Physical Education and Recreation for Emotionally Handicapped Children," *J. Hea. Phys. Educ. and Rec.* 44:73–76, 1973.

Walton, John N., and David Gardner-Medwin. "Progressive Muscular Dystrophy and the Myotonic Disorders." In *Disorders of Voluntary Muscle,* edited by John N. Walton. Edinburgh: Churchill Livingstone, 1974.

Webb, Ruth C. "Sensory-Motor Training of the Profoundly Retarded," *Amer. J. Ment. Def.* 74:283–295, 1969.

Webb, Wellington. "Physical Education Classes for the Emotionally Disturbed Child," *J. Hea. Phys. Educ. and Rec.* 43:79–81, 1972.

Weber, Elmer W. *Mentally Retarded Children and Their Education.* Springfield, Ill. Charles C Thomas, Publisher, 1963.

Weiner, Irving B. and David Elkind. *Readings in Child Development.* New York: John Wiley and Sons, Inc., 1972.

Wellman, Beth L. "Motor Performance of Preschool Children," *Child Educ.* 13:311–316, 1937.

Wellman, Beth L., and Carra Lou McCaskill. "Study of Common Motor Achievements at the Preschool Age," *Child Dev.* 9:141–150, 1938.

Werner, Peter H. "Effects of Integration of Physical Education with Selected Science Concepts Upon Science Knowledge and Selected Physical Performance Skills of Boys and Girls at the Fourth, Fifth, and Sixth Grade Levels," Doctoral dissertation, Indiana University, 1971.

Werner, Peter. "Integration of Physical Education Skills with the Concept of Levers at Intermediate Grade Levels," *Res. Quart.* 43:423–428, 1972.

Whelan, Richard F., and Norris G. Haring. "Modification and Maintenance of Behavior Through Systematic Application of Consequences," *Except. Child.* 32:281–289, 1966.

Whetnall, Edith, and D. B. Fry. *The Deaf Child.* Springfield, Ill.: Charles C Thomas, Publisher, 1971.

Wickstrom, Ralph L. *Fundamental Motor Patterns.* Philadelphia: Lea & Febiger, 1977.

Wight, Minnie G. "The Effect of Training on Rhythmic Ability and Other Problems Related to Rhythm," *Child Dev.* 8:159–172, 1937.

Wild, Monica R. "The Behavior Pattern of Throwing and Some Observations Concerning Its Course of Development in Children," *Res. Quart.* 9:20–24, 1938.

Williams, Judith R., and Roland B. Scott. "Growth and Development of Negro Infants: IV. Motor Development and Its Relationship to Child Rearing Practice in Two Groups of Negro Infants," *Child Dev.* 24:102–121, 1953.

Wilson, J., and H. M. Halverson. "Development of a Young Blind Child," *J. Genet. Psychol.* 71:155–175, 1947.

Winnick, Joseph P. "Planning Physical Activity for the Diabetic," *Phys. Educ.* 27:15–16, 1970.

Winnick, Joseph. "Issues and Trends in Training Adapted Physical Education Personnel," *J. Hea. Phys. Educ. and Rec.* 43:75–78, 1972.

Winnick, Joseph P. "Physical Activity and the Asthmatic Child," *Amer. Corr. Ther. J.* 31:148–151, 1977.

Winnick, Joseph P. "Early Movement Experiences and Program Components for the Stimulation of Cognitive Development." *Proceedings of The Seventh Annual Interdisciplinary International Conference on Piagetian Theory and The Helping Professions.* Los Angeles: University of Southern California, 1978.

Wohlwill, Joachim F., and Morton Wiener. "Discrimination of Form Orientation in Young Children," *Child Dev.* 35:1113–1125, 1964.

Wood, David W., Lillian P. Kravis, and Harold J. Lecks. "Physical Therapy for Children with Intractable Asthma," *J. Asth. Res.* 7:177–182, 1970.

Wright, Alex. "A Study to Determine the Effects of Physical Education on Educable Mentally Retarded Childrens' Motor Ability and Physical Fitness," Master's thesis, Springfield College, 1968.

Wright, Charles. "A Comparison of the Use of Traditional and Motor Activity Learning Media in the Development of Mathematical Concepts in Five and Six Year Old Children with an Attempt to Negate the Motivational Variable," Unpublished master's thesis, University of Maryland, 1969.

Zankle, Harry T. et al. "Physical Fitness Index Studies (PFI) in Hospitalized Diabetic Patients," *Arch. Phys. Med. and Rehab.* 38:250–253, 1957.

Zeigler, H. Philip, and H. Lebowitz. "Apparent Visual Size as a Function of Distance for Children and Adults," *Amer. J. Psych.* 70:106–109, 1957.

Ziter, Fred A. and Kent G. Allsop. "Comprehensive Treatment of Childhood Muscular Dystrophy," *Rocky Mount. Med. J.* 72:329–333, 1975.

Zohman, Lenore R. "Rehabilitation of Patients with Pulmonary Problems," in *Rehabilitation and Medicine,* edited by Sidney Licht. New Haven, Conn.: Elizabeth Licht, Publisher, 1968.

AUTHOR INDEX

SUBJECT INDEX

Page numbers in *italics* indicate illustrations. Page numbers followed by t indicate tables.

513